D0897386

**Footprint** Handbook
# Peru
ROBERT & DAISY KUNSTAETTER

# This is
## Peru

Ever since Hiram Bingham first set foot in Machu Picchu, the fabled Inca city has become one of the most recognized images in the world, so much so that it has come to represent Peru, acting as a magnet for every visitor. But for all its fame and glory, Machu Picchu is just the tip of the iceberg. Peru has more ancient archaeological sites than any other country in South America, and more are being found all the time. Most are still off the beaten path and offer the more intrepid visitor the thrill of genuine exploration. Trekking to such sites, be it with an organized group or on your own, is one of the finest experiences the country has to offer.

There is also much more to Peru than old stones. Of the 117 recognized life zones on the planet, Peru has 84, from mangroves to cloudforest, or from mist-fuelled oases in the desert to glacial lakes. It also has 28 out of 32 climate types. Amazingly, 60% of the country is jungle, even though less than 15% of its population lives there. Despite ongoing development, much of the Peruvian Amazon remains intact, and this vast green carpet is home to some of the greatest natural diversity on the planet. Not a year goes by without the recording of plants and animals previously unknown to science.

Peru is also a country of fiestas, and it would be an unusual visit that did not encounter at least one or two. Masks, costumes and dances tell centuries-old stories and reveal an intense spirituality that enriches daily life. Christian saints are carried through the streets as if they were the Inca emperors' sacred remains. Pachamama – Mother Earth – is offered a drop of every drink, and animal spirits and old combats come alive in masquerades.

The third largest country in South America, Peru is vast enough to accommodate this diversity. As a visitor you need time to take it in. So don't try to do too much at once, a relaxed and flexible itinerary is the best way to make the most of this amazing country. You will be sure to come back for more!

*Robert and*
*Daisy Kunstaetter*

# **Best of**
## Peru

## ❶ Lima

Peru's vibrant, sprawling and grimy capital is a world unto itself and the obligatory point of arrival for most visitors. The city's fine museums, colonial buildings, vibrant nightlife and world-famous dining will entertain, excite and inform. Page 34.

## ❷ Cordillera Blanca

A region of jewelled lakes and sparkling white mountain peaks, the Cordillera Blanca attracts mountaineers, hikers, cyclists and rafters in their thousands. Here stand some of the highest mountains in South America, with 30 snow-crested peaks over 6000 m. Page 78.

### ❸ Chavín de Huántar

This archaeological site belonged to one of the earliest and most influential cultures in pre-Inca Peru, and it has some extraordinary carvings and stonework. In the lee of the Cordillera Blanca, it is also one of the most spectacularly situated sites in the country. Page 91.

### ❹ Huaca de la Luna

The remains of the once-mighty Moche Empire are located near Trujillo on the north coast. They have revealed fabulous multicoloured friezes of gods from the first millennium AD and even the mummy of a tattooed woman. Page 116.

### ❺ North coast beaches

Peru's northern seaboard enjoys a rain-free climate all year, and boasts the country's finest beaches for bathing and surfing. When not riding the breakers, you can visit nature reserves or party into the small hours of the star lit night. Pages 118 and 120.

### ❼ Nazca Lines

The enigmatic Nazca Lines, whose origin and function continue to puzzle scientists, are etched into miles of barren southern desert. Their sheer scale and wonder can only be appreciated from the air. Page 210.

### ❻ Chachapoyas

Home to the mysterious 'Cloud People', the Chachapoyas region of the northern highlands boasts the enigmatic site of Kuélap, inaccessible cliff-side burial sites, the outstanding Leymebamba museum and the spectacular 771-m Gocta waterfall. Page 170.

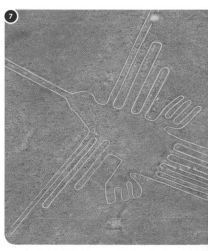

## ❽ Arequipa

Elegant Arequipa is known as the 'White City'. Spanish colonial churches, mansions and the Plaza de Armas all shine with pearly volcanic stonework. In contrast, the city's most famous jewel, the Santa Catalina Convent, is painted in bright colours, a gorgeous little city within a city. Page 222.

## ❾ Colca and Cotahuasi canyons

Come face to face with the majestic Andean condor, rising on morning thermals from the depths of the Colca or Cotahuasi canyon, two of the deepest in the world. Both offer world-class kayaking for those with a taste for profound adventure. Page 241.

## ❿ Lake Titicaca

The sapphire-blue waters of Lake Titicaca are bathed in a unique high-altitude light that no photograph can convey. Inhabiting its islands and the surrounding *puna* are Aymara, Quechua and Uros communities, many of whom remain faithful to their traditional cultures. Page 304.

## ⑪ Cuzco

Cuzco, navel of the ancient Inca world, is Peru's tourism central, and for good reason. Colonial churches, convents and extensive pre-Columbian ruins are interspersed with countless hotels, bars and restaurants that cater to the over one million tourists who visit every year from all over the world. Page 286.

## ⑫ Q'eswachaka

Every year in June, over 400 Quechua families from four communities join forces for four days to reconstruct the Inca rope bridge at Q'eswachaka using ancestral tools and materials. Witnessing this impressive feat of ancient civil and social engineering is an unforgettable experience. Page 320.

## ⑬ Machu Picchu

No amount of hype can dilute the tremendous feeling of awe on first arriving at Machu Picchu. A complete Inca city, for centuries it was buried in jungle until Hiram Bingham stumbled upon it in 1911. Page 339.

## ⑭ Manu and Tambopata

In the Manu and Tambopata reserves, large mammals, including tapirs, giant anteaters, otters and primates, are fairly easy to spot. Pages 419 and 429.

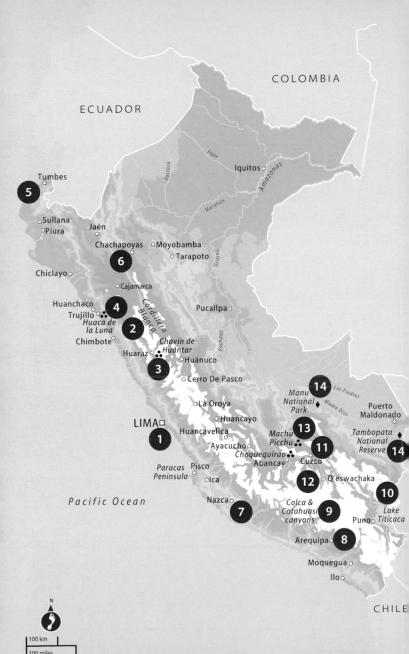

BRAZIL

BOLIVIA

Lima **1**

Cordillera Blanca **2**

Chavín de Huántar **3**

Huaca de la Luna **4**

North coast beaches **5**

Chachapoyas **6**

Nazca Lines **7**

Arequipa **8**

Colca and Cotahuasi canyons **9**

Lake Titicaca **10**

Cuzco **11**

Q'eswachaka **12**

Machu Picchu **13**

Manu and Tambopata **14**

# Route
## planner

The variety that Peru offers the visitor is enormous. The problem, if you're on a tight schedule, is how to fit it all in. Above all, don't attempt to do too much. Take it easy and give yourself time to appreciate one of the most beautiful and fascinating countries on Earth. Peru is larger than most visitors realize and has a great many different regions. The capital, Lima, is a world unto itself. On either side of this oversized metropolis, the north and south of the country are each divided into coast, highlands and jungle. Every region has its own special atmosphere and its own long list of attractions. From among them you can select the elements that most interest you and, depending on transport links, you can tailor your own itinerary.

For the following routes, all travel is by road unless indicated otherwise. However, if you're short of time, flying will be more efficient.

## One to two weeks

a whistle-stop tour of the country's highlights

**Southern highlights** This circuit covers some of the most popular destinations in the country. Spend a day or two in Lima, visiting the city's fascinating museums to gain an overview of the country's exceptionally rich history and culture. If your budget allows, you can also make the most of the capital's great gastronomy and vibrant nightlife. Then fly to Cuzco for a taste of its Inca and colonial heritage. On a short visit, you can catch the train from Cuzco directly to Machu Picchu, but if you prefer to hike the Inca Trail or any of the worthwhile alternatives, you need to consider additional time in the region. From Cuzco, travel to Puno to visit the shores and islands of beautiful Titicaca, the highest navigable lake in the world. Continue to the white city of Arequipa to take in its fine colonial architecture and more great dining opportunities. You can head out from the city to visit the awe-inspiring Colca Canyon, before flying back to Lima.

Above: Machu Picchu
Opposite page: Huascarán (6768 m),
the highest mountain in Peru.

**Northern highlights**  Alternatively, you might prefer to avoid the tourist honeypot of Cuzco and explore a different part of the country. Start, once again, in Lima, before travelling to Huaraz in the Cordillera Blanca. Only eight hours by road from the capital, it's one of the world's premier mountain recreation areas, with unparalleled ease of access. A few days hiking or climbing here could easily be combined with the coastal archaeological sites and fine museums near the colonial city of Trujillo and further north around Chiclayo and Lambayeque. From here, continue to the Chachapoyas region, which also contains a bewildering number of pre-Hispanic archaeological sites and the spectacular Gocta waterfall. For the final stage of your trip, either travel down the beautiful road that descends from the mountains to the subtropical city of Tarapoto, or take an even more magnificent ride to Cajamarca, surrounded by thermal baths, archaeological and historical sites and lovely countryside. From both Tarapoto and Cajamarca, you can catch a flight back to Lima.

## Three to four weeks

there's so much more to see

Adding an extra two weeks to your trip would allow you to combine the two itineraries above into a more comprehensive tour. Alternatively, try one of the following routes.

**Extended southern route**  A trip to the central Andes from Lima will take you off the beaten path, calling at Huancayo, Huancavelica and Ayacucho in a week to 10 days. Obviously the more time you allow, the more variety you'll see, especially in the Mantaro Valley near Huancayo, and the places of historical interest around Ayacucho. These are also two of the best

Above: Ferrocarril Central
Opposite page: Jungle in Madre de Dios

places to experience festivals and buy handicrafts. From Ayacucho, you can travel to Cuzco via Andahuaylas and Abancay. As an alternative to the highlands, head south from Lima on the Pan-American Highway for a week or so on the southern coast, taking in the Paracas Peninsula, with its marine birdlife, and the incredible Nazca Lines. A paved road runs from Nazca, via Abancay, to Cuzco.

On this extended itinerary you should have time to see much more of Cuzco and its surroundings, especially the Sacred Valley of the Incas. Instead of the trek to Machu Picchu, you could try the more demanding and rewarding hike to the Inca city of Choquequirao. From Cuzco, make a trip to the southern jungle, either by flying or travelling overland to Puerto Maldonado. Manu National Park and the Tambopata National Reserve provide wonderful opportunities for nature enthusiasts to enjoy the highest levels of biodiversity in the world. Fly back to Lima, either from Puerto Maldonado or Cuzco.

**Extended northern route** Travel overland from Lima to Huaraz for trekking in the Cordillera Blanca or Huayhuash. Both the Huayhuash and Alpamayo circuits (see page 14) are excellent long-distance high-altitude treks In this area. Head to Trujillo to visit the archaeological sites but break up a surfeit of sightseeing at the popular seaside resort of Huanchaco, before continuing to Chiclayo and Chachapoyas as above. Then descend from the mountains to Tarapoto and Yurimaguas, and travel by riverboat to Iquitos. The Amazonian city is the jumping-off point for the northern jungle, where there is a good network of jungle lodges. From Iquitos, catch a flight back to Lima.

# Best
## trekking
## destinations

**Huayhuash Circuit**
The Cordillera Huayhuash was made famous by Joe Simpson's mountaineering classic, *Touching the Void*. The Huayhuash trekking circuit has eight passes over 4700 m and requires plenty of stamina. You will be rewarded with views of massive ice faces rising out of the *puna*, azure lakes, deep gorges and high pastures. Page 101.

**Cordillera Blanca**
North of Lima, the Cordillera Blanca is the trekking heart of Peru. The most popular multi-day trek in this area takes three to five days from the **Santa Cruz Valley to Llanganuco** or vice versa. Less travelled and more demanding, but well worth the additional effort, is the **Alpamayo Circuit**, a seven- to 12-day trek around one of the most perfect peaks in the world. Both of these trekking routes are offered by many tour operators or they can be undertaken independently by those with sufficient experience. Pages 96 and 97.

Above: Cordillera Blanca
Right: Huayhuash Circuit

## Ausangate Circuit

Visible from Cuzco, the strikingly beautiful summit of Ausangate stands at 6384 m. The four- to six-day circuit of the mountain includes spectacular vistas of the heavily glaciated Cordillera Vilcanota, two passes over 5000 m, hot springs and beautiful turquoise lakes. The circuit rarely drops below 4000 m, so trekkers need to be fit and well acclimatized before attempting it. Page 319.

## Choquequirao

This Inca city is as spectacularly sited as Machu Picchu but far less visited. The four- to five- day hike starts at the village of Cachora (accessed from Cuzco) at 2875 m, descends into the seemingly bottomless Apurímac Canyon at 1500 m and climbs back up to Choquequirao at 3000 m, so you can figure out just how much climbing up and down is involved. Do this trek now, before the cable car arrives. Page 322.

## Capaq Ñan – the Great Inca Road

The world-famous trekking routes to Machu Picchu follow but a tiny fraction of the 25,000-km Inca road network. Vestiges of the Capaq Ñan can be found the length of the Andes and in Peru there are many well-preserved sections which make exceptional off-the-beaten-path trekking routes. The ancient road and stairway to Pariacaca in the central highlands and the 200-km stretch from Huari to Huánuco Viejo are but two examples. Pages 364 and 388.

## The classic Inca Trail

Peru's most famous trek is a four- or five-day organized hike through magnificent scenery, varied ecology and Inca ruins to Machu Picchu. For all its popularity, this is no easy stroll: it starts at 2600 m, climbs up to 4200 m, descends 1000 m on an Inca stairway, and, depending on the time of year, includes freezing nights and/or deep mud. Page 347-350.

Top: Ausangate Circuit
Above left: Choquequirao
Above middle: Classic Inca Trail
Above right: Capaq Ñan, near Huarautambo

Festival of La Virgen de la Candelaria, Puno

# When to go

## Climate

Peru's high season in the highlands is from May to September, when the weather is most stable for hiking and climbing. At this time the days are generally clear and sunny, though nights can be very cold at high altitude. During the wettest months in the highlands, November to April, some roads become impassable and hiking trails can be very muddy. April and May, at the end of the highland rainy season, is a beautiful time to see the Peruvian Andes in bloom, but the rain may linger, so be prepared.

On the coast, high season is September, and Christmas to February. The summer months are from December to April, but from approximately May to October much of this area is covered with *garúa*, a blanket of cloud and mist. At this time only the northern beaches near Tumbes are warm and pleasant enough for swimming.

The best time to visit the jungle is during the dry season, from April to October. During the wet season (November to April), it is oppressively hot (40°C and above) and while it only rains for a few hours at a time, which is not enough to spoil your trip, it is enough to make some roads virtually impassable, making travel more difficult.

The high season for foreign tourism is from June to September (but year-round in Cuzco, the Sacred Valley and Machu Picchu) while domestic tourism peaks on national holidays: Christmas, Carnaval, Semana Santa and Fiestas Patrias. Prices rise and accommodation and bus tickets are harder to come by. If you will be travelling during these time, buy your tickets in advance.

## Festivals

Every bit as important as knowing where to go and what the weather will be like is Peru's festival calendar. At any given time of the year there'll be a festival somewhere in the country, drawing people from miles around. Check the website of **iPerú** ⓘ *www.peru.travel*, and see the Festivals listings under each relevant town. For more information on the historic roots behind Peru's festivals, see page 465. For public holidays, see page 500.

**January   Marinera** festival, Trujillo. An opportunity to see performances of this emblematic dance.

**First week of February   Fiesta of the Virgen de la Candelaria**, takes place along the shores of Lake Titicaca near the Bolivian border and features dance groups from around the region.

**February/March/April   Carnaval** is held over the weekend before Ash Wednesday. **Semana Santa** (Holy Week) ends on Easter Sunday. Accommodation and transport is heavily booked and prices rise considerably. Book tickets and make hotel bookings early.

**1-3 May   Fiesta de la Cruz** is held over much of the central and southern highlands and on the coast.

**June   Festival del Andinismo**, in Huaraz, a week-long mountaineering festival held at the beginning of the month. In Cuzco, the entire month is one huge fiesta, culminating in **Inti Raymi**, on 24th, one of Peru's prime tourist attractions. This date is also celebrated for **San Juan** in the jungle lowlands.

**29 June   San Pedro y San Pablo** are celebrated throughout Peru, especially along the coast.

**30 August   Santa Rosa de Lima**, in Lima.

**September   Spring festival**, in Trujillo. Another opportunity to see Marinera dancers.

**October   Señor de los Milagros**, Lima, held on several dates throughout the month.

**1 November   Todos los Santos** (All Saints' Day).

**8 December   Festividad de la Inmaculada Concepción**.

# What to do

## Birdwatching

Peru is one of the top countries in the world for birdwatching. Its varied geography and topography, and its wilderness areas encompassing so many different life zones have endowed it with outstanding biodiversity. Peru vies with neighbouring Colombia for the highest number of bird species (over 1800) of any one country. Birds breed all year round, but there's a definite peak in breeding activity – and consequently birdsong – just before the rains come in October, and this makes it rather easier to locate many birds between September and Christmas. See http://perubirds.org and www.peru.travel for further details.

Details of the following key sites are given in the main travelling text: Paracas National Reserve; Lomas de Lachay; Huascarán Biosphere Reserve; Chiclayo and the route via Abra Patricia to Moyobamba; Iquitos; Manu Biosphere Reserve; and Tambopata National Reserve. More information on the birds of Peru is given in the Flora and fauna section on page 477.

## Climbing

The Cordillera Blanca is an ice climber's paradise. It takes just one or two days to reach the snowline on most mountains in the most intensive grouping of glaciated peaks in South America. The statistics are impressive: more than 50 summits between 5000 m and 6000 m (with over 20 surpassing 6000 m); and 663 glaciers. It is not unusual for climbers to reach three or more 6000-m summits, climbed Alpine-style, during a three-week trip. The degree of difficulty ranges from Pisco (5752 m), an excellent acclimatizer or novice's mountain (still demanding), to Copa (6173 m), of moderate difficulty, and the tremendous challenges of Alpamayo (5947 m), Artesonraju (6025 m), Quitaraju (6036 m) and Ranrapalca (6162 m). Huaraz is the main climbing centre in the Cordillera Blanca and has good infrastructure. It is home to the **Asociación de Guías de Montaña del Perú** (Peruvian Mountain Guide Association, www.agmp.pe).

The Huayhuash is a little more remote; Chiquián, northwest of the range, and Cajatambo to the south have fewer facilities for climbers. It is possible to contact guides, *arrieros*, porters and cooks in Chiquián, although it is best to enquire in Huaraz first. The Huayhuash is also accessible from Huánuco. It has some of the most spectacular ice walls in Peru. The Jirishancas and Yerupajas (Grande and Chico) are the most popular and demanding.

The cordilleras Vilcabamba and Vilcanota have the splendid peaks of Salkantay (6271 m) and Ausangate (6398 m), among others, but Cuzco is less developed for climbing. This is one of the genuine attractions of Peruvian *andinismo* – there is always another mountain more remote to feed the appetite. Huagurunchu (5730 m), for instance, in the central Andes, is barely known, and Coropuna, Peru's third highest at 6425 m, climbed in 1911 by Annie Smith Peck from the USA, is seldom visited these days.

Rock climbing is great in the *quebradas*, where the rock is most solid (frost-shattered higher up). This is becoming increasingly popular, particularly in the Quebrada de Llaca, near Huaraz, and for beginners at Monterrey. Other rock climbs in the Huaraz area include the boulders of Huanchac, the 'Sphinx' (or Torre de Parón), Hatun Machay, and routes in the Rurec Valley.

## Community tourism

*Turismo vivencial* is growing in popularity throughout Peru and provides worthwhile opportunities to stay with Peruvian families, participate in their daily activities and become acquainted with their customs and beliefs. By helping to weed the crops and tend the flocks, or dancing at a fiesta, you can gain a better appreciation for your hosts and their way of life. Community tourism programs are usually organized by rural communities in collaboration with agencies in nearby tourist centres. Look for them in the What to do sections throughout this book.

## Diving

Diving off the Paracas Peninsula is rewarding, as is the warmer tropical ocean with larger fish off Tumbes. It is also practised in the Bahía de Pucusana. The best season for visibility is March to November because the rivers from the mountains don't deposit silt into the sea at this time. Operators are listed in the What to do sections throughout the book; the website www.perudivers.com is a good place to start. If you plan to dive make sure that you are fit to do so. The **British Sub-Aqua Club (BSAC**, www.bsac. com) can put you in touch with doctors who will carry out medical examinations. Check that any dive companies you use are reputable and have the appropriate certification from the **Professional Association of Diving Instructors (PADI)**, www.padi.com, which has offices and centres worldwide.

## Kayaking

Peru offers outstanding whitewater kayaking for all standards of paddlers from novice to expert. Some first descents remain untested owing to logistical difficulties, though they are slowly being ticked off by a dedicated crew of local and internationally renowned kayakers. For the holiday paddler, it's probably best to join up with a rafting company (listed in the What to do sections throughout the book), who will carry your gear (plus any non-paddling companions) and provide you with food and camping gear while you enjoy the river from an unladen kayak. There is a small selection of kayaks available in Peru for hire from about US$25-35 a day. For complete novices, some companies offer two- to three-day kayak courses on the Urubamba and Apurímac rivers that can be booked locally. Kayaking is also offered on Lake Titicaca. For expedition paddlers, bringing your own kayak is the best option, though it is becoming increasingly expensive to fly with your boats around Peru. Knowledge of Spanish is indispensable in off-the-beaten-path locations.

## Mountain biking

With its amazing diversity of trails, tracks and rough roads, Peru is surely one of the last great mountain-bike destinations yet to be fully discovered. Whether you are interested in a two-day downhill blast from the Andes to the Amazon jungle or an extended off-road journey, then Peru has some of the world's best biking opportunities. The problem is finding the routes, as trail maps are virtually non-existent and main roads are often congested with traffic and far from fun to travel. A few specialist agencies run by dedicated mountain bikers offer single tracks and dirt roads that criss-cross the Andes, putting together exciting routes to suit every type of cyclist. Useful contacts include **Amazonas Explorer** (www.amazonas-explorer.com); **Beinhart Peru** (klaushartlperu@gmx.de); **Mountain Bike Adventures** (www.chakinaniperu.com) and **Perú Bike** (www.perubike.com). When signing up for a mountain-bike trip, remember that you are in the Andes so if you are worried about your fitness and the altitude, make sure you do a predominantly downhill trip.

Some companies offer imported high-quality, full-suspension mountain bikes with hydraulic disc brakes; others are less flash. Whatever the original quality of the bike, check that it has been properly and regularly maintained and that the guide gives you a full explanation of how to ride it properly. Poorly maintained bikes can be dangerous, and you may have very little come back after an accident, especially if booking and paying from overseas. Trips should have a support vehicle for the duration, not just to drop you off and meet you at the end. Guides should carry a first aid kit and a puncture repair kit at the very least (a comprehensive tool kit is preferable); they should also be knowledgeable about bike mechanics. Bikes do go wrong, punctures are frequent and people do fall off, so it is essential that your guide provides this minimum cover.

## Parapenting and hang-gliding

*Vuelo libre* is its name in Peru. Flying from the coastal cliffs is easy and the thermals are good. The Callejón de Huaylas is more risky owing to variable thermals, crosswinds and a lack of good landing sites, but there is a strong allure to flying at 6000 m in front of the glaciers of Huascarán. The area with the greatest potential is the Sacred Valley of Cuzco, which has excellent launch sites, thermals and reasonable landing sites. The season in the sierra is May to October, with the best months being August and September. Some flights in Peru have exceeded 6500 m.

While the attraction of parapenting or hang-gliding in the sierras is very great, with mountains on all sides and steep valleys below, most pilots are to be found in Lima. Arranging a tandem jump or a course is easy: just go to Parque del Amor in Miraflores in the afternoon and see who is hanging around waiting for the thermals and the breeze. Jumping off the cliff gives a completely different perspective on the city as you fly above the Pacific breakers and the traffic on the coastal highway, with a pelican's view of the blocks of flats and offices. There are other launch sites on the coast south of Lima, in the Callejón de Huaylas, Arequipa, the central highlands and in the Cuzco region.

Operators in Lima include **Aeroxtreme** (www.aeroxtreme.com), **Fly Adventure** (www.flyadventure.net), **Infinity** (www.infinitycross.com) and **Peru Fly** (www.perufly.com). Also see What to do, on page 68.

## Rafting

Peru is a premier destination for whitewater rafting. Several of its rivers are rated in the world's top 10 and a rafting trip, be it for one or 10 days, is now high on any adventurer's 'must-do' list of activities while travelling in Peru. It is not just the adrenalin rush of big rapids that attract, it is the whole experience of accessing areas beyond the reach of motor vehicles that few if any have ever visited. This may be tackling sheer-sided, mile-deep canyons, travelling silently through pristine rainforest, or canoeing across the stark altiplano, high in the Andes.

If you are looking to join a rafting expedition of some length, then it is definitely worth signing up before arriving in Peru. Some long expeditions

have fewer than two or three scheduled departures a year and the companies that offer them only accept bookings well in advance. For the popular day trips and expeditions on the Apurímac there are regular departures (the latter in the dry season only). If you can spare a couple of days to wait for a departure then it is fine to book in Cuzco. It also gives you the chance to talk to the company that will be operating your tour. There are day-trip departures all year and frequent multi-day departures in the high season. Note that the difficulty of the sections changes between the dry and rainy season; some become extremely difficult or impassable in the rainy season (December-March). The dry season is April/May to September (but can be as late as November).

For more information on staying safe when rafting, see box, page 237.

## Surfing

Peru is a top, internationally renowned surfing destination. Its main draws are the variety of waves and the year-round action. Point breaks, left and right reef breaks and waves of up to 6 m can all be found from September to February in the north and from March to December in the south, though May is often ideal south of Lima.

Ocean swells are affected by two currents: the warm El Niño in the north and the cold Humboldt current in the south arriving from Antarctica. Pimentel, near Chiclayo, is the dividing point between these two effects, but a wet suit is normally required anywhere south of Piura.

The biggest wave is at Pico Alto (sometimes 6 m in May), south of Lima, and the largest break is 800 m at Chicama, near Trujillo. There are more than 30 top surfing beaches. North of Lima these include: Chicama, Pacasmayo, Punta Tur, Punta Nonura, El Golf, Cabo Blanco, Los Organos and Máncora (all left break). South of Lima the best beaches are: Punta Hermosa, Punta Rocas (right break) and Pico Alto (right break, best in May), the pick of the bunch. Huaico/Santa Rosa (left break), Cabo Negro (left break), Sangallán (right break); El Olón and Piedras Negras (left breaks) and Caleta La Cruz (right break), are all near Ilo.

International competitions are held at Pico Alto (Balin Open in May) and Punta Rocas (during the summer months). For further information, contact **Eco-Innovation Tours** (www.eco-innovationtours.com); **Federación Deportiva Nacional de Tabla** (Fenta; www.surfingperu.com.pe); **Olas Peru Surf Travel** (www.olasperusurftravel.com and www.olasperu.com) and **Peru Surf Guides** (www.perusurfguides.com). A surfing magazine, *Tablista*, is published bimonthly. Also look out for the free *X3Mag*.

## Trekking

Peru has some of the finest trekking opportunities in all of South America. The best known routes around the *nevados* include the Llanganuco – Santa Cruz circuit in the Cordillera Blanca, the Ausangate circuit in the Cordillera Vilcanota, several Salkantay treks in the Cordillera Vilcabamba and a popular trek all around the Cordillera Huayhuash. Other good areas include the Colca and Cotahuasi canyons as well as the Nor Yauyos-Cochas Reserve in the upper Cañete Valley.

The other type of trekking for which Peru is justifiably renowned is walking among ruins and, above all, for the Inca Trail. However, there are very many other walks of this type in a country rich in archaeological heritage. Indeed, it is difficult to go hiking in Peru without stumbling on something of archaeological interest. Some of the best are: the valley of the Río Atuen near Leymebamba and the entire Chachapoyas region; the Tantamayo ruins above the Marañón; and beyond Machu Picchu to Vilcabamba and Choquequirao. People tend to think

of the Inca Trail to Machu Picchu as the only stretch of Inca roadway that can be walked. It is, however, just a tiny fraction of the vast Inca road network; see box, Stairway to heaven, page 364.

Most walking is on clear trails, well-trodden by the *campesinos* who populate most parts of the Peruvian Andes. If you camp on their land, ask permission first and, of course, do not leave any litter. Tents, sleeping bags, mats and stoves can easily be hired in Huaraz and Cuzco, but check carefully for quality. If you have your own trusted gear, it is best to bring it with you.

Some trekking and climbing companies show very little concern for their clients regarding acute mountain sickness, which is a risk in the Andes. Many commercial treks are unfortunately scheduled faster than would be ideal for acclimatization. If you trek independently, then you are free to go at your own pace.

See the colour section for more detailed descriptions of some of the treks listed above and **Trekking Peru** (www.trekkingperu.org) for complete background information and 30 trekking routes in nine regions of Peru. For additional advice, contact the **Asociación de Guías de Montaña del Perú** (www.agmp.pe).

## Volunteering

Devoting time to help an NGO or local community work with environmental or social projects is a great way to get to know the 'real Peru', warts and all. A more-than-basic knowledge of Spanish is essential and you should be prepared to spend at least one month to do anything worthwhile. The **Amauta Spanish School** (www.amautaspanish.com) offers various volunteering opportunities. In Huanchaco, **Otra Cosa Network** (www.otracosa.org) arranges volunteer placements in the north of the country. Projects which aim to get children away from the street and into schools include **Seeds of Hope, Huaraz** (www.seedsofhope.pe), and **Luz de Esperanza**, Huancayo (www.peruluz deesperanza.com). Additional volunteer opportunities are listed in the main text.

# Shopping tips

Almost everyone who visits Peru will end up buying a souvenir of some sort from the vast array of arts and crafts (*artesanía*) on offer. The best and cheapest place to shop for souvenirs, and pretty much anything else in Peru, is in the street markets that can be found absolutely everywhere. The country also has its share of shiny, modern shopping centres, but remember that the high overheads are reflected in the prices.

**What to buy and where to find it**

It is possible to find all kinds of **handicrafts** in Lima. Recommended buys are: hand-spun and hand-woven textiles; manufactured textiles in indigenous designs; llama and alpaca wool products such as ponchos, rugs, hats, blankets, slippers, coats and sweaters; *arpilleras* (appliqué pictures of Peruvian life), which are made with great skill and originality by women in the shanty towns; and fine leather products that are mostly handmade. Another good buy is clothing made from high-quality Pima cotton, grown in Peru.

The *mate burilado*, or engraved gourd found in every tourist shop, is cheap and one of the most genuine expressions of folk art in Peru. These are cheaper if bought in the villages of Cochas Grande or Cochas Chico near Huancayo in the central highlands. The Mantaro Valley is generally renowned for its folk culture, including all manner of *artesanía*.

**Alpaca clothing**, such as sweaters, hats and gloves, is cheaper in the sierra, especially in Puno. Another good source is Arequipa, where alpaca cloth for suits, coats, etc (mixed with 40% sheep's wool) can be bought cheaply from factories. Lima is more expensive, but may be the best bet in terms of quality. Note that if you want to make sure you're buying genuine alpaca, check that it is odourless when wet or dry; wet llama, in contrast, stinks.

One of the best places in Peru to look for *artesanía* is Ayacucho in the central highlands. Here you'll find excellent woven textiles, as well as the beautifully intricate **retablos**, or Saint Mark's boxes. Cuzco is one of the main weaving centres and a good place to shop for textiles, as well as excellent woodcarvings. Also recommended for textiles is Cajamarca. The island of Taquile on Lake Titicaca is a good place to buy *ch'uspas* (bags for coca leaves), *chumpis* (belts) and *chullos* (knitted hats with traditional ear flaps). For a more detailed look at Peruvian arts and crafts, see page 459. For tips on bargaining, see page 404.

## Improve your travel photography

Taking pictures is a highlight for many travellers, yet too often the results turn out to be disappointing. Steve Davey, author of Footprint's *Travel Photography*, sets out his top rules for coming home with pictures you can be proud of.

### Before you go
Don't waste precious travelling time and do your research before you leave. Find out what festivals or events might be happening or which day the weekly market takes place, and search online image sites such as Flickr to see whether places are best shot at the beginning or end of the day, and what vantage points you should consider.

### Get up early
The quality of the light will be better in the few hours after sunrise and again before sunset – especially in the tropics when the sun will be harsh and unforgiving in the middle of the day. Sometimes seeing the sunrise is a part of the whole travel experience: sleep in and you will miss more than just photographs.

### Stop and think
Don't just click away without any thought. Pause for a few seconds before raising the camera and ask yourself what you are trying to show with your photograph. Think about what things you need to include in the frame to convey this meaning. Be prepared to move around your subject to get the best angle. Knowing the point of your picture is the first step to making sure that the person looking at the picture will know it too.

### Compose your picture
Avoid simply dumping your subject in the centre of the frame every time you take a picture. If you compose with it to one side, then your picture can look more balanced. This will also allow you to show a significant background and make the picture more meaningful. A good rule of thumb is to place your subject or any significant detail a third of the way into the frame; facing into the frame not out of it.

This rule also works for landscapes. Compose with the horizon two-thirds of the way up the frame if the foreground is the most interesting part of the picture; one-third of the way up if the sky is more striking.

Don't get hung up with this so-called Rule of Thirds, though. Exaggerate it by pushing your subject out to the edge of the frame if it makes a more interesting picture; or if the sky is dull in a landscape, try cropping with the horizon near the very top of the frame.

### Fill the frame
If you are going to focus on a detail or even a person's face in a close-up portrait, then be bold and make sure that you fill the frame. This is often a case of physically getting in close. You can use a telephoto setting on a zoom lens but this can lead to pictures looking quite flat; moving in close is a lot more fun!

### Interact with people

If you want to shoot evocative portraits then it is vital to approach people and seek permission in some way, even if it is just by smiling at someone. Spend a little time with them and they are likely to relax and look less stiff and formal. Action portraits where people are doing something, or environmental portraits, where they are set against a significant background, are a good way to achieve relaxed portraits. Interacting is a good way to find out more about people and their lives, creating memories as well as photographs.

### Focus carefully

Your camera can focus quicker than you, but it doesn't know which part of the picture you want to be in focus. If your camera is using the centre focus sensor then move the camera so it is over the subject and half press the button, then, holding it down, recompose the picture. This will lock the focus. Take the now correctly focused picture when you are ready.

Another technique for accurate focusing is to move the active sensor over your subject. Some cameras with touch-sensitive screens allow you to do this by simply clicking on the subject.

### Leave light in the sky

Most good night photography is actually taken at dusk when there is some light and colour left in the sky; any lit portions of the picture will balance with the sky and any ambient lighting. There is only a very small window when this will happen, so get into position early, be prepared and keep shooting and reviewing the results. You can take pictures after this time, but avoid shots of tall towers in an inky black sky; crop in close on lit areas to fill the frame.

### Bring it home safely

Digital images are inherently ephemeral: they can be deleted or corrupted in a heartbeat. The good news though is they can be copied just as easily. Wherever you travel, you should have a backup strategy. Cloud backups are popular, but make sure that you will have access to fast enough WI-FI. If you use RAW format, then you will need some sort of physical back-up. If you don't travel with a laptop or tablet, then you can buy a backup drive that will copy directly from memory cards.

*Available in both digital and print formats, Footprint's Travel Photography by Steve Davey covers everything you need to know about travelling with a camera, including simple post-processing. More information is available at www.footprinttravelguides.com*

# Where to stay

from luxury hotels to wild camping and everything in between

Accommodation is plentiful throughout the price ranges and finding a hotel room to suit your budget should not present any problems, especially in the main tourist areas and larger towns and cities. The exception to this is during the Christmas and Easter holiday periods, during Carnival, Cuzco in June and for the Independence celebrations at the end of July, when all hotels are crowded and prices rise. It's advisable to book in advance at these times and also during school holidays and local festivals, see page 18. All accommodation registered with **iPeru** is listed on their website, www.peru.travel.

## Hotels, hostales, pensiones and hospedajes

There are many top-class hotels in Lima and Cuzco and in the main tourist centres, such as Arequipa, Puno, Iquitos and Trujillo. In less-visited places the choice of better-class hotels is more limited. Accommodation is more expensive in Lima, Cuzco and in jungle cities such as Iquitos and Puerto Maldonado. It also tends to be pricier in the north compared with the south, especially on the coast. If you want a room with air conditioning, expect to pay around 30% extra.

All hotels in the upper price brackets charge 18% sales tax (IGV) and 10% service on top of prices (foreigners should not have to pay the sales tax on hotel rooms; neither tax is included in prices given in the accommodation listings, unless specified). The more expensive hotels charge in dollars.

## Price codes

**Where to stay**

$$$$ over US$150

$$$ US$66-150

$$ US$30-65

$ under US$30

Price of a double room in high season, including taxes.

**Restaurants**

$$$ over US$12

$$ US$7-12

$ US$6 and under

Prices for a two-course meal for one person, excluding drinks or service charge.

Terms used to describe a place to stay in Peru are: *hotel*, *hostal*, *residencial* and *alojamiento*, in decreasing order of size and price, but good quality and value can be found in any category. Many larger hotels have their own restaurants serving lunch and dinner, as well as breakfast. Most hotels in our **$$** category and above will include breakfast. At the upper end this may be an excellent buffet while budget places may serve only a very basic breakfast or none at all; ask in advance. Most places are friendly and helpful, irrespective of the price, particularly smaller *alojamientos* and *hospedajes*, which are often family-run and might treat you as a member of the family.

The cheapest (and often the nastiest) hotels can be found near markets and bus stations. If you're just passing through and need a bed for the night, then they may be acceptable. Better-value accommodation is generally found on and around the main plaza.

Online hotel bookings are very common in Peru but almost always more expensive because the cost of commissions charged by booking sites is inevitably passed on to consumers. Bookings can also be made by phone, generally without paying a deposit. Also keep in mind that advance bookings are not indispensable outside peak travel periods (see above). Whenever possible, the authors prefer to choose their lodgings in person and on site.

## Youth hostels

The office of the Youth Hostel Association of Peru, **Asociación Peruana de Albergues Turísticos Juveniles** and **Administradora Peruana Hostelling International** ⓘ *Av Casimiro Ulloa 328, Miraflores, Lima T01-446 5488, www. hostellingperu.com.pe*, has information about youth hostels.

## Camping

Camping on trekking routes and in wilderness areas is delightful, but there can be problems with robbery when camping near towns or villages, where it is safer to ask permission to camp in someone's backyard or *chacra* (farmland). Most Peruvians are used to campers, but in some remote places people may never have seen a tent. Be casual about it; do not unpack all your gear, rather leave it inside your tent (especially at night), and never leave a tent unattended. Camping gas in screw-top containers is available in the main cities. Those with stoves designed for white-gas should use *bencina*, available from hardware stores (*ferreterías*) in larger towns.

# Food
# & drink

seafood, guinea pig and high-end gastronomy

## Food

### Coastal cuisine

The best coastal dishes are seafood-based, the most popular being *ceviche*. This is a dish of raw white fish marinated in lemon juice, onion and hot peppers. Traditionally, *ceviche* is served with corn-on-the-cob, *cancha* (toasted corn), yucca and sweet potatoes. *Tiradito* is *ceviche* without onions made with plaice. Another mouth-watering fish dish is *escabeche* – fish with onions, hot peppers, sweet red peppers, vinegar, cumin, hard-boiled eggs and olives (it can also be made vegetarian or with chicken). For fish on its own, don't miss the excellent *corvina*, or white sea bass. You should also try *chupe de camarones*, which is a shrimp stew made with varying ingredients. Other fish dishes include *parihuela*, a popular bouillabaisse which includes *yuyo de mar*, a tangy seaweed, and *aguadito*, a thick rice and fish soup said to have rejuvenating powers.

A favourite northern coastal dish is *seco de cabrito*, roasted kid (baby goat) served with beans and rice, or *seco de cordero* which uses lamb instead. Also good is *ají de gallina*, a rich and spicy creamed chicken. *Humitas* are sweet or savoury dumplings made with maize.

The *criollo* cooking of the coast has a strong tradition and can be found throughout the country. A dish almost guaranteed to appear on every restaurant menu is *lomo saltado*, a kind of stir-fried beef with onions, vinegar, ginger, chilli, tomatoes and fried potatoes, served with rice. Other popular examples of *comida criolla* are *cau cau*, made with tripe, potatoes, peas, carrots, peppers and parsley and served with rice, and *anticuchos*, which are grilled kebabs of beef heart with garlic, peppers, cumin seeds and vinegar. *Rocoto relleno* is a very spicy hot pepper stuffed with beef and vegetables, often served with *pastel de papas*, potato slices baked with eggs and cheese, to cool the fire. *Palta rellena* is avocado filled with chicken, tuna or potato salad. *Estofado de carne* is a beef stew and *carne en adobo* is a cut and seasoned steak.

*Causa* is made from mashed potatoes with lemon juice, layered with a filling of crabmeat, tuna or vegetable salad; it is served with marinated onions.

## Highland cuisine

The staples of highland cooking, corn and potatoes, come in a variety of shapes, sizes and colours. A popular potato dish is *papa a la huancaína*, which is topped with a spicy sauce made with *Leche Gloria* (the ubiquitous tinned evaporated milk) and cheese. The most popular corn dishes include *choclo con queso,* corn on the cob with cheese, and *tamales,* boiled corn dumplings filled with meat and wrapped in a banana leaf. Most typical of highland food is *pachamanca,* a combination of meats (beef, lamb, pork, chicken), potatoes, sweet potatoes, corn, beans, cheese and corn *humitas,* all slow-cooked in the ground, dating back to Inca times.

Meat dishes are many and varied. *Olluco con charqui* is a kind of potato with dried meat; *sancochado* is meat and all kinds of vegetables stewed together and seasoned with ground garlic; *chicharrones* are deep-fried chunks of pork or chicken or fish; and *lechón* is roast pork. A popular delicacy in the highlands is *cuy,* guinea pig. Very filling and good value are the many soups (*sopas*) and broths (*caldos*) on offer, such as *caldo de carnero, caldo verde* and *caldo de cabeza,* which includes a sheep's head cooked with corn and tripe. Also *yacu-chupe,* a green soup made from potato, with cheese, garlic, coriander, parsley, peppers, eggs, onions and mint, and *sopa a la criolla* containing thin noodles, beef heart, egg, vegetables and pleasantly spiced.

## Jungle cuisine

The main ingredient in jungle cuisine is river fish such as *dorado,* and especially the succulent, dolphin-sized *paiche,* which comes with the delicious *palmito,* or palm-hearts, yucca and fried bananas. *Tacacho* is plantain, cooked and ground to a chunky paste, usually served with pork (*cecina*) or sausage (*chorizo*). *Juanes* are a jungle version of *tamales,* filled with chicken and rice.

Peruvian **fruits** are of very good quality: they include bananas, citrus, pineapple (*piña*), avocado (*palta*), eggfruit (*lúcuma*), custard apple (*chirimoya*), quince (*membrillo*), papaya, mango, guava (*guayaba*), passion-fruit (*granadilla* and *maracuyá*) and soursop (*guanábana*).

## Drink

The most famous Peruvian drink is *pisco,* a clear brandy which, with egg white and lime juice, makes the famous pisco sour. The most renowned brands come from the Ica Valley. The best wines are also from Ica: *Tabernero, Tacama* (especially its Selección Especial and Terroix labels), *Ocucaje* and *Santiago Queirolo* (in particular its Intipalka label). Beer is of the lager type, the best known brands being *Cusqueña* and *Arequipeña* (lager) and *Trujillo Malta* (porter).

In Lima *Cristal* and *Pilsen* are the main commercial beers. Other brands, including some foreign beers, are on the market, but there is little difference between any of them. Seek out the microbreweries which are springing up in Huaraz, Cuzco and other tourist centres. *Chicha de jora* is a maize beer, usually home-made and served in highland communities during traditional celebrations, refreshing but strong; *chicha morada* is a very popular non-alcoholic beverage made with purple maize. The local rival to Coca Cola (but now owned by that US multinational) is the fluorescent yellow *Inca Kola*, see box, page 54. Peru produces very good coffee for export but instant remains the lowest common denominator for domestic consumption. There are many different kinds of *mate* (herbal tea): the most common are *manzanilla* (camomile), *menta* (mint) and *anís* (aniseed). *Mate de coca* is frequently served in the highlands to stave off the discomforts of altitude sickness.

## Eating out

A mid-range lunch or dinner costs US$5-8, but can go up to about US$80, with drinks and wine, in a first-class Lima restaurant (see Lima Restaurants, page 59, and Gastronomic Lima, page 60, for information on high-end dining). Middle- and high-class restaurants may add 10% service and 18% sales tax in the bill; this is not shown on the price list or menu, so check in advance. More economical restaurants usually charge only tax, while cheap simple eateries charge no taxes. Lunch (*almuerzo*) is the main meal and most restaurants serve one or two set lunch menus, called *menú ejecutivo* (US$4-5) or *menú económico* (US$2-3). Both have the advantage of being served almost immediately. The *menú ejecutivo* is a three-course meal with a drink and it offers greater choice and usually more interesting dishes. A *menú* may also be available for the evening meal (*cena*) but is usually less inspired.

*Pollerías*, serving *pollo a la brasa* (chicken roasted over coals or a wood fire) accompanied by chips and sometimes a salad bar, are ubiquitous and very popular with Peruvians in the evening. Chinese restaurants (*chifas*) are also common and some serve good food at reasonable prices. Simple economical vegetarian restaurants are increasingly present in larger towns and cities.

Most cheaper restaurants have blaring TVs, a must for local patrons but not conducive to relaxed dining.

# Menu reader

**Ají** Hot pepper, found on every table as either a sauce or pepper slices, served with lemon wedges meant for squeezing into the soup.

**Ají de gallina** Strips of chicken in a spicy cream sauce.

**Almuerzo** The midday meal. A set lunch is called *menú*, see Eating out, opposite.

**Anticuchos** Kebabs of beef heart, popular street food.

**Arroz** Rice. White rice accompanies most dishes in Peru.

**Cabrito** Goat stew, typical of the north coast.

**Caigua rellena** A local vegetable stuffed with ground meat.

**Cau cau** Tripe.

**Causa rellena** Cold mashed potatoes with lemon juice, tuna or chicken salad and mayonnaise.

**Cebada** A non-alcoholic drink made from barley.

**Cebiche (ceviche)** The flagship of Peruvian cooking. Raw fish (*cebiche de pescado*) or fish and seafood (*cebiche mixto*) marinated in lemon juice, served mid-morning to lunchtime. It doesn't keep well and is best avoided in the evening.

**Cena** Supper or the equivalent of *menú* served in the evening, but usually less inspired.

**Chicha morada** Very popular non-alcoholic drink make from purple corn.

**Desayuno** Breakfast.

**Escabeche de pescado o pollo** Fried fish or chicken seasoned with pickled onions and hot peppers. May be served warm or cold.

**Gaseosa** Any soft drink.

**Juanes** Rice or manioc with bits of chicken, pork or fish, wrapped and steamed in *bijao* leaves, typical of the jungle.

**Lomo saltado** Strips of beef stir fired with potatoes, onions, tomatoes and hot peppers. Very popular with Peruvians and visitors alike.

**Manjar blanco** Spreadable soft toffee.

**Mazamorra morada** A purple cornflour pudding served as a snack or light dessert.

**Menú** The set midday meal served at economical restaurants, not to be confused with the English word 'menu' which is '*la carta*' in Spanish.

**Olluquito** Strips of *olluco*, a small tuber related to the potato, cooked with ground meat.

**Pallares** Lima beans.

**Palta rellena** Avocado filled with tuna or chicken salad.

**Papa a la huancaína** Slices of cold boiled potato in a spicy creamy cheese sauce.

**Papa rellena** Mashed-potato fritters filled with ground meat.

**Parihuela** A hearty fish and seafood chowder.

**Pastel de papas** Potato and cheese casserole.

**Pollo a la brasa** Barbecued chicken, a very popular evening meal.

**Pollo broster** Deep-fried battered chicken.

**Rocoto relleno** Hot peppers stuffed with ground meat.

**Salteado de vainitas** Green beans and potatoes fried with eggs, a relatively common vegetarian option.

**Sopa a la minuta** Beef soup with thin noodles.

**Sopa criolla** A hearty beef soup.

**Sudado de pecado** Fish served in its broth.

**Tallarín verde** Spaghetti in a green herb sauce, usually served with beef or liver.

**Tamales** Ground corn with bits of pork or chicken, wrapped and steamed in banana leaves.

# Lima

Peru's much-maligned capital deserves a second look

It is a well-established cliché to call Lima a city of contradictions. In this sprawling metropolis of 10 million inhabitants you'll encounter grinding poverty and conspicuous wealth in abundance. The hardships of the poor are all too evident along the streets you pass on the traffic-clogged drive from the airport.

Lima's image as a place to avoid or quickly pass through is enhanced by the thick grey blanket of chilly fog that descends in May and hangs around for the next seven months. Wait until the blanket is pulled aside in November to reveal bright blue skies, and, suddenly, Limeños descend on the city's beaches for a raucous mix of sun, sea, salsa and ceviche.

Lima can entertain, excite and inform. It boasts some of the finest historical monuments and museums in the country, and its colonial centre is one of Peru's UNESCO World Heritage Sites. Strenuous efforts are being made to refurbish the historical districts. Most visitors choose to stay in Miraflores, San Isidro or Barranco, where plush hotels and shiny shopping centres rub shoulders with pre-Inca pyramids. Here, restaurants serve the city's famed cuisine, and bars keep the party going into the small hours. Scratch beneath that coating of grime and traffic fumes and you'll find that Lima is one of the most vibrant and hospitable cities anywhere.

**Best** for
Cuisine ▪ Museums ▪ Nightlife

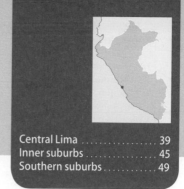

Central Lima . . . . . . . . . . . . . . . 39
Inner suburbs . . . . . . . . . . . . . 45
Southern suburbs . . . . . . . . . . 49

# Footprint picks

★ **Plaza de Armas**, page 39

Explore this square at the heart of colonial Lima.

★ **San Francisco**, page 40

Visit the catacombs and admire the lavish interior of this baroque church.

★ **Museo de la Nación**, page 46

Learn about the art and history of the aboriginal peoples of Peru at this unmissable museum.

★ **Museo Larco de Lima**, page 47

Gain an excellent overview of Peru's cultures through their pottery.

★ **Parque del Amor**, page 49

Escape the big city buzz for a stroll in this popular urban park.

★ **Barranco**, page 51

Discover Lima's contemporary art scene and then party the night away.

★ **Pachacámac**, page 53

Re-imagine the archaeological site as it was in its heyday, as the largest city and ceremonial centre on the coast of Peru.

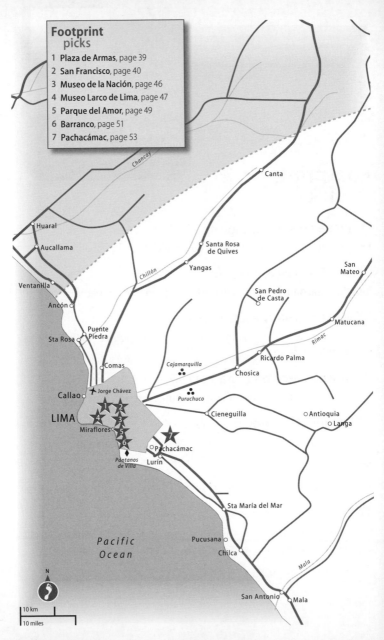

**Footprint**
picks

1  **Plaza de Armas**, page 39
2  **San Francisco**, page 40
3  **Museo de la Nación**, page 46
4  **Museo Larco de Lima**, page 47
5  **Parque del Amor**, page 49
6  **Barranco**, page 51
7  **Pachacámac**, page 53

*Chancay*

Canta

Huaral

Aucallama

Santa Rosa
de Quives

Ventanilla

*Chillón*

Yangas

San
Mateo

Ancón

San Pedro
de Casta

Sta Rosa

Puente
Piedra

*Rímac*

Matucana

Comas

*Cajamarquilla*

Ricardo Palma

Callao

Jorge Chávez

Chosica

**LIMA**

*Puruchuco*

4      3

Cieneguilla

Antioquia

Miraflores

5

Langa

6

Pachacámac

*Pantanos
de Villa*

Lurín

Sta María del Mar

*Pacific
Ocean*

Pucusana

Chilca

*Mala*

N

San Antonio

Mala

10 km
10 miles

# Essential Lima

## Finding your feet

All international flights land at Jorge Chávez airport in Callao, 16 km northwest of the centre; take a taxi or airport express bus. If arriving in Lima by bus, most of the terminals are just south of the historic centre on Avenida Carlos Zavala. This is not a safe area, take a taxi to and from there; better bus companies also have terminals in safer San Isidro. Miraflores is 15 km south of the centre. It has a good mix of places to stay, parks, great ocean views, bookstores, restaurants and cinemas. Neighbouring San Isidro is the poshest district, while Barranco, a little further south, is a centre for nightlife. Callao, Peru's major port, merges with Lima but is a city in its own right, with over one million inhabitants.

## Getting around

Downtown Lima can be explored on foot by day; at night a radio taxi is advised. Buses, combis and *colectivos* provide an extensive public transport system but are not entirely safe. Termini are posted above the windscreens, with the route written on the side. **Corredor Azul** buses run between Miraflores and downtown. There is also the Metropolitano rapid transit bus system and a limited metro service, neither of which is particularly useful for visitors. In most cases, taxis are the best way to travel between different districts. Bear in mind that Lima's roads are badly congested at all times of day, so allow plenty of time to get from A to B.

## Addresses

Several blocks, each with its own name, make up a *jirón* (often abbreviated to Jr). Street corner signs bear the names of both the *jirón* and the block. In the historic centre blocks also have their colonial names.

## Safety

Lima is a big metropolis with important public safety issues. Routine precautions and a street-smart attitude are advised. See page 500 for detailed suggestions on staying safe.

## When to go

Lima two distinct seasons. The winter is May to November, when a *garúa* (mist) hangs over the city, making everything grey, damp and cold. The sun breaks through around November and temperatures rise. The temperature in the coastal suburbs is lower than the centre because of the sea's influence.

## Time required

A few days are enough to see the highlights; a full week will allow more in-depth exploration.

## Weather Lima

| Month | Temp (high) | Temp (low) | Rain |
|-------|-------------|------------|------|
| January | 26°C | 20°C | 2mm |
| February | 26°C | 20°C | 1mm |
| March | 26°C | 20°C | 0.5mm |
| April | 24°C | 17°C | 0mm |
| May | 22°C | 15°C | 0mm |
| June | 20°C | 15°C | 4mm |
| July | 19°C | 15°C | 3mm |
| August | 18°C | 13°C | 9mm |
| September | 19°C | 13°C | 1mm |
| October | 20°C | 14°C | 1mm |
| November | 22°C | 16°C | 0.5mm |
| December | 24°C | 18°C | 0mm |

# Sights
## in Lima

Lima's colonial centre and suburbs, shrouded in fog which lasts eight months of the year, are fringed by the *pueblos jóvenes* which sprawl over the dusty hills overlooking the city. It has a great many historic buildings and some of the finest museums in the country and its food, drink and nightlife are second to none. Although not the most relaxing of South America's capitals, it is a good place to start before exploring the rest of the country.

## 1 Lima orientation

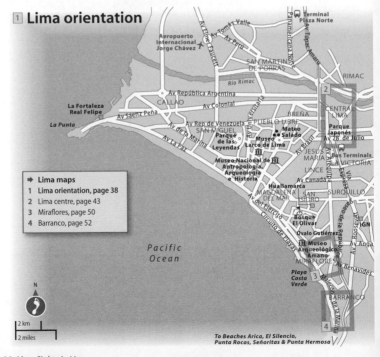

Lima maps
1 Lima orientation, page 38
2 Lima centre, page 43
3 Miraflores, page 50
4 Barranco, page 52

Pacific Ocean

N

2 km
2 miles

To Beaches Arica, El Silencio, Punta Rocas, Señoritas & Punta Hermosa

An increasing number of buildings in the centre are being restored and the whole area is being given a new lease of life as the architectural beauty and importance of the Cercado (as it is known) is recognized. Most of the tourist attractions are in this area. Some museums are only open 0900-1300 from January to March, and some are closed entirely in January.

## ★ Plaza de Armas (Plaza Mayor) and around

One block south of the Río Rímac lies the Plaza de Armas, or Plaza Mayor, which has been declared a World Heritage Site by UNESCO. Running along two sides are arcades with shops: Portal de Escribanos and Portal de Botoneros. In the centre of the plaza is a bronze fountain dating from 1650.

The **Palacio de Gobierno** ① *45-min tours in Spanish and English on Sat-Sun, book at least 2 days in advance at the palace tourist office (open Mon-Thu 0830-1900, T01-311 3900, ext 4308, or ask guard for directions)*, on the north side of the plaza, stands on the site of the original palace built by Pizarro. The changing of the guard is at 1145-1200.

The **cathedral** ① *T01-427 9647, Mon-Fri 0900-1700, Sat 1000-1300, Sun 1300-1700; entry to cathedral US$3, ticket also including Museo Arzobispado US$11,* was reduced to rubble in the earthquake of 1746. The reconstruction, on the lines of the original, was completed in 1755. Note the splendidly carved stalls (mid-17th century), the silver-covered altars surrounded by fine woodwork, mosaic-covered walls bearing the coats of arms of Lima and Pizarro and an allegory of Pizarro's commanders, the 'Thirteen Men of Isla del Gallo'. The remains of Francisco Pizarro, found in the crypt, lie in a small chapel, the first on the right of the entrance. The cathedral's **Museo de Arte Religioso** has sacred paintings, portraits, altar pieces and other items, as well as a café and toilets. Next to the cathedral is the **Archbishop's Palace and museum** ① *T01-427 5790, Mon-Sat 0900-1700*, rebuilt in 1924, with a superb wooden balcony. Permanent and temporary exhibitions are open to the public.

Just behind the Municipalidad de Lima is **Pasaje Ribera el Viejo**, which has been restored and is now a pleasant place, with several good cafés with outdoor seating. Nearby is the **Casa Solariega de Aliaga** ① *Unión 224, T01-427 7736, Mon-Fri 0930-1700 (daily with advance booking), US$11,*

*knock on the door and wait to see if anyone will let you in, or contact in advance for tour operators who offer guided visits.* It is still occupied by the Aliaga family and is open to the public and for functions. The house contains what is said to be the oldest ceiling in Lima and is furnished entirely in the colonial style. The **Casa de la Gastronomía Nacional Peruana**① *Conde de Superunda 170, T01-321 5627, Tue-Sun 0900-1700, www.limacultura.pe, US$1, behind the Correo Central,* has an extensive permanent collection of objects and displays on Peruvian food, historic and regional. It also has temporary exhibitions on the same theme. All signs are in Spanish.

## East of Plaza de Armas

The first two blocks of Calle Ancash, from Calle Carabaya (on the east side of the Palacio de Gobierno) to San Francisco church, have been designated the 'tourist circuit of the Calles El Rastro y Pescadería'. (These are the colonial names of these two blocks.) The circuit starts from **Desamparados railway station** (which now houses fascinating exhibitions on Peruvian themes) and includes the open-air **Museo de Sitio Bodega y Quadra** ① *Ancash 213, T01-420 2390, Tue-Sun 1000-1800, free* (which displays the foundations of an old building), the **Casa de la Literatura** ① *Ancash 207, T01-426 2573, www.casadelaliteratura.gob.pe, Tue-Sun 1000-1900, free* (with an exhibit about Peruvian identity and holds cultural events) and several historic houses. The area is fully pedestrianized.

At the end of the circuit is the baroque church of ★ **San Francisco** ① *1st block of Jr Lampa, corner of Ancash, T01-426 7377 ext 3, www.museocatacumbas.com, daily 0900-2015, guided tours only, US$2.75, students half price, US$0.40 children,* which was finished in 1674 and withstood the 1746 earthquake. The nave and aisles are lavishly decorated in Mudéjar style. The monastery is famous for the Sevillian tilework and panelled ceiling in the cloisters (1620). The catacombs under the church and part of the monastery are well worth seeing. The late 16th-century **Casa de Jarava** or **Pilatos** ① *Jr Ancash 390,* is opposite. Close by, **Casa de las Trece Monedas** ① *Jr Ancash 536,* still has the original doors and window grills. **Parque de la Muralla** ① *daily 0900-2000,* on the south bank of the Rímac, incorporates a section of the old city wall, fountains, stalls and street performers. There is a cycle track, toilets and places to eat both inside and near the entrance on Calle de la Soledad.

The **Palacio Torre Tagle** (1735) ① *Jr Ucayali 363, T01-204 2400, Mon-Fri 0830-1630, advance booking required,* is the city's best surviving example of secular colonial architecture. Today, it is used by the Foreign Ministry, but visitors are allowed to enter courtyards to inspect the fine Moorish-influenced wood-carving in balconies and wrought ironwork. At Ucayali 391 and also part of the Foreign Ministry is the Centro Cultural Inca Garcilaso, which holds cultural events. **Casa de la Rada**, or **Goyeneche** ① *Jr Ucayali 358,* opposite, is a fine mid 18th-century French-style town house which now belongs to a bank. The patio and first reception room are open occasionally to the public. **Museo Banco Central de Reserva** ① *Jr Ucayali at Jr Lampa, T01-613 2000 ext 22655, Tue-Sat 1000-1600, free, photography prohibited,* houses a large collection of pottery from the Vicus or Piura culture (AD 500-600) and gold objects from Lambayeque, as well as 19th- and 20th-century paintings: both sections are highly recommended. **San Pedro** ① *3rd block of Jr Ucayali, Mon-Sat 0800-1200, daily 1700-2000,* finished by Jesuits in 1638, has marvellous altars with Moorish-style balconies, rich gilded wood carvings in choir and vestry, and tiled throughout. Several Viceroys are buried here; the bell called La Abuelita, first rung in 1590, sounded the Declaration of Independence in 1821.

## BACKGROUND

### Lima

Lima, capital of Peru, is built on both sides of the Río Rímac, at the foot of Cerro San Cristóbal. It was originally named *La Ciudad de Los Reyes*, in honour of the Magi, at its founding by conquistador Francisco Pizarro in 1535. From then until the independence of the South American republics in the early 19th century, it was the chief city of Spanish South America. The name Lima, a corruption of the Quechua name *Rímac* (speaker), was not adopted until the end of the 16th century.

The Universidad de San Marcos was founded in 1551 and had a printing press in 1595, both among the earliest of their kind in South America. Lima's first theatre opened in 1563, and the Inquisition was introduced in 1569 (it was not abolished until 1820). For some time the Viceroyalty of Peru embraced Colombia, Ecuador, Bolivia, Chile and Argentina. There were few cities in the Old World that could rival Lima's power, wealth and luxury, which was at its height during the 17th and early 18th centuries. The city's wealth attracted many freebooters and in 1670 a protecting wall 11 km long was built round it, then destroyed in 1869. The earthquake of 1746 destroyed all but 20 houses, killed 4000 inhabitants and ended the city's pre-eminence. It was only comparatively recently, with the coming of industry and the arrival of migrants from the interior of Peru, that Lima began to change into what it is today.

Over the years the city has changed out of all recognition. The metropolitan area contains 10 million people, which equates to half the urban population of Peru and nearly one-third of the country's total population. Two-thirds of Peru's industries are located in the capital. Many of the hotels and larger businesses have relocated to the fashionable suburbs of Miraflores and San Isidro, thus moving the commercial heart of the city away from the Plaza de Armas. Modern Lima is seriously affected by smog for much of the year and is surrounded by poor grimy neighbourhoods. Many of these former squatters' camps of shacks in the desert have evolved into bustling working-class districts, home to millions of inhabitants and much of the city's commercial activity. They are generally not safe to visit on your own, but going accompanied by a local friend or guide can provide an eye-opening insight into the reality of life in Lima. See also page 48.

Between Avenida Abancay and Jirón Ayacucho is **Plaza Bolívar**, where General José de San Martín proclaimed Peru's independence. The plaza is dominated by the equestrian statue of the Liberator. Behind lies the Congress building which occupies the former site of the Universidad de San Marcos and is now the **Museo del Congreso y de la Inquisición** ① *Plaza Bolívar, C Junín 548, near the corner of Av Abancay, T01-311 7777, ext 5160, www. congreso.gob.pe/museo.htm, daily 0900-1700, free.* The main hall, with a splendidly carved mahogany ceiling, remains untouched. The Court of Inquisition was held here from 1584; between 1829 and 1938 it was used by the Senate. In the basement there is a recreation *in situ* of the gruesome tortures. A description in English is available at the desk and students will offer to show round for a tip.

Behind the Congress is the Mercado Municipal (or Central) and the Barrio Chino, with many *chifas* and small shops selling oriental items. Block 700 of Ucayali is pedestrianized in 'Chinese' style. The whole area is jam-packed with people.

## BACKGROUND

## Court of Inquisition

Established by Royal Decree in 1569, the Court of Inquisition in Lima soon proved to be a particularly cruel form of persecution, even by the standards of the day.

During its existence, the court meted out many horrific tortures on innocent people. Among the most fashionable methods of making the accused confess their 'sins' were burning, dismemberment and asphyxiation, to name but a few. The most common form of punishment was public flogging, followed by exile and death by burning. Up until 1776, 86 people were recorded as having been burned alive and 458 excommunicated.

Given that no witnesses were called except the informer and that the accused was not allowed to know the identity of the accuser, this may have been less a test of religious conviction than a means of settling old scores. This Kafkaesque nightmare was then carried into the realms of surreal absurdity during the process of judgement. A statue of Christ was the final arbiter of guilt or innocence but had to express its belief in the prisoner's innocence with a shake of the head. Needless to say, not too many walked free.

The Inquisition was abolished by the Viceroy in 1813 but was later reinstated before finally being proscribed in 1820.

### West of Plaza de Armas

The 16th-century **Santo Domingo church and monastery** ① *T01-426 5521, monastery and tombs daily 0930-1800; Sun and holidays morning only, US$1.65*, is on the first block of Jirón Camaná. The attractive first cloister dates from 1603. Beneath the sacristy are the tombs of San Martín de Porres, one of Peru's most revered saints, and Santa Rosa de Lima (see below). In 1669, Pope Clement presented the alabaster statue of Santa Rosa in front of the altar. Behind Santo Domingo is **Alameda Chabuca Granda**, named after one of Peru's greatest singers. In the evening there are free art and music shows and you can sample foods from all over Peru. A couple of blocks beyond Santo Domingo is **Casa de Osambela** or **Oquendo** ① *Conde de Superunda 298, T01-427 7987, Mon-Fri 0900-1245, 1400-1645, ask the caretaker if you can visit*. It is said that José de San Martín stayed here after proclaiming independence from Spain. The house is typical of Lima secular architecture with two patios, a broad staircase leading from the lower to the upper floor, fine balconies and an observation tower. It is now the Centro Cultural Inca Garcilaso de la Vega and headquarters of various academies. A few blocks west is **Santuario de Santa Rosa** ① *Av Tacna, 1st block, T01-425 1279, grounds open daily 0900-1300, 1500-1800, church daily 0800-1200, 1700-2000, free*, a small but graceful church and a pilgrimage centre, consisting of the hermitage built by Santa Rosa herself, the house in which she was born, a section of the house in which she attended to the sick, her well and other relics.

Due west of the Plaza de Armas is **San Agustín** ① *Jr Ica 251, T01-427 7548, daily 0830-1130, 1630-1900, ring for entry*, whose façade (1720) is a splendid example of churrigueresque architecture. There are carved choir stalls and effigies, and a sculpture of Death, said to have frightened its maker into an early grave. The church has been restored since the last earthquake, but the sculpture of Death is in storage. Further west, **Las Nazarenas church** ① *Av Tacna, 4th block, T01-423 5718, daily 0600-1300, 1600-*

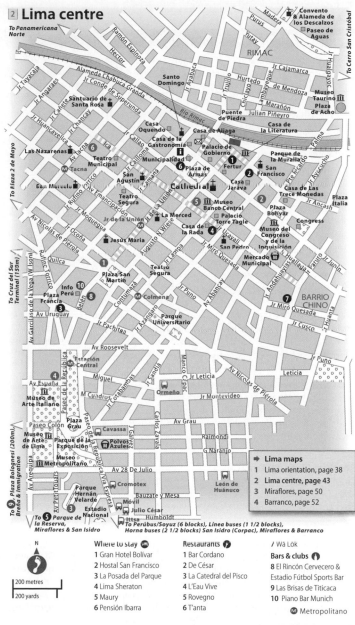

# 2 Lima centre

To Panamericana Norte

RIMAC

To Cerro San Cristóbal

Convento & Alameda de los Descalzos
Paseo de Aguas
Museo Taurino
Plaza de Acho

Alameda Chabuca Granda
Santo Domingo
Río Rímac
Puente de Piedra
Casa de la Literatura

Santuario de Santa Rosa
Casa Oquendo
Casa de Aliaga
Casa de la Trece Monedas
Plaza Italia

Las Nazarenas
Casa de la Gastronomía
Palacio de Gobierno
Parque de la Muralla
San Francisco

Teatro Municipal
Municipalidad
Plaza de Armas
Fertur
Casa Jarava

San Agustín
Catedral
Plaza Bolívar
Congress

Teatro Segura
Museo Banco Central
Museo del Congreso y de la Inquisición

La Merced
Palacio Torre Tagle
Mercado Municipal

Jesús María
Casa de la Rada
San Pedro

Plaza San Martín
Teatro Segura
BARRIO CHINO

Info Perú
Plaza Francia
Parque Universitario

Estación Central
Museo de Arte Italiano
Plaza Grau
Cavassa
Polvos Azules

Museo de Arte de Lima
Parque de la Exposición
Museo Metropolitano

Parque Hernán Velarde
Estadio Nacional
Cromotex

To Cruz del Sur Terminal (150m)
To Plaza 2 de Mayo
To Plaza Bolognesi (200m), Breña & Immigration
To Parque de la Reserva, Miraflores & San Isidro
To Perúbus/Soyuz (6 blocks), Línea buses (1 1/2 blocks), Horna buses (2 1/2 blocks) San Isidro (Corpac), Miraflores & Barranco

⇒ Lima maps
1 Lima orientation, page 38

2 Lima centre, page 43
3 Miraflores, page 50
4 Barranco, page 52

N

200 metres
200 yards

Where to stay
1 Gran Hotel Bolívar
2 Hostal San Francisco
3 La Posada del Parque
4 Lima Sheraton
5 Maury
6 Pensión Ibarra

Restaurants
1 Bar Cordano
2 De César
3 La Catedral del Pisco
4 L'Eau Vive
5 Rovegno
6 T'anta

7 Wà Lòk

Bars & clubs
8 El Rincón Cervecero & Estadio Fútbol Sports Bar
9 Las Brisas de Titicaca
10 Piano Bar Munich

Ⓜ Metropolitano

Lima Sights in Lima•43

## BACKGROUND

### Impressions of Lima

Ever since the earthquake of 1746 all but razed the city to the ground, descriptions of Lima have tended towards the unfavourable. Take the German naturalist and traveller Alexander Von Humboldt, for instance, who considered life in the city to be tedious with its lack of diversions, and described touring round the capital in 1802 thus: "The filthyness of the streets, strewn with dead dogs and donkeys, and the unevenness of the ground make it impossible to enjoy." Charles Darwin, who made a short visit in 1839 during his historic research trip on the *Beagle*, was no less graphic in his appraisal. He found it "in a wretched state of decay; the streets are nearly unpaved and heaps of filth are piled up in all directions where black vultures pick up bits of carrion."

Rather more complimentary was Jean Jacques Tschudi, the Swiss naturalist. He wrote: "The impression produced at first sight of Lima is by no means favourable, for the periphery, the quarter which the stranger first enters, contains none but old, dilapidated and dirty homes; but on approaching the vicinity of the principal square, the place improves so greatly that the miserable appearance it presents at first sight is easily forgotten."

The French feminist, Flora Tristan, who was Paul Gauguin's grandmother, came to Peru in 1834. She travelled extensively in the country and wrote a fascinating account of her experience, *Peregrinaciones de una Paria*, in which she painted Lima in a most favourable light: "The city has many beautiful monuments", she wrote: "The homes are neatly constructed, the streets well marked out, are long and wide." Paul Gauguin himself spent his formative years in Lima, where he was brought by his parents who were fleeing Napoleon Bonaparte's France. Towards the end of his life Gauguin wrote a collection of memoirs in which he included his impressions of Lima.

*2000,* is built around an image of Christ Crucified painted by a liberated slave in 1655. This is the most venerated image in Lima and is carried through the streets on a silver litter, along with an oil copy of El Señor de los Milagros (Lord of Miracles) encased in a gold frame (the whole weighing nearly a ton), on 18, 19 and 28 October and again on 1 November (All Saints' Day). *El Comercio* newspaper and local pamphlets give details of times and routes.

### South of Plaza de Armas

The Jirón de La Unión, the main shopping street, runs southwest from the Plaza de Armas. It has been converted into a pedestrian precinct which teems with life in the evening. In the two blocks south of Jirón Unión, known as Calle Belén, several shops sell souvenirs and curios. **La Merced** ① *Unión y Miró Quesada, T01-427 8199, Mon-Sat 0800-1245, 1600-2000, Sun 0700-1300, 1600-2000; monastery daily 0800-1200 and 1500-1730,* is in Plazuela de la Merced. The first Mass in Lima was said here on the site of the first church to be built. The restored façade is a fine example of colonial Baroque. Inside are some magnificent altars and the tilework on some of the walls is noteworthy. A door from the right of the nave leads into the Monastery. The cloister dates from 1546.

Jirón de la Unión leads to **Plaza San Martín**, which has a statue of San Martín in the centre. The plaza has been restored with colourful flower beds and is a nice place to sit and relax. On its west side is the refurbished **Gran Hotel Bolívar** ⓘ *Jr de la Unión 958, see Where to stay (page 55)*, which has a huge stained-glass dome over the entrance lobby. Its **El Bolivarcito** bar calls itself 'La Catedral del Pisco Sour'.

Further south, the **Museo de Arte Italiano** ⓘ *Paseo de la República 250, T01-321 5622, Tue-Sun 1000-1600, US$1,* is in a wonderful neoclassical building, given to Peru on the centenary of its independence. Note the remarkable mosaic murals on the outside. It consists of a large collection of Italian and other European works of art and houses the **Instituto de Arte Contemporáneo**, which has many exhibitions.

Across Avenida 9 de Diciembre from here is the **Parque de la Exposición**, inaugurated for the Lima International Exhibition in 1872. The **Palacio de la Exposición**, built in 1868, now houses the **Museo de Arte de Lima** ⓘ *Paseo Colón 125, T01-204 0000, www.mali.pe, Tue-Sun 1000-1900, Sat 1000-1700, US$9.35, students and over-65s half price, children under 8 free, reductions for Peruvians, free on Thu till 1500 and 1st Fri of month 1700-2200, bilingual guides available 1100-1600, signs in English.* There are more than 1200 exhibits from a collection of 17,000, giving a chronological history of Peruvian cultures and art from the Paracas civilization up to today. It includes excellent examples of 17th- and 18th-century Cuzco paintings, a beautiful display of carved furniture, heavy silver and jewelled stirrups and also pre-Columbian pottery. It also has theatre, film and concerts (see the website for details, or look in the museum itself), and a café.

The grounds now incorporate the **Gran Parque Cultural de Lima**. This large park has an amphitheatre, Japanese garden, food court and children's activities. Relaxing strolls through this green, peaceful and safe oasis in the centre of Lima are recommended. In the south of the park is the **Museo Metropolitano** ⓘ *Av 28 de Julio, www.limacultura.pe, Tue-Sun 1000-2000, US$2.50,* which has audiovisual displays and temporary exhibitions about the history of Lima; it also hosts lectures and has a library.

In **Parque de la Reserva** ⓘ *block 6 of Av Arequipa and Jr Madre de Dios opposite Estadio Nacional, Santa Beatriz, T01-424 0827, www.parquedelareserva.com.pe, Tue-Sun 0600-1000, 1530-2230,* is the **Circuito Mágico del Agua** ⓘ *displays at 1915, 2015, 2130, US$1.50,* a display of 13 fountains, the highest reaching 80 m, enhanced by impressive light and music shows. It's great fun and very popular.

## Inner suburbs
visit the major museums for an overview of Peru's history and culture

### Rímac and Cerro San Cristóbal
The **Puente de Piedra**, behind the Palacio de Gobierno, is a Roman-style stone bridge built in 1610, crossing the Río Rímac to the district of the same name. Although Rimac is experiencing a revival the area is not safe; go by taxi. On Jirón Hualgayoc is the bullring in the **Plaza de Acho**, inaugurated on 20 January 1766, with the **Museo Taurino** ⓘ *Hualgayoc 332, T01-481 1467, Mon-Sat 0900-1600, US$1, students US$0.50, photography US$2.* Apart from matador's relics, the museum contains good collections of paintings and engravings, some of the latter by Goya. There are two bullfight seasons: October to first week in December and during July.

The **Convento de Los Descalzos** ⓘ *Alameda de Los Descalzos, Rímac, T01-481 0441, Jan-Feb Mon-Sat 0930-1230, Mar-Dec daily 0930-1700, US$1, guided tour only, 45 mins in Spanish (worth it),* was founded in 1592. It contains over 300 paintings of the Cuzco, Quito and Lima schools which line the four main cloisters and two ornate chapels. The chapel of El Carmen was constructed in 1730 and is notable for its baroque gold leaf altar.

The museum shows the life of the Franciscan friars during colonial and early republican periods. The cellar, infirmary, pharmacy and a typical cell have been restored.

**Cerro San Cristóbal** dominates downtown Lima. It can be visited on a one-hour minibus tour ① *Camaná y Conde Superunda, every 15 mins daily 1000-2100, US$3*, departing from in front of Santo Domingo. The tour includes a look at the run-down Rímac district, passes the Convento de los Descalzos (see above), ascends the hill through one of the city's oldest shanties with its brightly painted houses and spends about 20 minutes at the summit, where there is a small museum and café. There are excellent views on a clear day. The second half of the trip is a historical tour. **Urbanito** buses ① *T01-424 3650, www. urbanito.com.pe,* also include Cerro San Cristóbal on their three-hour tour of central Lima, departing from the Plaza de Armas (weekends and holidays only).

## San Borja

★ **Museo de la Nación** ① *Javier Prado Este 2465, T01-618 9393 ext 2484, www.cultura. gob.pe. Tue-Sun 0900-1700, closed major public holidays. US$2.50, 50% discount with ISIC card.* Located in the huge **Banco de la Nación** building is the museum for the exhibition and study of the art and history of the aboriginal races of Peru. There are good explanations in Spanish and English on Peruvian history, with ceramics, textiles and displays of many ruins in Peru. It is arranged so that you can follow the development of Peruvian precolonial history through to the time of the Incas. A visit is recommended before you go to see the archaeological sites themselves. There are displays of the tomb of the Señor de Sipán, artefacts from Batán Grande near Chiclayo (Sicán culture), reconstructions of the friezes found at Huaca La Luna and Huaca El Brujo, near Trujillo, and of Sechín and other sites. 'Yuyanapaq' is a photographic record of the events of 1980-2000. Temporary exhibitions are held in the basement, where there is also a Ministerio de Cultura bookshop. The museum has a *cafetería*.

To get there, take a taxi from downtown Lima or Miraflores US$5. From Avenida Garcilaso de la Vega in downtown Lima take a bus to the 21st block of Javier Prado at Avenida Aviación. From Miraflores take a bus down Avenida Arequipa to Avenida Javier Prado (27th block), then take a **Corredor Azul** bus.

## Surco

The neighbourhood has a pleasant, well tended, plaza with several restaurants and bars nearby.

**Museo de Oro del Perú** ① *Alonso de Molina 1100, Monterrico, Surco (between blocks 18 and 19 of Av Primavera), Lima 33, T01-345 1292, www.museoroperu.com.pe. Daily 1030-1800, closed 1 Jan, 1 May, 28 Jul, 25 Dec. US$11.55, children under 11 US$5.60; multilingual audioguides available.* This museum houses an enormous collection of Peruvian gold, silver and bronze objects, an impressive array of arms and military uniforms from Spanish colonial times to the present and textiles from Peru and elsewhere. Allow plenty of time to appreciate everything. More than one hundred of its pieces can be seen in the **Sala Museo Oro del Perú**, in Larcomar.

## Breña and Pueblo Libre

**Mateo Salado archaeological site** ① *Corner of Av Tingo María (Breña) and Av M H Cornejo (Pueblo Libre), T01-476 9887, tours Wed-Sun 0900-1600, US$3.35.* West of the centre, adjacent to Plaza de la Bandera, is this large administrative and ceremonial centre from the Ychma culture (AD 1100-1450) with five terraced pyramids made of rammed earth.

South of here, in the Pueblo Libre district is a trio of important museums.

## BACKGROUND
### A fashion for passion

A unique form of women's clothing was worn by Lima's upper-class *mestizas* (women born in the colonies of Spanish origin) in the 18th century. Both the *saya* and the *manto* were of Moorish origin. The *saya* was an overskirt of dark silk, worn tight at the waist with either a narrow or wide bottom. The *manto* was like a thick black veil fastened by a band at the back of the waist where it joined the *saya*. It was brought over the shoulders and head and drawn over the face so closely that only a small, triangular space was left uncovered, sufficient for one eye to peep through. This earned them the title '*las tapadas*', or 'the covered ones'.

The fashion was created by Lima's *mestizas* in order to compete in the flirting stakes with their Spanish-born counterparts, whose tiny waists and coquettish fan-waving was turning men's heads. The *tapadas*, though veiled, were by no means modest. Their skirts were daringly short, revealing their appealingly tiny feet, and necklines plunged to scandalously low levels. The French feminist, Flora Tristan, was much taken with this brazen show. She commented: "I am sure it needs little imagination to appreciate the consequences of this time-honoured practice."

One consequence of this fashion, which ensured anonymity, was that Lima's *mestizas* could freely indulge in romantic trysts with their lovers. Often, however, they were content with flirting – sometimes with their unwitting husbands. Another consequence of their anonymity was political. Many *tapadas* used their afternoon strolls to pass notes and messages to the organizers of the independence movement. This romantic and political intrigue usually took place on the Paseo de Aguas, a walkway of pools and gardens built by the viceroy.

**Museo Nacional de Antropología, Arqueología e Historia** ① *Plaza Bolívar, Pueblo Libre (not to be confused with Plaza Bolívar in the centre), T01-321 5630 ext 5255, daily 0845 1630, Sun and holidays 0900-1600, US$4, students US$1.20, guides available for groups; taxi from downtown US$3; from Miraflores US$4.* The original museum of anthropology and archaeology has ceramics from the Chimú, Nazca, Mochica and Pachacámac cultures, a display on the Paracas culture, various Inca curiosities and works of art, and interesting textiles. **Museo Nacional de Historia** ① *T01-463 2009, Tue-Sat 0900-1700, Sun and holidays 0900-1600, US$3.65,* in a mansion occupied by San Martín (1821-1822) and Bolívar (1823-1826) is next door. It exhibits colonial and early republican paintings, manuscripts and uniforms.

To get there, take any public transport on Avenida Brasil with a window sticker saying 'Todo Brasil'. Get off at the 21st block called Avenida Vivanco. Walk about five blocks down Vivanco. The museum will be on your left. From Miraflores take bus SM 18 Caraballyo-Chorrillos, marked 'Bolívar, Arequipa, Larcomar', get out at block 8 of Bolívar by the Hospital Santa Rosa and walk down Avenida San Martín five blocks until you see a faded blue line marked on the pavement; turn left. The blue line is a pedestrian route (15 minutes) linking the Museo Nacional de Antropología, Arqueología e Historia to the Museo Larco de Lima.

★ **Museo Larco de Lima** ① *Av Bolívar 1515, T01-461 1312, www.museolarco.org, 0900-2200, 0900-1800 24 Dec-1 Jan, US$10.55 (half price for students, seniors US$8.75); texts*

## Lima's shanty towns

If you take a bus out of Lima, you will see many shanty towns along the highway. Variously known as *inavasiones*, *asentamientos humanos* or *pueblos jóvenes*, the shanty towns of Lima are monumental reminders of racial division and social inequality, and of the poverty in which more than half of the capital's population lives. Millions of people have no access to clean drinking water. Most of the Peruvians living in these settlements came from the provinces, escaping misery and the civil war of the 1980s and 1990s. They simply squatted on the hills surrounding Lima, only trying later to legalize their property.

There are old, 'established' shanty towns, like **Villa El Salvador**, with officially over 500,000 inhabitants, as well as newer, rapidly expanding ones. Some settlements consist of reed and bamboo shacks without roofs; others have developed an infrastructure, including markets, shops, restaurants and cafés.

Divisions in Peruvian society run deep. Early on, many of the shanty town dwellers did not even know of the existence of posh neighbourhoods like San Isidro and Miraflores. Needless to say, most inhabitants of the rich parts of Lima never visit shanty towns. With time and the pervasive influence of the media, however, this has begun to change.

Some visitors feel a voyeuristic fascination for Lima's poorest districts. Villa El Salvador, one of the oldest and biggest shanty towns, is now a municipality in its own right (www.munives.gob.pe) and is the only one that can be visited without much danger. It is at the southern end of the Tren eléctrico, so you can take a train there even if you don't feel the urge to wander around. The station is above street level, giving a general view of the place. Travel only by day, wear modest clothes and, if you venture out of the station, stick to the main street. Under no circumstances should you travel by public transport to other shanty towns. Almost without exception, they are dangerous, especially after dark.

*in Spanish, English and French, disabled access, photography not permitted; taxi from downtown, Miraflores or San Isidro, 30 mins, US$5.* Located in an 18th-century mansion, itself built on a seventh-century pre-Columbian pyramid, this unmissable museum has a collection which gives an excellent overview on the development of Peruvian cultures through their pottery. It has the world's largest collection of Moche, Sicán and Chimú pieces. There is a Gold and Silver of Ancient Peru exhibition, a magnificent textile collection and a fascinating erotica section. Don't miss the storeroom with its vast array of pottery, unlike anything you'll see elsewhere. There is a library and computer room for your own research and a good café open during museum hours, see page 59. It is surrounded by beautiful gardens, and has a park outside.

To get there, take any bus to the 15th block of Avenida Brasil. Then take a bus down Avenida Bolívar. From Miraflores, take the SM 18 Caraballlo-Chorrillos (see page 59), to block 15 of Bolívar.

San Isidro, Miraflores and Barranco are the hub of the capital's social life, with numerous hotels, restaurants and night spots (see pages 56-64). There are also beaches further south and a number of sights worth seeing. Avenida Arequipa runs south for 52 blocks from downtown Lima to Parque Kennedy in Miraflores. Alternatively, the Vía Expresa, a six-lane urban freeway locally known as 'El Zanjón' (the Ditch) is the fastest route across the city.

### San Isidro

To the east of Avenida La República, down Calle Pancho Fierro, is **El Olivar**, an olive grove planted by the first Spaniards which has been turned into a park. Some 32 species of birds have been recorded there. Between San Isidro and Miraflores is **Huallamarca** ① *C Nicolás de Rivera 201 and Av Rosario, T01-222 4124, Tue-Sun 0900-1700, US$1.75*. An adobe pyramid of the Maranga (Lima) culture, it dates from about AD 100-500, but has later Wari and Inca remains. There is a small site museum. To get there, take bus 1 from Avenida Tacna, or minibus 13 or 73 to Choquechaca, then walk.

### Miraflores

**Parque Kennedy** and the adjoining Parque Central de Miraflores are located between Avenida Larco and Avenida Mcal Oscar Benavides (locally known as Avenida Diagonal). The extremely well-kept park area has a small open-air theatre with performances Thursday to Sunday and an arts and crafts market most evenings of the week. To the north is the former house and now museum of the author **Ricardo Palma** ① *Gral Suárez 189, T01-445 5836, http://ricardopalma.miraflores.gob.pe, Mon-Fri 0915-1245, 1430-1700, US$2.20, includes video and guided tour.*

At the southern end of Avenida Larco and running along the Malecón de la Reserva is the renovated **Parque Salazar** and the modern shopping centre called **Centro Comercial Larcomar**. Here you will find expensive shops, hip cafés and discos and a wide range of restaurants, all with a beautiful ocean view. Don't forget to check out the Cosmic Bowling Alley with its black lights and fluorescent balls.

A few hundred metres to the north is the famous ★ **Parque del Amor**, a great place for a stroll where, on just about any night, you'll see at least one wedding party taking photos.

**Museo Arqueológico Amano** ① *Retiro 160, 11th block of Av Angamos Oeste, Miraflores, T01-441 2909, www.museoamano.org, daily 1000-1700, US$9 (photography prohibited),* has artefacts from the Chancay, Chimú and Nazca periods, which were owned by the late Mr Yoshitaro Amano. It has one of the most complete exhibits of Chancay weaving and is particularly interesting for pottery and pre-Columbian textiles, all superbly displayed and lit. To get there, take a bus or *colectivo* to the corner of Avenida Arequipa y Avenida Angamos and another one to the 11th block of Avenida Angamos Oeste. Taxi from downtown costs US$3.20; from Parque Kennedy, US$2.25.

**Tip...**

To travel by public transport between Miraflores and central Lima there is no shortage of Línea Azul buses along Avenida Arequipa. Buses to Barranco can be caught on Avenida Tacna, Avenida Wilson (also called Garcilaso de la Vega), Avenida Bolivia and Avenida Alfonso Ugarte.

Turn off Avenida Arequipa at 45th block to reach **Huaca Pucllana** ⓘ *General Borgoño, 8th block s/n, T01-445 8695, www.miraflores peru.com/huacapucllana/, Wed-Mon 0900-1700, 1900-2200, US$4.25, students US$2, includes small site museum and 45-min tour in Spanish or English*, a pre-Inca site which is under excavation. Originally a Lima culture temple to the goddesses of sea and moon (AD 200-700), it became a Wari burial site (AD 700-900) before being abandoned.

**Lugar de la Memoria, la Tolerancia y la Inclusion Social (LUM)** ⓘ *Bajada San Martín 151, T01-719 2065, www.lum.cultura.pe,* is a museum and documentation centre devoted to the victims of political violence in Peru during 1980-2000, one of several memorial

museums throughout the country (see also **Yalpana Wasi**, Huancayo, page 364, and **Museo de la Memoria de ANFASEP**, Ayacucho, page 377).

## ★ Barranco

The 45-minute walk south from Miraflores to Barranco along the Malecón is recommended in summer. This suburb was already a seaside resort by the end of the 17th century. There are many old mansions in the district, in a variety of styles, several of which are now being renovated, particularly on Calle Cajamarca and around San Francisco church. Barranco is quiet by day but comes alive at night (see Restaurants and Bars pages 63-64).

The attractive public library, formerly the town hall, stands on the plaza. It contains the helpful **municipal tourist office** ⓘ *T01-719 2046*. Nearby is the interesting *bajada*, a steep path leading down to the beach. The **Puente de los Suspiros** (Bridge of Sighs) crosses the *bajada* to the earthquake-damaged La Ermita church (only the façade has been restored)

100 metres
100 yards

**Where to stay** 🛏
1 Alemán *A3*
2 Antigua Miraflores *B1*
3 Belmond Miraflores Park *D1*
4 Blue House *C1*
5 Casa Andina Premium *C3*
6 Casa Andina Select *C2*
7 Casa Andina Standard *D2*
8 Casa de Baraybar *A1*
9 Casa Rodas *B3*
10 Condor's House *A1*
11 El Tambo Dos *C2*
12 Flying Dog &
    La Tasca Bar *B2, C2*
13 Girasoles *C3*
14 Hitchhikers B&B
    Backpackers *B1*
15 Hostal El Patio *C2*
16 HosteLima *A3*
17 Hotel de Autor *C1*
18 Inka Frog *A2*
19 José Antonio *C1*
20 JW Marriott *D1*
21 Lion Backpackers *C3*
22 Loki Backpackers *A1*
23 Pariwana *B3*
24 Pirwa *A3*
25 San Antonio Abad *D3*
26 Sonesta Posadas del Inca *C2*

**Restaurants** 🍴
1 Ache & Amaz *D2*
2 Alfresco *B1*
3 Café Café *B2*
4 Café de la Paz *B2, C2*
5 Central *D1*
6 El Parquetito *B2*
7 El Rincón Gaucho *D1*
8 Fiesta Gourmet *D2*
9 Govinda *D2*
10 Haiti *B3*
11 IK *A2*
12 La Estancia *C2*
13 La Gloria *B3*
14 La Lucha *B2*
15 Las Brujas de Cachiche *B1*
16 Las Tejas *C2*
17 La Tiendecita Blanca *B3*
18 Lobo del Mar –
    Octavio Otani *C1*
19 Maido *C2*
20 Manifiesto *B2*
21 Panchita *B3*
22 Pizza Street *B2*
23 Punto Azul *C2*
24 Rafael *C1*
25 Rosa Náutica *C1*
26 San Antonio *A3, D2*
27 Saqra *C2*
28 T'anta *D2*

**Bars & clubs** 🍸
29 Media Naranja *B2*
30 Murphy's *C3*
31 Treff Pub Alemán *C2*

➡ **Lima maps**
1 Lima orientation, page 38
2 Lima centre, page 43
3 **Miraflores, page 50**
4 Barranco, page 52

Ⓜ Metropolitano

# 4 Barranco

**To 3 &**
**Museo de Arte**
**Contemporáneo**

➡ **Lima maps**
1 Lima orientation,
page 38
2 Lima centre, page 43
3 Miraflores, page 50
4 Barranco, page 52

Pacific Ocean

Restaurants 🍴
1 Antica Pizzería
2 Expreso Virgen
de Guadalupe
3 La 73
4 Las Mesitas
5 Sóngoro Cosongo
6 Tío Mario
7 Tostería Bisetti

11 Del Carajo
12 El Dragón
13 Juanitos
14 La Candelaria
15 La Estación
de Barranco
16 La Noche
17 La Posada
del Mirador
18 Sargento Pimienta
19 The Lion's Head

Where to stay 🛏
1 'B'
2 Barranco 3B
3 Barranco's
Backpackers Inn
4 The Point

Bars & clubs 🍸
8 Ayahuasca
9 Barranco Beer
Company
10 Déjà Vu

Ⓜ Metropolitano

Founded in 1537, Callao used to be one of the most important cities in South America, the only seaport on the continent authorized to trade with Spain during the 16th and 17th centuries. During much of the 16th century Spanish merchants were plagued by threats from English privateers, such as Sir Francis Drake, who were all too willing to relieve the Spanish armada of its colonial spoils. The harbour was fortified in 1639 in order to prevent such attacks. In 1746, the port was completely destroyed by a tidal wave, triggered by the terrible earthquake of that year. According to some sources, all 6000 of Callao's inhabitants were drowned. The watermark is still visible on the outside of the 18th-century church of Nuestra Señora del Carmen de la Legua, which stands near the corner of Avenida Oscar Benavides and the airport road, Avenida Elmer Faucett. In 1850, the first railway in South America was opened between Lima and Callao. It was used not only as a passenger service but also, more importantly, for the growing import-export trade, transporting ore from the mines in the central highlands and manufactured goods from incoming ships.

Today, the most elegant area of Callao is Plaza Grau. It is well maintained and from here you can see a large part of the port and the Palomino Islands (inhabited by birds, seals and other marine species).

La Punta is a green peninsula next to Callao. It enjoys the relaxed, nostalgic atmosphere of a beach resort, with good local seafood restaurants, pleasant walks, friendly people and great views. It's an interesting place to come for lunch, but the ride back to Lima, even in a taxi, can be dangerous at night, as you have to drive through Callao proper.

and leads towards the Malecón, with fine views of the bay. A number of artists have their workshops in Barranco and there are several chic galleries.

The **Museo de Arte Contemporáneo de Lima (MAC Lima)** ① *Av Miguel Grau 1511, beside the municipal stadium, near Miraflores, T01-514 6800, www.maclima.pe, Tue-Sun 1000-1800, US$2, Sun US$0.35, with guided tour,* has permanent Latin American and European collections and holds temporary exhibitions. **MATE (Asociación Mario Testino)** ① *Av Pedro de Osma 409, T01-251 7755, www.mate.pe, Tue-Sun 1000-1900, US$5.55, with audio tour (no other explanations),* is the world-renowned fashion photographer's vision of modern art, with a shop and excellent café/restaurant. Next door, by contrast, and equally important is the **Museo de Arte Colonial Pedro de Osma** ① *Av Pedro de Osma 423, T01-467 0141, www.museopedrodeosma.org, Tue-Sun 1000-1800, US$6.75, students half price, guided tours in English or Spanish,* a private collection of colonial art of the Cuzco, Ayacucho and Arequipa schools.

## ★ Pachacámac
*T01-430 0168, http://pachacamac.cultura.pe, Tue-Sat 0900-1700, Sun 0900-1600; closed public holidays except by appointment, US$3.50, students US$1.75, guide US$7.*

When the Spaniards arrived, Pachacámac in the Lurín Valley was the largest city and ceremonial centre on the coast. A wooden statue of the creator-god, after whom the site is named, is in the excellent site museum. Hernando Pizarro was sent here by his brother

## ON THE ROAD

## Inca Kola

The high international profile currently enjoyed by upscale Peruvian gastronomy has tended to overshadow some of the country's less sophisticated tastes. Among the latter shines a fluorescent yellow, syrupy sweet soft drink, so brightly coloured that you might think it glows in the dark.

Invented by a British immigrant named Isaac Lindley, who arrived in Callao in 1910, it is said to be made from *hierba luisa* (lemon verbena), although sceptics would say it more closely resembles boiled lollipops. Be that as it may, the beverage has captured the national imagination and palate since its launch in 1935. The Lindley family business thrived for many decades, thanks to the Peruvian population's impressively sweet tooth. Even Coca Cola is reported to have added extra sugar to its formula in Peru in order to try to keep up with Inca Kola. Peru's 'golden kola' has been part-owned by its arch international rival since 1999, but it continues to be a hugely popular drink and an important icon of Peruvian national identity.

in 1533 in search of gold for Inca emperor Atahualpa's ransom. In their fruitless quest, the Spaniards destroyed images and killed the priests. The ruins encircle the top of a low hill, whose crest was crowned with a **Temple of the Sun**, now partially restored. Slightly apart is the reconstructed **House of the Mamaconas**, where the 'chosen women' spun fine cloth for the Inca and his court. An impression of the scale of the site can be gained from the top of the Temple of the Sun, or from walking or driving the 3-km circuit, which is covered by an unmade road for cars and tour buses.

The site is large and it is expected that tourists will be visiting by vehicle (there are six parking areas); taxis charge about US$20 each way.

### Lima's beaches

Even though the water of some beaches has been declared unsuitable for swimming, Limeños see the beach more as part of their culture than as a health risk. On summer weekends (December-April) the city's beaches get very crowded and lots of activities are organized. The beaches of **Miraflores**, **Barranco** and **Chorrillos** are popular, but the sand and sea here are dirty. It's much better to take a safe taxi south along the Circuito de Playas to Playa Arica (30 km south of Lima). There are many great beaches for all tastes between here and San Bartolo (45 km south). If you really want the height of fashion head to **Asia**, Km 92-104, where there are some 20 beaches with boutiques, hotels, restaurants and condos.

**Tip...**
Robbery is a serious threat on the beaches. Don't take any belongings of value with you; take care on the walkways down, and don't camp on the beach overnight.

## Tourist information

**iPerú** has offices at **Jorge Chávez international airport** (T01-574 8000, daily 24 hrs); **Casa Basadre** (Av Jorge Basadre 610, San Isidro, T01-421 1627/1227, Mon-Fri 0900-1800); and **Larcomar shopping centre** (La Rotonda nivel 2, stand 211-212, Miraflores, T01-445 9400, daily 1100-2100). The **Municipal tourist kiosk** is on Pasaje Escribanos, behind the Municipalidad, near the Plaza de Armas (T01-632 1542, www. visitalima.pe and www.munlima.gob.pe, daily 0900-1700); ask about guided walks in the city centre. There are 8 **kiosks** in Miraflores: Parque Central; Parque Salazar; Parque del Amor; González Prada y Av Petit Thouars; Av R Palma y Av Petit Thouars; Av Larco y Av Benavides; Huaca Pucllana (closed Sat pm); and Ovalo Gutiérrez. The **tourist police** (Jr Moore 268, Magdalena at the 38th block of Av Brasil, T01-460 1060/ T0800-22221, daily 24 hrs) are friendly and very helpful if you have your property stolen, English spoken. Also at Av España y Av Alfonso Ugarte; Colón 246, Miraflores, T01-243 2190, and at the airport. For English websites, see www.limaeasy.com and www. mirafloresperu.com and for an upmarket city guide see www.limainside.net.

## Where to stay

If you are only staying a short time and want to see the main sites, Central Lima is the most convenient place to stay. However, it is not as safe at night as the more upmarket areas of Miraflores, San Isidro and Barranco. All hotels in the upper price brackets charge 18% state tax and service on top of prices. In hotels foreigners pay no tax and the amount of service charge is up to the hotel. Neither is included in the prices below, unless otherwise stated. All those listed below have received good recommendations.

Lima has several international chain hotels: **Holiday Inn**, www.holidayinn.com; **JW Marriott**, www.marriott.com; **Sheraton**, www.sheraton.com; **Sofitel**, www.sofitel. com; **Swissôtel**, www.lima.swissotel.com; **Westin/Starwood**, www.starwoodhotels. com. Peruvian chain hotels in Lima include **Casa Andina**, www.casa-andina.com; **Costa del Sol**, www.costadelsolperu.com; and **Sonesta Posadas del Inca**, www. sonesta.com. There are dozens of hostels in Lima offering dormitory accommodation and charging US$10-17 pp, usually including a simple breakfast, hot water in shared bathrooms, kitchen facilities, bar and living room. Double rooms with private bathrooms start at about US$30. Some hostels are linked to travel agents or adventure tour companies.

---

### Central Lima

#### $$$$-$$$ Gran Hotel Bolívar
*Jr de la Unión 958, T01-619 7171, www.granhotelbolivar.com.pe.*
A refubished classic hotel which is one of the architectural attractions of downtown Lima. Huge stained-glass dome over the entrance lobby, Comfortable accommodation and first-class service. A pisco sour in their bar is a must. Provides all services including airport transfers and tourist information.

#### $$ La Posada del Parque
*Parque Hernán Velarde 60, near 1st block of Av Petit Thouars, Sta Beatriz, T01-433 2412, www.incacountry.com.*
A charmingly refurbished old house with a collection of fine handicrafts, in a safe area, comfortable rooms, breakfast 0830-0930, airport transfer 24 hrs for US$18 for 1-3 passengers (US$8 pp for larger groups), no credit cards, cash only. English spoken. Excellent value. Gay friendly.

#### $$ Maury
*Jr Ucayali 201, T01-428 8188.*

Formerly an upmarket hotel in the historical centre, but past its heyday. Some non-smoking rooms, a/c, frigobar, restaurant, airport transfers, secure. The bar is reputed to be the home of the 1st-ever *pisco sour* (this is, of course, disputed!).

### $ Hostal San Francisco
*Jr Azángaro 127, T01-426 2735.*
Dormitories with and without bathrooms, safe, Italian/Peruvian owners, good service, café.

### $ Pensión Ibarra
*Av Tacna 359, 1402 y 1502 (elevator to 14th/15th floors doesn't run all hours), no sign, T01-427 8603/1035, pensionibarra@gmail.com.*
Basic, economical, breakfast US$4, discount for longer stay, noisy, use of kitchen, balcony with views of the city, helpful owners (2 sisters), hot water, full board available (good small café almost next door). Reserve in advance; taxis can't stop outside so book airport pick-up (US$18.50) for safe arrival.

## Inner suburbs
San Miguel and Magdalena del Mar are on the seaward side of Pueblo Libre.

### $$ Mami Panchita
*Av Federico Gallessi 198 (ex-Av San Miguel), San Miguel, T01-263 7203, www.mamipanchita.com.*
Dutch/Peruvian-owned, English, Dutch and Spanish spoken, includes breakfast and welcome drink, comfortable rooms with bath, hot water, living room and bar, patio, book exchange, airport transfers, 15 mins from airport, 15 mins from Miraflores, 20 mins from historical centre. Frequently recommended.

## San Isidro

### $$$$ Country Club
*Los Eucaliptos 590, T01-611 9000, www.hotelcountry.com.*
Excellent, fine service, luxurious rooms, good bar and restaurant, buisness centre, gym, spa, golf, classically stylish with a fine art collection.

### $$$$ Sonesta El Olivar
*Pancho Fierro 194, T01-712 6000, www.sonesta.com/Lima.*
Excellent, one of the top 5-star hotels in Lima overlooking El Olivar park, modern, good restaurant and bar, terrace, gym, swimming pool, quiet, very attentive, popular.

### $$$ Garden
*Rivera Navarrete 450, T01-200 9800.*
Good beds, a/c, heating, small restaurant, ideal for business visitors, convenient, good value.

### $$ Chez Elizabeth
*Av del Parque Norte 265, San Isidro, T998-007557, http://chezelizabeth.typepad.fr.*
Family house in residential area 7 mins' walk from Cruz del Sur bus station. Shared or private bathrooms, TV room, laundry, airport transfers.

### $ Albergue Juvenil Malka
*Los Lirios 165 (near 4th block of Av Javier Prado Este), San Isidro, T01-442 0162, www.youthhostelperu.com.*
Dormitory style, 4-8 beds per room, also private doubles (**$$**), English spoken, laundry, climbing wall, nice café, airport transfer.

## Miraflores

### $$$$ Belmond Miraflores Park
*Av Malecón de la Reserva 1035, T01-610 4000, www.miraflorespark.com.*
An **Orient Express** hotel, excellent service and facilities, beautiful views over the ocean, top class. Rooftop, open-air, heated pool and spa which looks out over the ocean, open to the public when you buy a spa treatment.

### $$$$ Hotel de Autor
*Av 28 de Julio 562B, T01-396 2740; 2nd location at Av de la Aviación 316, T01-383 4268, www.hoteldeautor.com.*
Small hotel in a refurbished town house, in a courtyard off the street (no sign), 4 well-appointed suites and pleasant common areas, personalized service, English spoken.

### $$$ Alemán
*Arequipa 4704, T01-445 6999, www.hotelaleman.com.pe.*

No sign, comfortable, quiet, garden, excellent breakfast, smiling staff.

### $$$ Antigua Miraflores
*Av Grau 350 at C Francia, T01-201 2060, www.antiguamiraflores.com.*
A small, elegant hotel in a quiet but central location, excellent service, tastefully furnished and decorated, gym, good restaurant. Recommended.

### $$$ Casa de Baraybar
*Toribio Pacheco 216, T01-652 2262, www.casadebaraybar.com.*
1 block from the ocean, extra long beds, a/c or fan, colourful decor, high ceilings, 24-hr room service, laundry, airport transfers free for stays of 3 nights. Bilingual staff. Recommended.

### $$$ El Tambo Dos
*La Paz 720, T01-200 0100, www.eltamboperu.com.*
Comfortable rooms and social area. Perfectly located close to restaurants, bars and cafés (also has its own). Part of a small chain with 2 other locations in Lima (see website). Modern facilities, bilingual staff, parking.

### $$$ Girasoles
*Ernesto Diez Canseco 696, T01-446-6075, www.losgirasoleshotel.com.*
Family run hotel with bilingual staff, good location and service. Ample, well-appointed rooms, buffet breakfast served in **Sawa Café**, no extra charge for room service.

### $$$ José Antonio
*28 de Julio 398 y C Colón and C Colón 328, T01-445 7743, www.hotelesjoseantonio.com.*
Good in all respects, including the restaurant, large modern rooms, jacuzzis, swimming pool, business facilities, helpful staff speak some English.

### $$$ San Antonio Abad
*Ramón Ribeyro 301, T01-447 6766, www.hotelsanantonioabad.com.*
Secure, quiet, helpful, tasty breakfasts, 1 free airport transfer with reservation, justifiably popular, good value.

### $$$-$$ Casa Rodas
*Tarapacá 250, T01-242 4872, www.casarodas.com.*
Rooms for 2, 3 or 4, one with private bath, the rest with shared bath, good beds, helpful staff.

### $$$-$$ Hostal El Patio
*Diez Canseco 341, T01-444 2107, www.hostalelpatio.net.*
Very nice suites and rooms, comfortable, English spoken, convenient, *comedor*, gay friendly. Very popular, reservations are essential.

### $$$-$$ Inka Frog
*Gral Iglesias 271, T01-445 8979, www.inkafrog.com.*
Self-styled "Exclusive B&B", comfortable, nice decor, lounge with huge TV, rooftop terrace, good value.

### $$-$ Condor's House
*Martín Napanga 137, T01-446 7267, www.condorshouse.com.*
Award-winning, quiet hostel, 2 categories of dorm rooms with lockers, good bathrooms, also doubles, good meeting place, TV room with films, book exchange, *parrillada* prepared once a week, bar. Helpful staff.

### $$-$ Flying Dog
*Diez Canseco 117, T01-445 6745, www.flyingdogperu.com.*
Also at Lima 457 and Olaya 280, all with dorms, doubles, triples, quads. All are on or near Parque Kennedy, with kitchen, lockers, but all have different features. There are others in Cuzco, Iquitos and Arequipa.

### $$-$ Hitchhikers B&B Backpackers
*Bolognesi 400, T01-242 3008, www.hhikersperu.com.*
Located close to the ocean, mixture of dorms and private rooms with shared or private bath, nice patio, parking, bicycles to borrow, airport transfers. Also has a hostel in Cuzco.

### $$-$ HosteLima
*Cnel Inclán 399, T01-242 7034, www.hostelima.com.*
Private double rooms and brightly painted dorms, close to Parque Kennedy, helpful

staff, safe, bar/restaurant and snack shop, movie room, travel information.

### $$-$ Lion Backpackers
*Grimaldo del Solar 139, T01-447 1827, www.lionbackpackers.com.*
Quiet hostel in a convenient location, private and shared rooms (with lockers), all en suite, those on upper floor are the nicest, clean kitchen facilities, book exchange, helpful owner and staff, bus terminal pick-up.

### $$-$ Loki Backpackers
*José Galvez 576, T01-651 2966, www.lokihostel.com.*
In a quiet area, the capital's sister to the party hostel of the same name in Cuzco, doubles or dorms, good showers, cooked breakfast extra, Fri barbecues, lockers, airport transfers.

### $$-$ Pariwana
*Av Larco 189, T01-242 4350, www.pariwana-hostel.com.*
Party hostel with doubles and dorms in the heart of Miraflores, individual lockers with power outlets so you can leave your gadgets charging in a safe place. Always lots going on.

### $$-$ Pirwa
*Coronel Inclán 494, T01-242 4059, www.pirwahostels.com.*
Members of a chain of hostels in Peru (Cuzco, Arequipa, Puno, Nazca), choice of dorms and double rooms, lockers, transfers arranged, bike rental.

### $ Blue House
*José González 475, T01-445 0476, www.bluehouse.com.pe.*
A true backpacker hostel, most rooms with bath including a double, basic but good value for the location, *terraza* with *parrilla*, films to watch.

## Barranco

### $$$$ 'B'
*Sáenz Peña 204, T01-206 0800, www.hotelb.pe.*
Boutique hotel in an early 20th-century mansion. Beautifully redesigned as a luxury hotel in the original building and a contemporary wing, eclectic design features and a large collection of mostly modern art, next to Lucía de la Puente gallery and convenient for others, blog and Facebook give cultural recommendations, highly regarded Mediterranean/Peruvian restaurant, cocktail bar, plunge pool, parking, excellent service. 1 room for disabled travellers. In **Relais y Châteaux** group.

### $$$ Barranco 3B
*Jr Centenario 130, T01-247 6915, www.3bhostal.com.*
Small, modern B&B, simple comfortable rooms with fan.

### $$-$ Barranco's Backpackers Inn
*Mcal Castilla 260, T01-247 1326.*
Ocean view, colourful rooms, all en suite, shared and private rooms, tourist information.

### $ The Point
*Malecón Junín 300, T01-247 7997, www.thepointhostels.com.*
Rooms range from doubles to large dormitories, all with shared bath, very popular with backpackers (book in advance at weekends), laundry, gay friendly, restaurant, bar, party atmosphere most of the time, but also space for relaxing, weekly barbecues, travel centre.

## Callao (near the airport)
**Holiday Inn** (www.holidayinn.com) and **Costa del Sol** (www.costadelsolperu.com) have standard international hotels (**$$$$-$$$**) right by the airport.

### $$ Hostal Víctor
*Manuel Mattos 325, Urbanización San Amadeo de Garagay, T01-569 4662, Facebook:hostelvictor.*
15 mins from the airport by taxi, or phone or email in advance for free pick-up, large comfortable rooms, hot water, 10% discount for **Footprint** book owners, American breakfast (or packed breakfast for early departure), evening meals can be ordered locally, 2 malls with restaurants, shops, cinemas, etc nearby, very helpful but the area is not safe.

### $$-$ Pay Purix
*Av Japón (formerly Bertello Bolatti), Mz F,*
*Lote 5, Urbanización Los Jazmines, 1a Etapa,*
*Callao, T01-484 9118, www.paypurix.com.*
3 mins from airport, can arrange pick-up
(taxi US$6, US$2 from outside airport). Hostel
with doubles and dorms, convenient, English
spoken, CDs, DVDs, games and use of kitchen.

### Restaurants

18% tax and 10% service will be added to your
bill in middle- and top-end restaurants.
Chinese is often the cheapest at around US$5
including a drink. For the rise of Peruvian
cuisine, see Gastronomic Lima, opposite.

### Central Lima

### $$$ Wa Lok
*Jr Pururo 864 and 878, Barrio Chino,*
*T01-427 2656.*
Good dim sum, cakes and fortune cookies
(when you pay the bill). English spoken, very
friendly. Also at Av Angamos Oeste 700,
Miraflores, T01-447 1329.

### $$$-$$ De César
*Ancash 300, T01-428 8740. Open 0800-2300.*
Old-fashioned atmosphere, apart from the
3 TVs, breakfasts, snacks, seafood, meat
dishes, pastas, pizza, juices, coffees and teas.
Good food.

### $$ L'Eau Vive
*Ucayali 370, also opposite the Torre Tagle*
*Palace, T01-427 5612. Mon-Sat, 1230-1500*
*and 1930-2130.*
Run by nuns, lunch *menú*, Peruvian-style in
interior dining room, or à la carte in either of
dining rooms that open on to patio, excellent,
profits go to the poor, Ave María is sung
nightly at 2100.

### $$-$ Bar Cordano
*Ancash 202 y Carabaya (in Calles El Rastro y*
*Pescadería zone).*
Historic tavern serving Peruvian food
and drinks, great atmosphere, favoured
by politicians.

### $$-$ Rovegno
*Arenales 456 (near block 3 of Arequipa),*
*T01-424 8465.*
Italian and Peruvian dishes, home-made
pasta, also serves snacks and sandwiches
and has a bakery. Good value.

### $ La Catedral del Pisco
*Jr de la Unión 1100 esquina Av Uruguay 114,*
*T01-330 0079. Daily 0800-2200.*
*Comida criolla* and drinks, including free
Peruvian coffee (excellent) or *pisco sour* for
**Footprint Handbook** owners! Live music at
night, Wi-Fi.

### Breña and Pueblo Libre

### $$$ Café del Museo
*At the Museo Larco, Av Bolívar 1515, T01-462*
*4757. Daily 0900-2200, seating inside and on*
*the terrace.*
Specially designed interior, selection of
salads, fine Peruvian dishes, pastas and
seafood, a tapas bar of traditional Peruvian
foods, as well as snacks, desserts and
cocktails. Highly regarded.

### $$ Antigua Taberna Queirolo
*Av San Martín 1090, 1 block from Plaza Bolívar,*
*T01-460 0441, http://antiguatabernaqueirolo.*
*com. Mon-Sat 0930-2330, Sun 0930-1600.*
Atmospheric old bar with glass-fronted
shelves of bottles, marble bar and old
photos, owns bodega next door. Serves
lunches, sandwiches and snacks, good for
wine, does not serve dinner.

### San Isidro

### $$$ Antica Pizzería
*Av 2 de Mayo 732, T01-222 8437. 1200-2400.*
Very popular, great ambience, excellent food,
Italian owner. Also in Barranco at Alfonso
Ugarte 242, www.anticapizzeria.com.pe.

### $$$ Chifa Titi
*Av Javier Prado Este 1212, Córpac,*
*T01-224 8189, www.chifatiti.com.*
Regarded as the best Chinese restaurant in
Lima with over 60 years in operation.

## Gastronomic Lima *For locations, see maps, pages 43, 50 and 52.*

Lima attracts terms such "gastronomic capital of South America", which is reflected in the fact that the Mistura festival (www.mistura.pe) each September attracts hundreds of thousands of visitors. There are several restaurants that are championed as the height of culinary excellence. They are often priced beyond the average traveller's budget, but a meal at one of these could be the ideal way to celebrate a special occasion. Most serve à la carte and a tasting menu. At the heart of much of today's Peruvian gastronomy are traditional ingredients, from the coast, the Andes and the jungle. The star chefs all recognize the debt they owe to the cooks of the different regions. Their skill is in combining the local heritage with the flavours and techniques that they have learnt elsewhere, without overwhelming what is truly Peruvian.

Gastón Acurio is usually credited with being the forerunner of the evolution of Peruvian cuisine. He is also recognized for his community work. With **Astrid y Gastón Casa Moreyra** (Avenida Paz Soldán 290, San Isidro, www.astridygaston.com), Acurio and his wife Astrid have moved their flagship restaurant from Miraflores to this historic house in San Isidro. It has been completely remodelled and opened in 2014. Other ventures include ceviche at **La Mar** (Avenida Lar 770, Miraflores, T01-421 3365), *anticuchos* at **Panchita** (Avenida 2 de Mayo 298, Miraflores, T01-242 5957, see Facebook page) and his excellent and inexpensive chain of **T'anta** cafés, eg behind the Municipalidad in the city centre, at Pancho Fierro 115 in San Isidro, at Avenida Vasco Núñez de Balboa 660 and in Larcomar, in Miraflores, and at the airport.

**Central** (Santa Isabel 376, Miraflores, T01-446 9301, www.centralrestaurante.com. pe) presents Virgilio Martínez's award-winning, sophisticated recipes fusing Peruvian ingredients and molecular cuisine.

**Manifiesto** (Independencia 130, Miraflores, T01-249 5533, www.manifiesto.pe) is billed as "Tacna meets Italy", bringing together the birthplace and family roots of chef Giacomo Bocchio.

Rafael Osterling has two restaurants in the city: **Rafael** (San Martín 300, Miraflores, T01-242 4149, www.rafaelosterling.com), celebrated for its classic Peruvian dishes

---

### $$$-$$ Segundo Muelle
*Av Conquistadores 490, T01-717 9998, www.segundomuelle.com. Daily 1200-1700.*
Ceviches and other very good seafood dishes, including Japanese, *menú* and à la carte, popular.

### Cafés

#### Havanna
*Miguel Dasso 163, www.havanna.pe. Mon-Sat 0700-2300, Sun 0800-2200.*
Branch of the Argentine **Coffee and Alfajores** chain, others in the city include **Larcomar**.

### Miraflores
C San Ramón, known as **Pizza Street** (across from Parque Kennedy), is a pedestrian walkway lined with popular outdoor restaurants/bars/discos that are open until the wee small hours. Good-natured touts try to entice diners and drinkers inside with free offers.

### $$$ El Rincón Gaucho
*Av Armendáriz 580, T01-447 4778 and Av Grau 540, Barranco.*
Good grill, renowned for its steaks.

incorporating flavours from around the globe, especially the Mediterranean, and **El Mercado** (H Unanue 203, Miraflores, T01-221 1322), which concentrates on seafood, reflecting all the influences on Peruvian cooking.

At **IK** (Elías Aguirre 179, Miraflores, T01-652 1692, reservas@ivankisic.pe, see Facebook page), molecular gastronomy meets Peruvian ingredients at the late Ivan Kisic's restaurant.

**Lima 27** (Santa Lucía 295 – no sign, T01-221 5822, www.lima27.com) is a modern restaurant behind whose black exterior you will find contemporary Peruvian cuisine. It's in the same group as **Alfresco** (Malecón Balta 790, T01-242 8960), **Cala on Costa Verde** (http://calarestaurante.com), and a new sandwich bar, **Manduca**, in Jockey Plaza.

Pedro Miguel Schiaffino's **Malabar** (Camino Real 101, San Isidro, T01-440 5200, http://malabar.com.pe) takes the Amazon and its produce as the starting point for its dishes, as does Schiaffino's **Amaz** (Avenida La Paz 1079, Miraflores, T01-221 9393). This eatery is in a group of four places under the Hilton Hotel. Also here is **Ache** (Avenida La Paz 1055, T01-221 9315, achecocinanikkei on Facebook) which specializes in Japanese fusion cuisine.

**La Picantería** (Moreno 388 y González Prada, Surquillo, T01-241 6676, www.picanteriasdelperu.com) serves excellent seafood, first-class *ceviche*, has a fish-of-the-day lunch menu and a good bar.

**Maido** (San Martín 399, Miraflores, T01-447 9333, www.maido.pe) is a top-of-the-line restaurant specializing in Japanese-Peruvian fusion cuisine and the authentic 'Nikkei experience'. Considered one of the best in Latin America and booked months in advance.

**Fiesta Gourmet** (Avenida Reducto 1278, T01-242 9009, www.restaurantfiesta gourmet.com), specializes in dishes from Chiclayo and the north coast: superb food in elegant surroundings.

Beyond Lima there are many superb innovative restaurants in Arequipa (see www.festisabores.com), Cuzco, Ayacucho and elsewhere. Don't forget that the excellent regional cooking that provided inspiration for Peru's high-end international culinary fame is still very much alive and well, often in much more modest and affordable surroundings.

### $$$ Huaca Pucllana
*Gral Borgoño cuadra 8 s/n, alt cuadra 45 Av Arequipa, T01-445 4042, www.resthuaca pucllana.com. Daily 1200-1600, 1900-2400.*
Facing the archaeological site of the same name, contemporary Peruvian fusion cooking, very good food in an unusual setting, popular with groups.

### $$$ La Gloria
*Atahualpa 201, T01-445 5705, www.lagloriarestaurant.com. Mon-Sat 1300-1600, 2000-2400.*

Popular upmarket restaurant serving Peruvian food, classic and contemporary styles, good service.

### $$$ La Trattoria
*At Larcomar, T01-446 7002, www. latrattoriadimambrino.com.*
Italian cuisine, popular, good desserts. Has another branch, **La Bodega**, opposite entrance to Huaca Pucllana.

### $$$ Las Brujas de Cachiche
*Av Bolognesi 472, T01-447 1883, www.brujasdecachiche.com.pe. Mon-Sat 1200-2400, Sun 1230-1630.*

An old mansion converted into bars and dining rooms, fine traditional food (menu in Spanish and English), live *criollo* music.

### $$$ Rosa Náutica
*T01-445 0149, www.larosanautica.com.*
*Daily 1200-2400.*
Built on old British-style pier (Espigón No 4), in Lima Bay. Delightful opulence, fine fish cuisine, experience the atmosphere by buying a beer in the bar at sunset.

### $$$ Saqra
*Av La Paz 646, T01-650 88 84, www.saqra.pe.*
*Mon-Sat 1200-2400.*
Colourful and casual, indoor or outdoor seating, interesting use of ingredients from all over Peru, classic flavours with a fun, innovative twist, inspired by street food and humble dishes, vegetarian options, many organic products. Also good cocktail bar. Go with a group to sample as many dishes as possible.

### $$$-$$ Punto Azul
*San Martín 595, 01-T445 8078, Benavides 2711, T01-260 8943, with other branches in San Isidro, Surco and San Borja, http:// puntoazulrestaurante.com. Tue-Fri 1100-1600, Sat-Sun1100-1700 (San Martín 595 also open Mon-Sat 1900-2400).*
Popular, well-regarded chain of seafood and ceviche restaurants.

### $$ El Parquetito
*Lima 373 y Diez Canseco, T01-444 0490.*
*Daily 0900-0100.*
Peruvian food from all regions, good *menú* and à la carte, serves breakfast, eat inside or out.

### $$ La Estancia
*Schell 385, 01-444 2558. Sun-Thu 0800-2200.*
Café and restaurant, Peruvian dishes with a Mediterranean touch, salads, sandwiches, cocktails.

### $$ Las Tejas
*Diez Canseco 340, T01-444 4360.*
*Daily 1200-2400.*
Good, typical Peruvian food, especially ceviche, *menú* and à la carte.

### $$ Lobo del Mar – Octavio Otani
*Colón 587, T01-242 1871.*
Basic exterior hides one of the oldest *cevicherías* in Miraflores, excellent, a good selection of other seafood dishes.

### $ Al Toke Pez
*Av Angamos Este 886, Surquillo, across Paseo de la República from Miraflores. Tue-Sun 1130-1530.*
Small popular economical 'hole-in-the-wall' ceviche bar, also serves other seafood dishes, tasty, a real find.

### $ Govinda
*Schell 630.*
Vegetarian, from Hare Krishna foundation, lunch *menú* US$3.

## Cafés

### Café Café
*Martín Olaya 250, at the corner of Av Diagonal.*
Very popular, good atmosphere, over 100 different blends of coffee, good salads and sandwiches, very popular with 'well-to-do' Limeños. Also in Larcomar.

### Café de la Paz
*Lima 351, middle of Parque Kennedy and Pasaje Tarata 227, www.cafedelapazperu.com. Daily 0800-2400.*
Good outdoor café right on the park, expensive, great cocktails.

### Haiti
*Av Diagonal 160, Parque Kennedy. Mon-Thu 0700-0200, Fri-Sat 0700-0300.*
Great for people-watching, good ice cream.

### La Lucha
*Av Benavides y Olaya (under Flying Dog), on Parque Kennedy, with small branches between Olaya and Benavides, on Ovalo Gutiérrez and at Larcomar.*
Excellent hot sandwiches, limited range, choice of sauces, great juices, *chicha morada* and *café pasado*. Good for a wholesome snack. Very popular.

### La Tiendecita Blanca
*Av Larco 111 on Parque Kennedy.*
One of Miraflores' oldest, expensive, good people-watching, very good cakes, European-style food and delicatessen.

### San Antonio
*Av Angamos Oeste 1494.*
Fashionable *pastelería* chain with hot and cold lunch dishes, good salads, inexpensive, busy. Other branches at Rocca de Vergallo 201, Magdalena del Mar, and Av Primavera 373, San Borja.

## Barranco

### $$$ La 73
*Av Sol Oeste 176, casi San Martín, at the edge of Barranco, T01-2470780. Mon-Sat 1200-2400, Sun 1200-2200.*
Mostly meat dishes, has a lunch menu, look for the Chinese lanterns outside, good reputation.

### $$$ Sóngoro Cosongo
*Ayacucho 281, T01-247 4730, at the top of the steps down to Puente de Suspiros, www.songorocosongo.com. Mon-Sat 1200-2300, Sun from 2200.*
Varied *comida criolla*, "un poco de todo".

### $$$-$$ Tío Mario
*Jr Zepita 214, on the steps to the Puente de Suspiros.*
Excellent *anticuchería*, serving delicious Peruvian kebabs, always busy, fantastic service, varied menu and good prices.

### $$ Las Mesitas
*Av Grau 341, T01-477 4199. Open 1200-0200.*
Traditional tea rooms-cum-restaurant, serving *comida criolla* and traditional desserts which you won't find anywhere else, lunch *menú* served till 1400, US$3.

## Cafés

### Expreso Virgen de Guadalupe
*San Martín y Ayacucho.*
Café and vegetarian buffet in an old tram, also seating in the garden, more expensive at weekends.

### Tostería Bisetti
*Pedro de Osma 116, www.cafebisetti.com.*
Coffee, cakes and a small selection of lunchtime dishes, service a bit slow but a nice place.

## Bars and clubs

See also Entertainment (below) for a list of *peñas* offering live music and dancing.

### Central Lima
The centre of town, specifically Jr de la Unión, has numerous nightclubs, but it's best to avoid the nightspots around the intersection of Av Tacna, Av Piérola and Av de la Vega, as these places are rough and foreigners will receive much unwanted attention. For the latest gay and lesbian nightspots, check out www.gayperu.com.

### El Rincón Cervecero
*Jr de la Unión (Belén) 1045, T01-428 1422. Mon-Fri 1230-2400, Fri-Sat 1230-0030.*
German-style pub, fun.

### Estadio Fútbol Sports Bar
*Jr de la Unión (Belén) 1049, T01-427 9609. Mon-Wed 1215-2300, Thu 1215-2400, Fri-Sat 1215-0300, Sun 1215-1800.*
Beautiful bar with a disco, international football theme, good international and creole food.

### Piano Bar Munich
*Jr de la Unión 1044 (basement), T01-5737390. Mon-Sat from 1700.*
Small and fun.

### Miraflores

### La Tasca
*Av Diez Canseco 117, very near Parque Kennedy, part of the Flying Dog group and under one of the hostels (see Where to stay, page 57).*
Spanish-style bar with cheap beer (for Miraflores). An eclectic crowd including ex-pats, travellers and locals. Gay-friendly. Small and crowded.

### Media Naranja
*Schell 130, at bottom of Parque Kennedy.*
Brazilian bar with drinks and food.

### Murphy's
*Schell 619, T01-447 1082. Mon-Sat from 1600.*
Happy hours every day with different offers, lots of entertainment, very popular.

### Treff Pub Alemán
*Av Benavides 571-104, T01-444 0148 (hidden from the main road behind a cluster of tiny houses signed 'Los Duendes'). Mon-Thu 1200-0100, Fri-Sat 1800-0300, Sun 1900-0100.*
A wide range of German beers, plus cocktails, good atmosphere, darts and other games.

## Barranco
Barranco is the capital of Lima nightlife. The following is a short list of some of the better bars and clubs. The pedestrian walkway Pasaje Sánchez Carrión, right off the main plaza, has watering holes and discos on both sides. Av Grau, just across the street from the plaza, is also lined with bars, including the **Lion's Head Pub** (Av Grau 268, p 2) and **Déjà Vu** at No 294. Many of the bars in this area turn into discos later on.

### Ayahuasca
*San Martín 130. Mon-Sat 2000-0300 (opens 1800 Thu-Fri).*
In the stunning Berninzon House, which dates from the Republican era, a chilled out lounge bar with several areas for eating, drinking and dancing. Food is expensive and portions are small, but go for the atmosphere.

### Barranco Beer Company
*Grau 308, T01-247 6211, www. barrancobeer.com. Sun-Wed 1100-2400, Thu 1100-0200, Fri-Sat 1100-0300.*
Artisanal brewhouse.

### El Dragón
*N de Piérola 168, T01-221 4112.*
Popular bar and venue for music, theatre and painting.

### Juanitos
*Av Grau, opposite the park. Daily 1600-0400.*
Barranco's oldest bar, where writers and artists congregate, a perfect spot to start the evening.

### La Noche
*Bolognesi 307, at Pasaje Sánchez Carrión, T01-247 1012, www.lanoche.com.pe. Mon-Sat 2000-0200.*
A Lima institution. High standard live music, Mon is jazz night, all kicks off at around 2200.

### La Posada del Mirador
*Ermita 104, near the Puente de los Suspiros (Bridge of Sighs), see Facebook.*
Beautiful view of the ocean, but you pay for the privilege.

### Sargento Pimienta
*Bolognesi 757, www.sargentopimienta. com.pe. Tue-Sat from 2200.*
Live music, always a favourite with Limeños.

## Entertainment

Theatre and concert tickets can be booked through **Teleticket** (T01-613 8888, Mon-Fri 0900-1900, www.teleticket.com.pe). For cultural events, see **Lima Cultural** (www.lima cultura.pe), the city's monthly arts programme.

### Cinemas
The newspaper *El Comercio* lists cinema information in the section called *Luces*. Mon-Wed reduced price at most cinemas. Most films are in English with subtitles and cost from US$7-8.75 in Miraflores and malls, US$3-4 in the centre. The best cinema chains in the city are **Cinemark, Cineplanet** and **UVK Multicines**.
**Cinematógrafo de Barranco**, *Pérez Roca 196, Barranco, T01-264 4374.* Small independent cinema showing a good choice of classic and new international films.
**Filmoteca de Lima, Centro Cultural PUCP**, *Camino Real 1075, San Isidro, T01-616 1616, http://cultural.pucp.edu.pe.*

### Peñas
**Del Carajo**, *Catalino Miranda 158, Barranco, T01-247 7977, www.delcarajo.com.pe.* All types of traditional music.

**La Candelaria**, *Av Bolognesi 292, Barranco, T01-247 1314, www.lacandelariaperu.com. Thu-Sat 2000 onwards.* A good Barranco *peña* with a regular dance presentation and other shows.

**La Estación de Barranco**, *Pedro de Osma 112, T01-247 0344, www.laestacionde barranco.com. Mon-Sat 1900-0300.* Good, family atmosphere, varied shows.

**Las Brisas de Titicaca**, *Héroes de Tarapacá 168, at 1st block of Av Brasil near Plaza Bolognesi, T01-715 6960, www.brisasdeltiticaca. com.* A Lima institution. Tourist restaurant with lunch shows Fri-Sat 1300-1730, evening shows Tue-Wed 2100-0015, Thu 2145-0135, Fri-Sat 2200-0200.

### Theatres

**El Gran Teatro Nacional**, *corner of Avs Javier Prado and Aviación, San Borja.* Capable of seating 1500 people, it hosts concerts, opera, ballet and other dance as well as other events.

**Teatro Municipal**, *Jr Ica 377, T01-315 1300 ext 1767, see Facebook.* Completely restored after a fire, with full programmes and a theatre museum on Huancavelica.

There are many other theatres in the city, some of which are related to cultural centres. All have various cultural activities; the press gives details of performances: **CCPUCP** (see Cinemas, above); **Instituto Cultural Peruano-Norteamericano** (*Jr Cusco 446, Lima Centre, T01-706 7000, central office at Av Angamos Oeste 160, Miraflores, www. icpna.edu.pe*); **Centro Cultural Peruano Japonés** (*Av Gregorio Escobedo 803, Jesús María, T01-518 7450, www.apj.org.pe*).

## Festivals

**18 Jan** Founding of Lima.
**Mar/Apr** Semana Santa, or Holy Week, is a colourful spectacle with processions.
**28-29 Jul** Independence, with music and fire-works in the Plaza de Armas on the evening before.
**30 Aug** Santa Rosa de Lima.

**Mid-Sep** Mistura, www.mistura.pe, a huge gastronomy fair in Parque Exposición, with Peruvian foods, celebrity chefs, workshops and more.

**Oct** The month of **Our Lord of the Miracles**; see Las Nazarenas church, page 42.

## Shopping

### Bookshops

**Crisol**, *Ovalo Gutiérrez, Av Santa Cruz 816, San Isidro, T01-221 1010, below Cine Planet.* Large bookshop with café, titles in English, French and Spanish. Also in **Jockey Plaza Shopping Center** (*Av Javier Prado Este 4200, Surco, T01-436 0004, daily 1100-2300,* and other branches, www.crisol.com.pe).

**Ibero Librerías**, *Av Diagonal 500, T01-242 2798, Larco 199, T01-445 5520, in Larcomar, Miraflores, and other branches.* Stocks **Footprint Handbooks** as well as a wide range of other titles.

**SBS Librería Internacional**, *Av Angamos Oeste 301, Miraflores, T 01-206 4900, ext 210, www.sbs.com.pe, Mon-Fri 0900-1900, Sun 1000-1300.* Wide selection of imported English and Spanish titles. Several other locations in Lima and major provincial capitals.

### Camping equipment

It's better to bring all camping and hiking gear from home. Camping gas (the most popular brand is **Doite**) is available from any large hardware store or bigger supermarket. White gas (*bencina*) is available from hardware stores.

**Alpamayo**, *Av Larco 345, Miraflores at Parque Kennedy, T01-445 1671. Mon-Fri 1000-1930, Sat 1000-1300.* Sleeping mats, boots, rock shoes, climbing gear, water filters, tents, backpacks etc, very expensive but top-quality equipment. Owner speaks fluent English and offers good information.

**Altamira**, *Arica 880, Parque Damert, behind Wong on Ovalo Gutiérrez, Miraflores, T01-445 1286.* Sleeping bags, climbing gear, hiking gear and tents.

**Camping Center**, *Av Benavides 1620, Miraflores, T01-242 1779, www.campingperu.com. Mon-Fri*

*1000-1800*. Selection of tents, backpacks, stoves, camping and climbing gear.
**Tatoo**, *Av Prescott 295, San Isidro, T01-421 1562, www.tatoo.ws, Mon-Sat 1000-2030, Sun 1000-1800*. For top-quality imported ranges and own brands of equipment.
**Todo Camping**, *Av Angamos Oeste 350, Miraflores, near Av Arequipa, T01-242 1318. Mon-Fri 1000-2000, Sat 1000-1700*. Sells 100% deet, blue gas canisters, lots of accessories, tents, crampons and backpacks.

## Handicrafts
Miraflores is the place for high-quality, expensive handicrafts; there are many shops on and around the top end of Av La Paz (starting at Av Ricardo Palma). You will find much better value, however, in the provinces where the crafts are made.
**Agua y Tierra**, *Diez Canseco 298 y Alcanfores, Miraflores, T01-444 6980. Mon-Fri 1000-2000*. Fine crafts and indigenous art.
**Alpaca 859**, *Av Larco 859, Miraflores, T01-447 7163*. Good quality alpaca and baby alpaca products.
**Arte XXI**, *Av La Paz 678, Miraflores, T01-447 9777*. Gallery and store for contemporary and colonial Peruvian paintings.
**Artesanía Santo Domingo**, *Plazuela Santo Domingo, by the church of that name, in Lima centre, T01-428 9860*. Good Peruvian crafts.
**Kuna by Alpaca 111**, *Av Larco 671, Miraflores, T01-447 1623, www.kuna.com.pe. Daily 1000-2000*. High-quality alpaca, baby alpaca and vicuña items. Also in Larcomar (loc 1-07), Museo Larco, the airport, Jockey Plaza, at hotels and in San Isidro.
**Kuntur Wasi**, *Ocharán 182, Miraflores, opposite Sol de Oro hotel, T01-447 7173. Mon-Sat 1000-1900*. English-speaking owners are very knowledgeable about Peruvian textiles; often have exhibitions of fine folk art and crafts.
**Las Pallas**, *Cajamarca 212, Barranco, T01-477 4629. Mon-Sat 0900-1900*. Very high-quality handicrafts, English, French and German spoken.
**Luz Hecho a Mano**, *Berlín 399, Miraflores, T01-446 7098. Mon-Fri 1100-1330, 1400-1700, Sat*

*1030-1700*. Lovely handmade handbags, wallets and other leather goods including clothing which last for years and can be custom made.

## Jewellery
On Cs La Esperanza and La Paz, Miraflores, dozens of shops offer gold and silverware at reasonable prices.
**Ilaria**, *Av 2 de Mayo 308, San Isidro, T01-512 3530, www.ilariainternational.com. Mon-Fri 1000-1930*. Jewellery and silverware with interesting designs. There are other branches in Lima, Cuzco, Arequipa and Trujillo.

## Maps
**Instituto Geográfico Nacional**, *Av Aramburú 1190, Surquillo, T01-475 9960, www.ign.gob.pe. Mon-Fri 0830-1645*. It has topographical maps of the whole country at 1:100,000, political and physical maps of all departments and satellite and aerial photographs. You may be asked to show your passport when buying these maps.
**Lima 2000**, *Av Arequipa 2625 (near the intersection with Av Javier Prado), T01-440 3486, www.lima2000.com.pe. Mon-Fri 0900-1800*. Has excellent street maps of Lima, from tourist maps, US$5.55, to comprehensive books US$18. Also has country maps (US$5.55-9.25), maps of Cuzco, Arequipa, Trujillo and Chiclayo and tourist maps of the Inca Trail, Colca area and Cordillera Blanca.
**Limap**, *T01-444 2685, www.limap.pe*. Publishes various thematic maps (dining, shopping, beaches, etc.) and has a useful website.

## Markets
All are open 7 days a week until late(ish).
**Feria Nacional de Artesanía de los Deseos y Misterios**, *Av 28 de Julio 747, near junction with Av Arequipa and Museo Metropolitano*. Small market specializing in charms, remedies, fortune-telling and trinkets from Peru and Bolivia.
**Mercado 1**, *Surquillo, cross Paseo de le República from Ricardo Palma, Miraflores and go north 1 block*. Food market with a huge variety of local produce. C Narciso de

la Colina outside has various places to eat, including **Heladería La Fiorentina** (No 580), for excellent ice creams.

**Mercado Inca**, *Av Petit Thouars, blocks 51-54 (near Parque Kennedy, parallel to Av Arequipa), Miraflores*. An unnamed crafts market area, with a large courtyard and lots of small flags. This is the largest crafts arcade in Miraflores. From here to C Ricardo Palma the street is lined with crafts markets.

**Parque Kennedy**, the main park of Miraflores, hosts a daily crafts market from 1700-2300.

**Polvos Azules**, *on García Naranjo, La Victoria, just off Av Grau in the centre of town*. The 'official' black market, sells just about anything; it is generally cheap and interesting but unsafe.

## What to do

### Cycling
**Bike Tours of Lima**, *Bolívar 150, Miraflores, T01-445 3172, www.biketoursoflima.com. Mon-Fri 0930-1800, Sat-Sun 0930-1400.* Offer a variety of day tours through the city of Lima by bike, also bicycle rentals.

**Buenas Biclas**, *Domingo Elías 164, Miraflores, T01-241 9712, www.buenasbiclas.com. Mon-Fri 1000-2000, Sat 1000-1800.* Mountain bike specialists, knowledgeable staff, good selection of bikes, repairs and accessories.

**Cycloturismo Peru**, *T990-12 8105, www.ciclo turismoperu.com.* Offers good-value cycling trips around Lima and beyond, as well as bike rental. The owner, Aníbal Paredes, speaks good English, is very knowledgeable and is the owner of **Mont Blanc Gran Hotel**.

**Mirabici**, *Parque Salazar, T01-673 3903. Daily 0800-1900.* Bicycle hire, US$7.50 per hr (tandems available); they also run bike tours 1000-1500, in English, Spanish and Portuguese. Bikes to ride up and down Av Arequipa can be rented on Sun 0800-1300, US$3 per hr, leave passport as deposit, www.jahbike.com.

**Perú Bike**, *Punta Sal 506, Surco, T01-260 8225, www.perubike.com. Mon-Fri 0930-1930, Sat 0930-1500.* Experienced agency leading tours, professional guiding, mountain bike school and workshop.

### Diving
**Peru Divers**, *Av Defensores del Morro 175, Chorrillos, T01-251 6231, www.perudivers.com. Mon-Fri 0900-1700, call ahead.* Owner Lucho Rodríguez is a certified PADI instructor who offers certification courses, tours and a wealth of good information.

### Hiking
**Trekking and Backpacking Club**, *Jr Huáscar 1152, Jesús María, Lima 11, T01-423 5115, T943-866794, www.angelfire.com/mi2/ tebac.* Sr Miguel Chiri Valle, treks arranged, including in the Cordillera Blanca.

### Paragliding
**Aeroxtreme**, *Trípoli 345, dpto 503, T01-242 5125, www.aeroxtreme.com, call ahead.* One of several outfits offering parapenting in Lima, US$70, 20 years' experience.

**Andean Trail Perú**, *T998-363436, www. andeantrailperu.com.* For parapenting tandem flights, US$53, and courses, US$600 for 10 days. They also have a funday for US$120 to learn the basics. Trekking, kayaking and other adventure sports arranged.

### Textiles/cultural tours
**Puchka Perú**, *www.puchkaperu.com.* Web-based operator specializing in textiles, folk art and markets. Fixed-date tours involve meeting artisans, workshops, visit to markets and more. In association with Maestro Máximo Laura, world-famous weaver, http:// maximolauratapestries.com, whose studio in Urbanización Brisas de Santa Rosa III Etapa, Lima can be visited by appointment, T01-577 0952. See also Museo Máximo Laura in Cuzco.

### Tour operators
Do not conduct business anywhere other than in the agency's office and insist on a written contract.

**Aracari Travel Consulting**, *Schell 237, of 602, Miraflores, T01-651 2424, www.aracari.com. Mon-Sat 0800-1800.* Regional tours throughout Peru, also 'themed' and activity tours, has a very good reputation.

**Coltur**, *Av Reducto 1255, Miraflores, T01-615 5555, www.colturperu.com. Mon-Fri 0900-1800, Sat 0900-1200*. Very helpful, experienced and well-organized tours throughout Peru. Booking and customer service through their website.

**Condor Travel**, *Armando Blondet 249, San Isidro, T01-615 3000, www.condortravel.com. Mon-Fri 0900-1800*. Highly regarded operator with tailor-made programmes, special interest tours, luxury journeys, adventure travel and conventional tourism. One-stop shopping with own regional network. Booking and customer service through their website.

**Domiruth Travel Service**, *Av Rio de Janeiro 216, Miraflores, T01-610 6000, www.domiruth.com*. Tours throughout Peru, from the mystical to adventure travel. See also **Peru 4x4 Adventures**, part of Domiruth (*Jr Rio de Janeiro 216-218, www.peru4x4adventures.com*), for exclusive 4WD tours with German, English, Spanish, Italian and Portuguese-speaking drivers.

**Ecocruceros**, *Av Arequipa 4964, of 202, Miraflores, T01-226 8530, www.islaspalomino.com. Mon-Fri 0900-1900, Sat 0900-1300*. Daily departures from Plaza Grau in Callao (see page 53) to see the sea lions at Islas Palomino, 4 hrs with 30-40 mins wetsuit swimming with guide, snack lunch, US$48 (take ID), reserve a day in advance.

**Explorandes**, *C San Fernando 287, Miraflores, T01-200 6100, www.explorandes.com. Mon-Fri 0900-1750, Sat 0900-1200*. Award-winning company. Offers a wide range of adventure

and cultural tours throughout the country. Also offices in Huaraz and Cuzco (see pages 87 and 311).

**Fertur Peru Travel**, *C Schell 485, Miraflores, T01-242 1900; and Jr Junín 211, Plaza de Armas, T01-427 2626; USA/Canada T1-877 247 0055 toll free, UK T020-3002 3811, www.fertur-travel.com. Mon-Fri 0900-1900, Sat 0900-1600*. Siduith Ferrer de Vecchio, CEO of this agency, is highly recommended for tour packages, up-to-date tourist information and also great prices on national and international flights, discounts for those with ISIC and youth cards. Other services include flight reconfirmations, hotel reservations and transfers to and from the airport or bus or train stations. Also in Cuzco at Av El Sol 803, of 205, T084-221304.

**Il Tucano Peru**, *Elías Aguirre 633, Miraflores, T01-444 9361, 24-hr number T01-975 05375, www.iltucanoperu.com. Mon-Fri 0900-1800*. Personalized tours for groups or individuals throughout Peru, also 4WD overland trips, first-class drivers and guides, outstanding service and reliability.

**Info Perú**, *Jr de la Unión (Belén) 1066, of 102, T01-425 0414, www.infoperu.com.pe. Mon-Fri 0900-1800, Sat 0930-1400*. Run by a group of women, ask for Laura Gómez, offering personalized programmes, hotel bookings, transport, free tourist information, sale of maps, books and souvenirs, English and French spoken.

**InkaNatura Travel**, *Manuel Bañón 461, San Isidro, T01-203 5000, www.inkanatura.com. Mon-Fri 0900-1800, Sat 0900-1300*. Also in

Cuzco and Chiclayo, experienced company with special emphasis on both sustainable tourism and conservation, especially in Manu and Tambopata, also birdwatching, and on the archaeology of all of Peru.

**Lima Mentor**, *T01-243 2697, www.limamentor. com*. Contact through web, phone or through hotels. An agency offering cultural tours of Lima using freelance guides in specialist areas (eg gastronomy, art, archaeology, Lima at night), entertaining, finding different angles from regular tours. Half-day or full day tours.

**Lima Tours**, *N de Piérola 589, p 18, T01 619 6900, www.limatours.com.pe. Mon-Fri 0900-1745*. Very good for tours in the capital and around the country; programmes include health and wellness tours. Booking and customer service through their website.

**Peru Empire Co**, *Sáenz Peña 214, Barranco, T01-700 5137, www.pec.pe. Mon-Fri 0830-1815, Sat 0900-1200*. Offers tailor-made itineraries designed to match each traveller's personal interests, style and preferences to create ideal Peru trips.

**Peru For Less**, *ASTA Travel Agent, Luis García Rojas 240, Urbanización Humboldt, T01-273 2486, US office: T1-877-269 0309, UK office: T+44-203-002 0571, Cuzco office: T084-254800, www.peruforless.com*. Will meet or beat any published rates on the internet from outside Peru. Good reports.

**Peru Hop**, *Av Larco 812, p 3, corner with San Martín, T01-242 2140, www.peruhop.com. Daily 0900-2100*. A hop-on, hop-off bus service from Lima to Cuzco via Paracas,

Nazca, Arequipa, also to Puno and La Paz, daily departures, tours of places of interest, a variety of passes with different prices.

**Peru Rooms**, *Av Dos de Mayo 1545, of 205, San Isidro, T01-422 3434, www.perurooms.com*. Internet-based travel service offering 3- to 5-star packages throughout Peru, cultural, adventure and nature tourism.

**Rutas del Peru SAC**, *Av Enrique Palacios 1110, Miraflores, T01-445 7249, www.rutasdelperu. com*. Bespoke trips and overland expeditions in trucks.

**Vamos Expeditions**, *Av Alfredo León 114, of 1405, Miraflores, WhatsApp/T987-524304, www.vamosexpeditions.com*. Wide range of personalized 3- to 5-star packages: cultural, nature, adventure, special interest, alternative day tours, and off-the-beaten-path 4WD expeditions. Belgian/Peruvian-run by Annelies and Pablo.

**Viracocha**, *Av Vasco Núñez de Balboa 191, Miraflores, T01-447 1067, http://viracocha.pe. Mon-Fri 0900-1800, Sat 0900-1300*. Very helpful, especially for flights, adventure, cultural, mystical and birdwatching tours.

**Open-top bus tours** Mirabús (*Diagonal Oscar Benavides, block 3, T01-242 6699, www. mirabusperu.com, daily 0900-1900*), runs many tours of the city and Callao (from US$3.50 to US$30) – eg Lima half day by day, Lima by night, Costa Verde, Callao, Gold Museum, Miraflores, Pachacámac with Paso horses display and dance show, Caral. Similar services concentrating on the city are offered

by **Turibus**, from Larcomar, *T01-230 0909*, *www.turibusperu.com*.

**Private guides** The **MITINCI (Ministry of Industry Tourism, Integration and International Business)** certifies guides and can provide a list. Most are members of **AGOTUR** (Asociación de Guías Oficiales de Turismo, http://agoturlima.com). Book in advance. Most guides speak a foreign language.

## Transport

### Air

For details of flights see under destinations. A list of airlines is found in Getting around, page 488.

Jorge Chávez Airport (flight information T01-517 3500, www.lap.com.pe) is 16 km from the centre of Lima in Callao. It has all the facilities one would expect of an international airport. The **airport information desk** is by international Arrivals. **iPerú tourist information** desks at international arrivals, domestic departures and on the mezzanine (24 hrs, very helpful). The airport has car hire offices, public telephones, **Global Net** and other ATMs, *casas de cambio* and a bank (note that exchange rates are substantially poorer than outside, **Forex** exchange kiosk with fair rates in **Outlet Shopping Centre**, left of the airport as you step out, Mon-Sat 1100-1900, do not take any luggage with you). Internet facilities are more expensive in the city, but there is Wi-Fi at departure areas and all gates (10 mins free). Smart shops, restaurants and cafés are plentiful. Purchase airline tickets at the airport, not across from it, were fake airline agents are located.

**Transport from the airport** Airport Express Lima, T01-446 5539, www.airport expresslima.com, offers bus service between the airport and **Miraflores** from 0700-2400, every 30 mins in the morning and evening, hourly 1200-1800, US$8 one way, US$15 return (discounts for children 4-15 and for Peruvians). There are 7 stops in Miraflores; website has map and "stop finder". A more economical but less frequent van service is offered by **Quick Llama** (T960 165148, www. quickllama.com). Various taxi companies have desks at domestic and international arrivals, including **Taxi365** (T01 219 0271, taxi365@cmv.pe), **Taxi Directo** (T01-711 1111, servicioenlinea@taxidirecto.com) and **Taxi Green** (T01-484 4001, www.taxigreen.com.pe). All charge the same fares: US$17 to the centre, US$18.50 to Miraflores, fares to other destinations are posted. **Mitsu** (T01-261 7788, www.mitsoo.net) is more expensive and only operates from international arrivals. Independent taxi drivers also tout for passengers in the airport terminal, they are at least as expensive as the above and generally less secure. The least safe options are taxis and buses that stop by pedestrian exits outside the airport perimeter and armed robbery is a serious hazard.

If you must travel by public transport, avoid rush hour and travelling at night and pay more for a non-stop bus service. Combis to the centre (Av Abancay), lines '9',' C' or' Roma 1', charge US$0.60. Buses to Miraflores, line 'S' ('La S') or '18' and can be caught outside the airport on Av Faucett, US$0.85. Note that luggage is not allowed on public buses except very late at night or early in the morning, and they are not safe at any hour.

### Bus

**Local** Bus routes are shared by buses, combis (mid-size) and *colectivos* (mini-vans or cars). None is particularly safe; it is better to take a taxi (see below for recommendations). *Colectivos* run 24 hrs, although less frequently 0100-0600; they are quicker than buses and stop wherever requested. Buses and combis

**Tip...**
Do not go to the airport's car park exit to find a taxi without an airport permit outside the perimeter. Although these are much cheaper, they are not safe even by day, far less so at night. See Arriving at night, page 71.

## ON THE ROAD

### Arriving at night

A number of international flights arrive at Lima airport in the small hours of the morning. The iPerú tourist information office (upstairs in the departures area and very helpful), money-changing facilities and most other airport services operate around the clock. Don't change more money than you need though, as rates at the airport are very poor.

There are two international chain hotels by the airport (see page 58); if you don't want to stay there, the airport has ample seating areas and is safe. Most hotels can arrange for airport pick-up for between US$15 and US$30. Smaller hotels do not have their own vehicles and will usually just send a taxi driver to meet you. With any transport service, always confirm the price in advance. Airport Express buses (www.airportexpresslima.com) and Taxi Green (www.taxigreen.com.pe) are popular choices, providing safe service at posted prices. Independent taxi drivers who hang around outside the terminal building may be less safe and more expensive. Under no circumstances should you leave the airport perimeter to look for a taxi in the street. This is not safe even by day, far less so at night. It is worth noting that the ride to your hotel may be quicker in the middle of the night, as this is the only time when the streets of Lima are not completely clogged with traffic. See also Transport from the airport, page 70.

charge about US$0.40-0.45, *colectivos* a little more. On public holidays, Sun and from 2400 to 0500 every night, a small charge is added to the fare.

The **Metropolitano** (T01-203 9000, www.metropolitano.com.pe) is a system of articulated buses running on dedicated lanes north–south across the city from Naranjal in Comas to Estación Central (in front of the **Sheraton** hotel; estimated journey time 32 mins) and then south along the Vía Expresa/Paseo de la República to Matellini in Chorrillos (estimated journey time 32 mins); there are purpose-built stations along the route. The **Metropolitano** tends to be very crowded and is of limited use to visitors, but can be handy for reaching Miraflores (use stations between Angamos and 28 de Julio) and Barranco (Bulevar is 170 m from the Plaza). There are 2 branches through downtown Lima, either via Av Alfonso Ugarte and Plaza 2 de Mayo, or via Jr Lampa and Av Emancipación. Fares are paid using a prepaid and rechargeable card (minimum S/5, US$1.45), available from every station; each journey costs S/2.50 (US$0.70). Services

run Mon-Sat 0500-2300 with shorter hours on Sun and on some sections. There are express services Mon-Fri 0600-0900 and 1635-2115 between certain stations.

**Long distance** There are many different bus companies, but the larger ones are better organized, leave on time and do not wait until the bus is full, many are open 0700 to about 2200. Leaving or arriving in Lima by bus in the rush hour can add an extra hour or more to the journey. All bus companies have their own offices and terminals in the centre of the city, many around Carlos Zavala, but this is not a safe area. Many north-bound buses also have an office and stop at the Terminal Plaza Norte (http://granterminalterrestre.com, Metropolitano Tomás Valle), not far from the

**Tip...**

In the weeks either side of 28/29 July (Independence), and of the Christmas/New Year holiday, it is practically impossible to get bus tickets out of Lima, unless you book in advance. Bus prices double at these times.

airport, which is handy for those who need to make a quick bus connection after landing in Lima. Many south-bound buses are at the Terminal Terrestre Lima Sur, at Km 11-12 on the Panamericana Sur by Puente Atocongo (Metro Atocongo).

It is worth paying more for a safe, comfortable and reliable bus. The following are 3 large companies which currently have good reputations:

**Cruz del Sur** (T01-311 5050, www.cruzdel sur.com.pe) has its main terminal at Av Javier Prado 1109, La Victoria, with standard and luxury service to most parts of Peru. Another terminal is at Jr Quilca 531, Lima centre, for *Imperial* services to Arequipa, Ayacucho, Chiclayo, Cuzco, Huancayo, Huaraz, and Trujillo. There are sales offices throughout the city, including at Terminal Plaza Norte.

**Móvil**, Av Paseo de La República 749, Lima centre (near the national stadium); Av Alfredo Mendiola 3883, Los Olivos, and Terminal Terrestre Lima Sur, T01-716 8000, www.moviltours.com.pe. Serves major destinations throughout the country.

**Oltursa**, Aramburú 1160, San Isidro, T01-708 5000, www.oltursa.pe.Top-end services to **Nazca**, **Arequipa** and destinations in **northern Peru**, mainly at night.

There are a great many more companies (of varying quality) serving regional destinations, see Transport sections throughout the book.

**Cavassa**, Raimondi 129, Lima centre, T01-431 3200, www.turismocavassa.com.pe. Also at Terminal Plaza Norte. Services to **Huaraz**.

**Cial**, República de Panamá 2460, T01-207 6900 ext 119, and Paseo de la República 646, T01-207 6900 ext 170. Has national coverage.

**Cromotex**, Av Nicolás Arriola 898, Santa Catalina; Av Paseo de La República 659, T01-424 7575, www.cromotex.com.pe. To **Cuzco** and **Arequipa**.

**Flores**, T01-332 1212, www.floreshnos.pe. Has departures to many parts of the country, especially the south, from terminals at Av Paseo de le República 683, Av Paseo de le República 627 and Jr Montevideo 523. Nationwide coverage but poor service.

**Ittsa**, Paseo de la República 809, T01-423 5232, www.ittsabus.com. Also at Terminal Plaza Norte. Good service to the north, including **Chiclayo**, **Piura**, **Tumbes**.

**Julio César**, José Gálvez 562, La Victoria, T01-424 8060, www.transportesjuliocesar.com.pe. Also at Terminal Plaza Norte. Good service to **Huaraz**; recommended to arrive in Huaraz and then use local transport to points beyond.

**Línea**, Paseo de la República 941-959, Lima centre, T01-424 0836, www.transporteslinea.com.pe. Also at Terminal Plaza Norte (T01-533 0739). Among the best services to destinations in the north.

**Ormeño**, www.grupo-ormeno.com.pe, and its affiliated bus companies depart from and arrive at Av Javier Prado Este 1057, Santa Catalina, T01-472 1710, but the terminal at Av Carlos Zavala 177, Lima centre, T01-427 5679, is the best place to get information and buy any Ormeño ticket. Service has deteriorated in recent years.

**Soyuz**, Av México 333, T01-205 2370. To **Ica** every 7 mins, well organized. As **PerúBus**, www.perubus.com.pe, the same company runs north to **Huacho** and **Barranca**.

**Tepsa**, Javier Prado Este 1091, La Victoria; Av Gerardo Unger 6917, T01-617 9000, www.tepsa.com.pe. Also at Terminal Plaza Norte (T01-533 1524). Services to the north as far as **Tumbes** and the south to **Tacna**.

Transportes **Chanchamayo**, Av Nicolás Arriola 535, La Victoria, T01-265 6850. To **Tarma**, **San Ramón** and **La Merced**.

Transportes **León de Huánuco**, Av 28 de Julio 1520, La Victoria, T01-424 3893. Daily to **Huánuco**, **Tingo María**, **La Merced** and **Pucallpa**.

**International** Ormeño (see above) to **Guayaquil** (29 hrs with a change of bus at the border, US$56), **Quito** (38 hrs, US$75), **Cali** (56 hrs, US$131), **Bogotá** (70 hrs, US$141), **Caracas** (100 hrs, US$150), **Santiago** (54 hrs, US$102), **Mendoza** (78 hrs, US$159), **Buenos Aires** (90 hrs, US$148), **São Paulo** (90 hrs); a maximum of 20 kg is allowed pp. **Cruz del Sur** to **Guayaquil** (3 a week, US$85), **Buenos Aires** (US$201) and **Santiago** (US$130). **El Rápido** (Abtao 1279, La Victoria, T01-432 6380, www.elrapidoint.com.ar) to **Buenos Aires** Mon, Wed, Fri; connections in Mendoza to other cities in Argentina and Uruguay.

## Car hire

Most companies have an office at the airport, where you can arrange everything and pick up and leave the car. It is recommended to test drive before signing the contract as quality varies. It can be much cheaper to rent a car in a town in the Sierra for a few days than to drive from Lima; also companies don't have a collection service. Cars can be hired from: **Paz Rent A Car**, Av Diez Canseco 319, of 15, Miraflores, T01-446 4395, T999-939853. **Budget**, T01-204 4400, www.budgetperu.com. Prices range from US$35 to US$85 depending on type of car. Make sure that your car is in a locked garage at night.

## Metro

The 1st line of the **Tren Eléctrico** (www.lineauno.pe) runs from Villa El Salvador in the southeast of the city to Bayóvar in the northeast, daily 0600-2230. Each journey costs S/.1.50 (US$0.55); pay by swipe card S/.5 (US$1.75). Metro stations Miguel Grau, El Ángel and Presbítero Maestro lie on the eastern edge of the downtown area. Construction work has started on the next section.

## Taxi

Taxis do not use meters although some have rate sheets (eg **Satelital**, T01-355 5555, http://3555555satelital.com). Agree the price of the journey beforehand and insist on being taken to the destination of your choice. At night, on Sun and holidays expect a surcharge of 35-50%. The following are taxi fares for some of the more common routes, give or take a sol. From downtown Lima to: Parque Kennedy (Miraflores), US$5.50; Museo de la Nación, US$5.25; San Isidro, US$5.25; Barranco, US$6.25. From Miraflores (Parque Kennedy) to: Museo de la Nación, US$4.25; Archaeology Museum, US$5.25; Barranco, US$6.30. By law, all taxis must have the vehicle's registration number painted on the side. They are often white or yellow, but can come in any colour, size or make. Licensed and phone taxis are safest, but if hailing a taxi on the street, local advice is to look for an older driver rather than a youngster.

There are several reliable phone taxi companies, which can be called for immediate service, or booked in advance; prices are 2-3 times more than ordinary taxis: to the airport, about US$20; to suburbs, US$15. Try **Taxi Real**, T01-215 1414, www.taxireal.com; **Taxi Seguro**, T01-536 6956, www.taxisegurolima.com; **Taxi Tata**, T01-274 5151, www.tata-taxis.com. If hiring a taxi by the hour, agree on price beforehand, US$9-11. **Note** Drivers don't expect tips; give them small change from the fare.

## Train

Details of the service on the Central Railway to Huancayo are given on page 361.

# Huaraz & the cordilleras

trek among some of South America's loftiest peaks

The Cordillera Blanca is a region of lakes and mountain peaks that attracts mountaineers, hikers, cyclists and rafters in their thousands. Here stand some of the highest mountains in South America, with 30 snow-crested peaks over 6000 m, including Huascarán, the highest mountain in Peru at 6768 m.

This area contains the largest concentration of glaciers found in the world's tropical zone: a source of both beauty and danger. The turquoise lakes that form in the terminal moraines are the jewels of the Andes, and you should hike up to at least one during your stay, but their tranquility masks a frightening history, when dykes have broken, sending tons of water hurtling down the canyons. Earthquakes, too, have scarred the high valleys; the mass grave that was once the old town of Yungay is a very humbling place.

Southeast of Huaraz, the Cordillera Huayhuash equals the Cordillera Blanca in beauty and majesty and is also a very popular destination for trekkers and climbers, offering the best known long-distance trek in northern Peru. There are also various archaeological sites in the region, the most famous of which is the fortress-temple of Chavín de Huántar, on the east side of the Cordillera Blanca.

**Best** for
Scenery ▪ Solitude ▪ Trekking

Towards Huaraz &
  the cordilleras . . . . . . . . . . . . . 79
Huaraz . . . . . . . . . . . . . . . . . . . . . 79
Chavín & the Callejón
  de Conchucos . . . . . . . . . . . . . 90
Callejón de Huaylas . . . . . . . . . . 94
Cordillera Huayhuash . . . . . . 101

# Footprint
## picks

★ **Chavín de Huántar**,
page 91
This is one of Peru's most important pre-Inca archaeological sites.

★ **The bus ride through Punta Olímpica**, page 92
A spectacular tunnel at 4700 m connects Chacas with Carhuaz in the
Callejón de Huaylas.

★ **Yungay**, page 94
The old village is a haunting reminder of the sometimes merciless
power of nature.

★ **Laguna Parón**, page 97
A day trek (or taxi) from Caraz will take you to this exquisite lake
surrounded by majestic peaks.

★ *Puyas raimondii*, pages 97 and 98
Witness the flowering of these remarkable Andean plants.

★ **Llanganuco–Santa Cruz or Huayhuash**,
pages 97 and 101
Don't miss the chance to enjoy one of these classic treks.

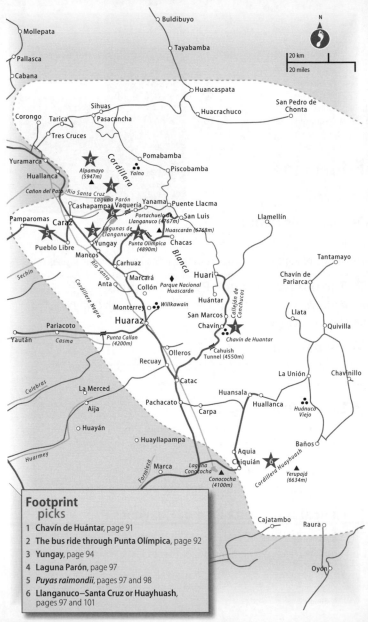

## Footprint
picks

1 Chavín de Huántar, page 91
2 The bus ride through Punta Olímpica, page 92
3 Yungay, page 94
4 Laguna Parón, page 97
5 *Puyas raimondii*, pages 97 and 98
6 Llanganuco−Santa Cruz or Huayhuash, pages 97 and 101

# Essential Huaraz and the cordilleras

## Finding your feet

Established in July 1975, **Parque Nacional Huascarán** includes the entire Cordillera Blanca above 4000 m, with an area of 3400 sq km. It is a UNESCO World Biosphere Reserve and part of the World Heritage Trust. The park's objectives are to protect the flora, fauna, geology, archaeological sites and scenic beauty of the Cordillera. Park fees: day-visit, US$9.25 (30 soles); two to three days, US$18.50 (60 soles); four to 30 days, US$46 (150 soles). Purchase tickets at the park office in Huaraz (Jr Federico Sal y Rosas 555, by Plazuela Belén, T043-422086, pnhuascaran@sernanp.gob.pe, Monday-Friday 0830-1300, 1430-1700), or at rangers posts at Llanganuco and Huascarán (for the Llanganuco–Santa Cruz trek), or at Collón for the Quebrada Ishinca. Current regulations state that local guides are mandatory everywhere in the park except designated 'Recreation Zones' (areas accessible by car). Tourists must hire a licensed tour operator for all activities and those operators may only employ licensed guides, cooks, *arrieros* and porters. Fees, regulations and their implementation change frequently; always confirm details in Huaraz

## Getting around

The best way to explore the Cordilleras is, of course, on foot. However, there are also numerous buses and minivans daily between Huaraz and Caraz in the Callejón de Huaylas, and more limited services to settlements on the eastern side of the Cordillera Blanca. The bus journey through the Punta Olímpica tunnel is an extraordinary experience that shouldn't be missed. For information on trekking in the cordilleras, see page 88.

## When to go

The months of May to September are the dry season and best for trekking, although conditions vary from year to year. From November to April the weather is usually wet, views may be restricted by cloud, and paths are likely to be muddy.

## Time required

You could spend anything from one to four weeks in this region, depending on how much trekking you want to do. Most circuits can be hiked in five days, but there are also worthwhile day hikes and longer routes, such as the Alpamayo Circuit.

## Weather Huaraz

| January | February | March | April | May | June |
|---|---|---|---|---|---|
| 13°C 1°C 122mm | 14°C 1°C 131mm | 14°C 0°C 126mm | 12°C -1°C 93mm | 11°C -1°C 55mm | 10°C -3°C 69mm |

| July | August | September | October | November | December |
|---|---|---|---|---|---|
| 9°C -3°C 61mm | 9°C -3°C 47mm | 9°C -3°C 62mm | 10°C -2°C 85mm | 11°C -2°C 96mm | 12°C -1°C 112mm |

# Cordillera
## Blanca

Apart from the range running along the Chile–Argentina border, the highest mountains in South America lie along the Cordillera Blanca and are perfectly visible from many spots. From Huaraz alone, you can see more than 23 peaks of over 5000 m, of which the most notable is Huascarán (6768 m), the highest mountain in Peru. Although the snowline is receding, the Cordillera Blanca still contains the largest concentration of glaciers found in the world's tropical zone; these are matched in splendour by the turquoise-coloured lakes that form in the terminal moraines. Here also is one of Peru's most important pre-Inca sites, at Chavín de Huántar.

North from Lima the Pan-American Highway parallels the coast and a series of roads branch off east for the climb up to Huaraz in the Callejón de Huaylas, gateway to Parque Nacional Huascarán.

Probably the easiest route to Huaraz is the paved road that branches off the highway north of Pativilca, 203 km from Lima. The road climbs increasingly steeply to the chilly pass at 4080 m (Km 120). Shortly after, Laguna Conococha, source of the Río Santa, comes into view. A road branches off from Conococha to Chiquián (see page 101) and the Cordilleras Huayhuash and Raura to the southeast. After crossing a high plateau the main road descends gradually for 47 km until Catac, where another road branches east to Chavín and on to the Callejón de Conchucos on the eastern side of the Cordillera Blanca. Huaraz is 36 km further on. From Huaraz the road continues north between the towering Cordillera Negra, snowless but rising above 5000 m and the snow-covered Cordillera Blanca.

The alternative routes to the Callejón de Huaylas are via the Callán Pass from Casma to Huaraz (fully paved, see page 110), and from Chimbote to Caraz via the Cañón del Pato (partly paved, rough and spectacular; page 110).

Located 420 km from Lima, Huaraz is the capital of Ancash department and the main town in the Cordillera Blanca, with a population of 127,000. It is a major tourist centre as well as a busy commercial hub, especially on market days. At 3091 m, it is a prime destination for hikers and a mecca for international climbers and trekkers.

### Sights

Huaraz's setting, at the foot of the Cordillera Blanca, is spectacular. The town was almost completely destroyed in the earthquake of May 1970. The Plaza de Armas has since been rebuilt, but the new **cathedral** is still under construction. **Museo Arqueológico de Ancash** ① *Ministerio de Cultura, Plaza de Armas, Mon-Sat 0900-1700, Sun 0900-1400*, contains stone monoliths and huacos from the Recuay culture, well labelled. The main thoroughfare, Avenida Luzuriaga, is bursting at the seams with travel agencies, climbing equipment hire shops, restaurants, cafés and bars. A good district for those seeking peace and quiet is La Soledad, six blocks uphill from the Plaza de Armas on Avenida Sucre. Here, along Sucre and Jirón Amadeo Figueroa, are many hotels and rooms for rent in private homes. The **Sala de Cultura SUNARP** ① *Av Centenario 530, Independencia, T043-421301, Mon-Fri 1700-2000, Sat 0900-1300, free*, often has interesting art and photography exhibitions by local artists.

**Tip...**

Huaraz has its share of crime, especially during the high season. Women should not go to surrounding districts and sites alone. Muggings have taken place on the way to Laguna Churup, to Mirador Rataquenua, on the trail from Wilcawain to Ahuac Cocha, and between the Monterrey thermal baths and Wilcawain. Enquire locally before visiting these areas.

## Around Huaraz

About 8 km to the northeast is **Willkawain** ① *Tue-Fri 0830-1600, Sat-Sun 0900-1330, US$1.75, take a combi from 13 de Diciembre and Jr Cajamarca, US$0.75, 20 mins, direct to Willkawain.* The ruins (AD 700-1100, Huari Empire) consist of one large three-storey structure with intact stone roof slabs and several small structures. About 500 m past Willkawain is Ichicwillkawain with several similar but smaller structures. A well-signed trail climbs from Wilkawain to Laguna Ahuac (Aguak Cocha, 4580 m); it's a demanding acclimatization hike (12 km return), with no services along the way.

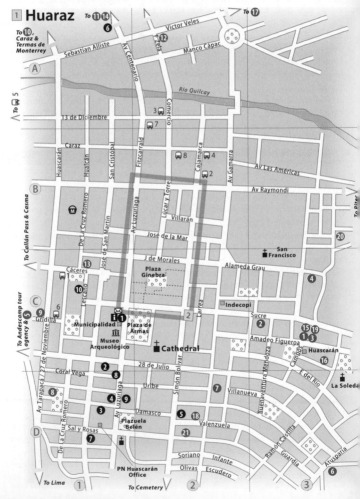

**Huaraz**

A popular excursion is to **Laguna Churup** ① *inside PN Huascarán, see page 77 for fees*, in a lovely setting beneath rocky peaks at 4500 m. This demanding 6-km full-day hike, climbs 600 m from the village of Pitec, 10 km east of Huaraz. There are no services in Pitec; take food, warm clothing, sun protection, etc. Most Huaraz operators offer this tour or take a taxi from to Pitec, US$15 one way (and hope for a ride back), US$35 with all-day wait.

## Listings Huaraz *maps below and page 82.*

### Tourist information

The national park office (see Essential box, page 77) is principally administrative, with no information for visitors.

#### Indecopi
*Av Gamarra 677, T043-423899, www.indecopi.gob.pe.*
Government consumer protection office. Very effective but not always quick. Spanish only.

#### iPerú
*Pasaje Atusparia, of 1, Plaza de Armas, T043-428812, iperuhuaraz@promperu.gob.pe. Mon-Sat 0900-1800, Sun 0900-1300.*
Also at Jr San Martín cuadra 6 s/n, daily 0800-1100, and at Anta airport when flights arrive.

#### Policía de Turismo
*Av Luzuriaga on Plaza de Armas, around the corner from iPerú, T043 422487, devtur.huaraz@policia.gob.pe. Mon-Sat 0730-2100.*
The place to report crimes and resolve issues with tour operators, hotels, etc. All female officers, limited English spoken.

### Where to stay

Hotels fill up rapidly in high season (May-Sep), especially during public holidays and special events when prices rise (beware overcharging). Touts meet buses and aggressively 'suggest' places to stay. Do not be put off your choice of lodging; phone ahead to confirm.

#### $$$$-$$$ Andino Club
*Pedro Cochachín 357, some way southeast of the centre (take a taxi after dark), T043-421662, www.hotelandino.com.*

**N**

| 200 metres |
| 200 yards |

**Where to stay** 🛏
1 Albergue Churup *C3*
2 Alojamiento El Jacal *C3*
3 Alojamiento Soledad *C3*
4 Alpes Huaraz *C3*
5 Andescamp Hostel *C1*
6 Andino Club *D3*
7 Angeles Inn *D2*
8 Benkawasi *D1*
9 Casa Jaimes *C1*
10 El Patio *A1*
11 Hatun Wasi *A1*
12 Hostal Colomba *A2*
13 Hostal Quintana *C1*
14 Jo's Place *A1*
15 La Cabaña *C3*
16 La Casa de Zarela *C3*
17 Lodging House Ezama *A3*
18 Res NG *D2*
19 Res Sucre *C3*
20 San Sebastián *B3*
21 Suiza Peruana *D2*

**Restaurants** 🍴
1 Bistro de los Andes *C2*
2 California Café *C1*
3 Chifa Jim Hua *D1*
4 El Fogón & Panadería Salazar *D1*
5 Huaraz Querido *D2*
6 Mi Comedia *A1*
7 Mi Comedia Gelatería *D1*
8 Pizza Bruno *D1*
9 Sala de Estar *D1*
10 Salud y Vida *C1*

**Transport** 🚌
1 Sandoval/Olguita Tours *C1*
2 Vans to Caraz & Yungay *A1, A2*
3 Vans to Wilcawain *A2*
4 Julio César *B2*
5 Móvil Tours terminal *A1*
6 Terminal de Transportistas Zona Sur *C1*
7 Trans Huandoy *A2*
8 Vans to Carhuaz *B2*

➡ **Huaraz maps**
1 Huaraz, page 80
2 Huaraz centre, page 82

Swiss-run hotel with very high standards, ample grounds, excellent restaurant, variety of rooms including panoramic views, balcony, fireplace, jacuzzi and sauna.

## 2 Huaraz centre

**Restaurants**
1 Café Andino & Familia Meza Lodging
2 Chilli Heaven
3 Creperie Patrick
4 El Horno Pizzería Grill
5 Encuentro
6 Frutelo
7 Pizza B&B
8 Pizzería Landauro
9 Rinconcito Minero
10 Rossonero
11 Trivio

**Bars & clubs**
12 13 Buhos
13 Taberna Tambo
14 Zona VIP

➡ Huaraz maps
1 Huaraz, page 80
2 Huaraz centre, page 82

### $$$ El Patio
*Av Monterrey, 250 m downhill from the Monterrey baths, T043-424965, www.elpatio.com.pe.*
Very colonial-style with lovely gardens, comfortable rooms, singles, doubles and triples, some with balconies, also 4 lodges with fireplaces. Meals on request, bar.

### $$$ Hostal Colomba
*Francisco de Zela 210, just off Centenario across the river, T043-421501, www.huarazhotel.com.*
Lovely old hacienda, family-run, garden with playground and sports, safe parking, gym and well-equipped rooms sleeping 1-6, comfortable beds, restaurant.

### $$$ The Lazy Dog Inn
*30 mins' drive from Huaraz (US$10 by taxi), close to the boundary of Huascarán National Park, 3.1 km past the town of Marian, close to the Quebrada Cojup, T971-448314, www.thelazydoginn.com.*
Eco-tourism lodge actively involved in community projects (see www.andean alliance.org), water recycling systems and composting toilets. Beautifully designed in warm colours, great location gives access to several mountain valleys. Organizes horse riding and hiking trips. Excellent home-cooked breakfast and dinner included. Canadian owned, English spoken. Recommended.

### $$$-$$ San Sebastián
*Jr Italia 1124, T043-426960, www.sansebastianhuaraz.com.*
Lovely out-of-the-way hotel, comfortable beds with duvets, bath tubs, restaurant, nice common areas, parking, helpful, good views. Recommended.

### $$ Suiza Peruana
*Jr Federico Sal y Rosas 843, T043-425263, www.suizaperuana.com.*
Central location, comfortable rooms, nice design, great views, elevator, garage, 24-hr service.

## $$-$ Albergue Churup
*Jr Amadeo Figueroa 1257, T043-424200, www.churup.com.*
13 rooms with private bath or 2 dorms with shared bath, hot water, fire in sitting room on 4th floor, cafeteria, use of kitchen 1800-2200, lots of information, laundry, book exchange, English spoken, Spanish classes, adventure travel tours, extremely helpful. Airport transfers and free pick-up from bus.

## $$-$ Alojamiento Soledad
*Jr Amadeo Figueroa 1267, T043-421196, info@quenualadventures.com.*
Private and shared bath, US$12 pp in dorm, abundant hot water, good breakfast, use of kitchen, family home and atmosphere, trekking information and tours, bus station pick-up. Warmly recommended.

## $$-$ Hatun Wasi
*Jr Daniel Villayzán 268, T043-425055.*
Family-run hotel next to **Jo's Place**. Spacious rooms, hot water, pleasant roof terrace, ideal for breakfasts, great views of the cordillera.

## $$-$ La Casa de Zarela
*J Arguedas 1263, T043-421694, www.lacasadezarela.hostel.com.*
Hot water, use of kitchen, laundry facilities, popular with climbers and trekkers, owner Zarela who speaks English organizes groups and is very knowledgeable.

## $$-$ Residencial NG
*Pasaje Valenzuela 837, T043-421831, www.residencialng.com.*
Breakfast, hot water, good value, helpful.

## $ Alojamiento El Jacal
*Jr Sucre 1044, T043-424612.*
With or without shower, hot water, helpful family, garden, laundry facilities.

## $ Alpes Huaraz
*Jr Ladislao Meza 112, up a cobblestone street past the San Francisco church, T043-428896, www.hostalalpeshuaraz.com.*
Rooms with private bath, hot water, fireplace, kitchen, terrace with views, garden, arrange tours, friendly atmosphere, good value.

## $ Andescamp Hostel
*Jr Huáscar 615, T043-423842, www.andescamphostel.com.*
Hostel with dorms and private rooms, some with bath, and snack bar. Tour agency, see What to do, page 86.

## $ Angeles Inn
*Av Gamarra 815, T043-422205, solandperu@yahoo.com.*
No sign, look for **Sol Andino** travel agency in same building (www.solandino.com), laundry facilities, garden, hot water, owners Max and Saul Angeles are official guides, helpful with trekking and climbing, rent equipment.

## $ Benkawasi
*Parque Santa Rosa 928, 10 mins from centre, T043-423150, http://huarazbenkawasi.com.*
Doubles, also rooms for 3, 4 and dorm, hot water, breakfast available, laundry, games room, pick-up from bus station.

## $ Casa Jaimes
*Alberto Gridilla 267, T043-422281, 2 blocks from the main plaza, www.casajaimes.com.*
Dormitory with hot showers, laundry facilities, has maps and books of the region. Noisy but economical.

## $ Familia Meza
*Lúcar y Torre 538, behind Café Andino (enquire here, see Restaurants, below), T943 695908.*
Shared bath, hot water, laundry facilities, popular with trekkers, mountaineers and bikers.

## $ Hostal Quintana
*Mcal Cáceres 411, T043-426060.*
English, French, Italian and Spanish spoken, mountain gear rental, 2 of the owner's sons are certified guides and can arrange itineraries, laundry facilities, café popular with trekkers.

## $ Jo's Place
*Jr Daniel Villayzan 276. T043-425505.*
Safe, hot water at night, nice mountain views, garden, terrace, English/Peruvian-run, warm atmosphere, popular.

## $ La Cabaña
*Jr Sucre 1224, T943-245024.*

Shared and double rooms, hot showers, laundry, popular, safe for parking, bikes and luggage, English and French spoken, good value.

### $ Lodging House Ezama
*Mariano Melgar 623, Independencia, 15 mins' walk from Plaza de Armas (US$0.50 by taxi), T043-423490.*
Light, spacious rooms, hot water, safe, helpful.

### $ Residencial Sucre
*Sucre 1240, T943-677560.*
Private house, kitchen, laundry facilities, hot water, English, German and French spoken, mountaineering guide, Filiberto Rurush, can be contacted here.

### Restaurants

### $$$ Creperie Patrick
*Luzuriaga 422, T043-426037, www.creperiepatrick.com. Mon-Sat 1600-2230, Sun 1800-2230.*
Excellent alpaca, *cuy*, crêpes, fish, quiche, spaghetti and good wine.

### $$$ Pizza Bruno
*Luzuriaga 834, T043-425689. Open from 1600-2300.*
Best pizza, excellent crêpes and pastries, good service, French owner Bruno Reviron also has a 4WD with driver for hire.

### $$$-$$ Mi Comedia
*Av Centenario 351, T043-587954. Open 1700-2300.*
Wood-oven pizzas, rustic European style, very good service.

### $$$-$$ Trivio
*Parque del Periodista,T943-613023. Daily 0800-0030.*
Creative international food, good coffee, nice view.

### $$ Bistro de los Andes
*Luzuriaga 702 y Sucre, Plaza de Armas, upstairs, T043-429556. Mon-Sat 1200-2200.*
Great food, owner speaks English, French and German. Plaza branch has a nice view of the plaza. Wide range of international dishes.

### $$ Chilli Heaven
*Parque Ginebra, T043-425532. Mon-Sat 1200-2145, Sun 1700-2100.*
Specializing in spicy food; Mexican, Indian and Thai.

### $$ El Horno Pizzería Grill
*Parque Ginebra, T043-421004. Daily 1200-2300.*
Good atmosphere, fine grilled meats and pizza, very popular.

### $$ Encuentro
*Parque del Periodista and Julian de Morales 650. Daily 0800-2300.*
Breakfast, lunch and dinners, very busy and very good.

### $$ Huaraz Querido
*Bolívar 981. Lunch only.*
Very popular place for great ceviche and other fish dishes.

### $$ Pizza B&B
*La Mar 674.*
Excellent traditional sauces for pizza and pasta, and desserts.

### $$ Pizzería Landauro
*Sucre, on corner of Plaza de Armas, T043-425651. Closed 1200-1800 and Sun.*
Very good for pizzas, Italian dishes, sandwiches, breakfasts, nice atmosphere.

### $$-$ Chifa Jim Hua
*Teófilo de Castillo 556, T043-429037. Daily 1100-2330.*
Large, tasty portions, economical lunch *menú* Mon-Sat.

### $$-$ El Fogón
*Luzuriaga 928, upstairs, T043-421267. Daily 1130-2300.*
Good value *menú*, wide selection of tasty Peruvian and international dishes, generous portions, good service, very popular with locals, go early.

### $$-$ Rinconcito Minero
*J de Morales 757. Open 0700-2300.*
Breakfast, popular lunch *menú*, vegetarian
options, coffee and snacks.

### $$-$ Sala de Estar
*Luzuriaga 923, upstairs. T043-456457.*
*Tue-Sun 1700-2300.*
Pasta dishes, home-made desserts, fruit
juices and drinks. Good creative meals.

### $$-$ Salud y Vida
*Lescano 632. Mon-Sat 0800-2100,*
*Sun 1230-1530.*
Vegetarian *menú* and à la carte,
sells home-made yoghurt.

## Cafés

### Café Andino
*Lúcar y Torre 530, 3rd floor, T043-421203,*
*www.cafeandino.com.*
Peruvian/American-owned café-restaurant-
bar with book exchange and extensive lending
library in many languages. A great place
to relax and meet other travellers, warmly
recommended. Owner Chris Benway also runs
**La Cima Logistics**, see What to do, page 87.

### California Café
*28 de Julio 562, T043-428354, http://*
*huaylas.com/californiacafe/california.htm.*
*Mon-Sat 0700-1900, Sun 0700-1400.*
Excellent breakfast, great sandwiches,
falafel, coffee and chocolate cake, book
exchange. Californian owner is a good source
of information on trekking in the Cordillera
Huayhuash and security issues.

### Frutelo
*Bolívar y Sucre, upstairs.*
*Open 0800-1200, 1700-2200.*
Fruit juices, coffee, creative sandwiches,
burgers and snacks.

### Mi Comedia Gelatería
*Jr San Martín 1213.*
"The best home-made *gelato* this side
of Milan."

### Panadería Salazar
*Av Luzuriaga 944, Gamarra 755 and*
*other locations.*
Good bakery and café, cheap, pleasant
atmosphere, good for a snack.

### Rossonero
*Luzuriaga 645 entre Sucre y J de Morales,*
*2nd floor, T043-421519. Daily 0700-2300.*
Café with extensive menu, coffee,
sandwiches, ice cream, reasonable prices.

## Bars and clubs

### 13 Buhos
*Parque Ginebra. Daily 0800-2300.*
Bar and restaurant. Daytime and nightspot,
very popular, owner makes his own craft
beer. Good music, games, nice ambience.

### Taberna Tambo
*José de la Mar 776. Open 1000-1600,*
*2000-early hours.*

Folk music daily, disco, full on, non-stop dance mecca. Very popular with both locals and gringos.

## Zona VIP
*José de la Mar y Bolívar.*
Lively disco.

## Festivals

**3 May** Patron saints' day, **El Señor de la Soledad**, celebrations last a week.
**Jun Festival del Andinismo**, international climbing week.
**Jun San Juan** and **San Pedro** are celebrated throughout the region during the last week of Jun.
**Aug Inkafest**, mountain film festival, dates change each year.

## Shopping

### Clothing
For local sweaters, hats, gloves and wall hangings at good value, try Pasaje Mcal Cáceres, off Luzuriaga; the stalls off Luzuriaga between Morales and Sucre; Bolívar cuadra 6, and elsewhere. **Last Minute Gifts** (Lucar Y Torre 530, 2nd floor) sells hats, clothing, souvenirs and jewellery.

### Markets
The central market offers various canned and dry goods, as well as fresh fruit and vegetables. Beware pickpockets in this area. There are also several supermarkets in town (see Huaraz centre map, page 82), do not leave valuables in your bags while shopping.

## What to do

Try to get a recommendation from someone who has recently returned from a tour, trek or climb. All agencies run conventional tours to Llanganuco (US$12 pp, very long day), Chavín (8-10 hrs, US$14 pp), Laguna Churup, Laguna 69, and Pastoruri. They all pool their clients and entry tickets are not included. Competition is fierce and the cheapest is not the best. Many agencies also hire equipment.

### Horse riding
**Posada de Yungar**, *Yungar (about 20 km from Huaraz on the Carhuaz road)*, T043-421267/967-9836. Swiss-run. Ask for José Flores or Gustavo Soto. US$7.50 per hr on good horses; good 4-hr trip in the Cordillera Negra.
**Sr Robinson Ayala Gride**, T043-423813. Contact him well in advance for half-day trips, US$36; enquire at **El Cortijo** restaurant, on Huaraz–Caraz road, Km 6.5. He is a master *paso* rider.

### Mountain biking
**Mountain Bike Adventures**, *Lúcar y Torre 530*, T043-424259, www.chakinaniperu.com. Contact Julio Olaza. US$60 pp for day trip, all inclusive, various routes, excellent standard of equipment. Julio speaks excellent English and also runs a book exchange, sells topo maps and climbing books.

### Trekking and climbing
Trekking tours cost US$50-70 pp per day, climbing US$100-160 pp per day. Many companies close in low season.
**Active Peru**, *Gamarra 699 y Sucre*, T043-429799, www.activeperu.com. Offers classic treks, climbing, plus standard tours to Chavín and Llanganuco, among others, good in all respects, Belgian owner speaks Dutch, German and English.
**Alpa-K**, *Parque Ginebra 30-B, above Montañero*, www.alpa-k.org. Owner Bertrand offers tours throughout Peru and has a B&B (**$**) on the premises. French, Spanish and some English spoken.
**Andean Footsteps**, *Cra Huaraz-Caraz Km 14, Paltay*, T943-121286. David Maguiña specializes in treks, climbs and tours with a commitment to using local personnel and resources. Local projects are sponsored.
**Andescamp**, *Jr Huáscar 615*, T043-423842, or T943-563424, www.andescamphostel.com. Popular agency and hostel (see Where to stay, above), especially with budget travellers. Only qualified guides used for climbing trips. Variety of treks, mountaineering expeditions and courses, rafting, paragliding and other adventure sports.

**Cordillera Blanca Adventures**, *run by the Mejía Romero family, Los Nogales 108, T043-421934, www.cordillerablanca.org.* Experienced, quality climbing/trekking trips, good guides/equipment.

**Explorandes**, *Gamarra 835, T043-421960, www.explorandes.com.*

**Galaxia Expeditions**, *Parque del Periodista, T043-425355, www.galaxia-expeditions.com.* Usual range of tours, climbing, hiking, biking, equipment hire, etc. Good budget option. Go to the office to buy tours direct, do not buy from unscrupulous sub-contractors.

**Huascarán**, *Jr Pedro Campos 711, Soledad, T043-424504, www.huascaran-peru.com.* Contact Pablo Tinoco Depaz, one of the brothers who run the company. Good 4-day Santa Cruz trip. Good food and equipment, professional service, free loan of waterproofs and *pisco sour* on last evening.

**La Cima Logistics**, *at Café Andino (see page 85), T943-914063, www.lacimalogistics. com.* Christopher Benway makes custom arrangements for climbing and trekking trips.

**Monttrek**, *Luzuriaga 646, upstairs, T920-227288, info@monttrek.com.pe.* Good trekking/climbing information, advice and maps, ice and rock climbing courses (at Monterrey), tours to Laguna Churup and the 'spectacular' Luna Llena tour; also hire mountain bikes, run ski instruction and trips, and river rafting. Helpful, conscientious guides. Next door in the pizzeria is a climbing wall, good maps, videos and slide shows. For new routes/maps contact Porfirio Cacha Macedo, 'Pocho', at Monttrek or at Jr Corongo 307, T043-423930.

**Peruvian Andes Adventures**, *José Olaya 532, T943-077736, www.peruvianandes.com.* Run by Hisao and Eli Morales, professional, registered mountain and trekking guides. All equipment and services for treks of 3-15 days, climbing technical and non-technical peaks, or just day walks. Vegetarians catered for.

**Quechuandes**, *Av Luzuriaga 522, T943-386147, www.quechuandes.com.* Trekking, mountaineering, rock climbing, ice climbing,

skiing, mountain biking and other adventure sports, guides speak Spanish, Quechua, English and/or French. Animal welfare taken seriously with weight limits of 40 kg per donkey.

**Guides** For details of the Casa de Guías, see page 89.

**Aritza Monasterio**, *through Casa de Guías.* Speaks English, Spanish and Euskerra.

**Augusto Ortega**, *Jr San Martín 1004, T043-424888.* Augusto has climbed Everest.

**Filiberto Rurush Paucar**, *Sucre 1240, T043-422264 (Lodging Casa Sucre).* Speaks English, Spanish and Quechua.

**Genaro Yanac Olivera**, *T043-422825.* Speaks good English and some German, also a climbing guide.

**Hugo Sifuentes Maguiña**, *Siex (Sifuentes Expeditions), Jr Huaylas 139, T043-426529.* Trekking, rock climbing and less adventurous tours.

**Koky Castañeda**, *T043-427213, or through Skyline Adventures, or Café Andino.* Speaks English and French, UIAGM Alpine certified.

**Max, Misael and Saul Angeles**, *T043-456891/422205 (Sol Andino agency).* Speak some English, know Huayhuash well.

**Máximo Henostrosa**, *T043-426040.* Trekking guide with knowledge of the entire region.

**Ted Alexander**, **Skyline Adventures**, *Pasaje Industrial 137, Cascapampa, Huaraz, T043-427097, www.skyline-adventures.com.* US outward bound instructor, very knowledgeable.

**Tjen Verheye**, *Jr Carlos Valenzuela 911, T043-422569.* Belgian and speaks Dutch, French, German and reasonable English, runs trekking and conventional tours and is knowledgeable about the Chavín culture.

**Camping gear** The following agencies are recommended for hiring gear: **Galaxia Expeditions**, **Monttrek**, **Kallpa** and **Montañero**. Also Skyline, **Andean Sport Tours** (Luzuriaga 571, T043-421612), and **MountClimb** (Jr Mcal Cáceres 421, T043-426060, mountclimb@yahoo.com). Casa de Guías rents equipment and sells dried food. Check all camping and climbing equipment

The Cordillera Blanca offers popular backpacking and trekking, with a network of trails used by the local people and some less well-defined mountaineers' routes. Most circuits can be hiked in five days. Although the trails are easily followed, they are rugged with high passes, between 4000 m and 5000 m, so backpackers should be fit, acclimatized to the altitude and able to carry all equipment. Essential items are a tent, warm sleeping bag, stove, and protection against wind and rain. The weather is unreliable and you cannot rule out rain and hail storms even in the dry season. Less stamina is required if you join a tour or hire mules to carry equipment.

**Safety** The height of the Cordillera Blanca and the Callejón de Huaylas ranges and their location in the tropics create conditions different from the Alps or the Himalayas. Fierce sun makes the mountain snow porous and glaciers move more rapidly. Deglaciation is rapidly changing the face of the Cordillera. Older maps do not provide a reliable indication of the extent of glaciers and snow fields (at least 15% of the range's glaciers have disappeared since the 1970s), so local experience is important. If the national park rules prohibiting independent treks or climbs have been lifted, move in groups of four or more, reporting to the Casa de Guías (see opposite) or the office of the guide before departing, giving the date at which a search should begin, and leaving your embassy's telephone number, with money for the call. International recommendations are for a 300 m per day maximum altitude gain. Be wary of agencies wanting to sell you trips with very fast ascents.

It is imperative that all climbers carry adequate insurance (it cannot be purchased locally). Be well prepared before setting out on a climb. Wait or cancel your trip when the weather is bad. Every year climbers are killed through failing to take weather conditions seriously. Climb only when and where you have sufficient experience.

Rescue services, while better than in the past, may not be up to international standards. In the event of an emergency try calling the **Casa de Guías**, T043-421811 or 941-946818; **Edson Ramírez** at the national park office, T944-627946 or T943-626627; or the **Police**, T043-422487 or 966-831514. Satellite phones can be rented

very carefully before taking it. Quality varies and some items may not be available, so it's best to bring your own. All prices are standard, but not cheap, throughout town. All require payment in advance, passport or air ticket as deposit and rarely give any money back if you return gear early. Many trekking agencies sell screw-on camping gas cartridges. White gas (*bencina*) is available from *ferreterías* on Raymondi below Luzuriaga and by Parque Ginebra.

**Tour operators**

**Chavín Tours**, *José de la Mar, T043-421578, www.chavintours.com.pe*. All local tours, long-standing agency with its head office in Lima.

**Mony Tours**, *San Martí n 643, T043-428949, www.monytoursperu.com*. Daily departures for local tours, uses its own vehicles, guiding in Spanish.

**Pablo Tours**, *Luzuriaga 501, T043-421145, www.pablotours.com*. For all local tours, also with many years of operation.

through the Casa de Guías and some agencies, ask around. There is cell-phone coverage in some (but not all) parts of the Cordillera Blanca. Confirm current emergency numbers locally as they change frequently, and try them before leaving town.

**Personal security and responsibility** Before heading out on any trekking route, always enquire locally about public safety. The Cordillera Blanca is generally safe, but robberies and muggings do occur. On all treks in this area, respect the locals' property, leave no rubbish behind, do not give sweets or money to children who beg and remember your cooking utensils and tent would be very expensive for a *campesino*, so be sensitive and responsible. Along the most popular routes, campers have complained that campsites are dirty, toilet pits foul and that rubbish is not taken away by groups. Do your share to make things better.

**Information** Casa de Guías, Plaza Ginebra 28-g in Huaraz, T043-421811, www.agmp.pe. Monday-Saturday 0900-1300, 1600-1800. This is the climbers' and hikers' meeting place. It has a full list of all members of the Asociación de Guías de Montaña del Perú (AGMP) throughout the country and has useful information, books, maps, arrangements for guides, *arrieros*, mules, etc. It also operates as an agency and sells tours. Notice board, postcards and posters for sale. Also see www.trekkingperu.org.

**Guides, arrieros and porters** The Dirección de Turismo issues qualified guides and *arrieros* (muleteers) with a photo ID. Note down the name and card number in case you should have any complaints. Most guides are hired in Huaraz or, to a lesser extent, in Caraz. Prices apply across the region, with some variations in the smaller towns: *arriero*, US$18 per day; donkey or mule, US$8 per day; trekking guides US$40-70 per day (more for foreign guides); climbing guides US$90-200 per day (more for foreign guides), depending on the difficulty of the peak; cooks US$30-40 per day; all subject to change. You are required to provide or pay for food and shelter for all *arrieros*, porters, cooks and guides. Associations of *arrieros*: Huarachuco-Llanganuco (for porters and cooks), T943-786497, victorcautivo@hotmail.com. Pashpa Arrieros, T043-830540/83319. Musho Arrieros, T043-230003/814416. Collon Arrieros (for llama trekking), T043-833417/824146.

**Quenual Adventures**, *at Alojamiento Soledad (see Where to stay, page 83)*, T943-603413, www.quenualadventures.com. Custom tailored trekking and conventional tours with multi-lingual guides. Owner Francisco Romero is knowledgeable and helpful.

### Transport

#### Air
**LC Peru** (Luzuriaga 904, T043-222003) flies 3 times a week to/from **Lima**, US$120-155, 1 hr.

#### Bus
Many of the companies have their offices along Av Raymondi, Jr Lúcar y Torre, and Bolívar (see map, page 80). Some recommended companies are: **Cavassa**, Jr Lúcar y Torre 446, T043-396215; **Cruz del Sur**, Bolívar y La Mar, T043-428726; **Empresa 14**, Bolívar 407, T043-421282; **Julio César**, Prol Cajamarca s/n, cuadra 1, T043-396443; **Línea**, Bolívar 450, T043-726666, **Móvil**, modern station at Av Confraternidad Internacional Oeste 451, T043-422555, ticket office on Bolívar 541, T043-429541; **Oltursa**,

Av Raymondi 825, T043-423717; **Z-Buss**, Bolívar 410, T043-428327.

**Long distance** To **Lima**, 7-8 hrs, US$15-25 (**Móvil** prices), large selection of ordinary service and luxury coaches throughout the day. To **Trujillo** via Callán Pass (sit on left for great views), Pariacoto, Casma, and Chimbote, **Línea** at 0930, 2200 and 2300, US$9-15, 7 hrs. To **Chimbote** (US$6, 4½ hrs) via **Casma** (same fare, 3½ hrs), 8 daily buses with **Yungay Express**. You can make connections from Chimbote at the Terminal Terrestre outside town, no need to enter the city.

**Within the Cordillera Blanca** Frequent minivans run daily, 0500-2000, between Huaraz and **Caraz**, 1¼ hrs, US$2, from Jr Cajamarca y Av Raimondi; no luggage racks, you have to pay an extra seat for your bag. To **Chavín**, 110 km, 3 hrs (sit on left side for best views), US$6 with **Sandoval/Olguita Tours**, Mcal Cáceres 338, 3 a day. Also **Trans Río Mosna**, Mcal Cáceres 265, T043-426632, 3 a day; buses go on to **Huari**, 4 hrs, US$7.50.

Vans and shared taxis to **Chacas**, US$7.50, 2½ hrs; and **San Luis**, US$9, 3 hrs; an unforgettable ride via the 4700-m-high Punta Olímpica tunnel, throughout the day with **Turismo Lince**, Villarán y Bolívar. **Renzo**, Raymondi 821, T043-425371, daily buses to Chacas via Punta Olímpica at 0615 and 1400; some continue to **Piscobamba** and **Pomabamba**. To **Sihuas**, Sandoval/Olguita Tours, Tue/Fri 0800; **Perú Andino**, 1 a week, 8 hrs, US$11.

*Colectivos* to **Recuay**, US$0.75, and **Catac**, US$0.85, daily at 0500-2100, from Gridilla, just off Tarapacá (Terminal de Transportistas Zona Sur). To **Chiquián** for the Cordillera Huayhuash, US$9, 120 km, 3½ hrs, with **Nazario**, Bolognesi 216, T043-422887, at 1345. To **Huallanca** (Huánuco) on the paved road through Conococha, Chiquián, Aquia to Huansala, then by good dirt road to Laguna Pachacoto and Huallanca. Departs Huaraz twice a day, 1st at 1300, with **Nazario**, as before, US$8. Frequent daily service from Huallanca to **Huánuco**.

**Taxi**
Standard fare in town is about US$1.20, more at night; radio taxis T043-421482 or 422512.

## Chavín and the Callejón de Conchucos

don't miss this pre-Inca fortress temple

From Huaraz it is possible to make a circuit by road, visiting Chavín de Huántar, Huari, San Luis, Yanama and Yungay, but bear in mind that the road north of Chavín is gravel and rough in parts and the bus service is less frequent. This area, known as the Callejón de Conchucos, sees less tourism than the Callejón de Huaylas and offers wonderful opportunities for off-the-beaten path exploration. Further west, and wilder still, lie the upper reaches of the Río Marañón, which can be accessed from Huari (see below) or Huánuco (see box, page 388).

### South of Huaraz

South of Huaraz is **Olleros**, from where the spectacular and relatively easy three- to four-day hike to Chavín, along a pre-Columbian trail, starts. Some basic meals and food supplies are available; for guides and prices, see Trekking and climbing in the cordilleras, above. Alternatively, if you're travelling by road to Chavín, head south from Huaraz on the main road for 38 km to **Catac** (two basic hotels and a restaurant), where a paved road branches east for Chavín.

Further south, the Pumapampa Valley is a good place to see the impressive *Puya raimondii* plants. A 14-km gravel road leads from Pachacoto to a park office at 4200 m,

## BACKGROUND
## The stone gods of Chavín

Based on physical evidence from the study of this 7-ha site, the temple of Chavín de Huántar is thought to have been a major ceremonial centre. Its architecture and sculpture had a strong impact on the artistic and cultural development of a large part of the coast and central highlands of Peru.

What first strikes visitors is the quality of the stonework. The sculptures have three functions: architectural, ornamental and cultist. Examples include the Lanzón, the Tello obelisk and the Raimondi stela; the latter two are currently held at the Museo Nacional de Antropología, Arqueología e Historia in Lima (see page 47).

At 5 m high, the **Lanzón** is the crowning glory of the Chavín religion and stands at the heart of the underground complex. Its Spanish name comes from the lance-, or dagger-like shape of the monolith which appears to be stuck in the ground. Carved into the top of the head are thin, grooved channels; some speculate that animals, or even humans, may have been sacrificed to this god. Others suggest that the Lanzón was merely the dominant figure for worship.

Named after the Peruvian scientist, Julio C Tello, the **Tello obelisk** belongs to the earliest period of occupation of Chavín (c 100 BC). It represents a complex deity – perhaps a caiman-alligator – connected with the earth, water and all the living elements of nature. Carved on the body are the people, birds, serpents and felines that the divine beast has consumed.

The **Raimondi stela** was named after the Italian naturalist, who also gave his name to the famous plant (see box, page 97) It shows a feline anthropomorphic divinity standing with open arms and holding a staff in each hand.

Together, the stone figures at Chavín indicate that the resident cult was based principally on the feline, or jaguar, and secondarily on serpents and birds.

where you can spend the night. Walking up the road from this point, you will see the gigantic plants, whose flower spike can reach 12 m in height and takes 100 years to develop. The final flowering (usually in May) is a spectacular sight. Another good spot, and less visited, is the **Queshque Gorge**, which is easy to find by following the Río Queshque from Catac.

From Catac to Chavín is a magnificent journey. The road passes Lago Querococha, and there are good views of the Yanamarey peaks. At the top of the route the road cuts through a huge rock face, entering the Cahuish tunnel at 4516 m. The tunnel has no light and is single lane with a small stream running through it. Cyclists must have powerful lights so that trucks and buses can see them. On the other side of the tunnel, the road descends into the Tambillo Valley, then the Río Mosna gorge before Chavín.

### ★ Chavín de Huántar *Colour map 3, B3.*
*Tue-Sun 0900-1600, US$3.50, students half price, guided tours in Spanish for groups available for an extra charge. You will receive an information leaflet in Spanish at the entrance.*

Chavín de Huántar, a fortress temple, was built about 800 BC. It is the only large structure remaining of the Chavín culture, which, in its heyday, is thought to have held influence from Cajamarca and Chiclayo in the north to Ayacucho and Ica in the south. In 1985, UNESCO designated Chavín a World Heritage Trust Site. The site is in good condition despite the effects of time and nature but becomes very crowded in high season. In order to protect the site some areas are closed to visitors. All the galleries open to the public have electric lights. The guard is also a guide and gives explanations of the ruins.

The main attractions are the marvellous carved stone heads (*cabezas clavas*), the designs in relief of symbolic figures and the many tunnels and culverts, which form an extensive labyrinth throughout the interior of the pyramidal structure. The carvings are in excellent condition, and the best are now in the Museo Nacional Chavín. The famous Lanzón dagger-shaped stone monolith of 800 BC is found inside one of the temple tunnels.

Just north of the ruins, the town of Chavín, painted colonial yellow and white, has a pleasant plaza with palm and pine trees. There are a couple of good, simple hotels and restaurants here and a local fiesta in mid-July. The **Museo Nacional Chavín** ⓘ *1 km north of town and 1.6 km from the site, Tue-Sun, 0900-1700, US$3.50,* has a comprehensive collection of items gathered from several deposits and museums, including the Tello obelisk dating from the earliest period of occupation of Chavín (c 100 BC), and many impressive *cabezas clavas*.

## Chavín to Huari
The road north from Chavín descends into the Mosna river canyon. The scenery is quite different from the other side of the Cordillera Blanca, very dry and hot. After 8 km it reaches **San Marcos**, the town that has been most heavily impacted by the huge **Antamina** gold mine. Hotels may be full with mine workers and public safety is a concern, so best press on for 32 km to Huari.

**Huari** is perched on a hillside at 3150 m and has various simple hotels ($ Huagancu 2, Jirón Sucre 335, T043-630434, clean and good value) and restaurants. The **fiesta of Nuestra Señora del Rosario** takes place on 7 October, with festivities during the first two weeks of the month. There is a spectacular two- to three-day walk from Huari to Chacas via Laguna Purhuay inside Parque Nacional Huascarán. Alberto Cafferata of Caraz writes: "The Purhuay area is beautiful. It has splendid campsites, trout, exotic birds and, at its north end, a 'quenual' forest with orchids. This is a microclimate at 3500 m, where the animals, insects and flowers are more like a tropical jungle, fantastic for ecologists and photographers." A pleasant alternative for those who don't want to do the longer walk to Chacas is a day walk to Laguna Purhuay, starting at the village of Acopalca; a taxi from Huari to Acopalca costs US$3.50, to Puruhuay, US$14. The lake has a visitor centre, food kiosk and boat rides.

## San Luis to Huaraz
From Huari the road climbs to the Huachacocha Pass at 4350 m and descends to **San Luis** at 3130 m, 60 km from Huari. Here you'll find the **$ Hostal Puñuri** (Ramón Castilla 151, T043-830408, with bath and hot water), a few basic restaurants, shops and a market.

Beyond San Luis there are a few options to take you back to Huaraz. The first is via **Chacas**, 10 km south of San Luis on a paved road. It has a fine church and celebrates the **Virgen de la Asunción** on 15 August, with bullfights, a famous *carrera de cintas* and fireworks. There are hostels ($), shops, restaurants and a small market. ★ A spectacular paved road and 4700-m-high tunnel through **Punta Olímpica** connect Chacas with Carhuaz in the Callejón de Huaylas north of Huaraz. Alternatively, it is a three-day hike west from Chacas to Marcará via the Quebradas Juytush and Honda (lots of condors to be seen). Quebrada Honda is known as the *Paraíso de las Cascadas* because it contains at least seven waterfalls.

The second road route heads some 20 km north of San Luis, to where a road branches left to **Yanama**, 45 km from San Luis, at 3400 m. It has a good comfortable hotel, **Andes Lodge Peru** ⓘ *T043-943 847423, www.andeslodgeperu.com*, **$$**, full board available, excellent food and services, fabulous views. The village retains many traditional features and is beautifully surrounded by snow-capped peaks. There are superb views from the ruins above the town, reachable on a day hike. From Yanama the road continues west via the Portachuelo de Llanganuco Pass to Yungay (see page 94).

## North of San Luis

A longer circuit to Huaraz can be made by continuing from San Luis for 62 km to **Piscobamba**, which has a couple of basic hotels, a few shops and small restaurants. Beyond Piscobamba by 22 km is **Pomabamba**, worth a visit for some very hot natural springs (the furthest are the hottest). There are various hotels ($) near the plaza and restaurants. Pomabamba is also the terminus of one of the variations of the **Alpamayo Trek**, see page 14.

From Pomabamba a dusty road runs up the wooded valley crossing the puna at Palo Seco, 23 km. The road then descends steeply into the desert-like Sihuas Valley, passing through the village of Sicsibamba. The valley is crossed half an hour below the small town of **Sihuas**, a major connection point between the Callejón de Conchucos, Callejón de Huaylas, the Upper Marañón and the coast. It has a few $ hotels and places to eat.

## Listings Chavín and the Callejón de Conchucos

### Where to stay

**Chavin**

**$$-$ La Casona**
*Wiracocha 130, Plaza de Armas, T043-454116.*
In a renovated house with attractive courtyard, single, double and triple rooms, some with balcony overlooking the plaza or courtyard, nice breakfast, laundry, parking.

**$$-$ R'ikay**
*On 17 de Enero 172N, T043-454068.*
Set around 2 patios, modern, best in town, variety of room sizes, hot water, restaurant does Italian food in the evening. Recommended.

**$ Inca**
*Wiracocha 170, T043-754021.*
Rooms are cheaper without bath, good beds, hot water on request, nice garden.

### Restaurants

**Chavín**

**$$-$ Chavín Turístico**
*Middle of 17 de Enero.*
The best in town, good *menú* and à la carte, delicious apple pie, nice courtyard, popular. Also run a *hostal* nearby.

**$$-$ La Portada**
*Towards south end of 17 de Enero.*
In an old house with tables set around a pleasant garden.

**$ La Ramada**
*Towards north end of main street, 17 de Enero.*
Regional dishes, also trout and set lunch.

### Transport

**Chavín**
It is much easier to get to Chavín (even walking!) than to leave the place by bus. All buses to **Huaraz** (2 hrs from Chavín), originate in Huari or further afield. They pass

through Chavín at irregular hours and may not have seats available. Buying a ticket at an agency in Chavín does not guarantee you will get a seat or even a bus. **Sandoval/Olguita Tours** goes through around 1200, 1600 and 1700 daily, **Río Mosna** at 0430 and then 4 between 1600-2200. There are also services to **Lima**, 438 km, 12 hrs, US$14, with **Trans El Solitario** and **Perú Andino** daily, but locals prefer to travel to Huaraz and then take one of the better companies from there.

In the other direction, buses from Huaraz or Lima (such as **El Solitario**, which passes through Chavín at 1800) go on to **Huari**, with some going on to **San Luis**, a further 61 km, 3 hrs; **Piscobamba**, a further 62 km, 3 hrs; and **Pomabamba**, a further 22 km, 1 hr. The other way to reach places in the Callejón de Conchucos is to hop on and off the cars and combis that leave regularly from Chavín's main plaza, every 20 mins and 30 mins respectively, to **San Marcos**, 8 km, and **Huari**, 38 km.

### Huari

Terminal Terrestre at Av Circunvalación Baja. Bus to **Huaraz**, 4 hrs, US$5.50, **Sandoval/Olguita Tours** 3 a day. Also runs to **San Luis** and **Lima**.

### San Luis to Huaraz

There are daily buses between Yanama and **Yungay** over the 4767-m Portachuelo de Llanganuco (3 hrs, US$7.50), stopping at **Vaquería** (at the end of the Santa Cruz Valley trek) 0800-1400, US$4, 2 hrs.

### North of San Luis
#### Pomabamba

To **Piscobamba**, combis depart hourly, 1 hr, US$1.50; also combis to Sihuas (see below). **El Solitario** has a service to **Lima** on Sun, Mon and Thu at 0800, 18 hrs, US$15, via **San Luis** (4 hrs, US$5), **Huari** (6 hrs, US$7.50) and **Chavín** (9 hrs, US$9); **La Perla del Alto Mayo** goes from Pomabamba to **Lima** via **Huaraz** on Wed, Thu, Sat, Sun, 16 hrs.

#### Sihuas

To **Pomabamba**, combi from Av 28 de Julio near the market at 1100, 4 hrs, US$7 (returns 0200). To **Huaraz**, via Huallanca, with **Cielo Azul**, daily at 0830, 10 hrs, US$11. To **Tayabamba**, for the Marañón route north to Huamachuco and Cajamarca: **Andía** passes through from Lima on Sat and Sun at 0100, **La Perla del Alta Mayo** passes through Tue, Thu 0000-0200; also **Garrincha** Wed, Sun around 0800; all 8 hrs, US$11, the beginning of a long wild ride. To **Huacrachuco**, **Andía** passes through Wed, Sat 0100. To **Chimbote**, **Corvival** on Wed, Thu and Sun morning, 9 hrs, US$9; **La Perla del Alta Mayo** Tue, Thu, Sun. To **Lima** (19 hrs, US$20) via Chimbote, **Andía** Tue, Sun 0200, Wed, Sat 1600; and 3 other companies once or twice a week each.

## Callejón de Huaylas

hike to beautiful mountain lakes

### Carhuaz and Mancos *Colour map 3, B2.*
Carhuaz is a friendly mountain town with a pleasant plaza. There is very good walking to thermal baths or up the Ulta Valley. Market days are Wednesday and Sunday (the latter is much larger). The local fiesta of **Virgen de las Mercedes**, 14-24 September, is rated as among the best in the region. From Carhuaz it is 14 km to Mancos at the foot of Huascarán. The village has a dormitory at La Casita de mi Abuela, some basic shops and restaurants. After Mancos, the main road goes to **Yungay** (8 km north, 30 minutes).

### ★ Yungay *Colour map 3, A2.*
The town of Yungay was completely buried by a massive mudslide during the 1970 earthquake; a hideous tragedy in which 20,000 people lost their lives. The original site

of Yungay, known as Yungay Viejo, is desolate and haunting; it has been consecrated as a *camposanto* (cemetery). The new settlement is on a hillside just north of the old town. It has a pleasant plaza and a concrete market, good on Wednesday and Sunday. The **Virgen del Rosario** fiesta is celebrated on 17 October, and 28 October is the anniversary of the founding of the town. The tourist office is on the corner of the Plaza de Armas. The main road continues 12 km north of Yungay to Caraz.

## Lagunas de Llanganuco

The Lagunas de Llanganuco are two beautiful lakes nestling beneath Huascarán and Huandoy. From Yungay, the first you come to is **Laguna Chinancocha** (3850 m), the second **Laguna Orconcocha** (3863 m). The park office is situated before the lakes at 3200 m, 19 km from Yungay. Accommodation is provided for trekkers who want to start the Santa Cruz Valley trek from here (see below). From the park office to the lakes takes about five hours (a steep climb). The last section is a nature trail, Sendero María Josefa (signed on the road), it takes 1½ hours to walk to the western end of Chinancocha where there is a control post, descriptive trail and boat trips on the lake. Walk along the road beside the lake to its far end for peace and quiet among the quenual trees, which provide shelter for 75% of the birdlife found in the park. The trailhead for a popular hike to **Laguna 69** is at Cebollapampa, 4 km past Orconcocha. This pretty route to a lake at 4600 m gets crowded in high season with groups (US$18 per person, quality varies). There is also public transport from Yungay, see Transport, page 100.

## Caraz *Colour map 3, A2.*

This pleasant town at 2290 m is a good centre for walking, a convenient access point for many excellent treks and climbs, and a more tranquil alternative to Huaraz. There are

**Caraz**

**Where to stay** 🛏
1 Apu Ecolodge
2 Caraz Dulzura
3 Chavín & San Marco
4 La Perla de los Andes
5 Los Pinos Lodge
6 O'Pal Inn

7 Pony's Lodge,
   Pony's Expeditions &
   Café de Rat
8 Yaku Rumi

**Restaurants** 🍴
1 El Turista
2 Entre Panes
3 La Pizza del Abuelo
4 La Terraza
5 Panificadora La Alameda

great views of Huandoy, Huascarán and surrounding summits from June to September. In other months, the mountains may be shrouded in cloud. On 20 January is the fiesta **Virgen de Chiquinquirá**. In the last week of July is **Semana Turística**.

The **Museo Arqueológico Municipal** is on San Martín, half a block up from the plaza. The ruins of **Tumshukaiko** are 1.5 km from the Plaza de Armas in the suburb of Cruz Viva, to the north before the turn-off for Parón. There are seven platforms dating from around 2000-1800 BC, but the site is in poor shape.

### Treks around Caraz

Caraz has a milder climate than Huaraz and is more suited to day trips. A good day walk goes from Caraz by the lakes of Miramar and Pampacocha to Tzatza, where you can get transport (US$1) back to Caraz. A longer full-day walk with excellent views of Huandoy and Huascarán follows the foothills of the Cordillera Blanca east along the main Río Santa

## Treks from Caraz

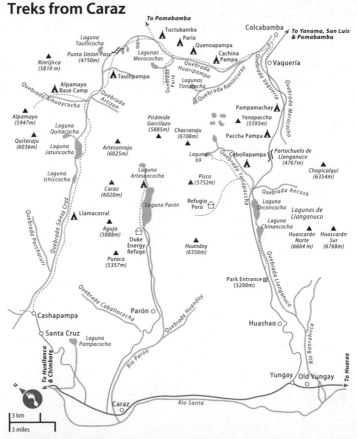

## ON THE ROAD

### ★ A blooming century

The giant *Puya raimondii*, named after Antonio Raimondi, the Italian scholar who discovered it, is a rare and strikingly beautiful plant.

Often mistakenly referred to as a cactus, it is actually the largest member of the bromeliad family (which includes the pineapple) and is found in only a few isolated areas of the Andes. One of these areas is Huascarán National Park, particularly the Ingenio and Queshque gorges, the high plateaus of Cajamarquilla, along the route leading to Pastoruri in the Pachacoto gorge and by the road from Caraz to Pamparomas.

At its base, the *Puya* forms a rosette of long, spiked, waxy leaves, 2 m in diameter. The distinctive phallic flower stalk of the plant can reach a height of 12 m. The plant takes an incredible 100 years to bloom, after which it withers and dies, but, during the flowering period, as many as 20,000 blooms can decorate a single plant. Groups of *Puya raimondii* blooming together create a spectacular picture against the dramatic backdrop of the Cordillera Blanca.

Valley, from Caraz south through the villages of Chosica and Ticrapa. It ends at Puente Ancash on the Caraz–Yungay road, from where frequent transport goes back to Caraz.

★ **Laguna Parón** From Caraz a narrow, rough road goes east 32 km to beautiful Laguna Parón in a cirque surrounded by several, massive snow-capped peaks, including Huandoy, Pirámide Garcilazo and Caraz. The gorge leading to it is spectacular. It is a long day's trek for acclimatized hikers (25 km) up to the lake at 4150 m, or a four- to five-hour walk from the village of Parón, which can be reached by combi (US$2). Camping is possible. There is no trail around the lake and you should not attempt it as it is slippery and dangerous, particularly on the southern shore; tourists have been killed here. Caraz agencies offer tours, US$15 per person. A taxi for up to four people with a two-hour wait costs about US$37.

★ **Santa Cruz Valley** One of the best known treks in the area is the beautiful three- to five-day route from Vaquería, over the 4750 m Punta Unión Pass, to Quebrada Santa Cruz and the village of Cashapampa. It can be hiked in either direction. Starting in Cashapampa, you climb more gradually to the pass, then down to Vaquería or the Llanganuco lakes beyond. Along this 'clockwise' route the climb is gentler, giving more time to acclimatize, and the pass is easier to find, although, if you start in Vaquería and finish in Cashapampa you ascend for one day rather than three in the other direction. You can hire an *arriero* (muleteer) and mule in Cashapampa; see box, page 88, for prices. Campsites are at Llamacorral and Taullipampa before Punta Unión, and Quenoapampa (or Huaripampa) after the pass. You can end the hike at Vaquería on the Yanama–Yungay road and take a minibus or, better, an open truck from there (a beautiful run). Or end the walk a day later with a night at the Yuraccorral campsite at the Llanganuco lakes, from where cars go back to Yungay. This trek is by far the most popular in the Cordillera Blanca and offered by all tour agencies in Huaraz and Caraz.

# ★ Puyas raimondii at Winchus

A stand of *Puya raimondii* can be seen near Winchus (also known as Carhuapunta), a 4300 m pass over the Cordillera Negra, 40 km (1½ hours) by road southwest of Caraz. From Pueblo Libre, 9 km from Caraz, a narrow paved road climbs west to the pass before dropping to Pamparomás and Moro to join the Panamerican highway south of Chimbote. The *Puya raimondii* plants are scattered along the road near the pass. There are splendid views of the Cordillera Blanca here, and west all the way down to the Pacific. The plants are usually in flower May or October, but may not flower at all on some years. Take warm clothing, food and water. The most popular way to visit is to rent a bike (US$18 per day), travel up by public transport (see below), and then ride back down to Caraz in four or five hours. Or form a group (eg via the bulletin board at **Pony's Expeditions**, Caraz) and hire a car which will wait for you (US$60 for five). From behind the market in Caraz, vans and buses leave for Pamparomás daily at 0730, 0800 and 0900 (1½ hours to Carhuapunta, US$3). Return transport passes Carhuapunta between 1200 and 1300 (confirm all times in advance). You can also walk back to either Pueblo Libre or Huata, north of Caraz; both have transport to Caraz until about 1700. Both are long full-day downhill hikes, about 20 km using shortcuts, much longer if you follow the road, so you should head back early and move fast. It is especially easy to get lost on the way down to Pueblo Libre.

## Listings Callejón de Huaylas *map page 95.*

### Tourist information

#### Caraz

The **tourist office** (Plaza de Armas, next to the municipality, T043-483860 ext 143), has limited information. There are several ATMs in the centre.

### Where to stay

#### Carhuaz

**$$ El Abuelo**
*Jr 9 de Diciembre 257, T043-394456,*
*www.elabuelohotel.com.*
Modern, comfortable hotel, nicely decorated with local tapestries and ceramics. Restaurant, garden with organic fruit and veg, parking, credit cards accepted. Knowledgeable owner is map-maker, Felipe Díaz.

**$** 4 family-run *hospedajes* operate as part of a community development project. All have private bath and hot water. The better 2 are: **Hospedaje Robri** (Jr Comercio 935, T043-224124), and **Alojamiento Las Torrestas** (Jr Amazonas 412, T043-394213).

#### Yungay

**$ Rima Rima**
*Grau 275, T043-393257,*
*www.hotelrimarima.com.*
Ample rooms with private bath, hot water, nice views from terrace.

**$ Sol de Oro**
*Santo Domingo 7, T043-393116.*
Simple rooms with private bath, hot water, kitchen and laundry facilities, good value.

#### Lagunas de Llanganuco

**$$$$-$$$ Llanganuco Mountain Lodge**
*Laguna Keushu, Llanganuco Valley,*
*T976-592524, www.llanganuco*
*mountainlodge.com.*
Standard and luxury rooms in a beautiful location, includes full board, great trekking opportunities (local guides available), low-season discounts. Enthusiastic British owner, Charlie Good. Contact well in advance.

## Caraz

### $$$-$$ Los Pinos Lodge
*Parque San Martín 103 (also known as Plazuela de la Merced), T043-391130, www.lospinoslodge.pe.*
Nice comfortable rooms, buffet breakfast, patio, gardens, parking, cosy bar, tourist information. Recommended.

### $$$-$$ O'Pal Inn
*Km 265.5, 5 mins south of Caraz, T043-391015, www.opalsierraresort.com.*
Scenic, family bungalows, suites and rooms, swimming pool, includes breakfast, restaurant, games room.

### $$ Apu Ecolodge
*Jabón Rumi, just off the main highway north of town, T995-194288, http://apuecolodge.com.*
Comfortable rooms and bungalows for 4 to 7 guests. Pleasant ample grounds set amid berry orchards. Lovely atmosphere, volunteer opportunities.

### $$-$ Pony's Lodge
*Sucre 1266, near the Plaza de Armas, T043-391642.*
Comfortable carpeted rooms with private bath and reliable hot water. Includes breakfast at **Café de Rat**. Part of **Pony's Expeditions** (see What to do, below). Attentive owners, English spoken.

### $ Caraz Dulzura
*Sáenz Peña 212, T043-392090, info@hostalcarazdulzura.com.*
Older, well-cared-for hotel, rooms with private bath, hot water (some have electric showers), patio and common areas, includes breakfast, friendly owner, quiet location away from the centre.

### $ Chavín
*San Martín 1135 just off the plaza, T043-391171.*
Get a room overlooking the street, many others have no window. Warm water, guiding service, tourist info, good popular restaurant for breakfast and lunch.

### $ La Perla de los Andes
*Daniel Villar 179, Plaza de Armas, next to the cathedral, T043-391767.*
Central location, adequate rooms, *pollería* downstairs, helpful staff, street noise.

### $ San Marco
*San Martín 1133, T043-391558.*
Several types of room with private or shared bath, electric showers, pleasant patios, clean, quiet, good value.

### $ Yaku Rumi
*In Shocsha, 1.5 km from Caraz along road to Laguna Parón, T940 215118, http://yakurumi.com.*
An innovative place for camping run by a small community of musicians and artists from Lima. New, eclectic and promising in 2018.

## Restaurants

### Carhuaz

### $$$-$$ La Bicharra
*Jr Comercio 1069, T943-780893. Daily from 1900.*
Innovative North African/Peruvian cooking.

### $$ JR
*Parque San Martín 165. Mon-Fri 1200-1500.*
Good varied *menú*, terrace seating, clean and popular.

### $$ La Cabaña
*In Acopampa, 3 km from Carhuaz, T04-394292.*
Pleasant garden seating with views of the Río Santa, tasty regional dishes, attentive service, vegetarian options.

### Yungay

### $$-$ Alpamayo
*Av Arias Graziani s/n. Daily 0730-1830.*
At north entrance to town, tasty local dishes, ice cream. Recommended.

### $ Café Pilar
*On the main plaza. Open 1000-2100, closed Wed.*
Good for juices, cakes and snacks, lunch *menú*.

## Caraz

### $$-$ Entre Panes
*Daniel Villar 211, half a block from the plaza.*
*Closed Tue.*
Variety of excellent sandwiches, also meals.
Good food, service and atmosphere.

### $$-$ La Pizza del Abuelo
*San Martín 1029, T987-318077. Open 1800-2200.*
Good pizzas, pastas, juices and desserts,
warm atmosphere, friendly owners.
Recommended.

### $$-$ La Terraza
*Jr Sucre 1107, T043-301226. Sun-Fri 0800-2130.*
Good *menú* as well as pizza, pasta, juices,
home-made ice cream, sandwiches, sweets,
coffee and drinks.

### Cafés

### Café de Rat
*Sucre 1266, above Pony's Expeditions.*
Breakfast, vegetarian dishes, good pizzas,
drinks and snacks, darts, travel books,
nice atmosphere.

### El Turista
*San Martín 1117. Open 0700-2030.*
Small, popular for breakfast, ham omelettes
and ham sandwiches are specialities.

### Panificadora La Alameda
*D Villar across the street from BCP bank.*
Good bread and pastries, ice cream, popular
with locals. The excellent *manjar blanco* for
which the town earned its nickname 'Caraz
dulzura' is sold here and at several other
shops on the same street.

## Shopping

### Caraz
Large market at Sucre y La Mar. Some
dried camping food is available from
**Pony's Expeditions**, who also sell
Camping Gaz canisters.

## What to do

### Caraz
Agencies in Caraz arrange treks in the
Cordilleras Blanca and Huayhuash, as well
as more local destinations.
**Apu-Aventura**, *Parque San Martín 103,
5 blocks west of plaza, T043-391130, www.
apuaventura.pe.* Range of adventure sports
and equipment rental.
**Pony's Expeditions**, *Sucre 1266, near the
Plaza de Armas, T043-391642, www.pony
expeditions.com. Mon-Sat 0800-2200.*
English, French, Italian and Quechua spoken.
Owners Alberto and Aidé Cafferata are
knowledgeable about treks and climbs. They
arrange local tours, offer accommodation
at **Pony's Lodge** (see Where to stay, above),
trekking, transport for day excursions,
and rental of a 4WD vehicle with driver.
Also maps and books for sale, equipment
hire and mountain bike rental (US$15 for
a full day). Well organized and reliable.
Highly recommended.

## Transport

### Carhuaz
Transport leaves from Av La Merced between
the plaza and the highway. To **Huaraz**,
*colectivos* 0500-2000, US$0.90, 40 mins. To
**Caraz**, 0500-2000, US$1, 1 hr. Buses from
Huaraz to **Chacas**, 87 km, 3 hrs, US$5.75, pass
through Carhuaz about 40 mins after leaving
Huaraz. The road works its way up the Ulta
Valley to the tunnel at Punta Olímpica from
where there are excellent views. **Renzo** daily
buses pass through en route to **San Luis** (see
page 92), 10 km past Chacas, 1½ hrs.

### Yungay
From the small terminal vans run all day to
**Caraz**, 12 km, 15 mins, US$0.50, and **Huaraz**,
54 km, 1 hr, US$2. To the **Llanganuco lakes**,
cars leave when full, especially 0700-0900,
from Av 28 de Julio 1 block from the
plaza, 1 hr, US$2.50. Taxi to Llanganuco,
US$40 with full-day wait. To **Yanama**, vans
run via the Portachuelo de Llanganuco

Pass, 4767 m, stopping at the trailhead for the Llanganuco–Santa Cruz trek, and Cebollapampa (for Laguna 69); leave 0700-0730, 58 km, 3½ hrs to Yanama, US$5.

## Caraz

To **Lima**, 470 km, daily, US$11-40, 10-11 hrs via Huaraz and Pativilca, 9 companies: **El Huaralino** (T996-896607), **Huaraz Buss** (T943-469736), **Zbuss** (T043-391050), **Cooperativa Ancash** (T043-391126), all on Jr Cordova, also **Rochaz** (Pasaje Olaya, T043-794375), **Cavassa** (Ctra Central, T043-392042), **Yungay Express** (Av Luzuriaga, T043-391492), **Móviltours** (east end of town, www.moviltours.com.pe).

To **Chimbote**, **Yungay Express**, via Huallanca and Cañón del Pato, 3 daily, US$9, 7 hrs, sit on right for best views. To **Trujillo**, via Casma with **Móviltours**. To **Huaraz**, combis leave from a terminal on the way out of town, where the south end of C Sucre meets the highway, daily 0400-2000, 1¼ hrs, US$2, no luggage racks, you might have to pay an extra seat for your bag. To **Yungay**, 12 km, 15 mins, US$0.70. To **Huallanca** and **Yuramarca** (for the Cañón del Pato), combis and cars leave from Córdova y La Mar, 0700-1600, US$2.50. To **Cashapampa** (for the Santa Cruz Valley) *colectivo*/minibus from Ramón Castilla y Jorge Chávez, Caraz, leave when full from 0600 to 1530, 1½ hrs, US$2. To **Parón** (for the walk to Laguna Parón), *colectivos* leave from Ramón Castilla y Jorge Chávez, close to the market, 1 hr, US$2.

## Cordillera Huayhuash

*remote mountains just waiting to be explored*

The Cordillera Huayhuash, lying south of the Cordillera Blanca, has azure trout-filled lakes interwoven with deep quebradas and high pastures around the hem of the range. It is perhaps the most spectacular cordillera for its massive ice faces that seem to rise sheer out of the puna's contrasting green. You may see tropical parakeets in the bottom of the gorges and condors circling the peaks. The area offers fantastic scenery and insights into rural life.

The cordillera can be approached from several points: **Chiquián** and **Llamac** in the north; **Oyón**, with links to Cerro de Pasco, lies to the southeast; **Churín** is to the south, and **Cajatambo**, a small market town with a beautiful 18th-century church and a lovely plaza, lies to the southwest. Note that the road out of Cajatambo is not for the faint-hearted. For the first three to four hours it is no more than a bus-width, clinging to the cliff edge. Many tour groups go via Matacancha on the road to Huallanca.

### ★ Huayhuash trekking circuit

The complete circuit is very tough; allow 10 to 12 days. There are up to eight passes over 4600 m, depending on the route. Fees are charged by every community along the way, adding up to about US$80 for the entire circuit; take soles in small denominations and insist on getting a receipt every time. A half-circuit is also possible, and there are many other options. The trail head is at **Cuartel Huain**, between Matacancha and the **Punta Cacanan Pass** (which marks the continental divide at 4700 m).

## Where to stay

There are various hotels (**$**) and some good restaurants around the plaza in Cajatambo. The following are all in Chiquián:

### $ Hostal San Miguel
*Jr Comercio 233, T043-447001.*
Nice courtyard and garden, clean, many rooms, popular.

### $ Hotel Huayhuash
*28 de Julio 400, T043-447049.*
Private bathroom, hot water, restaurant, laundry, parking, modern, great views, information and tours.

### $ Los Nogales de Chiquián
*Jr Comercio 1301, T043-447121, http://hotelnogaleschiquian.blogspot.com.*
Traditional design, with private or shared bath, hot water, cafeteria, parking. Recommended.

## Restaurants

### $ El Refugio de Bolognesi and Yerupajá
*Tarapacá, Chiquián.*
Both offer basic set meals.

### $ Panificadora Santa Rosa
*Comercio 900, on the plaza, Chiquián.*
For good bread and sweets, has coin-operated phones.

## Transport

Coming from Huaraz, the road is now paved beyond Chiquián to Huansala, on the road to Huallanca (Huánuco). Private vehicles can sometimes be hired in Chiquián or Llamac (less likely) to take you to the trailhead at Cuartel Huain; otherwise you'll have to walk.

# Cordilleras Huayhuash & Raura

## Chiquián

To **Huaraz**, buses leave the plaza at 0500 daily, US$1.75, except Trans **El Rápido**, Jr Figueredo 216, T043-447049, at 0500 and 1330, US$3.65. Also *colectivo* to Huaraz 1500, 3 hrs, US$2.45 pp. There is also a connection from **Chiquián to Huallanca** (Huánuco) with buses from Lima in the early morning and combis during the day, which leave when full, 3 hrs, US$2.50. From Huallanca there are regular combis on to **La Unión**, 1 hr, US$0.75, and from there transport to **Huánuco**.

## Cajatambo

Buses to **Lima** daily at 0600, US$9, with **Empresa Andina** (office on plaza next to Hostal Cajatambo), **Tour Bello** (1 block off the plaza) and Turismo Cajatambo (Jr Grau 120; or Av Carlos Zavala 124 corner of Miguel Aljovin 449, Lima, T01-426 7238).

# North coast

imposing ruins and some serious waves

Peru's north coast could well be described as the Egypt of South America. This is a region of numerous monumental ruins, built by the many highly skilled pre-Inca cultures that once thrived here.

The ground-breaking discovery at Caral is open to visitors. Not far from Trujillo, Chan Chán was the capital of the Chimú Kingdom; its crumbling remains still represent the largest adobe city in the world. The Huaca de la Luna and the Huaca Cao Viejo of the Moche Empire reveal fabulous, multicoloured friezes of gods from the first millennium AD. Further north, near Chiclayo, the adobe brick pyramids of Túcume, Sipán and Sicán rise massively from the coastal plains. The wealth from some of their tombs is displayed in state-of-the-art museums.

But it's not all pyramids and royal tombs. The elegant city of Trujillo is one of the finest examples of colonial architecture in the country. There are charming towns, such as Huanchaco, with its bizarre-looking reed fishing rafts, and Chulucanas, with its famous pottery. Up and down the coast the seafood is wonderful and the hospitality unrivalled. In addition, the northern seaboard enjoys a rain-free climate all year and has Peru's finest beaches for bathing and surfing. Around Tumbes, the most northerly regional capital, four reserves protect mangroves, equatorial dry forest and tropical forest, each with its share of endangered species.

**Best** for
Archaeology ■ Beaches ■ Seafood

North of Lima . . . . . . . . . . . . . . 108
Trujillo & around . . . . . . . . . . . 112
Chiclayo & around . . . . . . . . . 130
Piura & around . . . . . . . . . . . . . 142
North to Ecuador . . . . . . . . . . . 146

# Footprint picks

★ **Caral**, page 108

This may be the oldest city in South America.

★ **Sechín**, page 109

The 500 monoliths here depict a gruesome battle in graphic detail.

★ **Trujillo**, page 112

The city's mansions, with their elaborately carved wooden balconies, are among the finest in Peru.

★ **El Brujo**, page 118

This ancient complex was a ceremonial centre for up to 10 cultures.

★ **Huanchaco**, page 118

Hang out with other travellers at this fishing village turned surfing village.

★ **Lambayeque and Ferreñafe**, pages 132 and 136

These colonial towns are a good base for exploring the surrounding sites.

★ **Northern beaches**, page 146

Enjoy some of the best surf and warmest water in Peru.

★ **Tumbes' natural parks and reserves**, page 147

Four protected natural areas are home to unique ecosystems.

ECUADOR

Santuario Nacional
los Manglares de Tumbes
Puerto Pizarro
Tumbes
Aguas Verdes

Zona Reservada
de Tumbes

Cancas
Zorritos
Punta Sal
Máncora
Los Organos
Cabo Blanco
Talara
Sullana
Colán
Paita
Catacaos
Sechura
Bayovar

Parque Nacional
Cerros de Amotape
Alamor
Tambo
Grande
Frias
Chulucanas
Chira
Piura
Vice

La Tina

Ayabaca
Espíndola

Namballe
Chiriaco

Huancabamba
Canchaque

Aramango

Jaén
Chamaya
Pucará

Bagua
Bagua Grande

Santa María
de Nieva

Samariza

San Ramón

Barranca

La Libertad
Jeberos

Nueva Cajamarca

Moyobamba

Sechura
Desert
Olmos

Sto Tomas
Chochope

Lonya Grande

Pedro Ruiz

Chachapoyas

Lamas
Tarapoto

Reventazón

Motupe
Apurlec
Túcume
Mórrope
Lambayeque
Pimentel
Sta Rosa
Puerto Etén

Chota

Leymebamba

Sipán
Chiclayo
Sipán
Zaña
Monsefú

San Miguel
de Pallaques
Celendín

Cajamarca

Sacanche

Ferreñafe

San Juan

Pacasmayo

Chepén
Contumazá

Cajabamba

Pto Chicama
Ascope
Otusco
Huamachuco

El Brujo
Huanchaco
Chan Chán
Simbal
Santiago
de Chuco

Retamas

Huacas del Sol
& de la Luna
Trujillo

Tayabamba

Salaverry

Tauca

Mollepata

Sihuas
Huancaspata

Virú
Tangurhe

Chuquicara

Tres Cruces

Huallanca
Cashapampa

Chacas

Chimbote
Nepeña
Pamparomas
Caraz

Huari

Playa Tortugas
Pariacoto

Huaraz
Quivilla
Chavinillo

Casma
Sechín
La Merced
Culebras
Huarmey
Marca

Recuay

Huayllapampa
Chiquián

Chasquitambo
Conococha (4100m)
Raurá

Paramonga
Pativilca
Barranca
Supe
Cajatambo
Cochas
Churín
Huancahuasi

Caral
Huaura
Huacho

Sayán

Reserva Nacional
Loma de Lachay

Aucallama
Chancay

Chillón

Callao
LIMA

Pacific Ocean

## Footprint picks

1 **Caral**, page 108
2 **Sechín**, page 109
3 **Trujillo**, page 112
4 **El Brujo**, page 118
5 **Huanchaco**, page 118
6 **Lambayeque and Ferreñafe**, pages 132 and 136
7 **Northern beaches**, page 146
8 **Tumbes' natural parks and reserves**, page 147

N

50 km
50 miles

# Essential North coast

## Finding your feet

The transport hubs of the region are Trujillo, Chiclayo and Piura. All have regular flights and bus services to and from Lima. It can be a long haul across the desert, so if you are short on time then flying to the north coast is convenient.

## Getting around

Once you are up north, bus travel is the best way to get around. Trujillo is best explored on foot, although taxis are readily available. The major sites outside the city, Chan Chán, the Moche pyramids and Huanchaco, are easily reached by public transport, but take care when walking around. A number of recommended guides run tours to these and other places. From Chiclayo it is easy to visit Lambayeque's museums, Sipán and Túcume by public transport or on a local tour; Sicán is a full-day tour from Chiclayo including Ferreñafe and Pómac. Public transport is your best bet for travel from Piura north to the beaches and Ecuador.

## When to go

The summer months are December to April and can be very hot, especially around Piura. Hotels around Máncora are heavily booked at this time and prices can increase by 100% or more, especially for Christmas, Easter and other holidays. Surfing is best from November to March. There may be sea mists from May to October, especially south of Trujillo, but Piura's climate is very pleasant at this time, although nights can be cold and the wind piercing. This is also a good time to visit the nature reserves around Tumbes. Keep an eye on weather reports; El Niño events tend to affect the north coast more adversely than elsewhere.

## Time required

One to three weeks, depending on how many centres you choose to visit.

## Weather Trujillo

| January | February | March | April | May | June |
|---|---|---|---|---|---|
| 26°C 19°C 2mm | 25°C 18°C 10mm | 27°C 19°C 15mm | 25°C 17°C 0mm | 23°C 16°C 1mm | 22°C 16°C 0mm |

| July | August | September | October | November | December |
|---|---|---|---|---|---|
| 22°C 15°C 1mm | 21°C 15°C 6mm | 21°C 15°C 0mm | 22°C 15°C 0mm | 23°C 15°C 2mm | 23°C 17°C 8mm |

# North
## of Lima

The north of Peru has been described as the Egypt of South America, as it is home to countless pre-Inca treasures. Along a seemingly endless stretch of desert coast lie many of the country's most important pre-Inca sites: Chan-Chán, the Moche pyramids, Túcume, Sipán, Batán Grande and El Brujo. The main city is Trujillo, while Chiclayo is more down to earth, with one of the country's largest witchdoctors' markets. The coast is also famous for its deep-sea fishing, surfing and the unique reed fishing boats at Huanchaco and Pimentel.

## North from Lima

awesome prehistoric ruins along the Panamericana

### Huacho and around

The Pan-American Highway is four-lane (several tolls, about US$2.65) to Km 101. Here it by-passes both **Huacho** and **Puerto Huacho**, 19 km to the west. There are several hotels in Huacho. The beaches south of the town are clean and deserted.

### ★ Caral

*25 km east of the Panamericana (Km 184); after 18.5 km, a track leads across the valley to the ruins (30 mins), though the river may be impassable Dec-Mar. Information: Proyecto Especial Caral, T01-205 2500 (Lima), www.caralperu.gob.pe. Daily 0900-1600. US$4, US$7 per group; all visitors must be accompanied by an official guide and not stray from the marked paths.*

A few kilometres before Barranca, a signed turning to the east at Km 184 leads up the Supe Valley to the UNESCO World Heritage Site of Caral. This ancient city, 26 km from the coast, dates from about 2600 BC. Many of the accepted theories of Peruvian archaeology have been overturned by Caral's age and monumental construction. It appears to be the oldest city in South America (a claim disputed by the Miravalles site, in the department of Cajamarca). The dry desert site lies on the southern fringes of the Supe Valley, along whose flanks are 32 more ruins, 19 of which have been explored. Caral covers 66 ha and contains eight significant pyramidal structures. To date seven have been excavated by archaeologists from the University of San Marcos, Lima, who are undertaking careful restoration on the existing foundations to re-establish the pyramidal tiers.

It is possible to walk around the pyramids on marked paths. A viewpoint provides a panorama of the whole site. Allow at least two hours for your visit. Handicrafts are sold in the car park. You can stay or camp at the **Casa del Arqueólogo,** a community museum in Supe (at the turn-off to Caral), which provides information on the Caral culture and the progress of the excavations.

## Barranca to Huarmey

Barranca is by-passed by the highway but is an important transport hub for the region so you may find yourself there to change buses. There are hotels and restaurants if you wish to stay overnight ($$-$ **Hotel Chavín**, José Gálvez 222, T01-235-2253, www.hotelchavin. com.pe, ageing but good) and transport connections to Huaraz via Conococha for the Cordillera Blanca; and to Chiquián for the Cordillera Huayhuash. Some 4 km beyond the turn-off to Huaraz at Pativilca, beside the Panamericana, are the well-preserved ruins of the Chimú temple of **Paramonga** ⓘ *US$1.80; caretaker may act as guide.* Set on high ground with a view of the ocean, the fortress-like mound is thought to be of Huari origin and resembles a llama when seen from above.

Between Pativilca and Chimbote the mountains come down to the sea. The road passes by a few very small protected harbours in tiny rock-encircled bays, such as **Huarmey**, with a fine beach and active hostel.

## ★ Sechín

*5 km north of Casma, off the road to Huaraz. Daily 0800-1700 (photography best around midday). US$1.80 (children US$0.35, students US$1.40); ticket also valid for the Max Uhle Museum by the ruins and other sites in the Casma Valley. Mototaxi from Casma, US$2.85 each way for 2 passengers, US$8.55 return including wait.*

This archaeological site in the Nepeña Valley, north of Casma, is one of the most important ruins on the Peruvian coast. It consists of a large square temple completely faced with about 500 carved stone monoliths narrating, it is thought, a gruesome battle in graphic detail. The style is unique in Peru for its naturalistic vigour. The complex as a whole is associated with the pre-Chavín Sechín culture, dating from about 1600 BC. Three sides of the large stone temple have been excavated and restored, but you cannot see the earlier adobe buildings inside the stone walls because they were covered up and used as a base for a second storey, which has been completely destroyed.

## Casma and around *Colour map 3, B2.*

Sechín is accessed from the city of Casma (population 22,600), which has a pleasant Plaza de Armas, several parks and two markets including a good food market. While safer than Chimbote, you should still take care if staying in Casma. Tortugas, 10 minutes away, is a better option and is a pleasant place to spend a day at the seaside and enjoy the seafood.

## Chimbote to Callejón de Huaylas *Colour map 3, A2.*

The port of Chimbote (population 375,000) serves the national fishing industry; the smell of its fishmeal plants is overpowering. If that's not enough to put you off staying here, the city is also dangerous. Take extensive precautions; always use taxis from the bus station, and avoid staying overnight if possible. You can make transport connections directly at the Terminal Terrestre without going into the city.

Just north of Chimbote, a road branches northeast off the Pan-American Highway and goes up the Santa Valley following the route of the old Santa Corporation Railway which used to run as far as **Huallanca** (not to be confused with the town southeast of

Huaraz), 140 km up the valley. At Chuquicara, three hours from Chimbote (paved, but very narrow thereafter), is **Restaurante Rosales**, a good place to stop for a meal (you can sleep here, too, but it's very basic). There are also places to stay and eat at Huallanca, and fuel is available. At the top of the valley by the hydroelectric centre, the road goes through the very narrow and spectacular **Cañón del Pato**. You pass under tremendous walls of bare rock and through almost 40 tunnels, but the flow of the river has been greatly reduced by the hydroelectric scheme. After this point the road is paved to the Callejón de Huaylas and south to Caraz and Huaraz. For bus services along this route, see Transport, in Listings section, below.

A faster route to Huaraz, paved and also very scenic, branches off the Pan-American Highway at **Casma**. It climbs to **Pariacoto**, with basic lodging, and crosses the Cordillera Negra at the **Callán Pass** (4224 m). The descent to Huaraz offers great views of the Cordillera Blanca. This beautiful trip is worth taking in daylight; sit on the right for the best views. The road has many dangerous curves requiring caution. For bus services along this route, see Transport, opposite.

An alternative road for cyclists (and vehicles with a permit) is the 50-km private road known as the 'Brasileños', used by the Brazilian company Odebrecht which has built a water channel from the Río Santa to the coast. The turn-off at Km 482 on the Pan-American Highway is 35 km north of the Santa turning and 15 km south of the bridge in Chao. It is a good all-weather road via Tanguche. Permits are obtainable from the Chavimochic HQ at San José de Virú, US$7.50, or from the guard at the gate on Sunday.

## Listings North from Lima

### Where to stay

#### Barranca to Huarmey

**$ Jaime Crazy**
*Manuel Scorza 371 y 373, Sector B-8, Huarmey, T043-400104, JaimeCrazyPeru on Facebook.*
A hostel offering trips to beaches, archaeological sites, farming communities, volunteering and all sorts of activities.

#### Casma and around
Hotel prices are higher in Jan and Feb.

**$$ Hostal El Farol**
*Túpac Amaru 450, Casma, T043-411064, www.elfarolinn.com.*
Very nice, rooms and suites, swimming pool, pleasant garden, very good restaurant, parking, information.

**$$ Hostal Gabriela**
*Malecón Grau Mz 6, Lt 18, Tortugas, T043-631302, misateinversiones@gmail.com.*
Pleasant 10-room hotel, lounge with ocean views, good restaurant with extensive menu, seafood, local and international dishes.

**$$ Tarawasi**
*1a Línea Sur, Centro, Tortugas, T043-782637, tarawasitortugas@hotmail.com.*
Small family-run *hospedaje*, pleasant atmosphere, 2 terraces with ocean views, good restaurant serves Peruvian and Mediterranean food.

**$ El Dorado**
*Av Garcilazo de la Vega Mz J, Lt 37, 1 block from the Panamericana, Casma, T043-411795, http://eldoradocasma.blogspot.com.*
With fan, pool, restaurant and tourist information.

**$ Las Dunas**
*Luis Ormeño 505, Casma, T043-711057.*
An upgraded and enlarged family home, welcoming.

## Chimbote to Callejón de Huaylas

There are plenty of hotels in Chimbote, so try to negotiate a lower rate.

### $$ Cantón
*Bolognesi 498, T043-344388.*
Modern, higher quality than others, has a good but pricey *chifa* restaurant.

### $$ Ivansino Inn
*Av José Pardo 738, T043-321811.*
Includes breakfast, comfortable, modern.

### $ Hostal El Ensueño
*Sáenz Peña 268, 2 blocks from Plaza Central, T043-320662.*
Cheaper rooms without bath, very welcoming, safe.

### $ Hostal Karol Inn
*Manuel Ruiz 277, T043-321216.*
Hot water, good, family-run, laundry, *cafetería*.

### $ Residencial El Parque
*E Palacios 309, on plaza, T043-345572.*
Converted old home, hot water, nice, secure.

## Restaurants

### Huacho and around
Good restaurants in Huacho include **Cevichería El Clásico** (C Inca s/n, daily 1000-1800), and **La Estrella** (Av 28 de Julio 561).

### Casma and around
The best restaurants are at **Hostal El Farol** and at the hotels in Tortugas. Cheap restaurants are on Huarmey. The local ice cream, *Caribe*, is available at Ormeño 545.

### $$ Tío Sam
*Huarmey 138.*
Specializes in fresh fish, good ceviche.

## What to do

### Casma and around
**Akela Tours**, *Lima A3-3, T990-283145, Facebook: akelatours*. Good tours of Sechín, trips to the desert and beaches, sandboarding; run by Monika, an archaeologist.

**Sechín Tours**, *Hostal Monte Carlo, Casma, T043-411421, renatotours@yahoo.com.* Organizes tours in the local area. The guide, Renato, only speaks Spanish but has knowledge of local ruins.

## Transport

### Huacho and around
**AméricaMóvil** (Av Luna Pizarro 251, La Victoria, Lima, T01-423 6338; in Huacho T01-232 7631) and **Zeta** (Av Abancay 900, Lima, T01-426 8087; in Huacho T01-239 6176) run every 20-30 mins **Lima–Huacho**, daily 0600 to 2000, 2½ hrs, US$6 (more expensive at weekends).

### Caral
**Empresa Valle Sagrado Caral** buses to the site leave the terminal in Barranca (Berenice Dávila, cuadra 2), US$2.75 shared, or US$35 private service with 1½ hrs at the site. A taxi from Barranca to the ruins costs US$10 one way. Tours from Lima usually allow 1½ hrs at Caral, with a 3-hr journey each way, stopping for morning coffee and for lunch in Huacho on the return. If you don't want to go back to Lima, you'll have to get to Barranca to continue your journey.

### Barranca to Huarmey
Bus companies have their offices in Barranca, so buses tend to stop there (opposite El Grifo service station at the end of town) rather than at Pativilca or Paramonga. To **Lima**, 3½ hrs, US$7.50. To **Casma**, 155 km, several daily, 2½ hrs, US$6. To **Huaraz**, combis to Conococha from José Gálvez 336, US$3.75, 3 hrs; from Conococha take a combi to Huaraz. To **Chiquián**, **Trans Santiago** combis, US$4.60, 3½ hrs, twice a day. From Barranca buses run only to Paramonga port (3 km off the highway, about 15 mins from Barranca); from there you can get a taxi to the **Paramonga ruins**, US$9 (including wait); otherwise it's a 3-km walk along the Panamericana.

## Casma and around

**América Express** and **Tres Estrellas** run frequent services from **Lima** to **Chimbote** (see Chimbote, below) stopping in Casma, 370 km, 6 hrs, US$11-18; other companies going to Chimbote or Trujillo might drop you off by the highway. In the other direction, many of the buses to **Lima** stop briefly opposite the petrol station, block 1 of Ormeño or, if they have small offices, along blocks 1-5 of Av Ormeño.

To **Chimbote**, 55 km, it is easiest to take the **Los Casmeños** *colectivos*, which depart when full from between the Plaza de Armas and Banco de la Nación, 45 mins, US$2.15. To **Trujillo** and Chiclayo, it is best to go first to Chimbote bus station and then take an **América Express** bus.

To **Huaraz**, 150 km via **Pariacoto**, 4 hrs, US$9, with **Transportes Huandoy** (Ormeño 166, T043-712336) daily 0700, 1100 and 1400, or **Yungay Express** (by the Ovalo near the Repsol petrol station) daily 0600, 0800 and 1400; also *colectivos* from the same Ovalo, US$11, 3 hrs.

## Chimbote

The bus station is 4 km south of town on Av Meiggs. Under no circumstances should you walk to the centre: minibus, US$0.50, taxi US$1.50. There are no hotels near the terminal; some companies have ticket offices in the centre.

To/from **Lima**, 420 km, 5½ hrs, US$15-20, frequent service with many companies, eg hourly with **América Express**, several daily with **Tres Estrellas**. To **Trujillo**, 130 km, 2 hrs, US$6, **América Express** every 20 mins till 2100, these continue to **Chiclayo**.

To **Huaraz**, most companies, with the best buses, go the 'long way round': down the Panamericana to Pativilca, then up the main highway, 7 hrs, US$14; the main companies start in Trujillo and continue to **Caraz**. The fastest route, however, is via Pariacoto, 5 hrs, US$11, with **Trans Huandoy** (Etseturh, T043-354024) at 0600, 1000 and 1300, and **Yungay Express** at 0500, 0700 and 1300. Alternatively, you can travel to **Caraz** via the Cañón del Pato, 6 hrs, US$12, with **Yungay Express** at 0830; sit on the left-hand-side for the best views.

---

## ★ Trujillo and around  *Colour map 3, A1.*

a colonial city with ancient archaeology on its doorstep

---

The capital of La Libertad Department, 548 km from Lima, Trujillo disputes the title of second city of Peru with Arequipa. It has an urban population of over 1.5 million, but the colonial centre is compact. The greenness surrounding the city is a delight against the backcloth of brown Andean foothills and peaks. Founded by Diego de Almagro in 1534 as an express assignment ordered by Francisco Pizarro, it was named after the latter's native town in Spain. Nearby are some of Peru's most important Moche and Chimú archaeological sites and a stretch of the country's best surfing beaches.

## Sights

The focal point is the pleasant and spacious **Plaza de Armas**, whose buildings, and many others in the vicinity, are painted in bright pastel colours. The prominent sculpture represents agriculture, commerce, education, art, slavery, action and liberation, crowned by a young man holding a torch depicting liberty. Fronting it is the **cathedral** ① *daily 0700-1230, 1700-2000*, dating from 1666, with religious paintings and sculptures displayed next door in the **museum** ① *Mon-Fri 0900-1300, 1600-1900,*

**Tip...**
The city is generally safe, but take care beyond the inner ring road, Avenida España, as well as at bus stops, terminals, ATMs and internet cafés.

# BACKGROUND
## Masters of sculpture

One of the most remarkable pre-Inca civilizations was that of the Moche people, who evolved during the first century AD and lasted until around AD 750. Though these early Peruvians had no written language, they left a vivid record of their life and culture in beautifully modelled and painted ceramics.

Compared with the empires of their successors, the Chimú and Inca, the realm of the Moche was very small, covering less than 400 km of coast from the valleys of Lambayeque to Nepeña, south of present-day Chimbote. The Moche harnessed rivers spilling from the Andean cordillera, channelling them into a network of irrigation canals that watered the arid valleys along this seemingly inhospitable stretch of coast. The resultant lush fields produced plentiful crops, which, along with the sea's bountiful harvest of fish and seafood, gave the Moche a rich and varied diet. With the leisure allowed by such abundant food, Moche craftsmen invented new techniques to produce their artistic masterpieces. It is these ancient pottery vessels that have made the greatest contribution to our understanding of this civilization.

These masters of sculpture used clay to bring to life animals, plants and anthropomorphic deities and demons. They recreated hunting and fishing scenes, combat rituals, elaborate ceremonies and sexual intercourse (sometimes with contraception). They depicted the power of their rulers as well as the plight of the sick and disabled.

Ritual combat is a common theme in their work: prisoners of war are apparently brought before congregations where their throats are cut and their blood offered to those present. Decapitation and dismemberment are also shown.

Moche potters were amazingly skilled at reproducing facial features, specializing in the subtle nuances of individual personality. In addition to these 3D sculptures, the Moche potter was skilled at decorating vessels with low-relief designs. Among the most popular scenes are skeletal death figures holding hands while dancing in long processions to the accompaniment of musicians. The potters also developed a technique of fine-line painting scenes on ceramic vessels. Over a period of several centuries the painters became increasingly skillful at depicting complex and lively scenes with multiple figures. Because of their complexity and detail, these scenes are of vital importance in reconstructing Moche life.

The early introduction of moulds and stamps brought efficiency to the production of Moche ceramics. By pressing moist clay into the halves of a mould, it was possible to produce an object much more rapidly than by hand. Similarly, the use of stamps facilitated the decoration of ceramic vessels with elaborate low-relief designs. Mould-making technology thus resulted in the repeated duplication of individual pieces. Since there were almost no unique ceramic objects, elaborate ceramics became more widely available and less effective as a sign of power, wealth and social status of the élite.

Although among the most sophisticated potters in Spanish America, the Moche did not use ceramics for ordinary tableware. Neither do their ceramics show many everyday activities, such as farming, cooking and pottery making. This is because Moche art expresses the religious and supernatural aspects of the culture.

Sat 0900-1300, US$1.45. Also on the plaza are the **Hotel Libertador**, the colonial-style Sociedad de Beneficencia Pública de Trujillo and the Municipalidad (great views from Salón Dorado on second floor, ask at the gate). The **Universidad de Trujillo** ① *Independencia y Almagro*, second only to that of San Marcos at Lima, was founded in 1824. The colonial-style **Casa Urquiaga** (or **Calonge**) on the plaza now houses the **Banco Central de**

# Trujillo

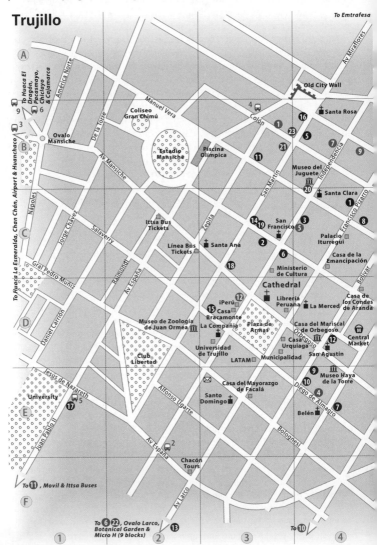

**Reserva** ① *Pizarro 446, Mon-Fri 0930-1500, Sat-Sun 1000-1330.* Another beautiful colonial mansion is **Casa Bracamonte (or Lizarzaburu)** ① *Independencia 441*, which houses the Seguro Social de Salud del Perú and has occasional exhibitions. Opposite the cathedral on Independencia, is the **Casa Garci Olguín** (Caja Nuestra Gente), recently restored but boasting the oldest façade in the city and Moorish-style murals. Two blocks from Plaza de

**Where to stay** 😴
1 Bona Nit &
  Munay Wasi Hostel *B3*
2 Casa de Clara *F6*
3 Chan Chán Inn *A5*
4 Chimor *E4*
5 Colonial *C4*
6 El Gran Marqués *F2*
7 El Mochilero *B4*
8 Gran Bolívar *B5*
9 Gran Recreo *B4*
10 Hostal El Centurión *F4*
11 Kallpa *F1*
12 Libertador *D3*

**Restaurants** 🍴
1 Asturias, Demarco,
  Oviedo & Romano *C4*
2 Café Amaretto *C3*
3 Casona Deza *C4*
4 Cevichería Puerto Mori *B4*
5 Dulcería Doña Carmen *B4*
6 El Celler de Cler *C3*
7 El Chileno *E4*
8 El Kluv *C4*
9 El Mochica *E4*
10 Fitopán *E4*
11 Galera Central *B3*
12 Juguería San Agustín *D4*
13 Mar Picante *F2*
14 Muya Vegano *C3*
15 Olé Café *D3*
16 Patio Rojo *B4*
17 Pizzería Pizzanino *E1*
18 Rincón de Vallejo *C3*
19 Trujillo Señorial *C3*

**Bars & clubs** 🎵
20 Bar/Café Juguete *C4*
21 Canana *B3*
22 El Boticario *F2*
23 El Estribo *B3*

**Transport** 🚌
1 Buses to Huaca del Sol y
  de la Luna *D6*
2 Combi A to Chan Chan &
  Huanchaco *E2, E5*
3 Combis A & B; & Micros B, H
  & H-Corazón: to Chan Chán
  & Huanchaco *B1*
4 Combi B & Micro B: to
  Chan Chán &
  Huanchaco *A4, B3*
5 Micro H to Chan Chán &
  Huanchaco *E1*
6 El Dorado *B1*
8 Oltursa & Flores *A5*
9 Turismo Díaz *B1*
10 Cruz del Sur *A4*

Armas is the spacious 18th-century **Palacio Iturregui**, now occupied by the **Club Central** ① *Jr Pizarro 688, restricted entry to patio, daily 0830-1000, US$1.85,* an exclusive social club with a private collection of ceramics. **Casa Ganoza Chopitea** ① *Independencia 630,* which now houses a café/bar, is considered architecturally the most representative of the viceroyalty in the city. It combines baroque and rococo styles and is also known for the pair of lions that adorn its portico.

Other mansions still in private hands include **Casa del Mayorazgo de Facalá** ① *Pizarro 314 (Scotiabank),* another entrance on Bolognesi, Mon-Fri 0915-1230. **Casa de la Emancipación** ① *Jr Pizarro 610 (Banco Continental), Mon-Sat 0900-1300, 1600-2000,* is the building where independence from Spain was planned and was the first seat of government and congress in Peru. The **Casa del Mariscal de Orbegoso** now houses the **Museo de la República** ① *Orbegoso 553, daily 0930-2000.* It is owned by the BCP bank and holds temporary exhibitions. **Museo Haya de la Torre (Casa del Pueblo)** ① *Orbegoso 664, Mon-Sat 0900-1300, 1600-2000,* is a small, well-presented museum about the life of the founder of the APRA party who was one of the leading 20th-century socialists in the Americas. He was born in the house, which now holds a cinema club once a week.

One of the best of the many churches is the 17th-century **La Merced** ① *Pizarro 550, daily 0800-1200, 1600-2000,* with picturesque moulded figures below the dome. The church and monastery of **El Carmen** ① *Colón y Bolívar, Mass Sun 0700-0730,* has been described as the 'most valuable jewel of colonial art in Trujillo', but is rarely open except for Mass. **La Compañía** ① *near Plaza de Armas,* is now an auditorium for cultural events.

**Museo de Arqueología** ① *Junín 682 y Ayacucho, Casa Risco, T044-249322, Mon-Fri 0830-1430, US$1.85,* houses a large and interesting collection of thematic exhibits of Moche and Chimú culture. The **Museo del Juguete** ① *Independencia 705 y Junín, Mon-Sat 1000-1800, Sun 1000-1300, US$1.85, children US$0.70,* is a toy museum containing examples from prehistoric times to 1950, collected by painter Gerardo Chávez. **Museo de Zoología de Juan Ormea** ① *Jr San Martín 368, T044-205011, Mon-Fri 0900-1800, US$0.70,* has interesting displays of Peruvian animals.

Gerardo Chávez also opened the **Museo de Arte Moderno** ① *Prolongación Av Federico Villarreal, esquina Carretera Industrial, 3.5 km from centre, T044-215668, Mon-Fri 0800-1300, 1345-1745, Sat-Sun 0800-1500, US$3, students half price,* which has some fine exhibits, a peaceful garden (Jardín de los Sentidos) and friendly staff. In the central square of the Moche district (6 km south of the centre) is the **Museo de Moche** ① *daily 0900-1600, US$1.65,* that houses the Cassinelli Collection of Mochica and Chimú pottery. There is also a small park ① *Mon-Sat 0800-1700, free,* about half a block beyond the Ovalo Larco, southwest of the city centre.

## Huacas del Sol and de la Luna

*Information: Proyecto Huaca de la Luna, Jr San Martín 380, Trujillo, T044-221269, www. huacas.com. Daily 0900-sunset (last entry 1600); access by 1-hr guided tour only (English, French or Spanish); groups can be up to 25 people and quite rushed. US$4 (students US$2, children US$0.40), booklet in English or Spanish US$2.85; all tickets are sold at the Museo Huacas de Moche – see below.*

A few kilometres south of Trujillo are the huge and fascinating Moche pyramids, the Huaca del Sol and the Huaca de la Luna. Until the Spaniards destroyed a third of it in a vain search for treasure, Huaca del Sol was the largest man-made structure in the western hemisphere, at 45 m high. It consisted of seven levels, with 11 or 12 phases of construction over the first six centuries AD. Today, about two thirds of the pyramid have been lost and it is closed to the public.

Huaca de la Luna, 500 m away, received scant attention until extensive polychrome moulded decorations were uncovered in the 1990s. The colours on these remarkable geometric patterns and deities have faded little and it is now possible to view impressive friezes of the upper four levels on the northern exterior wall of the *huaca*. The highest mural is a 'serpent' which runs the length of the wall; beneath it are several levels of repeated motifs depicting victorious warriors, 'felines', 'fishermen' holding fish and huge 'spider/crab' images. Combined with intricate, brightly painted two-dimensional motifs in the sacrificial area atop the huaca, and with new discoveries in almost every excavation, Huaca de la Luna is a truly significant site well worth visiting.

The **Templo Nuevo**, or Plataforma III, represents the period 600 to 900 AD and has friezes in the upper level showing the so-called Rebellion of the Artefacts, in which weapons take on human characteristics and attack their owners. Also visit the **Museo Huacas de Moche** ① *5 mins' walk from Huaca de la Luna, www.huacasdemoche.pe, daily 0900-1600, US$1, students US$0.75, children US$0.40,* the site museum. Three halls display objects found in the huacas, including beautiful ceramics, arranged thematically around the Moche culture, the cermonial complex, daily life, the deities of power and of the mountains and priests who worshipped them. In the nearby **Campiña de Moche** are craft workshops (open irregular hours) and several outdoor restaurants with swimming pools.

The **visitor centre** ① *T044-834901,* has a café showing videos and a souvenir shop and good toilets. In an outside patio, craftsmen reproduce ceramics in designs from northern Peru.

## Chan Chán
*5 km from Trujillo centre. Daily 0900-1600. Site may be covered up if rain is expected. Tickets cost US$3.80 (US$2 with ISIC card), children US$0.35, and are valid for Chan Chán (site and museum), Huaca El Dragón and Huaca La Esmeralda for 2 days. Official guides, US$10, wait by the souvenir shops; toilets here too.*

The imperial city of the Chimú domains was once the largest adobe city in the world. The vast, crumbling ruins consist of 10 great compounds built by Chimú kings, with perimeter walls up to 12 m high surrounding sacred enclosures with usually only one narrow entrance. Inside, rows of storerooms contained the agricultural wealth of the kingdom, which stretched 1000 km along the coast from near Guayaquil to the Carabayllo Valley, north of Lima. The Incas almost certainly copied this system and used it in Cuzco where the last Incas continued building huge enclosures. The Chimú surrendered to the Incas around 1471 after 11 years of siege.

Most of the compounds contain a huge walk-in well which tapped the ground water, raised to a high level by irrigation further up the valley. Each compound also included a platform mound which was the burial place of the king, his women and his treasure, presumably maintained as a memorial.

The dilapidated city walls enclose an area of 28 sq km containing the remains of palaces, temples, workshops, streets, houses, gardens and a canal. What is left of the adobe walls bears either well restored or modern fibreglass fabrications of moulded decorations showing small figures of fish, birds, fishing nets and

**Tip...**
There are police at the entrance to the site, but it is a 25-minute walk from there to the ticket office. If you're not on a tour, you are advised to take one of the vehicles that wait at the entrance as it is not safe to walk to the ticket office. On no account should you walk beyond Chan Chán to Buenos Aires beach, nor walk on the beach itself, as there is serious risk of robbery and of being attacked by dogs.

various geometric motifs. Painted designs have been found on pottery unearthed from the debris of a city ravaged by floods, earthquakes and *huaqueros* (grave looters). The **Ciudadela de Nik-An** (formerly called Tschudi) is the only palace open to visitors.

The **site museum** ① *on the main road, 100 m before the turn-off, daily 0830-1630, US$1*, has objects found in the area, with displays and signs in Spanish and English.

The partly restored temple, **Huaca El Dragón** ① *daily 0930-1630 (in theory); combis from Huayna Cápac y Los Incas, or Av España y Manuel Vera marked 'Arco Iris/La Esperanza', taxi US$2*, is on the west side of the Pan-American Highway in the district of La Esperanza. It dates from Huari to Chimú times (AD 1000-1470) and is also known as **Huaca Arco Iris** (rainbow), after the shape of friezes which decorate it.

The poorly preserved **Huaca La Esmeralda** is at Mansiche, between Trujillo and Chan Chán, behind the church and near the Mall Aventura shopping centre. Buses to Chan Chán and Huanchaco Pass the church at Mansiche.

## ★ El Brujo
*3 km from Magdalena de Cao. Daily 0900-1600. US$4 (US$2 with ISIC card, children US$0.35). Shops and toilets at the entrance. See www.fundacionwiese.com.*

A complex collectively known as El Brujo, 60 km north of Trujillo, is considered one of the most important archaeological sites on the north coast. Covering 2 sq km, it was a ceremonial centre for up to 10 cultures, including the Moche. Excavations here will, no doubt, continue for many years. Trujillo travel agencies run tours and there is a trail system for exploring the site.

Huaca Cortada (or El Brujo) has a wall decorated with stylized figures in high relief. Huaca Prieta is, in effect, a giant rubbish tip dating back 5000 years, which once housed the original inhabitants of the area. It was first investigated by the US archaeologist Junius Bird in the late 1940s, leading him to establish the chronology of prehistoric Peru that prevails today and cementing the place of this unremarkable *huaca* in Peruvian history.

Huaca Cao Viejo has extensive friezes, polychrome reliefs up to 90 m long, 4 m high and on five different levels. The mummy of a tattooed, woman, La Señora de Cao, dating from AD 450, was found here. Her mausoleum, with grave goods, can be visited in an excellent purpose-built museum. In front of Cao Viejo are the remains of one of the oldest Spanish churches in the region. It was common practice for the Spaniards to build their churches near these ancient sites in order to counteract their religious importance. Demonstrations of shamanism, including immersion in a ceremonial Moche well, are offered by the visitor centre.

## ★ Huanchaco
An alternative to Trujillo is this fishing and surfing village, full of hotels, guesthouses and restaurants. It is famous for its narrow pointed fishing rafts, known as *caballitos* (little horses) *de totora*, made of totora reeds and depicted on the pottery of Mochica, Chimú and other cultures. Unlike those used on Lake Titicaca, they are flat, not hollow, and ride the breakers rather like surfboards. You can see fishermen returning in their reed rafts at about 0800 and 1400 when they stack the boats upright to dry in the fierce sun. Fishermen offer trips on their *caballitos* for US$1.75; be prepared to get wet. Groups should contact Luis Gordillo (El Mambo, T044-461092). Overlooking Huanchaco is a huge church (1535-1540), whose belfry has extensive views. **El Quibishi**, at the south end of the beach, is the main *artesanía* market and also has a food section.

Although Puerto Chicama has a longer wave (see below), Huanchaco claims to be the best place in Peru to learn to surf. There are more surfing spots here, with no crowding and good waves for varying levels of difficulty.

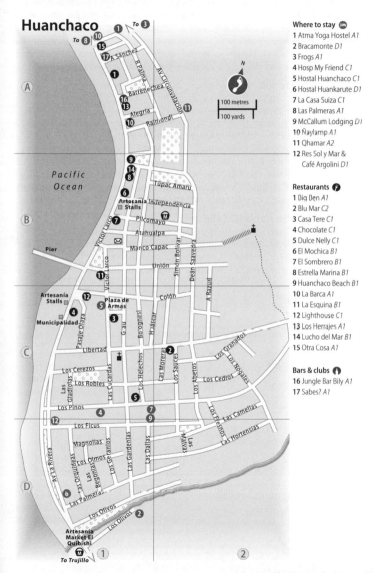

# Huanchaco

**Where to stay** 🛏
1 Atma Yoga Hostel *A1*
2 Bracamonte *D1*
3 Frogs *A1*
4 Hosp My Friend *C1*
5 Hostal Huanchaco *C1*
6 Hostal Huankarute *D1*
7 La Casa Suiza *C1*
8 Las Palmeras *A1*
9 McCallum Lodging *D1*
10 Ñaylamp *A1*
11 Qhamar *A2*
12 Res Sol y Mar &
Café Argolini *D1*

**Restaurants** 🍴
1 Big Ben *A1*
2 Blu Mar *C2*
3 Casa Tere *C1*
4 Chocolate *C1*
5 Dulce Nelly *C1*
6 El Mochica *B1*
7 El Sombrero *B1*
8 Estrella Marina *B1*
9 Huanchaco Beach *B1*
10 La Barca *A1*
11 La Esquina *B1*
12 Lighthouse *C1*
13 Los Herrajes *A1*
14 Lucho del Mar *B1*
15 Otra Cosa *A1*

**Bars & clubs** 🍸
16 Jungle Bar Bily *A1*
17 Sabes? *A1*

## Puerto Chicama

Surfers claim that Puerto Chicama (Malabrigo), 70 km north of Trujillo (turn off the Panamericana at Paiján) is the best surf beach in Peru, with the longest left-hand point-break in the world. The best waves are from March to October (high point May/June). The town has a 1-km-long fishing pier, huge, abandoned warehouses and the remains of a railway to Casa Grande cooperative left over from the town's sugar-exporting days. There are a few *hospedajes* and simple places to eat in town itself (shop early by the market for fresh seafood), but the best places to stay and eat are in Distrito El Hombre, the clifftop south of town (eg **Chicama**, Arica 625); avoid the shacks that line the beach.

### Pacasmayo and around *Colour map 3, A1.*

**Pacasmayo**, 102 km north of Trujillo, is the port for the next oasis north. It has a nice beachfront with an old Customs House and a very long pier. Away from the seafront Pacasmayo is a busy commercial centre. Resort El Faro is 1 km away, with surfing at the point and kite- and windsurfing closer to town. There are maritime festivals at New Year and Semana Santa. **Bosque de Cañoncillo**, 23 km northeast of Pacasmayo (40 minutes by taxi, US$15 with one-hour wait, public transport also available), has trails through carob forests and lakes with endemic birds; two hours' walk from entrance to lakes, take water and sun protection. **Puemape** is a long beach with good waves and basic restaurants, 15 km south of Pacasmayo, 40 minutes by taxi, US$10.

## Santuario y Reserva Nacional Calipuy

These two adjacent highland nature reserves are home to impressive stands of *Puya raimondii* and the largest herd of guanaco in Peru, respectively. Both reserves reach elevations above 4000 m and are not easy to get to, but well worth the effort (Cristian at SERNANP is a helpful contact, T968-218433, sncalipuy@sernanp.gob.pe, rncalipuy@sernanp.gob.pe). Entry is free. Access is either through Chao (more direct), along the Panamericana south of Virú, or the regional centre of Santiago de Chuco, which has simple places to stay and eat, see Transport (page 130).

---

**Listings** Trujillo and around *maps pages 114 and 119.*

### Tourist information

Useful websites include http://trujilloperu.xanga.com, http://vivetrujillo.com and www.conocetrujillo.com.

**Gobierno Regional de la Libertad**
*Dirección de Turismo, Av España 1800, T044-296221.*
Information on regional tourism.

**Indecopi**
*Santo Toribio de Mogrovejo 518, Urbanización San Andrés II etapa, T044-295733, sobregon@indecopi.gob.pe.*
For tourist complaints.

**iPerú**
*Jr Independencia 467, of 106, T044-294561, iperutrujillo@promperu.gob.pe. Mon-Sat 0900-1800, Sun 0900-1300. Also at Huaca de La Luna, daily 0900-1300.*

**Municipalidad de Trujillo**
*Sub-Gerencia de Turismo, Av España 742, T044-244212, anexo 119, sgturismo@munitrujillo.gob.pe. Mon-Fri 0900-1600.*
Information about museums, official tour agencies and cultural activities.

**Tourist police**
*Diego de Almagro 480, Plaza de Armas, policia_turismo_tru@hotmail.com. Mon-Sat 0800-2000.*

Provide useful information and can help with reports of theft, some staff speak English.

## Where to stay

### Trujillo
The city is well supplied with hotels in all price categories. Chains include **Casa Andina** (www.casa-andina.com).

#### $$$$-$$$ Libertador
*Independencia 485, Plaza de Armas, T044-232741, www.libertador.com.pe.*
Modern hotel in historic building, lovely place to stay. Comfortable rooms, excellent service, swimming pool in a flower-filled patio, sauna, *cafetería* and restaurant, breakfast extra, excellent buffet lunch on Sun.

#### $$$$-$$$ Moche Sanctuary Lodge
*Camino a la Campiña de Moche Km 5, T947-736177, www.mochelodge.com.*
Comfortable upmarket colonial-style lodge with a huge wide-open garden and swimming pool, some rooms have their own large jacuzzi. Located next to the museum of Huacas del Sol y de la Luna. Spectacular views of the ancient Moche pyramids, an original, quiet and inspirational place to stay.

#### $$$ Chimor
*Diego de Almagro 631, T044-202252.*
A small modern hotel, comfortable and welcoming, includes buffet breakfast.

#### $$$ El Gran Marqués
*Díaz de Cienfuegos 145-147, Urbanización La Merced, T044-481710, www.elgranmarques.com.*
Price includes breakfast, modern, minibar, pool, sauna, jacuzzi, restaurant.

#### $$$ Gran Recreo
*Estete 460, T044-230303, http://granrecreohotel.com.*
Modern stylish hotel, good location, small swimming pool, good restaurant, bar, parking. Good value for this category.

#### $$$-$$ Kallpa
*Díaz de las Heras s/n, Urbanización Vista Hermosa, T044-281266, www.kallpahotel.pe.*
A smart boutique hotel, welcoming, English spoken, below usual boutique hotel prices.

#### $$ Colonial
*Independencia 618, T044-258261, www.hostalcolonial.com.pe.*
Attractive but small rooms, hot showers, basic breakfast, good restaurant, especially for set lunch. Recommended.

#### $$ Gran Bolívar
*Bolívar 957, T044-222090, www.granbolivarhotel.net.*
In a converted 18th-century house, restaurant and room service, café, bar, laundry, gym, parking.

#### $$ Hostal El Centurión
*Paraguay 304, Urbanización El Recreo, T044-201526, www.hostalelcenturion.com.*
About 20 mins' walk from the plaza, modern, good rooms, well kept, safe but no a/c, simple restaurant, good service.

#### $ Bona Nit
*Colón 257, T044-298530, www.bonanithostal.com.*
Well located economy hotel, rooms with fan and frigobar, includes simple breakfast, good value.

#### $ Casa de Clara
*Cahuide 495, T044-243347, http://trujilloperu.xanga.com.*
Friendly backpackers' *hostal*, hot water, good food, helpful, information, lodging packages with meals and tours, laundry service, use of kitchen with permission and charge for gas, meeting place and lots going on, many languages spoken (see Clara Bravo and Michael White, What to do, page 127). Restaurants nearby. Good economy option.

#### $ Chan Chán Inn
*Av Ejército 307, T044-791515, chanchaninn@hotmail.com.*

Close to several bus terminals so noisy, includes breakfast, popular with backpackers, café, laundry, money exchange, information.

### $ El Mochilero
*Independencia 887, T044-297842, Elmochilerotrujilloperuoficial on Facebook.*
A variety of basic dorms and rooms, only one with bath, electric showers, breakfast available, fridge for guests' use. Tours arranged, information.

### $ Munay Wasi Hostel
*Jr Colón 250, T044-231462, www.munaywasihostel.com.*
Family-run hostel within Av España, private and shared rooms (US$10 pp with breakfast), shared bath, book exchange, tourist information, fully equipped kitchen.

## El Brujo

### $ Hospedaje Jubalu
*Libertad 105, Magdalena de Cao, T995-670600.*
With hot water. There's no internet in town and limited shopping.

## Huanchaco

### $$$-$$ Bracamonte
*Los Olivos 160, T044-461162, www.hotelbracamonte.com.pe.*
Comfortable, modern, contemporary decor, pool and garden, secure, good restaurant offers lunch *menú* and some vegetarian dishes, English spoken, laundry service, games room, garage. Highly recommended.

### $$ Hostal Huanchaco
*Larco 185 on the plaza, T044-461272.*
With hot water, pool, good but pricey cafeteria, breakfast extra, video, pool table.

### $$ Hostal Huankarute
*La Rivera 312, T044-461705, www.hostalhuankarute.com.*
On the seafront, with small pool, bar, sun terrace, bicycle rental; some rooms larger, more luxurious and more pricey, all with ocean view.

### $$ Las Palmeras
*Av Larco 1624, sector Los Tumbos, T044-461199, Facebook: laspalmerasdehuanchaco.*
Rooms with terrace, hot water, dining room, pool and gardens. Rooms on top floor with sea view cost more than ground floor rooms with pool view. Basic breakfast extra.

### $$ Qhamar
*Av Circunvalación 140, Urbanización El Boquerón, T044-462366, www.qhamarhotel.com.*
Modern quiet hotel away from the centre. All rooms with sea view, a bit small but bright and comfortable. Small swimming pool, pool table, table football, bar, garden, airport pick-up available.

### $$ Residencial Sol y Mar
*La Rivera 400, T044-461120.*
Ample rooms, large pool, garden, terrace, event room, no breakfast but **Café Argolini** next door.

### $ Atma Yoga Hostel
*Ricardo Palma 442, T 044-664507, WhatsApp +51-972-444260, www.atmahuanchaco.com.*
Hostel in a quiet neighbourhood with yoga studio and instructor, classes open to non-guests. Rooms with private or shared bath, US$7.50 in dorm, kitchen, TV room, patio, balconies, no breakfast but coffee and tea in the morning. Dutch/Peruvian-run.

### $ Frogs
*C El Pescador 308, Los Tumbos, www.frogsperu.com.*
Located in a quiet area, big bright rooms, some with with sea view. Yoga area, terrace with hammocks and bean bags, sunset views, bar, pool table, ping pong, ample kitchen facilities and TV room. Popular meeting place, organize daily activities, Peruvian/German-owned.

### $ Hospedaje My Friend
*Los Pinos 533, T044-461080.*
Dorm rooms (US$6 pp with breakfast) with bath upstairs, hot water, TV room, information. Tours arranged but service is

erratic. Popular with surfers, good meeting place, restaurant/bar open 0800-2230.

### $ La Casa Suiza
*Los Pinos 308, T044-639713,*
*www.lacasasuiza.com.*
This Huanchaco institution has a variety of rooms with/without bath, breakfast US$3, occasional barbecues on the roof, book exchange.

### $ McCallum Lodging
*Los Ficus 460, T044-626923, http://*
*mccallumlodginghouse.wordpress.com.*
Private rooms and dorms (US$6 pp, no breakfast), hot water, hammocks, home-cooked meals available and recipes shared, laundry, baggage and surfboard storage, family atmosphere, highly considered by locals and tourists.

### $ Ñaylamp
*Av Larco 1420, northern end of seafront*
*in El Boquerón, T044-461022,*
*www.hostalnaylamp.com.*
Rooms set around a courtyard with garden, others have sea view, dorms, hammocks, good beds, hot water, kitchen facilities, camping, tents for hire, laundry, safe, Italian food, good breakfasts.

## Puerto Chicama
The following are in Distrito El Hombre (several close out of season).

### $$$ Chicama Surf Resort
*T044-576206, www.chicamasurf.com.*
*All year.*
Exclusive, with surfing classes, boats to the waves, spa, restaurant, infinity pool.

### $$ Hostal Los Delfines
*T943-296662.*
Owner is Tito Venegas. Guests can use well equipped kitchen, rooms with balcony, hot water, spacious.

### $$-$ Iguana Inn
*C Progreso, Pto Malabrigo, T04-57622,*
*www.hoteliguanainn.com.*

Good mid-range option, well equipped rooms with fridge and coffee/tea maker, no breakfast.

### $ Hostel El Hombre
*C Arica 803, T044-576077.*
Legendary surfers' hangout and meeting spot. Basic dorms (US$5 pp). Owner Doris prepares food. In town there are several cheaper places; **Hostal El Naipe**, Tacna 395, is arguably the best.

## Pacasmayo

### $$$ El Faro
*Urbanización La Perla, T044-311802,*
*www.elfaropacasmayo.com.*
Well known surf resort on the coast, simple rooms, large pool, good restaurant, bar, surf-board and other gear rentals, organizes tours.

### $$ El Mirador
*Aurelio Herrera 10, www.perupacasmayo.com.*
Variety of rooms and prices, all with private bath, fan and safe box. Well located, popular and good value.

### $ Da Vincy
*Ayacucho 44, T044-521889.*
Rooms with private bath, no breakfast, good-value economy option.

### $ Duke Kahanamoku
*Ayacucho 44, T044-521889.*
Old house close to the beach with private and shared rooms, backpakers' surfing place, classes and board rental, breakfast extra, hot water.

## Restaurants

Trujillo offers very good, varied dining. A speciality is *shambar*, a thick minestrone made with pork. On sale everywhere is *turrón*, a nougat-type sweet. All along Pizarro are restaurants to suit all tastes and budgets, most popular are **Asturias**, **Demarco**, **Oviedo** and **Romano** (see below). On the west side of the central market at Grau y Ayacucho are several small, cheap eateries.

## Trujillo

### $$$ El Celler de Cler
*Independencia 588, upstairs. Open 1830-0100.*
One of the best restaurants of Trujillo, located in an old colonial house in the centre, some seating on a nice little balcony. Peruvian and international dishes, mostly meat, no fish.

### $$$-$$ El Mochica
*Bolívar 462, also Mochica de Doña Fresia, Santa Marina 146, Urbanización La Merced, T044-659214, www.elmochica.com.pe.*
Good traditional northern Peruvian cuisine, with live music on special occasions. La Merced branch is more upscale.

### $$ Demarco
*Pizarro 725.*
Popular at midday for lunchtime *menús* and for its cakes and desserts, good service.

### $$ Mar Picante
*Húsares de Junín 412, T044-20846.*
Very good local seafood in a family-run restaurant.

### $$ Pizzería Pizzanino
*Av Juan Pablo II 183, Urbanización San Andrés, opposite University. Evening only.*
Good for pizzas, pastas, meats, desserts.

### $$ Romano
*Pizarro 747.*
International food, good *menú*, breakfasts, coffee, excellent milkshakes, cakes.

### $$-$ Cevichería Puerto Mori
*Estete 482, T044-346752.*
Very popular, they serve only good seafood. At the same location are 2 more fish restaurants, but not of the same quality.

### $ Asturias
*Pizarro 741.*
Nice café with a reasonable *menú*, good pastas, cakes and sandwiches.

### $ Galera Central
*Junín 235, T044-294142. Closed Sun.*
Good economical *menú* and *comida criolla*, friendly service.

### $ Juguería San Agustín
*Bolívar 526.*
Good juices, good *menú*, sandwiches, ice creams, popular, excellent value. Also at Av Larco Herrera y Husares de Junín.

### $ Muya Vegano
*San Martín 600 esquina Gamarra.*
A good healthy restaurant with vegan *menú* options starting around US$2.

### $ Olé Café
*Diego de Almagro 349.*
Small, rustic restaurant serving menu and sandwiches. Paintings on the wall and a lounge area with Moche pottery.

### $ Oviedo
*Pizarro 737.*
With soups, vegetarian options, good salads and cakes, helpful.

### $ Patio Rojo
*San Martín 883. Mon-Thu 0800-2300, Fri-Sat 0800-0100, Sun 1000-1600.*
NIce little restaurant with a peaceful patio serving inexpensive vegetarian and organic *menú*.

### $ Rincón de Vallejo
*Orbegoso 303.*
Good *menú*, typical dishes, very crowded at peak times. 2nd branch at Av España 736.

### $ Trujillo Señorial
*Gamarra 353, T044-204873. Mon-Sat 1300-1530.*
Restaurant and hotel school, good *menú*, food nicely presented, good value.

## Cafés

### Café Amaretto
*Gamarra 368.*
Smart, good selection of real coffees, "brilliant" cakes, sweets, snacks and drinks.

### Casona Deza
*Independencia 630. Tue-Sun 1600-2300.*
Comfortable café/bar selling home-made pasta and pizza and good coffee in an old mansion.

**Dulcería Doña Carmen**
*San Martín 814.*
Serves local specialities such as *alfajores*,
*budín, king kong*, etc.

**El Chileno**
*Ayacucho 408.*
Café and ice cream parlour, popular.

**El Kluv**
*Junín 527 (next to Metro Market).*
Italian-owned, fresh, tasty pizzas at noon
and in the late afternoon.

**Fitopán**
*Bolívar 406, www.fitopan.com.*
Good selection of breads, also serves
lunches. Has 3 other branches.

## El Brujo

**$ Café Antojitos**
*At entrance to Plaza de Armas,*
*Magdalena de Cao.*
Run by a women's cooperative, specializing
in sugar-based snacks.

**$ El Brujo**
*Plaza de Armas, Magdalena de Cao.*
Best place to eat in town and accustomed
to providing meals for tourists.

## Huanchaco

There are about 30 restaurants on the
beachfront. Recommended on Av Larco are
**Estrella Marina** at No 740, **Los Herrajes** at
No 1020, and **Lucho del Mar** at No 750; all **$$**.
Many keep shorter hours or close altogether
in low season. Av Los Pinos is the place for
cheap fast food.

**$$$ Big Ben**
*Av Larco 1884, El Boquerón, T044-461378,*
*www.bigbenhuanchaco.com. Daily 1200-1700.*
Seafood and international cuisine, very good.

**$$$ El Mochica**
*Av Larco 700, T044-461963. Open 0900-2300.*
Same owners and good quality as the
restaurant in Trujillo.

**$$$ Huanchaco Beach**
*Av Larco 800, T044-461484. Open 1200-1700.*
One of the best quality in town, popular
with tours.

**$$$-$$ El Sombrero**
*Av Larco 510, T044-462283, www.*
*elsombrero.com.pe. Open 1100-2300.*
Good ceviche and seafood, most tables
have a great sea view. Popular with tour
groups. Has its own hotel (**$$**) upstairs with
big modern rooms, but noisy. Has another
branch at Av Mansiche 267, Trujillo.

**$$ Casa Tere**
*Plaza de Armas, T044-461197.*
For best pizzas in town, also pastas, burgers
and breakfasts. Has a beautiful collection of
old pictures of Huanchaco.

**$$ La Barca**
*Raimondi 117, T044-461855.*
Very good seafood, well-run, popular.

**$$ Lighthouse**
*Av La Rivera y Colón, T044-461055.*
*Mon-Sat 1830-2330.*
Argentine-owned restaurant with a nice
vibe and good innovative cooking. Chicken,
kebabs, also vegetarian and organic dishes.
Most food is prepared on their big barbecue
or in *El Cilindro* (a smoker in an old oil drum).

**$ Blu Mar**
*Jr Libertad 354. Open 0800-1700, closed Tue.*
Good inexpensive *menú* with
generous portions.

**$ Chocolate**
*Av Rivera 752. Daily 0830-1800.*
Swiss management, serves breakfast and lunch,
vegetarian options, good coffee and cakes.

**$ La Esquina**
*Jr Unión 120. Open 1200-2200.*
Small place serving very good barbecued fish.

**$ Otra Cosa**
*Av Victor Larco 1312. Open 0800-2200.*
Dutch/Peruvian vegetarian restaurant serving
a variety of dishes including falafel, burritos

and *menú*. Good organic coffee, fruit salads, juices and the best Dutch apple pie in Peru.

## Cafés

### Café Argolini
*Av Rivera 400.*
Convenient for people staying in the Los Pinos/Los Ficus area for fresh bread, cakes, ice cream, coffee and juices.

### Dulce Nelly
*Los Pinos y Los Helechos.*
Small café with good desserts and a variety of breads baked daily at 1700 (very popular).

## Bars and clubs

### Trujillo

#### Bar/Café Juguete
*Junín y Independencia. Until midnight.*
An classic French-style café serving good coffee as well as alcohol. Has a pasta restaurant attached.

#### Canana
*San Martín 788, T044-232503.*
Bars and restaurant, disco, live music at weekends (US$1.50-3), video screens (also has travel agency). Recommended, but take care on leaving.

#### El Boticario
*Av Larco 962, T044-639346. Open from 2000.*
A small but very elegant upmarket bar with great service and original cocktails. You have to go well dressed but it's worth it.

#### El Estribo
*San Martín 809, T044-204053.*
A club playing a wide variety of genres and attracting a mixed crowd.

### Huanchaco

#### Jungle Bar Bily
*Av Larco 420. Open 1000-0200.*
Well known popular cocktail bar, happy hour 1800-2200. Also a good restaurant.

### Sabes?
*Av Larco 920, http://sabesbar.com.
Open 1900-0200.*
Well established British-owned pub, good pizzas and cocktails (happy hour 1900-2100), pool table and tranquil atmosphere. Popular with tourists and Trujillanos alike.

## Festivals

**End Jan National Marinera Festival**.
**Last week of Sep Festival Internacional de La Primavera**.
Both festivals have cultural events, parades, beauty pageants and Trujillo's famous **Caballos de Paso**.

**Huanchaco**
**1st week of May Festival del Mar**, a celebration of the disembarkation of Taycanamo, the leader of the Chimú period. A procession is made in Totora boats.
**29 Jun San Pedro**, patron saint of fishermen. His statue is taken out to sea on a huge totora-reed boat. There are also surf competitions. **Carnival** and **New Year** are also popular celebrations.

## Shopping

### Trujillo
#### Bookshops
**Librería Peruana**, *Pizarro 505, just off the plaza.* Has the best selection in town, plus postcards; ask for Sra Inés Guerra de Guijón.
   There are also 3 branches of **SBS**: on Jr Bolívar 714; in Mall Aventura, Av Mansiche block 20, and in Plaza Real Mall, Prol Av César Vallejo (behind UPAO University), California (take taxi or green California micro A).

#### Handicrafts
**120 Artesanía por Descubrir**, *Las Magnolias 403, California, www.tienda120.blogspot.com.* Art gallery designs and handmade crafts, near Real Plaza.

**APIAT**, *Av España y Zela*. The largest craft market in the city, good for ceramics, totora boats, woodwork and leather, competitive prices.
**Artesanía del Norte**, *at Dulcería La Libertad, Jr Pizarro 758, and at the Huacas del Sol y de la Luna*. Sells items mostly designed by the owner, Mary Cortijo, using traditional techniques.
**Trama Perú**, *Pizarro 754, T044-243948, www.tramaperu.com. Daily 1000-2200*. High-quality, handmade art objects, authorized Moche art replicas.

### Markets
**Mercado Central**, *Gamarra, Ayacucho and Pasaje San Agustín*.
**Mercado Unión**, *between Av Santa and Av Perú*. A little safer than others; also repairs shoes, clothes and bags.

## What to do

### Trujillo
### City tours
**Mirabus**, *tickets from Multidestinos, Orbegoso 311, of 36, T044-291861, US$4.50, departs from Plaza de Armas at 1000, 1200, 1700, 1800, 1900 in summer, 1200 and 1700 in winter*. 1-hr ride through the colonial centre in a double-decker bus with Spanish commentary.

### Horse shows
**Casa Campo Alcor**, *Vía de Evitamiento Km 567, Víctor Larco, T948-315055. Open 1330-1430, US$9*. These horses, typical of northern Peru, have been bred for their special gait which makes them more comfortable to ride. In the show they dance to the sounds of *marinera*.

### Tour operators
Prices vary and competition is fierce so shop around. During low season (Mar-Apr and Dec) some tours only run in the afternoon or with a minimum number of participants. During peak season (a week before and after Jul 28 and at Easter) English guides are scarce. At all times, groups are usually large and quality varies. To Chan Chán, El Dragón and Huanchaco, 4-4½ hrs for US$8-9 pp. To

Huacas del Sol and de la Luna, 2½-3 hrs for US$8-9 pp. To El Brujo, 4-5 hrs for US$13-17 pp. Prices do not include entrance fees.
**Chacón Tours**, *Av España 106-112, T044-255212. Sat afternoon and Sun morning*. Recommended for flights etc, not local tours.
**Colonia Tours**, *Independencia 618 (Hotel Colonial), T044-25826*. Local tours including Chan Chán, Las Huacas and El Brujo.
**Domiruth**, *Diego de Almagro 539, T044-299 0952, www.domiruth.com*. For airline tickets.
**North Perú Tours**, *Gamarra 432, of 301, T044-310423, www.north-peru.com*. Organizes tours around Trujillo and throughout northern Peru.
**Trujillo Tours**, *Pizarro 478, of 101, T044-200412*. Organizes good tours (more time, better guides) to Chan Chán and the Huacas for around US$25.

### Tour guides
Many hotels work on a commission basis with taxi drivers and travel agencies. If you decide on a guide, make your own direct approach and always agree what is included in the price. The tourist police (see Tourist information) has a list of guides; average cost US$8 per hr. Beware of cowboy outfits herding up tourists around the plazas, especially Plaza de Armas, and bus terminals for rapid, poor quality tours. Also beware scammers offering surfing or salsa lessons and party invitations.
**Alfredo Ríos Mercedes**, *T949-657978, riosmercedes@hotmail.com*. Speaks English.
**Clara Bravo and Michael White**, *Cahuide 495, T044-243347, http://trujilloperu.xanga.com, microbewhite@yahoo.com*. Clara is an experienced tourist guide who speaks Spanish, English, German and understands Italian and runs small group tours daily: archaeological tour US$20 for 6 hrs, city tour US$7 pp, US$53 per car to El Brujo, with extension to Sipán, Brüning Museum and Túcume possible (tours in Lambayeque involve public transport, not included in cost). Clara works with **Michael White**, who provides transport and is very knowledgeable about tourist sites.

**Henry Valiente**, *T949-547132, ysaac_hnr9@ hotmail.com*. An experienced English-speaking guide.

**Jannet Rojas Sánchez**, *Alto Mochica Mz Q 19, Trujillo, T949-344844*. Speaks English, enthusiastic. Also works for **Guía Tours** (Av Nicolás de Piérola 1208, T998-460330).

**Luis Ocas Saldaña**, *Jr José Martí 2019, T954-042086, guianorteperu@hotmail.com*. Very knowledgeable, helpful, covers all of northern Peru.

**William Alvarado**, *T947-006070, william_alvarado_gotur@hotmail.com*. An experienced English-speaking guide.

### Volunteering

There are many social and volunteer projects in Trujillo, but not all are recommendable. Try to get a personal recommendation from other volunteers before signing up.

**Supporting Kids in Peru**, *www.skipperu.org*. Works with poor children and their families in Trujillo.

### Huanchaco
### Language classes

**Sam Owen**, *T967-992775, skypispanish@ gmail.com*. Originally from Wales and married to a Peruvian, he offers unique and very practical Spanish lessons.

### Massage

**Aroma's Thai**, *in Huanchaquito on the main road to Trujillo, T044-635360, 991-175954*. Professional massages, good for after that first surf lesson.

### Surfing

There are plenty of surf schools, competition is fierce and there have been conflicts with hotels who rent boards. Enquire locally about the current situation and who is considered safe and reputable. Equipment rental is US$9 per day; single lesson, about US$22 for 2 hrs.

**Muchik**, *Independencia 100, next to El Mochica restaurant, T 04-633487, www. escueladetablamuchik.com*. Instructors

Chicho and Omar Huamanchumo are former surf champions. They arrange trips to other surf sites and also offer repairs. Recommended.

### Volunteering

**Esperanza Canina**, *in Huanchaquito on the main road to Trujillo, www.esperanzacanina. com*. Cares for abandoned dogs and tries to find homes for them.

**Fairmail**, *www.fairmail.info*. An innovative social enterprise that teaches poor kids to use a camera, sells their photo-art and returns the profits to them.

## Transport

### Trujillo
### Air

The **airport** is west of the city; access to town is along Av Mansiche. Taxi to city hotels, US$7-9.

To **Lima**, 1 hr, several daily flights with **LATAM**, **LC Perú** and **Avianca/TACA**.

### Bus

**Local** Micros (small buses with 25 or more seats) and combis (up to 15 passengers) on all routes within the city cost US$0.50-0.60; colectivos (6 passengers) charge US$0.50 and tend to run on main avenues starting from Av España. In theory, they are not allowed in the city centre. For transport to the archaeological sites, see below.

To **Huanchaco**, there are 2 combi routes (A and B; both take 25 mins), run by the **Caballitos de Totora** company (white and black), and 4 micros (A, B, H and H-Corazón; 45-60 mins), run by **Transportes Huanchaco** (red, yellow and white). They run 0500-2030, every 5-10 mins, US$0.75. The easiest place to pick up any of these combis or micros is Ovalo Mansiche, 3 blocks northwest of Av España in front of the Cassinelli museum. Combi A takes the southerly route on Av España, before heading up Av Los Incas. Combi B takes the northerly route on Av España.

**Long distance** The **Terminal Terrestre de Trujillo** (TTT), or Terrapuerto, is to the southeast of the centre, at Km 558 on the Panamericana Norte, beyond Ovalo La Marina. Bus companies also continue to operate from their private terminals as well. Always ask where the bus leaves from when buying your ticket. On arrival, take a taxi from the terminal and insist on being taken to your hotel of choice.

To **Lima**, 561 km, 9-10 hrs in the better class buses, average fare US$22-32; 10 hrs or more in the cheaper buses, US$11-16. There are many bus companies doing this route, among those recommended are: **Cruz del Sur** (Amazonas 437, between Av Ejército and Miraflores, T044-720444; **Línea** (Av América Sur 2857, T044-297000), 3 levels of service; **Flores** (Av Ejército 346, T044-208250); **Ittsa** (TTT and Av Juan Pablo 1110, T044-284644), frequent service, good value; **Móvil** (TTT, T044-245523, and Av América Sur 3959, T044-286538); **Oltursa** (TTT, T044-263055), 3 *bus cama* services to Lima; **Ormeño** (Av El Ejército 233, T044-259782).

To **Puerto Chicama**, combis from Santa Cruz terminal (Av Santa Cruz, 1 block from Av América Sur), US$2, 1½ hrs; also **Dorado** buses (Av N de Piérola 1062, T044-291778), US$2, via Chocope (US$0.75) and Paiján (US$0.60). Small **Pakatnamú** buses leave when full, 0400-2100 (from Av N de Piérola 1092, T044-206594), to **Pacasmayo**, 102 km, 1¼ hrs, US$5.50.

To **Chiclayo**, 4 hrs from Trujillo, from US$5.50, several companies, including **Emtrafesa** (Av Túpac Amaru 185, T044-471521) and **Ittsa** (see above), both hourly. To **Jaén**, 9 hrs. To **Piura**, 6 hrs, US$10-15 (**Ittsa**'s 0900, 1330, or **Línea**'s 1415 buses are good choices). **Ittsa** also goes to **Talara**, 2200, 9 hrs, US$16.

Direct buses to **Huaraz**, 319 km, via Chimbote and Casma (169 km), with **Línea**, 0900 and 2130; **Móvil**, 2240 and 2300; and **Julio Cesar**, www.transportesjuliocesar. com.pe; 8 hrs, US$17-30. There are also several buses and *colectivos* to **Chimbote**, with **América Express** (from Av La Marina 315), 135 km, 2 hrs, US$6, departures every 30 mins from 0530 (ticket sales from 0500); leave Trujillo before 0600 to make a connection to Huaraz from 0800 in Chimbote (see page 112). Ask Clara Bravo and Michael White (see Tour guides, above) about transport to Caraz avoiding Chimbote: a worthwhile trip via the Brasileños road and Cañon del Pato.

To **Cajamarca**, 300 km, 7-8 hrs, US$10-27, with **Línea** (1030, 2200, 2300), **Turismo Díaz** (1320, 2230) and **Emtrafesa** (2145). To **Huamachuco**, 181 km, 5-6 hrs, see page 160.

## Taxi

Taxis in town charge US$1.30 within Av España and US$1.50 within Av América; always use official taxis, which are mainly black, or cooperative taxis, which have the company logo on the side (eg **Sonrisas**, T044-233000). Beware of overcharging; check fares with locals.

## Huacas del Sol and de la Luna

There are combis every 15 mins from Ovalo Grau in Trujillo and, less safe, from Galvez y Los Incas, but they drop you a long walk from the site. Taxis charge about US$5; there are few at the site so ask your driver to wait.

## Chan Chán

Take any transport between Trujillo and Huanchaco (see above) and ask to get out at the turn-off, US$0.50; then get onward transport from the entrance to the ticket office, US$1. Do not walk from the turn-off to the ticket office. A taxi from Trujillo to the site is US$5; from Huanchaco, US$3.

## El Brujo

The complex can be reached by taking one of the regular buses from Trujillo to Chocope, US$1.25, every 10 mins, 1 hr, and then a *colectivo* to Magdalena de Cao, US$0.75 (leave when full), 15 mins, then a mototaxi taking up to 3 people to the site, US$7.50 including 1½-hr wait. Unless you particularly like Peruvian public transport, it is more convenient to go on a tour.

## Huanchaco

From Huanchaco, micro A goes to the 28 de Julio/Costa Rica junction in Trujillo where it turns west along Prolongación César Vallejo, passing the UPAO university and Plaza Real shopping centre, continuing to the Av El Golf (the terminus for the return to Huanchaco on almost the same route). On other routes from Huanchaco to Trujillo centre, ask the *cobrador* to let you off near C Pizarro on Av España. To reach the **Línea**, **Móvil Tours** and southern bus terminals in Trujillo, take micro H from Huanchaco; it also goes to Ovalo Grau where you can catch buses to the Huacas del Sol and de la Luna. For **Cruz del Sur**, **Ormeño** and **Flores** bus services, take combi or micro B from Huanchaco.

## Puerto Chicama

Buses stop just off Plaza Central, opposite the Comisaria.

## Santuario y Reserva Nacional Calipuy

Buses from Terminal Santa Cruz in Trujillo to **Santiago de Chuco**, US$6, 4 hrs. Private 4WD from Santiago de Chuco to the reserves, about US$85 return. To hire a 4WD in Trujillo to the reserves via Chao, contact Manuel Rubio, T948-312400, about US$150 for 1 day, US$215 for 2.

---

## Chiclayo and around *Colour map 1, C2.*

witches' brews and Moche treasures

---

Lambayeque Department, sandwiched between the Pacific and the Andes, is a major agricultural zone, especially for rice and sugar cane. It boasts a distinctive cuisine and musical tradition, and an unparalleled ethnographic and archaeological heritage. Excavations at the region's adobe pyramid cities are uncovering fabulous treasures.

## Chiclayo

Since its foundation in the 16th century, Chiclayo has grown to become a major commercial hub with a population of 800,000. Its witchcraft market is famous, but it is best known for the spectacular cache of pre-Hispanic archaeological treasures found on its doorstep.

On the Plaza de Armas is the 19th-century neoclassical **cathedral**, designed by the English architect Andrew Townsend. The private **Club de la Unión** is on the plaza at the corner of Calle San José. Continue five blocks north on Balta, the busiest commercial street, to the **Mercado Modelo**, one of northern Peru's liveliest and largest daily markets. Don't miss the market stalls off Calle Arica on the south side, where ritual paraphernalia used by traditional curers and diviners (*curanderos*) are sold: herbal medicines, folk charms, curing potions and exotic objects, including dried llama fetuses, to cure all manner of real and imagined illnesses. At **Paseo Artesanal Colón**, south of the plaza, shops sell handicrafts in a quiet, custom-built open-air arcade. Other relaxing spots are the **Paseo de las Musas**, with its gardens and imitation Greek statues, and **Paseo Yortuque**, with 80 fiberglass statues representing the history of the area.

> **Tip...**
> The ruined Spanish town of Zaña, 51 km south of Chiclayo, was destroyed by floods in 1720, and sacked by English pirates on more than one occasion. There are ruins of 5 colonial churches and the convents of San Agustín, La Merced and San Francisco.

## Monsefú and the coast

The traditional town of **Monsefú**, southwest, is known for its music and handicrafts; there's a good market, four blocks from the plaza. The stalls open when potential customers arrive (see also Festivals, page 140).

Beyond Monsefú are three ports serving the Chiclayo area. **Pimentel**, 8 km from Chiclayo, is a beach resort which gets very crowded on Sundays and during the summer (US$4 to rent a chair and sunshade). Most of the seafront has been

# Chiclayo

To Combis to Túcume (2 blocks)
To Combis to Batán Grande (1 block)

Arica

Mercado de Brujos

Mercado Modelo

Amazonas

Simón Bolívar

Civiles

P nglo

Av José Balta

7 De Enero

A

Pedro Ruiz

Diego Ferre

7

8 De Octubre

Leticia

Leoncio Prado

Leoncio Prado

Lora y Cordero

Angamos

Av Luis Gonzales

Lora

10

Vicente De La Vega

9

1

Mercado Central

San Martín

11

San José

B

To 6

Plaza Elías Aguirre

Elías Aguirre

Club de la Unión

9

Plaza de Armas

Cathedral

Av Sáenz Peña

12

Av Leonardo Ortiz

M Grau

María Izaga

6

Av Ugarte

Garcón

10 11 12

8

4

13 8 10

1

iPerú

Airaga

2

Torres Paz

F Cabrera

Juan Cuglievan

Alfredo Lapoint

Colón

Av José Balta

2

7 De Enero

To A'irport

C

Tacna

Dall'Orso

9

Scotiabank

Av Bolognesi

11

8

3

7 To 4 5 15

6

To Trujillo

N

100 metres
100 yards

1 To 2

To 5 14 16

2

3

**Where to stay**
1 Alfonso Ugarte B2
2 Costa del Sol Wyndham C3
3 Embajador A3
4 Hosp Concordia C3
5 Hosp San Eduardo C3
6 Intiotel B2
7 Paraíso A3
8 Pirámide Real C3
9 Santa Rosa B2
10 Sicán C2
11 Sol Radiante C2
12 Sunec C2

**Restaurants**
1 Boulevar B2
2 Café 900 C3
3 Café Astoria C2
4 Chifa Lam Yiu C3
5 El Huaralino C1
6 Fiesta B1
7 Govinda B3
8 Hebrón C3
9 Kango Café B2
10 La Parra C3
11 La Plazuela B1
12 Las Américas B3
13 Roma C3
14 Sabores Peruanos C1
15 Tradiciones C3
16 Vichayo Restobar C1

**Transport**
1 Brüning Express to Lambayeque B1
2 Cial C1
3 Civa C3
4 Colectivos to Lambayeque A2
5 Colectivos to Puerto Etén A3
6 Cruz del Sur C3
7 Emtrafesa C3
8 Línea C2
9 Móvil C1
10 Oltursa B1
11 Tepsa C2
12 Transportes Chiclayo B1

## ON THE ROAD

### King Kong in Lambayeque

Vintage movie fans will wonder what the icon of early cinema is doing in all the confectionary shops of northern Peru. King Kong, it seems, is alive and well here in the 21st century.

Back in the 1920s, the story goes, one Señora Victoria Mejía de García, who lived on Calle San Roque in Lambayeque, used to prepare and sell home-made sweets in order to finance her charity work. Among these delicacies were giant *alfajores* (biscuits filled with toffee and other sweets), which were soon dubbed 'King Kong' in the heyday of the popular film.

Señora Victoria's family eventually built her cottage industry into a major enterprise and their San Roque brand of King Kongs (www.sanroque.com.pe) is considered by many to be the best, among countless others. You will see them in the shops and hear them being touted by many loud vendors at the bus stations: "*Hay kinkones!*" – "gorilla biscuits for sale".

bought up by developers, but the main plaza is an oasis of green. There are several seafood restaurants (**El Muelle de Pimentel**, Rivera del Mar cuadra 1, T074-453142, is recommended). You can walk along the restored pier for US$0.75. Sea-going reed boats (*caballitos de totora*) are used by fishermen and may be seen from the pier returning late morning or afternoon on the beach.

The surfing between Pimentel and the Bayovar Peninsula is excellent, reached from Chiclayo (14.5 km) by a road branching off from the Pan-American Highway. Nearby **Santa Rosa** has little to recommend it, other than to see the realities of fishing life, and it is not safe to walk there from Pimentel. The most southerly port, 24 km by road from Chiclayo, is **Puerto Eten**, a quaint place with some wooden buildings on the plaza. Its old railway station has been declared a national heritage monument. The adjacent roadstead, Villa de Eten, is a centre for panama hat-making, but is not as picturesque.

### ★ Lambayeque

About 12 km northwest of Chiclayo is Lambayeque, a good base from which to explore the Chiclayo area. Its narrow streets are lined by colonial and Republican houses, many retaining their distinctive wooden balconies and wrought-iron grillwork over the windows, although many are in very bad shape. On Calle 2 de Mayo don't miss **Casa de la Logia o Montjoy**, whose 67-m-long balcony is said to be the longest in the colonial Americas. It has been restored and can be visited (free). At 8 de Octubre 345 is **Casona Descalzi** ① *T074-283433, daily 1100-1700*, which is well preserved as a good restaurant. It has 120 carved iguana heads on the ceiling. **Casona Iturregui Aguilarte**, at No 410, is, by contrast, seriously neglected. Also of interest are the 16th-century **Complejo Religioso Monumental de San Francisco de Asís** and the baroque **Iglesia de San Pedro**, which stands on Plaza de Armas 27 de Diciembre.

The reason most people visit is to see the town's two museums. The older of the two is the **Brüning Archaeological Museum** ① *daily 0900-1700, US$2.75, a guided tour costs an extra US$10*, in a modern building, which specializes in Mochica, Lambayeque/Sicán and Chimú cultures. Three blocks east is the more recent **Museo de las Tumbas Reales de Sipán**

## ON THE ROAD

### Old Lord of Sipán

The excavations at Sipán by the archaeologist Walter Alva revealed a huge number of riches in the shape of 'El Señor de Sipán'. This well-documented discovery was followed by an equally astounding find dating from AD 100. The tomb of the 'Old Lord of Sipán', as it has come to be known, predates the original Lord of Sipán by some 200 years, and could well be an ancestor of his.

Some of the finest examples of Moche craftsmanship have been found in the tomb of the Old Lord. One object in particular is remarkable; a crab deity with a human head and legs and the carapace, legs and claws of a crab. The gilded piece is over half a metre tall – unprecedented for a Moche figurine. This crab-like figure has been called Ulluchu Man, because the banner on which it was mounted yielded some of the first samples yet found of this ancient fruit.

The ulluchu fruit usually appears in scenes relating to war and the ritual offering of a prisoner's blood. One theory is that the ulluchu, part of the papaya family, has anticoagulant properties that are useful in preventing clotting before a man's blood is offered.

---

① *Av Juan Pablo Vizcardo y Guzmán 895, T074-283977, www.museotumbasrealessipan.pe, Tue-Sun 0900-1700, US$3.55, guides US$13 (some speak English), mototaxi from plaza US$0.60, shaped like a pyramid.* The magnificent treasure from the tomb of the 'Old Lord of Sipán', and a replica of the Lord of Sipán's tomb are displayed here (see below). A ramp from the main entrance takes visitors to the third floor, from where you descend, mirroring the sequence of the archaeologists' discoveries. There are handicrafts outside and in the museum shop, also a branch of **Arte y Joyas Arqueológicas del Perú** ① *T9-8512 2539, ciecsipanarqueojoyas@gmail.com (also at Museo Amano in Lima and Museo Inkariy, Urubamba Km 53, Cuzco),* selling jewellery inspired by pre-Inca and Inca art. There is also a tourist office ① *Tue-Sun 1000-1400.*

From Lambayeque the Pan-American Highway heads north for 190 km to cross the **Sechura Desert**, a large area of shifting sands separating the oases of Chiclayo and Piura. If you're travelling this route, stop off in **Mórrope**, 20 km north of Lambayeque, to see one of the earliest churches in northern Peru. **San Pedro de Mórrope** (1545), an adobe and *algarrobo* structure on the plaza, contains the tomb of the cacique Santiago Cazusol.

> **Tip...**
>
> Solo cyclists should not cross the desert as muggings have occurred. Take the safer, inland route to Piura via Olmos. In the desert, there is no water, fuel or accommodation. Do not attempt this alone.

### Sipán

*Turn-off is well signposted in the centre of Pomalca. Daily 0900-1700. Tombs and museum, US$3.50; guide at site US$10 (may not speak English). To visit the site takes about 2-3 hrs. There are comedores in front of the museum.*

At this imposing complex, about one hour southeast of Chiclayo excavations since 1987 in one of three crumbling pyramids have brought to light a cache of funerary objects considered to rank among the finest examples of pre-Columbian art. Peruvian archaeologist Walter Alva, former leader of the dig, continues to probe the immense mound that has revealed no less than 16 elite tombs filled with 1800-year-old offerings worked in precious metals, stone, pottery and textiles of the Moche culture (circa AD 1-750). In the most extravagant Moche tomb El Señor de Sipán was discovered, a priest clad in gold (ear ornaments, breast plate, etc), with turquoise and other valuables.

In another tomb were found the remnants of what is thought to have been a priest, sacrificed llama and a dog, together with copper decorations. In 1989 another richly appointed, unlooted tomb contained even older metal and ceramic artefacts associated with what was probably a another warrior-priest, called 'The Old Lord of Sipán'. Three tombs are on display, with replicas of the original finds. **Museo de Sitio Huaca Rajada** ① *daily 0900-1700, US$2.85*, concentrates on the finds at the site, especially Tombs 14, 15 and 16 containing 'Priest-Warriors', the decorative techniques of the Moche and the roles that archaeologists and local communities play in protecting these precious discoveries. You can wander around the previously excavated areas of the Huaca Rajada to get an idea of the construction of the burial mound and adjacent pyramids. For a good view, climb the large pyramid across from the excavated Huaca Rajada.

## Ventarrón

A 4000-year-old temple, Ventarrón, was uncovered about 20 km from Sipán in 2007 by Walter Alva; his son, Ignacio, is in charge of the dig. It predates Sipán by some 2000 years and shows at least three phases of development. Its murals, which appear to depict a deer trapped in a net, are claimed to be the oldest in the Americas and there is evidence of cultural exchange with as far away as the Amazon. The site was closed in early 2018 following a fire, it is expected to re-open in 2019.

## Chaparrí Reserve

*75 km from Chiclayo, for day visits T074-433194, www.chaparri.org. US$10.50 entry to the reserve; groups of 10 accompanied by a local guide. Mototaxi from Chongoyape to Chaparrí, US$15.*

East from Pomalca, just before Chongoyape, is the turning to the Chaparrí private ecological reserve, 34,000 ha, set up and run by the Comunidad Muchik Santa Catalina de Chongoyape. Visitors can go for the day or stay at the **EcoLodge Chaparrí** (see Where to stay, page 138). All staff and guides are locals, which provides work and helps to prevent littering. There are no dogs or goats in the area so the forest is recuperating; it contains many bird and mammal species of the dry forest, including white-winged guan and spectacled bear. There is a Spectacled Bear Rescue Centre where bears rescued from captivity live in semi-wild enclosures. The Tinajones reservoir is good for birdwatching.

## Túcume

*T074 835625. Daily 0830-1630. US$4.50, students US$1, children US$0.30, plus guide US$15. Mototaxi from highway/new town to ruins, US$0. 75. Allow at least 3 hrs to visit the whole site and museum.*

About 35 km north of Chiclayo, not far from the old Panamericana and Túcume Nuevo, lie the ruins of this vast city built over 1000 years ago. A short climb to the two *miradors* on **Cerro La Raya** (or **El Purgatorio**) offers the visitor an unparalleled panoramic vista of 26 major pyramids, platform mounds, walled citadels and residential compounds flanking a ceremonial centre and ancient cemeteries. One of the pyramids, Huaca Larga, where excavations are still being undertaken, is the longest adobe structure in the world,

# BACKGROUND
## A tale of fish and demons

Among the many legends that abound in this part of northern Peru are stories about the hill that dominates the site at Túcume and the origins of its two names: Cerro La Raya (Ray Hill) or El Purgatorio (Purgatory).

The first name, Cerro La Raya, refers to the indigenous legend of a manta ray that lived in a nearby lake. The local children constantly tormented the fish by throwing stones at it, so, to escape this torment, the poor creature decided to move to the hill and become part of it. The lake then disappeared and, ever since, the hill has been enchanted.

The second name derives from the conquering Spaniards' attempts to convert the indigenous people to the Christian faith. The Spanish invaders encountered fierce local resistance to their religion and came up with the idea of convincing the people of Túcume that the hill was, in fact, purgatory. They told the locals that there was a demon living on the hill, who would punish anyone not accepting the Roman Catholic faith.

In order to lend some credence to this tale, a group of Spaniards set out one dark, moonless night and built a huge bonfire at the foot of 'El Purgatorio', giving it the appearance of an erupting volcano and convincing the locals that any unbelievers or sinners would be thrown alive into the flames of this diabolical fire.

As if that wasn't enough to terrify the local populace, the Spanish also concocted the fiendish tale of 'El Carretón', an enormous wagon pulled by four great horses that would supposedly speed forth from the bowels of 'El Purgatorio' on the darkest of nights. Driven by a dandily dressed demon boss, and carrying his equally dandy demon buddies, this hellish vehicle careered round the town of Túcume making a fearsome racket. Any poor unbelievers or sinners found wandering the streets would immediately be carted off and thrown into the flames of purgatory.

measuring 700 m long, 280 m wide and over 30 m high. There is no evidence of occupation at Túcume before the Sicán or Lambayeque people who developed the site AD 1000-1375. Thereafter the Chimú conquered the region, establishing a short reign until the arrival of the Incas around 1470. The Incas built on top of the existing structure of **Huaca Larga** using stone from Cerro La Raya.

Among the other pyramids which make up this huge complex are: **Huaca El Mirador** (90 m by 65 m, 30 m high), **Huaca Las Estacas**, **Huaca Pintada** and **Huaca de las Balsas**, which is thought to have housed people of elevated status such as priests. A walkway leads around the covered pyramid and you can see many mud reliefs including fishermen on rafts.

Apart from the miradors and Huaca Las Balsas, not much of the site is open to view, as lots of archaeological study is still going on. However, a site museum displays many objects found here, including miniature offerings relating to the pre-Hispanic gods and mythology of Lambayeque, items relating to the last Inca governor of Túcume and a room detailing the history of the region from pre-Columbian times to the present. There is also a shop.

The town of **Túcume Viejo** is a 20-minute walk beyond the site. Look for the side road heading towards a park, opposite which is the ruin of a huge colonial church made of adobe and some brick. The surrounding countryside is pleasant for walks through mango trees and fields of maize. **Fiesta de la Purísima Concepción**, the festival of the town's patron saint, takes place eight days prior to Carnival in February, and also in September.

## ★ Ferreñafe

The colonial town of Ferreñafe, 20 km northeast of Chiclayo, is worth a visit, especially for the **Museo Nacional Sicán** ⓘ *Av Batán Grande cuadra 9, T074-246469, Museo-Nacional-Sican-109965152373661 on Facebook, Tue-Sun 0900-1700, US$4, students half price, good explanations in Spanish, café and gift shop.* This excellent museum on the outskirts of town houses objects of the Sicán (Lambayeque) culture from near Batán Grande. To get there, take a mototaxi from the centre, five minutes, US$1.75, or, from Chiclayo, catch a *colectivo* from Calle 8 de Octubre 300, towards Ferreñafe; these leave every 15-20 minutes, taking 20 minutes, US$1.

## Sicán (El Santuario Histórico Bosque de Pómac)

*20 km beyond Ferreñafe along the road to Batán Grande (from the old Panamericana another entrance is near Túcume), dalemandelama@gmail.com. Daily 0900-1700. US$4; a guide (Spanish only) can be hired with transport, US$12, or horses for hire US$7. Food and drinks are available at the visitor centre, and camping is permitted.*

El Santuario Histórico Bosque de Pómac includes the ruins of Sicán. Visiting is not easy because of the arid conditions and distances involved: it is 10 km from the visitor centre to the nearest *huaca* (pyramid). A two-hour guided tour of the area includes at least two *huacas*, some of the most ancient carob trees and a mirador that has a beautiful view across the emerald-green tops of the forest with the enormous pyramids dramatically breaking through.

Sicán has revealed several sumptuous tombs dating to AD 900-1100. The ruins comprise some 12 large adobe pyramids, arranged around a huge plaza, measuring 500 m by 250 m, with 40 archaeological sites in total. The city of the Sicán (or Lambayeque culture) was probably moved to Túcume (see above), 6 km west, following 30 years of severe drought and then a devastating El Niño-related flood in AD 1050-1100. These events appear to have provoked a rebellion in which many of the remaining temples on top of the pyramids were burnt and destroyed. The forest itself has good birdwatching possibilities.

> **Tip...**
> There is a pleasant dry forest walk to Huaca I, with shade and the chance to do some bird- and lizard-watching.

## Olmos and around

On the old Pan-American Highway 885 km from Lima, Olmos is a tranquil place surrounded by endless lemon orchards and vineyards; there are several hotels and a **Festival de Limón in the** last week in June. A paved road runs east from Olmos over the Porculla Pass, branching north to Jaén and east to Bagua Grande (see page 188). Olmos is the best base for observing the critically endangered white-winged guan, a bird thought extinct for 100 years until its rediscovery in 1977.

## Tourist information

### Chiclayo

**Indecopi**
*Los Tumbos 245, Santa Victoria, T074-206223, aleyva@indecopi.gob.pe.
Mon-Fri 0800-1300, 1630-1930.*
For complaints and tourist protection.

**iPerú**
*Palacio Municipal, C San José 823, T074-205703, iperuchiclayo@promperu.gob.pe.
Mon-Sat 0900-1800, Sun 0900-1300.*
Also in Lambayeque at **Museo de las Tumbas Reales de Sipán**, Tue-Sun 1000-1400. There are tourist kiosks on the plaza and on Balta.

**Tourist police**
*Av Sáenz Peña 830. Daily 24 hrs.*
Very helpful and may store luggage and take you to the sites themselves.

### Ferreñafe

**Mincetur**
*On the Plaza de Armas, T074-282843, citesipan@mincetur.gob.pe.*
Helpful.

## Where to stay

### Chiclayo
Chain hotels include **Casa Andina** (www.casa-andina.com) and **Costa del Sol Wyndham** (www.costadelsolperu.com).

**$$$ Intiotel**
*Luis Gonzales 622, T074-235931, www.intiotel.com.*
More expensive rooms with jacuzzi, family rooms available, welcome cocktail, airport transfer included, parking, safe and fridge in room, restaurant, helpful staff.

**$$$ Sunec**
*Izaga 472, T074-205110, www.sunechotel.com.pe.*

Modern hotel in a central location, parking, small pool, **Milenario** restaurant.

**$$ Embajador**
*7 de Enero 1368, 1½ blocks from Mercado Modelo, T074-204729, https://hotelchiclayoembajador.com.*
Modern, bright, good facilities, 10 mins' walk from centre, small comfortable rooms, small restaurant, excellent service, free pick-up from bus office, tours arranged.

**$$ Paraíso**
*Pedro Ruiz 1064, T074-228161, www.hotelesparaiso.com.pe.*
Modern rooms with fan, restaurant, 24-hr cafeteria, meeting rooms, parking, very good service.

**$$ Santa Rosa**
*L González 927, T074-224411, www.santarosahotelchiclayo.com.*
Rooms with windows are bright and spacious, best at rear. Hot water, fan, laundry, good value.

**$ Alfonso Ugarte**
*Alfonso Ugarte 1193, T074-222135.*
No meals, small but comfortable double and single rooms.

**$ Hospedaje Concordia**
*7 de Enero Sur 235, Urbanización San Eduardo, T074-209423.*
Rooms on 2nd floor bigger than 3rd, modern, pleasant, no meals, laundry service, view of Parque San Eduardo.

**$ Hospedaje San Eduardo**
*7 de Enero Sur 267, Urbanización San Eduardo, T074-208668.*
No meals, colourful decor, modern bathrooms, fan, Wi-Fi, public phone, quiet, hot water.

**$ Pirámide Real**
*MM Izaga 726, T074-224036.*
Compact and spotless, good value, no meals, safe in room, fan, very central.

### $ Sicán
*MM Izaga 356, T074-208741,*
*hsican@hotmail.com.*
With breakfast, hot water, fan, comfortable, restaurant and bar, laundry, parking, welcoming and trustworthy.

### $ Sol Radiante
*Izaga 392, T074-237858.*
Hot water, comfortable, pleasant, family-run, laundry, tourist information. Pay in advance.

## Lambayeque

### $$ Hostería San Roque
*2 de Mayo 437, T074-282860,*
*www.hosteriasanroque.com.*
In a fine, extensive colonial house, beautifully refurbished, helpful staff, bar, swimming pool, lunch on request. Single, double, triple, quad rooms and dorm for groups of 6, $.

### $ Hostal Libertad
*Bolívar 570, T074-283561,*
*www.hostallibertad.com.*
1½ blocks from plaza, big rooms, fridge, secure.

### $ Hostal Real Sipán
*Huamachuco 664, opposite Brüning Museum.*
Modern, an option if arriving late at night.

## Mórrope

### $$-$ La Casa del Papelillo
*San Pedro 357, T955-624734,*
*lacasadelpapelillo@gmail.com,*
*www.airbnb.es/rooms/89079.*
3 rooms in a remodelled 19th-century home, 1 with private bath, includes breakfast, communal areas, cultural events, discounts for community volunteer work. Owner Cecilia is knowledgeable and helpful.

## Chaparrí Reserve

### $$$$ EcoLodge Chaparrí
*T984-676249 or in Chiclayo T074-452299,*
*www.chaparrilodge.com.*
A delightful oasis in the dry forest, 6 beautifully decorated cabins (more being built) and 5 double rooms with shared bath, built of stone and mud, nice and cool, solar power. Price is for 3 meals and a local guide for 1 day, first-class food. Sechuran foxes in the gardens; hummingbirds bathe at the pool about 0600 every day. Recommended.

## Túcume

### $$ pp Los Horcones
*T951-831705, www.loshorcones*
*detucume.com. Closed Feb-Mar.*
Rustic luxury in the shadow of the pyramids, adobe and *algarrobo* rooms set in lovely garden with lots of birdlife, pool. Good food, pizza oven, breakfast included. Note that if rice is being grown nearby in Jan-May there can be a serious mosquito problem.

## Olmos

### $$$ Los Faiques
*9 km from old Panamericana on road to*
*Salas, can arrange a taxi from Chiclayo or*
*take Salas combi from Chiclayo, T979-299932,*
*www.losfaiques-salas.com.*
Very pretty place in a quiet forest setting, buffet breakfast, dinner on request.

### $ El Remanso
*San Francisco 100, T074-427046,*
*elremansolmos@yahoo.com.*
Like a hacienda, with courtyards, small pool, whitewashed rooms, colourful bedding, flowers and bottled water in room, hot water (supposedly). Price is full board, good restaurant. Charming owner. There are several other places to stay in town.

## Restaurants

### Chiclayo
For delicious, cheap ceviche, go to the **Nativo** stall in the Mercado Central, a local favourite. For ice cream, try **Kango Café**, Elías Aguirre 580.

### $$$ El Huaralino
*La Libertad 155, Santa Victoria.*
Wide variety, international and creole, but mixed reports of late.

### $$$ Fiesta
*Av Salaverry 1820 in 3 de Octubre suburb, T074-201970, www. restaurantfiestagourmet.com.*
Gourmet local dishes, excellent food and service, beautifully presented, daily and seasonal specials, fabulous juices, popular business lunch place.

### $$$ Sabores Peruanos
*Los Incas 136. Tue-Sun 1200-1700.*
Great Peruvian seafood and meat dishes.

### $$ Boulevar
*Colón entre Izaga y Aquirre.*
Good, friendly, *menú* and à la carte.

### $$ Hebrón
*Balta 605.*
For more upmarket than average chicken, but also local food and *parrilla*, good salads. Also does an excellent breakfast and a good buffet at weekends.

### $$ Las Américas
*Aguirre 824. Daily 0700-0200.*
Good service.

### $$ Roma
*Izaga 706. Open all day.*
Wide choice, breakfasts, snacks and meals.

### $$ Tradiciones
*7 de Enero Sur 105, T074-221192. Daily 0900-1700.*
Good variety of local dishes, including ceviche, and drinks, pleasant atmosphere and garden, good service.

### $$ Vichayo Restobar
*Los Alamos 230, Urbanización Santa Victoria, T074-227664. Wed-Fri until 1630, longer hours Sat-Sun.*
Excellent fish and seafood dishes.

### $ Café 900
*MM Izaga 900, www.cafe900.com.*
Appealing atmosphere in a remodelled old house, good food, popular with locals, sometimes has live music.

### $ Café Astoria
*Bolognesi 627. Daily 0800-1200, 1530-2100.*
Breakfast, good-value *menú*.

### $ Chifa Lam Yiu
*María Izaga 645. Daily 1700-2200.*
Very good Chinese food, generous portions.

### $ Govinda
*Vicente de la Vega 982. Open until 1900.*
Vegetarian food, good variety and friendly service.

### $ La Parra
*Izaga 746.*
Chinese and creole *parrillada*, very good, large portions, cheerful.

### $ La Plazuela
*San José 299, Plaza Elías Aguirre.*
Good food, seats outside.

### Panadería El Padrino
*Luis Gonzales 740.*
Has a good choice of breads, including *integral*.

---

### Lambayeque
A Lambayeque speciality is the 'King Kong', a giant *alfajor* biscuit filled with *manjar blanco* and other sweets. San Roque brand (www.sanroque.com.pe), sold throughout Peru, is especially good.

### $$ Casona Descalzi
*8 de Octubre 345. Lunch only.*
Good menu, including traditional northern dishes.

### $$ El Cántaro
*2 de Mayo 180. Lunch only.*
For traditional local dishes, à la carte and a good *menú*.

### $$ El Pacífico
*Huamachuco 970, T074-283135. Lunch only.*
Renowned for its enormous plates of *arroz con pato* and *causa norteña*.

### $$ El Rincón del Pato
*A Leguía 270. Lunch only.*
Offers 40 different duck dishes and very good seafood, wide variety, large portions.

**$$-$ Sabor Norteño**
*Bolívar 440.*
One of the few restaurants open in the early evening.

**$ Café Cultural La Cucarda**
*2 de Mayo 263, T074-284155.*
*Tue-Sun, evenings only.*
Small alternative café, decorated with antiques, delicious pastries, pies and cakes. Recommended.

## Festivals

**6 Jan Reyes Magos** in Mórrope, Illimo and other towns, a recreation of a medieval pageant in which pre-Columbian deities become the Wise Men.
**4 Feb Túcume** devil dances.
**14 Mar and 14 Sep El Señor Nazareno Cautivo**, in Lambayeque and Monsefú, whose main celebration of this festival is 14 Sep.
**Mar/Apr Holy Week**, traditional Easter celebrations and processions in many villages.
**2-7 Jun Divine Child of the Miracle**, Villa de Eten.
**27-31 Jul Fexticum** in Monsefú, traditional foods, drink, handicrafts, music and dance.
**6 Aug** Pilgrimage from the mountain shrine of **Chalpón** to **Motupe**, 90 km north of Chiclayo; the cross is brought down from a cave and carried in procession through the village.
**24 Dec-1 Jan Christmas** and **New Year** processions and children dancers (*pastorcitos*

and *seranitas*) can be seen in many villages, including **Ferreñafe**, **Mochumi**, **Mórrope**.

## What to do

### Chiclayo
**Tour operators**
Lambayeque's museums, Sipán and Túcume can easily be visited by public transport (see below). Local operators run 3-hr tours to Sipán; Túcume and Lambayeque (5 hrs); Sicán is a full-day tour including Ferreñafe and Pómac. There are also tours to Zaña and coastal towns.
**InkaNatura**, *Manuel María Izaga 730, of 203, T979-995024, www.inkanatura.net. Mon-Fri 0915-1315, 1515-1915, Sat 0915-1315.* Historical and nature tours throughout northern Peru. Good service.
**Runa turismo**, *T969-777942 (WhatsApp), info@runaturismo.com.* Owner Julio Porras organizes bicycle, nature and archaeology tours. He knows the area well and speaks fluent English.

### Sicán (El Santuario Histórico Bosque de Pómac)
**Horse riding**
**Rancho Santana**, *Pacora, T979-712145, www.cabalgatasperu.com. Mar-Dec.* Relaxing tours on horseback, half-day (US$15.50), 1-day (US$22.50) or 3-day tours to Santuario Bosque de Pómac, Sicán ruins and Túcume, Swiss-run (Andrea Martin), good horses. Also

$ a bungalow, a double room and camping (tents for hire) at the ranch with safe parking for campervans. Frequently recommended.

## Transport

### Chiclayo
#### Air
**José Abelardo Quiñones González airport** 1 km from town, T074-233192; taxi from centre US$4. Arrive 2 hrs before flight; be prepared for manual search of hand luggage; only a small café in departure lounge.

Daily flights to/from **Lima** and **Piura** with **LATAM** (MM Izaga 770), **StarPerú** (MM Izaga 459, T074-225204), **LC Perú** and **Viva Air** (these 2 have no office in Chiclayo), direct or via **Trujillo**.

#### Bus
**Local** Combis to **Monsefú** cost US$0.75 from Bolognesi y Sarmiento, or Terminal Epsel (Av Castañeda Iparraguirre s/n). Combis to **Pimentel** leave from Av L Ortiz y San José, US$1.10. *Colectivos* to **Lambayeque**, US$0.75, 25 mins, leave from Pedro Ruíz at the junction with Av Ugarte; also **Brüning Express** combis from Vicente de la Vega entre Angamos y Av L Ortiz, every 15 mins, US$0.50, or **Trans Lambayeque** *colectivo* from Plaza Elías Aguirre, US$0.90. Combis to Sipán leave from terminal Epsel, US$1, 1 hr. To **Chongoyape** for Chaparrí Reserve, take a public bus from Leoncio Prado y Sáenz Peña (1¼ hrs, US$1.50), then a mototaxi to **Chaparrí**, US$10. Combis to Tucumé leave from Av Leguía, 15 m from Angamos, US$1, 45 mins. *Colectivos* to the centre of Ferreñafe leave from Terminal Epsel every few mins, or from 8 de Octubre y Sáenz Peña, 40 mins, U$1. Combis to **Batán Grande** depart from Av N de Piérola, and pass the museum in Ferreñafe every 15-20 mins, 40 mins, US$1.

**Long distance** There is no central terminal; most buses stop outside their offices on Bolognesi. To **Lima**, 770 km, US$25-36, with **Civa** (Av Bolognesi 714, T979-778176); **Cruz del Sur** (Bolognesi 888, T074-380100); **Ormeño** (Haya de la Torre 242, 2 blocks south of Bolognesi, T074-234206); **Ittsa** (Av Grau 497, T074-233612); **Línea** (Bolognesi 638, T0801-00015), *especial* and *bus cama* service; **Móvil** (Av Bolognesi 195, T074-271940), goes as far as Tarapoto; **Oltursa** (ticket office at Balta e Izaga, T992-365962, terminal at Vicente de la Vega 101, T074-225611); **Tepsa** (Bolognesi 504-36 y Colón, T074-236981) and **Transportes Chiclayo** (Av L Ortiz 010, T074-503548). Most companies leave from 1900 onwards.

To **Trujillo**, 209 km, with **Emtrafesa** (Av Balta 110, T074-225538), every 15 mins, 4 hrs, US$5.50, and **Línea**. To **Piura**, 4 hrs, US$5.50, **Transportes Chiclayo** leave 15 mins throughout the day; also **Línea** and **Emtrafesa**. To **Sullana**, US$8.50. To **Tumbes**, US$9, 9-10 hrs; with **Cial**, **Cruz del Sur** or **El Dorado**. To **Cajamarca**, 260 km, US$9-20, eg **Línea**, 4 a day; others from Tepsa terminal (Bolognesi y Colón, eg **Días**, T074-224448). To **Chachapoyas**, US$13.50-25, with **Civa**, 1730 daily, 10-11 hrs; **Transervis Kuelap** (Tepsa station), 1830 daily; **Móvil**, at 2000. To **Jaén**, US$7.75-9.60, many companies; **Móvil charges** US$11.55-15.50. To **Tarapoto**, 18 hrs, US$25-29, with **Móvil**, also **Tarapoto Tours** (Bolognesi 751, T074-636231). To **Guayaquil**, with **Civarun** at 1825, *semi-cama* US$34.75, *cama* US$42.50, also **Super Semería**, US$25, 12 hrs, via Piura, Máncora, Tumbes; they also go to Cuenca.

#### Taxi
Mototaxis are a cheap way to get around: US$1 anywhere in city. Chiclayo to Pimentel, US$6, 20 mins. Taxi *colectivos* to Eten leave from Mariscal Nieto and José Quiñones.

### Lambayeque
Some major bus lines have offices in Lambayeque and can drop you off there. There are numerous combis between Lambayeque and **Chiclayo** (see above). Combi to **Túcume**, US$1.25, 25 mins.

Piura was founded in 1532, three years before Lima, by the conquistadors left behind by Pizarro. The city of half-a-million inhabitants has public gardens and two well-kept parks, Cortés and Pizarro (also called Plaza de las Tres Culturas); the

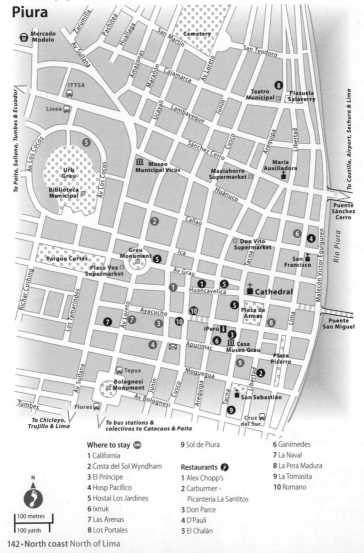

# Piura

**Where to stay** 🛏
1 California
2 Costa del Sol Wyndham
3 El Príncipe
4 Hosp Pacífico
5 Hostal Los Jardines
6 Ixnuk
7 Las Arenas
8 Los Portales
9 Sol de Piura

**Restaurants** 🍴
1 Alex Chopp's
2 Carburmer -
   Picantería La Santitos
3 Don Parce
4 D'Pauli
5 El Chalán
6 Ganímedes
7 La Naval
8 La Pera Madura
9 La Tomasita
10 Romano

latter has a statue of the man himself. Old buildings are kept in repair and new buildings blend with the Spanish style of the old city. Several bridges cross the Río Piura to Castilla, two are pedestrian.

## Sights

On the **Plaza de Armas** is the **cathedral** ① *daily 0800-1200,1700-2030*, with a gold-covered altar and paintings by Ignacio Merino. A few blocks away is **San Francisco** ① *Mon-Sat 0900-1200, 1600-1800*, where the city's independence from Spain was declared on 4 January 1821, nearly eight months before Lima. **Casa Museo Grau** ① *C Tacna 662, opposite the Centro Cívico, T073-326541, Mon-Fri 0800-1300, 1500-1800, Sat-Sun 0800-1200, US$0.70*, is the birthplace of Admiral Miguel Grau, hero of the War of the Pacific with Chile. The museum contains a model of the *Huáscar*, the largest Peruvian warship in the War of the Pacific, which was built in Britain. It also contains interesting old photographs. The small **Museo Municipal Vicús** ① *Sullana, near Huánuco, Tue-Sat 0900-1645, Sun 0900 1300*, includes a Sala de Oro (closed weekends, US$1.45) with 60 gold artefacts from the local Vicús culture and an art section.

## Catacaos

Twelve kilometres southwest of Piura, Catacaos is famous for its *chicha, picanterías* (local restaurants, some with music) and for its crafts, including tooled leather, gold and silver filigree jewellery, wooden articles and straw hats (expensive). The town has splendid celebrations during Holy Week. About 2 km south of Catacaos is the **Narihuala archaeological site** ① *Tue-Sun 0830-1630, US$0.70, children will guide you for a tip, mototaxi from Catacaos US$1.80*, which consists of deteriorated adobe pyramids of the Tallán culture (AD 900-1400) and a site museum.

## Paita and around

Paita, 50 km from Piura, is the major fishing port for the area and is flanked on three sides by a towering, sandy bluff. Looming over Paita is a small colonial fortress built to repel pirates, who attacked it frequently. Several colonial buildings survive. Bolívar's mistress, Manuela Sáenz, lived the last 24 years of her life in Paita, after being exiled from Quito. She supported herself until her death in 1856 by weaving, embroidering and making candy, after refusing the fortune left her by her husband. Nearby beaches include **Colán**, to the north, with the oldest church in South America – built on top of a pyramid, various hotels, restaurants and a long sandy beach (beware the stingrays); and less developed **Yasila**, a fishing village to the south. **Isla Foca**, with a great diversity of sea birds and a pelican rookery (November-Dec ember), is reached from Paita. Fishermen offer boat tours around the island, 40 minutes, US$25 per boat, contact Asociación Cristo te Ama, T968-198924.

## Listings Piura and around *map page 142.*

### Tourist information

**iPerú**
*Ayacucho 459, of 102, ½ block from Plaza de Armas, T073-320249, iperupiura@promperu. gob.pe. Mon-Sat 0900-1800, Sun 0900-1300; there's another office in Arrivals at the airport.*
Very helpful staff, English spoken.

### Where to stay

**$$$$-$$$ Costa del Sol Wyndham**
*Av Loreto 649, T073-302864, www.costadelsolperu.com.*
Centrally located, part of the Peruvian first-class hotel chain, pool, restaurant.

#### $$$$-$$$ Los Portales
*Libertad 875, Plaza de Armas, T073-321161,*
*www.losportaleshoteles.com.pe.*
Elegantly refurbished *casona* in the heart of
the city, luxurious suites and rooms, includes
welcome cocktail, the city's social centre
pleasant terrace, nice pool.

#### $$$ Ixnuk
*Ica 553, T073-322205, www.ixnuk.com.*
Modern hotel with bright ample rooms, a/c,
fridge, airport transfers.

#### $$$-$$ El Príncipe
*Junín 930, T073-324868.*
Comfortable suite and rooms with a/c, fridge,
airport transfers.

#### $$ Las Arenas
*Loreto 945, T073-305554.*
Older well maintained hotel in a central
location, variety of rooms, a/c, cheaper with
fan, small pool, IYHF discounts.

#### $$ Sol de Piura
*Tacna 761, T073-332395,*
*www.soldepiura.com.*
Centrally located modern hotel, comfortable
rooms with a/c, fridge, airport transfers.

#### $$-$ Hostal Los Jardines
*Av Los Cocos 436, Urbanización Club Grau,*
*T073-520699, www.hotellosjardines.com.*
Not far from the centre, rooms with ceiling
fan, no breakfast, ageing but OK, parking,
good value.

#### $ California
*Jr Junín 835, upstairs, T073-328789.*
Shared or private bath, own water-tank,
mosquito netting on windows, roof terrace.

#### $ Hospedaje Pacífico
*Apurimac 717, T073-303061.*
Simple comfortable rooms with fan, the
newer ones on the top floors are the nicest,
no breakfast, good value.

## Restaurants

#### $$$ Carburmer – Picantería La Santitos
*Libertad 1001, T073-309475. Daily 1100-2200.*
Very good fish, regional dishes and pizza in a
renovated colonial house with a/c.

#### $$$ La Tomasita
*Tacna 853, T073-321957. Daily 1100-1730.*
Very good *picantería* serving regional dishes
including ceviche, *arroz con cabrito* (goat)
and *seco de chavelo* (sun-dried meat). A/c.
Recommended.

#### $$$-$$ Don Parce
*Tacna 642, T073-300842. Daily 0700-2400.*
Upmarket restaurant serving varied
international food, pork is their speciality.
Economical 3-course *menú* Mon-Sat.

#### $$ Alex Chopp's
*Huancavelica 544, T073-322568.*
*Daily 1200-2400.*
A la carte dishes, seafood, fish,
and especially beer.

#### $$-$ Romano
*Ayacucho 580, Mon-Sat 0730-2300, and*
*Ayacucho 609. Tue-Sun 0900-1600.*
Popular with locals, wide selection of
*menú* options.

#### $ El Zurdo
*Av Chulucanas y C 14. Daily 0800-1600.*
Outdoor restaurant famous for its *ceviche* and
seafood. Far from centre but worth the trip,
good service and value.

#### $ Ganímedes
*Apurimac 468-B. Mon-Sat 0800-2230,*
*Sun 0800-2100.*
Vegetarian lunch *menú*, pizza and à la carte
from 1800, very good bakery.

#### $ La Naval
*Apurímac 836 (no sign). Mon-Sat 0700-1600.*
Tasty economical *menú*, good selection,
family-run and friendly.

## Cafés and snack bars

### D'Pauli
*Lima 541. Mon-Sat 0900-2100, Sun 0930-1600.*
Sweets, cakes and sandwiches.

### El Chalán
*Several branches including Tacna 520 on Plaza de Armas, Grau 173, Grau 452 and others. Daily 0730-2200.*
Sandwiches, sweets, fruit salad, *cremoladas* and very good ice cream. Very popular, a Piura institution.

### La Pera Madura
*Arequipa 168, next to Teatro Municipal, no sign. Daily 2000-2300.*
For turkey sandwiches, *tamales* and other local specialities.

### Catacaos
Among the town's *picanterías*, **La Chayo** (Jr Paita 313) and **El Ganso Azul** (Jr Josefina Ramos 504) are very good, both open daily 1000-1700.

## What to do

City tours, visits to craft towns, beaches, adventure sports (including surfing and sandboarding) and nature tours in the Piura highlands and desert are all available.

**Canechi Tours**, *Luis Montero 490, T073-344602, www.canechitours.com.*
**Pirhua Tours**, *Av Corpac 208, in front of the airport, T958-101934, www.pirhuatours.com.*

## Transport

### Air
**Capitán Guillermo Concha** airport is in Castilla, 10 mins from the centre by taxi (US$2-3; airport taxis charge more); airport taxi to Máncora, US$75. It has gift shops and car rental agencies (see below). 10 daily flights to **Lima** with **Avianca/TACA** (Sánchez Cerro 234), **LATAM** (Centro Comercial Open Plaza), **Peruvian Airlines** (Libertad 777) and Viva Air (T073-640003).

## Bus

**Local** *Colectivos* have their stops near the Piura stations; they leave as they fill up. To **Catacaos**, *colectivos* from Jr Loreto 1292, 1 block from Ovalo Bolognesi, US$0.90, 20 mins. To **Paita**, **Trans Dora** (T968-158086) from Prolongación Sánchez Cerro, next to Club de Tiro, every 20 mins, 1 hr, US$1.50; also from **Terminal Gechisa** (Prolongación Sánchez Cerro, opposite Proyecto Chira, T073-399322) and *colectivos* from Av Loreto block 12, by Jr Tumbes. Transfer in Paita for **Colán** and **Yacila**. To **Chulucanas** from **Terminal Castilla**, every 30 mins (less often in wet season), US$1.20, 1 hr. To **Huancabamba**, with **San Pedro y San Pablo** (T073-349271), from **Terminal El Bosque**, Castilla, at 0730, 1330, 1830, 6 hrs; also **Civa** (T073-397991) from same terminal at 1030, 1800; and **Turismo Express Norte** (073-344330) from Terminal Castilla, at 0730, 1400, 1830.

**Long distance** Interprovincial bus companies are on Av Sánchez Cerro, blocks 11-13, and Av Loreto, blocks 11-14; the latter is in a more pleasant area and closer to the centre. Some regional services run from **Terminal Gechisa**, Prolongación Sánchez Cerro (the road to Sullana), west of the city.

To **Lima**, 973 km, 14-15½ hrs, US$30-48. Most buses stop at the major cities on route: **Cruz del Sur** (Av Circunvalación 160, T073-480100); **Oltursa** (Bolognesi & Sullana Norte, T073-326666); **ITTSA** (Sánchez Cerro 1142, T073-333982); **Tepsa** (Loreto 1191, T948-915074); several others.

To **Chiclayo** and **Lambayeque**, 209 km, 4 hrs, from US$5.50, with **Trans Chiclayo** (Sánchez Cerro 1121), every 30 min; **Línea** (Sánchez Cerro 1215, www.linea.pe), hourly; several others. To **Trujillo**, 7 hrs, 420 km, US$12.50-15, **Línea** at 1330 and 2300; **Emtrafesa** (Los Naranjos 255, T073-337093) daily at 2200; several others in the afternoon and around 2300.

To **Sullana**, 38 km, 30 mins, US$0.50, frequent service from **Terminal Gechisa** 0500-2200. To **Ayabaca**, 6 hrs, with

Transporte Vegas (Panamericana C1 Lt 10, Urbanización San Ramón, T073-308729) at 0730, 0830 and 1400, or El Poderoso Cautivo (Sullana Norte 7, Urbanización San Ramón, T073-309888) at 0730, 0840 and 1500.

To **Tumbes**, 282 km, 4½ hrs, US$7-8.50, **El Dorado** (Sánchez Cerro 1119, T073-325875), every 1-2 hrs; several others originating in cities to the south eg **Cruz del Sur**, **Cial** (Bolognesi 817, T073-304250), **CIVA** (Av Loreto 1401, T073-345451) and **Emtrafesa** (Los Naranjos 255, T073-337093, also to Chiclayo and Trujillo); also *colectivos*, US$12. To **Máncora**, 187 km, US$5.50, 3 hrs, with **Eppo** (Av Panamericana 243, behind CC Real Plaza, T073-304543, www.eppo.com.pe), every 30 mins; or buses to Tumbes or Ecuador; **SERTUR** *colectivos* from Sanchéz Cerro cuadra 11, US$11. To **Cajamarca**, 467 km, US$18, 10 hrs, at 1845, 1930, 2130, 2230, with **Dias** (Av Loreto 1485, T969-381108), also to Lima at 1500; also to **Tarapoto**, 1230 daily, US$21, 16 hrs.

**To Ecuador** To **Guayaquil** via Tumbes, US$15-20, 10-11 hrs, with **CIFA**, from the same terminal as Dias (Av Loreto 1485, T972-894616), at 1030, 1800, 2030, 2200; also **Super Semeria** (from the same terminal), at 2200, and **CIVA**, from Av Loreto 1465, at 1945. To **Loja** via Macará, with **Transportes Loja**, from the same terminal as Ronco (Av Loreto 1241, T073-333260), at 1300 and 2100, US$14, 8-9 hrs; or with **Unión Cariamanga**, from Dias terminal (T969-493907), at 2000. To **Cuenca**, US$15, 10 hrs, with **Azuay**, from Ronco terminal, T976-900101), at 2030; or **Super Semeria**, from Dias terminal, at 2030.

**Car hire**
**Ramos**, T073-348668; and **Vicus**, T073-342051, both outside the airport, several others.

beach resorts and nature reserves en route to the border

## Sullana to La Tina
The Pan-American Highway forks at **Sullana**, 38 km north of Piura. Built on a bluff over the fertile Chira Valley, the city is neither clean nor safe, so there is no reason to stop here. Turning east at the fork, the Panamericana runs to to Tambo Grande, then heads north to cross the Peru–Ecuador border at La Tina (see below) and continues via Macará to Loja and Cuenca. The excellent paved road is very scenic and is the best option if you want to visit the southern or central highlands of Ecuador.

**Border at La Tina–Macará** The border crossing is problem-free and both sides are open 24 hours. Immigration, customs and other services are currently on either side of the international bridge. An integrated bi-national border complex has been built on the Ecuadorean side, 200 m from the bridge, but was not yet operational in mid-2018. On the Peruvian side, there is one *hospedaje* and several eating places on the road down to the bridge. On the Ecuadorean side, Macará is a small city with all services, 2.5 km past the bridge. There are no money changers or ATMs right at the bridge, only at the park in Macará where vehicles leave for the border.

## Sullana to Máncora
The second branch of the Pan-American Highway is the coastal road which goes from Sullana northwest towards the Talara oilfields, and then follows the coastline to Máncora and Tumbes. From Talara, the Panamericana goes a few kilometres inland but the old Panamericana gives access to lovely beaches and fishing towns that are a peaceful alternative to Máncora. Roads here were seriously affected by flooding in 2017 but they are open and the area is worth visiting.

## Máncora

Máncora, a resort stretching along the Pan-American Highway, is popular with young Limeños, Chileans and Argentines and also as a stop-off for travellers, especially surfers, on the Peru-Ecuador route. Development here has been rapid and haphazard. The resort is crowded and noisy during the December-February high season; beaches can get dirty; drugs and scams (many involving mototaxis) abound. The centre is patrolled but outlying areas are not, enquire locally about safety. There is one bank and various ATMs in Máncora but take some cash, exchange rates are better in Piura. **Vichayito**, 7 km south of Máncora, is accessed from Km 1155 or from Las Pocitas and is a lovely beach well suited to swimming, kite-surfing (April to November) and diving. Separated by a headland from Vichayito is **Las Pocitas**, a stretch of beautiful beach with rocks, behind which little pools (or *pocitas*) form at low tide. It is another alternative to Máncora, just 4 km away, for those looking for tranquillity. East of Máncora is **Fundo La Caprichosa** (www.ecofundolacaprichosa.com), run by a Swiss artist, offering accommodation, trekking, zip-line, climbing wall and various other activities.

## Punta Sal to Tumbes

At Km 1187, 22 km north of Máncora, is the turn-off for **Punta Sal**, marked by a large white arch (El Arco) over the road (2 km). Punta Sal boasts a 3-km-long white sandy beach and a more upmarket clientèle than Máncora, with accommodation (and prices) to match. There is no town centre and no banks, ATMs or restaurants independent of hotels, so it is very quiet in the low season.

**Zorritos**, 62 km north of Punta Sal and 27 km south of Tumbes, is an important fishing centre with a good beach. **Caleta La Cruz**, 16 km southwest of Tumbes, is the only part of the Peruvian coast where the sea is warm all year. It was here that Pizarro landed in 1532. There are regular *colectivos*, US$0.30 each way, from Tumbes.

## ★ Tumbes and around *Colour map 1, A2.*

Capital of the eponymous department and the most northerly Peruvian city, Tumbes (population 120,000) is 265 km north of Piura. Few tourists stop here since international buses take you directly north to Ecuador or south to the beaches or Piura.

> **Warning...**
> Beware of pickpockets in Tumbes.

The most striking aspect of the town itself is its bright and cheery modern public buildings: the **Malecón Benavides**, a long promenade beside the Tumbes river, has rainbow-coloured archways and a monstrous statue called El Beso (the Kiss); the Plaza de Armas sports a large structure of many colours, and even the **cathedral**, built in 1903 and restored in 1985, has green and pink stripes. Calles Bolívar and San Martín (Paseo de la Concordia) make for a pleasant wander, and there is a small artisans' market at the top end of San Martín (approaching Plaza Bolognesi). On Calle Grau, there are the tumble-down colonial houses, many of which are no longer in use.

Tumbes provides access to important protected areas, administered by **Sernanp** ⓘ *Panamericana Norte 1739, Tumbes, T072-526489; Los Cocos H-23, Urbanización Club Grau, Piura, T072-321668*, which, due to the latitude, are rich in fauna and flora found nowhere else in Peru. The best time to visit the parks is the dry season, April to December. On the coast, the **Santuario Nacional los Manglares de Tumbes** (permit required to visit) protects 3000 ha of Peru's remaining 4750 ha of mangrove forest. Inland, the **Parque Nacional Cerros de Amotape** protects 90,700 ha of varied habitat, but principally the best-preserved area of dry forest on the west coast of South America. Adjoining it is the

**Zona Reservada de Tumbes** (75,000 ha), which protects dry equatorial forest and tropical rainforest. The Río Tumbes crocodile, which is a UN Red-data species, is found at the river's mouth, where there is a small breeding programme, and in its upper reaches.

**Tip...**
The mangroves can be visited any time of the year, but the dry season is best. To have the complete experience, stay long enough to visit the mangrove at both high and low tide. Be sure to take repellent.

**Border with Ecuador** The best way to cross this border is on one of the international buses that run between Peru (Piura, Máncora or Tumbes) and Ecuador (Huaquillas, Machala, Guayaquil or Cuenca). If travelling from further south in Peru, do not take a bus all the way to the border; change to an Ecuador-bound bus in Piura, Máncora or Tumbes. Formalities are only carried out at the new bridge, far outside the border towns of **Aguas Verdes** (Peru) and **Huaquillas** (Ecuador). There are two border complexes called CEBAF (**Centro Binacional de Atención Fronteriza**), open 24 hours on either side of the bridge. Both complexes have Peruvian and Ecuadorean immigration officers so you get your exit and entry stamps in the same place. If crossing with your own vehicle however, you may have to stop at both border complexes for customs.

If you do not take one of the international buses then the crossing is hot, harrowing and transport between the two sides via the new bridge and border complex is inconvenient and expensive (see Transport, page 153). Travellers often fall victim to thefts, muggings, shakedowns by minor officials and countless scams on both sides. Never leave your baggage unattended and do your own arithmetic when changing money. Those seeking a more relaxed crossing to or from Ecuador should consider La Tina–Macará or Namballe–La Balsa.

## Listings North to Ecuador

### Tourist information

#### Máncora

**Municipio**
*Municipalidad Provincial de Tumbes,*
*Jr Bolognesi 194, T01-616-7300 ext 3049.*
See also www.vivamancora.com.

#### Tumbes

**iPerú**
*Malecón III Milenio, p3, T072-506721,*
*iperutumbes@promperu.gob.pe.*
*Mon-Sat 0900-1800, Sun 0900-1300.*

### Where to stay

#### Máncora
There are at least 50 hotels in and around Máncora, heavily booked in high season (Dec-Mar) when prices can increase by 100% or more and 1-day bookings are not accepted. Many hotels have even higher rates for Christmas, New Year, Easter and Independence Day holidays when the resort is full to bursting. The main strip of the Panamericana is known as Av Piura from the bridge for the 1st couple of blocks, then Av Grau to the end of town. The better hotels are at the southern end of town, with a small concentration of mid-range hotels just over the bridge. Hotels to the left look onto the beach directly in front of the best surf and often have beach entrances as well as road entrances. They are the most popular with tourists and are all noisy at night from nearby discos, which last until around 0200 Mon-Thu and 0600 Fri-Sun. Cheaper hotels close to the village have no direct beach access. When

checking into a cheaper hotel, expect to pay up front and make sure you get a receipt or you might to be asked to pay again the next time the receptionist sees you. Take every precaution with your valuables, theft is common. Mosquitoes are bad Dec-Mar and dengue fever is a concern, so protect against bites day and night.

## Máncora town

### $$$ Don Giovanni
*Pje 8 de Noviembre s/n, T073-258525, www.dongiovannimancora.com.*
3-storey Indonesian-style beachfront hotel, includes breakfast, restaurant and ice cream parlour, kitesurfing classes available.

### $$$ DCO Suites
*Ex Panamericana norte Km1214+800, T073258171, www.hoteldco.com.*
Boutique hotel with excellent food, very good service, and a spa.

### $$ Del Wawa
*Beachfront, T073-258427, www.delwawa.com.*
This relaxed and spacious Spanish-owned hotel is popular with serious surfers and kitesurfers. Hotel service poor, rooms noisy, food average, but great location and nice restaurants round the corner.

### $$ Kon Tiki Bungalows
*Los Incas 200, T073-258138, www.kontikimancora.com.*
On hill with lighhouse, great views, cabins with thatched roofs, hammocks, kitchen facilities, bar. Transport to/from bus station provided. Advance booking required.

### $$ Las Olas
*Av Piura 135, on the beach, T073-258099, www.lasolasmancora.com.*
Smart, cabin-style rooms, top floor rooms have best view of ocean, hammocks and gardens, includes breakfast.

### $$ Punta Ballenas Inn
*Km 1164, south of Cabo Blanco bridge at the south entrance to town, T072-630844, www.puntaballenas.com.*

Lovely setting on beach, garden with small pool, expensive restaurant.

### $$-$ Laguna Surf Camp
*Acceso Veraniego s/n, T994-015628, www.vivamancora.com/lagunacamp.*
50 m from the sea, thatched roofs, cabins sleeping up to 6 people (US$11 pp), also cabins around small communal area with hammocks, pool and restaurant. Good surf lessons, helpful staff.

### $$-$ Loki del Mar
*Av Piura 262, T073-258484, www.lokihostel.com.*
In the **Loki** group of hostels, seafront, bright white and modern muti-storey building, doubles with private bath or dorms with 4-6 beds and lockable closets, bar, restaurant, pool, lots of activities. Be ready for loud music and parties. Advance booking required.

### $ Arena Blanca
*Off the Malecón, T073-411420.*
Good economy option, no breakfast but it has a restaurant, swimming pool, can get noisy at weekends, good service and value.

## Quebrada Cabo Blanco
Crossing the bridge into Máncora, a dirt track leads downhill to the right, to the Quebrada Cabo Blanco, signed to **La Posada Youth Hostel**. The many hotels at the end of the track are badly lit for guests returning at night (robberies have occurred) but are relatively quiet and relaxing.

### $$ Kimbas Bungalows
*T073-258373, www.kimbasbungalows mancora.com.*
Relaxed spot with charming thatched bungalows, Balinese influences, nice garden with hammocks, pool, some rooms have hot water, good value. Recommended.

### $$ La Posada
*Calle Principal del Barrio Industrial s/n, T073-258328.*
IYHF affiliated hostel, dorms (US$20 pp), camping (US$12 pp) and rooms with private

bath, fan, garden with hammocks, pool, cooking facilities, parking,

## Las Pocitas and Vichayito
There are over 40 hotels in this area, south of Máncora. Most are more upmarket than those in town.

### $$$$ Las Arennas
*Antigua Panamericana Norte, Km 1213, T073-283800, www.arennasmancora.com.*
Smart, luxury pool or beachfront suites, all modern facilities, with central bar and restaurant serving imaginative dishes, beautiful pool, palm-lined beach frontage, very romantic.

### $$$ Las Pocitas B&B
*Acceso Máncora 101, T969-037359, www.laspocitas.pe.*
Great location, rooms with ocean views, lovely palm-lined beach, terrace, pool, restaurant and bar.

### $$$ Máncora Beach Bungalows
*Antigua Panamericana Norte, Km 1215, Lima T01-201 2060, www.mancora-beach.com.*
Comfortable rooms with ceiling fan, terrace and hammocks, good restaurant, good value for this price range.

### $$$ Puerto Palos
*Antigua Panamericana Norte, 2 km south of Máncora (10 mins by mototaxi, US$2), T073-258199, www.puertopalos.com.*
Variety of rooms, fan, suites have a/c. Excellent, nice pool overlooking ocean, hammocks, sunbeds, umbrellas, good restaurant. Friendly and hospitable.

### $$ Marcilia Beach Bungalows
*Antigua Panamericana Norte, Km 1212, T991-212 831, www.marciliadevichayito.com.*
Nice rustic bamboo cabins with ocean views, includes breakfast, family-run.

---

## Punta Sal to Tumbes
There is a huge resort of the Colombian **Royal Decameron** group in Punta Sal, www.decameron.com.

### $$$$ Punta Sal Suites & Bungalows Resort
*Panamericana Norte, Km 1192, Punta Sal Chica, T072-596700/540088, www.puntasal.com.pe.*
A beautiful complex of bungalows along a fine sandy beach, with pool, bar decorated with photos of big game fishing, fine restaurant. Most deals are all-inclusive, but massages and whale-watching trips are extra. Good food and service.

### $$$-$ Waltako Beach Town
*Panamericana 1199, Canoas de Punta Sal, T964-171289, www.waltakoperu.com.*
Thatched cabins for 2, 4 or 6 people, with kitchenette, porch and hammock. Camping on the beach if you bring your own tent. Restaurant and bar, bicycles, quad bikes and horses for hire. Volunteers welcomed for conservation and reforestation work.

### $$ Hospedaje El Bucanero
*At the entrance to Playa Punta Sal, set back from the beach, T988-288481.*
The most happening place in Punta Sal, popular with travellers, rates rise in high season, a variety of rooms, pool, restaurant, bar and gardens.

### $$ Huá
*On the beach at the entrance to Playa Punta Sal, T072-540023, www.hua-puntasal.com.*
A rustic old wooden building, pleasant terrace overlooking ocean, hammocks, quiet, restful, good food, friendly service.

### $$-$ Las Terrazas
*Ex Panamericana norte Km 1187, T072-540 043.*
One of the more basic and cheaper hotels in Punta Sal in operation since 1989, restaurant has sea view, some rooms better than others, those with own bath and sea view twice the price. Helpful owners.

### $ Hospedaje Orillas del Mar
*San Martín 496, Cancas.*
A short walk from Punta Sal Chica beaches, this is the best of the basic *hostales* lining the beach and Panamericana.

## $ Hostal Grillo Tres Puntas
*Panamericana Norte, Km 1235, Zorritos,*
*T072-794830, www.casagrillo.net.*
On the beach, rustic bamboo cabins, quiet
and peaceful. Great food prepared by
Spanish chef-owner, León, who breeds
Peruvian hairless dogs. Lukewarm showers,
Wi-Fi in dining area, camping possible on
the beach.

### Tumbes
Note that Av Tumbes is still sometimes
referred to by its old name of Teniente
Vásquez. At holiday times it can be very
difficult to find a room.

## $$$ Wyndham Costa del Sol
*San Martín 275, Plazuela Bolognesi,*
*T072-523991, www.costadelsolperu.com.*
The only high-class hotel in town, minibars,
a/c, good restaurant, garden, pool, excellent
service. Parking for an extra fee. Rooms which
look onto the Plaza Bolognesi are noisy.

## $$ Lourdes
*Mayor Bodero 118, 3 blocks from main plaza,*
*T072-522966.*
Welcoming place. Narrow corridor leading to
cell-like rooms which are plushly decorated
with a mixture of antique and modern
furniture. Good bathrooms, fans in each room.

## $$-$ Asturias
*Av Mcal Castilla 305.*
Comfortable, hot water, a/c or fan, restaurant,
bar and laundry. Accepts credit cards.

## $ Hostal Tumbes
*Filipinas s/n, off Grau, T072-522203,*
*or T972-852954.*
Small, dark, basic but cleanish rooms with
fans and bath. Good cheap option.

### Restaurants

#### Máncora
Máncora is packed with restaurants: plenty
of sushi, pizza and grills. Most are pricey;
the cheaper places are north along Av Piura.

## $$$ Pizzería Mamíferos
*Av Piura 346, T073-258 386. Tue-Sun 1800-2300.*
Wood-fired pizzas and lasagne.

## $$$-$$ Josil
*Av Piura, near The Birdhouse. Closed Sun.*
Very good Sushi bar.

## $$$-$$ Tao
*Av Piura 240. Closed Wed.*
Good Asian food and curries.

## $$ Angela's Place/Cafetería de Angela
*Av Piura 396, www.vivamancora.com/*
*deangela. Daily 0900-2300.*
A great option for a healthy breakfast or
lunch and heaven for vegetarians and whole-
food lovers: home-made bread, yoghurts,
fresh fruit, etc.

## $$ Don César
*Micaela Bastidas 1416 (hard to find, ask*
*around or take a mototaxi). Closed Tue.*
Good fresh seafood, very popular with locals.

## $ The Birdhouse
*Av Piura.*
This small open-air commercial centre
incorporates **Green Eggs and Ham**, daily 0730-
2300 for great breakfasts (US$3.35), including
waffles, pancakes or eggs and bacon, plus
juice or coffee. Directly underneath is **Papa
Mo's** milk bar, with comfy seats next to the
sand and a selection of drinks.

## $ Café La Bajadita
*Av Piura 424.*
Has an impressive selection of delicious
home-made desserts and cakes.

#### Tumbes
There are cheap restaurants on the Plaza
de Armas, Paseo de la Concordia and near
the markets.

## $$-$ Budabar
*Grau 309, on Plaza de Armas, T072-525493.*
One of a kind chill-out lounge offering
traditional food and comfy seating with
outdoor tables and cheap beer, popular in
the evenings.

## $$-$ Chifa Wakay
*Huáscar 413. Evenings only.*
A large, well-ventilated smart restaurant offering the usual *chifa* favourites.

## $$-$ Classic
*Tumbes 185.*
Look for it almost under the bridge over the river, heading south. Popular for local food.

## $$-$ Los Gustitos
*Bolívar 148.*
Excellent *menús* and à la carte. Popular, good atmosphere at lunchtime.

## $ Cherry
*San Martín 116. Open 0800-1400, 1700-2300.*
Tiny café offering an amazing selection of cakes and desserts, also fresh juices, shakes, sandwiches, hot and cold drinks and traditional *cremoladas* (fruit juice with crushed ice).

## $ Sí Señor
*Bolívar 119 on the plaza.*
Good for snacks, cheap lunch menus.

## What to do

### Máncora
Surfing on this coast is best Nov-Mar; boards and suits can be hired from several places on Av Piura, US$10 per day. Many agencies on Av Piura offer day trips to **Manglares de Tumbes**, to **El Ñuro** where you can swim with green turtles, and whale-watching trips Jul-Dec, as well as private transport in cars and vans.

**Iguanas Trips**, *Av Piura 306, T073-632762, www.iguanastrips.com.* Run by Ursula Behr, offers a variety of adventure tourism trips, horseriding and camping in the nearby national parks and reserve zones.

**Samana Chakra**, *in the eponymous hotel, T073-258604, www.samanachakra.com.* Yoga classes, US$5 per hr.

**Surf Point Máncora**, *on the beach next to Hostal del Wawa.* Surf lessons US$17.50 per hr, kitesurfing (season Mar-Sep) US$50 per hr. Surfboard, bodyboard and paddle board rentals.

## Transport

### Sullana
#### Bus
The long-distance Terminal Terrestre is outside the centre; always take a taxi or mototaxi. To **Tumbes**, 244 km, 4-5 hrs, US$8, several buses daily. To **Chiclayo** and **Trujillo** (see under Piura). To **Lima**, 1076 km, 14-16 hrs, several buses daily, most coming from Tumbes, luxury overnight via Trujillo with **Ittsa** (Av Grau 624, T073-290651), also with **Ormeño** and **Tepsa** (Av Grau 113, T073-258672). To **Máncora**, **Eppo** (from its own terminal), frequent, 2½ hrs, US$4.50. To **Piura**, from **Terminal Gechisa**, José de La Mar, in the centre, US$0.50, 30 mins.

To the international bridge at **La Tina** (see page 146), shared taxis leave when full from the Terminal Terrestre La Capullana, off Av Buenos Aires, several blocks beyond the canal, US$5, 1¾ hrs. Pick-up from border to **Macará**, US$1.50. Buses leave frequently from Macará for Loja, so even if you are not taking the through bus (see Piura, page 145), you can still go from Sullana to Loja in a day.

### Máncora
#### Bus
To **Sullana** with **Eppo**, every 30 mins, 0400-1830, US$3.50, 2½ hrs; continue to **Piura**, US$6, 3 hrs; also *colectivos* to Piura, 2 hrs, US$11. To **Tumbes** (and points in between), vans and *colectivos* leave when full, US$3.50, 1½ hrs. Several companies to **Lima**, US$28-70, 18 hrs. To **Chiclayo**, **Tran Chiclayo**, US$17.50, 6 hrs. To **Trujillo**, US$25, 9 hrs.

**To Ecuador** To **Machala** (US$14, 5 hrs) and **Guayaquil** (US$17.50, 8 hrs), with **CIFA** and **Super Semería** at 0800, 1100 and 1300; Guayaquil direct at 2300 and 2330; several others, via Piura Transport. To **Cuenca**, **Super Semería** at 2300, US$20; or **Azuay** at 2330.

## Punta Sal

Taking a taxi from Máncora to Punta Sal is the safest option, 20 mins, US$14; mototaxi 40 mins, US$10.

## Tumbes
### Air

Daily flights to and from **Lima** with **LATAM**.

### Bus

Daily to and from **Lima**, 1320 km, 18-20 hrs, depending on stopovers, US$34-45 regular fare; and **Cruz del Sur** (Teniente Vásquez 315, T973-984175), VIP service US$60. **Civa** (Av Tumbes 518, T072-525120) has several buses daily. Cheaper buses usually leave 1600-2100, more expensive ones 1200-1400. Except for the luxury service, most buses to Lima stop at major cities en route. Tickets to anywhere between Tumbes and Lima sell quickly, so if arriving from Ecuador you may have to stay overnight. Piura is a good place for connections in the daytime.

To **Sullana**, 244 km, 3-4 hrs, US$8, several buses daily. To **Piura**, 4-5 hrs, 282 km, US$7-8.50, with **El Dorado** (Piura 459, T972-687391) every 1-2 hrs; **Trans Chiclayo** (Auxiliar Panamericana 584) and **Cruz del Sur**. *Colectivos* **Tumbes/Piura** (Tumbes N 308, T072-525977) are a faster option, 3½ hrs, US$12 pp, leave when full. To **Chiclayo**, 552 km, 7-8 hrs, US$9, several each day with **Cruz del Sur**, **El Dorado** and others. To **Trujillo**, 769 km, 10-11 hrs, from US$15, with **Ormeño** (Av Tumbes s/n, T072-522228), **Cruz del Sur**, **El Dorado**, **Emtrafesa** (Tumbes Norte 596, T072-522894).

**To Ecuador** CIFA (Av Tumbes 958) runs to **Machala**, US$4, and **Guayaquil**, 5 hrs, 4 a day, luxury bus at 1000, US$8.50. For other options, see Piura Transport (page 145). If you cannot cross on an international bus (the preferred option), then take a taxi from Tumbes to the new international bridge and border complex beyond Aguas Verdes, 17 km, US$12, and from there to **Huaquillas** across the border, US$2.50-5. See Border with Ecuador, page 148.

# Northern highlands

This vast area stretches from the western foothills of the Andes across the mountains and down to the fringes of the Amazon jungle. It contains spectacular pre-Columbian ruins, some of them built on a massive scale unequalled anywhere in the Americas.

A good road rises from the coast to the city of Cajamarca, where the Inca Atahualpa was captured by the Spanish. Despite the proximity of a huge gold mine, the city has a pleasant colonial centre, with comfortable hotels and good restaurants. Close by are the hot springs where Atahualpa used to bathe and a number of pre-Inca sites.

Beyond Cajamarca, an exceptionally tortuous road winds its way east to Chachapoyas. This is a pleasant, friendly small city at the centre of a region full of fantastic archaeological treasures whose mysteries are only just being uncovered. There are fortresses, enigmatic cities and strange burial sites; not to mention spectacular waterfalls such as 771-m-high Gocta and great trekking opportunities.

From Chachapoyas there are three options: continue east on one of Peru's most beautiful roads to the tropical city of Tarapoto and the port of Yurimaguas, from where you can sail to the Amazon; return to the coast at Chiclayo, or head north to Ecuador via Jaén and San Ignacio.

**Best** for
Archaeology ■ Birdwatching ■ Trekking ■ Waterfalls

Cajamarca & around. . . . . . . . 158
Chachapoyas region . . . . . . . 167

# Footprint picks

## ★ Marca Huamachuco, page 159

One of the top 10 archaeological sites in Peru, this is home to the oldest-known buildings to have more than two storeys.

## ★ Los Baños del Inca, page 162

Atahualpa tried the effect of these waters on a war wound and his bath is still there.

## ★ Museo Leymebamba, page 168

One of the finest archaeology museums in the country houses superb collections of mummies and *quipus*.

## ★ Kuélap, page 170

Ride the cable car to this spectacular pre-Inca walled city. It is said to contain three times more stone than the Great Pyramid at Giza in Egypt.

## ★ Gocta, page 173

This gorgeous 771-m waterfall surrounded by cloudforest may be the third highest in the world.

## ★ Road to the jungle, page 181

The ride from Chachapoyas to Yurimaguas via Moyobamba and Tarapoto is as spectacular as any in Peru.

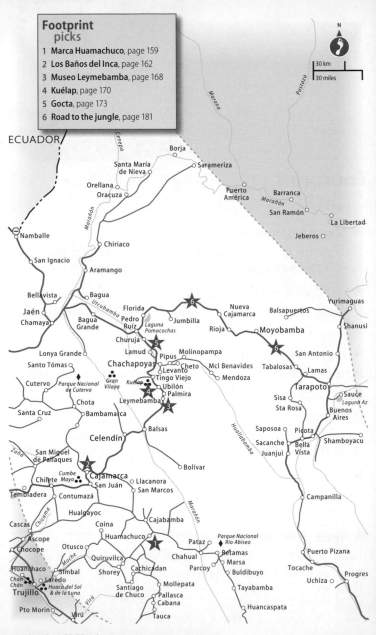

**Footprint picks**

1 **Marca Huamachuco**, page 159
2 **Los Baños del Inca**, page 162
3 **Museo Leymebamba**, page 168
4 **Kuélap**, page 170
5 **Gocta**, page 173
6 **Road to the jungle**, page 181

N

30 km
30 miles

ECUADOR

Borja
Santa María
de Nieva          Sarameriza
Orellana
Oracuza              Puerto
                     América      Barranca
                          Marañón      San Ramón
Namballe                                          La Libertad

San Ignacio                                    Jeberos

        Chiriaco
Aramango
Bellavista      Bagua
        Bagua                                    Yurimaguas
Jaén    Grande   Florida      Nueva
Chamaya         Pedro  Jumbilla  Cajamarca  Balsapuertos
        Bagua    Ruíz                              Shanusi
        Grande  Laguna                    Moyobamba
              Pomacochas
        Churuja              Rioja
Lonya Grande  Lamud   Pipus
              Chachapoyas  Molinopampa      San Antonio
Santo Tómas         Levanto  Cheto  Mcl Benavides  Tabalosas  Lamas
Cutervo  Parque Nacional  Gran  Tingo Viejo        Tarapoto
        de Cutervo  Vilaya  Kuélap  Mendoza
Chota           Ubilón                    Sisa  Laguna Az
        Bambamarca  Palmira              Sta Rosa  Buenos
Santa Cruz      Leymebamba                        Aires
                     Balsas          Saposoa  Picota
                                Sacanche  Bella  Shamboyacu
        San Miguel  Celendín          Juanjui  Vista
        de Pallaques
Tembladera  Chilete  Cumbe  Bolívar
              Mayo  Cajamarca  Llacanora
Cascas    Contumazá  San Juán  San Marcos
                                Campanilla
        Hualgayoc
Cascas           Coina  Cajabamba
Ascope    Otusco  Huamachuco
Chocope  Quiruvilca  Pataz  Parque Nacional  Puerto Pizana
Huanchaco  Simbal  Cachicadan  Chahual  Río Abiseo
Chan  Laredo  Shorey      Retamas
Chán  Huaca del Sol  Santiago  Marsa  Tocache  Progres
Trujillo  & de la Luna  de Chuco  Mollepata  Buldibuyo
        Pallasca    Tayabamba  Uchiza
Pto Morin  Virú  Cabana
              Tauca  Huancaspata

# **Essential** Northern highlands

## Getting around

Long-distance buses connect the major centres and crossroads, including Cajamarca, Celendín, Chachapoyas, Pedro Ruíz, Moyobamba, Tarapoto and Jaén. Cars and vans are convenient and increasingly common, serving near and far destinations. The archaeological sites around Chachapoyas are spread over a large area, so the easiest way to visit them is on a tour. Some of the more remote sites can only be reached by trekking.

## When to go

Cajamarca has a pleasant climate year round, with warm days and chilly nights. Carnival in Cajamarca can be particularly messy and violent, so it is not the best time for sightseeing around the city. Hotels are also likely to be fully booked at this time. More sedate festivals in the city include Easter and Corpus Christi in May. November to April is the wet season in the northern highlands when travel can be difficult, although the Chachapoyas area may be cloudy at any time of year. The climate becomes more tropical the further east you go.

## Time required

One to three weeks, depending on how many areas you choose to visit.

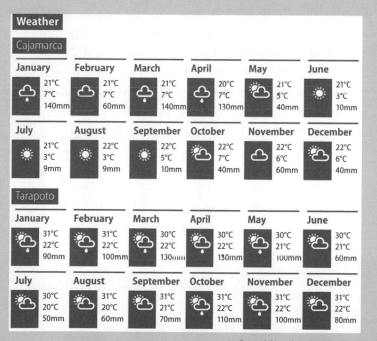

| Weather | | | | | |
|---|---|---|---|---|---|
| **Cajamarca** | | | | | |
| **January** | **February** | **March** | **April** | **May** | **June** |
| 21°C 7°C 140mm | 21°C 7°C 60mm | 21°C 7°C 140mm | 20°C 7°C 130mm | 21°C 5°C 40mm | 21°C 3°C 10mm |
| **July** | **August** | **September** | **October** | **November** | **December** |
| 21°C 3°C 9mm | 22°C 3°C 9mm | 22°C 5°C 10mm | 22°C 7°C 40mm | 22°C 6°C 60mm | 22°C 6°C 40mm |
| **Tarapoto** | | | | | |
| **January** | **February** | **March** | **April** | **May** | **June** |
| 31°C 22°C 90mm | 31°C 22°C 100mm | 30°C 22°C 130mm | 30°C 22°C 130mm | 30°C 21°C 100mm | 30°C 21°C 60mm |
| **July** | **August** | **September** | **October** | **November** | **December** |
| 30°C 20°C 50mm | 31°C 20°C 60mm | 31°C 21°C 70mm | 31°C 22°C 110mm | 31°C 22°C 100mm | 31°C 22°C 80mm |

# Cajamarca
## & around

To the northeast of Trujillo is Cajamarca, an attractive colonial town surrounded by lovely countryside. It was here in 1532 that Pizarro ambushed and captured Atahualpa, the Inca emperor. This was the first showdown between the Spanish and the Incas and, despite being greatly outnumbered, the Spanish emerged victorious. Only one Inca building remains in the city, the so-called Ransom Chamber, but the city has a pleasant colonial centre and some interesting archaeological sites nearby. Change has come fast to Cajamarca: the nearby Yanacocha gold mine (www.yanacocha.com.pe) has brought new wealth to the town but also major ecological disruption and social problems. The city is also the hub of tourism development for the whole *Circuito Turístico Nororiental*, which encompasses Chiclayo, Cajamarca and Chachapoyas.

The main route from the coast to Cajamarca is via Ciudad de Dios, a junction some 20 km north of Pacasmayo (see page 120) on the Panamericana. The 175-km paved road branches off the highway soon after it crosses the Río Jequetepeque. Terraced rice fields and mimosas may often be seen in bloom, brightening the otherwise dusty landscape. The old road (also paved) via Huamachuco and Cajabamba is longer and higher but more interesting, passing over the bare *puna* before dropping to the Huamachuco Valley.

## Huamachuco and around *Colour map 3, A2.*

This colonial town is located at 3180 m, 181 km from Trujillo. It was on the royal Inca Road and has the largest main plaza in Peru, with fine topiary and a controversial modern **cathedral**. On Sundays there is a colourful **market**, with dancing in the plaza. **Museo Municipal Wamachuko** ⓘ *Sucre 195, Mon-Sat 0900-1300, 1500-1900, Sun 0900-1200, free,* displays artefacts found at nearby **Cerro Amaru** and **Marca Huamachuco** (see below). The extensive Huari ruins of **Wiracochapampa** are 3 km north of town (45 minutes' walk), but much of the site is overgrown. There are good thermal baths at **El Edén** with several open-air pools, 45 minutes by combi via Sausacocha.

★ **Marca Huamachuco** ⓘ *Access along a poor road, off the road to Sanagorán, 5 km from Huamachuco (there is an archway at the turn-off). Daily 0900-1700; a minimum of 2 hrs is needed, or 4 hrs to really explore. Carry all food and drink with you. Mototaxi from Huamachuco to the turn-off, US$2, or combi to Sanagorán.* These hilltop pre-Inca fortifications rank in

**Tip...**
In dry weather, 4WDs can make it to the top of the site, but it is generally much faster to walk on the mule trail that starts just after the archway.

the top 10 archaeological sites in Peru. They are 3 km long, dating back to at least 300 BC though many structures were added later. Its most impressive features are: El Castillo, a remarkable circular structure with walls up to 8 m high located at the highest point of the site, and El Convento complex, five circular structures of varying sizes towards the northern end of the hill. The largest one has been partially reconstructed.

## Cajabamba

Cajabamba is a small market town and a useful stop-over point between Huamachuco and Cajamarca (places to eat include **Cafetería La Otuscana**, Grau 929, and **Don Lucho**, L Prado 227). A thermal bath complex, **La Grama**, is 30 minutes by combi (US$1) from Cajabamba, with a pool, very hot individual baths and an adjoining small *hostal*.

## Where to stay

### Huamachuco

**$$ Real**
*Bolívar 250, T044-441402,*
*www.hotelrealhuamachuco.com.*
Modern, sauna, majority of fittings are wood,
pleasant with good service.

**$$ Santa María**
*Grau 224, T044-348334.*
An enormous, sparsely furnished edifice
offering the best-quality rooms in town,
with restaurant.

**$$-$ Hostal Santa Fe**
*San Martín 297, T044-441019,*
*www.actiweb.es/luisnv83/.*
Good value, hot water, parking, restaurant.

**$ Hostal Huamachuco**
*Castilla 354, on the plaza, T044-440599.*
With private or shared hot showers, small
rooms but large common areas, good value,
has parking.

### Cajabamba

**$ Hostal Flores**
*Leoncio Prado 137, Plaza de Armas,*
*T076-551086.*
With electric shower, cheaper without
bath, clean but rooms are gloomy,
nice patio; no breakfast.

## Restaurants

### Huamachuco

**$$-$ Bull Grill**
*R Castilla 364.*
Smart place specializing in meat dishes,
with a cool bar at the back.

**$ Café Somos**
*Bolognesi 665.*
Good coffee, large turkey/ham sandwiches
and excellent cakes.

**$ Doña Emilia**
*Balta 384, on Plaza de Armas.*
Good for breakfast and snacks.

**$ El Viejo Molino**
*R Castilla 160.*
Specializes in local cuisine, such as *cuy*
(guinea pig).

## Transport

### Huamachuco
**Trujillo**, 181 km, 5-6 hrs, US$9-15 (see
page 129): the best service is **Fuentes**
(J Balta 1090, Huamachuco, T044-441090
and Av R Palma 767, Trujillo, T044-204581);
**Tunesa** (Suárez 721, T044-441157). To
**Cajabamba**, with **Trans Los Andes** (Pje
Hospital 109), 3 combis a day, 2 hrs, US$7.50.

### Cajabamba
Several companies run buses and combis to
**Cajamarca**, 127 km, US$7.50-8, 3 hrs.

Cajamarca (population 226,000) is an attractive colonial town surrounded by lovely countryside. It was here in 1532 that Pizarro ambushed and captured Atahualpa, the Inca emperor. This was the first showdown between the Spanish and the Incas and, despite being greatly outnumbered, the Spanish emerged victorious. Change has come fast to Cajamarca: the nearby Yanacocha gold mine (www.yanacocha.com.pe) has brought new wealth to the town but also major ecological disruption and social problems. The city is also the hub of tourism development for the whole Circuito Turístico Nororiental, which encompasses Chiclayo, Cajamarca and Chachapoyas.

### City centre

The **Plaza de Armas**, where Atahualpa was executed, has a 350-year-old fountain, topiary and gardens. The **cathedral** ⓘ *daily 0800-1000, 1600-1800*, opened in 1776 and is still missing its belfry, but the façade has beautiful baroque carving in stone. On the opposite

# Cajamarca

**Where to stay**
1 Cajamarca
2 Costa del Sol Wyndham
3 El Cabildo
4 El Cumbe Inn
5 El Ingenio
6 El Portal del Marqués
7 Hosp Los Jazmines
8 Hostal Becerra
9 Hostal Perú
10 La Casona del Inca
11 Los Balcones de La Recoleta

**Restaurants**
1 Cascanuez
2 D'Cava & Parilla
3 De Buena Laya
4 El Pez Loco
5 El Zarco
6 Heladería Holanda
7 Las Tullpas
8 Om Gri
9 Pizzería El Marengo
10 Pizzería Vaca Loca
11 Qillpu Café Lounge
12 Querubino
13 Salas
14 Sanguchón.com

N

100 metres
100 yards

side of the plaza is the 17th-century church of **San Francisco** ⓘ *Mon-Fri 0900-1200, 1600-1800*, older than the cathedral and with more interior stone carving and elaborate altars. The attached **Museo de Arte Colonial** ⓘ *entrance is behind the church on Amalia Puga y Belén, Mon-Sat 1000-1200,1400-1800, US$1.55*, is filled with colonial paintings and icons. The guided tour of the museum includes entry to the church's spooky catacombs.

The group of buildings known as **Complejo Belén** ⓘ *Tue-Sat 0900-1300, 1500-2000, Sun 0900-1300. US$1.55 (valid for more than 1 day and for the Cuarto de Rescate; see below), guided tour for all the sites, US$9-12*, comprises the tourist office and Institute of Culture, two museums and the beautifully ornate church of Belén, considered the city's finest. The arches, pillars and walls of the nave are covered in lozenges (*rombos*), a design picked out in the gold tracery of the altar. Look up to see the inside of the dome, where eight giant cherubs support an intricate flowering centrepiece. The carved pulpit has a spiral staircase and the doors are intricately worked in wood. In the same courtyard is the **Museo Médico Belén**, which has a collection of medical instruments. Across the street on Junín and Belén is a maternity hospital from the colonial era, now the **Archaeological and Ethnological Museum** ⓘ *T076-362601*. It has a range of ceramics from all regions and civilizations of Peru.

To the east, the **Cuarto de Rescate (Ransom Chamber)** ⓘ *entrance at Amalia Puga 750, Tue-Sat 0900-1800, Sun 0900-1300*, is the room where Atahualpa was held prisoner. A red line on the wall is said to indicate where Atahualpa reached up and drew a mark, agreeing to have his subjects fill the room to that height, once with gold and twice with silver.

You can also visit the stone altar set high on **Santa Apolonia hill** ⓘ *US$0.60, take bus marked Santa Apolonia/Fonavi, or micro A*, from where Atahualpa is said to have surveyed his subjects. There is a road to the top, or you can walk up from Calle 2 de Mayo, using the steep stairway. The view is worth the effort, especially at sunrise (but go in a group).

Around the city centre are many fine old houses, with garden patios and 104 elaborately carved doorways. Look out for the **Bishop's Palace**, across the street from the cathedral; the **Palace of the Condes de Uceda**, at Jirón Apurímac 719 (now occupied by BCP bank, photography prohibited); and the **Casa Silva Santiesteban** (Junín y 2 de Mayo).

The Universidad Nacional de Cajamarca maintains an experimental arboretum and agricultural station, the **Museo Silvo-agropecuario** ⓘ *Km 2.5 on the road to Baños del Inca*, with a lovely mural at the entrance.

## Around Cajamarca

★ **Los Baños del Inca** ⓘ *6 km from Cajamarca. Daily 0500-2000, T076-348385, www.ct binca.com.pe, entry US$0.70, baths US$1.75-2.10, sauna US$3.50, massage US$7. Combis marked Baños del Inca cost US$0.20, 15 mins; taxis US$2.30*. These sulphurous thermal springs are where Atahualpa bathed to try to cure a festering war wound; his bath is still there. The water temperature is at least 72° C, and the main baths are divided into five categories, all with private tubs and no pool (take your own towel); many of the facilities are open to men- or women-only at certain times. Obey the instructions and only spend 20 minutes maximum in the water. The complex is renewed regularly, with gardens and various levels of accommodation (see Where to stay, below). A nice 13-km walk downhill from the Baños del Inca will bring you to **Llacanora** after two hours, a typical Andean village in beautiful scenery.

**Ventanillas** Head north from the baños to the **Ventanillas de Otusco** ⓘ *8 km from Cajamarca, daily 0800-1800, US$1.10, combi US$0.20*, part of an old pre-Inca cemetery that has a deteriorating gallery of secondary burial niches. There are good day walks in this area and local sketch maps are available. From Otusco, a road leads 20 km to **Ventanillas de Combayo** ① *occasional combis on Mon-Sat; more transport on Sun when a market is held nearby, 1 hr.* These burial niches are more numerous and spectacular than those at Otusco, being located in an isolated, mountainous area and distributed over the face of a steep, 200-m-high hillside.

**Cumbe Mayo** This site, 20 km southwest of Cajamarca, is famous for its extraordinary, well-engineered pre-Inca channels, running for 9 km across the mountain tops at 3600 m. This hydraulic irrigation system is said to be the oldest man-made construction in South America. The sheer scale of the scene is impressive, backed by the huge rock formations known as Los Frailones ('big monks') and others. On the way to Cumbe Mayo is the Layzón ceremonial centre. It is possible to walk from Cajamarca to Cumbe Mayo in three to four hours, although you're advised to take a guide or join a tour group. The trail starts from the hill of Santa Apolonia (see above) and goes straight through city streets for about 1 km and up the hill. At the top of the pass, leave the trail and take the road to the right to reach the canal. The walk is not difficult and you do not need hiking boots, but it is cold (best weather May to September). Take warm clothing and a good torch. The locals use the trail to bring their goods to market. There is no bus service to Cumbe Mayo; taxi US$15. Guided tours run from 0830 to 1400 and are recommended in order to see all the pre-Inca sites.

**Porcón** The rural cooperative, with its evangelical faith expressed on billboards, is a popular excursion, 30 km northwest of Cajamarca. It is a tightly organized community, with carpentry, bakery, cheese and yoghurt-making, zoo and vicuñas. A good guide helps to explain everything. If you're not taking a tour, contact **Cooperativa Agraria Atahualpa Jerusalén** ① *Chanchamayo 1355, Fonavi 1, T076-825631.* At Km 8 along the road to Porcón is **Huambocancha**, a town specializing in stone sculptures. Combis run from Cajamarca market, US$0.75, 30 minutes.

**Kuntur Wasi** ① *21 km north of Chilete, site museum in San Pablo US$1.75, ruins US$2.50.* Some 93 km west of Cajamarca is the mining town of Chilete, near which is Kuntur Wasi, a site devoted to a feline cult. It consists of a pyramid and stone monoliths. There are two basic *hostales* in Chilete.

## Listings Cajamarca *map page 161.*

### Tourist information

Information is available from: **iPerú** (Jr Cruz de Piedra 601, T076-365166, iperucajamarca@ promperu.gob.pe, Mon-Sat 0900-1800, Sun 0900-1300); **Dirección Regional de Turismo** and **Ministerio de Cultura**, in the Conjunto Monumental de Belén (Belén 631, T076-362601, Mon-Fri 0900-1300, 1500-1730), and the **Sub-Gerencia de Turismo** (Av Alameda de los Incas, Complejo Qhapac Ñan, opposite

UNC university on the road to Baños del Inca, T076-363626, www.municaj.gob.pe).

### Where to stay

**$$$$ Costa del Sol Wyndham**
*Cruz de Piedra 707, T076-362472, www.costadelsolperu.com.*
On the Plaza de Armas, part of a Peruvian chain, with airport transfer, welcome drink;

restaurant, café and bars, pool, spa, casino, business centre.

### $$$ El Ingenio
*Av Vía de Evitamiento 1611-1709, T076-368733, www.elingenio.com.*
Colonial style buildings 1½ blocks from El Quinde shopping mall. With restaurant, solar-powered hot water, spacious, quiet and relaxed, generous breakfast.

### $$ Cajamarca
*Dos de Mayo 311, T076-362532, www.hotelcajamarca.com.pe.*
3-star in beautiful colonial mansion, sizeable rooms, food excellent in **Los Faroles** restaurant.

### $$ El Cabildo
*Junín 1062, T076-367025.*
In historic monument with patio and modern fountain, full of character, elegant local decorations, comfortable.

### $$ El Cumbe Inn
*Pasaje Atahualpa 345, T076-366858, www.elcumbeinn.com.*
Comfortable, variety of rooms, evening meals on request, small gym, very helpful.

### $$ El Portal del Marqués
*Del Comercio 644, T076-368464, www.portaldelmarques.com.*
Attractive converted colonial house, safe, parking, leased restaurant **El Mesón del Marqués** has good lunch *menú*. Casino with slot machines.

### $$ La Casona del Inca
*2 de Mayo 458-460, Plaza de Armas, T076-367524, http://casonadelinca.pe.*
Upstairs, old building, traditional style, some rooms overlooking plaza, some with interior windows, good beds, breakfast in café on top floor, tours, laundry.

### $$ Los Balcones de la Recoleta
*Amalia Puga 1050, T076-363302, http://hostalbalcones.jimdo.com.*
Beautifully restored 19th-century house, central courtyard full of flowers, some rooms with period furniture.

### $ Hospedaje Los Jazmines
*Amazonas 775, T076-361812, www.hospedajelosjazmines.com.pe.*
In a converted colonial house with courtyard and café, 14 rooms with hot water, all profits go to disabled children, guests can visit the project's school and help.

### $ Hostal Becerra
*Del Batán 195, T076-367431.*
With hot water, modern, pleasant, will store luggage until late buses depart.

### $ Hostal Perú
*Amalia Puga 605, on the plaza, T076-365568.*
Old building around central patio used by **El Zarco** restaurant, functional rooms with wooden floors, hot water, credit cards taken.

---

## Los Baños del Inca

### $$$$-$$$ Laguna Seca
*Av Manco Cápac 1098, T076-584300, www.lagunaseca.com.pe.*
In pleasant surroundings with thermal streams, private hot thermal baths in rooms, swimming pool with thermal water, restaurant, bar, health spa with a variety of treatments, disco, horses for hire.

### $$$ Hacienda Hotel San Antonio
*2 km off the Baños road (turn off at Km 5), T076-348237, Facebook: Hacienda-Hotel-San-Antonio-258452027710.*
An old *hacienda*, wonderfully restored, with open fireplaces and gardens, 15 mins walk along the river to Baños del Inca, riding on *caballos de paso*, own dairy produce, fruit and vegetables, catch your own trout for supper; try the *licor de sauco*.

### $$-$ Los Baños del Inca
*See page 162, T076-348385.*
Various accommodation options: bungalows for 2 to 4 with thermal water, fridge; **Albergue Juvenil**, not IYFH, hostel rooms with bunk beds or double rooms, private bath, caters to groups, basic. Camping possible. Restaurant offers full board.

## Restaurants

### $$$ Querubino
*Amalia Puga 589, T076-340900.*
Mediterranean-style decoration, a bit of everything on the menu, including pastas, daily specials, breakfasts, cocktails, coffees, expensive wines otherwise reasonable, popular.

### $$ D'Cava & Parrilla
*Comercio esquina Cruz de Piedra.*
*Daily 1200-2200.*
Steak house in a traditional house on the main plaza, some tables on the upper floor have views of the square. Good-sized portions, economical *menú* at midday, popular with locals and tourists.

### $$ El Pez Loco
*Cruz de Piedra 631.*
Recommended for fish dishes.

### $$ Las Tullpas
*2 de Mayo 390.*
Good selection of Peruvian and international dishes; tasty.

### $$ Om-Gri
*Amazonas 856. Opens 1300 (1830 Sun).*
Delicious Italian dishes, small, informal and plenty of character, French spoken.

### $$ Pizzería El Marengo
*Junín 1201, T076-368045 for delivery.*
Good pizzas and warm atmosphere.

### $$ Salas
*Amalia Puga 637, on the main plaza and Cruz de Piedra 639, T076-362867. Open 0800-2200.*
A Cajamarca tradition: fast, attentive service, excellent local food (try their *cuy frito*), best *tamales* in town, very popular.

### $$-$ De Buena Laya
*Jr del Batán 258.*
With a rustic interior offers Novo Cajamarquino cuisine; lunchtime *menú* US$3.50.

### $$-$ El Zarco
*Jr del Batán 170, T076-363421.*
*Sun-Fri 0700-2300.*
Breakfast, good vegetarian dishes, excellent fish, also has short *chifa* menu, very popular.

### $ Pizzería Vaca Loca
*San Martín 330.*
Popular, best pizzas in town.

## Cafés

### Cascanuez
*Amalia Puga 554.*
Great cakes, extensive menu including *humitas*, breakfasts, ice creams and coffees, highly regarded.

### Heladería Holanda
*Amalia Puga 657 on the Plaza de Armas, T076-340113.*
Dutch-owned, easily the best ice creams in Cajamarca, 50 flavours (but not all on at the same time); try *poro poro*, *lúcuma* or *sauco*, also serves coffee. Four branches, including at Baños del Inca. Ask if it is possible to visit their factory.

### Qillpu Café Lounge
*Belén 624. Mon-Sat 0800-1300, 1500-2200.*
Popular central café for good coffee and snacks.

### Sanguchón.com
*Junín 1137.*
Best burgers in town, sandwiches, also popular bar.

---

## Los Baños del Inca

### $$ Villa Rica Churrasquería
*Av Manco Capac 1055.*
Lively and popular with great Peruvian food and good service.

## Festivals

**Feb Carnaval.** Cajamarca's pre-Lent festivities are spectacular and regarded as among the best, if the most raucous, in the country.
**Mar Palm Sun.** The processions in Porcón, 16 km to the northwest, are worth seeing.
**24 Jun San Juan** in Cajamarca, Chota, Llacanora, San Juan and Cutervo.

**Jul** Agricultural fair is held at Baños del Inca.
**Oct** **Festival Folklórico** in Cajamarca on the 1st Sun.

## Shopping

### Handicrafts

Specialities including gilded mirrors and cotton and wool saddlebags (*alforjas*). Items can be made to order. The **Mercado Central** at Amazonas y Apurímac is colourful and worth a visit for *artesanía*. There are also stalls at the Belén complex (Belén and/or 2 de Mayo) and along the steps up to Santa Apolonia hill. Other options for a good range of local crafts are the **Feria Artesenal** (Jr El Comercio 1045, next to the police office) and **El Molino** (2 de Mayo).

## What to do

Agencies around the Plaza de Armas offer trips to local sites and further afield, trekking on Inca trails, riding *caballos de paso* and handicraft tours. Approximate prices: Cumbe Mayo, US$6.50-8.50, 4-5 hrs at 0930; Porcón, US$6.50-8.50, 4-5 hrs at 0930; Otusco, US$4.50-7, 3-3½ hrs at 1530; city tour, US$7, 3 hrs at 0930 or 1530. Kuntur Wasi is a full day trip. There are also 2 day/3 night tours to Kuélap and Cutervo National Park.

**Cumbemayo Tours**, *Amalia Puga 635 on the plaza, T076-362938*. Standards tours, guides speak English and French.
**Mega Tours**, *Amalia Puga 691 on the plaza, T076-341876, www.megatours.org*. Conventional tours, full day and further afield, ecotourism and adventures.

## Transport

### Air

The airport is 5 km from town; taxi US$8. There are flights to/from **Lima**, 2 daily with LC Peru (Jr del Comercio 964, T076-366539) and 3 daily with **LATAM** (Jr del Comercio 832, Plaza de Armas).

### Bus

Buses in town charge US$0.35. Bus companies have their own ticket offices and terminals; many are on Av Atahualpa blocks 2-6, a 20-min walk from the Plaza de Armas.

To **Lima**, 870 km, 12-14 hrs, US$27-53, many daily with **Civa** (Ayacucho 753, T076-361460), **Cruz del Sur** (Atahualpa 606, T076-361737) and **Línea** (Atahualpa 318, T076-363956), **Móvil Tours** (Atahualpa 686 T076-280093), **Tepsa** (Sucre y Reina Forje, T076-363306) and **Turismo Días** (Av Evitamiento s/n, T076-344322), including several luxury services.

To **Trujillo**, 295 km, 7 hrs, US$10-27, regular buses daily 0900-2230, with **Emtrafesa** (Atahualpa 315, T076-369663), **Línea** and **Turismo Días**; most continue to Lima via Chimbote. To **Chiclayo**, 265 km, 6 hrs, US$9-20, several buses daily with **Línea** and **Turismo Días**; change here for Piura and Tumbes. To **Celendín**, 107 km, 2 hrs, US$6, usually 2 a day with **CABA** (Atahualpa 299, T076-366665), 1 daily with **Royal Palace's** (Reina Forje 130, T076-343063) and 3 a day with **Rojas** (Atahualpa 309, T076-340548). To **Chachapoyas**, 336 km, 8-9hrs, US$14-15.50, with **Virgen del Carmen** (Atahualpa 333A, T983-915869), small bus at 0530 and 1700, via **Leymebamba**, US$10.80, 6-8 hrs; also 1 small bus daily with **Amazonas Express**; paved road through beautiful countryside.

### Taxi

US$2 within city limits. Mototaxis, US$0.75. Radio taxi: **El Sol**, T076-368897, 24 hrs; **Taxi Super Seguro**, T076-507090.

# Chachapoyas
## region

Cajamarca is a convenient starting point for the trip east to the department of Amazonas, which contains the archaeological riches of the Chachapoyans. Here lie the great pre-Inca cities of Vilaya (not yet developed for tourism) and the immense citadel of Kuélap, among many others. It is also an area of great natural beauty with waterfalls, notably Gocta, cliffs and caves. The road is paved but prone to landslides in the rainy season. It follows a winding course through the mountains, crossing the deep canyon of the Río Marañón at Balsas. The road climbs steeply with superb views of the mountains and the valleys below. The fauna and flora are spectacular as the journey alternates between high mountains and low forest.

## Celendín *Colour map 1, C4.*

East from Cajamarca, this is the first town of note, with a pleasant plaza and cathedral that is predominantly blue. The fascinating local market on Sunday is held in three distinct areas. From 0630 till 0730 there's a **hat market** by the Alameda, between Ayacucho and 2 de Mayo at Jorge Chávez, at which you can see hats at every stage of production. Then, at 0930 the **potato market** takes place at 2 de Mayo y Sucre, and, at the other end of town, there's a **livestock market** on Túpac Amaru. The **Virgen del Carmen** festival takes place from 16 July to 3 August. The most popular local excursion is to the hot springs and mud baths at **Llanguat**, 20 km away (US$2.75 by limited public transport).

## Leymebamba and around *Colour map 1, C4.*

There are plenty of ruins – many of them covered in vegetation – and good walking possibilities around this pleasant town at the source of the Utcubamba River. **La Congona**, a Chachapoyan site, is well worth the effort, with stupendous views. It consists of three hills: on the vegetation-covered conical hill in the middle, the ruins are clustered in a small area, impossible to see until you are right there. The other hills have been levelled. La Congona is the best preserved of three sites in this area, with 30 round stone houses (some with evidence of three storeys) and a watch tower. The two other sites, **El Molinete** and **Cataneo**, are nearby. All three sites can be visited in a day but a guide is advisable. It is a brisk three hours' walk from Leymebamba, first along the rough road to Fila San Cristóbal, then a large trail. The road starts at the bottom of Jirón 16 de Julio.

In 1996 six burial chullpas were discovered at **Laguna de los Cóndores**, a spectacular site in a lush cloudforest setting. The chullpas contained 219 mummies and vast quantities of ceramics, textiles, woodwork, quipus and everyday utensils from the late Inca period, now housed in the excellent ★ **Museo Leymebamba** ① *outside San Miguel, on the road to Celendín, T968-986 888, www.museoleymebamba.org, daily 0800-1700, entry US$5.75.* It is beautifully laid out and very informative, and the collection of mummies and quipus is superb. To get there from Leymebamba, walk to the village of 2 de Mayo, ask for the trail to San Miguel, then take the footpath uphill; the road route is much longer (taxi from Leymebamba US$2.75, mototaxi US$2).

It is also possible to visit Laguna de los Cóndores itself; the trip takes 10 to 12 hours on foot and horseback from Leymebamba. An all-inclusive tour for the three-day muddy trek can be arranged at Leymebamba hotels (ask for Sinecio or Javier Farge) or with Chachapoyas operators, US$70 per person.

## Around Yerbabuena

The road to Chachapoyas follows the Utcubamba River north. In the mountains rising from the river at **Yerbabuena** (important Sunday market, basic *hospedaje*) are a number of archaeological sites. Before Yerbabuena, a road heads east to **Montevideo** (basic hospedaje) and beyond to the small village of **San Pedro de Utac**, where you can hike up to the impressive but overgrown ruins of Cerro Olán.

On the other side of the river, west of Yerbabuena, are burial chullpas from the Revash culture (AD 1250), entry US$3. They are reached from either **San Bartolo** (30-45 minutes' walk, horses can be rented) or along a trail starting past **Puente Santo Tomás** (1½ to two hours' walk).

The town of **Jalca Grande** (or La Jalca), at 2800 m, is reached along a road going east at **Ubilón**, north of Yerbabuena. Jalca Grande has the remains of a Chachapoyan roundhouse, a stone church tower, a small **museum** with ceramics and textiles, and one very basic *hospedaje*.

# Sites around Chachapoyas

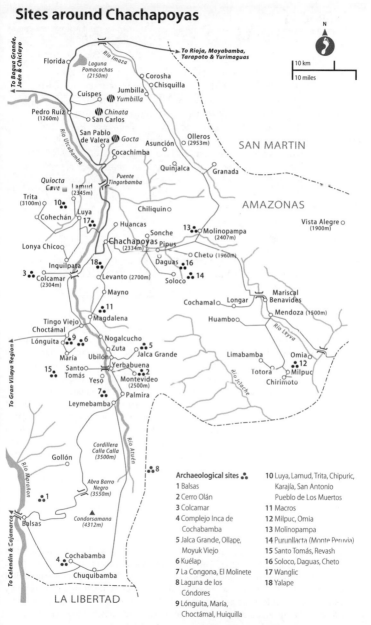

**N**

10 km
10 miles

To Bagua Grande, Jaén & Chiclayo

Florida

*Rio Imaza*

To Rioja, Moyabamba, Tarapoto & Yurimaguas

Laguna Pomacochas (2150m)

Corosha
Chisquilla

Jumbilla
Yumbilla

Cuispes

Pedro Ruiz (1260m)

Chinata
San Carlos

San Pablo de Valera  Gocta

Cocachimba

Asunción

Olleros (2953m)

**SAN MARTIN**

Quinjalca

Granada

*Rio Utcubamba*

Quiocta Cave

Lamud (2345m)

Puente Tingorbamba

Trita (3100m)

**10**

Luya

Cohechán

**17**

Huancas

Chiliquin

**AMAZONAS**

Sonche

Chachapoyas (2334m)

Pipus

**13** Molinopampa (2407m)

Vista Alegre (1900m)

Lonya Chico

**18**

Cheto (1960m)

Daguas **16**

**3** Colcamar (2304m)

Inquilpata

Levanto (2700m)

Soloco

**14**

Mayno

**11** Magdalena

Cochamal

Longar

Mariscal Benavides

Tingo Viejo
Choctámal

**9 6**

Nogalcucho

Huamboo

Mendoza (1500m)

*Rio Leyva*

Lónguita

María

Zuta

Ubilón

**5**

Jalca Grande

Limabamba

Omia

**12**

**15**

Santo Tomás

Yeso

Yerbabuena

**2**

Montevideo (2500m)

Totora

Milpuc

Chirimoto

*Rio Jebche*

**7**

Palmira

Leymebamba

Cordillera Calla Calla (3500m)

*Rio Atuén*

Gollón

**8**

Abra Barro Negro (3550m)

*Rio Marañón*

**1**

Balsas

Condorsamana (4312m)

To Celendín & Cajamarca

**4** Cochabamba

Chuquibamba

**LA LIBERTAD**

To Gran Vilaya Region

## Archaeological sites

1 Balsas
2 Cerro Olán
3 Colcamar
4 Complejo Inca de Cochabamba
5 Jalca Grande, Ollape, Moyuk Viejo
6 Kuélap
7 La Congona, El Molinete
8 Laguna de los Cóndores
9 Lónguita, María, Choctámal, Huiquilla

10 Luya, Lamud, Trita, Chipuric, Karajía, San Antonio Pueblo de Los Muertos
11 Macros
12 Milpuc, Omia
13 Molinopampa
14 Purunllacta (Monte Peruvia)
15 Santo Tomás, Revash
16 Soloco, Daguas, Cheto
17 Wanglic
18 Yalape

## Chachapoyas

The Chachapoyan Empire began about AD 0 and covered an area bounded by the rivers Marañón and Huallaga, as far as Pataz in the south and Bagua in the north. Theories about the culture suggest that its cities, highways, terracing, irrigation, massive stonework and metal-craft were all fully developed. Socially the Chachapoya were organized into chiefdoms, which formed war alliances in the case of external aggression. Archaeologists claim that this region overwhelms even Machu Picchu and its neighbouring Inca sites in grandeur and mystery. By some counts, its 'lost' and uncharted cities, such as Pueblo Alto, near the village of Pueblo Nuevo (25 km from Kuélap) and Saposoa in the northeast of San Martín department, exceed three dozen. By far the majority of these cities, fortresses and villages were never discovered by the Spanish. In fact many had already returned to the jungle by the time the conquistadors arrived in 1532.

The German ethnologist and former mayor of Chachapoyas (2006-2010), Doctor Peter Lerche, has carried out extensive research on Chachapoyan cultures. In an article in *National Geographic*, September 2000, 'Quest for the Lost Tombs of the Peruvian Cloud People', Doctor Lerche writes about the discovery of a Chachapoya tomb named the 'White House' and gives a good general introduction to the history and archaeology of the region.

### Tingo to Kuélap *Colour map 1, C4.*

Situated at the junction of the Tingo and Utcubamba rivers, 40 km north of Leymebamba and 37 km south of Chachapoyas, is **Tingo Viejo** (altitude 1800 m). Heading up a side valley the road climbs steeply up to the the pretty village of **Tingo**. Just up the hill from the plaza is the ticket office for the **Kuélap cable car** ① *www.telecabinaskuelap.com, US$6.25pp including bus from car park at the ticket office to cable car station, every 10 mins 0800-1600.* The cable car takes 20 minutes to cross the valley. It can get very busy from 0900 when the tour groups from Chachapoyas generally arrive and it is important to get there early during Easter week and Peruvian Independence Day holiday. Most Mondays the cable car is closed for maintenance, so alternatively, you can follow the road from Tingo, round the valley via the villages of Choctámal, Lónguita, María and Quizango to arrive at the Kuélap ticket office (2½ hours from Chachapoyas). For fit hikers only, there is a four- to five-hour strenuous hike from Tingo Viejo to Kuélap (1200 m of ascent). It is recommended that you start early and take plenty of water as it can be very hot.

### ★ Kuélap *Colour map 1, C4.*

*Daily 0800-1700. US$6.25, guides available for US$10-15 per group. The ticket office at the car park has a small but informative Sala de Interpretación.*

Kuélap is a spectacular pre-Inca walled city at 3000 m which was re-discovered in 1843. It was built continuously from AD 500 up to Inca times and is said to contain three times more stone than the Great Pyramid at Giza in Egypt. The site lies along the summit of a mountain crest, more than 1 km in length. The massive stone walls, 585 m long by 110 m wide at their widest, are as formidable as those of any pre-Columbian city. Some reconstruction has taken place, mostly of small houses and walls, but the majority of the main walls on all levels are original, as is the inverted, cone-shaped main temple. The structures have been left in their cloudforest setting, the trees covered in bromeliads and moss, the flowers visited by hummingbirds.

## Chachapoyas *Colour map 1, C4.*

The capital of the Amazonas region (population 29,900) was founded in 1538 and retains its colonial character. The city's importance as a crossroads between the coast and jungle began to decline in the late 1940s, but archaeological and ecological tourism have grown gradually since the 1990s and have brought increasing economic benefits to the region.

The cathedral, with a lovely modern interior, stands on the spacious Plaza de Armas. **Ministerio de Cultura Museum** ⓘ *Ayacucho 904, T041-477045, Mon-Fri 0800-1300, 1500-1700, free*, contains a small collection of artefacts and mummies, with explanations in Spanish. The **Museo Santa Ana** ⓘ *Jr Santa Ana 1054, T041-790988, Mon-Fri 0900-1700,*

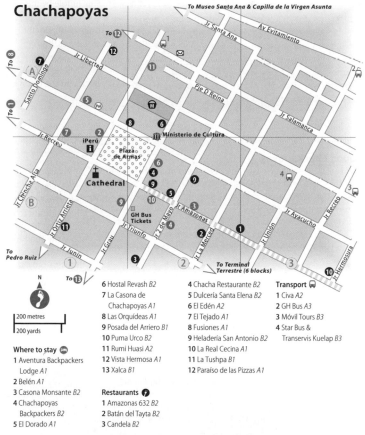

# Chachapoyas

**N**

200 metres
200 yards

### Where to stay 🛏
1 Aventura Backpackers Lodge *A1*
2 Belén *A1*
3 Casona Monsante *B2*
4 Chachapoyas Backpackers *B2*
5 El Dorado *A1*
6 Hostal Revash *B2*
7 La Casona de Chachapoyas *A1*
8 Las Orquídeas *A1*
9 Posada del Arriero *B1*
10 Puma Urco *B2*
11 Rumi Huasi *A2*
12 Vista Hermosa *A1*
13 Xalca *B1*

### Restaurants 🍴
1 Amazonas 632 *B2*
2 Batán del Tayta *B2*
3 Candela *B2*
4 Chacha Restaurante *B2*
5 Dulcería Santa Elena *B2*
6 El Edén *A2*
7 El Tejado *A1*
8 Fusiones *A1*
9 Heladería San Antonio *B2*
10 La Real Cecina *A1*
11 La Tushpa *B1*
12 Paraíso de las Pizzas *A1*

### Transport 🚌
1 Civa *A2*
2 GH Bus *A3*
3 Móvil Tours *B3*
4 Star Bus & Transervis Kuelap *B3*

## ON THE ROAD

### Vikings in the cloudforest?

The province of Rodríguez de Mendoza is home to fair-skinned, blond-haired, blue-eyed people who seem incongruous in this part of the world. Where did they come from?

For many decades, their origin was the subject of much speculation. One theory suggested they were the descendants of Vikings who arrived in South America via Easter Island around AD 1000. Another claimed they were the offspring of dissident conquistadors, who had strayed far from the mainstream of the conquest. Yet another hypothesis claimed that they might be descendants of Marrano Jews who fled the Inquisition in Lima during the 16th century.

DNA analysis eventually stripped away some of the romance. The inhabitants of Guayabamba were traced to one Spanish family who lived in the region for a long time. There is evidence that the people of Chirimoto were originally Italian and Spanish settlers from the 1820s. More wide-ranging but related research has compared the DNA of the mummies found at Laguna de Cóndores with Scandinavian bog people and other European mummies. This does not, however, explain everything. Why, for example, do married women here always cover their heads with a scarf, an uncommon custom in this part of the world?

Whatever their origin, you will find the people of the Guayabamba Valley to be very friendly and welcoming. Enjoy getting to know them.

*US$2*, has colonial religious art and pre-Hispanic ceramics and textiles. Jirón Amazonas, pedestrianized from the Plaza de Armas uphill to Plaza Burgos, makes a pleasant stroll.

### Around Chachapoyas

**Huancas** ① *Autos leave from the terminal and from the corner of Av Aeropuerto and Evitamiento in Chachapoays, daily 0600-1800, 20 mins, US$1.15, or 2-hr walk.* Huancas is a small village to the north of Chacha where rustic pottery is produced. Walk uphill from the plaza to the **mirador** ① *1 km, US$1,* for magnificent views into the deep canyon of the Río Sonche, with tumbling waterfalls. There are crafts on sale here. At **Huanca Urco** ① *5 km from Huancas, past the large prison complex, US$1,* are ruins, remains of an Inca road and another mirador with fine views to Gocta waterfall in the distance.

**Levanto** Due south of Chachapoyas, Levanto was built by the Spaniards in 1538, directly on top of the previous Chachapoyan structures, as their first capital of the area. Nowadays Levanto is an unspoilt colonial village overlooking the massive canyon of the Utcubamba River. On a clear day, Kuélap can be seen on the other side of the rift. A 30-minute walk from Levanto towards Chachapoyas will bring you to the overgrown ruins of **Yalape**, which seems to have been a massive residential complex, extending over many hectares. Local people can guide you to the ruins.

### Mendoza and around

A paved road heads east from Chachapoyas, reaching Mendoza after 2½ hours. The town is the centre of the coffee-producing region of Rodríguez de Mendoza. Close by are the caves at Omia, the Tocuya thermal baths, Mirador Wimba and the Santa Natalia waterfall. Also of interest is the Guayabamba Valley, where there is an unusually high incidence of fair-skinned people. It is a worthwhile four-hour hike from Mendoza to Huamanpata, a very pretty valley surrounded by forest; there's a lake here in the wet season, but this reduces down to a river in drier months. Robert Cabrera (T949-305401) has cabins and camping, and he offers two-day tours from US$35 per person; contact him well in advance.

**Tip...**
South of the road from Chachapoyas to Mendoza, in the district of Soloco, is Parjugsha, Peru's largest cave complex, about 300 m deep and with some 20 km of galleries (10 km have been explored and connected). Spelunking experience is essential.

## Lamud and around

At Km 37 on the Chachapoyas–Pedro Ruiz road an unpaved road leads to the village of **Luya** where it divides. One branch goes north to **Lamud**, a convenient base for several interesting sites, such as San Antonio and Pueblo de los Muertos. **EcoMuseo Molino de Pledra San José** ⓘ *1 km north of Lamud, daily 0900-1600*, has a fascinating display of traditional rural life with demonstrations of milling, baking, weaving, etc. Also worth visiting is the **Quiocta cave** ⓘ *30 mins by car from Lamud, then a 10-min walk, US$2, 0800-1600, closed Thu.* The cave is 560 m long, 23 m deep, and has four chambers with stalactites and stalagmites and a stream running through it. There are petroglyphs at the mouth, and partly buried human remains. Tours to the cave can be arranged in Chachapoyas or through the Lamud tourist office.

The second road from Luya goes south and west to Cruzpata for access to **Karajía** ⓘ *2½ hrs' walk from Luya or 30 mins from Cruzpata, US$2, take binoculars*, where remarkable, 2.5-m-high sarcophagi are set into an impressive cliff-face overlooking the valley. Other sites nearby include **Chipuric**, 1½ hours' walk from Luya, and **Wanglic**, a funeral site with large circular structures built under a ledge in a lush canyon with a beautiful waterfall nearby: a worthwhile excursion (1½ hours). Ask for directions in Luya, or take a local guide (US$10 a day). The road to Luya and Lamud is unpaved; see Chachapoyas Transport for how to get there.

## ★ Gocta

*Access from San Pablo de Valera or Cocachimba. Entry fee US$4, guides (compulsory), US$15 for up to 15 passengers.*

South of Pedro Ruíz is the spectacular **Gocta waterfall**, one of the highest in the world at 771 m. From Chachapoyas, take the Pedro Ruiz road for 35 km to Cocahuayco (about 18 km before Pedro Ruiz) where there are two roads up to Gocta, along either bank of the Cocahuayco River. The first turn-off coming from Chachapoyas leads to the village of **Cocachimba** at 1796 m (5.3 km from the main road, 20 minutes). From here, it is a 1½- to 2½-hour walk (5.5 km) to the base of the lower waterfall, of which there is an impressive view. The second turn-off, 100 m further along the main road, leads to the village of **San Pablo de Valera** at 1934 m (6 km from the main road, 20 minutes by car). From here, it is a one- to 1½-hour walk to a mirador with excellent views of both falls, and then 30 to 60 minutes to the base of the upper falls, 6.3 km in total. Both routes go through about 2 km of lovely forest; the San Pablo trail is somewhat flatter. A path connecting both banks starts on the San Pablo side at the mirador. This is a much smaller trail, quite steep and not signposted past the mirador. There is a suspension footbridge over the main river before the trail joins the Cocahimba trail about three quarters of the way to the base of the lower falls. To see both sides in one day you need to start very early, but this is a great way to get the full experience. Each community offer similar services: horses can be hired for US$14 (they can only go part of the way); rubber boots and rain ponchos are available

## ON THE ROAD
### Gocta Falls

Secrets of this size are hard to keep, yet the residents of the District of Valera, northwest of Chachapoyas, did not reveal the existence of Gocta, a 771-m waterfall, until the German Stefan Zimmendorff came across it in 2002. This spectacular waterfall, surrounded by cloudforest, is the source of the Río Cocahuayco, a tributary of the Utcubamba, and has two tiers: the upper waterfall is 231 m high, and the lower waterfall is 540 m high. The National Geographic Society's ranked Gocta third in the list, after Angel Falls in Venezuela and Tugela Falls in South Africa. Although there are other contenders for this distinction and no consensus on exactly where Gocta ranks in the world's waterfall hierarchy, the falls' great natural beauty make them unquestionably worth a visit.

Good trails on both sides of the river lead to the falls, with magnificent views along the way. Located on the eastern slopes of the Andes, the area is rich in fauna and flora: 20 species of mammals have been identified here, including two endemic primates; as well as 110 bird species and 355 plant species, including 41 species of orchid. In the words of Miles Buesst, "The World Waterfall Database gives Gocta itself a 'scenic rating' of 96%, which I think is ungenerous!"

Most operators in Chachapoyas offer tours of Gocta, and you can visit on your own from either Pedro Ruíz or Chachapoyas (see page 171). A local guide is compulsory and can be hired in the villages of Cocachimba or San Pablo de Valera.

for US$1.20 (it is always wet by the falls). The best time to visit is during the dry season from May to September; in the wet season the falls are more spectacular, but it is cold, rainy and the trails may be slippery.

Several more waterfalls in this area are increasingly accessible, including **Yumbilla** ① *entry US$3*, which is 895 m (124 m higher than Gocta) in four main tiers. Access is from the village of **Cuispes**, northeast of Pedro Ruíz (25 minutes by mototaxi, US$1.50 per person, minimum US$3). The **Asociación de Turismo Yacu Urco** ① *T979-605381*, offers transport, guiding (US$9-12) and canyoning equipment rentals. **Chinata** (540 m high in four main tiers) is best reached from **San Carlos** (20 minutes southeast of Pedro Ruíz, mototaxi minimum US$3). Both falls are accessed along paths in the cloudforest. **Canyoning Explorer** ① *Jr Bongará 220, Cuispes, T997-583804, www.canyoning explorer.com*, offers abseiling, with bilingual guides, down these and other waterfalls (from US$40 pp for a full day, depending on the size of the group and level of difficulty, minimum two passengers).

**Tip...**

If you start the Gocta hike at San Pablo and finish at Cocachimba, arrange transport to return to San Pablo at the end of the day. Or, if you are staying in Cocachimba, arrange transport to San Pablo to begin the hike. The ride is about 30 minutes.

## Tourist information

### Chachapoyas

#### iPerú
*On the Plaza de Armas, Jr Ortiz Arrieta 582,*
*T041-477292, iperuchachapoyas@promperu.*
*gob.pe. Mon-Sat 0900-1800, Sun 0900-1300.*

### Mendoza
For information on the area, ask for Michel
Ricardo Feijoó Aguilor in the Mendoza
municipal office, mifeijoo@gmail.com; he can
help arrange guides and accommodation.
A recommended guide is Alfonso Saldana
Pelaez, fotoguiaalsape@gmail.com.

### Gocta
Community tourist information is available
in both San Pablo, T041-631163, daily
0800-1730, and Cocachimba, T041-630569,
daily 0800-1730.

## Where to stay

### Celendín

#### $$-$ Hostal Celendín
*Unión 305, Plaza de Armas, T076-555041,*
*hcgustavosd1@hotmail.com.*
Some rooms with plaza view, central patio
and wooden stairs, hot water, pleasant, has
2 restaurants: **Rinconcito Shilico** (2 de Mayo
816), and **Pollos a la brasa Gusys**.

#### $ Hostal Imperial
*Jr Dos de Mayo 568, 2 blocks from the plaza,*
*T076-555492.*
Large rooms, good mattresses, hot water,
Wi-Fi, parking, decent choice.

#### $ Loyer's
*José Gálvez 410, T076-555210.*
Patio with wooden balcony all round, nice,
singles, doubles and family rooms.

#### $ Maxmar
*Dos de Mayo 349, T076-555330.*

Cheaper without bath, hot shower extra,
basic, parking, good value, owners Francisco
and Luis are very helpful.

#### $ Mi Posada
*Pardo 388, next to Atahualpa bus,*
*T074-979-758674.*
Includes breakfast, small cheerful rooms,
family atmosphere.

#### $ Raymi Wasi
*Jr José Gálvez 420, T976-551133.*
With electric shower, cheaper without, large
rooms, has patio, quiet, parking, good value,
restaurant and karaoke.

### Leymebamba and around

#### $$$$-$$$ Kentitambo
*Across the road from Museo Leymebamba,*
*T971-118273, www.kentitambo.com.*
Accommodation in 3 comfortable cabins,
lovely grounds with hummingbirds, meals
made from local produce. **Kentikafe** offers
sandwiches, cake, tea and coffee.

#### $$ La Casona
*Jr Amazonas 223, T041-630301,*
*www.casonadeleymebamba.com.*
Nicely refurbished old house with balcony,
attractive common area, simple rooms with
solar hot water, arrange tours and horses.

#### $$ La Joya Hostal Cafetín
*Jr 16 de Julio, T990-168715.*
Modern hotel, ample rooms, good café on
1st floor.

#### $ La Petaca
*Jr Amazonas 426, on the plaza, T999-020599.*
Good rooms with hot water, breakfast
available, café, helpful.

### Tingo to Kuélap

#### $$$ Estancia Chillo
*5 km south of Tingo Viejo towards*
*Leymebamba, T041-630510/979-340444.*

On a 9-ha farm, dinner and breakfast included, with bath, hot water, transport, horse riding. Friendly family, a lovely country retreat.

### $$$-$$ La Casa de Doña Lola
*9 km south of Tingo Viejo, Km 282 on the road to Leymebamba, T991-929 218, Milpuj on Facebook.*
Small lodge on **Milpuj Reserve** (www.conservamospornaturaleza.org/area/milpuj-la-heredad/), a seasonally dry forest at 1800-2500 m altitude. Private or shared bath, option including breakfast and dinner recommended since there is nowhere else to eat nearby.

### $$ Choctámal Marvelous Spatuletail Lodge
*3 km from Choctámal towards Kuélap at Km 20, T941-963327, www.marvelousspatuletail.com.*
Book in advance. Heated rooms, hot showers, hot tub, telescope for star-gazing. Meals US$8-10. Offers horse riding and a chance to see the endangered marvellous spatuletail hummingbird.

### $ Albergue León
*Along the south bank of the Río Tingo, Tingo Viejo, just upriver from the highway, T941-715685, hildegardlen@yahoo.es.*
Basic, private or shared bath, electric shower, guiding, arrange horses, run by Lucho León who is knowledgeable.

___

### Chachapoyas

### $$$ Casona Monsante
*Amazonas 746, T041-477702, www.casonamonsante.com.*
Converted colonial house with patio, orchid garden, comfortable rooms decorated with antiques.

### $$$-$$ La Casona de Chachapoyas
*Chincha Alta 569, T041-477353, www.lacasonadechachapoyasperu.com.*
Converted old house with lovely courtyard, very nicely decorated, all rooms different,

comfy beds, family atmosphere, good service, living room and *comedor* with open fire, library. Repeatedly recommended.

### $$$ Xalca
*Jr Grau 940, T041-479106, www.laxalcahotel.com.*
Built in colonial style with central patio, large comfortable rooms, parking, good service.

### $$$-$$ Hostal Revash
*Grau 517, Plaza de Armas, T041-477391, revash9@hotmail.com.*
Traditional house with patio, stylish decor, steaming hot showers, breakfast available, helpful owners, good local information and tours, popular.

### $$ Las Orquídeas
*Ayacucho 1231, T041-478271, www.hostallasorquideas.com.*
Converted home, pleasantly decorated rooms, large garden.

### $$ Posada del Arriero
*Grau 636, T041-478945, www.posadadelarriero.net.*
Old house with courtyard nicely refurbished in modern style, although rooms are a bit plain, helpful staff.

### $$ Puma Urco
*Amazonas 833, T041-477871, www.hotelpumaurco.com.*
Comfortable rooms, includes breakfast, TV, frigobar, **Café Café** next door, hotel and café receive good reports, run tours.

### $ Aventura Backpackers Lodge
*Jr Amazonas 1416, T959-555939, Facebook: AventuraBackpackersLodge.*
Dorms with bunk beds, use of kitchen, good value.

### $ Belén
*Jr Ortiz Arrieta 540, Plaza de Armas, T041-477830.*
Nicely furnished rooms with bath and hot water, pleasant sitting room overlooking the plaza.

### $ Chachapoyas Backpackers
*Jr Dos de Mayo 639, T041-478879,*
*www.chachapoyasbackpackers.com.*
Nice private rooms with or without bath
and 2- and 3-bed dorms with shared
bath, electric showers, well-equipped
kitchen, laundry facilities, a good budget
option, same owners as **Turismo Explorer**
tour operator. Popular family-run place.
Recommended.

### $ El Dorado
*Ayacucho 1062, T041-477047,*
*ivvanovt@hotmail.com.*
With bathroom, electric shower, helpful
staff, a good economical option.

### $ Rumi Huasi
*Ortiz Arrieta 365, T041-791100.*
With and without bath, electric shower,
small rooms, simple and good.

### $ Vista Hermosa
*Puno 285, T041-477526.*
Pleasant ample rooms, some have balconies,
electric shower, good value.

## Levanto

### $ Levanto Marvelous Spatuletail Lodge
*Behind the church, T041-478838,*
*www.marvelousspatuletail.net.*
2 circular buildings with tall thatched roofs,
4 bedrooms with 2 external bathrooms can
accommodate up to 12 people, hot shower,
lounge with fireplace and kitchen, meals
US$8-10, must book ahead.

## Lamud and around

### $$$ Tambo Sapalanchan
*500 m north of Lamud, T987-936003,*
*tambosapalanchan@gmail.com.*
Comfortable bungalows overlooking
attractive farmland, restaurant.

### $ Hostal Kuélap
*Garcilaso de la Vega 452, on the plaza, Lamud.*
With or without bath or hot water, basic.

## Gocta
## San Pablo

### $ Hospedaje Las Gardenias
*T941-718660.*
Basic rooms with shared bath, cold water,
economical meals available.

### $ Hotel Gocta Camping
*T941-718660.*
Camping with hot showers and lovely views
at the site of a hotel under construction.

## Cocachimba

### $$$$-$$$ Gocta Natura Cabins
*www.goctanatura.com.*
Five spacious bungalows, each with private
terrace and fine views of Gocta waterfall.

### $$$ Gocta Andes Lodge
*Cocachimba, T041-630552 (Tarapoto*
*T042-522225), www.goctalodge.com.*
Beautifully located lodge overlooking the
waterfall, ample rooms with balconies, lovely
terrace with pool, restaurant. Packages
available with other hotels in the group.

### $ Hospedaje Gallito de la Roca
*T041-630048.*
Small simple rooms with or without bath,
hot water, economical meals available.

### $ Hospedaje Las Orquídeas
*T041-631265.*
Simple rooms in a family home, shared bath,
cold water, restaurant.

## Cuispes

### $$ Hospedaje Rocío
*Contact Asociación de Turismo Yacu Urco.*
Small rooms with private bath, no breakfast.

### $$ Posada de Cuispes
*Contact Asociación de Turismo Yacu Urco.*
Comfortable with private bath, hot water.

## San Carlos

### $ Hospedaje Masuma
*T958 949013.*

Modern, comfortable with private bath and hot water, good service.

## Restaurants

### Celendín

**$$-$ La Reserve**
*José Gálvez 313.*
Good quality and value, extensive menu, from Italian to *chifa*.

**$ Carbón y Leña**
*2 de Mayo 410.*
For chicken, *parrillas* and pizzas.

**$ Juguería Carolin**
*Bolognesi 384. Daily 0700-2200.*
One of the few places open early, for juices, breakfasts and *caldos*.

### Chachapoyas

**$$$ Batán del Tayta**
*La Merced 604. Closed Sun.*
Excellent innovative local cuisine, generous portions. Recommended.

**$$ Candela**
*Dos de Mayo 728, on Facebook.*
*Tue-Sun 1800-2300.*
Pizzas and pasta with local Chachapoyas ingredients, baked in an adobe oven.

**$$ El Tejado**
*Santo Domingo 424. Daily 1200-1600.*
Excellent upscale *comida criolla*. Large portions, attentive service, nice atmosphere and setting. Good-value *menú* on weekdays.

**$$ La Real Cecina**
*Jr Hermosura 676 on Plaza Burgos.*
*Daily 1100-2300.*
Popular with locals for lunch and dinner with typical Chachapoyas beef jerky (*cecina*) cuisine.

**$$ La Tushpa**
*Ortiz Arrieta 753. Open 1800-2200,*
*closed Sun.*
A restaurant for carnivores. Great steaks and chicken dishes.

**$$ Paraíso de las Pizzas**
*Chincha Alta 355. Open till 2200.*
Good pizzas and pastas, family-run.

**$ Chacha Restaurante**
*Grau on Plaza de Armas. Daily.*
Huge portions of typical Peruvian food.

**$ El Edén**
*Grau 448 by the market. Sun-Thu 0700-2100,*
*Fri 0700-1700.*
Good economical vegetarian set meals, and à la carte.

### Cafés

**Amazonas 632**
*Amazonas 632. Mon-Sat 1700-2300.*
A nice hangout with good snacks, main courses and desserts.

**Dulcería Santa Elena**
*Amazonas 800. Daily 0900-2230.*
Very good old-fashioned home-made desserts.

**Fusiones**
*Ayacucho 952, Plaza de Armas.*
*Mon-Sat 0700-2230.*
Breakfast, fair-trade coffee, juices, snacks, Wi-Fi, book exchange, volunteer opportunities, occasional live music.

**Heladería San Antonio**
*2 de Mayo 521 and Amazonas 856.*
Good home-made ice cream; try the *lúcuma* and *guanábana* flavours.

## What to do

### Chachapoyas
The cost of full-day trips depends on season (higher Jul-Sep), distance, number of passengers and whether meals are included. Several operators have daily departures to Kuélap (US$20-25, include transport to Tingo, cable car and lunch in Tingo; Gocta, US$13.50-15; Quiocta and Karajía, US$19-27, and Museo de Leymebamba and Revash, US$31-39. All-inclusive trekking tours to Gran Vilaya cost about US$46-50 pp per day.

**Amazon Expedition**, *Jr Ortiz Arrieta 508, Plaza de Armas, T041-798718, http://amazonexpedition.com.pe*. Day tours and multi-day treks.

**Andes Tours**, *at* **Hostal Revash**, *on Facebook*. Daily trips to Kuélap and Gocta, other tours to ruins, caves and trekking. Also less-visited destinations, combining travel by car, on horseback and walking.

**Chachapoyas Trip Adventures**, *Jr Amazonas 770. T958-641621, www.chachapoyastrip adventures.com*. Daily tours, include night tour of the city.

**Cloudforest Expeditions**, *Jr Puno 368, T041-477610, www.kuelapnordperu.com*. Tours to ruins, trek to Yumbilla, English and German spoken.

**Nuevos Caminos**, at **Café Fusiones**, *T041-479170, www.nuevoscaminostravel. com*. Alternative community tourism, volunteer opportunities.

**Turismo Explorer**, *Jr Grau 549, T041-478162, www.turismoexplorerperu.com*. Daily tours to Kuélap, Gocta and other destinations, trekking tours including Laguna de los Cóndores and other archaeological sites, transport, good service.

**Vilaya Tours**, *Jr Amazonas 261, T941-708798, www.vilayatours.com*. All-inclusive treks to off-the-beaten-path destinations throughout northern Peru. Run by Robert Dover, a very experienced and knowledgeable British guide. Book ahead.

## Transport

### Celendín
To **Cajamarca**, 107 km, 2 hrs, with **Royal Palace's** (Jr Unión y José Gálvez, by Plaza de Armas), 1400 daily; also **CABA**, 2 a day, and **Rojas**, 3 a day. Cars to Cajamarca leave when full from Ovalo Agusto Gil, Cáceres y Amazonas, 2 hrs, US$9 pp. They also go from the same place to **Chachapoyas**, 6 hrs, US$18 pp. Small bus with **Virgen del Carmen** (Cáceres 112 by Ovalo A Gil, T076-792918) to Chachapoyas, daily at 0830 and 2030, US$9.25, 6-7 hrs, via **Leymebamba**, 4-5 hrs, US$6.15; also 2 daily combis with **Rojas**, US$9.25.

### Leymebamba and around
To **Chachapoyas** (fills quickly, book ahead), 2½-3 hrs, cars US$6.15, combis US$3, best with **Raymi Express**, at 0500, 0600, 0630, 1200; several other companies. To **Celendín**, US$6.15, 4-5 hrs and **Cajamarca**, US$10.75, 6-8 hrs, service originating in Chachapoyas.

### Tingo to Kuélap
The easiest way to visit Kuélap is on a tour from Chachapoyas (see above). To reach the cable car or go to Kuélap by shared car or van, transport goes from the Terminal Terrestre in Chachapoyas. To **Tingo** (US$2.15, 1 hr) with **Tours Tella**, 0600-1700, as they fill. To **Kuélap** (US$4, 2½ hrs) with **Tours Tella**

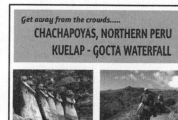

at 0900 and 1400, return from Kuélap at 0500 and 1400; with **Trans Roller's** at 0400, return 0700. Cars bound for Magdalena, Yerbabuena or Leymebamba Pass through **Tingo Viejo**, but there is no local transport from there to Tingo.

## Taxi

To **Tingo** US$20 one way or US$35 to wait for your return from Kuélap.

## Chachapoyas
### Air

To **Tarapoto**, Mon-Sat 3 daily flights in a 9-seater aircraft with **SAETA** (Jr Grau 293, T953600621, www.saetaperu.com), US$68, 25 mins, 10 kg luggage allowance. To/from **Lima**, with **ATSA** (reservations and tickets at **Chachapoyas Backpackers**, www.atsaairlines.com) 3 weekly, US$70-100, 1¾ hrs. See also under Jaén, page 191, for daily flights to Lima; see below for shuttle service to Jaén airport.

### Bus
**Regional** The **Terminal Terrestre**, a regional transport terminal, is 9 blocks from the Plaza de Armas, at Jr Triunfo, block 1. For services to **Tingo**, **Choctámal** and **Kuélap**, see above. To **Leymebamba**, 83 km, 3 hrs, car US$6.15, combi US$3 (reserve ahead), the best service is with **Raymi Express**, at 0900, 1200, 1400, 1600; also **Mi Cautivo**, 4 a day. For **Revash**, to **Santo Tomás**, **Comité Santo Tomás** at 1000, 1300, 1500 (return at 0300, 0400, 0500), US$3, 3 hrs; get off at **Cruce de Revash** (near Puente Santo Tomás), US$3, 2½ hrs; or with the same company to **San Bartolo** at 1400 (return 0600), US$4.30, 3 hrs. To **Yerbabuena** with **Mi Cautivo** and **Trotamundos**, hourly 0600-1600, US$2.50. To **Jalca Grande** with **Tours Tello**, Mon-Sat at 1200, 1430, 1600, Sun at 1500 (return 0400, 0500, 0600, Sun at 1100) US$3, 3 hrs. To **Levanto**, **MW Megawil** at 0500 and 1100. To **Mendoza** (86 km), with **Guayabamba**, 0400-1900, cars US$6, 2 hrs, also combis US$3, 2½ hrs. To **Luya** and **Lamud**, several

companies, cars 0400-2000, US$1.55; there are cars from Luya to Cruzpata, 0600-1700, US$3, 1 hr.

Also from the Terminal Terrestre, to **Pedro Ruiz** (for connections to Chiclayo, Jaén, or Tarapoto), cars depart as they fill 0500-2200, US$3, 1 hr; combis every 2 hrs 0600-1800, US$1.55; and vans, as they fill 0500-1900. To **Bagua Grande** (for connections to Jaén), cars US$6.25, 2 hrs; combis/vans US$3. To **Jaén**, with **Turismo Dias** (www.descubreperu.pe), at 0700 daily, Mon and Thu also at 1030, US$6.15, 4 hrs, continues to **Shumba airport**, US$9.20;also with **Móvil Tours** (from its private station, see below), at 0700 (from Jaén at 1400), US$15.40. To **Moyobamba**, vans US$6.15-7.70, 5 hrs, with **Turismo Selva**, about every 2 hrs 0630-1630, those 0630-1230 continue to **Tarapoto** (US$10.80, 8 hrs); Moyobamba with **Evangelio Poder de Dios** (www.turismoevangelio.com) at 0430, 0800, 0930, 1500; additional departures with **Cruz Hermanos**. To **Tarapoto** US$12-14, 8 hrs, with **Virgen del Carmen** at 1900, **Turismo Das** at 2000. To **Celendín** (6-7 hrs, US$9.25) and **Cajamarca** (8-9 hrs, US$14-15.50) with **Amazonas Express** (small bus), at 1900 daily; **Virgen del Carmen** (small bus), at 1830 to Celendín, 1930 to Cajamarca; **Turismo Rojas** (combi), at 0530 and 1830 to Celendín, transfer for Cajamarca.

**Long distance** The recommended companies serving Chachapoyas are: **MóvilTours** (Libertad 464, T041-478545), **GH Bus** (tickets from Jr Grau entre Triunfo y Amazonas, T041-479200; station at C Evitamiento, take a taxi) and **Transervis Kuélap** (Jr Unión 330, T041-478128). To **Lima** (20-22 hrs, US$37-48) with **Móvil Tours** at 1000 and1300 (from Lima at 1400 and 1600); with **GH Bus** at 1030. To **Chiclayo** (9 hrs, US$15-25) at 2000 and 2015 with **Móvil Tours** (2030 and 2100 from Chiclayo), 1930 with **GH Bus**; 2000 with **Transervis Kuélap**. Other options to Chiclayo are **Civa** (Salamanca y Ortiz Arrieta, T041-478048) at 1815 and **Star Bus** (Jr Unión 330) at 1930. To **Trujillo** (12 hrs,

US$23-29), at 1930 with **Móvil Tours** (1600 from Trujillo) or **GH Bus**.

## Gocta

The easiest way to get to Gocta is with a tour from Chachapoyas; in high season there are also tours from Pedro Ruiz. A taxi from Chachapoyas costs US$30, or US$38 with 5-6 hrs' wait. A taxi from Pedro Ruiz costs US$2 pp (there are seldom other passengers to share) or US$10 for the vehicle. Sr Fabier,

T962-922798, offers transport service to San Pablo; call ahead to find out when he will be in Pedro Ruiz. A mototaxi from Pedro Ruiz (5 Esquinas, along the road to Chachapoyas, 4 blocks from the highway) costs US$6, beware of overcharging and dress warmly; it is windy and cold. Arrange return transport ahead or at the tourist offices in San Pablo or Cocachimba, as it is difficult to get transport back from Cocahuayco to either Chachapoyas or Pedro Ruiz.

## ★ Chachapoyas to the Amazon
look out for birdlife on this dramatic journey to the jungle

From Chachapoyas the road heads north through the beautiful Utcubamba Canyon for one hour to a crossroads at Pedro Ruíz, which has two hotels, other lodgings and some basic restaurants. From here, you can return to the coast, head to Jaén for Ecuador, or continue east to Tarapoto and Yurimaguas, making the spectacular descent on a paved road from high Andes to jungle.

## Pedro Ruiz to Moyobamba

In the rainy season, the road east of Pedro Ruiz may be subject to landslides. This is a very beautiful journey, first passing Laguna Pomacochas, then leading to where the high Andes tumble into the Amazon Basin before your eyes. The descent from the heights of the Abra Patricia Pass to the Río Afluente at 1400 m is one of the best birdwatching areas in northern Peru. **ECOAN** ① *T084-227988, www.ecoanperu.org*, has two bird reserves: **Huembo** ① *Km 315.5, 20 mins east of Pedro Ruíz before Pomacochas, T973-955697, 2070 m altitude, 47 ha community reserve with 3 km of trails and birdfeeders*, protecting the marvellous spatuletail hummingbird (*Loddigesia mirabilis*), US$10 day visit, $$$$ full board in 12-person lodge; and, at Abra Patricia, **Owlet** ① *Km 364.5, 2½ hrs from Chachapoyas, 3 hrs from Moyobamba, T984-903605, 1950-2350 m altitude, 3300 ha private reserve*, aimed at conserving the critically endangered long-whiskered owlet (*Xenoglaux loweryi*) and other rare species such as the yellow-tailed woolly monkey, 430 species of bird have been

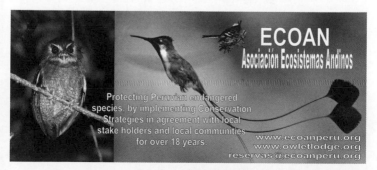

ECOAN
Asociación Ecosistemas Andinos

Protecting Peruvian endangered species, by implementing Conservation Strategies in agreement with local stake holders and local communities for over 18 years.

www.ecoanperu.org
www.owletlodge.org
reservas@ecoanperu.org

identified here, **$$$$** full board in 18-person lodge (includes use of 7.5 km of trails and 15-m-high observation tower), guide service US$35-50 per day depending on group size, guide to observe the owlet US$25. Further along, Nueva Cajamarca (reported unsafe), Rioja (198 km, with several hotels) and Moyobamba are growing centres of population, with much forest clearance, despite the designation of 182,000 ha of cloudforest as the **Bosque de Protección Alto Mayo** ① *Cra a Posic, Rioja, T042-558467, bpaltomayo@sernanp.gob.pe.*

## Moyobamba *Colour map 1, B5.*

Moyobamba, capital of the San Martín region (population 56,500), is a pleasant town in the attractive Río Mayo Valley. The area is renowned for its orchids: there is a **Festival de la Orquídea** during the last weekend of October, the festival is international every second year (next 2019). Among several places to see the plants is **Orquideario Waqanki** ① *2.6 km from the centre, T942-651363, www.waqankilodge.pe, orquideario and mirador daily 0600-1700, US$3 (includes 1-hr guided tour); birdwatching trails 0500-2200, US$6 (full day)*, an impressive small reserve with trails through the woods and a birdwatching mirador, more than 200 species of regional orchids and other plants, also has hummingbird feeders and many interesting birds can be seen. Run by knowledgeable conservationist José Altamirano. Bungalows on the premises (**$$$** including breakfast, other meals available) are ideal for nature lovers; also offer tours of organic coffee farms in the area. Beyond are **Baños Termales San Mateo** ① *5 km southeast, US$1.55 by mototaxi, daily 0500-2000, US$0.90*, which are worth a visit. Boat trips can be taken from **Puerto de Tahuishco** ① *US$9.25 for 30-min ride, up to 10 passengers*, the town's harbour, a pleasant walk north of the centre; there is a chocolate museum here. Along the way are the miradors Punta San Juan and Boulevard Punta de Tahuishco, with views of the Río Mayo below.

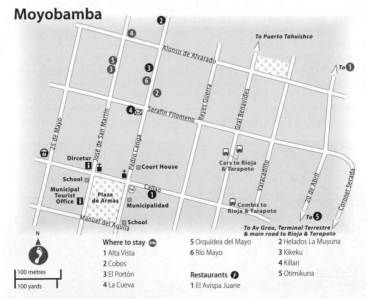

## Moyobamba

**Where to stay** 🛏
1 Alta Vista
2 Cobos
3 El Portón
4 La Cueva
5 Orquídea del Mayo
6 Río Mayo

**Restaurants** 🍴
1 El Avispa Juane
2 Helados La Muyuna
3 Kikeku
4 Killari
5 Otimikuna

**Morro de Calzada** ① *entry US$0.95, 13.5 km west of Moyobamba via Calzada, Rioja-bound combi to the Calzada turn-off, US$0.60, mototaxi from turn-off to the trailhead US$2.50, van to Calzada village US$.80 from Jr Cusco below the market, car to Calzada US$1.55 from Manuel del Aguila y Sargento Tejada, taxi from Calzada to the trailhead US$1.55*, is an isolated outcrop in white sand forest that is good for birdwatching. A path through forest leads to a lookout at the top (1½ hours) but enquire about safety beforehand.

## Tarapoto and around *Colour map 1, C5.*

Tarapoto, the largest commercial centre in the region, with a population of 144,200, is a very friendly place. It stands at the foot of the forested hills of the **Area de Conservación Regional Cordillera Escalera** (149,870 ha), which is good for birdwatching and walking. Within this conservation area are the Ahuashiyacu Falls (see Tarapoto to Yurimaguas, below), Cascada de las Golondrinas (contact the community association Alto Ahuashiyacu, T042-523075/942-031550, acpeceaa_2002@hotmail.es) and the Alto Shilcayo area with more waterfalls (contact Asociación de Protección de Flora y Fauna, T042-532063/951-533850. Next to the conservation area and within easy reach of town is the 20-ha private reserve **Wayrasacha** ① *6-km walk (10 km by car) from the city, T042-522261/942-903257, http://wayrasacha2.wixsite.com/wayrasacha*, run by Peruvian/Swiss couple César Ramírez and Stephanie Gallusser, who offer day trips and volunteer opportunities (English and French spoken). Orchids and other regional plants and some exotic carnivorous specimens

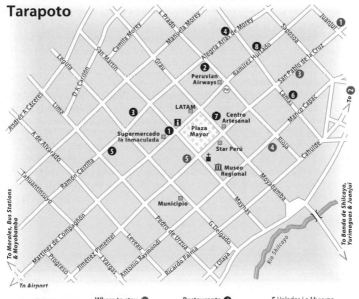

**Tarapoto**

| Where to stay 🛏 | Restaurants 🍴 | 5 Helados La Muyuna |
|---|---|---|
| 1 El Mirador | 1 Café Plaza | 6 La Patarashca Restaurant |
| 2 Huingos Lodge | 2 Chalet Venezia & | 7 Real Grill |
| 3 La Patarashca | La Maison du Pain | 8 Zygo |
| 4 Luna Azul | 3 Chifa Cantón | |
| 5 San Antonio | 4 El Callejón de las Parrillas | |

100 metres
100 yards

can be seen at **Las Cattleyas** ① *Jr Moyobamba 164, T942-941881, ViveroJardinLasCattleyas on Facebook, Mon-Sat 0900-1300, 1500-2100, Sun 0900-1300, US$1.55.*

## Lamas

Off the main road, 22 km northwest of Tarapoto, Lamas is a small hill town with a Quechua-speaking native community, descendants of the Chancas people from the distant central highlands. Lamas is known as 'la ciudad de los tres pisos' (the city of three storeys). On the top level is a lookout with good views, a hotel-restaurant and a *recreo turístico*. The main town occupies the middle level, where there is a small **Museo Los Chankas** ① *Jr San Martín 1157, daily 0830-1300, 1430-1800, US$1.55,* with ethnological and historical exhibits. Uphill from the museum is **El Castillo de Lamas** ① *Mon-Sat 0900-1230, 1400-1800, Sun 0930-1830, US$1.85,* an art gallery and café set in an incongruous medieval castle. On the lower level is the neighbourhood of **Wayku**, where the native Chancas live. Lamas' **Easter** celebrations draw many Peruvian visitors, as do the **Fiestas Patronales** in honour of Santa Rosa de Lima in the last week in August.

## Tarapoto to Yurimaguas

From Tarapoto it is 129 km to Yurimaguas on the Río Huallaga (see page 404), along a spectacular paved road. The road climbs through lush country reaching the 50-m **Ahuashiyacu Falls** ① *US$1.85, taxi US$3 one way, ½-day tour from Tarapoto US$11,* within the **Cordillera Escalera** conservation area after 15 km. This is a popular place with locals. Tours are available or there's transport from La Banda de Shilcayo, a Tarapoto neighbourhood. Past Ahuashiyacu, the road climbs to a tunnel – stop at the police control for good birdwatching (taxi US$5) – after which you descend through beautiful forest perched on rocky cliffs to Pongo de Caynarachi (several basic *comedores*), where the flats start. From Yurimaguas launches go to Iquitos (see page 407).

## Tarapoto to Tingo María

The Carretera Belaunde Terry heads south from Tarapoto, crosses the Río Mayo and follows the Río Huallaga. The resort of **Sauce**, on the shores of the large **Laguna Azul**, popular for water sports, is 52 km from Tarapoto. Further south, around **Picota**, are waterfalls, thermal baths and a cave with oilbirds. Beyond are the larger towns of **Juanjui** (123 km from Tarapoto) and **Tocache** (177 km from Juanjui). Some 169 km further south is Tingo María (see page 399). This road, paved except for 92 km between Juanjui and Tocache, gives access to the 1,350,000 ha, **Parque Nacional Cordillera Azul** ① *headquarters Jr Angel Delgado Morey 565, Tarapoto, T042-529844, pncordilleraazul@sernanp.gob.pe,* the fourth largest in Peru, with 1.38 million ha, spanning four departments. Before travelling this road, enquire about safety.

**Listings** Chachapoyas to the Amazon *maps pages 182 and 183.*

### Tourist information

**Moyobamba**
See www.moyobamba.net and www.turismosanmartin.gob.pe.

**Dircetur**
*Jr San Martín 301, T042-562043. Mon-Fri 0800-1300, 1430-1730.*
Has leaflets and map, English spoken.

**Oficina Municipal de Información**
*Jr San Martín, at the plaza, T042-563164 ext 542, informacionturistica@munimoyo bamba.gob.pe. Mon-Fri 0800-1300, 1430-1800, Sat 0900-1300, 1500-1800, Sun 0900-1300.*
Very helpful, but no English spoken.

## Tarapoto

**Dircetur**
*Jr Angel Delgado Morey, cuadra 1,*
*T042-522567.*

**Oficina Municipal de Información and
Policía de Turismo**
*Jr Ramírez Hurtado, at plaza, T042-526188.*
*Daily 0700-2300.*
Helpful, English spoken.

## Where to stay

### Moyobamba

**$$$ Alta Vista**
*Jr Sucre 184, near Mirador Punta San Juan,*
*T042-562258, www.altavistacasahotel.com.*
Pleasant setting overlooking the river valley,
large grounds, pool, nice rooms, cafeteria.

**$$ Orquídea del Mayo**
*Jr San Martín 432, T042-561049,*
*orquideadelmayohostal@hotmail.com.*
Modern comfortable rooms with bath,
hot water.

**$$ Río Mayo**
*Jr Pedro Canga 415, T042-564193.*
Central, modern comfortable rooms,
frigobar, small indoor pool, parking.

**$$-$ El Portón**
*Jr San Martín 449, T042-562900,*
*www.casahospedajeelporton.com.*
Pleasant modern rooms with fan, hot water,
kitchen facilities, breakfast available, nice
grounds with hammocks and common areas,
orchid garden, good location, quiet, family-run.

**$ Cobos**
*Jr Pedro Canga 404, T042-562153.*
Private bath, cold water, simple but good.

**$ La Cueva**
*Jr Alonso de Alvarado 870, T042-563761,*
*hospedaje.lacuevadejuan on Facebook.*
Small courtyard and garden, private bath,
hot water, newer rooms on upper floor are
particularly nice, central but reasonably quiet,
family-run, helpful owners, good value.

### Lamas

**$ Hospedaje Girasoles**
*Opposite the mirador in the upper part of*
*town, T042-543439, stegmaiert@yahoo.de.*
Breakfast available, nice views, pizzeria and
friendly, knowledgeable owners.

### Tarapoto and around
There are several **$** *alojamientos* on Alegría
Arias de Morey, cuadra 2, and cheap basic
hotels by the bus terminals.

**$$$ Puerto Palmeras**
*Cra Belaúnde Terry, Km 614 towards Sauce,*
*T042-524100.*
Private 25-ha reserve outside town.
Large, modern complex, popular
with families, lots of activities and
entertainment. Nice rooms, helpful staff,
good restaurant, pleasant grounds with
pool, mountain bikes, horses and small
zoo, airport transfers.

**$$$ Puma Rinri Lodge**
*Cra Shapaja–Chasuta, Km 16, T042-526694,*
*www.pumarinri.com.*
Lodge/resort hotel on the shores of the
Río Huallaga, 30 km east of Tarapoto.
Offers a variety of all-inclusive packages.

**$$ El Mirador**
*Jr San Pablo de la Cruz 517, 5 blocks*
*uphill from the plaza T042-522177,*
*www.elmiradortarapoto.blogspot.com.*
Newer rooms with a/c, others with fan,
hot water, laundry facilities, breakfast
served on rooftop terrace with good
views and hammocks, small garden,
tours arranged. Family-run, very
welcoming and recommended.

**$$ Huingos Lodge**
*Prolongación Alerta cuadra 6, Sector Takiwasi,*
*T042-524171, www.huingoslodge.com.*
Nice cabins in lovely grounds by the Río
Shilcayo. Fan, electric shower, frigobar,
kitchen facilities, hammocks, HI-affiliated,
mototaxi from bus stations US$1.55-2.

## $$ La Patarashca
*Jr San Pablo de la Cruz 362, T042-527554, www.lapatarashca.com.*
Very nice hotel with large rooms, rustic decor, a/c or fan (cheaper), electric shower, includes buffet breakfast, restaurant, large garden with hammocks, pool, tours arranged.

## $$-$ Luna Azul
*Jr Manco Capac 276, T042-525787, www.lunaazulhotel.com.*
Modern, central, includes breakfast and airport transfers, with bath, hot water, a/c or fan, frigobar.

## $ San Antonio
*Jr Jiménez Pimentel 126, T042-525563.*
Screened rooms with private bath, hot water, a/c or fan, breakfast available, patio with tables, good value.

## Restaurants

### Moyobamba

#### $$-$ El Avispa Juane
*Jr Callao between Pedro Canga and Reyes Guerra. Daily 0715-1600, 1830-2200.*
Good regional specialities including *juane* and *comida criolla*, *menú* Mon-Sat, snacks, popular.

#### $$-$ Kikeku
*Jr Pedro Canga 450, next to casino. 24 hrs.*
Good *chifa*, also *comida criolla*, large portions, noisy.

#### $$-$ Otimikuna
*Jr 20 de Abril 555. Mon-Sat 1100-1500.*
Varity of *menú* dishes and regional and Peruvian specialities à la carte. Very popular, go early.

#### Helados La Muyuna
*Jr Pedro Canga 529.*
Good natural jungle fruit ice cream.

#### Killari
*Jr Serafín Filomeno y Pedro Canga, next to Serpost. Mon-Sat 0800-1145, 1830-2245.*
Very popular café for breakfast, regional and other snacks, burgers and light meals.

### Tarapoto
There are several restaurants and bars around Jr San Pablo de la Cruz on the corner of Lamas – a lively area at night.

#### $$$-$$ Chalet Venezia
*Jr Alegría Arias de Morey 298. www.restaurant cafechaletvenezia.com. Tue-Sun 1200-2300.*
Upmarket Italian-Amazonian fusion cuisine, wine list, elegant decor, interior or terrace seating, varied *menú* and à la carte. A Tarapoto tradition, French/Peruvian-run.

#### $$$-$$ Real Grill
*Jr Moyobamba on the plaza. Daily 0830-2400.*
Regional and international food. One of the best in town.

#### $$-$ Chifa Cantón
*Jr Ramón Castilla 140. Mon-Fri 1200-1600, Sat-Sun 1200-2400.*
Chinese, very popular and clean.

#### $$-$ El Callejón de las Parrillas
*Jr Alegría Arias de Morey 391. Mon-Sat 1130-1500, 1830-2300.*
Very popular restaurant serving *menú* at midday and grill and regional specialities in the evening.

#### $ Zygo
*Jr Ramírez Hurtado 417. Mon-Thu 0800-2000, Fri-Sat 0800-2100.*
Vegetarian restaurant/café, quality ingredients (organic when possible), breakfast all day, *menú* 1200-1500, vegan options, salads, snacks, a variety of coffees and juices. French/Peruvian-run.

### Cafés

#### Café Plaza
*Jr Maynas corner Martínez, at the plaza. Daily 0730-2300.*
Breakfast, coffee, snacks, juices, Wi-Fi, popular.

#### Helados La Muyuna
*Jr Ramón Castilla 271. Sun-Fri 0730-2330, Sat 1800-2400.*
Good natural ice cream, fruit salads and drinks made with jungle fruits.

## La Maison du Pain
*Jr Leoncio Prado 179. Mon-Fri 0600-2100, Sat-Sun 0630-1300, 1530-2100.*
Very good French bread and pastries.

### Pedro Ruíz
#### Bus
Many buses on the **Chiclayo–Tarapoto** and Chiclayo–**Chachapoyas** routes pass through town. Bus fare to Chiclayo, US$11.50-19; to Tarapoto, US$11.50-15.50. Cars or combis are more convenient for Chacha or Bagua Grande. To **Jaén**, **Trans Fernández** buses from Tarapoto or take a car to Bagua Grande and transfer there.

#### Car, combi and van
To **Chachapoyas**, cars US$3, combis US$1.55, 1 hr. To **Bagua Grande**, cars US$4.75, combis US$4, 1 hr. To **Moyobamba**, cars US$10.70, 4 hrs. To **Nueva Cajamarca**, cars US$9.75, combis US$7.75, 3-3½ hrs. From Nueva Cajamarca it's a further 20 mins to **Rioja** by car, US$1.15, or combi, US$0.75. From Rioja to **Moyobamba**, 21 km, 20 mins, car US$1.15, combi, US$0.75.

### Moyobamba
#### Bus
The bus terminal is 12 blocks from the centre on Av Grau (mototaxi US$0.55). No services originate in Moyobamba; all buses are en route to/from Tarapoto. Several companies head west to **Pedro Ruiz** (US$9, 4 hrs), **Jaén** (US$9, 7 hrs), **Chiclayo** (US$15-US$23, 12 hrs). To reserve a seat on a long-haul bus, you may have to pay the fare to the final destination even if you get off sooner.

#### Car, combi and van
**Empresa San Martín** (Benavides 276), **ETRISA** (Benavides 244) and **Empresa Cajamarca** (Serafín Filomeno 275) run cars (US$1.15) and vans (US$0.75) to **Rioja**, 20 mins; to **Nueva Cajamarca**, 40 mins (US$2, US$1.55), **Bagua Grande**, 5-6 hrs

(US$15, US$8), and **Tarapoto**, 2 hrs (US$6.15, US$3); combis with **Turismo Selva** (Callao y Benavides) cost about 50% less than cars on all routes. To **Chachapoyas**, vans US$6.15-7.70, 5-6 hrs, with **Evangelio Poder de Dios** (Grau 640, www.turismoevangelio.com), at 0600, 1200, 1500; with **Turismo Selva** at 0530 and 0730; also with **Cruz Hermanos**.

### Tarapoto
#### Air
Taxi to town, US$3; mototaxi US$1.55. To **Lima**, 4 daily with **LATAM** (Ramírez Hurtado 183, on the plaza, T042-529318), 2-3 daily with **Peruvian Airlines** (Ramírez Hurtado 277, T042-529969) and 1 daily with **Star Perú** (Jiménez Pimentel 325, Plaza de Armas, T042-528765) and 2 weekly with **Viva Air**. To **Iquitos** 1 daily with **Star Perú**, 3 weekly with **SAETA** (Jr Aviación 639, opposite the airport, T942-694483, www.saetaperu.com), via **Yurimaguas**. To **Chachapoyas**, Mon-Sat 3 daily flights in a 9-seater aircraft with **SAETA**, US$68, 25 mins, 10-kg luggage allowance. To **Pucallpa**, 3 weekly with each of **SAETA** and **North American** (T061-579418, www.northamerican.pe).

#### Bus
Buses depart from Av Salaverry, blocks 8-9, in Morales; mototaxi from centre, US$1.20, 20 mins.

To **Moyobamba**, 116 km, US$3.85, 2 hrs; to **Pedro Ruiz**, US$11.50-15.50 (companies going to Jaén or Chiclayo), 6 hrs; to **Chiclayo**, 690 km, 15-16 hrs, US$25-29; and **Lima**, US$46-52, *cama* US$64, 30 hrs with **Móvil Tours**, **GH Bus**, **Civa** and others. To **Trujillo**, $26, 12-13 hrs, with **Móvil Tours**, **GH Bus** and **Turismo Días**. To **Chachapoyas**, US$12-14, 6 hrs, with **Virgen del Carmen** at 0900 and **Turismo Días** at 2000, with **Turismo Selva** (Av Alfonso Ugarte, cuadra 11) at 0700, 1000, 1200 and 1400, US$7.70, or transfer in Moyobamba. To **Jaén**, US$13.50-15.50, 9-10 hrs, with **Fernández**, 2 a day. To **Piura** US$23, 14-15 hrs, with **Sol Peruano**, at 1200 and **Turismo Días** at 1230. To **Tingo María** (paving in progress in 2018 between Tocache and Juanjui), US$17, 10 hrs, and **Pucallpa**, US$22, 15-16 hrs, with **Transamazónica** daily; and **Transmar** (www.transmar.com.pe) 3 times a week.

## Car, combi and van
To Lamas, cars from Av Alfonso Ugarte, cuadra 10-13, US$1.55, 30 mins. To **Moyobamba**, cars with **Empresa San Martín** (Av Alfonso Ugarte 1456, T042-526327), **ETRISA** (Av Alfonso Ugarte 1096, T042-521944) and **Cajamarca** (Av Alfonso Ugarte 1438, T042-529122); they will pick you up from your hotel, US$6.15, 2 hrs;

combis with **Turismo Selva** (Av Alfonso Ugarte, cuadra 11), US$3, 2½ hrs. To **Yurimaguas**, cars with **Empresa San Martín** and ETRISA, US$6.15, 2 hrs; **Turismo Selva** vans, US$3, 2½ hrs, 8 daily. To **Bagua Grande**, with **Turismo Selva** at 0800, 1100, 1300, US$11, 8 hrs. To **Juanjui**, frequent service with **Turismo Selva**, US$4, 2 hrs; to **Tocache**, with **Turismo Selva**, at 0700, 0930, 1200 and 1400 (from Tocache at 0200, 0400, 0730 and 0900), US$12.30, 7 hrs; also with **Euro Sac** (Jr Humberto Pinedo 100, Morales). To **Tingo María** with **Pizana Express** vans, US$21.50, 9 hrs; several others.

## Chachapoyas to Ecuador
*a scenic route and a straightforward border crossing*

### Bagua Grande and further west
This is the first town of note heading west from Pedro Ruiz. It has several hotels but is hot, dusty and unsafe; Pedro Ruiz or Jaén are more pleasant places to spend the night. Note that Bagua Grande is not the same as Bagua (Bagua capital), the district's capital, on a side road to the northwest. From Bagua Grande the road follows the Río Chamaya, climbing to the Abra de Porculla (2150 m) before descending to join the old Pan-American Highway at Olmos (see page 136). From Olmos you can go southwest to Chiclayo, or northwest to Piura.

### Jaén *Colour map 1, B3.*
Some 50 km west of Bagua Grande, a road branches northwest at Chamaya to Jaén, a convenient place to take a flight to and from Lima or make a stopover en route to Ecuador. It is a rapidly growing modern city (less safe than it used to be) surrounded by rice fields, with a population of about 100,000. The **Museo Hermógenes Mejía Solf** ① *2 km south of centre, T976-719590, Mon-Fri 0800-1400, mototaxi US$0.60*, displays pre-Columbian artefacts from a variety of cultures. Newly discovered temples at Monte Grande and San Isidro, close to Jaén, are revealing more finds, dating back possibly to 3500 BC.

### San Ignacio to the border
A paved road runs north for 109 km to **San Ignacio**, a pleasant town with steep streets in the centre of a coffee-growing area. The nearby hills offer excursions to waterfalls, lakes, petroglyphs and ancient ruins. West of San Ignacio is the **Santuario Tabaconas-Namballe** ① *Sernanp, Jr Jaén 505, San Ignacio, T076-437457 or 968-218439, dcotrina@sernanp.gob.pe, access from the town of Tabaconas (see Transport)*, a 32,125-ha reserve at 1700-3800 m protecting the spectacled bear, mountain tapir and several ecosystems including the southernmost Andean *páramo*. A two-hour walk from Tabaconas leads to Lagunas Arreviatadas and the Chichilapa information centre and shelter.

From San Ignacio the paved road runs 41 km through green hills to **Namballe**, with several simple hotels and restaurants. The border is 7 km from Namballe at **La Balsa** (mototaxi, US$1.55, 15 minutes), which has a basic *comedor*, a few small shops and money changers. Peruvian immigration is open 0730-1430, 1600-1930, Ecuadorean immigration (T07-3059815) 0600-2200 (24 hours in an emergency). **Sur Oriente** has a daily direct bus La Balsa–Vilcabamba–Loja at 1000 (from Loja at 0500, passes Vilcabamba at 0600), US$11, nine hours to Loja; otherwise experience riding the more folkloric *rancheras* (open-sided buses), from La Balsa to Zumba at 1200, 1730 and 1900 (US$2.25, 1½ hours) and from Zumba to La Balsa at 0800, 1430 and 1730. Taxi La Balsa–Zumba US$20. From Zumba there is onward transport to Vilcabamba and Loja. This crossing is relaxed and straightforward.

## Chachapoyas - Vilcabamba (Ecuador)

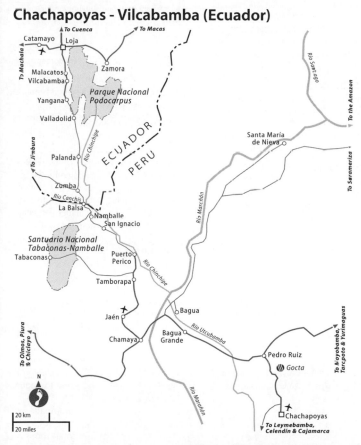

## Where to stay

### Bagua Grande

**$$-$ Río Hotel**
*Jr Capac Malku 115, www.riohotel baguagrande.blogspot.com.*
A good choice if you can't avoid staying in Bagua Grande.

### Jaén

**$$$ Urqu**
*Av La Colina, north of the centre, T947-934688, www.urquhotel.com.*
Modern hotel on a hill overlooking Jaén Valley. Bungalows and suites, well-appointed rooms, restaurant, pool, spa.

**$$ Casa del Sol**
*Mcal Castilla 140, near Plaza de Armas, T076-317110, hotelcasadelsol@hotmail.com, on Facebook.*
Modern confortable rooms with frigobar, parking, suites with jacuzzi (**$$$**).

**$$ El Bosque**
*Mesones Muro 632, T076-431492, hoteleraelbosque@speedy.com.pe.*
On main road by bus terminals. Quiet rooms at back, gardens, frigobar, pool, restaurant.

**$$ Prim's**
*Diego Palomino 1341, T076-432970, www.primshotel.com.*
Includes breakfast, good service, comfortable, a/c, some single rooms with fan, frigobar, friendly, small pool.

**$ Danubio**
*V Pinillos 429, T076-433110.*
Older place, nicely refurbished, many different rooms and prices, some cheaper rooms have cold water only, fan, good.

### San Ignacio to the border

**$ Flores**
*On the main road, Namballe, T076-830011 (community phone).*
Simple, with bath. Several others on the same street.

**$ Gran Hotel San Ignacio**
*Jr José Olaya 680 at the bottom of the hill, San Ignacio, T076-356544, granhotel-sanignacio@hotmail.com.*
Restaurant for breakfast and good lunch *menú*, modern comfortable rooms, upmarket for here.

**$ La Posada**
*Jr Porvenir 218, San Ignacio, T076-356180.*
A good economy option refurbished in 2016, with bath and hot water, restaurant, breakfast extra.

**$ Sol de la Frontera**
*1 km north of Namballe, 5 km from La Balsa, T997-827766, isabelayub@yahoo.es.*
British-run by Isabel Wood. Comfortable bungalows set in 2.5 ha of countryside, bathtubs, gas water heaters, no restaurant, bring food. A good place to break the trip, the best option near the border. Camping and campervans welcome.

## Restaurants

### Jaén

**$$-$ La Cabaña**
*San Martín 1521. Daily 0700-0000.*
Upmarket restaurant with daily specials at noon, à la carte in the evening, popular.

**$$-$ Lactobac**
*Bolívar 1378 at Plaza de Armas. Daily 0730-0000.*
Variety of à la carte dishes, snacks, desserts, good *pollo a la brasa*. Very popular.

## $ El Pimpollo
*Villanueva Pinillos 208. Daily 1100-0200.*
Small place on the main plaza, good *menú*
at midday, à la carte and *pollo a la brasa* in
the evening.

## $ Gatizza
*Diego Palomino 1503. Mon-Sat*
*0600-1500, 1800-2200.*
Simple place, tasty and varied *menú*.

## Transport

### Bagua Grande
Many buses pass through **Bagua Grande**
en route to/from Chiclayo, Tarapoto or
Chachapoyas, ask for Terminal Leyva. Cars
to **Jaén** from Mcal Castilla y Angamos at the
west end of town, US$4, combis US$2.50,
1 hr. From R Palma 308 at the east end of
town, cars leave to **Pedro Ruiz**, US$4.60,
combis US$4, 1 hr; to **Chachapoyas**, US$6.25,
combis US$3, 2 hrs; to **Moyobamba**, US$15,
combis US$8, 5-6 hrs; to **Tarapoto**, combi
US$11, 8 hrs.

### Jaén
### Air
The airport is at **Shumba**, 17 km north,
on the road to San Ignacio. To/from **Lima**,
1-2 daily with **LATAM** (on the Plaza de Armas,
T01-213 8200, Mon-Fri 1000-2200), US$180.

### Bus, car and combi
Terminals are strung along Mesones Muro,
blocks 4-8, south of centre; there are many
ticket offices, so always enquire where the
bus actually leaves from. On block 8 is the
**Terminal Terrestre Sur** which has many
companies. To **Chiclayo**: US$6.15-12.30, 6 hrs,
many companies, **Móvil** more expensive
than others. Cars to Chiclayo from Mesones

Muro, cuadra 4, US$10, 5 hrs. To **Lima** (via
**Trujillo**), with **Móvil** at 1500, 16 hrs, *bus cama*
US$38.50, *semi-cama* US$31; with **Civa**
(tickets from Mcal Ureta 1300 y V Pinillos;
terminal at Bolívar 935), 1700, US$27-31.
To **Piura** via Olmos, with **Sol Peruano**, at
2200, US$15.50, 8 hrs. To **Tarapoto**, 490 km,
US$12.30, 10 hrs, with **Fernández** (Mesones
Muro 705) at 2100 and 2130, with **Turismo
Dias** (www.descubreperu.pe) at 1930. To
**Moyobamba**, US$10.75, 7 hrs, same service
as Tarapoto, likewise to **Pedro Ruiz**, US$6.15,
3½ hrs. To **Chachapoyas**, with **Turismo Dias**,
at 1400 daily and an extra departure after
the second flight on Mon and Thu, US$6.15
from Jaén, US$9.20 from the airport, 4 hrs;
also with **Móvil Tours**, at 1400, US$15.40,
both companies start at **Shumba airport**.
To **Bagua Grande**, cars from Mesones Muro
cuadra 6, 0400-2000, US$4, 1 hr; combis
from cuadra 9, US$2.50. To **Chamaya**, cars
from Mesones Muro, cuadra 4, 0500-2000,
US$1, 15 mins. To **San Ignacio** (for Ecuador),
from Av Pacamuros, block 19, 0400-1800,
2 hrs, cars US$6.15, vans US$5; combis from
Jr Contisuyo, 1 block from Av Pacamuros
block 18, US$3.70, 3 hrs.

### San Ignacio to the border
**Terminal Sur** is 1 km south of the centre.
To **Chiclayo**, with **Civa** at 1915, with **Trans
Chiclayo** at 1945, US$9.25, 10-11 hrs. To
**Lima**, with **Divino Señor** at 1230, US$31.
To **Jaén**, 2-3 hrs, cars US$6.15, vans US$5,
combis US$3.70. To **Namballe** and **La Balsa**
(border with Ecuador), cars leave from
**Nuevo Terminal** at Prolongación Comercio,
just south of the centre, US$4.60, 1½-2 hrs.
From Nuevo Terminal, at 0830 daily, combis
to **Tabaconas**, US$10.75, 4½ hrs, and
**Huancabamba**, US$15, 7½ hrs.

# South coast

The desert coastline south of Lima has some distinctive attractions. The most famous, and perhaps the strangest, are the enigmatic Nazca Lines, whose origin and function continue to puzzle scientists.

Further north, the Ica Valley, with its wonderful climate, produces that equally wonderful grape brandy known as *pisco*. Nearby, the oasis resort of Huacachina attracts a lively young crowd. And, on the coast, the Paracas Peninsula, once home to one of Peru's most important ancient civilizations is now an internationally recognized marine reserve. As you bob in a boat to the Ballestas Islands, part of another national reserve, to watch the seabirds, look for the giant Candelabra, drawn on the cliffs by unknown hands.

West of Nazca are the pyramids of Cahuachi, a pre-Inca ceremonial site, and, to the south on a small bay, is Puerto Inca, the seaport and fishing harbour for Cuzco in pre-colonial times. The major Inca road from here through the canyons to the sierra may have fallen into disuse, but important paved roads now climb up from the coast to the highlands from Pisco, Nazca and Camaná. The Sondondo Valley, a true gem off the beaten path, lies north of the road between Nazca and Cuzco. A rougher route from coast to sierra starts in the Cañete Valley, not far south of Lima, and climbs through the Cordillera Yauyos to Huancaya and Huancayo.

**Best** for
Archaeological mysteries ▪ Birdwatching ▪ Pisco

South from Lima . . . . . . . . . . . . 196
Nazca & around . . . . . . . . . . . . 209

# Footprint picks

★ **Cañete Valley**, page 196

Follow a rough road from the coast to the sierras, through miles of pre-Columbian terracing and spectacular natural scenery.

★ **Bodegas**, pages 198 and 202

Watch *pisco* being made in the traditional way before sampling a glass.

★ **Ballestas Islands**, page 200

Spot sea birds, sealions, dolphins and evidence of an ancient culture.

★ **Huacachina**, page 201

Let the adrenalin flow as you descend the dunes in a sandboard or buggy.

★ **Nazca Lines**, page 210

Puzzle over these mysterious designs in the desert.

★ **Sondondo Valley**, page 213

Leave the crowds and discover a beautiful land of working ancient terraces, the largest concentration of condors and much more.

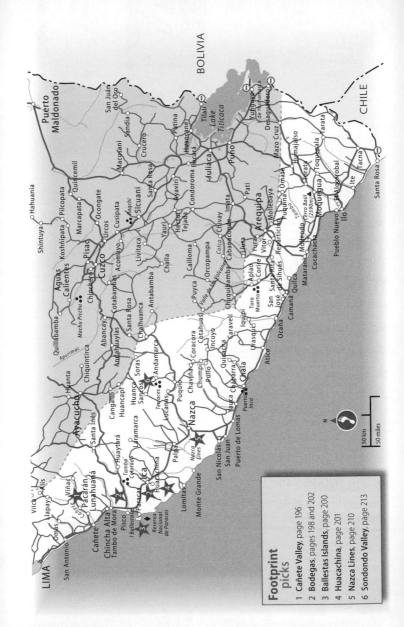

## Footprint picks

1 Cañete Valley, page 196
2 Bodegas, pages 198 and 202
3 Ballestas Islands, page 200
4 Huacachina, page 201
5 Nazca Lines, page 210
6 Sondondo Valley, page 213

# Essential South coast

### Finding your feet

The Pan-American Highway runs along the coast all the way south from Lima to the Chilean border and is the main transport artery for the South Coast. The highway from Lima to Pisco is a dual carriageway. There are several important roads branching off it, east to the highlands: the highway from Nazca to Abancay is the main overland route from Lima to Cuzco; north of Nazca, another paved road runs from Pisco to Ayacucho in the central highlands, while to the south a highway leads from Camaná to Arequipa and Juliaca.

### Getting around

There are frequent bus services south along the Pan-American Highway from Lima. Cars and vans provide local transport, although you will need a taxi to visit the bodegas around Ica. The Paracas Peninsula is best visited on a tour from either Pisco or Paracas. Huacachina is reached by taxi or *colectivo* from Ica. The Nazca Lines are best seen from the air. However, flights tend to be turbulent and can be dangerous. The lines can also be seen from an observation tower reached on a land-based tour, by taxi or by bus. Land-based tours also include visits to archaeological sites. The Sondondo Valley can be visited on a tour or using minivans which go from one town to another.

### When to go

The summer months are December to April. There may be sea mists May to October, although the Nazca Lines are far enough inland not to be affected. Here, the sun blazes year round by day and the nights are crisp. Ica has a very pleasant climate that allows grapes to thrive. Sandstorms can be a problem around the Paracas Peninsula, especially in August, when they can last for days.

### Time required

You'll need one to two weeks thoroughly to explore, but a few days is enough time to see one of the attractions, such as the Nazca Lines, en route to elsewhere.

## Weather Nazca

| January | February | March | April | May | June |
|---|---|---|---|---|---|
| 26°C 19°C 5mm | 27°C 19°C 9mm | 27°C 18°C 14mm | 25°C 17°C 0mm | 23°C 16°C 0mm | 21°C 14°C 0mm |

| July | August | September | October | November | December |
|---|---|---|---|---|---|
| 19°C 13°C 0mm | 19°C 13°C 0mm | 20°C 14°C 0mm | 21°C 14°C 0mm | 22°C 16°C 0mm | 24°C 17°C 0mm |

# South from
## Lima

Beyond the beaches which are popular with Limeños the road passes near several towns, including Cañete and Chincha, with its Afro-Peruvian culture. The surrounding desert, interrupted by the occasional oasis, is magnificent. The Paracas Peninsula, near Pisco, is one of the world's great marine bird reserves and was home to one of Peru's most important ancient civilizations. Further south, the Ica Valley, with its wonderful climate, is home to that equally wonderful grape brandy, pisco. Most beaches have very strong currents and can be dangerous for swimming; if unsure, ask locals.

## Cañete province

*beaches, vineyards and a forgotten valley*

### Cañete and Quebrada de Lunahuaná

About 150 km south of Lima, on the Río Cañete, is the prosperous market centre of **San Vicente de Cañete**. All the main services are within a few blocks of the plaza. A paved road runs inland, mostly beside the Río Cañete, through Imperial and Nuevo Imperial to **Lunahuaná** (40 km). This town is located 8 km beyond the Inca ruins of **Incawasi**, which dominate the valley. In the week Lunahuaná is very quiet, but on Sunday the town is full of life, with pisco tastings from the valley's bodegas, food and handicrafts for sale in the plaza and lots of outdoor activities. Throughout February and March you may still be able to see traditional methods of treading the grapes to the beat of a drum.

### ★ Upper Cañete Valley

Beyond Lunahuaná the road ascending the Cañete Valley leaves the narrow floodplain and runs 41 km, paved, through a series of gorges to the San Jerónimo bridge. A side road heads to Huangáscar and the village of Viñac, where **Mountain Lodges of Peru** has its **Viñak-Reichraming Lodge** (see Where to stay, opposite). The road beyond Huangáscar, from which you can see extensive areas of pre-Columbian agricultural terracing, is impassable from January to mid-March.

The main road carries on to the market towns of **Yauyos** (basic accommodation, 5 km off the road) and **Llapay**, a good base in the middle of the valley. Beyond Llapay, the Cañete Valley narrows to an exceptionally tight canyon; the road squeezes between rock and rushing water. Near **Alis**, the road forks. The eastern branch climbs steeply to a 4600-m pass then drops down to Huancayo (see page 363), while the northern branch follows the Río Cañete deeper into the **Reserva Paisajística Nor Yauyos-Cochas (RPNYC)** ⓘ *contact the Sernanp regional office: Av Francisco Solano 107, Covica, El Tambo, Huancayo, T064-213064, www.sernanp.gob.pe/nor-yauyos-cochas, rpnycperu.blogspot.com, or guide Juan Carlos Pilco (pilco_traveler@hotmail.com).* After the attractive village of **Huancaya**, the valley is transformed into one of the most beautiful upper valleys in all Peru. The river passes through high Andean terrain and descends through a series of absolutely clear, turquoise pools and lakes, interrupted by cascades and whitewater rapids. Culturally, the valley is fascinating for its dying indigenous languages and traditional ways of life, including impressive pre-Columbian terraces. Further north, a remarkable ancient road with intact stone steps goes from Pachacamac, near Lima (see page 53), across RPNYC, to Jauja in the highlands; see box, Stairway to heaven, page 364.

## Listings Cañete province

### Tourist information

**Cañete and Quebrada de Lunahuaná**
For information on Cañete town, see www. municanete.gob.pe, or the Oficina de Turismo's Facebook page. There's a **tourist office** in Lunahuaná in the Municipalidad, opposite the church, T01-284 1006, daily.

### Where to stay

**Cañete and Quebrada de Lunahuaná**
There are places to stay in San Vicente de Cañete, and a range of options in and around Lunahuaná, from large family resorts and *casas de campo* to campsites, plus many *restaurantes campestres*. Note that prices may rise at weekends and holidays.

**Upper Cañete Valley**
For details of accommodation in Huancaya, call T01-810 6086/7, or see www.huancaya. com. For accommodation and restaurants in Alis, Llapay, Yauyos and other towns, see parroquianoryauyos.blogspot.com/2013/08/hospedajes-y-restaurantes-en-la.html. For towns in RPNYC reserve, download list from rpnycperu.blogspot.com/p/turismo.html.

**$$$ Viñak-Reichraming Lodge**
*Mountain Lodges of Peru, T01-421 6952, www.refugiosdelperu.com (see page 312).*
A wonderful place to relax or go horse riding or walking, with superb views and excellent food. Prices are per person for full board.

**$ Hostal Llapay**
*Llapay. Will open at any hour.*
Basic but very friendly, restaurant.

### Festivals

**Cañete and Quebrada de Lunahuaná**
**Feb** A festival of adventure sports is held in Lunahuaná.
**1st weekend of Mar** Fiesta de la Vendimia (grape harvest) in Lunahuaná.
**Last week of Aug** **Cañete festival**, with regional music and dancing.

### What to do

**Cañete and Quebrada de Lunahuaná**
Several agencies in Lunahuaná offer rafting and kayaking on the Río Cañete, especially at the anexo of San Jerónimo: Nov-Apr rafting is at Grades IV-V; May-Oct is low water, Grades I-II only.

## Transport

### Cañete and Quebrada de Lunahuaná

Soyuz bus runs between Lima and **Cañete** every 7 mins, US$5. There are combis between Cañete and **Lunahuaná**, US$2.75.

### Upper Cañete Valley

Cars run from the Yauyos area to **Huancayo**, US$7.50. Ask locally where and when they leave. Public transport between villages is scarce and usually goes in the morning. When you get to a village you may have to wait till the early evening for places to open up.

## Ica region

vineyards, archaeological sites, coastal and marine reserves

### Pisco and around *Colour map 5, B2.*

An important coastal city, Pisco (population 105,000, www.pisco.info) is located a short distance west of the Pan-American Highway and 237 km south of Lima. Once a key port, Pisco gave the famous Peruvian brandy its name. Puerto San Martín, in the Paracas Peninsula to the southwest, is today the regional port. Major earthquakes struck the coast of Peru south of Lima in 2007 and again in 2011, causing substantial loss of life and property damage; Pisco and surroundings have since recovered. Tours to Paracas, vineyards and *bodegas* (wineries and distilleries, see From Pisco to the sierra, below) and archaeological sites are on offer.

Criollo culture is celebrated at local festivals (see page 206) in **Chincha Alta** (population 177,000, www.chincha.net), 35 km north of Pisco, where African slave labour once allowed the great haciendas to thrive. Chincha is also a good place to sample locally produced wine and pisco at **Bodega Tabernero** (Km 198 Panamericana Sur, www.tabernero.com) and **Viñas de Oro** (Km 211, T01-706 2241, ext 2342, idaga@bvo.com.pe).

### ★ From Pisco to the sierra

A 317-km paved road, known as Los Libertadores, goes up the Pisco Valley from the suburb of San Clemente (El Cruce) to Ayacucho in the sierra, with a branch to Huancavelica. At Abra Apacheta it reaches 4750 m. The scenery on this journey is superb. There are vineyards and bodegas known as the **Ruta del Pisco en Pisco**, as far as **Humay**, 31 km inland. The following can be visited: **Piscos Polanco** (Km 24.7, T988-700652, rubenpolancodelcarpio@gmail.com) and La Encañada (off Km 30.6, T985-928531).

At Km 39 is one of the best-preserved Inca ruins in coastal Peru: **Tambo Colorado** ① *T056-234383, site museum entry US$2.50, daily 0900-1700, see www.facebook.com/TamboColorado for details of a French research project here.* This 1.2-ha site, dating to the Pachacutec reign, is thought to have been an administrative centre. It has three sectors of impressive buildings around a trapezoidal plaza. Most unusual for an Inca site, the walls are built of adobe blocks, many retain their original colours. Guided tours are available from Pisco (these may visit the vineyards and bodegas along the way), Paracas or Ica, or travel independently (see Transport, page 206).

### Paracas

Down the coast from Pisco is the bay of Paracas, sheltered by the large Paracas Peninsula to the south and west. Paracas also refers to strong winds bringing sand storms; the resort town; the pre-Hispanic

> **Tip...**
> Paracas means 'sandstorm' in Quechua; these can last for up to three days, especially in August. The wind gets up every afternoon, peaking at around 1500.

## BACKGROUND

## An economic mess

The islands lying off the coast of Peru are the breeding grounds for millions of sea birds, whose droppings have accumulated over the centuries. These piles of mineral-rich excrement were turned into piles of cash during the last century.

Though the ancient Peruvians knew of the benefits of guano – the name given to the natural fertilizer – and used it on their crops, it wasn't until 1840 that the vast deposits were exploited for commercial purposes. It was at this time that Peru began to trade abroad, particularly with France and England. Almost simultaneously, guano began to replace rare metals as the country's main export.

However, with the economy heavily based on the sales of bird droppings, Peru was caught in a vicious circle of borrowing money on future sales, then having to repay loans at vastly inflated rates. This unhealthy state of affairs was exacerbated in 1864 when Spain decided to occupy the guano islands of Chincha, thereby leaving the Peruvian government really up to its neck in it.

The main producers of guano are the guanay cormorant and the Peruvian booby. They gather in colonies on the islands, attracted by the huge shoals of anchovy that feed on the plankton in the cold water of the Humboldt current.

culture which thrived here; and the **Paracas National Reserve** ⓘ *Ctra Pisco–Puerto San Martín Km 27, T968-218617, www.sernanp.gob.pe/de-paracas, daily 0800-1700, entry US$3.40, group tours cost US$9-12 per person, US$38-46 private tour for 4*. The reserve protects an area with one of the highest biodiversities on the Peruvian coast. This 335,000-ha reserve (35% land, 65% marine) is a Ramsar site very rich in marine birds; sea lions and dolphins may also be seen. The scenery and beaches are lovely, there are also fossilized shells and archaeological sites.

Paracas can be reached from Pisco by the coast road (6 km) via San Andrés, passing the fishing port and a large proportion of Peru's fishmeal industry. Alternatively, go down the Pan-American Highway for 14.5 km past the Pisco turning, and take the road to Paracas, 11 km across the desert.The entrance to the reserve is at the south end of town on the main road. Two kilometres beyond is the **Interpretation Centre** ⓘ *entry with reserve ticket, daily 0800-1700*, with natural history information and, next to it, the **Julio C Tello Site Museum** ⓘ *museojuliotello@cultura.gob.pe, recorrido360.cultura.pe/paracas/, Tue-Sun 0900-1700, US$2.30, students US$1.75* (named after the Peruvian archaeologist who first researched the Paracas culture), with textiles, ceramics and funerary objects. Tours follow a route through the reserve, including to a mirador overlooking **La Catedral** rock formation, part of which collapsed in 2007. Longer tours venture into the deserts to the south. The tiny fishing village of **Lagunilla** is 5 km from the museum across the neck of the peninsula. Eating places there are poor value (watch out for prices in dollars), but almost all tours stop for lunch here. About 14 km from the museum is the pre-Columbian image known as '**El Candelabro**' (the candelabra), which has been carved into the hillside. It's at least 50 m long, access by land is forbidden and it must be seen from the sea.

**Tip...**

It's advisable to see the peninsula as part of a tour from either Pisco or Paracas: it is not safe to walk alone and it is easy to get lost.

# BACKGROUND
## Textiles and trepanation

The Paracas culture, which inhabited this region between 200 BC and AD 200, is renowned for its finely woven textiles, in particular *mantos*, large decorated cloths, embroidered with anthropomorphic, zoomorphic and geometric designs. These *mantos* were used to wrap mummified bodies in their funerary bundles. Their discovery by anthropologists and archaeologists provided vital clues to this civilization. The bodies were often found to have trepanned skulls. Trepanation was a form of brain surgery performed by the Paracas people in which metal plates were inserted to replace broken sections of skull – a common injury among warring factions at that time. In addition, the Paracas culture practised the intentional deformation of infants' skulls for aesthetic reasons.

Once a small fishing village, the town of Paracas (www.paracas.com) is now a bustling tourist centre with more than 60 hotels and as many restaurants and tour operators; most of them are located around El Chaco, the fishing port. A couple of blocks north is the Marina Turística, a modern pier with several services as well as the **Museo Histórico de Paracas** ① T955-929514, whose exhibits include information about the trepanation and cranial deformation practised by the Paracas.

★ **Islas Ballestas**, three islands opposite the Paracas Reserve, are part of the **Sistema de Islas, Islotes y Puntas Guaneras (SIIPG) National Reserve** ① T01-2262300, rnislasypuntas@sernanp.gob.pe, entry US$3.40 payable at either dock or through Teleticket. The islands are spectacular, eroded into numerous arches and caves which give the islands their name (*ballesta* means archer's bow) and provide shelter for thousands of seabirds. You will see, close up, guano birds, pelicans, penguins, hundreds of inquisitive sea lions and, if you're lucky, dolphins swimming in the bay. Birdlife here includes some very rare species. *Islas Ballestas Guía de Fauna*, with information about the species commonly seen, can be downloaded from the Sernanp website and the book *Las Aves del Departamento de Lima* by Maria Koepcke is also useful. Tours to the islands leave from the Marina Turística or the Embarcadero El Chaco (dock fee US$1.55 at both piers), departures at 0800, 1000 and 1200; the trip takes about two hours and costs US$12-28. Most boats are speedboats, equipped with life jackets, although they are without toilets and some are very crowded; wear warm clothing and protect against the sun. The boats pass Puerto San Martín and the Candelabra en route to the islands.

## Ica *Colour map 5, B2.*

Ica (population 244,000), 70 km southeast of Pisco, is Peru's chief wine centre and is also famous for its *tejas*, a local sweet of *manjar blanco* (*dulce de leche*). A wine and pisco festival takes place during the vintage (end February to early March). The **Museo Regional** ① Av Ayabaca, 895 (take bus 17 from the Plaza de Armas, US$0.50), T056-234383, recorrido360. cultura.pe/ica/ica.html, Tue-Fri 0800-1900, Sat and Sun 0830-1830, US$2.30, students US$1.20, tip guide, has mummies, ceramics, textiles and trepanned skulls from the Paracas, Nazca and Inca cultures. There's also a good, well-displayed collection of Inca *quipus* and clothes made of feathers. Behind the building is a scale model of the Nazca Lines with an observation tower, which is useful for orientation before visiting the lines themselves. Ica is neither safe nor pleasant, Huacachina, only 10 minutes away, is a better option.

## Pisco: a history in the making

A visit to Peru would not be complete without savouring a pisco sour, a cocktail made from *pisco* (a clear brandy, similar to *grappa*), mixed with lime or lemon juice, syrup, egg white and Angosturas bitters. Peruvians are mighty proud of their national tipple, which has turned out to be one of the few positive results of conquest (see also page 31).

Peru was the first conquered territory in Spanish America to produce wines and brandies. The cultivation of grapes began with the import of vine stalks from the Canary Islands, which were planted on the outskirts of Lima. The crop later reached Cuzco and Ayacucho in the Andes but it was in Ica that the enterprise really took off, owing to the region's exceptional climate.

A hundred years after the conquest, the wine and *pisco* trade had grown considerably. Ica sent its wine to Huamanga, Cuzco, Lima and Callao. And ships left from Pisco for ports in Central America, as well as Valparaíso and Buenos Aires.

Royal bans tried to halt the expansion of Peruvian vineyards because it endangered the Spanish wine industry. In 1629, the prohibition included the transport of Peruvian wines aboard Atlantic-bound ships. But despite the restrictions, the industry continued to expand during the 17th and 18th centuries.

Today several firms utilize modern procedures to manufacture and market larger quantities of *pisco*, but there are still many small, independent producers. Here the grapes are crushed by foot and the fermented grape juice is emptied into traditional Peruvian stills, called *falcas*, which are crucial to the process of true *pisco* production. More conventional wineries still rely on wood from the carob tree, a slow-burning fuel whose constant source of heat makes for a finer flavour, rather like food cooked over a charcoal fire.

Another important factor is the type of grape used. The Quebranta, brought to the Americas by the Spaniards, lends its unique characteristics to the making of renowned 'pure' *pisco*. There are also 'fragrant' *piscos* from Moscatel and Albilla varieties, 'Creole' *piscos* made with prime fragrant grapes and 'green' *piscos* made with partially fermented grape juice.

The Ica Valley is still Peru's foremost producer of pisco and, together with Chincha, is the heart of a touristic Ruta del Pisco which comprises a number of bodegas (both industrial and artesanal), a museum and a school of technology and innovation. Nearby producer valleys are Pisco and Lunahuaná, while other centres include Moquegua, Vitor in Arequipa, Locumba in Tacna and Surco in Lima.

## ★ Huacachina

*From Ica, take a taxi for US$2.50-3 or colectivo from Bolívar block 2, return from behind Hotel Mossone, US$0.75. Tourist information at http://huacachinaperu.pe.*

About 5 km from Ica, around a palm-fringed sulphurous lake amid amazing sand dunes, is the oasis and resort of Huacachina, a trendy hang-out for people seeking a change from the archaeology and chill of the Andes. A popular health spa for rich Iqueños in the first half of the 20th century, it is once again a fashionable destination among Peruvian and international visitors making the most of adrenalin sports by day and the vibrant nightlife. Paddle boats can be rented, sandboarding on the dunes is a major pastime (for the inexperienced, note that sandboarding can be dangerous) and dozens of sandbuggies (*tubulares*) plough the dunes at high speed (take a formal tour even if it is more expensive; there have been fatal accidents caused by inexperienced drivers).

## ★ Bodegas around Ica

The best time to visit wineries is during harvest season, from late February to early March. **La Ruta de los Lagares** is a circuit of 10 vineyards offered by tour operators during the vintage; a different bodega is visited every day, you can see the entire process of pisco and wine making, from harvest and the traditional way of treading grapes to bottling; check with iPeru for current dates. The tourist information office also has a list of local wine and pisco bodegas that you can visit at any time of the year. These include the following: **Tacama** ① *Distrito La Tinguiña, 7 km northeast of the city, T056-581030 ext 1039, www. tacama.com,* the first vineyard in South America. In the same area is **El Carmelo** ① *T056-232191, www.elcarmelohotelhacienda.com,* which also has a hotel (**$$$-$$**) and is right in the old hacienda. **El Catador** ① *Subtanjalla, 10 km northeast from Ica, T056-403295, www. elcatador.pe, good tours in Spanish,* has a shop selling wines, pisco and crafts associated with winemaking. In the evening there's a restaurant-bar with dancing and music. **Viñas Queirolo** ① *Ctra Los Molinos Km 11, T056-403295, www.hotelvinasqueirolo.com,* with an upmarket hotel (**$$$**). **Ocucaje** ① *Ctra Panamericana Sur, Km 335.5, Ocucaje, T01-251 4570, www.ocucaje.com,* a bodega 33 km south of Ica.

## Listings Ica region

### Tourist information

**Paracas**

**iPeru**
*Av Libertadores s/n – Ingreso Bulevar, El Chaco. Wed-Sun 0700-1600.*

**Ica**

**Dircetur**
*Av Grau 148, T056-238710.*
Some tourist information is also available at travel agencies.

### Where to stay

**Pisco**

**$$ San Jorge Residencial**
*Jr Barrio Nuevo 133, T056-532035, on Facebook.*
Smart and modern. Hot water, restaurant, café/bar in garden with pool, secure parking. Swanky and spacious.

**$$-$ El Candelabro**
*Callao y Pedemonte, T056-532620, www.hoteleselcandelabro.com.*
Modern and pleasant, with restaurant. All rooms have bath and fridge. Also run **Hospedaje Pardo** in Pisco and furnished apartments by the sea in San Andrés.

**$$-$ Hostal San Isidro**
*San Clemente 103, T056-536471, http://sanisidrohostal.com.*
Rooms with bath, hot water, safe, nice pool and cafeteria, breakfast extra, kitchen and laundry facilities, games room, parking, English spoken, welcoming. Arranges dune buggy tours and other excursions.

**$$-$ Posada Hispana Hostal**
*Bolognesi 222, T056-536363, www.posadahispana.com.*
Some rooms with loft, all with bath, hot water, can accommodate groups, comfortable, **Café de la Posada** offers *menú,*

information service, English and French spoken. Very good service.

### $ Hostal Tambo Colorado
*Av Bolognesi 159, T056-531379, www.hostaltambocolorado.com.*
Nice *hostal* with pleasant common areas, hot water, small café/bar, use of kitchen, parking. Welcoming, helpful owners are knowledgeable about the area.

## Paracas
Note that the main street is referred to as Av Libertadores or Av Principal.

### $$$$ Hotel Paracas Luxury Collection Resort
*Av Paracas 173, T056-581333, www.libertador.com.pe.*
The famous Hotel Paracas, now part of the Libertador chain of hotels, has been reincarnated as a resort, with spa, pools, excellent rooms in cottages around the grounds, access to beach, choice of top restaurants (**$$$**) including a trattoria, bar, kayaking.

### $$$$ La Hacienda Bahía Paracas
*Lote 25, Urbanización Santo Domingo, 1056-581370, www.hoteleslahacienda.com.*
By the beach in a neighbourhood to the south of the centre, part of a Peruvian chain of luxury hotels, rooms and suites, some with access straight to pool, spa, choice of restaurants, bar.

### $$$$-$$$ Doubletree Guest Suites Paracas
*Lote 30-34, Urbanización Santo Domingo on the outskirts, T01-617 1000, www.doubletree.com.*
Low rise, clean lines and a comfortable size, built around a lovely pool, on beach, water sports, spa, all mod cons and popular with families.

### $$$ Gran Palma
*Av Principal, half block from plaza, T01-665 5933, www.hotelgranpalma.com.*

Elegant hotel in central location convenient for boats, best rooms have sea view, fridge, buffet breakfast on a nice terrace with ocean views, tours.

### $$$-$$ 360 Lagoon Hotel/ Eco Hostel Paracas
*Av Libertadores s/n, T994-816815, www.360lagoonhotel.com.*
Hotel with well-equipped rooms and hostel with 2-room campers with a sitting area and private or shared bath and no shower. Nice common areas are shared by both establishments: artificial lagoon, small pool, restaurant serving breakfast (included) and lunch. Pet friendly. Here too are **Argos Disco** and the excellent and elegant **Il Covo Restaurant** (**$$$**, open 1700-2200, 10% discount for 360 Lagoon Hotel guests), serving authentic Italian food.

### $$$-$$ Bamboo Lodge
*Malecón El Chaco, near Marina Turística, T056-507017, hotelbamboolodge.com/en/paracas/.*
Small rooms with balconies and the best views of the bay, terrace with jacuzzi, **La Muña Restaurant** (**$$**) with good food and atmosphere, nice selection of dishes including vegetarian.

### $$$-$$ Los Frayles
*Av Paracas Mz D lote 9, T056-536255, www.hotelresidenciallosfrayles.com.*
Spacious hotel with terraces, 2 pools, cafeteria, central location just south of El Chaco pier. Across the street is the simpler **Hostal Los Frailes** (www.hostallosfrayles.com) with a variety of simple, well-kept rooms, ocean view. Breakfast included in hotel but extra in *hostal*, tourist information, transfers to/from bus arranged.

### $$-$ Kokopelli
*Av Paracas 128 next to the artisan's market, T056-311824, www.hostel kokopelli.com/paracas.*
Very popular beachfront chain hostel, private rooms with or without bath, 4- to 14-bed dorms with lockers, some with pods (US$9-12), all include breakfast, hot

showers, bar/grill, pool, games room, kayaks and paddle boards, pleasant atmosphere.

### $ Hostal El Amigo
*Oposite Parque Quñones, El Chaco, T056-545042, hostalelamigo@hotmail.com.*
Simple, hot water, very helpful staff. Good value.

### $ Paracas Backpackers House
*Av Los Libertadores, 3 blocks from El Chaco pier, T056-536700, www.paracasbackpackershouse.com.pe.*
Comfortable rooms with and without bath, private and dorms, kitchen facilities, tourist information; at high season prices rise to **$$-$**. Good value and service. Many imitators.

## Ica
Hotels are fully booked during the harvest festival and prices rise. Many hotels are in residential neighbourhoods; insist taxis go to the hotel of your choice.

### $$$$-$$$ Las Dunas
*Av La Angostura 400, T056-256224, www.lasdunashotel.com.*
Variety of rooms and suites. Prices are reduced on weekdays. Packages available. Complete resort with restaurant, bars, swimming pools, many sporting activities and full-day programmes, telescope, playground. Very popular with Peruvians.

### $$$ Villa Jazmin
*Los Girasoles Mz C-1, Lote 7, Res La Angostura, T056-258179, www.villajazmin.net.*
Modern hotel in a residential area near the sand dunes, 8 mins from the city centre, solar heated water, restaurant, buffet breakfast, heated pool, tours arranged, airport and bus transfers, helpful staff, tranquil and very good.

### $$ Princess
*Santa Magdalena D-103, Urbanización Santa María, T056-215421, www.hotelprincess.com.pe.*
Taxi ride from the main plaza, small rooms, frigobar, pool, tourist information, helpful, peaceful, very good.

### $$ Torontel
*JJ Salas 232, a few blocks from the plaza, T056-229073, hoteltorontel.com.*
Ample rooms with tile floors, ceiling fan and a/c, restaurant, parking, good service.

## Huacachina
Note that Malecón Picasso is also known as El Boulevard.

### $$$ Hostería Suiza
*Malecón 264, T056-238762, www.hosteriasuiza.com.pe.*
Overlooking lake, lovely grounds pool and terraces, attracts a more mature crowd, quiet, safe parking.

### $$$ Mossone
*East end of the lake, T056-213630, www.dmhoteles.pe.*
Elegant hacienda-style with a view of the lagoon, occupies 1-5th of the resort, includes good buffet breakfast, full board available, spacious rooms, lovely courtyard and large pool, bilingual staff, bicycles and sandboards.

### $$ Banana's Adventure Hostel
*Av Perotti s/n, T056-237129, www.bananasadventure.com.*
Well-equipped popular hostel with private rooms and 4- to 6-bed dorms (US$23 pp), price includes breakfast and 1 tour, small pool, restaurant with vegetarian and vegan options.

### $$ Carola del Sur
*Av Perotti s/n, T056-237398, www.carolalodge.com.*
Lively popular hotel, large pool, restaurant/bar and disco (open until 0400 at weekends), hammocks, noisy at night, pressure to buy tours. New wing built in 2017. Good value.

### $$ El Huacachinero
*Av Perotti, north of the lagoon, T056-217435, www.elhuacachinero.com. Run by Desert Adventures (see What to do, below).*
One of the more elegant hotels, spacious sparsely furnished but comfortable rooms

overlooking a large pool, comfortable beds, good outside bar and restaurant, ping-pong tables, parking, nice atmosphere offers tours and buggy rides.

### $$-$ Desert Nights
*Near the south shore of the lagoon, T9426 56 261.*
Nice popular hostel with good views of the lagoon, rooms with or without bath and simple dorms, good restaurant (**$$**)/bar, young crowd, run tours. Good reputation, English spoken. In the same group are **Desert Adventures**, **El Huacachinero**, **Huacachina Backpackers House**, **Wild Olive** and **Desert Nights Ecocamp** ($$-$ ecocamphuacachina.com, spacious tents by a pool and restaurant/bar).

### $$-$ Wild Olive
*Av Perotti 154, next to the library, T956-000326, wildolivehuacachina.com.*
Nice guesthouse with private rooms and 4- to 10-bed dorms (sex specific or mixed, US$12 pp) with lockers, ample common areas, kitchen facilities, Italian trattoria (**$$**, 0800-2200) serving pasta and international food on a terrace with views of the lagoon, good service.

### $ Casa de Arena
*Av Perotti s/n, T056-215274, www.hotelcasadearena.com.*
A choice of rooms, some ample and well furnished, other older ones are basic, alsodorms, breakfast extra, Wi-Fi in common areas bar, pool, board hire, popular with backpackers' disco at weekends, party atmosphere, good service.

## Restaurants

### Pisco
**Meqaplaza Mall**, at the entrance to town has a food court, supermarket and other services.

### $$ As de Oro
*San Martín 472, T056-531693, www. asdeoros.com.pe. Closed Mon.*

Wide selection of excellent Peruvian and international food, not cheap but always full at lunchtime, swimming pool, disco some evenings.

### $ Café Maky Neko
*Progreso 297. Open 0900-1500, 1800-2300.*
Cosy restaurant serving juices, sandwiches, ice cream, pizza and pasta, grill, desserts, good coffee.

### $ Enkasa
*Callao 163, T933-910089. Daily 1700-2300.*
Artesanal pizza and pasta, tacos, good coffee. Good personalized service.

---

### Paracas
There are several eating places on the Malecón by Playa El Chaco, all with similar menus (mainly seafood) and prices (in our **$$** range), vegetarian options and open for breakfast, including **Bahía**; **El Ancla**, **Bruce's Restobar**, **Karamba** (has craft beer) and **Muelle Viejo** (restobar). Better-value *menús* are available at lunchtime on the main road. Very good restaurants are found at **Hotel Paracas**, **Bamboo Lodge** and **360 Lagoon Hotel** (see Where to stay, above).

### $$ Paracas
*Av Paracas, near the entrance to the pier, T056-535138, www.restaurantparacas.com. Daily 1000-2300.*
Lovely setting, 2 terraces with excellent view of the bay. Wide selection of dishes, especially seafood.

### Arena Café
*Av Principal, next to Paracas Backpackers. Open 0700-2300.*
Good coffee, snacks, fine desserts, breakfast, pleasant atmosphere.

---

### Ica

### $$ Venezia
*Los Manzanos 146, 8 blocks from the plaza, T056-210372, www.restaurantvenezia.com. Closed Mon.*

Italian and international food, pleasant atmosphere and excellent service.

### $ D'lizia
*Lima 155, Plaza de Armas, T056-237733, www.delizia.com.pe. Open 0700-2300.*
Also in the *patio de comidas* at Plaza Vea mall and in Urbanización Moderna. Modern and bright, for breakfasts, lunches, sandwiches, snacks, ice cream, cakes and sweets, juices and drinks.

### $ Plaza 125
*Lima 125, Plaza de Armas, T056-211816. Open 0700-0100.*
On the plaza, regional and international food as well as breakfast, good-value set lunches.

### Lora Café
*Lima 135, Plaza de Armas. Open 0700-0100.*
Nice café with good food, desserts and coffee.

### Tejas Helena
*Cajamarca 137.*
Sell the best *tejas* and locally made chocolates.

### Huacachina
There are many restaurants around the lagoon, all serving similar fare. Those at hotels **El Huacachinero**, **Desert Nights**, **Wild Olive** and **Banana's Adventure** are good.

### $$ La Casa de Bamboo
*Av Perotti s/n, next to Hostería Suiza, T944-255871.*
Café-bar with wide selection of good food, English breakfast, Marmite, Thai curry, falafel, vegetarian and vegan options, book exchange, games. Also a simple reliable hotel upstairs (**$$**).

## Festivals

### Pisco and around
**End Feb  Verano Negro**. Famous festival in Chincha Alta celebrating black and criollo culture.
**Sep 8  Semana Turística Pisco**. A week of festivities commemorating San Martín's arrival in Peru.

**Nov  Festival de las Danzas Negras** is held in El Carmen, 10 km south of Chincha Alta.

### Ica
**Early Mar  Festival Internacional de la Vendimia** (wine harvest).
**Oct**  The image of **El Señor de Luren** draws pilgrims from all Peru to a fine church in Parque Luren on the 3rd Mon, when there are all-night processions; celebrations start the week before.

## What to do

### Paracas
There are agencies all over town offering trips to the Islas Ballestas, the Paracas reserve, Ica, Nazca and Tambo Colorado. A 2-hr boat tour to the islands costs US$13-15 pp, including park entrance fee and tax, departure 0800. Usually, agencies will pool 40 clients together in 1 boat. An agency that does not pool clients is **Huacachina**, based in Ica, with an office in Paracas, T056-215582, www.huacachinatours.com. Do not book tours on the street.
**Zarcillo Connections**, *Av Principal de Ingreso a El Chaco 101, Paracas, T056-536636, www.zarcilloconnections.com*. With long experience for trips to the Paracas National Reserve, Tambo Colorado, trekking and tours to Ica, Chincha and the Nazca Lines and surrounding sites. Agent for **Cruz del Sur** buses. Also has its own hotel, **Zarcillo Paradise**, in Paracas.

### Ica
Agencies offer city tours (US$11), trips to the Nazca Lines, Paracas and Islas Ballestas, plus dune buggies and sandboarding.
**AV Dolphin Travel**, *C Lima 176, Plaza de Armas, T056-218920, www.av-dolphintravelperu.com*.
**Desert Travel**, *Lima 171, inside Tejas Don Juan on the plaza, T056-227215, www.agenciadeserttravel.blogspot.com*.
**Ica Desert Trip**, *Bolívar 178, T056-237373, www.icadeserttrip.com*. Roberto Penny

Cabrera (speaks Spanish and English) offers 1-, 2- and 3-day trips off-road into the desert, archaeology, geology, etc. 4 people maximum, contact by email in advance. Take toilet paper, something warm for the evening, a long-sleeved loose cotton shirt for daytime and long trousers. Recommended, but "not for the faint-hearted".

## Huacachina

Dune buggies (*tubulares*) do white-knuckle, rollercoaster tours for US$12-15 (plus a small municipal fee); some start at 1000 but most between 1600 and 1700 to catch the sunset, 2½ hrs. Taking a tour with an official operator is recommended, there have been fatal accidents with inexperienced drivers. **Desert Adventures**, *Huacachina, T056-228458, www.desertadventure.net*. Frequently recommended for sandboarding and camping trips into the desert by 4WD and buggies, French, English and Spanish spoken. Also to beaches, Islas Ballestas and Nazca Lines flights. In the same group are several hotels (see Where to stay, above).

### Pisco
### Air

Capitán RE Olivera airport, originally a military base, has a new passenger terminal. **LATAM** flies twice weekly to Cuzco. **Aerodiana** (T01-447 6824, aerodiana.com.pe) and **Alas Peruanas** (T056-522444, http://alasperuanas.com) offer Nazca Lines overflights.

### Bus

Buses drop passengers at San Clemente on Panamericana Sur (**El Cruce**); many bus companies and tour agencies have their offices here. It's a 10-km taxi ride from the centre, US$8, or US$10 to Paracas. *Colectivos* leave from the 1st block of San Juan de Dios, near the plaza, for El Cruce when full, US$0.15. From town to **Paracas** via San Andrés, *colectivos* from first block of Callao when full, US$1.25 (US$0.50 to San Andrés),

30 mins; taxi US$7. From El Cruce to Paracas, **Soyuz** at 0700, US$2.50, 40 mins.

To **Lima**, 242 km, 4 hrs, US$7.70. The best company is **Soyuz**, every 2 hrs from El Cruce. **Flores** is the only company that goes into Pisco town (Piedemonte corner San Martín), from Lima (12 daily) and Ica (7 daily), but buses are poor and services erratic. To **Ica**, US$1.55, 45 mins, 70 km, also *colectivos*. To **Nazca**, 210 km, take a bus to Ica and then change to another bus or a *colectivo*. To **Ayacucho**, 220 km, 6 hrs, US$11-1610, several buses daily with **Palomino, Antezana** and **Oropesa** leave from El Cruce; book in advance and take warm clothing as it gets cold at night. To **Huancavelica** via Castrovirreyna at 4600 m, 269 km, 6-7 hrs, US$10, with **Oropesa** and **Oro Bus** coming from Ica; car service with **Palomino**, T948 016767, US$10.80, 5 hrs. To **Arequipa**, US$17, 12 hrs, many daily.

To **Tambo Colorado**, buses depart from near the plaza in Pisco at 0800, US$2.50, 3 hrs; also *colectivos*. Alight 20 mins after the stop at Humay; the road passes right through the site. For buses back to Pisco in the afternoon, wait at the caretaker's house. By taxi about US$24 one way or US$36 return.

### Paracas

To **Lima**, US$14-31, 4½ hrs, 5 daily with **Cruz del Sur**; at 1025 with **Soyuz** (1640 from Lima); at 0950 with **Oltursa** (0630 from Lima). To **Ica** US$3.70-13, 1¼ hrs, at 0720 and 1635 with **Soyuz**; 5 daily with **Cruz del Sur**. To **Nazca** US$15-22, 3½-4 hrs, 5 daily with **Cruz del Sur**), at 1015 with **Oltursa**, or transfer in Ica. Agencies in Paracas sell direct transfers between Paracas and Huacachina, with **Pelican Perú**, www.pelicanperu.com, at 1050 daily, US$7, comfortable and secure.

### Ica
### Air

Aeródromo Las Dunas is to the northwest of the city. **Aerodiana** (T01-447 6824, aerodiana.com.pe), **Alas Peruanas** (T056-522444, http://alasperuanas.com) and **Móvil**

**Air** (T940-495155, www.movilair.com.pe) offer Nazca Lines overflights from Ica.

## Bus

Most bus offices are on Lambayeque block 1 and Av Matías Manzanilla. To **Pisco**, 70 km, US$1.55-2.50, 45 mins, 11 daily with **Soyuz** (Av Manzanilla 130, www.soyuzonline.com.pe), also *colectivos*.To **Paracas**, US$3.70-13, 1¼ hrs, at 0915 and 1500 with **Soyuz**; 5 daily with **Cruz del Sur** (C Fray Ramón Rojas y Sebastián Barranca). To **Lima**, 302 km, 4½ hrs, US$9-26 several daily including **Soyuz** about every hour 0030-2130, **Cruz del Sur**, 16 daily and **Oltursa** (Av Ayabaca 974), 8 daily. To **Arequipa**, 706 km, US$28-46, 11½ hrs, with **Cruz del Sur** (6 daily), **Oltursa** (1 daily) and

6 others, via Nazca. To **Nazca**, 140 km, 2½ hrs, US$3.70, several companies including: **Cueva** (Huánuco 479), every 40 mins, 0630-2000; **Palomino** (Lambayeque 135), hourly 0510-1810; and **Soyuz** every 45 mins (0330-2130); with **Cruz del Sur**, 9 daily (US$13-18). Also minivans US$4.60 and *colectivos*, US$6.15, from Av JJ Elías, opposite Colegio San Luis Gonzaga, leave when full, 2 hrs. To **Cuzco**, US$28-57, 17 hrs, with **Cruz del Sur** (2 daily), **Oltursa** (1 daily), **Palomino** (Lambayeque 135, 2 daily) and others. To **Huancavelica**, US$11, 7-8 hrs, with **Oro Bus** (Lambayeque 135) and **Oropesa** (Huánuco 497). To **Ayacucho**, US$12-17, 7 hrs, with **Palomino**, **Antezana** (Lambayeque 135) and **Oropesa**.

# Nazca
## & around

Set in a green valley amid a perimeter of mountains, Nazca's altitude puts it just above any fog which may drift in from the sea. Nearby are the mysterious, world-famous Nazca Lines and numerous other ancient sites.

**Nazca town** *Colour map 5, B3.*

Nazca town lies 140 km south of Ica via the Pan-American Highway (444 km from Lima) and is the tourist centre for visiting the Nazca Lines. Jirón Bolognesi, west of the Plaza de Armas, is a promenade where locals stroll; many services are concentrated here. **Museo Antonini** ① *Av de la Cultura 600, eastern end of Jr Lima (10 min walk from the plaza), T056-523444, CISRAP@numerica.it, daily 0900-1900 (ring the bell), US$4.60, students US$2.15, guiding extra (about US$6 for group of 10), US$1.60 to take photos,* houses the discoveries of Professor Orefici and his team from the huge pre-Inca city at Cahuachi (see page 212),

**Nazca**

| Where to stay | Restaurants | |
|---|---|---|
| 1 Alegría | 1 Coffee Break | 9 Mamashana & |
| 2 Casa Andina Standard | 2 El Huarango | Vía La Encantada |
| 3 DM Hoteles Nasca | 3 Kañada | 10 Mom's Café |
| 4 Hostal Guillens | 4 La Choza | |
| 5 Majoro | 5 La Kasa Rústika | |
| 6 Oro Viejo | 6 La Maison Blanche | |
| 7 Posada de Don Hono | 7 La Taberna | |
| 8 Posada Guadalupe | 8 Los Angeles | |
| 9 Wasipunko | | |

N

200 metres
200 yards

which, Orefici believes, holds the key to understanding the Nazca Lines. Many tombs survived the *huaqueros* (tomb robbers), and there are displays of mummies, ceramics, textiles, amazing *antaras* (pan pipes) and photos of the excavations. In the garden is a pre-Hispanic aqueduct. Recommended.

The **Maria Reiche Planetarium** ① *DM Hoteles Nasca, T056-522293, show daily usually at 1930 in English, 2030 in Spanish, US$6.15*, offers introductory lectures every night about the Nazca Lines, based on Reiche's theories, which cover archaeology and astronomy. The show lasts about 45 minutes, after which visitors are able to look at the moon, planets and stars through telescopes.

Viktoria Nikitzki, a colleague of Maria Reiche, gives one-hour lectures about the Nazca Lines at **Dr Maria Reiche Centre** ① *Av de los Espinales 300, 1 block from Ormeño bus stop, T965-888056, viktorianikitzki@hotmail.com, US$5*. She also organizes tours in June and December (phone in advance to confirm times or to ask about volunteer work).

Just south of town are the **Paredones ruins and aqueduct** ① *entry US$3 (including El Telar Geoglyphs, Acueductos de Cantayoc and Las Agujas Geoglyphs), tour to all these sites US$12-15 pp, taxi to Paredones US$2.50 or US$12-15 to visit all the sites*. The ruins, also called Cacsamarca, are Inca on a pre-Inca base but are not well preserved. However, the underground aqueducts, built 300 BC-AD 700, are still in working order and worth seeing. A 30-minute to one-hour walk through Buena Fe (or organize a taxi from your hotel) will bring you to the Cantayoc, Las Agujas and El Telar sites, which consist of markings in the valley floor and ancient aqueducts descending in spirals into the ground. The markings consist of a triangle pointing to a hill and a telar (cloth) with a spiral depicting the threads. Climb the mountain to see better examples.

## ★Nazca Lines

Cut into the stony desert above the Ingenio valley north of Nazca are the famous Nazca Lines, thought to have been etched onto the Pampa Colorada sands by three different groups: the Paracas people (700 BC-AD 200), the Nazcas (200 BC-AD 600) and the Huari settlers from Ayacucho (about AD 630); see Origins of the Lines, below. There are large numbers

> **Tip...**
> Maria Reiche's book, *Mystery on the Desert*, is on sale in Nazca for US$10 (proceeds to conservation work). Another good book is *Pathways to the Gods: the mystery of the Nazca Lines*, by Tony Morrison (Michael Russell, 1978).

of lines, not only parallels and geometrical figures, but also recognizable designs, including a dog, an enormous monkey, birds (one with a wing span of over 100 m), a spider and a tree. They are best seen from the air (see What to do, page 216), but three of the huge designs – the Hand, the Lizard (bisected by the Pan-American Highway) and the Tree – can also be viewed from the **Mirador Metálico** ① *25.3 km northwest of Nazca town on the Pan-American Highway, entry US$1, Mon-Fri 0800-1730*, a metal tower paid for by Maria Reiche in 1976. Go early before it is too hot and allow enough time, queues are long and the lookout is always crowded. There is also a good view of some Lines from the hill 300 m back to Nazca known as **Mirador Natural**. In 1994 Maria Reiche also opened a small site museum in the cottage she occupied for many years, **Museo Maria Reiche** ① *Panamericana Sur Km 421, 29.3 km from Nazca, entry US$1.55, students US$0.75, 0800-1800*, with information about Reiche's studies, maps, photos and scale models of the figures. María and her sister Renata are buried in the garden. Tours to the natural and tower lookouts and the museum cost US$24-26 per person, not including entry fees; taxis

## BACKGROUND
## Guardian of the Lines

The greatest contribution to our awareness of the Nazca Lines was made by Maria Reiche, who was born in Dresden in 1903 and died in Lima in 1998. The young German mathematician arrived in Peru in the early 1930s and lived and worked on the pampa for over 50 years, dedicating her life to removing centuries of windswept debris and carrying out painstaking survey work. She even used to sleep on the pampa.

Maria Reiche's years of meticulous measurement and study of the Lines led her to the conclusion that they represented a huge astronomical calendar. She also used her mathematical knowledge to determine how the many drawings and symbols could have been created with such precise symmetry. She suggested that those responsible for the Lines used long cords attached to stakes in the ground. The figures were drawn by means of a series of circular arcs of different radius. Reiche also contended that they used a standard unit of measurement of 1.30 m, or the distance between the fingertips of a person's extended arms.

As well as the anthropomorphic and zoomorphic drawings, there are a great many geometric figures. Reiche believed these to be a symbolic form of writing associated with the movements of the stars. In this way, the Lines could have been used as a kind of calendar that not only recorded celestial events but also had a very important practical function, indicating the times for harvest, fishing and festivals.

Whatever the real purpose of the Nazca Lines, one fact remains indisputable: that their status as one of the country's major tourist attractions is largely due to the selfless work of Maria Reiche, the unofficial guardian of the Lines.

charge US$24 per person; alternatively, take one of the frequent buses on the Nazca–Ica line (see Transport, page 216, US$1.25 to the attractions; note that the fancier services do not stop here).

**Origins of the Lines** The Nazcas had a highly developed civilization which reached its peak about AD 600. Their polychrome ceramics, wood carvings and adornments of gold are on display in many of Lima's museums. The Paracas people represented an early phase of the Nazca culture, renowned for their superb technical quality and stylistic variety in weaving and pottery. The Nazcas were succeeded by the Huari Empire, in conjunction with the Tiahuanaco culture, which dominated much of Peru from AD 600-1000.

The German expert, Dr Maria Reiche, who studied the Lines for over 40 years, mostly from a step ladder, maintained that they represent some sort of vast astronomical pre-Inca calendar. Other theories abound, that the Lines are the tracks of running contests (Georg A von Breunig, 1980, and English astronomer Alan Sawyer); that they were used for ritualized walking (Anthony Aveni); that they represent weaving patterns and yarns

**Tip...**
The best times to fly over the Nazca Lines are between 0800 and 1000 and again between 1500 and 1630, when there is less turbulence and better light (assuming there is no fog). Flights are bumpy with many tight turns; many people get airsick, so it's wise not to eat or drink just before a flight.

(Henri Stierlin) and that the plain is a map of the Tiahuanaco Empire (Zsoltan Zelko). Johan Reinhard proposes that the Lines conform to fertility practices throughout the Andes, in common with the use of straight lines in Chile and Bolivia. William H Isbell proposed that the Lines are the equivalent of pyramid-building in other parts of Peru in the same period, with the added purpose of controlling population growth through mass labour.

Another theory, based on the idea that the Lines are best seen from the air, is that the ancient Nazcas flew in hot-air balloons (Jim Woodman, 1977, and, in part, the BBC series *Ancient Voices*). A related idea is that the Lines were not designed to be seen physically from above, but from the mind's eye of the flying shaman. Both theories are supported by pottery and textile evidence which shows balloonists and a flying creature emitting discharge from its nose and mouth. There are also local legends of flying men. The depiction in the desert of creatures such as a monkey or killer whale suggests the qualities needed by the shaman in his spirit journeys.

After six years' work at La Muña and Los Molinos near Palpa (43 km north of Nazca) using photogrammetry, Peruvian archaeologist Johny Isla and Markus Reindel of the Swiss-Liechtenstein Foundation deduced that the Lines on both the Palpa and Nazca plains were offerings dedicated to the worship of water and fertility, two elements which also dominate on ceramics and on the engraved stones of the Paracas culture. Isla and Reindel believe that the Palpa Lines predate those at Nazca and that these lines and drawings are themselves scaled-up versions of the Paracas drawings. This research proposes that the Nazca culture succumbed not to drought, but to heavy rainfall, probably during an El Niño event.

In all probability, there was no single, overriding significance to the Lines for the people who made them. Some of the theories attached to them may capture parts of their meaning, and, no doubt, more theories and new discoveries will be tested to cast fresh light on the puzzle.

## Other excursions

Overlooking Nazca town to the east is **Cerro Blanco**, the highest sand dune in the world at 2078 m. Tours to the dune start very early in the morning and involve a three-hour hike to the summit. Descents can be made on dune buggies, or by sandboarding or parapenting.

The Nazca area is dotted with over 100 ancient cemeteries, where the dry, humidity-free climate has perfectly preserved invaluable tapestries, cloth and mummies. At **Chauchilla** ① *27 km south of Nazca, last 12 km a sandy track, US$2.50, open 0600-1800, taxi US$25,* huaqueros ransacked the tombs and left bones, skulls, mummies and pottery shards littering the desert. A tour takes about two hours and usually includes a visit to a small family gold-processing shop where very old-fashioned techniques are still used.

One hour west of the Nazca Lines along a rough dirt track, **Cahuachi** ① *24 km northwest of Nazca town, open 0800-1730, entry free, US$21-24 pp on a tour (including Acueductos de Ocongalla and Chauchilla cemetery, US$24-28 per vehicle in private taxi,* is a Nazca ceremonial site comprising some 30 pyramids. About 8% of the site has been excavated so far and work continues in 2018, some of it has been reconstructed. Some believe it could be larger than Chan Chán, making it the largest adobe city in the world (see also Museo Antonini, page 209). Some 4 km beyond Cahuachi is a site called **Estaquería** ① *open 0800-1730, entry free,* thought to have been a series of astronomical sighting posts; more recent research suggests the wooden pillars were used to dry dead bodies and therefore it may have been a place of mummification.

On the coast, 70 km west of Nazca, **Reserva Nacional de San Fernando** ① *entry free, request permit from Sernanp, Calle Arica 494, Nazca, T968-218448, rnsanfernando@sernanp. gob.pe, 4WD vehicle recommended,* was established in 2011 to protect migratory and local land and oceanic wildlife, such as the Humboldt penguin, sea lions, the Andean fox, dolphins and whales. Condors are usually seen here and guanacos may also be spotted, which is unusual for the coast. San Fernando is located in the highest part of the Peruvian coastal desert, where the Nazca Plate lifts the continental plate, generating moist accumulation in the ground with resulting seasonal winter flora and a continental wildlife corridor between the high coastal mountains and the sea. Full-day and two-day/ one-night tours are offered by some agencies in town.

## ★ Towards Cuzco: Sondondo Valley

Two hours out of Nazca on the paved road to Abancay and Cuzco is the **Reserva Nacional Pampa Galeras Bárbara D'Achille** ① *Calle Grau 494, Nazca, T056 522770, www.sernanp. gob.pe/pampa-galeras-barbara-d-achille, entry free,* at 4100 m, with the largest population of vicuñas in Peru It has an interesting site museum, an interpretation centre and a basic shelter. At Km 155 is **Puquio**, an uninspiring commercial centre which provides access to **Andamarca** and the surrounding villages of the splendid **Sondondo Valley** ① *T931-219013, valledelsondondo@gmail.com, valledelsondondo.turismo on Facebook,* in the south of the department of Ayacucho. Sondondo offers 5600 ha of ancient terraced slopes (many still in use), the largest population of condors in Peru (with luck, some 35 birds can be spotted from the Mirador de Mayobamba), *Puyas raimondii*, rock formations, thermal springs, lakes and waterfalls, Wari, Chanka and Inca archaeological sites, small friendly villages and great walking opportunities. This off-the-beaten-path area is gradually opening up to tourism and infrastructure is improving in Andamarca, Aucará, Cabana, Chipao and Mayobamba. There are minivans and buses from Puquio and Ayacucho. Beyond Puquio, it's another 185 km to **Chalhuanca**. There are wonderful views on this stretch, with lots of small villages, valleys and alpacas.

## Puerto Inca

*Taxi from Chala US$8, or colectivo or bus towards Nazca as far as the turn-off at Km 610.*

On the coast 143 km southeast of Nazca and 10 km north of the fishing village of **Chala**, are the large pre-Columbian ruins of Puerto Inca. This was the port for Cuzco during Inca times. The site is in excellent condition: the drying and store houses can be seen as holes in the ground (be careful where you walk), there are also remains of dwellings. On the right side of the bay is a cemetery and on the hill starts the Inca road from the coast to Cuzco. The road was 240 km long, with a staging post every 7 km so that, with a change of runner at every post, seafood could be sent in 24 hours. The site is best appreciated when the sun is shining. On the beach near the ruins is the resort of **Puerto Inka** ($$$-$$, www. puertoinka.com.pe), with cabins (hot), camping and watersports.

## Tourist information

**iPerú** is located at the airport (iperunasca@
promperu.gob.pe, daily 0700-1600). The
**tourist police** and regular police are at
Av Los Incas cuadra 1, T056-522084 (T105
for emergencies).

## Where to stay

If arriving by bus, beware of touts who tell
you that the hotel of your choice is closed,
or full. If you phone or email, the hotel
should pick you up at the bus station free
of charge, day or night.

**$$$ DM Hoteles Nasca (Nazca Lines)**
*Jr Bolognesi 147, T056-522293,*
*www.dmhoteles.pe.*
Former **Nazca Lines Hotel**, now part of the
Peruvian chain. Lovely facilities and rooms
conserving the original style, a/c, rooms with
private patio, peaceful, restaurant, parking,
pool (US$9-10.50 pp includes sandwich and
drink), tours.

**$$$ Majoro**
*Panamericana Sur Km 452, T056-522490,*
*www.hotelmajoro.com.*
A charming old hacienda about 5 km from
town past the airstrip so quite remote,
elegant rooms, beautiful gardens, pool,
slow and expensive restaurant, quiet and
welcoming, good arrangements for flights
and tours.

**$$$ Wasipunko**
*Panamericana Sur Km 462, 15 mins south of*
*Nazca, T056-631183, www.wasipunko.com.*
Ecolodge in an old ranch with adobe buildings,
rustic rooms, highly regarded restaurant
(especially the *pachamanca*), camping
US$8 pp. Run by Olivia Sejuro, a painter
who aims to rescue local cuisine and other
cultural traditions. Expensive for the simple
infrastructure, but the value is in experiencing
the tranquillity of the dry forest in the desert
and the authentic food. Recommended.

**$$$-$$ Casa Andina Standard**
*Jr Bolognesi 367, T01-213 9739,*
*www.casa-andina.com.*
Part of the Peruvian hotel chain. Bright,
modern decor, central patio with palm trees,
pool, restaurant and the very good **Sama
Café**, overlooking Jr Bolognesi.

**$$ Alegría**
*Jr Lima 166, T056-522702,*
*www.hotelalegria.net.*
Popular with large groups, rooms with hot
water, restaurant, cafeteria, pool, garden,
English, Hebrew, Italian and German spoken,
laundry facilities, book exchange, ATM,
parking, bus terminal transfers. OK but can
be noisy from disco and traffic. Also has a
tour agency where guests are encouraged
to buy tours (see What to do), flights and
bus tickets.

**$$ Oro Viejo**
*Callao 483, T056-521112,*
*hoteloroviejo@hotmail.com.*
Has a suite with jacuzzi and comfortable
standard rooms, nice garden, swimming
pool, restaurant and bar. Recommended.

**$$ Posada de Don Hono**
*Av María Reiche 112, T056-523991,*
*laposadadedonhono1@hotmail.com.*
Close to the plaza yet quiet and with a
country feeling. Nice bungalows with
terrace surrounded by plants, small rooms,
good restaurant, parking. Good value.
Recommended.

**$ Hostal Guillens**
*Av Los Incas 117, T056-522497.*
Basic, hot water, hammocks, nice garden,
camping, restaurant.

**$ Posada Guadalupe**
*San Martín 225, T056-522249.*
Very economical, family-run, lovely courtyard
and garden, hot water, with or without bath,
good breakfast, relaxing. (Touts selling tours
are nothing to do with the hotel.)

## Restaurants

A choice of restaurants is found along the promenade of Jr Bolognesi.

### $$$-$$ La Kasa Rústika
*Bolognesi 372, T056-32463, lakasarustika.com.pe.*
Upmarket restaurant and bar with extensive menu of Peruvian and international dishes, especially meat and seafood, good ambiance and service.

### $$$-$$ Vía La Encantada
*Bolognesi 282, 1056-524216, on Facebook.*
Modern, stylish with great food – fish, meat or vegetarian, good-value lunches; also hotel.

### $$ Mamashana
*Bolognesi 270, T056-521286, www.mamashana.com.*
Rustic style with a lively atmosphere, for breakfast, grills, Peruvian dishes, pastas (including several vegetarian choices) and pizzas. Varied menu, good food and service.

### $$-$ La Choza
*Bolognesi 290, T981-620 870.*
Nice rustic decor with woven chairs and thatched roof, Peruvian and other types of food.

### $$-$ La Maison Blanche
*Bolognesi 388, T056-522361, on Facebook.*
European-style crêperie, café, bar. Tasty dishes and desserts, excellent vegetarian options, some outdoor seating.

### $$-$ La Taberna
*Jr Lima 321, T056-521411.*
Excellent food, live music, popular with gringos, it's worth a look just for the graffiti on the walls. A bit dated but still good.

### $ El Huarango
*Arica 602, T056-522141.*
National and international (including Cajun) cuisine. Relaxed family atmosphere and deliciously breezy terrace.

### $ Kañada
*Lima 160, nazcanada@yahoo.com.*

Cheap cevichería, good *menú*, excellent *pisco sours*, nice wines, a bit run down but food is good, popular, display of local artists' work, English spoken, helpful.

### $ Los Angeles
*Bolognesi 266.*
Good, cheap, vegetarian options, try the *sopa criolla* and the chocolate cake.

## Cafés

### Coffee Break
*Bolognesi 219. Sun-Fri 0700-2300.*
For real coffee and good pizzas; bright somewhat gaudy.

### Mom's Café
*Lima 168, next to Hotel Alegría.*
Pleasant café, good coffee, breakfast, sandwiches, milkshakes, salads, desserts.

## Festivals

**29 Aug-10 Sep** **Virgen de Guadalupe** festival.

## What to do

**Land-based tours**
All guides must be approved by the Ministry of Tourism and should have an official identity card. Touts (*jaladores*) operate at popular hotels and the bus terminals using false ID cards and fake hotel and tour brochures. Better buy your tour from agencies at their office, or phone or email the company you want to deal with in advance. Many hotels also offer tours with approved guides, some are not above pressurising guests to purchase tours at inflated prices. Taxi drivers usually act as guides, but most speak only Spanish and their prices are similar to those from agencies. Do not take just any taxi on the plaza for a tour; always ask your hotel for a reputable driver.
**Alegría Tours**, *Lima 186, T056-522497, http://alegriatoursperu.com*. Tours to local and regional destinations, also throughout southern Peru. Guided hikes to nearby sites.

Guides speak English, German, French and Italian. They also offer adventure tours, such as mountain biking from 4000 m in the Andes down to the plain, sandboarding, and more.

**Huarango Travel Service**, *Arica 602, T056-522141, huarangotravel@yahoo.es.* Tours around Ica, Paracas, Huacachina, Nazca and Palpa.

**Mystery Peru**, *Simón Bolívar 221, T01-435 0051, T956-691155, www.mysteryperu.com.* Owned by Enrique Levano Alarcón, based in Nazca with many local tours, also packages throughout Peru.

**Nazca Perú 4x4**, *in a suburb south of the city, T975-017029, on Facebook.* Tubular (buggy) 4WD tours to San Fernando National Reserve and other off-the-beaten-track locations.

### Sightseeing flights

10 companies operate small planes for 2-12 passengers to see the Nazca Lines. There are different options, depending on the number of figures included; 12-13 figures are seen in a 30-min flight, for about US$80; 20-24 figures are seen in a 1-hr flight, running about US$170; there are options to fly over the Nazca Lines plus other attractions such as the Palpa Lines (equally impressive as those of Nazca, 1 hr, US$200) or the Cahuachi and Paredones archaeological sites (45 mins, USD$180). Packages combining flights and visits to other attractions in the region (ie Paracas, Ballestas, sandboarding, buggy rides) are also on offer, as are full-day trips out of Lima combining bus travel plus flights. Shop around, there are many promotions. A US$10 airport tax must be added to the cost. Most tours include transport to the airport; otherwise it's US$5 by taxi or US$0.25 by bus. It is best to organize a flight with the airlines themselves at the airport. They will weigh you and select a group of passengers based on weight, so you may have to wait a while for your turn. Passengers 95 kg or over must pay for 2 seats.

**Aero Diana**, *T01-447 6824, www.aerodiana.com.pe.* Daily flights aboard 12-passenger planes over the Lines, from Nazca, Ica and Pisco.

**Aero Paracas**, *T01-641 7000, www.aeroparacas.com.* Daily flights over the Nazca and Palpa Lines, since 1992.

**Alas Peruanas**, *T056-522444, http://alasperuanas.com, or through Hotel Alegría.* Experienced pilots offer flights over the Nazca and Palpa Lines and over archaeological sites, starting in Nazca, Ica or Pisco. All **Alas Peruanas** flights include the BBC film of Nazca.

**Móvil Air**, *T940 495155, www.movilair.com.pe.* Flights over Nazca and Palpa Lines from Nazca and Ica in 4- to 12-passenger planes; also full-day tours starting in Lima.

## Transport

### Air
The airport caters only for sightseeing flights.

### Bus
It is worth paying extra for a good bus; there are reports of robbery on the cheaper services. Over-booking is common. Several transport companies share a private station known as **Terminal Terrestre**, at Lima 155; others have their own stations.

To **Lima**, 446 km, 7½ hrs, several buses daily, US$11-40. **Cruz del Sur** (Lima y San Martín, next to Terminal Terrestre, T056-523713), via Ica, some also via Paracas, 10 daily, **Oltursa** (Terminal Terrestre, T056-522265), 3 daily, **Móvil Tours** (Terminal Terrestre, T940 495155), at 0600 (4 daily from Lima). To **Ica**, 2½ hrs, US$3.70, several companies including: **Cueva** (Av Los Incas 108, T056-523846), every 40 mins, 0630-2000; **Palomino** (Terminal Terrestre, T056-524220), hourly 0510-1810; **Soyuz** (Terminal Terrestre, T056-521464) every 40 mins, 0430-2100; with **Cruz del Sur**, 9 daily (US$13-18). Also minivans US$4.60 and *colectivos*, US$6.15, from Av los Incas next to Primax petrol station, Ovalo Nasca, as they fill, 2 hrs. For **Pisco** (210 km), 3 hrs, buses stop at El Cruce, 5 km outside town (see under Pisco, Transport), so change in Ica for direct transport into Pisco or take a *colectivo* from

El Cruce. To **Paracas**, US$15-22, 3½-4 hrs, 5 daily with **Cruz del Sur**; at 0630 with **Oltursa**, or transfer in Ica.

To **Arequipa**, 565 km, 9 hrs, US$19-22.50, or US$28-52 for *bus cama* services: **Cruz del Sur** 4 daily and **Oltursa** at 1400 and 2200, reliable, comfortable and secure on this route. Delays are possible out of Nazca because of drifting sand across the road or because of mudslides in the rainy season. Travel in daylight if possible. Book your ticket the previous day. To **Cuzco**, 659 km paved, via **Puquio**, **Chalhuanca** and **Abancay**, US$26-48, 14-15 hrs, several companies (service originating in Lima) depart Nazca 2000-2400, including **Cruz del Sur**, **Oltursa**, **Palomino**, **Tepsa** (Terminal Terrestre), **Civa** (Terminal Terrestre).

# Arequipa &
## the far south

The colonial city of Arequipa is the ideal place to start exploring southern Peru. The distinctive volcanic sillar stone used for building its churches, mansions and Plaza de Armas has given it the nickname 'White City'. In contrast, Arequipa's most famous colonial jewel, the Santa Catalina Convent, is painted in bright colours, a gorgeous little city within a city.

Urban Arequipa is, however, only one attraction in a region of towering volcanoes, deep canyons, terraced valleys and clear rivers well suited to rafting. Arequipa is the gateway to the Cotahuasi Canyon, the world's deepest at 3354 m, and its more popular neighbour, Colca. There is excellent trekking and riding on the canyons' terraces and the calendar is full of festivals. Above all, Colca is an easy place to get a close-up view of the majestic condor rising on the morning thermals. On the altiplano there are lakes, herds of alpaca and vicuña and, at the World Heritage Site of Toro Muerto, the largest field of petroglyphs in the world.

From Arequipa routes lead west to Lake Titicaca and south to the Chilean border near Tacna via the pleasant city of Moquegua.

**Best** for
Architecture ▪ Food ▪ Scenery ▪ Trekking

Arequipa & around . . . . . . . . . . 222
Colca & Cotahuasi canyons . . 241
South of Arequipa . . . . . . . . . . 253

# Footprint picks

## ★ Santa Catalina Convent, page 223

This beautifully restored convent and its treasure trove of art allows you to travel back in time and step into a Spanish colonial town.

## ★ Museo Santuarios Andinos, page 223

Meet 'Juanita', the Inca child mummy from the glaciers of Ampato, and learn about human sacrifice in pre-Columbian times.

## ★ Casa Museo Vargas Llosa, page 226

Let the Nobel laureate Mario Vargas Llosa tell you about his life, and meet some of the characters in his novels at this innovative modern museum.

## ★ Colca Canyon, page 241

Known as the easiest place in Peru to see the majestic condor, Colca also offers stunning scenery, quaint indigenous villages set on pre-Columbian terraces and very popular trekking.

## ★ Cotahuasi Canyon, page 249

Still an off-the-beaten-path destination, but not for much longer, the deepest canyon in the world is a land of green oases and hanging valleys amid arid slopes. It offers waterfalls, thermal baths and archaeological sites as well as great trekking and challenging kayaking.

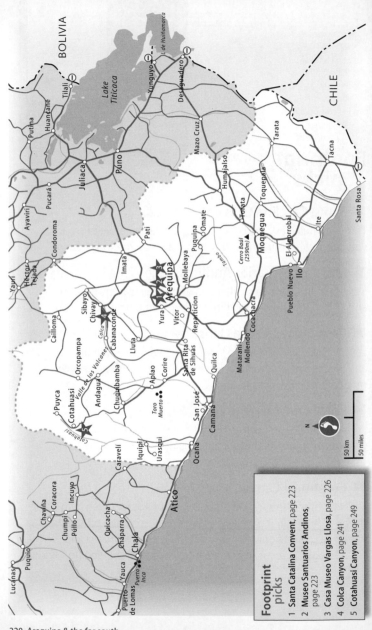

BOLIVIA

CHILE

Lake Titicaca

## Footprint picks

1 Santa Catalina Convent, page 223
2 Museo Santuarios Andinos, page 223
3 Casa Museo Vargas Llosa, page 226
4 Colca Canyon, page 241
5 Cotahuasi Canyon, page 249

N

50 km
50 miles

# Essential Arequipa and the far south

## Finding your feet

Arequipa is the main commercial centre and transport hub for the south, with flights and long-distance buses to/from Lima and other major cities. **4M Express** (www.4m-express.com), provides a useful service from Arequipa or Chivay east to Puno or north Cuzco. Head south from Arequipa to reach Moquegua and the coast, where both the Vía Costenera and the Pan-American Highway run down to the Chilean border.

## Best Arequipeño restaurants
**Crepísimo**
**Hatunpa**
**La Nueva Palomino**
**Tío Darío**
**Zig Zag**
For details of these restaurants and information on Arequipeña cuisine, see pages 231-232.

## Getting around

In Arequipa, the main places of interest and the hotels are within walking distance of the Plaza de Armas. If you are going to the suburbs, take a bus or taxi. Traffic can be chaotic, making the city noisy; perhaps a planned public transit system will help. Public buses run from Arequipa to both the Colca and Cotahuasi canyons, although tourist services may be more reliable. Buses and colectivos connect villages in the canyon areas; there are also numerous trekking opportunities.

## When to go

The climate in Arequipa is delightful, with a mean daytime temperature in the low 20s. The sun shines on 360 days of the year and average annual rainfall is just 100 mm.

## Time required

One week is enough time to explore the city and its immediate surroundings.

## Weather Arequipa

| January | February | March | April | May | June |
|---|---|---|---|---|---|
| 20°C | 20°C | 20°C | 21°C | 21°C | 20°C |
| 10°C | 10°C | 10°C | 9°C | 8°C | 7°C |
| 20mm | 10mm | 10mm | 0mm | 0mm | 0mm |

| July | August | September | October | November | December |
|---|---|---|---|---|---|
| 20°C | 20°C | 21°C | 21°C | 21°C | 21°C |
| 7°C | 7°C | 8°C | 8°C | 8°C | 9°C |
| 0mm | 0mm | 0mm | 0mm | 0mm | 0mm |

# Arequipa
## & around

The city of Arequipa (population one million) stands in a beautiful valley 1011 km from Lima, at the foot of the perfect cone of El Misti volcano (5822 m), guarded on either side by the mountains Chachani (6057 m), and Pichu-Pichu (5669 m). The city has fine Spanish buildings and many old and interesting churches built of sillar, a pearly white volcanic stone almost exclusively used in the construction of Arequipa. The city was re-founded on 15 August 1540 by an emissary of Pizarro, but it had previously been occupied by Aymara peoples and the Incas. It is the main commercial centre for the south and is a busy place. Arequipeños have an independent spirit and many resent Lima's domination of Peruvian affairs. Arequipa has been declared a World Cultural Heritage Site by UNESCO.

*beautiful buildings and fascinating museums in the 'White City'*

## Plaza de Armas

The elegant Plaza de Armas is faced on three sides by arcaded buildings with many restaurants, and on the fourth by the massive **cathedral**, founded in 1612 and largely rebuilt in the 19th century. It is remarkable for having its façade along the whole length of the church (entrances on Santa Catalina and San Francisco 0700-0900, 1700-1900). Inside is the fine Belgian organ and elaborately carved wooden pulpit. The cathedral has a **museum** ① *www.museocatedralarequipa.org.pe, Mon-Sat 0900-1630, US$3*, which outlines the history of the building, its religious objects and art and the bell tower. Behind the cathedral is an alley with handicraft shops and places to eat.

## ★ Santa Catalina Convent

*Santa Catalina 301, T054-2212132, www.santacatalina.org.pe. Mon, Wed, Fri-Sun 0800-1700 (last admission 1600), Tue and Thu 0800-2000, US$12, 1-hr tour US$6 for group up to 4, many guides speak English or German.*

This is by far the most remarkable sight, opened in 1970 after four centuries of mystery. It is a complete miniature walled colonial town of over 2 ha in the middle of the city, where about 450 nuns lived in total seclusion, except for their women servants. The few remaining nuns have retreated to one section of the convent, allowing visitors to see a maze of cobbled streets and plazas bright with geraniums and other flowers, cloisters and buttressed houses. These have been painted in traditional white, orange, deep red and blue. The convent has been beautifully refurbished, with period furniture, paintings of the Cuzco school and fully equipped kitchens. On Tuesday and Thursday evenings the convent is lit with torches, candles and blazing fireplaces: very beautiful. There is a good café, which sells cakes, sandwiches, baked potatoes and a special blend of tea.

## ★ Museo Santuarios Andinos

*La Merced 110, T054-286614, ext 105. Mon-Sat 0900-1800, Sun 0900-1500, US$6 includes a 20-min video in English; 40-min guided tour US$3, discount with university student card (not ISIC).*

This museum contains the frozen Inca mummies of child sacrifices found on Mount Ampato. To the Incas, Nevado Ampato was a sacred god, who claimed the highest tribute: human sacrifice. The mummy known as 'Juanita', found in 1995, is particularly fascinating as both the body and the Inca textiles it is wearing are so well preserved; it reveals a huge amount of information about Inca life and ritual practices. From January to April, Juanita is often jetting round the world and is replaced by other child sacrifices unearthed in the mountains.

## Monasterio de Santa Teresa

*Melgar 303, T054-281188, www.museo carmelitas.com. Tue-Sat 0900-1700, Sun 0900-1300, US$6, multilingual guides available (tip suggested), check website for events.*

**Tip...**

There have been reports of taxi drivers colluding with criminals to rob both tourists and locals. Ask hotels, restaurants, etc, to book a safe taxi for you. Theft can be a problem in the market area and the park at Selva Alegre at quiet times. Be very cautious walking anywhere at night. The police are conspicuous, friendly, courteous and efficient, but their resources are limited.

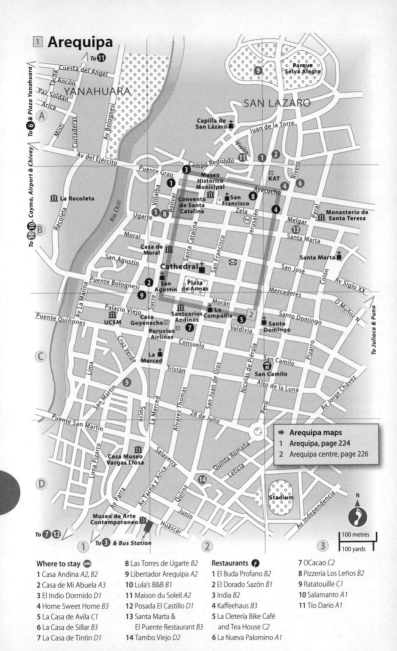

# Arequipa

**Where to stay**
1 Casa Andina *A2, B2*
2 Casa de Mi Abuela *A3*
3 El Indio Dormido *D1*
4 Home Sweet Home *B3*
5 La Casa de Avila *C1*
6 La Casa de Sillar *B3*
7 La Casa de Tintin *D1*
8 Las Torres de Ugarte *B2*
9 Libertador Arequipa *A2*
10 Lula's B&B *B1*
11 Maison du Soleil *A2*
12 Posada El Castillo *D1*
13 Santa Marta &
   El Puente Restaurant *B3*
14 Tambo Viejo *D2*

**Restaurants**
1 El Buda Profano *B2*
2 El Dorado Sazón *B1*
3 India *B2*
4 Kaffeehaus *B3*
5 La Cletería Bike Café
   and Tea House *C2*
6 La Nueva Palomino *A1*
7 OCacao *C2*
8 Pizzería Los Leños *B2*
9 Ratatouille *C1*
10 Salamanto *A1*
11 Tío Darío *A1*

→ Arequipa maps
1 Arequipa, page 224
2 Arequipa centre, page 226

Smaller, less known, but as impressive as Santa Catalina, is the Monastery of Santa Teresa, dating to 1710. This living monastery is the home of Carmelite nuns and one of Arequipa's hidden treasures. Housed in one cloister the **Museo de Arte Virreinal**, which also includes an exhibit about the techniques and materials used in colonial art. If you are there at noon, you can listen to the nuns singing Angelus and other prayers. Sweets, rose soap and other things made by the nuns are sold at the gift shop.

## Colonial houses

Arequipa is said to have the best preserved colonial architecture in Peru, apart from Cuzco. As well as the many fine churches, there are several seignorial houses with large carved tympanums over the entrances. Built as single-storey structures, they have mostly withstood earthquakes. They have small patios, no galleries, flat roofs and small windows, disguised by superimposed lintels or heavy grilles. Good examples are the 18th-century **Casa Tristán del Pozo**, or **Gibbs-Ricketts house** ⓘ *San Francisco 108, Mon-Fri 0900-1800, Sat 0900-1200*, with its fine portal and puma-head waterspouts. It houses a bank and art gallery. **Casa de Moral** ⓘ *Moral 318 y Bolívar, Mon-Sat 0900-1700, Sun 0900-1300, US$1.80, US$1 for students*, also known as Williams house is now a bank and has a museum. **Casa Goyeneche** ⓘ *La Merced 201 y Palacio Viejo*, is also a bank office, but the guards will let you view the courtyard and fine period rooms.

The oldest district of Arequipa is **San Lázaro**, a collection of tiny climbing streets and houses quite close to the **Hotel Libertador**, where you can find the ancient **Capilla de San Lázaro** ⓘ *daily 0900-1700, US$1.80.*

## Arequipa's churches

Among the many fine churches is **La Compañía** ⓘ *General Morán y Alvarez Thomas*, whose main façade (1698) and side portal (1654) are striking examples of the florid Andean *mestizo* style. To the left of the sanctuary is the **Capilla San Ignacio de Loyola** or **Capilla Real** (Royal Chapel) ⓘ *Mon-Sat 0900-1300, 1500-1800, Sun 0900-1300, Mass daily 1200, US$1.50*, with a beautiful polychrome cupola. Also well worth seeing is the church of **San Francisco** ⓘ *Zela 103, Mon-Sat 0715-0900, 1500-2000, Sun 0715-1245, 1800-2000*. There are religious art **museums** ⓘ *Mon-Sat 0900-1200, 1500-1800, US$1.80*, on either side of it, and also at the convent and at Templo de la Tercera Orden.

Opposite San Francisco is the interesting **Museo Histórico Municipal** ⓘ *Plaza San Francisco 407, Mon-Sat 0800-1600, US$3*, with scale models of the façades of Arequipa's churches, much war memorabilia, some impressive photos of the city in the aftermath of several notable earthquakes, and some items from the important pre-Inca Chiribaya culture (AD 800-1350) which extended from southern Peru to northern Chile and had its centre in Ilo, on the coast.

## Beyond the city centre

a 17th-century monastery and a 21st-century interactive museum

## La Recoleta

*Jr Recoleta 117, T054-270966, www.museolarecoleta.com. Mon-Sat 0900-1200, 1500-1700, open until 2000 Wed and Fri. US$3.*

This Franciscan monastery, built in 1647, stands on the other side of the river. A seldom-visited gem, it contains a variety of sights, including several cloisters, a religious art museum and a pre-Columbian art museum with ceramics and textiles produced by

## ② Arequipa centre

**➡ Arequipa maps**
1 Arequipa, page 224
2 Arequipa centre, page 226

**Where to stay** 🛏
1 Casa Andina *B1*
2 Casablanca Hostal *B1*
3 Casa de Melgar &
  Il Fornellino Restaurant *A2*
4 Hostal Santa Catalina *A1*
5 Hostal Solar *A2*
6 La Casa de Margott *A2*
7 La Casona de Jerusalén *A1*
8 La Posada del Cacique *A2*
9 Le Foyer *A1*
10 Los Andes B&B *B1*

**Restaurants** 🍴
1 Bóveda San Agustín *B1*
2 Café Capriccio *B1, B2*
3 Café Valenzuela *B2*
4 Chicha *B1*
5 Crepísimo, Chaqchao,
  Gud & Alianza Francesa *A1*
6 El Turko *B2*
7 Entre Libros y Café *A2*
8 Gonzalette Asador *A1*
9 Hatunpa *A1*
10 Istanbul *B1*
11 La Canasta *B2*
12 La Lucha Sanguchería
   Criolla *B2*
13 La Trattoria del
   Monasterio *A1*
14 Lo'kanta *A2*
15 Pura Fruta *A1*
16 Zig Zag *B2*

**Bars & clubs** 🍸
17 Casona Forum &
   Déjà Vu *A1*
18 Farren's *B1*
19 Museo del Pisco *B1*

cultures of the Arequipa area. Most impressive however is the museum of Amazon exploration featuring artifacts and photos of early Franciscan missionaries in the Amazon. The library, containing many antique books, is open for supervised visits during museum hours.

### ★ Casa Museo Vargas Llosa
*Av Parra 101, south of the centre, T054-283574. Tours Tue-Sun at 1000, 1030, 1400 and 1430 (3-10 visitors), or at any time if booked in advance for a minimum of 6 people, US$3.*

The birthplace of Peru's Nobel laureate in literature, Mario Vargas Llosa (1936- ) is now an innovative, modern museum. In holographic displays the writer himself tells you about the highlights of his life and career; during the 90-minute tour, you even get to meet some of the characters in his novels. Vargas Llosa's private library is now found at the **Biblioteca Regional** ① *San Francisco 308, Mon-Sat 0830-2030.*

**Other sights** Museo de Arte Contemporáneo Arequipa ① *Tacna y Arica 201, T054-221068, Mon-Fri 0900-1400, US$1.50,* in the old railway station, is dedicated to painting and photography from 1950 onwards. The building is surrounded by gardens. **Museo de Arqueología Universidad Católica de Santa María UCSM** ① *Cruz Verde 303, T054-221083, Mon-Fri 0830-1600, donations welcome,* has a small collection of textiles, ceramics and mummies, tracing the region's history from pre-Columbian times to the Republican era.

### Yanahuara
In the district of Yanahuara, northwest of the centre across Puente Grau, is the mestizo-style church of **San Juan Bautista** ① *Plaza de Yanahuara, open Sun and for mass Mon-Sat 0700, Sun 0700 and 1100,* completed in 1750, with a magnificent churrigueresque façade, all in sillar. On the same plaza is a mirador through whose arches there is a

## ON THE ROAD
## Appeasing the gods

To the Incas, Nevado Ampato was a sacred god, described as one of the principal deities in the Colca Canyon region, who brought water and good harvests and, as such, claimed the highest tribute: human sacrifice.

In September 1995, Johan Reinhard of the Chicago Field Museum of Natural History, accompanied by Peruvian climber Miguel Zárate, whose brother Carlos is a well-known mountain guide, were climbing Ampato when they made a startling discovery. At about 6000 m they found the perfectly preserved mummified body of an Inca girl, wrapped tightly in textiles. They concluded that she had been ritually sacrificed and buried on the summit.

Mummies of Inca human sacrifices had been found before on Andean summits, but the girl from Ampato, nicknamed Juanita, was the first frozen Inca female to be unearthed and her body may be the best preserved of any found in the Americas from pre-Columbian times. The intact tissues and organs of naturally mummified, frozen bodies are a storehouse of biological information. Studies reveal how she died, where she came from, who her living relatives are and even yield insights about the Inca diet.

Juanita's clothes are no less remarkable. The richly patterned textiles serve as a model for depictions of the way noble Inca women dressed. Her *lliclla* – a bright red and white shawl beneath the outer wrappings – has been declared "the finest Inca woman's textile in the world".

A subsequent ascent of Ampato revealed a further two mummies at the summit. One is a young girl and the other, though badly charred by lightning, is believed to be a boy.

Nowadays, villages in the Colca region continue to make offerings of chicha to the mountain gods for water and good harvests.

fine view of El Misti with the city at its feet, a popular spot in the late afternoon. Yanahuara has many fine restaurants.

## Around Arequipa

the great volcanoes

Some 3 km beyond the southwestern suburb of Tingo, beside the Río Sabandía on the Huasacanche road, is La Mansión del Fundador (T054-225200, www.la mansiondelfundador.com, daily 0900-1700, US$4.50). Originally owned by the founder of Arequipa, Don Garcí Manuel de Carbajal, it has been restored as a museum with original furnishings and paintings; it also has a cafeteria and bar.

About 8 km southeast of Arequipa is the **Molino de Sabandía** ① *US$3, ring bell for admission; taxi US$7*. This was the first stone mill in the area, built in 1621. It has been fully restored, and the guardian diverts water to run the grinding stones when visitors arrive. Adjoining Sabandía is the Inca site of **Yumina** ① *free, taxi US$7.50 or take a bus to Characato or Sabandía from Av La Paz by Mercado Siglo XX*, with many Inca terraces which are still in use.

## Climbing El Misti and Chachani

At 5822 m, El Misti volcano offers a relatively straightforward opportunity to scale a high peak. There are three routes for climbing the volcano; all take two days. The northeast route starts from the Aguada Blanca reservoir, reached by 4WD, from where a four-hour hike takes you to the Monte Blanco camp at 4800 m. Then it's a five- to six-hour ascent to the top. Two hours takes you back down to the trail. The southwest route involves taking a 4WD vehicle to the trailhead at Pastores (3400 m), followed by a hike of five or six hours to a camp at 4700 m. A five-hour climb takes you to the summit, before a three-hour descent to the trail. A southern route (Grau) also starts at 3400 m, with a camp at 4610 m, followed by a five-hour hike to the summit and a two-hour descent.

Climbing Chachani (6057 m), northwest of El Misti, is also popular. This peak retains its icy covering longer than El Misti, though this is fast disappearing.

Remember that both summits are at a very high altitude and that this, combined with climbing on scree, makes it hard going for the untrained. Great care must be taken on the unstable rock left by deglaciation; serious accidents have occurred. Be prepared for early starts, and take plenty of water, food and protection against the weather. Favoured months are May to September. Always contact an experienced guiding agency or professional guide in Arequipa as you should never climb alone. The price range is US$75-90 per person for a group of three to five people (see What to do, page 236).

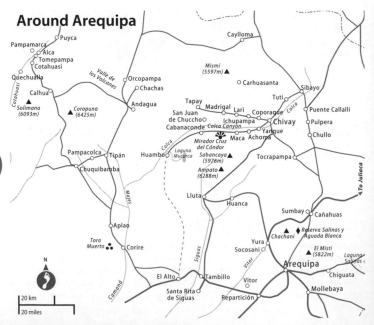

## Around Arequipa

## Tourist information

### Indecopi
*Hipólito Unanue 100-A,*
*Urbanización Victoria, T054-212054,*
*mlcornejo@indecopi.gob.pe.*

### iPerú
*Portal de la Municipalidad 110, on the*
*south side of Plaza de Armas, T054-223265,*
*iperuarequipa@promperu.gob.pe. Mon-Sat*
*0900-1800, Sun 0900-1300, also in the airport*
*Arrivals hall, at flight times.*

### Municipal tourist office
*Portal de la Municipalidad 112 next to iPerú.*
*Mon-Fri 0830-1700.*

### Tourist police
*Jerusalén 315, T054-201258. Daily 24 hrs.*
Very helpful dealing with complaints or
giving directions.

## Where to stay

There are 3 hotels of the **Casa Andina**
chain (www.casa-andina.com) as well as
several hostel chains, including **Flying Dog**
(www.flyingdogperu.com), **Pirwa** (www.
pirwahostels.com) and **Wild Rover** (www.
wildroverhostels.com). Economical *hostales*
of varying quality are located along Puente
Grau and Ayacucho, near Jerusalén.

### $$$$ Libertador Arequipa
*Plaza Simón Bolívar, Selva Alegre,*
*T054-215110, www.libertador.com.pe.*
Large comfortable rooms, good service,
swimming pool (cold), gardens, good meals,
pub-style bar, cocktail lounge, squash court.

### $$$ Casa de Melgar
*Melgar 108, T054-222459,*
*www.lacasademelgar.com.*
18th-century building, excellent rooms, solar
hot water, courtyard, good breakfast buffet,
Italian restaurant (**Il Fornellino**) next door.

### $$$-$$ La Casa de Avila
*San Martín 116, Vallecito, T054-213177,*
*www.casadeavila.com.*
Rooms around spacious, sunny garden,
computers for guests' use, can arrange
airport/bus station pick-up, recommended
Spanish courses held in the garden and
other activities.

### $$ Casablanca Hostal
*Puente Bolognesi 104, a few metres*
*from the Plaza de Armas, T054-221327,*
*www.casablancahostal.com.*
Super stylish *hostal*, lovely minimalist rooms in
a colonial building. Ambient lighting, rooms
with exposed stone walls, most with balcony.

### $$ Casa de Mi Abuela
*Jerusalén 606, T054-241206,*
*www.lacasademiabuela.com.*
An Arequipa tradition, in the same family for
several generations, suites with bathtub and
rooms, small swimming pool, therapeutic
massage area, rooms at the back are
quieter and overlook the garden, English
spoken, parking, restaurant and piano
bar, buffet breakfast or evening snacks on
patio or in beautiful gardens, tour operator.
Warmly recommended.

### $$ Hostal Solar
*Ayacucho 108, T054-241793,*
*www.hostalsolar.com.*
Colonial building, newer rooms in back
are bright, good breakfast served in nice
patio, sun lounge on roof, very secure,
multilingual staff.

> **Tip...**
> On arrival, do not believe taxi drivers
> who say the hotel of your choice is
> closed or full in order to take you to
> another hotel which pays them a high
> commission. Instead, phone your
> preferred hotel in advance, or ring
> the doorbell and check for yourself.

## $$ La Casa de Margott
*Jerusalén 304, T054-229517,*
*www.lacasademargott.com.*
Family-run in a refurbished 19th-century
house, bright with a massive palm tree in patio,
spacious, convenient, small bar/café, small
sauna, security box, heaters in fancier rooms.

## $$ La Casa de Tintin
*Urbanización San Isidro F1, Vallecito,*
*T054-284700, www.hoteltintin.com.*
20 mins' walk, 5 mins by taxi from the Plaza
de Armas, Belgian/Peruvian-owned, garden,
terrace, sauna, massage, laundry service, café
and bar, very pleasant and comfortable.

## $$ La Casona de Jerusalén
*Jerusalén 306-A, T054-205453,*
*lacasonadejerusalen@hotmail.com.*
Centrally located colonial house with garden,
ample bright rooms with or without bath,
private bath rooms include breakfast, terrace,
parking. English, German and Italian spoken.

## $$ Las Torres de Ugarte
*Ugarte 401A, T054-283532,*
*www.torresdeugarte.com.*
Round the corner from Santa Catalina
convent, some rooms are bungalow style in
colonial part at the back, roof terrace, safe,
luggage store, reflexology.

## $$ Maison du Soleil
*Pasaje Violín 102, Plazoleta Campo*
*Redondo, San Lázaro, T054-212277,*
*www.maisondusoleil.com.pe.*
Nice hotel in a quiet, pleasant location,
comfortable rooms, lovely common areas
and terrace, includes buffet breakfast,
attentive service, **Arthur** restaurant (www.
arthurestaurant.com.pe, closed Sun) features
molecular cuisine and offers cooking lessons
(www.peruvianflavor.com).

## $$ Posada El Castillo
*Pasaje Campos 105, Vallecito, T054-201828,*
*www.posadaelcastillo.com.*
Dutch/Peruvian-owned, in an old house
decorated with utensils found in the
renovation, 5 mins by taxi from city centre.

Variety of rooms and suites, some with
balcony and view of El Misti, wonderful
breakfast in annexe, pool, lovely gardens,
a good choice.

## $$ Santa Marta
*Santa Marta 207, T054-243925,*
*www.hostalsantamarta.com.*
Pleasant, comfortable hotel with nice patio,
modern rooms in back, arrange airport and
bus terminal transfers. Renovated and under
new management in 2017.

## $$-$ Le Foyer
*Ugarte 114, T054-286473, www.hlefoyer.com.*
Nicely refurbished old house, pleasant
common areas, terrace bar, colourfully
decorated, private rooms and US$10 pp in
dorm, book exchange, arrange tours, popular.

## $$-$ Los Andes Bed & Breakfast
*La Merced 123, T054-330015,*
*www.losandesarequipa.com.*
Good value, kitchen use, hot water, large
rooms with waxed wood floors and
minimalist decor, TV rooms, pleasant roof
terrace, tour agency.

## $ El Indio Dormido
*Av Andrés Avelino Cáceres B-9, T054-427401,*
*http://members.tripod.com/h_indio_dormido/.*
Close to bus terminals, kitchen, cafeteria,
parking, laundry, TV room, very helpful,
family-run.

## $ Home Sweet Home
*Rivero 509-B, T054-405982,*
*www.homesweethome-peru.com.*
Family-run, Cathy, who runs a travel
agency speaks Spanish, English, French,
very helpful, warm and inviting atmosphere,
substantial fresh breakfast included. Private
or shared bath, US$6 pp in dorm, hot water
all day, simple rooms, kitchen and laundry
facilities, parking.

## $ Hostal Santa Catalina
*Santa Catalina 500, T054-221766,*
*www.hostalsantacatalinaperu.com.*
On busy corner, simple rooms arranged
around a courtyard, private or shared bath,

kitchen facilities, security box, roof terrace with great views, helpful staff, organizes tours.

### $ La Casa de Sillar
*Rivero 504, T054-284249, www.lacasadesillar.com.*
Nice refurbished 17th-century stone house, comfortable rooms, private or shared bath, nice patio with plants, ample kitchen facilities, terrace with views, tour operator.

### $ Lula's B&B
*In Cayma, T054-272517, www.bbaqpe.com.*
Same owners as **Ari Quipay** language school, Lula (Peruvian) and her husband (Swiss) speak Spanish, English, German and French, with airport/bus terminal pick-up, modern, charming, quiet, meals available.

### $ Tambo Viejo
*Av Mariscal Cáceres 107, IV Centenario, 5 blocks south of the plaza near the rail station, T054-288195, www.tamboviejo.com.*
Noisy and less-than-safe area. 12-room guesthouse, quiet inside, English and Dutch spoken, walled garden, choice of 8 fresh breakfasts (extra), vegetarian restaurant, safe deposit, coffee shop, bar, book exchange (2 for 1), money changed, tourist information for guests, luggage store extra, tours and volcano climbs arranged, discounts for long stays. For a small fee, you can use the facilities if passing through. Free pick-up from bus terminal 0700-2300 (call when arriving).

### Restaurants

Arequipa is proud of its gastronomy. Typical dishes, many of them spiced with the hot *rocoto* pepper, accompanied by a glass of local *chicha* or an Arequipeño wine, are available in *picanterías* and at San Camilo market. There are also regional sweets and excellent chocolate, see Shopping, below. AGAR, the local gastronomy association, organizes a recommended yearly FestiSabores event, see Festivals, page 235.

### $$$ Chicha
*Santa Catalina 210,Casona Santa Catalina int 105, T054-287360. Mon-Sat 1200-2300, Sun 1200-1800.*
The menu of mostly local and fusion dishes is created by Gastón Acurio, fine dining in a historic building opposite Santa Catalina. In the same patio and also with an Acurio menu is **Tanta**, serving breakfast and snacks.

### $$$ La Trattoria del Monasterio
*Santa Catalina 309, T054-204062, www.latrattoriadelmonasterio.com. Mon-Sat 1200-1600, 1900-2300, Sun 1200-1600.*
A fusion of Italian and Arequipeño styles and ingredients, in a cloister in Convento de Santa Catalina.

### $$$ Salamanto
*San Francisco 211, T054-577061, www. salamanto.com. Mon-Sat 1230-1630, 1830-2330.*
Gourmet Peruvian cuisine, the menu changes every 3 months, bar specializing in local brands of pisco, good service, popular among foreigners. Tasting menu with 7 dishes for US$30, or US$50 with drinks.

### $$$ Zig Zag
*Zela 210, T054-206020, www.zigzag restaurant.com. Daily 1200-2300.*
Lovely atmosphere and decor in a colonial house with arched ceilings, gourmet European/Peruvian fusion cuisine, specializes in meat (alpaca is recommended) and fish cooked on volcanic rock. Also offer a choice of set meals at midday. Delicious, very popular, book in advance. Recommended.

### $$$-$$ Crepísimo
*Santa Catalina 208, at Alianza Francesa, T054-206620, www.crepisimo.com. Daily 0800-2300.*
Over 100 different sweet and savoury crêpes with traditional and Peruvian flavours, plus salads, sandwiches, *menú* at lunch, great coffee and juices, draft beer, magazines and board games, pleasant ambiance. Very tasty and recommended.

## ON THE ROAD

## Arequipa's gastronomy

One of the most important elements of the Arequipeño identity is its food. Very tasty and often spicy, Arequipa's dishes are a major component of internationally acclaimed Peruvian cuisine. Some of the better known dishes include:

**adobo** spicy pork stew served with *pan de tres puntas*, a local bread, and hot *rocoto* peppers.

**chancho al palo** pork roasted on a spit.

**chupe de camarón** freshwater shrimp chowder

**cuy chactado** crispy guinea pig with a corn breading, fried under stones and served with potatoes, *habas* (broad beans) and a hot *rocoto* sauce.

**queso helado** frozen milk with cinnamon.

**rocoto relleno** hot pepper stuffed with beef, vegetables, black olives and raisins, topped with cheese and served with *pastel de papa*, a potato pie, also topped with cheese and anis.

**soltero** a mixed vegetable and cheese salad.

These traditional dishes or *comida criolla* are served with *chicha*, a fermented corn drink, which in Arequipa, unlike other areas, is often made with purple corn. *Picanterías* are the restaurants specializing in traditional food and many good choices are found in and around the city. Local sweets include: marzipan, *alfajores arequipeños* (a crispy pastry filled with molasses) and fine chocolates.

The culinary delights of Arequipa go well beyond the *picantería*, with a fine selection of restaurants offering a fusion of Peruvian and international food. Since 2007, the Asociación Gastronómica de Arequipa, AGAR, has hosted FestiSabores, an annual gastronomic festival held for four days around the last weekend in October; the first of its kind in Peru. It is a great place to sample much of what Arequipa has to offer: traditional as well as fusion cuisine, regional sweets, wine and *pisco*, an organic food market, exhibits, music and folklore. Check www.festisabores.com for exact dates, location and additional information.

¡Buen provecho!

### $$$-$$ La Nueva Palomino
*Pje Leoncio Prado 122, Yanahuara, T054-252393. Daily 1130-1730.*
An Arequipa institution that has been in the same family for 3 generations. Very popular, large *picantería*, with a wide selection of local dishes, such as *rocoto relleno*, *cuy chactado* and *chupe de camarones*, accompanied by *chicha arequipeña*, made with purple corn, large portions. Expect queues at weekends. Recommended.

### $$$-$$ Tío Darío
*Callejon del Cabildo 100, Yanahuara, T054-270473, www.tiodario.com. Daily 1100-1630.*

Very good ceviche and other seafood specialities with an Arequipeño touch, as well as grilled meats, outdoor seating in pleasant gardens with views. 1-hr cooking show plus 1 dish for US$22, minimum 2 customers.

### $$ Bóveda San Agustín
*Portal San Agustín 127-129, T054-243596. Daily 0800-2300.*
Attractive bar downstairs, with an upstairs balcony overlooking the Plaza de Armas. Good breakfasts, lunches and evening specials.

### $$ Pizzería Los Leños
*Jerusalén 407, T054-281818. Daily 1700-2300.*

The 1st wood-fired pizza in the city, plus pasta, *empanandas* 0800-1300, original flavours with a touch of Peruvian home cooking, pleasant atmosphere and music.

### $$-$ Gonzalette Asador
*Zela 201-B. Mon-Sat1730-2400, and Villa Hermosa 1009, Av Aviación. Sat-Sun and holidays 1100-1700.*
Good value for alpaca steaks, *parrillada*, lamb, pleasant atmosphere, good music.

### $$-$ Hatunpa
*Ugarte 207 and 208 (across the street). Mon-Sat 1230-2130, Sun 1200-1600.*
Small place serving tasty dishes prepared with Andean native potatoes with a choice of toppings, craft beer, warm personalized service, very popular.

### $$-$ La Lucha Sanguchería Criolla
*Calle Mercaderes 116, www.lalucha.com.pe. Daily 0700-2200.*
Traditional place for great sandwiches, best bread in town, good service, informal rustic atmosphere.

### $$-$ Lo'kanta
*San Francisco 216, T054-231146. Mon-Wed 0730-2330, Thu-Sun 0700-2400.*
Breakfast and meals all day long, pizza, pasta, *empanadas*, sandwiches with home-made bread, desserts and coffee. All tasty and well prepared.

### $ El Buda Profano
*Bolívar 425, www.elbudaprofano.com. Daily 1200-2200.*
Tasty vegan sushi bar, soups, drinks, desserts, English spoken.

### $ El Dorado Sazón
*Puente Bolognesi 203, T054-284595. Daily 1300-2200.*
Good choice for *pollo a la brasa* prepared on a wood fire, large salad bar, a favourite of Arequipeños.

### $ El Puente
*Santa Marta 207-A, Mon-Sat 0830-1700, and Bello Horizonte C-11B, across Puente*
*Quiñones, behind Umacollo stadium. Daily 0830-1800.*
A choice of tasty vegetarian dishes, good value.

### $ El Turko
*San Francisco 223-25. Sun-Thu 0730-2400, Fri and Sat 0730-0600 (open all night).*
Bright café/bar selling kebabs, coffee, sweets, recommended breakfasts and good sandwiches, outdoor seating available.

### $ India
*Bolívar 502. Mon-Sat 1200-2100.*
Very small restaurant serving tasty Indian cuisine, prepared by an Indian cook, many vegetarian dishes.

### $ Istanbul
*San Francisco 231. Sun-Wed 0900-2400, Thu-Sat 0900-0200.*
Middle Eastern fast food, including a delicious falafel and other vegetarian dishes Also good coffee. In the same group as **El Turko**.

### $ Ratatouille
*Puente Bolognesi 214, T958-794192, http://ratatouillearequipa.wix.com/home.*
French/Peruvian-owned, colourful, serves typical Mediterranean dishes, as the name implies, based on fresh produce, good value, popular.

## Cafés

### Café Capriccio
*Mercaderes 121. Daily 0800-2200.*
Not that cheap, but excellent coffee, cakes, etc. Very popular with local business people. **Capriccio Gourmet**, on Santa Catalina 120, San Francisco 135 and at several shopping centres, is also good.

### Café Valenzuela
*Morán 114 and other locations. Mon-Sat 0800-2200, Sun 1630-2030*
Fantastic coffee (also sells beans and ground coffee), locals' favourite.

### Chaqchao
*Santa Catalina 204, p2, T054-234572, www. chaqchao-chocolates.com. Daily 0930-2330.*

Coffee, pizza, desserts, organic chocolate. At 1100 and 1445 they offer fun chocolate-making classes (US$20, 2 hrs), reserve ahead.

### Entre Libros y Café
*Jerusalén 307. Mon-Sat 1030-2100.*
Coffee from various regions of Peru, teas, juices, fraps, sandwiches, library, books for sale, musical and other cultural events.

### Gud
*Santa Catalina 206-A. Mon-Sat 0900-2100.*
*Paninis*, salads, waffles, desserts, chocolates and craft beer.

### Kaffeehaus
*Melgar 117, www.kaffeehaus.org.*
*Mon-Fri 0730-2000, Sat 0800-2000.*
Variety of excellent coffees roasted on the premises, waffles, sandwiches, German desserts, terrace and garden seating. German/Peruvian-run.

### La Canasta
*Jerusalén 115 in courtyard, no sign.*
*Mon-Sat 0830-2000.*
Excellent bakery, great baguettes twice daily, also serves breakfast and delicious apple and brazil nut pastries, courtyard seating. Recommended.

### La Cletería Bike Café and Tea House
*San Juan de Dios 206, Galerías Coloniales, tienda 21 y 22. Mon 1500-2030, Tue-Fri 1000-1400, 1530-2030, Sat 1000-2030.*
Innovative combination of a café and bike shop. Coffee, tea, juices, craft beer, sandwiches, and sweets. Owner Claudia makes the best scones this side of the Atlantic. Also bike tours (4-hr city tour, US$10) and rentals. *Cine pedal* movies Sat at 1900. Warmly recommended.

### OCacao
*Palacio Viejo 205 A. Mon-Fri 0900-2130, Sat 1000-2030.*
Small café run by a Belgian *chocolatier*: coffee, sweets, excellent truffles and bonbons.

### Pura Fruta
*Mercaderes 131 and Av Trinidad Morán 205, Cayma. Mon-Sat 0800-2200, Sun 0900-1400.*

A great variety of fruit juices and smoothies, coffee, frappés, yoghurt, salads, sandwiches, desserts.

## Bars and clubs

### Casona Forum
*San Francisco 317, www.casonaforum.com. Entry US$7.50.*
Huge complex incorporating the **Retro Bar** (live music Tue-Sat from 1930), **Zero** pool bar for rock music, **Club Latino** for salsa dancing, Club de los 80 (Thu-Sat from 2200) for 1980s music and lovely views, and **Forum**, an underground club with imitation waterfall and plants (Thu-Sat from 2200).

### Déjà Vu
*San Francisco 319-B. Daily 1900-0300.*
Popular rooftop bar, hosts DJ electronic music evenings and live music, weekend drinks specials. During the day (1100-1800), **Deja Vu** fish restaurant (**$$**) operates in the terrace, lovely setting and food.

### Farren's
*Pasaje Catedral 107.*
Good meeting place, great music.

### Museo del Pisco
*Moral 229A. Daily 1700-2400.*
Bar where you can learn about the pisco culture and history, also snacks, tastings and mixology classes (US$11.50, 45 mins).

## Festivals

A full list of the region's many festivals is available locally from **iPerú**, see Tourist information, above.

**10 Jan  Sor Ana de Los Angeles y Monteagudo**, festival for the patron saint of Santa Catalina monastery.
**Mar-Apr  Semana Santa** celebrations involve huge processions every night, culminating in the burning of an effigy of Judas on Easter Sun in the main plazas of Cayma and Yanahuara, and the reading of his will, containing criticisms of the city authorities.

## ON THE ROAD
### Ancient apparel

Four thousand years before the Spanish conquistadors set foot on Peruvian soil, the indigenous peoples excelled at the textile arts. Cotton was cultivated on the arid coast, but, up on the high Andean plain, there was a ready supply of fibre from native camelids: llamas, alpacas, vicuñas and guanacos. Alpacas and llamas were domesticated as early as 4000 BC and the wild camelids (guanacos and vicuñas) were used as clothing even further back by hunters who roamed the bleak, high Andean plateau. By 1500-1000 BC llamas were being used for ritual burial offerings, indicating their prestige.

Camelid fibre is easy to spin and dye and allowed the ancient weavers to develop extraordinarily fine spinning techniques. The pre-Columbian peoples prized the silky soft fibre of the alpaca, in particular. Living at altitudes of 4000 m, where temperatures can drop to -15°C, these animals have developed a coat that not only has thermal properties but is also soft and resistant. The majority of Peru's alpacas are in the hands of small breeders and indigenous communities who still herd and manage their animals in much the same way as their ancestors.

Alpaca-breeding and herding is the main economic activity of high-altitude regions, such as the Province of Carabaya in Puno. The textile arts tradition also continues. Fine woven and knitted garments can be found in specialized shops in main cities and tourist centres, see Shopping, below.

**27 Apr** The celebration of the apostle Santiago.

**May** Known as the **Mes de Las Cruces**, with ceremonies on hilltops throughout the city.

**3 Aug** A procession through the city bearing the images of Santo Domingo and San Francisco.

**6-31 Aug Fiesta Artesanal del Fundo El Fierro** is a sale and exhibition of *artesanía* from all parts of Peru, taking place near Plaza San Francisco.

**6-17 Aug** Celebration of the city's anniversary on 15th, many events including a mass ascent of El Misti.

**Oct-Nov FestiSabores**, www.festisabores. com, gastronomic festival held at Plaza Yanahuara for 4 days around the last weekend in Oct (confirm dates in advance as they may vary from year to year). A good place to sample the local food, wine, pisco and music; check www.festisabores.com for exact dates.

**2 Nov Day of the Dead** celebrations in cemeteries.

**Dec Hay Festival**, www.hayfestival.org/ arequipa, week-long cultural festival, offshoot of the UK literary festival.

### Shopping

The central San Camilo market, between Perú, San Camilo, Piérola and Alto de la Luna, is worth visiting.

#### Alpaca goods, textiles and crafts

**Claustros de La Compañía**, *Morán 140*. Handicrafts shopping centre in a colonial setting, containing many alpaca knitwear outlets including a factory outlet in the 2nd patio.

**El Ekeko**, at *Patio del Ekeko, Mercaderes 141, www.elekeko.pe*. A variety of crafts, T-shirts, Panama hats, gourmet foodstuffs.

**Fundo del Fierro**, large handicraft market behind the old prison on Plaza San Francisco; it's worth a visit.

**Ilaria**, *at Patio del Ekeko*. Fine jewellery.

**Kuna by Alpaca 111**, *at Patio del Ekeko, www.kuna.com.pe or www.incalpaca.com*.

High-quality alpaca and wool products. Also at Casona Santa Catalina, Santa Catalina 210, Local 1-2; in **Hotel Libertador** and at the airport. Shops in Lima, Cuzco and Puno.
**Michell y Cia**, *Juan de la Torre 101, www. michell.com.pe*. Factory outlet, excellent place for alpaca and other wool yarn in huge variety of colours, also a clearance room for baby and adult alpaca yarn. Alpaca and pima cotton garments also for sale at **Sol Alpaca** (Casona Santa Catalina, Santa Catalina 210). 1920s machinery on display. Branches in Lima and Cuzco.
**Millma's Baby Alpaca**, *Pasaje Catedral 112 and 117, also at Santa Catalina 225, millmas@ hotmail.com*. 100% baby alpaca goods, run by Peruvian family, high-quality, beautiful designs, good prices.

### Bookshops
**Librería El Lector**, *San Francisco 213*. Wide selection, including Peruvian authors, book exchange in various languages (2 for 1), stocks **Footprint**.
**Librerías San Francisco** *has branches at Portal de Flores 138 and San Francisco 102-106*. Books on Arequipa and Peru, some in English, also expensive regional topographical maps.
**SBS Book Service**, *San Francisco 125, T054-205317*. Has a good selection of travel books, etc.

### Climbing and hiking gear
**Andesgear**, *Santa Catalina 210, Casona Santa Catalina, local 21 y 22, T054-418644. Daily 0900-2100*. Clothing, footwear, backpacks and equipment. Wide selection of international brands.

### Shopping centres
There are several international style malls in the suburbs of Cayma, Paucarpata, Cerro Colorado and others.
**Patio del Ekeko**, *Mercaderes 141*. A commercial centre with upmarket restaurants and shops.

### Sweets
**Antojitos de Arequipa**, *Morán 129*. An Arequipa institution. Sells traditional sweets. Also at Jerusalén 120, Portal de Flores 144, the airport and all shopping centres.
**La Ibérica**, *Jerusalén 136, www.laiberica. com.pe*. Another Arequipa stalwart since 1909. Top-quality chocolate, but expensive. Outlets at Mercaderes 102, Morán 112, Portal de Flores 130, the airport and all shopping centres.

## What to do

### City tours
There are 4 guides' associations, one of which (**Adegopa**, Morán 118,Claustros de la Compañía, tienda 11http://adegopa. blogspot.com) offers free promotional tours.
**Panoramic bus tours** are offered by several companies (eg www.bustour.com.pe), US$11 for 2 hrs, US$14 for 3-4 hrs. Most depart from C Zela by Santa Catalina convent, several daily. **Free walking tours** are offered daily at 1000 and 1500 by tourism students from the Universidad Nacional San Agustín (UNSA), meet at Santa Catalina 204; information from Municipal Tourist office at Plaza de Armas; also with **Free Walking Tour Peru** (T998-959566, www.fwtperu.com), depart Plaza San Francisco at 1145; several others, tips expected.

### Climbing, cycling, rafting and trekking
Be wary of agencies offering climbing trips with very fast ascents.

## ON THE ROAD

## Rafting around Arequipa

**Río Chili** (year-round, Grade II-IV): just outside Arequipa but highly water dependent and relying on dam releases to make it worthwhile. A fun half-day out if you need a break from the heat.

**Río Colca** (June, Grade IV-V): possibly even harder than the Cotahuasi, this rarely run expedition river has had its fair share of casualties in the past. Be prepared for rocks falling off the cliffs almost continuously, sandflies, storms and out-of-this-world whitewater. Recent seismic activity around Arequipa has caused major changes to several rapids; definitely book with the local experts.

**Río Cotahuasi** (May-June, Grade IV-V): this is a total expedition, including a long drive past Coropuna mountain, followed by six days of non-stop technical whitewater. The scenery is out of this world, including Wari terracing and ruins all in an incredibly deep desert canyon. Probably the best whitewater river on offer in Peru, only a handful of operators offer this trip and only one or two depart each year. Book early and only with companies who have plenty of experience.

**Río Majes** (all year, Grade II-III): where the Colca emerges from its gorge it joins the Río Majes and some day trips can be organized locally or from Arequipa. Good freshwater shrimp make up for the pretty average whitewater.

**Beinhart Peru**, *T928 841740, www. beinhart-peru.page4.com (in German)*. Custom tailored multi-day or multi-week cycling and trekking expeditions for small groups. Run by Klaus Hartl, a very dynamic and knowledgeable guide based in Puerto Maldonado and Arequipa. German, English and Czech spoken, contact well in advance. Warmly recommended.

**Carlos Zárate Aventuras**, *Jerusalén 505-A, T054-202461, www.zarateadventures.com/en*. Run by Carlos Zárate of the Asociación de Guías de Montaña de Perú. Good family-run business that always works with qualified mountain guides. A specialist in mountaineering and exploring, with a great deal of information and advice and some equipment rental. Carlos also runs trips to one of the supposed sources of the Amazon, Nevado Mismi, as well as trekking in the Cotahuasi Canyon, climbing tougher peaks such as Ampato and Coropuna, mountain biking, rock climbing and rafting.

**Colca Trek**, *Jerusalén 401 B, T054-206217, www.colcatrek.com.pe*. Knowledgeable and

English-speaking Vlado Soto is one of the best guides for the Cotahuasi Canyon and is recommended for climbing, trekking and mountain biking in the Colca Canyon. He also rents equipment and has topographical maps.

**Cusipata**, *Jerusalén 402-A, T054-203966, www.cusipata.com*. Recommended as a very good local rafting operator, very popular half-day trips. Also 6-day trips on the Río Colca. Río Chili 1-day kayak courses, as well as mountain bike tours.

**Expediciones y Aventuras**, *Rivero 504 at La Casa de Sillar, T958 326432, www.expediciones yaventuras.com*. Family-run adventure sports operator led by Gustavo Rondón. Experienced guides for rafting, kayaking, biking, climbing, trekking, sand-boarding, body-boarding and horse riding tours. Innovative 4WD routes and camping tours to Colca, Valle de los Volcanes, Cotahuasi, protected areas and the coast; very helpful.

**Naturaleza Activa**, *Santa Catalina 211, T988 227723, naturactiva@yahoo.com*. Experienced guides, knowledgeable, climbing, trekking and mountain biking.

**Sacred Road Xtreme**, *Jerusalén 400 AB2, T054-212332, www.sacredroad.com.* Arranges hiking, climbing, biking, and rock climbing in Colca Canyon and elsewhere, experienced guides led by Arcadio Mamani, equipment available.

## Language classes

**Centro de Intercambio Cultural Arequipa (CEICA)**, www.ceica-peru.com; **Escuela de Español Ari Quipay (EDEAQ)**, www.edeaq. com; **Instituto Cultural Peruano Alemán**, www.icpa.org.pe; **Llama Education**, www. arequipaspanish.com; **Spanish School Arequipa**, www.spanishschoolarequipa.com.

## Tour operators

Many agencies on Jerusalén, Santa Catalina and around Plaza de Armas sell air and bus tickets and offer tours of Colca, Cotahuasi, Toro Muerto and the city. Prices vary greatly so shop around; check carefully what is included in the cheapest of tours and that there are enough people for the tour to run. Travel agents frequently work together to fill buses. Many tourists prefer to contract tours through their hotel. If a travel agency puts you in touch with a guide, make sure he/she is official. The following have been recommended as helpful and reliable:
**Andina Travel Service**, *Jerusalén 309-A, T054-285477.* Good 1- to 4-day tours of Colca Canyon, climbing and other adventure sports, guide Gelmond Ynca Aparicio is very enthusiastic.

**Colca Explorer**, *Mariscal Benavides 201, Selva Alegre (north of the centre), T054-282488, www. colca-explorer.com.* Agency associated with **Amazonas Explorer** in Cuzco, with many options in Colca and southern Peru: from classic local tours to horse riding, mountain biking, fishing in remote lakes, climbing, treks and visiting alpaca farms on the altiplano.
**Colca Journeys**, *C Rodríguez Ballón 533, Miraflores (northeast of the centre), T973-901010, www.colcajourneys.com.* Specializes in and operates tours to the Colca and Cotahuasi canyons as well as Valle de los Volcanes.
**Giardino Tours**, *at Casa de Mi Abuela (see page 229), T054-221345, www.giardinotours.com.* Professional company offering tours and transport, has own properties in Arequipa, Colca (eg delightful **La Casa de Mamayacchi** in Coporaque) and Valle de Los Volcanes, community tourism options, good information.
**Kuntur Adventure and Tourism (KAT)**, *Jerusalén 524B, T054-281864, www.katperu tours.com.* Offers a variety of standard, alternative and adventure tours (small groups, up to 7 persons) including Colca and half-day Ruta del Sillar. Also bike rentals. Run by Gerardo Pinto, very knowledgeable and helpful, English and German spoken.
**Land Adventure**, *Residencial La Peña A-20, Sachaca (southwest of the centre), T947-376345, www.landadventures.net.* 'Sustainable' tour operator with good guides for communities in Colca, trekking (including a 5-day Salkantay trek and Lares), climbing, downhill biking; private tours only.

**Pablo Tour**, *Jerusalén 400-AB-1*, *T054-203737*, *www.pablotour.com*. Family-run agency, has connections with several *hostales* in Cabanaconde and knows the area well, 3-day mixed tours in the Colca Canyon with mountain biking, trekking and rafting, also climbing and sandboarding, free tourist information, topographical maps for sale, bus and hotel reservation service. Son Edwin Junco Cabrera can sometimes be found in the office; he speaks fluent French and English and is very helpful.

**Tierra Etnica**, *Jerusalén521B*, *T054-286927*, *www.tierraetnica.com*. Culinary tours, community tourism in Colca.

**Vita Tours**, *Jerusalén 302*, *T054-284211*, *www.vitatours.com.pe*. Good value tours in the Arequipa area, including to the coast, and in the Colca Canyon where they have a hotel, **La Casa de Lucila in Chivay**.

### Volunteering

**Paz Holandesa**, *Villa Continental, Calle 4, No 101, Paucarpata, T054-432281, www.pazholandesa.com*. Dutch foundation dedicated to helping the impoverished (see their website if you are interested in volunteering). Also has a travel clinic for tourists, Dutch and English spoken, 24 hr service, highly recommended.

**Volunteers Peru**, *www.volunteersperu.org*. Runs social projects in a home for abandoned girls in the city and teaching English in Cotahuasi.

## Transport

Taking a taxi from the airport or bus terminals to your hotel is recommended.

### Air

Rodríguez Ballón airport is 7 km from the centre, T054-434834. 2 desks offer hotel reservations; also car rentals. Take a taxi to/from your hotel, 30 mins. Airport taxis charge US$7-9 to the centre; other taxis charge US$4-6 to/from the centre; best to use a radio taxi company, listed below. The stop for local

buses and combis (eg 'Río Seco', 'Cono-Norte' or 'Zamacola') is about 500 m from the airport, but this is not recommended with luggage.

To **Lima**, 1½ hrs, several daily with **Avianca/TACA** (Centro Comercial Real Plaza, Av del Ejército, Cayma), **LATAM** (Santa Catalina 118-C), **Peruvian Airlines** (La Merced 202-B) and **LC Perú** (Moral 223-225, T054-214746). **LATAM** also serves **Juliaca**, 30 mins. **Avianca/TACA and LATAM** also serve **Cuzco**, 1 hr from Arequipa. **Peruvian Airlines** also serves **Tacna**. **Amaszonas** (La Merced 121-B, www.amaszonas.com) sells tickets between Cuzco and **La Paz**, Bolivia.

### Bus

There are 2 terminals at Av Arturo Ibáñez Hunter, south of the centre, 30 mins by city bus (not recommended with luggage, US$0.50), or 20 mins by taxi, US$2.50-3.60. The older **Terminal Terrestre**, T054-427792, has shops and places to eat. The newer **Terrapuerto**, across the car park, T054-348810, has a travel agency (**Inca Travel**, T054-427852, www.incatravelperu.com, daily 0600-1500, 1600-2100), which gives information and makes hotel reservations. Most luxury class services leave from the Terrapuerto. Terminal tax is US$0.55-0.90. Some companies have offices in both terminals. Flores, with frequent service to Lima and throughout southern Peru, is in both terminals and also has a private terminal nearby at Av Forga y Av Los Incas. Note that buses may not depart from the terminal where you bought your ticket.

To **Lima**, 1011 km, 15-18 hrs, standard services US$18-29, luxury US$36-56. **Cruz del Sur** (T054-427375), **Enlaces** (T054-430333),

> **Tip...**
> Theft is a serious problem in the bus station area. Take a taxi to and from the bus station and do not wander around with your belongings. It is best not to arrive at night as you may find yourself stranded at the bus station.

**Tepsa** (T054-608079), **Oltursa** (T01-708-5000) are recommended; many others. The road is paved but drifting sand and breakdowns may prolong the trip.

To **Nazca**, 566 km, 9-11 hrs, US$19-22.50 (US$30-52 on luxury services), several buses daily, mostly at night; most buses continue to Ica (US$30-42) and Lima. Also US$12-15 to **Chala**, 400 km, 6 hrs, 5 daily with **Llamosas** from the Terrapuerto. Note that some companies charge a full fare to Lima for intermediate destinations. To **Moquegua**, 213 km, 4 hrs, US$6.50-12, hourly buses (**Moquegua** is recommended) and frequent *colectivos*. To **Tacna**, 320 km, 6-7 hrs, US$9-11, hourly with **Flores**, direct luxury service without stopping in Moquegua, US$16; overnight service with **Cromotex**.

To **Cuzco**, all buses go via Juliaca, US$11-46, 10-11 hrs. Most companies go overnight (eg **Enlaces**, **Cial**, **Cruz del Sur**, **Oltursa**), but Flores and others travel in daytime, at 0715 and 1230.

To **Juliaca**, US$5.50 normal, US$7 *semi-cama*, US$9-27 *cama*, 5 hrs with **Julsa** (T054-430843, poor safety record), hourly 24 hrs a day, with **Flores**, 6-8 daily; some buses continue to Puno. To **Puno**, 297 km, 5-6 hrs, US$7-11, hourly with **Julsa**, 4 daily with **Flores**, at 0800 with **Cruz del Sur** (US$21-27), **Tour Perú** (www.tourperu.com.pe) at 2230 with connections to La Paz (Bolivia), several others. **4M Express** (La Merced 125 Int 111, T054-452296, www.4m-express.com) offers a tourist service to Puno with stops at Pampa Cañahuas (vicuña observation), Vizcachani (rock formations) and Lagunillas (flamingo and other bird observation) daily at 1245, 6 hrs, US$35 (high season), includes bilingual guiding, snack and hotel pick-up in Arequipa. They offer a similar service from Chivay to Puno and Cuzco (see Colca transport, page 248),

so you don't necessarily have to travel via Arequipa. To **Puerto Maldonado** via Juliaca, US$18-24, 16 hrs, at 1530 with **Julsa**, 1600 with **Power** and **Reyna**, 1700 with **Wayra** (T959-390512) or 1630 with **Mendivil** (T974-210329); more frequent departures from Juliaca. Avoid overnight travel to and from Puerto Maldonado as holdups have taken place.To **Chivay**, with **Andalucía** (Terrapuerto, T959 448412) at 0930*, 1500, 2400*, **Reyna** (Terminal Terrestre, T958 793712) at 0100*, 0830, 1100*,and **Trans Milagros** (T054-298090) at 0330*, 0530, 1400*, US$4, 3 hrs; those with an asterisk (*) continue to **Cabanaconde**, US$5.50, a further 56 km, 2 hrs. **4M Express** provide private transport between Arequipa and Chivay on request and tour vans will also take extra passengers, pick-up starting 0300, arrange with a tour operator. **Rutas del Sur**, C Jerusalén 519, T951-024751, www.tourrutasdelsur.com, provides tourist transport between Arequipa, **Chivay** (Colca Canyon), **Puno**, and **Cuzco**.

### Taxi

From US$1 for trips around town. Companies include: **Alo 45**, T054-454545; **Taxitel**, T054-266262; Real T054-426161; **Turismo Arequipa**, T054-458888.

### Train

The train station is 7 blocks south of the Plaza de Armas (Huáscar y Quiroz, www.perurail.com). The railway runs from Arequipa to Juliaca (279 km), where it divides, to Cuzco (381 km) and Puno (44 km). For **PeruRail**'s *Belmond Andean Explorer*, see page 316. *Andean Plains and Islands of Discovery* service to **Cuzco** (2 days/2 nights, US$1225-1755) departs Sat 2000, includes excursion on Lake Titicaca (Uros, Taquile and Playa Collata) and stops at Marangoni and Raqchi.

# Colca &
# Cotahuasi canyons

watch condors cruising above this spectacular canyon

The Colca Canyon is deep: twice as deep as the Grand Canyon. The Río Colca descends from 3650 m above sea level at Chivay to 3287 m at Cabanaconde. In the background looms the grey, smoking mass of Sabancaya (5976 m), one of the most active volcanoes in the Americas, and its more docile neighbours, Ampato (6265 m) and Hualca Hualca (6025 m). Unspoiled Andean villages lie on both sides of the canyon, inhabited by the Cabana and Collagua peoples, and some of the extensive pre-Columbian terraced fields are still in use. High on anyone's list when visiting the canyon is an early-morning trip to the Cruz del Cóndor to see these majestic birds at close quarters.

## Arequipa to Chivay

From Arequipa there are two routes to **Chivay**, the first village on the eastern edge of the canyon. The old dirt route goes through Cayma and then runs north between Misti and Chachani to the altiplano. The newer paved route is longer but quicker. It goes through Yura, following the railway. The two routes join at Cañahuas, one of the access points to Reserva Nacional Salinas y Aguada Blanca, where you will have to purchase or show your tourist ticket. Both routes afford fine views of the volcanoes Misti, Chachani, Ampato and Sabancaya; if you're lucky, you can see herds of vicuñas near the road. Cyclists should use the Yura road, as it's in better condition and has less of a climb at the start. At Cañahuas, you can change buses to/from Juliaca or Chivay if you want to bypass Arequipa; the road from Cañahuas to Puno via Patahuasi, Imata and Juliaca is paved and has a daily tourist transport service (see Transport, page 248). It can be cold in the morning, reaching 4825 m in the Pata Pampa Pass, but the views are worth it.

## Chivay and around

**Chivay** (3650 m) is the gateway to the canyon, and its road bridge is the main link between the north and south sides (others are at Yanque and Lari). Crossing the river at Chivay going west to follow the canyon on the north side, you pass the villages of **Coporaque**, **Ichupampa** (a footbridge crosses the river between the two villages), **Lari**, **Madrigal** and **Tapay**.

In Chivay, the **Maria Reiche Planetarium and Observatory** ① *in the grounds of the Casa Andina hotel, 6 blocks west of the plaza between Huayna Capac and Garcilazo, www.casa-andina.com, US$5.70, discounts for students*, makes the most of the Colca's clear Southern Hemisphere skies with a powerful telescope and two 55-minute presentations per day at 1830 (Spanish) and 2000 (English). There is a Globalnet ATM close to the plaza. Thse hot springs of **La Calera** ① *US$4.30 to bathe, half price to visit, regular colectivos (US$0.30), taxi*

# **Essential** Colca Canyon

## Finding your feet

To enter the canyon you must buy a tourist ticket for US$25 (valid for 10 days) at a checkpoint on the road to Chivay; you may be required to show this ticket at Mirador Cruz del Cóndor. Tour prices generally do not include the Colca entry ticket, meals other than breakfast nor entry to the baths.

From Arequipa a one-day tour to the mirador costs US$20-25. It departs Arequipa at 0300-0330, arrives at the Cruz del Cóndor at 0730-0830, followed by an expensive lunch stop at Chivay and back to Arequipa by 1800-1900. For many, especially for those with altitude problems, this is too much to fit into one day (the only advantage is that you don't have to sleep at high altitude). Two-day tours start at US$25-35 per person with an overnight stop in Chivay or Yanque; more expensive tours range from US$45 to US$90. Most agencies will have a base price for the tour and then different prices depending on which hotel you pick.

## Trekking around the canyon

There are many hiking possibilities in the area, with *hostales* or camping for longer treks. Make sure to take enough water, or purification tablets, as it gets very hot and there is not a lot of fresh water available. Sun protection is also a must. Ask locals for directions as there are hundreds of confusing paths going into the canyon.

Buy food for longer hikes in Arequipa. Topographical maps are available at the **Instituto Geográfico Nacional** in Lima, and at **Colca Trek** or **Pablo Tour** in Arequipa. Economical trekking tours from Arequipa cost US$45-55 for two days, US$55-65 for three days; entry tickets and lunch on the last day are not included. Agencies pool their passengers and quality varies; ask around for a personal recommendation. A private three-day trekking tour for two passengers costs about US$450 per person.

## When to go

January to April is the rainy season, which makes the area green with lots of flowers. This is not the best time to see condors, however, or to go hiking. May to December is the dry, cold season.

## Time required

Allow at least two to three days to appreciate the Colca Canyon fully, more if you plan on doing some trekking.

---

*(US$1.70) or a 1-hr walk from town,* are 4 km away and are highly recommended after a hard day's trekking.

Beyond the baths, the road continues northeast to **Tuti**, which has a small handicrafts shop and is the starting point for the trek to **Nevado Mismi** (5598 m). After Tuti is **Sibayo** (*pensión* and grocery store) from where a long circuit leads back to Arequipa, passing through **Puente Callalli**, **Chullo** and **Sumbay**. This is a little-travelled road, but the views, with vicuña, llamas, alpacas and Andean duck are superb.

### Chivay to Cruz del Cóndor

From Chivay, the main road goes west along the south side of the Colca Canyon. The first village encountered is **Yanque** (8 km, excellent views), with an interesting church containing superbly renovated altar pieces and paintings; there's a museum on the opposite side of the plaza. A large thermal swimming pool (entry US$4.50) is 20 minutes' walk from the plaza, beside the renovated colonial bridge that leads to the villages of Coporaque and Ichupampa on the other side of the canyon. The road west continues

## ON THE ROAD

## How deep is that canyon?

The people of the Colca Canyon region were more than a little disgruntled when it was announced that the neighbouring Cotahuasi Canyon was deeper than Colca, taking its place as the deepest in the world, a distinction many Colca guides cling to tenaciously. But, how can you actually determine the depth of a canyon when there are different ways of measuring and no obvious international convention to follow?

Gonzalo de Reparaz Ruiz, a French-Basque geographer, was the first to study the hydrography of southern Peru in the 1960s. He was the one to crown Colca the deepest canyon, perhaps overlooking its neighbour. The depth of Cotahuasi was later determined by measuring the height of Nevado Solimana, the highest point on the eastern rim, then the highest point on the western rim opposite Solimana. The average of these two points is 3354 m above the Río Cotahuasi.

Cotahuasi's honour as the world's deepest canyon is disputed, with a long list of contenders in the Himalayas, Tibet and elsewhere. Generally, however, the depth of these canyons has been determined as the difference between the height of one high peak and the river, without taking into account the second rim; and some peaks are actually very far from the river.

Regardless of the exact depth of Cotahuasi and Colca, they are both spectacular canyons with much to offer the visitor.

paved to **Achoma** and **Maca** (footbridge to Madrigal on the north side), which barely survived an earthquake in 1991. Then comes the tiny village of **Pinchollo**. From here it is a 30-minute walk on a dirt track to the **Hatun Infiernillo** geyser.

The mirador at **Cruz del Cóndor**, where you may be asked to show your tourist ticket, overlooks the deepest point of the canyon. The view is wonderful and condors can be seen rising on the morning thermals (0900, arrive by 0800 to get a good spot) and sometimes in the late afternoon (1600-1800). Camping here is officially forbidden, but if you ask the tourist police in Chivay they may help. **Reyna**'s 0430 bus from Chivay stops here very briefly (ask the driver), or try hitching with a tour bus at around 0600. Buses from Cabanaconde stop at about 0700 (**Andalucía**) or 0830 (**Reyna**); they leave Cabanaconde's plaza 30 minutes earlier.

### Cabanaconde

From the mirador it is a 20-minute ride in tourist transport or 40 minutes by local bus on a paved road to Cabanaconde at 3287 m. You can also walk: three hours by the road, or two hours via a short cut following the canyon. This is the last village in the Colca Canyon, friendly, smaller and less touristy than Chivay. The views are superb and condors can be seen from the hill just west of the village, a 15-minute walk from the plaza. You'll also see agricultural terraces, arguably the most attractive in the valley, to the south of the village. Cabanaconde is an excellent base for visiting the region, with interesting trekking, climbing, biking and horse riding.

### Treks around Cabanaconde

Two hours below Cabanaconde is **Sangalle**, an 'oasis' of palm trees and swimming areas where there are three campsites with basic bungalows and toilets. It's a beautiful spot, recommended. (It's three to 4½ hours back up; ask for the best route in both directions. Horses can be hired to carry your bag, US$5.85.)

A popular hike involves walking east on the Chivay road to the Mirador de Tapay (before Cruz del Cóndor), then descending to the river on a steep track (four hours, take care). Cross the bridge to the village of San Juan de Chuccho on the north bank, where you can stay and eat at a basic family hostel, of which there are several. From here, pass **Tapay** (also possible to camp here, minivan to Cabanaconde at 0400 and 1100) and the small villages of Cosñirhua and Malata, all the time heading west along the north side of the Río Colca (take a guide or ask local directions). After about three hours' walking, cross another bridge to the south bank of the Río Colca, follow signs to Sangalle, spend the night and return to Cabanconde on the third day. This route is offered by many Arequipa and local agencies.

Another nice hike, which can be combined with the one above, goes west past the stadium to Mirador de Achachihua, then steeply downhill to a road and, along it to a pedestrian or a car bridge over the Río Colca (three to four hours). Before crossing, look for geysers upstream from the pedestrian bridge. On the north side, continue on the road for about 30 minutes. At a hairpin bend where the road turns northeast, go left and follow a large trail northwest, cross a pedestrian bridge over the Río Huaruro, just ahead is **Llahuar** (30 minutes from the road) with nice rustic thermal baths next to the Colca River and two places to stay. Minivans from Tapay to Cabanaconde Pass the Llahuar turn-off around 0500 and 1200. From Llahuar, you can continue steeply uphill to the villages of Llatica and Fure and the Fure and Huaruro Falls (five to six hours). From Fure you can reach the Tapay–Cabanaconde road.

# Trekking around Cabanaconde

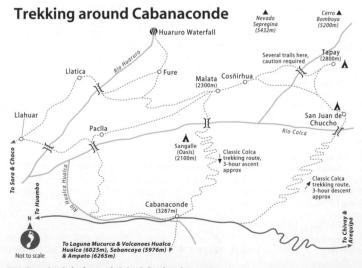

## Tourist information

Tourist information and a map are available in Arequipa from the **Autoridad Autónoma del Colca** (Puente Grau 116, T054-203010, Mon-Fri 0900-1700, Sat 0900-1200). In Chivay, there is a very helpful **tourist office** in the Municipalidad on the west side of the plaza (closed at weekends). The tourist police, also on the plaza, can give advice about local guides. There's a traveller's **Medical Center (TMC)** (Ramón Castilla 232, T054-531037). There's also a friendly tourist information office in Cabanaconde (T054-280212) that is willing to give plenty of advice, if not maps. It's a good place to find trekking guides and muleteers (US$25 a day mule and guide).

## Where to stay

Note that only the fancier hotels and *hostales* have Wi-Fi and it is very slow.

### Chivay and around

#### $$$ Casa Andina
*Huayna Cápac s/n, Chivay, T054-531020, www.casa-andina.com.*
Attractive cabins with hot showers and a cosy bar/dining area, a member of the recommended hotel chain, heating, parking.

#### $$$ Pozo del Cielo
*C Huáscar B-3, Sacsayhuaman–Chivay, T054-531041 (Alvarez Thomas 309, Arequipa, T054-346547), www.pozodelcielo.com.pe.*
Very comfortable option, located over the Puente Inca from Chivay amid pre-Inca terraces. Warm rooms, good views, good service and restaurant.

#### $$ Casa de Lucila
*M Grau 131, Chivay, T054-531109, http://vitatours.com.pe.*
Large 4-storey hotel, comfortable rooms, guides available, reserve ahead in high season.

#### $$ Colca Inn
*Salaverry 307, Chivay, T054-531111, www.hotelcolcainn.com.*
Good mid-range option, modern, decent restaurant, basic breakfast included or US$2.50 for buffet breakfast, some rooms with heaters, nice views from upper rooms. Also run the more upmarket **Hotel Colcallacta**.

#### $$ La Casa de Mamayacchi
*In Coporaque, 6 km from Chivay on the opposite side of the river, T054-531004, www.lacasademamayacchi.com, reservations through Giardino Tours in Arequipa.*
Part of the hotel is in an original Inca structure, nice rooms with heaters, lovely dining area, terraced garden, multi-day packages including transport.

#### $$ Posada del Colca
*Salaverry 325, Chivay, T054-531040, laposadadelcolca@hotmail.com, also on Facebook.*
Central, good rooms.

#### $ Hospedaje Restaurant Los Portales
*Arequipa 603, Chivay, T054-531101, losportalesdechivay@hotmail.com, also on Facebook.*
Good value, though beds have rather 'floppy' mattresses. Restaurant downstairs.

#### $ La Pascana
*Puente Inca y C Siglo XX 106, Chivay, T054-531001, hrlapascana@hotmail.com.*
Excellent value on the northwest corner of the plaza. Spacious en suite rooms overlook a pleasant garden, hot water, parking and a good restaurant.

#### $ Rumi Wasi
*Sucre 714, 6 blocks from plaza (3 mins' walk), Chivay.*
Good rooms, hot water, parking, helpful staff. Worthwhile economy option.

## Chivay to Cruz del Cóndor

### $$$$ Colca Lodge
*Across the river from Yanque, T054-531191 (office: Mariscal Benavides 201, Selva Alegre, Arequipa, T054-202587), www.colca-lodge.com.*
Very relaxing, with beautiful hot springs beside the river, spend at least a day to make the most of the activities on offer. Day passes available. Rooms heated with geothermal energy, solar-heated water.

### $$$$ Las Casitas del Colca
*Av Fundo La Curiña s/n, Yanque, T996 998355, www.lascasitasdelcolca.com.*
Luxury cottages made of local materials with underfloor heating and plunge pools. Has a gourmet restaurant, bar, vegetable garden and farm, offers cookery and painting courses, the spa offers a variety of treatments, swimming pool.

### $$$ Collahua
*Av Collahua cuadra 7, Yanque (office: Mercaderes 212, Galerías Gamesa, Arequipa, T054-226098), www.hotelcollahua.com.*
Modern bungalows just outside Yanque, with heating, solar-powered 24-hr hot water and plush rooms, restaurant.

### $$$ Eco Inn
*Lima 513, Yanque, T054-837112, www.ecoinnhotels.com.pe.*
Perched high on a bluff with incredible views over the valley and restored Uyo Uyo ruins. Large, comfortable rooms in cabins, restaurant open from 0530 for buffet breakfast, Wi-Fi in lobby and restaurant.

### $$ Tradición Colca
*Av Colca 119, Yanque, T054-781178 (office: C Argentina 108, Urbanización Fecia JL Bustamante y Rivero, T054-424926), www.tradicioncolca.com.*
Adobe construction, gas stove, garden spa, massages, sauna. Restaurant, bar, games room, observatory and planetarium (free for guests), horse riding from 2 hrs to 2 days, hiking tour to Ullu Ullu, bike rentals, travel agency in Arequipa.

### $ Casa Bella Flor Sumaq Wayta Wasi
*Cuzco 303, Yanque, T054-774505, www.casabellaflor.com.*
Charming small lodge run by Sra Hilde Checca, flower-filled garden, tasteful rooms, good meals (also open to non-residents). Hilde's uncle, Gregorio, guides visitors to pre-Columbian sites.

### $ Hospedaje Refugio del Geyser
*C Melgar s/n, behind municipality, Pinchollo, T959-007441.*
Basic with good local information.

### $ Rijchariy Colca Lodge
*On the track leading down to the footbridge over the river, Yanque, T054-764610.*
Great views, garden, comfortable rooms, restaurant.

---

## Cabanaconde

### $$ Kuntur Wassi
*C Cruz Blanca s/n, on the hill above the plaza, T054-233120, www.arequipacolca.com.*
Excellent 3-star, restaurant with fine traditional meals. Creative design, with rooms with heaters spaced between rock gardens and waterfalls. Viewing 'tower' and conference centre above. Owners Walter and María very welcoming and knowledgeable about treks.

### $$ La Casa de Santiago
*Grau, 3 blocks from the plaza, T941 414048, www.lacasadesantiago.com.*
Upmarket small *hostal*, with views of the mountains and a large garden.

### $$ Posada del Conde
*C San Pedro, T054-440197, pdelconde@yahoo.com.*
Smart hotel and lodge. Cheaper in low season, with hot shower, comfortable beds, good food. Local guides and horses for hire.

### $ Hostal Valle del Fuego
*1 and 2 blocks from the plaza on C Grau y Bolívar, T054-668910, www.valledelfuego.com.*
Rooms with comfortable beds and dorms (US$7 pp, breakfast extra), laundry facilities,

good restaurant. Can arrange guides, pack animals, bike rentals. The Junco family have plenty of information and work with related establishments, including: **Pablo Tour** in Arequipa, where you can make reservations and get a Colca map; **Oasis Paraíso** in Sangalle (discounts for clients of Valle del Fuego and related hotels); **Casa de Pablo Club** at the end of the street, and **La Casa de Santiago** (see above). They usually meet the incoming buses. Popular.

### $ La Posada de San Felipe
*At Anglican Church, Camino al Mirador Achachihua, 4 blocks from the plaza, T983 855648.*
Nice ample rooms with bath and reliable hot water, quiet location.

### $ Pachamama Home
*San Pedro 209, T054-767277, www.pachamamahome.com.*
Backpacker hostel, rooms with and without bath, family atmosphere, hot water, lots of information, good bar/pizzeria **Pachamama** next door, try the Colca Sour, made from a local cactus. You can help with teaching and activities for village children.

### $ Virgen del Carmen
*Av Arequipa s/n, 5 blocks up from the plaza*
Hot showers, may even offer you a welcoming glass of *chicha*.

### Trekking around Cabanaconde
Sangalle has 3 campsites with basic bungalows and toilets. In San Juan de Chuccho, **Hostal Roy** and **Casa de Rebelino** (**$**) are both good. US$2 will buy you a decent meal. Llahuar hostels (**$**) fill up, reserve ahead, **Llahuar Lodge** (T956 271333, llahuar.lodge@hotmail.com), rustic cabins with shared cold shower, nice camping area above hot pools (US$3 pp), good meals; next door and more economical is **Casa de Virginia** (T973 559851), rooms with shared bath with solar hot shower, camping (US$2.30 pp) meals on request, use of pools at Llahuar Lodge.

## Restaurants

### Chivay and around
Several restaurants serve buffet lunches for tour groups, US$5 pp, also open to the general public. Of the few that open in the evening, most have folklore shows and are packed with tour groups. When walking in the valley meals and drinks can be taken in any of the larger lodges. For local cheeses and dairy products, visit **Productos del Colca** (Av 22 de Agosto), in the central market.

### $$ El Balcón de Don Zacarías
*Av 22 de Agosto 102 on plaza, T054-531108.*
Breakfast, the best lunch buffet in town, à la carte menu, *Novo Andino* and international cuisine.

### $$ Yaraví
*Plaza de Armas 604.*
Arequipeña food, vegetarian options and the most impressive coffee machine in town.

### $$-$ McElroys's Irish Pub
*On the plaza.*
Warm bar, good selection of drinks (sometimes including expensive Guinness), sandwiches, pizza, pasta and music. Also buffet lunch and à la carte at night. Accepts Visa.

### $ Aromas Caffee
*Plaza de Armas 101, www.aromascaffee.com.*
Very good regional coffee, juices, sandwiches and sweets.

### $ Innkas Café-Bar
*Plaza de Armas 706.*
Coffee, sandwiches, *menú*, pizzas, pool table, good atmosphere.

### Cabanaconde

### $$-$ Casa de Pablo Club
*C Grau.*
Excellent fresh juices and *pisco sour*, cable TV (football!), small book exchange and some equipment hire.

### $ Café de Mirko
*At Plaza de Armas. Opens early.*
Small café serving coffee, teas and snacks.

**$ Rancho del Colca**
*On the plaza.*
Mainly vegetarian.

## Festivals

There are numerous festivals in the Colca region, many of which last several days and involve traditional dances and customs.

**2-3 Feb Virgen de la Candelaria**, celebrated in Chivay, Cabanaconde, Maca and Tapay.
**Feb Carnaval** in Chivay.
**3 May Cruz de la Piedra** in Tuti.
**13 Jun San Antonio** in Yanque and Maca.
**14 Jun San Juan** in Sibayo and Ichupampa.
**21 Jun Anniversary of Chivay**.
**29 Jun San Pedro y San Pablo** in Sibayo.
**14-17 Jul La Virgen del Carmen** in Cabanaconde.
**25 Jul Santiago Apóstol** in Coporaque.
**26 Jul-2 Aug Virgen Santa Ana** in Maca.
**15 Aug Virgen de la Asunta** in Chivay.
**8 Dec Immaculada Concepción** in Yanque and Chivay.
**25 Dec Sagrada Familia** in Yanque.

## What to do

See also Essential Colca Canyon, page 242.

### Chivay
Several tour agencies are located near the church on Plaza de Armas. All offer similar services: visits to Cruz del Cóndor, trekking, bike rentals, bus tickets, etc.

### Cabanaconde
Local guides charge US$15 pp per day to Sangalle, US$20 pp per day to Llahuar, minimum 3 passengers. A muleteer with 1 mule charges US$25 per day.
**Agotour Colca**, *T951 526615 (Alejandro Maque).* An association of regional guides.
**Chiqui Travel & Expeditions**, *Plaza de Armas s/n, next to the Municipalidad, T958-063602.* Edizon Gomosio, private guide, professional and reliable, organizes trekking, biking

and horse riding, can also arrange for pack animals and make reservations.

## Transport

### Bus
The bus station in Chivay is 3 blocks from the main plaza, next to the stadium for service to Arequipa, Cabanaconde and Pinchollo. Vans and *colectivos* leave from the terminal behind the market to other villages in the area.

See Arequipa Transport, page 239, for service originating there. To **Arequipa**, buses start at the Plaza de Armas in **Cabanaconde**, US$5.50, 5 hrs; **Reyna** at 0700 and 1400, **Andalucía** at 0900 and 1300 and **Trans Milagros** at 1130 and 2200; they pass **Cruz del Cóndor** (20 mins, US$2.20), then **Chivay** 2 hrs after departure; Chivay–Arequipa US$4, 3 hrs. Tour buses take extra passengers if they have room, enquire with tour operators. **4M Express** (see below) offers private transport to Arequipa on request. **Chivay** to/from **Cabanaconde**, 56 km, US$1.45, 2 hrs, through buses depart from/to Arequipa; also hourly minibuses depart half a block from the Chivay terminal. To **Cuzco**, take the **4M Express** tourist service (see below) or a regular bus to Cañahuas and change there for a bus to Juliaca, then carry on to Cuzco. Note, however, there are no bus stations in Cañahuas, it is cold and buses to Juliaca are often full.

**Tourist service 4M Express**, www.4m-express.com, has several routes departing from Hotel La Pascana on Chivay's plaza, all stop at places of interest along the way and include a snack. To **Puno** Terminal Terrestre, daily 1315, US$50, 7 hrs, stopping at Patapampa lookout, Chucura Volcano and Lagunillas (birdwatching). To **Cuzco**, direct route along a paved road via Tuti, Sibayo and Sicuani, Mon, Wed and Fri at 0700, US$65 (lunch extra), 10½ hrs, stopping at Castillos de Callalli rock formations, Yauri rock forest, Laguna de Langui (25 km long), Sicuani (lunch break) and dropping off at 4M's private station.

# ★ Cotahuasi Canyon

how low can you go?

At its deepest, at Ushua (just below the village of Quechualla), the Cotahuasi Canyon measures 3354 m from rim to river, making it 163 m deeper than the Colca Canyon and the deepest canyon in the world. From this point, the only way along the canyon is by kayak, and it is through kayakers' reports that the area has come to the notice of tourists.

The Reserva Paisajística Cañón de Cotahuasi protects the extensive Cotahuasi drainage, from the icy summits of Solimana and Huanzo (5445 m) to where it joins the Río Ocoña at 950 m. The canyon is very dry, especially from April to October when the contrast between the desert slopes and the green irrigated oases along the wider sections of the river valley and on the hanging valleys of its tributaries is particularly striking. Grapes, organic *kiwicha* (amaranth) and quinoa for export, avocados, citrus and other fruits are grown here. The side canyons are very impressive in their own right. Despite the arid climate and rugged geography, the canyon has been populated for centuries. There are a number of pre-Inca and Inca remains perched on terraces cut into the vertical canyon walls and segments of Inca trade routes from the coast to the highlands can still be seen. The area has several thermal baths, waterfalls, impressive rock formations, cacti and *Puya raimondii* bromeliad forests, and amazing views. A good *turismo vivencial* programme with homestays in many villages allows you to access all the attractions.

## Towards Cotahuasi: Río Majes Valley
Southwest of Arequipa, a paved road branches off the Pan-American to the impressive Siguas Canyon and on to the agricultural valley and canyon of the Río Majes, a rafting destination. At the linear roadside town of **Corire** are several hotels and restaurants serving excellent freshwater shrimp.

Nearby is the world's largest field of petroglyphs at **Toro Muerto** ① *6.5 km from Corire, US$1.45, van from the plaza in Corire to La Candelaria Mon-Fri 0700, returning 1400, US$0.60, or taxi, US$14 incl 2-hr wait, tours available from Arequipa.* Access to the UNESCO World Heritage Site is signposted off the main road 1.5 km south of Corire, where a road turns east to the village of La Candelaria, 2 km from the main road. One block above the plaza is the archaeological site's office where the entry fee is collected. From here it is 3 km on a dirt road to the site entrance which provides the only shade in the area; the immense field of 5000 sculpted rocks in the desert lies beyond. The sheer scale of the 5-sq-km site is awe-inspiring and the view is wonderful. The higher you go, the more interesting the petroglyphs, though some have been ruined by graffiti. Don't believe the guides who, after the first few rocks, say the others are all the same. The designs range from simple llamas to elaborate human figures and animals. There are several styles which are thought to be Wari (AD 700-1100), Chuquibamba (AD 1000-1475) and Inca in origin. An extensive review of the designs is found in *Memorias del Arqueólogo Eloy Linares Málaga* (Universidad Alas Peruanas, 2011). Take plenty of water, sunglasses and sun cream. At least an hour is needed to visit the site.

From Corire an unpaved road follows the Río Majes to Camaná on the coast. Upriver from Corire, the paved road goes past a park with dinosaur prints to the regional centre of **Aplao**, which has a small museum containing Wari cultural objects from the surrounding area. A side road to the north leads to **Andagua** (several places to stay) in the fascinating **Valle de los Volcanes**, while the main paved road continues northwest to **Chuquibamba** (several places to stay and eat) in a scenic terraced valley, where the paving ends. Beyond Chuquibamba, the road climbs steeply to traverse the *puna* between Nevado Coropuna (6425 m) and Nevado Solimana (6093 m). The views are awe-inspiring, so it is well worth the effort to travel this route by day.

The once precarious road to the Cotahuasi Canyon has been improved and there is talk of paving the remaining 120 km between Chuquibamba and Cotahuasi town, which would cut travel time from Arequipa to under six hours and end the region's splendid isolation.

## Cotahuasi and the upper canyon

From **Mirador Allhuay** (3950 m) at the rim of the Cotahuasi Canyon, the road, already paved, winds down to the peaceful colonial town of **Cotahuasi**, nestled in a sheltered hanging valley at 2680 m, beneath Cerro Huinao. Its streets are narrow, with whitewashed houses. The Río Cotahuasi flows 1500 m below the town at the bottom of its great canyon.

Following the Río Cotahuasi to the northeast up the valley, you come to **Tomepampa** (10 km), a small town at 2700 m, with painted houses and a colonial church. The attractive hot springs of **Luicho** ① *16.5 km from Cotahuasi, daily 0330-2130, US$1.80, 1 simple room for rent*, are a short walk from the road, across a bridge. There are three pools (33° to 38°C). The paved road ends at **Alca**, 20 km from Cotahuasi, at 2750 m, with several simple places to stay and eat. Above it are the small ruins of Kallak, Tiknay and a 'stone library' of rock formations. All these places are connected by hourly mini-buses from Cotahuasi (see Transport). **Puyca** ① *23 km beyond Alca, bus from Alca at 0530, return at 1200, 1½ hrs, US$2.50, www.canyoncotahuasi.com*, is the last village of any significance in the valley, hanging on a hillside at 3560 m. Locals can guide you on treks in the area, and horses can be hired. Nearby, at 3700 m, are the extensive Wari ruins of Maucallacta (20-minute walk), the most important in the Cotahuasi area. Beyond is **Churca** ① *24 km from Puyca, van from Alca at 0530, return at 1200, 2-3 hrs, US$3.20*, from where you can walk to Lauripampa at about 4000 m in 20 minutes to see a vast prairie of *Puya raimondii* plants. On the opposite side of the river from Churca is Chincayllapa from where you can drive to the Occoruro geysers at 4466 m, also reached in a full-day walk from Puyca.

Along a tributary of the Cotahuasi, in a beautiful terraced side canyon north of Cotahuasi, is the village of **Pampamarca** ① *at 3397 m, 28 km from Cotahuasi, no vehicle access following a 2016 landslide, enquire locally about hiking to Pampamarca and accommodation in homestays*. There are excellent walking possibilities here. Attractions include the Wito rock formations, 90-m-high Uskune waterfall, Josla thermal baths and, a bit further afield, the Fuysiri waterfalls.

## Downstream from Cotahuasi

A rough, narrow road follows the Río Cotahuasi downriver for 28 km to Mayo. At Km 13 is the access to the powerful, 150-m **Cataratas de Sipia** ① *2 km from the road, bus from Terminal Terrestre Tue-Thu and Sat 0630, Mon and Sun 0630 and 1330, Fri 0630 and 1400, US$1.45, 30 mins (return 2½-3 hrs later)*. A good trail leads from the road to several lookouts over the three-tiered falls, which are the most visited attraction in the canyon; take care near the edge, especially if it is windy. The best light is at midday. You can also get an overview of the falls from the road, continuing past the turn-off to the top of the hill.

From Sipia the road, carved into the canyon wall, leads to the hamlets of Chaupo and Rosariopampa and, at Km 23, the impressive cactus forest of **Judiopampa**, before climbing to **Velinga** (with homestays). The road continues to the charming little village of **Quechualla** at 1665 m (9 km from Velinga, more homestays). Beyond Quechualla, a trail leads to Ushua, the deepest part of the canyon.

## Tourist information

Tourist information is available from
**CONSETUR**, represented in Cotahuasi by
**Purek Tours** (C Arequipa 103, daily 0900-
1300, 1400-2000). A map of Cotahuasi may
be available at **iPerú** in Arequipa. See also
www.municipiolaunion.com. There are no
ATMs in Cotahuasi but **Banco de la Nación**
(C Cabildo) changes US$ cash.

## Where to stay

**Río Majes Valley**

**$ Hostal Willy's**
*Av Progreso opposite the market, Corire,
T054-472046 and Progreso y Morán,
at the plaza, Aplao, T959-476622.*
Both modern buildings with comfortable
rooms, no breakfast.

**$ La Casa de Mauro**
*La Central, 12 km north of Aplao
(combi service), T054-631076,
www.star.com.pe/lacasademauro.*
Simple cabins and camping (US$5.50 per
tent) in a lovely rural setting, restaurant
with 60 different shrimp dishes, run by the
friendly Zúñiga family, rafting, trekking and
conventional tours.

**$ Montano**
*Ramón Castilla s/n, Corire, T054-472122.*
Best rooms are at the back away from the
road, some rooms are small, no breakfast,
good value.

**Cotahuasi and the upper canyon**
For information about homestays in
the villages outside Cotahuasi, contact
CONSETUR (see above).

**$$ Valle Hermoso**
*Tacna 108-110, Cotahuasi, T054-581057,
www.hotelvallehermoso.com.*

Nice and cosy, includes breakfast, beautiful
views of the canyon, comfortable rooms,
large garden, meals with home-grown fruit
and veg require advanced notice.

**$ Casa Primavera**
*Main street, Tomepampa, T954-734056.*
Family-run hostel with a flower-filled
courtyard, some rooms with private bath,
price includes breakfast, other meals on
request, kitchen facilities, common areas,
good value.

**$ Don Justito**
*Arequipa 110, ½ block below the plaza,
Cotahuasi, T973-698053.*
Ample functional rooms with and without
bath, plenty of solar-heated water, popular,
good-value economy option.

**$ El Mirador**
*Centenario 100-A, Cotahuasi, T054-489417.*
Pleasant rooms, great views, parking,
no breakfast.

**$ Hatun Huasi**
*Centenario 309, Cotahuasi, T054-581054,
www.hatunhuasi.com.*
Popular *hostal* with a variety of rooms, nice
small garden and common areas, parking,
breakfast extra, helpful owner Catalina Borda
speaks some English. Recommended.

## Restaurants

**Cotahuasi and the upper canyon**
There are many *tiendas* well-stocked with
fruit, vegetables and local wine.

**$$-$ Buen Sabor**
*C Arequipa, up from the plaza, Cotahuasi.*
A la carte Peruvian dishes, caters to tourists.

**$ La Chocita Cotahuasina**
*Av Independencia, ½ block from the church,
Cotahuasi. Open 0700-2100, closed Wed.*
Good set meals, pleasant patio seating.

## What to do

Several tour operators in Arequipa (see page 238), organize tours to Cotahuasi. Also see **Purek Tours** in Cotahuasi town, under Tourist information, above.

**Amazonas Explorer**, *in Cuzco (see page 313), www.amazonas-explorer.com*. Can organize 5-day kayaking expeditions on the Cotahuasi for experienced kayakers only.

### Río Majes Valley
**La Casa de Mauro Tours**, *see Where to stay, T959-362340, www.star.com.pe/ lacasademauro*. Pancho Zúñiga offers rafting, trekking and 4WD tours in the Majes, Cotahuasi and Colca areas.

### Cotahuasi and the upper canyon
**Purek Tours**, *C Arequipa 103, Cotahuasi, T054-698081, cotahuasitours@gmail.com*. Biking, horse riding and 2- to 3-day trekking tours.

## Transport

### Río Majes Valley
**Empresa Del Carpio** buses to **Corire** and **Aplao** leave from the Terrapuerto in **Arequipa** about every 1½ hrs 0430-1900, 3-4 hrs, US$4.30; to **Chuquibamba** at 0515 and 1615, return 0500 and 1200, US$7.50, 6-7 hrs. For **Toro Muerto**, ask to be let out at the turn-off to La Candelaria. Cotahuasi-bound buses from Arequipa stop at the plaza in Corire (near the Del Carpio station), at the highway in Aplao and at the terminal in Chuquibamba. To **Camaná** on the coast (transfer here for Nazca and Lima), van from Aplao at 0800, passes Corire 0830, US$5.40, 2 hrs; returns from Camaná at 0400-0500. To **Andagua**, **Reyna** from Arequipa at 1600, via Corire and Aplao, return about 1500. There is a daily minivan from Andagua to **Chacas**.

### Cotahuasi and the upper canyon
Destinations along the canyon are connected Mon-Sat 0600-1800 by hourly combis from Cotahuasi, fewer on Sun. Cotahuasi has a modern bus station (terminal fee US$0.35) 10 mins' walk from the plaza. Buses daily from **Arequipa** Terminal Terrestre, 8-9 hrs, US$11: **Cromotex** at 1900; **Reyna** at 1700 and 1900; they stop for refreshments in Chuquibamba, about halfway. Both companies continue to **Tomepampa** and **Alca;** buses leave Alca for Arequipa around 1400 (you can get off at Cotahuasi). Return Cotahuasi to Arequipa, **Cromotex** at 1900, **Reyna** at 1700 and 1900. From **Lima**, **Trans López** (Sebatián Barranca 158, La Victoria, T01-332 1015), Sun at 0900, US$36, 20 hrs (passes Chuquibamba Mon 0500-0630); return Cotahuasi to Lima Tue 0700. This is the only public transport daytime option to/from Cotahuasi, offering magnificent views; you can board in Corire, Aplao or Chuquibamba.

# South of
Arequipa

From Arequipa, the main road to the coast goes southwest for 37 km to Repartición where it divides. One branch goes west from here for 54 km through a striking arid landscape before dividing again: northwest to the Majes and Cotahuasi areas (see above) or southwest to Camaná (170 km from Arequipa) on the coast. The second branch from Repartición goes south and, in 15 km, divides south to Mollendo and southeast towards Moquegua.

**Moquegua and around** *Colour map 6, C2.*

This city lies 213 km from Arequipa in the narrow Moquegua river valley and enjoys a subtropical climate. The old centre, a few blocks above the Pan-American Highway, has winding, cobbled streets and 19th-century buildings. The Plaza de Armas, with its mix of ruined and well-maintained churches, colonial and republican façades and fine trees, is one of the most interesting small-city plazas in the country. Within the ruins of Iglesia Matriz is the **Museo Contisuyo** ① *Jr Tacna 294, on the Plaza de Armas, T053-461844, www. museocontisuyo.com, Daily 0800-1300, 1430-1730, US$0.50,* which focuses on the cultures that thrived in the Moquegua and Ilo valleys, including the Huari, Tiahuanaco, Chiribaya and Estuquiña, who were conquered by the Incas. Artefacts are well displayed and explained in Spanish and English.

A highly recommended excursion is to **Cerro Baúl** (2590 m) ① *20 mins by colectivo, US$1,* a huge limestone plateau with marvellous views and many legends. A steep path leads up to the summit, allow three hours round trip and take plenty of water and sunscreen. Nearby is the pleasant and attractive town of **Torata** (24 km northeast of Moquegua, combis from Moquegua stadium, US$1.25), renowned for its traditional bread. **La Ruta del Pisco,** mainly to the south of the city, connects about a dozen *bodegas* such as Biondi, producing pisco in the Moquegua Valley. The area is also known for its excellent olives.

One of the most breathtaking stretches of the **Carretera Binacional** from Ilo to La Paz runs from Moquegua to Desaguadero at the southeastern end of Lake Titicaca. The road is fully paved and should be travelled in daylight. It skirts Cerro Baúl and climbs through zones of ancient terraces to its highest point at 4755 m. On the altiplano there are herds of llamas and alpacas, lakes with waterfowl, strange mountain formations and snow-covered peaks. At Mazo Cruz there is a PNP checkpoint where all documents and bags are checked. Approaching Desaguadero the magnificent Cordillera Real of Bolivia comes into view.

## Tacna *Colour map 6, C2.*

Thanks to its location, only 36 km from the Chilean border and 56 km from the international port of Arica, Tacna has free-trade status. It is an important commercial centre, and Chileans flock here for shopping and inexpensive medical and dental treatment. Around the city the desert is gradually being irrigated for agriculture; fishing is also important. Tacna was in Chilean hands from 1880 to 1929, when its people voted by plebiscite to return to Peru. Above the city (8 km away, just off the Panamericana Norte) is the **Campo de la Alianza**, scene of a battle between Peru and Chile in 1880. The cathedral, designed by Eiffel, faces the Plaza de Armas, which contains huge bronze statues of Admiral Grau and Colonel Bolognesi. They stand at either end of the Arca de los Héroes, the triumphal arch which is the symbol of the city. The bronze fountain in the plaza is said to be a duplicate of the one in the Place de la Concorde (Paris) and was also designed by Eiffel. The **Parque de la Locomotora** ① *knock at the gate under the clocktower on Jr 2 de Mayo for entry, daily 0700-1700, US$0.30,* near the city centre, has a British-built locomotive, which was used in the War of the Pacific. There is a very good railway museum at the station.

### Border with Chile

It is 56 km from Tacna to the Chilean city of Arica. The border post is 30 minutes from Tacna at Santa Rosa, open 0800-2300 Sunday to Thursday and 24 hours on Friday and Saturday. You need to obtain a Peruvian exit stamp at Santa Rosa before proceeding a short distance to the Chilean post at Chacalluta where you will get a Chilean entrance stamp. Formalities are straightforward and should take about 30 minutes in total. All luggage is X-rayed in both directions. No fruit or vegetables are allowed across the border. If you need a Chilean visa, get it from the Chilean consulate in Tacna (Presbítero Andía block 1, T052-423063, Monday-Friday 0800-1300). Money-changers can be found at counters in the international bus terminal; rates are much the same as in town. Remember that Peruvian time is one hour earlier than Chilean time from March to October; two hours earlier from September/October to February/March (varies annually).

**Crossing by bus** It takes one to two hours to travel from Tacna to Arica, depending on waiting time at the border. Buses charge US$2.50, and *colectivo* taxis, which carry five passengers, charge US$7.50 per person. All leave from the international terminal in Tacna throughout the day, although *colectivos* only leave when full. As you approach the terminal you will be grabbed by a driver or his agent and told that the car is "just about to leave". This is hard to verify as you may not see the *colectivo* until you have filled in the paperwork. Once you have chosen a driver/agent, you will be rushed to his company's office where your passport will be taken from you and the details filled out on a Chilean entry form. It is then 30 minutes to the Peruvian border post at Santa Rosa. The driver will hustle you through all the exit procedures. A short distance beyond is the Chilean post at Chacalluta, where again the driver will show you what to do. It's a further 15 minutes from Chacalluta to Arica's bus terminal. A Chilean driver is more likely to take you to any address in Arica.

**Crossing by private vehicle** Those leaving Peru by car must buy *relaciones de pasajeros* (official forms, US$0.45) from the kiosk at the border or from a bookshop; you will need four copies. At the border, return your tourist card to immigration (Migraciones), visit the PNP (police) office, return the vehicle permit to the SUNAT/Aduana office and finally depart through the checkpoints.

## Tourist information

### Moquegua

**Dircetur**
*Ayacucho 1060, T053-462236.*
*Mon-Fri 0800-1630.*
The regional tourist office.

### Tacna

**Dircetur**
*Blondell 50, p 2, T052-246944, www.*
*turismotacna.com. Mon-Fri 0730-1530.*
Provides a city map and regional information.

**Immigration**
*Av Circunvalación s/n, Urbanización El*
*Triángulo, T052-243231.*

**iPerú**
*San Martín 491, Plaza de Armas, T052-*
*425514. Mon-Sat 0830-1800, Sun 0830-1300,*
*iperutacna@promperu.gob.pe.*
Also in the Arrivals hall at the airport (usually
open when flights are scheduled to arrive),
at the Terminal Terrestre Internacional (Mon-
Sat 0830-1500) and at the border (Fri-Sat
0830-1600).

**OGD Tur Tacna**
*Deústua 364, of 107, T052-242777.*

**Tourist police**
*Pasaje Calderón de la Barca 353, inside the*
*main police station, T052-414141 ext 245.*

## Where to stay

### Moquegua

A Casa Andina (www.casa-andina.com)
opened in 2017.

**$$ Colonial**
*Urbanización San Fernando, behind the*
*football stadium, T053-461569, www.*
*hotelcolonialmoqueguaperu.com.*
Good rooms (some have a grandstand view
of the football pitch!), nice quiet setting, pool
and garden, helpful staff, buffet breakfast.

**$$-$ Principado**
*Moquegua 249, T053-463540.*
Clean, comfortable lodgings, opened in 2017,
popular and often full, book in advance.

**$ Alameda**
*Junín 322, T053-463971.*
Includes breakfast, large comfortable
rooms, welcoming.

**$ Hostal Carrera**
*Jr Lima 320-A (no sign), T053-462113.*
With or without bath, solar-powered hot
water (best in afternoon), laundry facilities
on roof, good value.

### Tacna

**$$$ Gran Hotel Tacna**
*Av Bolognesi 300, T052-424193,*
*www.dmhoteles.pe.*
Disco, gardens, safe car park. The pool is
open to non-guests who make purchases
at the restaurant or bar. English spoken.

**$$ Copacabana**
*Arias Aragüez 370, T052-421721,*
*www.copahotel.com.*
Good rooms, also has a restaurant and pizzeria.

**$$ Dorado**
*Arias Aragüez 145, T052-415741,*
*www.doradohoteltacna.com.*
Modern and comfortable, good
service, restaurant.

**$$ El Mesón**
*H Unanue 175, T052-425841,*
*www.mesonhotel.com.*
Central, modern, comfortable, safe.

**$ Hostal Anturio**
*28 de Julio 194 y Zela, T052-244258.*
Cafeteria, breakfast extra, good value.

**$ La Posada del Cacique**
*Arias Aragüez 300-4, T052-247424.*
Antique style in an amazing building
constructed around a huge spiral staircase.

## $ Roble 18 Residencial
*H Unanue 245, T052-241414,*
*roble18@gmail.com.*
1 block from Plaza de Armas. Hot water,
English, Italian, German spoken.

## Restaurants

### Moquegua

#### $$ El Punto de Paisa
*Urbanización Primavera H-1, T053-462331.*
Excellent open-air fish restaurant. Try
a *fuente* (plate for 2) of delicious mixed
seafood for US$20.

#### $ Moraly
*Lima y Libertad. Mon-Sat 1000-2200,*
*Sun 1000-1600.*
Serves breakfast and good *comida criolla*
throughout the day. A reliable choice.

#### Café La Palacette
*Ancash 572.*
Prepares large juices and very creamy
cakes, as well as offering a shot of pisco
for under US$1.

#### Café Valeria
*Ancash 260.*
An alternative café with good coffee and
delicious *lechón* sandwiches in a Louis
XV-inspired red velvet and gold furnished
setting, where stand-up comedy or theatrical
shows take place from time to time. A nice
little surprise for Moquegua!

### Tacna

#### $$ Da Vinci
*San Martín 596 y Arias Araguez,*
*T052-744648. Mon-Sat 1100-2300,*
*bar Tue-Sat 2000-0200.*
Pizza and other dishes, nice atmosphere.

#### $ Cusqueñita
*Zela 747. Daily 1100-1600.*
Excellent 4-course lunch, large
portions, good value, variety of choices.
Recommended.

#### $ Koyuki
*Bolívar 718. Closed Sun evening.*
Generous set lunch daily, seafood and
à la carte in the evening. Several other
popular lunch places on the same block.

#### $ Salón Chifa
*San Martín 962.*
Said to be the best Chinese food in town.

#### $ Un Limón
*Av San Martín 843, T052-425182.*
Ceviches and variety of seafood dishes.

### Cafés

#### Café Zeit
*Deústua 150, CafeZeit on Facebook.*
German-owned coffee shop, cultural
events and live music as well as quality
coffee and cakes.

#### Verdi
*Pasaje Vigil 57.*
Café serving excellent *empanadas* and
sweets, also set lunch.

## Festivals

### Moquegua
**25 Nov Día de Santa Catalina.**
The anniversary of the founding
of the colonial city.

## Transport

### Moquegua
**Bus**
All bus companies are on Av Ejército,
2 blocks north of the market at Jr Grau,

> **Tip...**
> If you're travelling to La Paz, Bolivia,
> the quickest and cheapest route is
> via Moquegua and Desaguadero; it
> involves one less border crossing than
> via Arica and Tambo Colorado. There is
> a **Bolivian Consulate** in Tacna (Avenida
> Bolognesi 175, Urbanización Pescaserolli,
> T052-245121, Monday-Friday 0830-1630).

except **Ormeño** (Av La Paz casi Balta). To **Lima**, US$30-42, 15 hrs, many companies with executive and regular services. To **Tacna**, see Tacna to Moquegua, below; colectivos leave from the corner of Ancash y El Ejercito. To **Arequipa**, 3½ hrs, US$7.50-12, several buses daily. Colectivos for Tacna and Arequipa leave when full from Av del Ejercito y Andrés Aurelio Cáceres; they charge almost double the bus fare – negotiate. To **Desaguadero** and **Puno**, San Martín–Nobleza, 4 a day, 6 hrs, US$12; colectivos to Desaguadero, 4 hrs, US$20, with **Mily Tours** (Av del Ejército 32-B, T053-464000).

## Tacna
### Air
The airport (T052-314503) is at Km 5 on the Panamericana Sur, on the way to the border. To go from the airport directly to Arica, call the bus terminal (T052-427007) and ask a colectivo to pick you up on its way to the border, US$7.50. Taxi from airport to Tacna centre US$6.

To **Lima**, 1½ hrs; 4 daily flights with **LATAM** (Apurímac 101, esquina Av Bolognesi, T01-213 8200) and **Peruvian Airlines** (Av Bolognesi 670, p2, T052-412699), also to **Arequipa**.

### Bus
There are 2 bus stations (T052-427007; local tax US$0.50) on Hipólito Unánue, 1 km from the plaza (colectivo US$0.35, taxi US$1.25). One terminal is for international services (ie Arica), the other for domestic; both are well organized, with baggage stores. It is easy to make connections to the border,

**Tip...**
Bus passengers' luggage is checked at **Tomasiri**, 35 km north of Tacna. Do not carry anything on the bus for anyone else. Passports may be checked at Camiara, a police checkpoint some 60 km from Tacna. **Sernanp** also has a post where any fruit will be confiscated in an attempt to keep fruit fly out of Peru.

Arequipa or Lima. To **Moquegua**, 2.5 hrs, US$3; and **Arequipa**, 6 hrs, frequent buses with **Flores** (Av Saucini behind the Terminal Nacional, T052-426691), **Trans Moquegua Turismo** and **Cruz del Sur**. Ask at the **Flores** office about buses along the Vía Costanera to Ilo. Colectivos to Moquegua from roundabout near the bus station, US$6, 2 hrs. To **Nazca**, 793 km, 12 hrs, several buses daily, en route to Lima (fares US$3 less than to Lima). Several companies daily to **Lima**, 1239 km, 21-26 hrs, US$26-62 bus-cama with **Oltursa** or Civa; **Cruz del Sur** (T052-425729) charges US$43.

Buses to **Desaguadero**, **Puno** and **Cuzco** leave from Terminal Collasuyo (Av Internacional, Barrio Altos de la Alianz, T052-312538); taxi to centre US$1. San Martín–Nobleza in early morning and at night to **Desaguadero**, US$22, and **Puno**, US$18, 8-10 hrs.

### Train
The station is at Av Albaracín y 2 de Mayo. 2 trains daily at 0600 and 1630, US$4.50, 1½ hrs, immigration formalities at the respective stations.

# Lake Titicaca

the birthing pool for the Inca Empire

Straddling Peru's southern border with Bolivia are the deep, sapphire-blue waters of mystical Lake Titicaca, a favourite of school geography lessons. This gigantic inland sea covers up to 8500 sq km and is the highest navigable lake in the world, at an average 3810 m above sea level.

The Straits of Tiquina divide the lake in two: to the north, the larger Lago Mayor or Chucuito, and to the south, the smaller and shallower Lago Menor or Huiñamarca (Wiñaymarca). Titicaca's shores and islands are home to the Aymara, Quechua and Uros peoples. Here you can wander through old traditional villages where Spanish is a second language and where ancient myths and beliefs are still held dear.

The main city on the lake is Puno, where chilled travellers gather to stock up on warm woollies to keep the cold at bay. The high-altitude city is the departure point for the islands and is also well placed to visit the remarkable funeral towers of Sillustani and the peaceful Capachica Peninsula. When it is time to move on, make the beautiful journey from Puno to Cuzco, or visit some parts of Peru that other travellers rarely reach: the remote northeastern shore of the lake and the magnificent cordilleras of Carabaya and Apolobamba.

**Best** for
Boat trips ▪ Festivals ▪ Handicrafts ▪ Local customs ▪ Scenery

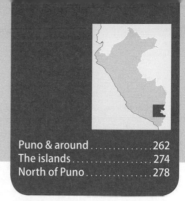

Puno & around . . . . . . . . . . . . . 262
The islands . . . . . . . . . . . . . . . . 274
North of Puno . . . . . . . . . . . . . . 278

# Footprint
## picks

★ **Fiesta de la Virgen de la Candelaria**, pages 263 and 270
Early February is the time to experience Puno's folklore at its best.

★ **Sillustani**, page 264
Set on a beautiful peninsula on Lake Umayo, these impressive stone
burial towers are up to 12 m high.

★ **Capachica Peninsula**, page 264
The community tourism programme gives visitors the opportunity to
experience rural life around Lake Titicaca first hand.

★ **Juli and Pomata**, pages 265 and 266
Anybody interested in religious architecture should visit these villages
along the southwestern shore of Lake Titicaca.

★ **Amantaní**, page 276
Explore the ruins and take in the magnificent views from the
top of Pacha Mama or Pacha Tata, the peaks of this beautiful
and tranquil island.

★ **Isla Suasi**, page 281
Leave the crowds and visit the northeast shore of Titicaca where you'll
find Isla Suasi, a private island with a luxury hotel.

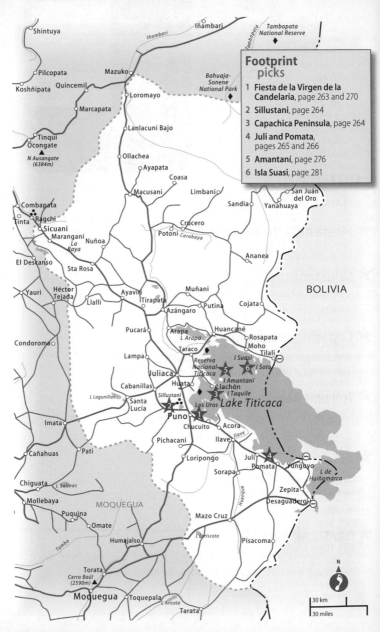

## Footprint picks

1 **Fiesta de la Virgen de la Candelaria**, page 263 and 270
2 **Sillustani**, page 264
3 **Capachica Peninsula**, page 264
4 **Juli and Pomata**, pages 265 and 266
5 **Amantaní**, page 276
6 **Isla Suasi**, page 281

# **Essential** Lake Titicaca

### Finding your feet

The regional airport is in Juliaca, 44 km north of Puno. Paved roads climb from the coastal deserts and oases to the high plateau around Lake Titicaca, either from Arequipa via Yura, Santa Lucía and Juliaca or from Moquegua via Desaguadero. The steep ascents lead to wide open views of pampas with agricultural communities, desolate mountains, small lakes and salt flats. It is a rapid change of altitude, so be prepared for some discomfort and breathlessness. The route to or from Cuzco, whether by rail or road, is also very beautiful and although the gradient is not as steep, it also reaches an altitude of 4321 m.

### Getting around

In Puno, the main places of interest and many hotels are within walking distance of Jirón Lima and the plazas. Three-wheel *trici-taxis* are the best way to get to the train station, port or local van stations (about 10 to 15 minutes from the centre) and a taxi to the bus station, especially if you have luggage or are not acclimatized to the altitude. Boats run regularly from the port to the most popular islands on the lake, and

villages along the western shore are easily reached by public transport. Northwest of Puno, Juliaca is a major transport hub with the only airport in the region and paved roads to Cuzco Arequipa, Puerto Maldonado and the scenic and under-visited north shore of the lake. There is good public transport to all these areas.

### When to go

Being so high up, Puno gets bitterly cold at night, and from June to August the temperature regularly drops below freezing. Days are bright and the midday sun is hot, but you can never be quite sure what weather is going to come off the lake. There is more rain from November to April. The first two weeks in February, when the Fiesta de la Candelaria takes place, and 4-5 November, when the emergence of the founding Incas from the lake is celebrated, are good times to visit, but crowded, too.

### Time required

One to two weeks will give you the chance to explore the area around Puno including the most popular islands. Add more time to venture along the northeastern shore.

## **Weather** Puno

| January | February | March | April | May | June |
|---------|----------|-------|-------|-----|------|
| 16°C | 16°C | 16°C | 17°C | 16°C | 16°C |
| 4°C | 3°C | 3°C | 1°C | -2°C | -4°C |
| 117mm | 81mm | 72mm | 36mm | 3mm | 3mm |

| July | August | September | October | November | December |
|------|--------|----------|---------|----------|----------|
| 16°C | 16°C | 17°C | 18°C | 17°C | 17°C |
| -6°C | -4°C | -1°C | 1°C | 2°C | 3°C |
| 0mm | 9mm | 12mm | 24mm | 45mm | 51mm |

Located on the northwest shore of Lake Titicaca at 3855 m, Puno is capital of its region and Peru's folklore centre, with a vast array of handicrafts, festivals and costumes and a rich tradition of music and dance. The city has a noticeable vitality, helped by the fact that students make up a large proportion of the 140,000-strong population.

### Sights

The **cathedral** ⓘ *Sun-Fri 0800-1200, 1500-1800, Sat 0800-1300, 1500-1900,* completed in 1657, has an impressive baroque exterior, but an austere interior. Across the street from the cathedral is the **Balcony of the Conde de Lemos** ⓘ *Deustua y Conde de Lemos, art gallery open Mon-Fri 0830-1230, 1330-1730,* where Peru's Viceroy stayed when he first arrived in the city. The **Museo Carlos Dreyer** ⓘ *Conde de Lemos 289, Mon-Fri 0900-1900,*

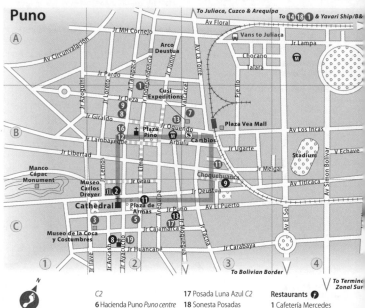

**Puno**

200 metres
200 yards

**Where to stay**
1 Casa Andina *A4, B2*
2 Casona Colón Inn *Puno centre*
3 Conde de Lemos *C2*
4 El Buho *Puno centre*
5 Hacienda Plaza de Armas *C2*
6 Hacienda Puno *Puno centre*
7 Hostal Imperial & Los Uros *B3*
8 Hostal Los Pinos *B2*
9 Hostal Margarita *B2*
10 Hostal Pukara *Puno centre*
11 Inka's Rest *B3*
12 Intiqa *B2*
13 Italia *B2*
14 Libertador Lago Titicaca *A4*
15 Plaza Mayor *Puno centre*
16 Posada Don Giorgio *B2*
17 Posada Luna Azul *C2*
18 Sonesta Posadas del Inca *A4*
19 Tayka & Vylena Hostels *C1*
20 Tierra Viva Puno Plaza *Puno centre*

**Restaurants** 🍴
1 Cafetería Mercedes *Puno centre*
2 Casa del Corregidor *C2*
3 Incabar *Puno centre*
4 La Casona *Puno centre*
5 La Cayma *Puno centre*
6 La Estancia *Puno centre*
7 La Hostería *Puno Centre*
8 La Table del'Inca *C2*
9 Loving Hut *C3*
10 Machupizza *Puno centre*
11 Mojsa *C2*

*Sat 0900-1300, US$4.60 includes 45-min guided tour,* has eight halls with archaeological and historical artefacts from pre-Inca to republican times. Around the corner is the **Casa del Corregidor** ① *Deusta 576,* a beautifully restored 17th-century home housing a nice café (see Restaurants, page 269) and shops. A block south of the cathedral at Jirón Ilave 581 is the **Museo de la Coca y Costumbres** ① *T051-2019420, www.museodelacoca.com, Mon-Sat 0900-1900, US$3, Spanish and English explanations,* with information about the pharmacological properties, history and use of coca, the history of Puno's dances and a display of costumes used during ★ **Virgen de la Candelaria** (early February) celebrations.

A short walk up Independencia leads to the **Arco Deustua**, a monument honouring those killed in the battles of Junín and Ayacucho. Nearby is a mirador giving fine views over the town, the port and the lake beyond. The walk from Jirón Cornejo following the Stations of the Cross up Cerro Azoguini, with fine views of Lake Titicaca, has been recommended, but be careful and don't go alone or after dark; the same applies to any of the hills around Puno, including Huajsapata and Kuntur Wasi. For a taste of rural life in the *puna*, visit **Fundo Chincheros** ① *9 km from Puno on the road to Juliaca, T051-35192, http://fundo.casadelcorregidor.pe, English and Dutch spoken,* which offers day visits and overnight stays in an old hacienda house.

**Puno centre**

From the Plaza de Armas, Avenida Titicaca leads 12 blocks east to the lakeshore and port. From its intersection with Avenida Costanera towards the pier, one side of the road is lined with the kiosks of the **Artesanos Unificados de Puno**, selling crafts. Closer to the port are food kiosks. On the opposite side of the road is a shallow lake where you can hire **pedal boats** ① *US$1.55 pp for a 20-min ride.* At the pier are the ticket counters for transport to the islands. The **Malecón Bahía de los Incas**, a lovely promenade along the waterfront, extends to the north and south; it has a sundial and is a pleasant place for a stroll and for birdwatching.

The **Buque Museo Yavarí** ① *anchored in Puno Bay, visits Mon-Sat 0800-1700 with advanced booking only, contact Asociación Yavarí, T01-467 6609, yavari.puno@gmail. com, donations appreciated; bed and breakfast service not operating in early 2018, consult www.yavari.org for updates,* is the oldest ship on Lake Titicaca. It was built in England in 1862 and was shipped in kit form to Arica, then by rail to Tacna and by mule to Lake Titicaca, a journey that took six years. The *Yavarí* was finally launched on Christmas Day 1870. Berthed in Puno

12 Pizzería/Trattoria El Buho *Puno centre*
13 Ricos Pan *C2, centre*
14 Tradiciones del Lago *Puno centre*
15 Tulipan's *Puno centre*
16 Ukukus *Puno centre*

**Bars & clubs** 🎵
17 Dómino *Puno centre*
18 Pachas *Puno centre*
19 Positive *Puno centre*

harbour, is the **MS Ollanta** ① *not open to the public in 2018*, which was built in Hull (UK) and sailed the lake from 1926 to the 1970s. Another old ship is the **MN Coya** ① *anchored near the Hotel Sonesta Posadas del Inca, no longer sailing, occasionally hired for special events*, built in Scotland and launched on the lake in 1892.

## ★ Sillustani

*34 km from Puno off the road to Juliaca. Daily 0830-1730. US$4.60. Tours from Puno, US$12-14, last about 3-4 hrs, some stop at a Colla house on the way, to see local products. Or take a van towards Juliaca as far as the turn-off for Sillustani (US$1), where taxis wait (mostly in the morning), US$1 pp for the 14-km-ride to the site. It's cold and windy; make sure you have return transport.*

Near Puno are the chullpas (pre-Columbian funeral towers) of Sillustani in a beautiful setting on a peninsula in Lake Umayo (3850 m). The scenery is barren, but impressive. John Hemming writes: "Most of the towers date from the period of Inca occupation in the 15th century, but they are burial towers of the Aymara-speaking Colla tribe. The engineering involved in their construction is more complex than anything the Incas built – it is defeating archaeologists' attempts to rebuild the tallest 'lizard' chullpa."

> **Tip...**
> Photography at Sillustani is best in the afternoon light, though this is when the wind is strongest.

Artefacts found in the tombs can be seen at the Museo Carlos Dreyer in Puno (see page 262). Handicraft sellers wait at the exit. There is community tourism at **Atuncolla**, near the lake, US$21.50 per person for homestays with full board, contact T951-905006.

There are more chullpas from the Lupaca and Colla kingdoms (AD 1100-1450) in **Cutimbo** ① *turn-off at Km 17 on the Puno–Moquegua road, daily 0830-1730, US$4.60*, where rock art and Inca ruins are also to be found.

## ★ Península de Capachica

The Península de Capachica encloses the northern side of the Bahía de Puno and is a great introduction to Lake Titicaca. The scenery is very pretty, with sandy beaches, pre-Inca terracing, trees and flowers. It is also good for hiking and mountain biking, and sailing boats can be hired. The view of the sunset from Auki Carus hill rivals that from Taquile (see page 274). The dress of the local women is very colourful, with four-cornered hats called *monteras*, matching vests and colourful *polleras*. Towns and villages throughout the peninsula are involved in community-based tourism: at the southern end, the farming villages of **Llachón**, **Santa María** and **Ccotos**; in the centre of the peninsula **Chifrón** and further north **Escallani**. Each community organization has links to different tour operators in Puno, Cuzco or abroad; iPerú in Puno has a list of updated contact information for the participating organizations. Visitors share in local activities and, when possible, the produce served is from the residents' farms. Off the east coast of the peninsula is the island of **Ticonata**, whose community tourism association offers accommodation in round houses and various activities. It's a short boat ride from Ccotos, or from Amantaní (see page 276); motorboats from Puno take 3½ hours.

> **Tip...**
> Capachica is a great place to start your exploration of Lake Titicaca: it's relatively close to the airport and you can get to the islands by boat.

## ON THE ROAD
## Sacred lake

Lake Titicaca has played a dominant role in Andean beliefs for over two millennia. This, the highest navigable body of water in the world, is the most sacred lake in the Andes.

From the lakes profound, icy depths emerged the Inca creator deity, Viracocha. Legend has it that the sun god had his children, Manco Cápac and his sister, Mama Ocllo, spring from its waters to found Cuzco and the Inca dynasty.

The name Titicaca derives from the word *titi*, a mountain cat, and the Quechua word *caca*, meaning rock. The rock refers to the Sacred Rock on the Isla del Sol (on the Bolivian side), which was worshipped by the pre-Inca people on the island. The mountain cat inhabited the shores of the lake and is said to have visited the Isla del Sol occasionally. The ancient indigenous people saw the eyes of the mountain cat gleaming in the Sacred Rock and so named it Titicaca, or Rock of the Mountain Cat.

The *titi* has characteristics – such as its aquatic ability and the brilliance of its eyes – that conceptually link it with a mythological flying feline called *ccoa*. The role of the *ccoa* remains important in some part of the Andes. It was originally associated with the gods that controlled the weather and was believed to throw lightning from its eyes, urinate rain, spit hail and roar thunder. Among indigenous people today, the *ccoa* is believed to live in the mountains as one of the mountain god's servants. It is closely involved in daily life and is considered the most feared of the spirits as it uses lightning and hail.

## Western shore: Chucuito to the border

An Inca sundial can be seen near the village of **Chucuito** ① *19 km from Puno, vans from 1 de Mayo y Banchero Rossi, US$0.50, 25 mins*, which has houses with carved stone doorways and two interesting colonial churches: 16th-century Santo Domingo, the first in the region, and 17th-century La Asunción. Also here is the Inca Uyo, a fertility plaza filled with stone phalli. Further south is the larger town of **Acora** (34 km), which provides access to a lovely peninsula with luxury hotels and the Charcas beaches. At the north end of the peninsula the village of **Luquina Chico** has a community tourism programme, similar to those in Capachica. The important commercial centre of **Ilave** is 55 km from Puno.

★ **Juli** ① *www.munijuli.gob.pe, 80 km, colectivo from Terminal Zonal Sur in Puno, US$1.40, 1½ hrs; returns from outside Juli market at Ilave 349; taxi US$50 return including a stop at Vilcauta*, has some fine examples of religious architecture. **San Pedro church** ① *on the plaza, daily 0800-1700, free, donations appreciated*, contains a series of paintings of the saints, with the Via Crucis scenes in the same frame, and gilt side altars above which some of the arches have baroque designs. **San Juan Letrán** and **La Asunción** ① *both Tue-Sun 0800-1700, US$4.60 each,* are now museums containing paintings by artists from the Cuzco School of Art and from Italy. San Juan has two sets of 17th-century paintings of the lives of St John the Baptist and St Teresa, contained in sumptuous gilded frames, as well as intricate *mestizo* carving in pink stone. The nave at La Asunción is empty, but its walls are lined with unlabelled paintings. The original murals on the walls of the transept can be seen. Its fine bell tower was damaged by earthquake or lightning. Outside is an archway and atrium which date from the early 17th century. Needlework, other weavings, handicrafts and antiques are offered for sale in town. Ten minutes from town towards

Puno is **Vilcauta** (or Arama Muru), rock formations including one in the shape of a large doorway, where celebrations are held during the solstices.

A further 20 km along the lake, atop a hill, is ★ **Pomata**, whose red sandstone church of **Santiago Apóstol** ① *daily 0800-1200, 1300-1600, US$90 (if guardian is not there, leave money on table),* has a striking exterior and beautiful interior, with superb carving and paintings from the Escuela Cusqueña. To get there, take a bus from Juli (US$0.90) or from Puno (US$2.50).

Past Pomata, the road south along the lake divides; one branch continues straight towards the Bolivian border at Desaguadero, via **Zepita**, where the 18th-century Dominican church is worth a visit. **Desaguadero** is a bleak place with simple restaurants and accommodation. Friday is the main market day, when the town is packed. There is a smaller market on Tuesday but at other times it is deserted.

The other branch of the road from Pomata follows the lakeshore to the border crossing at Kasani near **Yunguyo** (see page 284 for border crossings). Vans depart from Yunguyo to Punta Hermosa, where you can catch a boat to Anapia in Lago Menor (see page 276).

## Listings Puno and around *map page 262.*

### Tourist information

Useful websites include www.munipuno. gob.pe (the municipal site) and www. titicaca-peru.com (in Spanish and French).

#### Indecopi
*Jr Ancash 146, T051-363667.*
Consumer protection bureau.

#### iPerú
*Jr Lima y Deustua, near Plaza de Armas, T051-365088, iperupuno@promperu.gob.pe. Mon-Sat 0900-1800, Sun 0900-1300. Also at Terminal Terrestre, daily 0600-2000, and at Juliaca airport.*
Very helpful English-speaking staff, good information and maps.

#### Tourist police
*Jr Deustua 588, T051-352303. 24 hrs.*
Report robberies here, and scams (such as unscrupulous price changes) to Indecopi and iPerú.

### Where to stay

There are over 80 places to stay in Puno, including a number of luxury hotels in and around the city. Prices vary according to season. Many touts try to persuade tourists to go to a hotel not of their own choosing;

be firm. Chain hotels include **Casa Andina** Premium and Standard (www.casa-andina. com), **Sonesta Posadas del Inca** (www. sonesta.com/laketiticaca/), **Tierra Viva Puno Plaza** (www.tierravivahoteles.com),

#### $$$$ Libertador Lago Titicaca
*On Isla Esteves linked by a causeway 5 km northeast of Puno (taxi US$3), T051-367780, www.libertador.com.pe.*
Modern hotel with every facility, built on a Tiahuanaco-period site, spacious, good views, bar, restaurant, disco, good service, parking.

#### $$$ Hacienda Plaza de Armas
*Jr Puno 419, T051-367340, www.hhp.com.pe.*
Tastefully decorated modern hotel overlooking the Plaza de Armas, small comfortable rooms, all with bathtub or jacuzzi, heater, safety box, restaurant.

#### $$$ Hacienda Puno
*Jr Deustua 297, T051-356109, www.hhp.com.pe.*
Refurbished colonial house, with buffet breakfast, rooms and suites with good bathrooms, restaurant with local specialities, comfortable.

#### $$$ Intiqa
*Jr Tarapacá 272, T051-366900, www.intiqahotel.com.*

Built around a sunny courtyard. Stylish, rooms have heaters, dinner available, professional staff.

### $$$ Plaza Mayor
*Deustua 342, T051-368728,*
*www.plazamayorhotel.com.*
Comfortable, well-appointed, good big beds, buffet breakfast, heating, restaurant.

### $$ Casona Colón Inn
*Tacna 290, T051-351432, www.coloninn.com.*
Colonial style, good rooms, some with bathtub, heating, good service. Le Bistrot serves international and Peruvian cuisine.

### $$ Conde de Lemos
*Jr Puno 681, Plaza de Armas, T051-369898,*
*www.condelemosinn.com.*
Convenient, comfy suites and rooms with bathtubs, heating, elevator, buffet breakfast, restaurant.

### $$ El Buho
*Lambayeque 142, T051-366122,*
*www.hotelbuho.com.*
Nice carpeted rooms, most with bathtubs, heating, buffet breakfast, tour agency, parking extra.

### $$ Hostal Imperial
*Teodoro Valcarcel 145, T051-352386,*
*www.hostalimperial.com.*
Simple but big rooms, good hot showers, safety box, helpful, stores luggage, comfortable.

### $$ Hostal Pukara
*Jr Libertad 328, T051-368448,*
*www.pukaradeltitikaka.com.*
Excellent, English spoken, helpful service, heating, central, quiet, free coca to drink in evening, American breakfast included, dining room on top floor, lots of stairs.

### $$ Italia
*Teodoro Valcarcel 122, T051-367706,*
*www.hotelitaliaperu.com.*
Cheaper in low season, good restaurant, buffet breakfast, small rooms, helpful staff.

### $$ Posada Don Giorgio
*Tarapacá 238, T051-363648, on Facebook.*

Comfortable large rooms, nicely decorated, traditional architecture, heater extra.

### $$ Posada Luna Azul
*Cajamarca 242, T051-364851,*
*www.posadalunaazul.com.*
Comfortable carpeted rooms, heating, parking, luggage storage.

### $ Hostal Los Pinos
*Tarapacá 182, T051-367398,*
*hostalpinos@hotmail.com.*
Family-run, helpful, breakfast available, heater on request, reliable hot water, laundry facilities, small book exchange, tours organized, good value. Warmly recommended.

### $ Hostal Margarita
*Jr Tarapacá 130, T051-352820.*
Large building, family atmosphere, cold rooms, private or shared bath, heaters on request, helpful owner, tours can be arranged.

### $ Hostal Vylena
*Jr Ayacucho 503, T051-351292,*
*hostalvylena20@hotmail.com.*
Functional rooms, hot water during limited hours, breakfast available, luggage storage, economical.

### $ Inka's Rest
*Pasaje San Carlos 158, T051-368720.*
Several sitting areas, heating, double or twin rooms with private or shared bath and US$9 pp in dorm, cooking and laundry facilities, a place to meet other travellers, reserve ahead.

### $ Los Uros
*Teodoro Valcarcel 135, T051-352141.*
Private or shared bath, breakfast available, quiet at back, small charge to leave luggage, laundry, heating costs extra.

### $ Tayka Hostel
*Jr Ayacucho 515, T951-633355,*
*www.taykahostel.com.*
Simple lodging, private rooms and 4-bed dorms (US$11 pp), all include breakfast, electric showers, luggage storage.

## Península Capachica

Local families offer accommodation in their homes, lists available from iPerú in Puno and the Municipalidad in Capachica town. All hosts can arrange private boat transport (US$24-31 per boat) to Amantaní and Uros Titino (1½ hrs from Puno), a less visited, more authentic, part of the Uros Islands; for public boat service see Transport. Among those who offer lodging in Llachón (**$** per bed, meals extra) are: **Tomás Cahui Coila** (T951-691501); **Felix Turpo Coila** (T951-664828); **Valentín Quispe** (T951-821392, llachon@yahoo.com); other families also accept guests.

## Western shore: Chuchito to the border

Local families offer accommodation in their homes in Luquina Chico, tip of Chucuito Peninsula, US$25-28 pp full board.

### $$$$ Castillo del Titicaca
*Playa de Charcas, 45 mins from Puno, T950-308000, www.castillo.titicaca-peru.com.*
Exclusive 5-room hotel on a rocky promontory overlooking the lake and surrounded by extensive terraced gardens. Luxurious apartments and rooms, 1 inside a castle, restaurant with lake views, full board. Belgian manager Christian Nonis is known for his work on behalf of the people of Taquile.

### $$$$ Titilaka Lodge
*Comunidad de Huencalla s/n, on a private peninsula near Chucuito, T01-700 5111 (Lima), www.titilaka.com.*
Luxury boutique hotel in Relais et Châteaux group offering all-inclusive packages in an exclusive environment on the edge of the lake. Plenty of activities available on land and on the water; works with local Uros communities.

### $$$ Taypikala Lago
*Sandia s/n, Chucuito, T051-792266, www.taypikala.com.*
Upmarket hotel near the lakeshore, suites with jacuzzi, fridge and fireplace, and heated rooms with bathtub and safety box; restaurant, pool, spa, water sports, gym, meditation and yoga areas.

### $$ Las Cabañas
*Jr Tarapacá 538, Chucuito, T951-751196, www.chucuito.com.*
Rooms and ample cottages in nice grounds, breakfast included, other meals available. Owned by Sr Juan Palao, a knowledgeable local historian, busy at weekends, events held here; will collect you from Puno if you phone in advance.

### $ Hostal Isabel
*San Francisco 110, near Plaza de Armas, Yunguyo, T951-794228.*
With or without bath, nice rooms and courtyard, electric shower, parking, friendly. Several other cheap places to stay.

### $ Sra Nely Durán Saraza
*Chucuito Occopampa.*
2 nice rooms, 1 with lake view, shared bath, breakfast and dinner available, very welcoming and interesting.

## Restaurants

Tourist restaurants and their touts, all offering alpaca, trout, *cuy* and international dishes, are clustered along Jr Lima.

### $$$ La Table del'Inca
*Jr Ancash 239, T994-659357. Mon-Sat 1800-2200, Sun in high season.*
Upscale restaurant serving French/Peruvian fusion cuisine, nice decor and ambiance, *menú* with your choice of 3 courses and a glass of wine for US$25.

### $$$ Mojsa
*Lima 635 p 2, Plaza de Armas, www.mojsarestaurant.com. Daily 1200-2130.*
Resto-bar with nice views over the plaza, good international and *Novo Andino* dishes, nice wood decor, also has an arts and crafts shop.

### $$$-$$ La Casona
*Lima 423, p2, T051-351108, www.lacasona-restaurant.com. Daily 1200-2130.*
Upmarket tourist restaurant serving a wide choice of international dishes.

### $$$-$$ Tradiciones del Lago
*Lima 418, T051-368140, www.tradiciones delago.com. Daily 1200-2200.*
Popular tourist restaurant serving a great variety of à la carte dishes.

### $$ Incabar
*Lima 348, T051-368031. Daily 0800-2200.*
Open for breakfast, lunch and dinner, interesting dishes in creative sauces, fish, pastas, curries, café and couch bar, nice decor.

### $$ La Estancia
*Libertad 137. Daily 1100-2200.*
Grilled meat and à la carte Peruvian dishes, large portions, very popular.

### $$ La Hostería
*Lima 501, T051-365406. Mon-Sat 1100-2200, Sun 1700-2200.*
Good set meal and à la carte dishes including local fare such as alpaca and *cuy*, pizza, also breakfast.

### $$ Tulipan's
*Lima 394. Daily 1000-2200.*
Sandwiches, juices and a lunchtime menu are its staples. One of the few places in Puno with outdoor seating in a pleasant colonial courtyard, a good option for lunch.

### $$-$ La Cayma
*Libertad 216, T051-634226. Open 0900-2200, closed Sat.*
Good pizza, Peruvian and international dishes, tasty set lunch, pleasant atmosphere, good service.

### $$-$ Loving Hut
*Pje Choquehuanca 188, www.lovinghutco/pe. Mon-Sat 0900-1900.*
Daily choice of very tasty, creative vegan dishes and salad bar, good value *menú* 1130-1530. Popular and recommended.

### $$-$ Machupizza
*Arequipa 409 and Tacna 279, T951-246001. Daily 1730-2300.*
Tasty pizza and other Italian dishes, good value, warm atmosphere, popular with locals, delivery.

### $$-$ Pizzería/Trattoria El Buho
*Jr Libertad 240, T051-356223. Daily 1700-2230.*
Excellent pizza, lively atmosphere.

### $$-$ Ukukus
*Pje Grau 146, T051-369504. Sun-Fri 1000-2200.*
Good combination of Andean and *Novo Andino* cuisine as well as pizzas and some Chinese *chifa* style.

## Cafés

### Cafetería Mercedes
*Jr Arequipa 111.*
Good menú, bread, cakes, snacks, juices.

### Casa del Corregidor
*Deustua 576, aptdo 2, T051-365603. Mon-Sat 0900-2100.*
In restored 17th-century building, sandwiches, good snacks, main dishes, coffee, good music, great atmosphere, nice surroundings with patio. Also has a Fairtrade store offering products directly from the producers.

### Ricos Pan
*Jr Arequipa 332 and Jr Moquegua 334. Mon-Sat 0600-2130, Sun 1500-2130.*
Café and bakery, great cakes, excellent coffees, juices and pastries, breakfasts and other dishes.

## Bars and clubs

### Dómino
*Libertad 443.*
Happy hour Mon-Thu 2000-2130. "Megadisco", good.

### Pachas
*Lima 370.*
Innovative bar.

### Positive
*Lima 382. Daily 0600-0100.*
Drinks, snacks, large-screen TV, reggae and rock. Also serves breakfast all day.

## ON THE ROAD
### Pot luck

One of the most intriguing items for sale in Andean markets is Ekeko, the symbol of good fortune and plenty, and one of the most enduring and endearing of the Aymara folk legends.

He is a cheery, avuncular little chap, with a happy face to make children laugh, a pot belly because of his predilection for food, and short legs so he can't run away. His image, usually in plaster of Paris, is laden with sacks of grain, sweets, household tools, baskets, utensils, suitcases, confetti and streamers, rice, noodles and other essentials. Dangling from his lower lip is the ubiquitous lit cigarette. Believers say that these little statues only bring luck if received as gifts, not purchased. You can get one for your best friend at the Alacitas festival of miniatures, held in Puno around the first week of May.

## Festivals

**Last week in Jan-1st week in Feb   Virgen de la Candelaria**. On the 1st Sun, some 100 communities compete in an indigenous dance contest. The dances include *llameritos*, *wifala* and *ayarachis*. The following Sun and Mon colourfully attired dancers participate in a contest of *mestizo* costumes (*trajes de luces*) and folk dances such as *diablada*, *morenada*, *llamerada*, *caporales* and *saya*. A large procession takes place on 2 Feb, the main day. The nighttime festivities on the streets are better than the official functions in the stadium.

**Mar/Apr   Good Fri**. A candlelit procession through darkened streets.

**3 May   Festividad de las Cruces**. Celebrated with masses, a procession and the Alasitas festival of miniatures.

**29 Jun**   Colourful festival of **San Pedro**, several venues, including Ichu (between Puno and Chucuito) and Zepita (see page 266).

**4-5 Nov**   Pageant dedicated to the founding of Puno and the emergence of Manco Cápac and Mama Ocllo from the waters of Lake Titicaca.

## Shopping

Puno is the best place in Peru to buy alpaca wool articles; bargaining is appropriate. There are numerous outlets selling alpaca garments, paintings and other handicrafts in the centre. You will be hassled to buy along Jr Lima, so keep your wits about you.

### Markets
**Mercado Artesanal Asociación de Artesanos Unificados** (see page 263, daily 0700-1800). Closer to the centre is **Central Integral de Artesanos del Perú (CIAP;** Jr Deustua 792, Mon-Sat 0900-2100). The **Mercado Central** (in the blocks bound by Arbulú, Arequipa, Oquendo and Tacna), has all kinds of food, including good cheeses as well as a few crafts. Beware pickpockets.

## What to do

Touts (*jalagringos*) approach tourists at the bus terminal and at Jr Lima; to find a tour with a reputable agency and avoid paying above the odds, ask for their card, then arrange your tour at the agency. Only use agencies with named premises, compare prices and never hand over money on the street.

Agencies organize trips to the Uros floating islands (½ day from US$9), the islands of Taquile (full day including Uros from US$14, US$31 on a fast boat) and Amantaní (2 days, see page 276), as well as to Sillustani (½ day from US$14) and other places. The standard tour is 2 days, 1 night, visiting the Uros, staying in either Taquile or Amantaní and then visiting the other island the next day (US$31-49 pp). Some agencies pool tourists, especially in low season. We have received good reports on the following:

**All Ways Travel**, *Casa del Corregidor, Deustua 576, p 2, T051-353979, T051-355552, www.titicacaperu.com*. Good quality tours, very helpful, kind and reliable, speak German, French, English and Italian, towards the upper end of the price range. Among their tours is a unique cultural tour to the islands of Anapia and Yuspique in Lake Wiñaymarka, beyond the straits of Tiquina.

**CEDESOS**, *Centro para el Desarrollo Sostenible, Jr Moquegua 348 Int p 3, T051-367915, www.cedesos.org*. A non-profit NGO which offers interesting tours of Capachica and Chucuito peninsulas with overnight stops in family homes, going also to the less visited islands where there are few tourists.

**Cusi Expeditions**, *Jr T Valcarcel 155, T051-369072, cusitravel@hotmail.com*. Experienced operator that runs most of the standard tour boats to the islands. Good prices, accurate information.

**Edgar Adventures**, *Lima 328, T051-353444, www.edgaradventures.com*. English, German and French spoken, very helpful and knowledgeable, work with organized groups. Constantly exploring new areas, lots of off-the-beaten-track tours. Community-minded, promote responsible tourism. Consistently recommended.

**Inca Lake Travel**, *Jr Cajamarca 619, of 4, T956-060988, www.incalake.com*. Standard

tours as well as bike tours and rentals; also tours to Bolivia.

**Kontiki Tours**, *Jr Melgar 188, T051-353473, www.kontikiperu.com*. Large tour agency specializing in spiritual tourism and special interest excursions.

**Nayra Travel**, *Lima 419, of 105, T051-337934, www.nayratravel.com*. Small agency run by Lilian Cotrado and her helpful staff, traditional local tours and a variety of options in Llachón. Can organize off-the-beaten track excursions for a minimum of 2 people. Recommended.

**Pirámide Tours**, *no storefront, www.titikakalake.com*. Sells out of the ordinary and classic tours, flexible, personalized service, modern fast launches, very helpful, works only via internet.

**Titikaka Explorers**, *Jr Puno 633 of 207, T951-522633, www.titikaka-explorers.com*. Good service, helpful, works with organized groups.

## Transport

### Air

The regional airport is in Juliaca (see Transport page 282). Airport transfers from/to **Puno** US$4.60 pp with hotel pick-up: **América Tours** (Jr Tacna 313, T951 568624) and **Rossy Tours** (Jr Tacna 308, T051-366709); many hotels also offer airport transfers; leave Puno at least 2 hrs before your flight. Taxi from Puno to the airport, about US$25-30. Alternatively, take regular public transport to Juliaca (US$1.10, see page 278) and then

a taxi to the airport from there (US$6.15), but allow extra time. **LATAM** office in Puno at Jr Tacna 299, T051-367227.

### Boat
Boats to the islands (see page 278) leave from the terminal at the harbour; *trici-taxi* from centre, US$1, mototaxi US$1.25.

**To Bolivia Crillon Tours**, Camacho 1223, La Paz, T+591 2-233 7533, www.titicaca.com, run luxury services by bus and hydrofoil between La Paz and Puno, with onward tours to Cuzco and Machu Picchu. Similar services, by catamaran, are run by **Transturin** (León Tours, Ayacucho 152, p2, T051-352771, Puno, www.transturin.com).

### Bus
**Local** Small buses and vans for Juliaca, Ilave and towns on the lakeshore as far as Desaguadero and Yunguyo, leave from the **Terminal Zonal Sur** (Av Costanera Sur; taxi to the centre, US$1.55). To **Juliaca**, 44 km, 1 hr, vans US$1.10, also from **Terminal Virgen de Fátima** (Jr Ricardo Palma 225) and **Dorado** (Jr Lampa y Pje Ilo); they all go to the *Salida a Cuzco*, outside the centre of Juliaca or to Terminal Tupac; for long-distance bus services via Juliaca, see page 278. To **Yunguyo**, 0600-1900, 2½ hrs, US$3.10; if there are enough passengers, they may continue to the border at **Kasani**, US$3.60 (taxi from Puno to Kasani US$55). To **Desaguadero**, vans 0300-1900, 2½ hrs, US$3.10 (taxi US$55).

**Long distance** All long-distance buses leave from the **Terminal Terrestre** (1 de Mayo 703 y Victoria, by the lake). It has a tourist office. Platform tax, US$0.50. Taxi to the centre, US$1.55.

To **Puerto Maldonado**, 595 km, direct with Santa Cruz Fri and Sun at 1700, US$14-15, 13 hrs, or change in Juliaca (see page 278). To **Arequipa**, 5-6 hrs via Juliaca, 310 km, US$6-15, hourly with **Julsa** (poor safety record); 4 daily with **Flores**; at 1500 and 2230, with **Cruz del Sur** (city office at

Jr Lima 394, T051-368524, *bus cama* US$23); at 1445 (*semi-cama*) and 2230 (*cama*) with **Transzela** (www.transzela.com.pe); at 2230 with **Tour Peru** (city office at Jr Tacna 285, T051-206088); several others. **Tourist service** with 3 stops (see Arequipa transport, page 239), with **4M Express** (no office in Puno, contact through Arequipa, www.4m-express.com and www.busperu4m.com) and **Tour Rutas del Sur** (city office Jr Lima 440, T951-024755, www.tourrutasdelsur.com), from the Terminal Terrestre at 0600, 6 hrs, US$35 includes bilingual guiding, snack and hotel drop-off in Arequipa. Both companies also offer service with 3 stops direct to **Chivay** on the **Colca Canyon** (see Transport, page 248), without going to Arequipa, from the Terminal Terrestre at 0600, US$18-50, 7 hrs; **Rutas del Sur** also offers 1- to 4-day tours on the Puno–Colca Canyon–Arequipa route. To **Moquegua**, 6 hrs, US$6-12, and **Tacna**, 7-8 hrs, US$8-18, 5 daily with **San Martín Nobleza** (note they go directly to Tacna);. at 0830, 2030, 2115 with **Sol Andino**; at 0900, 2030, 2100 with **Héroes del Pacífico**; several others between 2030 and 2130. To **Lima**, 1011 km, 21-24 hrs, US$30-68, all buses go through Arequipa, sometimes with a change of bus; with **Cruz del Sur** at 1500, with **Civa** at 1400.

To **Cuzco**, 388 km, 6-7 hrs, there are 3 levels of service, all via Juliaca: Regular, stopping in Juliaca, US$7-12; Direct, US$15-23, from Terminal Terrestre with **Tour Perú** (city office at Jr Tacna 285, T051206088, www.tourperu. com.pe) at 2200, with **Cruz del Sur** at 0800 and 2200, with **Transzela** (www.transzela. com.pe) at 0815 and 2200, with **Turismo Mer** (city office at Jr Tacna 336, T051-367223, www.turismomer.com) at 0830 and 2200, and with **Huayruro Tours** (city office at Jr Arequipa 624, T051-351294, at 2230; and

> **Tip...**
> It is advisable to travel between Puno and Cuzco by day, for safety as well as for the views.

tourist service with 5 stops (Pucará, La Raya, Sicuani for lunch, Raqchi and Andahuaylillas), US$60-65 (includes lunch, and entry tickets), 10 hrs. Several companies offer the tourist service; all depart from the Terminal Terrestre where they have offices (except Turismo Mer): **Inka Express** (city office at Jr Tacna 346, T051-365654), leaves 0700; **Turismo Mer** (city office Jr Tacna 336) leaves from private terminal at Av Costanera 430, past the Terminal Zonal Sur, at 0730; **Wonder Perú** (city office Jr Tacna 344, T051-353388, www.wonderperuexpedition.com) leaves 0715. In high season, reserve 2 days ahead.

**To Bolivia**  To **Copacabana** (via **Kasani border**), US$4.60-7.70, 3½ hrs, departures at 0700 or 0730 and 1430; continuing to **La Paz**, US$9.25-15.50 (from Puno), 10 hrs (including border and lunch stops); most services involve transferring to a Bolivian company in Copacabana. All companies have offices at the Terminal Terrestre from where they leave; some also have offices in the centre; some provide hotel pick-up. The better companies include: **Tour Peru** (see above); **Panamericano** (Jr Tacna 245, T051-354001); **Huayruro Tours** (Jr Arequipa 624, T051-366009), and **Titicaca** (Jr Tacna 285, of 104, T051-363830, www.titicacabolivia. com), which also has a 0600 departure. **Litoral**, at the Terminal Terrestre, is cheaper, but thefts have been reported on its night buses. To **La Paz**, direct via **Desaguadero**, US$12-19 (high season), 5-6 hrs, with **Tour Peru** at 0645; with **Panamericana/Nuevo Continente** at 0530.

**Taxi**
In addition to regular cabs, and mototaxi, Puno also has 3-wheel rickshaw *trici-taxis*.

## Train
The train station is 3 blocks from Plaza Pino (La Torre 224, T051-369179, www.perurail. com, Mon-Fri 0700-1200, 1500-1800, Sat 0700-1500). The railway runs from Puno to Juliaca (44 km), where it divides, to Cuzco (381 km) and Arequipa (279 km). **PeruRail**'s *Belmond Andean Explorer* luxury sleeper trains with private bath and shower operate on this route (no service in Feb). Includes stops at points of interest. Buy tickets well in advance; passport required. To **Cuzco** (1 day/1 night, US$1140-1460 double occupancy) departs Wed 1200, stopping at La Raya and Cusipata.

## Península Capachica
### Boat
Passenger service from **Chifrón** to **Amantaní** 0800-1300 (Amantaní to Chifrón 0700-1400), US$2.50-3; from Chifrón to **Capachica Village**, mototaxi US$0.80, 15 mins or 30-min walk. In Santa María (**Llachón**), boats can be hired for trips to **Amantaní** (US$24-31, 40 mins) and **Taquile** (US$37, 50 mins).

### Road
Vans run daily 0700-1600 from Av Costanera y Jr Lampa in Puno to **Capachica**, 1½ hrs, US$155, where you get another van to **Llachón**; these leave when full, 30 mins, US$0.80; by mototaxi costs US$4.60, by taxi US$6.15. If there are enough people, vans will go direct from Puno to Llachón, US$2.15.

### Western shore
Minibuses to **Puno** depart from Jr Cusco esquina Arica, 1 block from Plaza 2 de Mayo, in **Yunguyo**, 0600-1900, 2½ hrs, US$3.10; taxi US$55. For transport to other towns in this area, see above.

### The Uros
*US$2.50 to land, 5 km northeast of Puno.*

Of the estimated 80 Uros or 'floating islands' in Puno Bay, only about 15 are regularly visited by tourists. Today we can talk about two kinds of Uros people; those close to the city of Puno and easily accessible to tourism, and those on islands that remain relatively isolated. On the more far-flung islands, reached via narrow channels through the reed beds, the Uros do not like to be photographed and continue to lead relatively traditional lives outside the monetary economy. They hunt and fish and depend on trade with the mainland for other essentials. They also live off the lake's plants, the most important of which are the reeds they use for their boats, houses and the very foundations of their islands.

Visitors to the floating islands will encounter more Uros women than men. These women wait every day for the tour boats to sell their handicrafts, while most of the men are out on the lake, hunting and fishing, although you may see some men building or repairing boats or nets. They glean extra income from tourists offering overnight accommodation in reed houses, selling meals and providing Uro guides for two-hour tours. Organized tour parties are usually given a boat-building demonstration and the chance to take a short trip in a reed boat (US$3 extra). Some islanders will also greet boatloads of tourists with a song and will pose for photos. The islanders, who are very friendly, appreciate gifts of pens, paper, and other items for their two schools. This form of tourism on the Uros Islands is now well-established and, whether it has done irreparable harm or will ultimately prove beneficial, it takes place in superb surroundings. Take drinking water as there is none on the islands.

**Tip...**
The Uros people cannot live from tourism alone, so it is better to buy their handicrafts or pay for services rather than just to tip them.

### Taquile
*US$6.15 to land, 37 km east of Puno.*

Isla Taquile is just 1 km wide but 6-7 km long. It has numerous pre-Inca and Inca ruins, and Inca terracing. The sunset from the highest point of the island (3950 m) is beautiful. Full-day tours usually include a stop in Taquile along with Uros, and two-day tours to Amantaní also stop here either on the way there or back. This means there are lots people on the island around midday. For a more authentic experience, get a tour that stays overnight in Taquile, or go independently to have time to explore the island's six districts or *suyos* and to observe the daily flurry of activity around the boatloads of tourists: demonstrations of traditional dress and weaving techniques, the preparation of trout to feed the hordes. When the boats leave, the island breathes a gentle sigh and people slowly return to their more traditional activities.

On Sunday, people from all the districts gather for a meeting in the main plaza after mass (in Quechua once a month). There is an (unmarked) **museum of traditional costumes** on the plaza and a co-operative shop that sells exceptional

**Tip...**
There are four docks on Taquile, so if you have trouble walking up many steps at high altitude, ask to be taken to a landing stage which requires less climbing.

## ON THE ROAD
## Like the fish and birds of the water

Titicaca's waters nourished great civilizations like the Tiahuanaco and Pukará and drew the Incas south in search of new lands and the origin of their own creation legend. But very little is known about a third people who made Titicaca their home. They were the Uros, the people of the floating islands. The ephemeral nature of their totora reed constructions and the watery world they inhabit make archaeological study impossible, and only their myths remain.

In their oral histories, the Uros say that their forefathers came from the south. We cannot know for certain when the Uros first arrived at Lake Titicaca, but it is thought that a great drought around AD 1200 provoked a series of massive migrations of entire peoples across the *altiplano*. In a scenario similar to the one predicted for parts of the world in the 21st century, conflicts arose as competition increased for water and fertile land.

The Uros found the fertile shores of the great lake occupied by other, much larger ethnic groups. According to Uro tradition, facing defeat by their established rivals, the Uros hid in the water among the reeds. Tired and cold, they cut the *totora* and, by binding the reeds together, made a number of rafts on which they slept.

Legend has it that when the Inca Pachacútec arrived to conquer the lake region he asked the Uros who they were. These people who had hunted and fished in the same way for generations replied as they always had, saying:
We are the founders of the world, the first inhabitants of the planet. Our blood is black and we cannot drown. We are like the fish and birds of the water.

With the arrival of the Spanish in the 16th century, the Uros isolated themselves even more from the mainland. Persecuted by the invaders, they began to meld themselves more than ever to their lake environment and their only outside contact was with other ethnic groups onshore, with whom they exchanged fish and birds for agricultural products.

Recalling their childhood, some old Uros islanders still remember when the first tourists arrived. Fearing that the Spanish had returned, their grandparents told them to run and hide.

Times have changed on some of the floating islands where the Uros smile, pose for photographs, and then ask for a tip. After generations of intermarriage with their Aymara neighbours, one of South America's most ancient tribal groups is in fact now ethnically extinct. The last Uro died in 1959, and the Uros language died with her.

woollen goods; they are not cheap, but of very fine quality. Each week different families sell their products. Other shops on the plaza sell postcards, water and dry goods. If you are staying over, you are advised to bring some food with you, particularly fruit, bread and vegetables, as well as water, plenty of small-value notes, candles, a torch, toilet paper and a sleeping bag. Take precautions against sunburn and take warm clothes for the cold nights.

## ON THE ROAD

## A lasting tradition

One of the most enduring textile traditions in Peru is found among the people of Taquile. Each family possesses at least four different types of costume: for work, leisure, weddings and festivals.

For weddings, which all take place on 3 May, when the planet Venus – Hatun Chaska – is visible, the bridegroom wears a red poncho provided by the best man. As a single man he wore a half red, half white cap, but to signify his married status he wears a long red hat and a wide red wedding belt, or *chumpi*. His bag for coca leaves, *ch'uspa*, is also filled.

The bride wears a wide red hat (*montera*) and her hands are covered with a ritual cloth (*katana-oncoma*). A *quincha*, a small white cloth symbolizing purity, is hidden in her skirt. With her red wedding blouse (*gonna*), she wears a gathered skirt (*pollera*), made from 20 different layers of brightly coloured cloth. She also wears a belt (*faja*) and black cloak known as a *chukoo*.

The wool used for weaving is usually spun by the women, but on Taquile men spin wool, as well as knitting their conical hats (*chullos*). In fact, only the men on Taquile know how to knit. By the age of 10, a boy can knit his own Chullo Santa María, which is white-tipped to show single status. When he marries, or moves in with a woman, he adopts the red-tipped *chullo*, which is exclusive to the island. Today, much of the wool for knitting is bought ready-spun from factories in Arequipa.

## ★ Amantaní
*US$2.50 to land, 44 km northeast of Puno.*

Another island worth visiting is Amantaní. It is very beautiful, peaceful and arguably less spoiled and friendlier than Taquile. There are three docks; the one on the northwest shore is closest to Pueblo de Amantaní, the main village. There are seven other villages on the island and ruins on both of its peaks, **Pacha Tata** (4115 m) and **Pacha Mama** (4130 m), from which there are excellent views. There are also temples. On the northwest shore, 30 minutes from the Pueblo, is the **Inkatiana**, a throne carved out of stone, eroded from flooding. The residents make beautiful textiles and sell them quite cheaply at the Cooperativa de Artesanos. They also make basketwork and stoneware. The people are Quechua speakers, but understand Spanish. Islanders arrange dances for tour groups for which visitors are invited to dress up in local clothes and join in. Small shops sell water and snacks.

## Anapia and Yuspique
*18 km from Punta Hermosa (past Yunguyo), contact Asociación de Turismo Anapia, Sra María Chávez Segales, T951-991164.*

In the Peruvian part of the Lago Menor or Huiñamarca, are the islands of **Anapia**, inhabited by a friendly, Aymara-speaking community which maintains its traditions, and **Yuspique**, on which are ruins and vicuñas. These are seldom visited. The community has organized committees for tourism, motorboats, sailing boats and accommodation with families (from US$9 per person). You can visit Anapia independently (see Transport, below) or take a tour with **All Ways Travel**, see page 271. On the island ask for José Flores, who is very knowledgeable about Anapia's history, flora and fauna. He sometimes acts as a guide.

## Where to stay

For independent travel, the **iPerú** office in Puno has a list of families offering accommodation in their homes and the contact information for the community leaders in charge of tourism. Puno agencies offer tours including overnight stays on the islands.

### The Uros

Some of the islands offering accommodation are: Kantati, Aruma, Qhanan Pacha and Kamisaraki. Quality and price vary greatly, from US$6.15 for a bed in a very basic place to US$65 pp full board including transport and tour.

### Taquile

The Community Tourism Agency **Munay Taquile** (T051-351448, www.taquile.net) can arrange accommodation on the island. Someone will approach you when you get off the boat if you don't have anything booked in advance. Rates are from US$8 pp for bed only, from US$22 pp full board, or US$43 pp including transport and guiding. Some families have become popular with tour groups and so have been able to build bigger and better facilities (with showers and loos), classified as Albergue Rural or Hotel Rural. As a result, families with more basic accommodation (Casa Rural) are often losing out on valuable tourist income. There are 8 communities in Taquile, instead of staying in the busy part of the island around the main square, consider staying in one of the outlying communities, for example in Huayllano, on the south side of the island; contact **Alipio Huatta Cruz** (T951-668551 or T951-615239) or arrange a visit with **All Ways Travel**, see page 271.

### Amantaní

Rates are US$9-14 for just a bed, US$11-30 pp full board, or from US$31 pp including a tour. If you are willing to walk to more distant communities, you might get a better price and you are helping to share the income. Options include: **$$ Kantuta Lodge** (T051-630238, 951-636172, www.kantutalodge.com), run by Segundino Cari and family, full board; **Hospedaje Ccolono** (Occosuyo, T951-675918); **Eduardo Yucra Mamani** (Jatari, Comunidad Pueblo, T951-664577); or **Victoriano Calsin Quispe** (T051-360220/363320).

## Restaurants

### Taquile

There are many small restaurants around the plaza and on the track to the Puerto Principal, including Gerardo Huatta's **La Flor de Cantuta**, on the steps, and **El Inca** on the main plaza. Meals are generally fish, rice and chips, omelette and *fiambre*, a local stew. Meat is rarely available and drinks often run out. Breakfast consists of pancakes and bread.

### Amantaní

The artificially low price of tours allows families little scope for providing anything other than basic meals, so take your own supplies.

## Festivals

### Taquile

**Jun-Aug** The principal festivals are **2-7 Jun** and the **Fiesta de Santiago 25 Jul-2 Aug**, with many dances in between.

### Amantaní

**15-20 Jan** **Pago a la Tierra** (3rd Thu of Jan at Pacha Tata) and **San Sebastián** (20 Jan) are celebrated on the hills of the island. The festivities are very colourful, musical and hard-drinking.
**9 Apr** **Aniversario del Consejo** (the local council).
**8-16 Aug** **Feria de Artesanías**.

## Transport

Purchasing one-way tickets gives you more flexibility if you wish to stay longer on the islands, but joining a tour is the most convenient way to visit, especially as it will include transport between your hotel and the port. 2-day tours to Uros, Amantaní and Taquile, including simple lodging and meals, start at US$31.

### The Uros
**Asociación de Transporte los Uros** (T051-368024, aeuttal@hotmail.com, daily 0800-1600) runs motorboats from Puno to the islands, daily 0600-1600 or whenever there are 10 people, US$3. Agencies charge US$7.70-9.25 for a ½-day tour.

### Taquile
**Operaciones Comunales Taquile** (T051-205477, daily 0600-1800) has boats at 0730 and 0800 in high season, stopping at the **Uros** on the way, returning at 1400 and 1430; in low season only 1 boat travels, US$7.70 return. Organized tours cost US$14-25.

### Amantaní
**Transportes Unificados Amantaní** (T051-369714, daily 0500-1800) has 2 boats daily at 0815, 1 direct, the 2nd stopping at Uros; they return at 0800 the next day, 1 direct to **Puno**, the 2nd stopping at **Taquile** and continuing to Puno at 1200. Rates are US$7.50 Puno to Amantaní direct one way; US$9.25 return including stops at **Uros** and Taquile; US$3 Amantaní to Taquile one way. If you stop in Taquile on the way back, you can choose to continue to Puno at 1200 with the Amantaní boat or take a Taquile boat at 1400 (also 1430 in high season). Note they can be very crowded.

### Anapia
Take a van from Parque Primero de Mayo in **Yunguyo** towards Tinicachi and alight at **Punta Hermosa**, just after Unacachi, US$0.55, 35 mins. Boats leave **Anapia** for Punta Hermosa on Sun and Thu around 0600-0800, returning from Punta Hermosa to Anapia on the same days between 1200 and 1300, US$1.25, 1½ hrs each way. To hire a boat from Punta Hermosa to Anapia costs US$25 for a small fishing boat, US$46 for a *lancha* (larger boat).

## North of Puno

routes to Cuzco, the jungle and Bolivia

Heading north from Puno, the road crosses a range of hills to another coastal plain, which leads to Juliaca. This town is the main transport hub for journeys north to Cuzco or the jungle, southwest to Arequipa or east along the unspoiled northern shores of the lake.

### Juliaca *Colour map 6, B2.*
Freezing cold at night, hygienically challenged and less than safe, Juliaca (population 273,000, 44 km north of Puno and 289 km northeast of Arequipa, is not particularly attractive. As the commercial focus of an area bounded by Puno, Arequipa and the jungle, it has grown very fast into a noisy chaotic place, lots of contraband and a great many *trici-* and mototaxi. Monday, market day, is the most disorganized of all.

### Lampa
The unspoiled friendly little colonial town of Lampa, 31 km northwest of Juliaca along an old road to Pucará, is known as the 'Pink City'. Being so close to Juliaca, it is a fine alternative place to stay for those seeking tranquility. It has a splendid

## ON THE ROAD
## Lampa: living in the past

Walking past Lampa's imposing pink-stone church and the colonial *casonas* with their terracotta finish which give the town its nickname, you can't help but wonder why this town is so different from others in the region. In the late 19th and early 20th centuries, the Lampa aristocracy did not allow the iron horse to trample upon its plains, so the Cuzco–Arequipa railway had to make a detour and go to Juliaca. With it went change and development. Lampa lost the importance it had held since colonial times becoming a tranquil town that time forgot, but always clinging tightly to its aristocratic air.

church, La Inmaculada ① *daily 0900-1200, 1400-1600, US$3.60*, containing a copy of Michelangelo's 'Pietà' cast in aluminium, many Cuzqueña school paintings and a carved wooden pulpit. A plaster copy of the 'Pietà' and a mural depicting local history can be seen in the Municipalidad. **Museo Kampac** ① *Jr Alfonso Ugarte 462 y Ayacucho, T951-820085, daily 0700-1800, US$1.80*, a small private museum featuring an eclectic collection of sculptures and ceramics from a number of Peruvian cultures; the owner, Profesor Jesús Vargas, can be found at the shop opposite. Lampa has a small Sunday market and celebrates a fiesta of **Santiago Apóstol** on 6-15 December. There is a fine colonial bridge just south of the town and La Cueva del Toro cave with petroglyphs at Lensora, 4 km past the bridge. The Tinajani rock formations and stands of *Puya raimondii* plants south of Ayaviri (see below) can also be accessed from Lampa.

### Juliaca to Cuzco
The road Puno–Juliaca–Cuzco is fully paved. There is much to see on the way, but neither the regular nor the direct daytime buses make frequent stops. Tourist buses stop at the most important attractions, but to see these and other sights at a more relaxed pace, you will need to take local transport from town to town, or use your own car. There are plenty of places to stay and eat en route.

The road and railway cross the altiplano, gradually climbing. Along the way is **Pucará**, 65 km northwest of Juliaca, which has pre-Inca ruins, a museum and produces ceramic bulls which are placed on roofs throughout the region. Accessed from **Ayaviri** (33 km from Pucará), whose speciality is a mild, creamy cheese, are the Tinajani rock formations, stands of *Puya raimondii* plants and Laguna Orurillo. Knitted alpaca ponchos and pullovers and miniature llamas are made in **Santa Rosa** (42 km from Ayaviri), which has access to Nuñoa where more *Puyas raimondii* can be seen. Nearby, at the foot of the snow-covered Kunurana peak, is **Tambo Queque Norte** (T958795751, www.tamboquequenorte.com, comfortable rooms in $$$ range, good restaurant, horse riding), a working cattle ranch and dairy, open to visitors.

At **La Raya** (4350 m), the highest pass between Juliaca and Cuzco, there is a crafts market by the railway. Trains stop here so passengers can admire the scenery. Up on the heights breathing may be a little difficult, but the descent along the Río Vilcanota is rapid. At **Aguas Calientes**, 10 km from La Raya along the railway, are steaming springs reaching 40°C, with thermal pools for bathing; the beautiful deposits of red ferro-oxide in the middle of the green grass is a startling sight. At **Maranganí**, the river is wider and the fields greener, with groves of eucalyptus trees.

Located 38 km beyond La Raya Pass at 3690 m is **Sicuani**, the main city in eastern Cuzco and a good base from which to visit the easternmost attractions of the region. It is an important commercial and agricultural centre and a transport hub. Excellent llama and alpaca wool products and skins are sold next to the pedestrian walkway and at the Saturday market. Around Plaza Libertad there are several hat shops. The tourist office (see Tourist information, below) has an excellent display of traditional outfits from all the districts of Canchis, which are among the most colourful in Cuzco. For information about places between Sicuani and Cuzco, see Raqchi and around, page 319.

## Puno to the jungle

A branch of the Interoceanic Highway, fully paved, runs together with the Juliaca–Cuzco road, before branching north across the vast alpaca-grazed altiplano. **Azángaro** (73 km from Juliaca) has the Templo de Tintiri, an adobe colonial church rich in art. Beyond is the cold regional centre of **Macusani**, 192 km from Juliaca, at 4400 m. The dramatic road then descends past the mining supply towns of **Ollachea** (with simple accommodation and eateries, a waterfall, thermal baths and pre-Inca ruins) and **San Gabán** (with petroglyphs and waterfalls) to **Puente Iñambari** (or Loromayo), where it converges with the other branches of the Interoceánica from Cuzco and Puerto Maldonado (see page 422). **Mazuko** (360 km from Juliaca), another mining town, is 5 km north of the junction. This off-the-beaten-path route over the **Cordillera Carabaya** connects Lake Titicaca and the southern jungle (see Transport, below).

This is an excellent area for those who want to explore. Along the way are rock formations, petroglyphs and the glaciated summits of Allin Cápac surrounded by lakes and

# Cuzco - Puno - La Paz (Bolivia)

valleys ideal for trekking. Richar Cáceres (T946-680485) in Macusani, is a recommended English-speaking mountaineer and guide, who is knowledgeable about the area. There are reasonable places to stay in Macusani (**Apu** and **El Arca de Noé** are good choices) and a government Tambo in **Aymaña**, northwest of Macusani.

Further east, leading north from the northeastern shore of Titicaca near Huancané, another road goes towards the jungle. At **Putina**, 92 km from Juliaca, are **thermal baths** ⓘ *Tue-Sun 0400-2100, US$0.70*. Vicuñas can be seen at Picotani nearby, and *Puya raimondii* plants at Bellavista, 5 km from town. The road then crosses the beautiful Cordillera Apolobamba to **Sandia** (125 km from Putina), **San Juan del Oro** (80 km from Sandia) and **Putina Punco**, 40 km ahead. Beyond lies the remote **Parque Nacional Bahuaja-Sonene** ⓘ *Sernanp, Libertad 1189, Puno, T051-363960, day visit US$9.25*, with restricted access requiring a Sernamp permit for overnight stays (US$55). It is difficult to reach the park from this side and involves paddling a canoe through serious rapids; access is easier from the Río Tambopata side, see page 429.

> **Tip...**
> Detailed information about this area is found in *Carabaya: Paisajes y cultura milenaria* by Rainer Hostnig, 2010 (rainer.hostnig@gmail.com).

## Huancané to Bolivia

A paved road goes northeast from Juliaca across the *puna* for 56 km to **Huancané** (altitude 3825 m), which has a massive adobe church by its attractive plaza and good birdwatching possibilities nearby in the **Reserva Nacional del Titicaca**, where the road crosses the Río Ramis. Nearby, a road goes north to Putina and the jungle, see above. East of Huancané, the shore of Titicaca is beautiful, with terraced hills rising above coves on the lake. There are many Inca and pre-Inca ruins as well as pre-Inca roads to follow. In the warmer coves, where the climate is tempered by the lake, people lead traditional lives based on fishing and subsistence farming. Around the town of **Moho**, the garden of the altiplano, fruit and flowers are grown. At Cambria, near the town of **Conima**, there is access from the shore to idyllic ★ **Isla Suasi** (www.islasuasi.pe, see Where to stay, below). Beyond are the village of **Sucuni**, access to the Siani archaeological site, and **Tilali**, with basic lodging and eateries, before reaching the Bolivian border.

## Listings North of Puno

### Tourist information

#### Juliaca
Information is available from **Dircetur** (Jr Noriega 191, p 3, T051-321839, Mon-Fri 0730-1530) and **iPerú** (at the airport, iperupunoapto@promperu.gob.pe, open when flights arrive).

#### Juliaca to Cuzco
The **Sicuani tourist information office** (at the Municipio, Plaza de Armas, T084-509257, Mon-Fri 0800-1300, 1430-1800) has pamphlets and very helpful staff.

### Where to stay

#### Juliaca
The town has water problems in dry season.

**$$$-$$ Hotel Don Carlos**
*Jr 9 de Diciembre 114, Plaza Bolognesi, T051-323600, www.hotelesdoncarlos.com.*
Comfortable, modern facilities, heater, good service, breakfast, restaurant and room service. Also has **Suites Don Carlos** (Jr M Prado 335, T051-321571).

**$$ Amerón**
*Mariano Núñez 254-B, near Plaza Vea, T051-322378, www.ameron.com.pe.*

Multi-storey hotel with comfortable rooms with heaters, those in front have traffic noise.

### $$ Royal Inn
*San Román 158, T051-321561, www.royalinnhoteles.com.*
Rooms and suites with heater and bathtub, good restaurant (**$$-$**).

### $$ Sakura
*San Román 133, T322072, hotelsakura@hotmail.com.*
Quiet, basic rooms in older section with shared bath.

### $$-$ Hostal Luquini
*Jr Brasesco 409, Plaza Bolognesi, T051-321510.*
Comfortable, patio, helpful staff, reliable hot water in morning only, motorcycle parking.

## Lampa

### $$ La Casona
*Jr Tarapacá 271, Plaza de Armas, T999-607682, patronatolampa@yahoo.com.*
Lovely refurbished 17th-century house, nice ample rooms with heaters and duvets, advanced booking required, tours arranged.

### $ Hospedaje Estrella
*Jr Municipalidad 540, T980-368700, juanfrien@hotmail.com.*
Appealing rooms, with or without private bath, solar hot water, very friendly, breakfast available, parking.

## Huancané to Bolivia

### $$$$ Hotel Isla Suasi
*T992-699848 (reservations), T951-3100701 (reception), www.islasuasi.pe.*
The hotel is the only occupant on this small, tranquil, private island, being reforested with native trees. There are beautiful terraced gardens. You can circumnavigate the island either on a motorized zodiac or paddling a canoe or kayak to see nesting birds. The island has vicuñas, a small herd of alpacas and vizcachas. The sunsets from the highest point are beautiful. Facilities are spacious, comfortable and solar-powered, price

includes buffet breakfast, guided walk and birdwatching. Excellent gourmet cuisine. Service is personalized and very attentive. Transport costs US$100 pp return by private boat from Puno, including stops in Uros and Taquile, or US$500 for a 5-passenger vehicle.

## Restaurants

### Juliaca

### $$ El Asador
*Unión 113. Daily 1200-0100.*
Regional dishes, chicken, grill and pizza, good food and service, pleasant atmosphere.

### $ Delycia's
*M Núñez 168. Closed Fri evening and Sat.*
Good vegetarian set lunch with small salad bar.

### $ Nuevo Star
*Bolívar 121. Daily 0600-2000.*
Decent set meals.

### $ Ricos Pan
*Jr San Román y Jorge Chávez.*
Good bakery with café, popular.

## Transport

### Juliaca
#### Air
Manco Cápac airport, is small but well organized. To/from **Lima**, 1¾ hrs, 5 a day with **LATAM** (Jr San Román 125, T051-322228, airport T051-328485) via **Arequipa** (30 mins), **Cuzco** and direct; and 2 a day direct with **Avianca/TACA** (Real Plaza mall, Jr Tumbes 391, T051-326415, airport T051-327966). Beware over-charging for ground transportation. If you have little luggage, regular taxis and vans stop just outside the airport parking area. Taxi from Plaza Bolognesi, US$2.75; taxi from airport to centre US$3.60, or less from outside airport gates. For transfers to/from **Puno**, see page 271.

#### Bus
**Local** To **Puno**, minibuses leave when full from Jr Brasesco near Plaza Bolognesi

throughout the day and from Terminal Tupac (Jr Benigno Ballón cuadra 7 y San Martín, by Mercado Tupac), US$1.10, 1 hr. To **Capachica**, they leave when full from Cerro Colorado market, 0500-1700, US$2, 1½ hrs. To **Lampa**, cars (US$1.25) and vans (US$0.90) leave when full from the Mercado Santa Bárbara area, eg **El Veloz** (Jr Huáscar 672 y Colón) or **Ramos** (2 de Mayo y Colón), others nearby, 30 mins. Vans to **Pucará** (US$1.25, 45 min), **Ayaviri** (US$1.80, 1½ hrs) and **Azángaro** depart from Terminal Virgen de Las Mercedes (Jr Texas, corner San Juan de Dios); they also stop at Paseo Los Kollas by the exit to Cuzco to pick up passengers. To **Sicuani**, take a bus bound for Cuzco (see below) or **Chasquis** vans leave when full from 8 de Noviembre 1368, by Paseo de Los Kollas, US$5.40, 2½-3 hrs. Minibuses for **Moho** via **Huancané** depart when full 0500-1800 from Jr Moquegua y Circunvalación, north of Mercado Tupac Amaru, US$2.15, 1½ hrs. Minibuses for **Conima** and **Tilali** depart when full from Jr Lambayeque y Av Circunvalación Este, also near the market, US$3, 3 hrs; these may continue to the Bolivian border on market days.

**Long distance** The Terminal Terrestre is at the east end of San Martín (cuadra 9, past the Circunvalación). To **Lima**, US$38 normal, US$43-70 *cama*, 20-22 hrs; direct service with **Flores** at 1500 and 1700 or **Civa** at 1530, several others via Arequipa. To **Cuzco**, US$6-9 normal, US$12-17 *semi-cama*, US$17-23 *cama*, 5-6 hrs, with **Cruz del Sur** (T051-502536) at 0900, **Transzela** (T051-330056) at 0915 and 2300, **Power** (T051-322531) about every 2 hrs, 0600-2330, **Flores** at 1200, several others; also vans from salida a Cuzco. To **Arequipa**, US$4.60-6 normal, US$7-9 semi-cama, US$19-25 *cama*, 4-5 hrs, with

Cruz del Sur at 1130 and 1615, **Transzela** at 0700, 1000, 1230, 1600, 2130, **Julsa** (T051-331952) every 2 hrs 0300-0015, with **Flores** at 0930, 1145, 1245, several others; also vans from **Terminal Tupac** (Benigno Ballón cuadra 7 y San Martín), US$8, 3½ hrs. To **Moquegua** (7 hrs) and **Tacna** (8-9 hrs), US$8-9 normal, US$9-12 *semi-cama*, US$12.50-15 *cama*, several depart 0715-0830 and around 2000. To **Puerto Maldonado** US$9-15, 12 hrs; several companies leave from the Terminal Terrestre and then pick up passengers at private terminals around M Nuñez cuadra 11, 'El Triángulo', by the exit to Cuzco: **Santa Cruz** (Av Ferrocarril 154 y M Núñez, T051-331857) at 1230,1530, 1830; **Julsa Angeles** (T051-326602) at 2100; **Wayra** (Ferrocarril 154) at 0930; **Realeza** at 0630 and 2000, **San Martín** (Jr Tumbes 920, T951-614124) at 0715. Buses originating in Arequipa only stop at their own stations. To **Macusani**, **Alianza** (Av Ferrocarril y Cahuide) 1300, 1700, 1815, US$3.50, 3 hrs; **Jean** (M Núñez y Pje San José), 0845, 1330, 1800; also minibuses from Pje San José, leave when full, US$4.25.

## Juliaca to Cuzco
### Sicuani
The bus terminal is in the newer part of town, which is separated from the older part and the plaza by 3 bridges, the middle one has a pedestrian walkway. To **Juliaca**, Chasquis vans leave when full, US$5.40, 2½-3 hrs. To **Cuzco**, 137 km, US$3.60, 3 hrs. (The Sicuani terminals in Cuzco are at Av Huayruropata, Wanchaq, near Mercado Tupac Amaru.)

### Puno to the jungle
From Macusani to **Juliaca**, US$3.50, 3 hrs; also minibuses US$4.25. Vans go as they fill from Macusani to San Gabán; some continue to Puente Iñambari.

## Borders with Bolivia

**Puno–La Paz via Yunguyo and Copacabana** The most frequently travelled route is along the southwest coast of Titicaca, from Puno to La Paz via **Yunguyo** (Peru) and **Copacabana** (Bolivia). The border villages on either side are called Kasani. This route is very scenic and involves crossing the Straits of Tiquina on a launch (there are barges for the vehicles) between Copacabana and La Paz. Almost all the tourist class bus services use this route.

**Peruvian immigration** (daily 0700-1930, Peruvian time) is five minutes' drive from **Yunguyo** and 500 m from the Bolivian immigration post (daily 0830-2000, Bolivian time). Minibuses go from the Terminal Zonal Sur in Puno to Yunguyo may continue to the border at Kasani if there are enough passengers; there are also shared taxis (US$0.40 per person) and private taxis (US$2.50) from Yunguyo (Jirón Titicaca y San Francisco, one block from Plaza de Armas) to Kasani. Minibuses (US$0.50) and taxis (US$3 or US$0.60 per person) run from Kasani to Copacabana (8 km, 15 minutes). Peruvian time is one hour behind Bolivian time. If you need a visa for Bolivia go to the **Bolivian consulate** in Puno (Jirón Aymaraes G-5, Urbanización APROVI, Barrio Llaviri, T051-205400, consuladopuno@hotmail.com, Monday-Friday 0800-1600; allow about 48 hours).

There is one ATM at Plaza 2 de Mayo in Yunguyo and a couple in Copacabana, as well as *cambios* at the Plaza de Armas in Yunguyo and on both sides of the border; rates are better on the Peruvian side.

**Puno–La Paz via Desaguadero** A more direct route between Puno and La Paz is via the bleak town of **Desaguadero** (same name on both sides of the border), on the southwest coast of the lake. The Carretera Binacional, which joins La Paz with Moquegua and the Pacific port of Ilo, goes through Desaguadero, see page 266, but there is no need to overnight here, as all roads to Desaguadero are paved and, if you leave La Paz, Moquegua or Puno early enough, you should be at your destination before nightfall. This particular border crossing allows you to stop at the ruins of Tiahuanaco in Bolivia along the way. The **Peruvian border office** is open daily 0700-1930; the Bolivian office, daily 0800-2030 (both local time). It is easy to change money on the Peruvian side where there are many changers by the bridge.

**Puno–La Paz via Tilali and Puerto Acosta** The most remote route to Bolivia is along the scenic northeast shore of the lake, via Huancané, Moho, **Tilali** (Peru) and **Puerto Acosta** (Bolivia). The Peruvian immigration office for entry and exit formalities is in Tilali, on the plaza, open 0800-1700. Customs control is 2 km further on and Bolivian immigration and customs are in Puerto Acosta, at the police control (*tranca*) just outside town on the road to La Paz; immigration is open 0830-1230 and 1430-1830. From Juliaca there are vans to Tilali, the last village in Peru; these may continue to the border on market days (Wednesday and Saturday). Three dirt tracks cross the border, via Janko Janko (4 km from Tilali, 10 km from Puerto Acosta, the most direct, little used), via Chaqawara (3 km from Tilali) and via Vilupaya (with the busiest market). On non-market days getting rides on both sides of the border is more difficult, consider walking; there are fragments of ancient road along the Janko Janko route. To hire a car Tilali–Puerto Acosta (if you can find one) costs US$25-30. From Puerto Acosta vans run to Terminal del Altiplano in El Alto, near **La Paz**, US$3, 3½ hours.

# Cuzco

Cuzco stands at the head of the Sacred Valley of the Incas and is the jumping-off point for the Inca Trail and legendary archaeological site of Machu Picchu. It's not surprising, therefore, that this is the prime destination for the vast majority of first-time visitors to Peru.

The ancient capital is today a city of 450,000 inhabitants. Almost every central street has remains of Inca walls and doorways; the perfect Inca stonework serves as the foundations for more modern dwellings. The curved stonework of Qoricancha, the Temple of the Sun, for example, is probably unequalled in the entire world.

Yet Cuzco today is not some dead monument; the local Quechua people bring the city to life, with a fascinating combination of pre-Hispanic and Christian beliefs, and a long list of colourful festivals. Tourism is as much a part of Cuzco's personality as its Inca and colonial treasures. Colonial churches and extensive pre-Columbian ruins are interspersed with countless hotels, bars and restaurants that cater to the over one million international tourists who visit every year. Road and rail links climb east to Lake Titicaca through the scenic Upper Vilcanota Valley. This region offers fine archaeology, beautiful churches, congenial towns and excellent trekking. West of Cuzco is access to one of the area's greatest gems, the beautifully restored Inca city of Choquequirao.

**Best** for
Colonial architecture ▪ Inca archaeology ▪ Museums

Cuzco city . . . . . . . . . . . . . . . . . . . 290
Upper Vilcanota Valley . . . . . . 316
Cuzco to Choquequirao . . . . . 322

# Footprint
## picks

★ **Plaza de Armas**, page 290
The heart of Cuzco since Inca and colonial times.

★ **Qoricancha**, page 291
The Inca Temple of the Sun, once filled with fabulous treasures.

★ **San Pedro market**, page 295
A lively colourful working market popular with tourists.

★ **San Blas**, page 295
A district of steep, narrow streets filled with shops, galleries,
hotels and restaurants.

★ **Museo Inka**, page 295
This museum features impressive cultural exhibits dating to pre-Inca times.

★ **Sacsayhuaman**, page 296
Mysterious walls made of immense stones, just outside Cuzco.

★ **Ausangate Trek**, page 319
Are you fit enough to tackle one of the most demanding treks in Peru?

★ **Choquequirao**, page 322
It's worth every drop of sweat required to trek there.

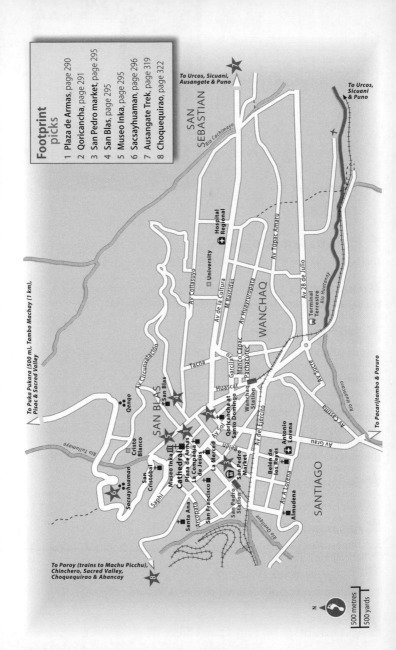

**Footprint picks**

1 Plaza de Armas, page 290
2 Qoricancha, page 291
3 San Pedro market, page 295
4 San Blas, page 295
5 Museo Inka, page 295
6 Sacsayhuaman, page 296
7 Ausangate Trek, page 319
8 Choquequirao, page 322

To Urcos, Sicuani, Ausangate & Puno

To Urcos, Sicuani & Puno

SAN SEBASTIAN

Hospital Regional

Río Cachimayo

Av Collasuyo

University

Av de la Cultura

M Bastidas

Av Topac Amaru

Av 28 de Julio

Terminal Terrestre

Río Huatanay

WANCHAQ

García

Av Sucre

Río Huantaro

To Pacarijtambo & Paruro

Tacna

Pachacutec

Manco Capac

Arthuaynopata

Huascar

Wanchaq Station

Qoricancha Santo Domingo

Av Garcilaso

Santo Domingo

Antonio Lorena

SANTIAGO

Belén de los Reyes

Av A Lorena

Av del Ejercito

Almudena

Río Quillque

San Pedro Station

San Pedro Market

La Merced

San Francisco

Santa Ana

Accopata

Av El Sol

Plaza de Armas

Cathedral

La Compañia de Jesús

Museo Inka

San Cristóbal

Saphi

Av A Castilla

Av Castilla

Av Grau

SAN BLAS

San Blas

Qenqo

Cristo Blanco

Av Circunvalación

Sacsayhuaman

Río Tullumayo

To Puka Pukara (500 m), Tambo Machay (1 km), Pisac & Sacred Valley

To Poroy (trains to Machu Picchu), Chinchero, Sacred Valley, Choquequirao & Abancay

N

500 metres
500 yards

288·Cuzco

# Essential Cuzco

### Finding your feet

Respect the altitude: rest for several hours after arrival; eat lightly; don't smoke; avoid alcohol; drink plenty of water, and remember to walk slowly. There are too many sights in the city to see on a single visit; limit yourself to the highlights or to areas of particular interest. Note that many churches close to visitors on Sunday, and photography inside churches is generally not allowed.

### Getting around

The **airport** is to the southeast of the city. The **bus terminal** is near the Pachacútec statue in Ttio district. If transport has not been arranged by your hotel on arrival, you are advised to travel by taxi from the airport or bus stations. You are also advised to take a taxi when returning to your hotel at night. During the day, the centre of Cuzco is quite small and easy to explore on foot. Agencies offer guided tours of the city and surrounding archaeological sites, but visiting independently is not difficult. There are regular buses from Cuzco to villages and towns throughout the region.

### Visitors' tickets

A combined entry ticket, called **Boleto Turístico de Cusco** (**BTC**), is available to several sites of historical and cultural interest in and around the city, and costs as follows: 130 soles (US$39.40) for 14 sites for 10 days; or 70 soles (US$21.20) for the included city sites (valid for two days); or Sacsayhuaman, Qenqo, Puka Pukara and Tambo Machay (one day); or Pisac, Ollantaytambo, Chinchero and Moray (two days). The BTC can be bought at **iCusco/Dircetur** (Portal Mantas 117-A, Monday-Saturday 0800-2000, Sun 0800-1300) and **Cosituc** (Avenida El Sol 103, of 102, Galerías Turísticas, T084-261465, daily 0800-1800, www.cosituc.gob.pe), or at any of the sites included in the ticket. For students with an ISIC card the 10-day BTC costs 70 soles (US$25), only available at the Cosituc office upon presentation of the ISIC card. Take your ISIC card when visiting the sites.

Two other combined entry tickets apply to churches and religious museums, and can be purchased at any of the included sites. The **Circuito Religioso Arzobispal** (**CRA**, http://cra.org.pe) costs 30 soles (US$12 for 30 days) and includes the cathedral, Museo Arzobispal, San Blas and San Cristóbal. The **Ruta del Barroco Andino** (**RBA**, http://rutadelbarrocoandino.com) costs 25 soles (US$7.60 for seven days) and includes La Compañía in Cuzco and churches in Adahuayllillas, Huaro and Canincunca, all southeast of Cuzco. To visit only La Compañía the cost is 15 soles (US$4.55); to visit the three out-of-town churches or any one of them, you need the **RBA Valle Sur Este** ticket for 15 soles (US$4.55). Other churches and museums have individual entry fees.

Machu Picchu entrance tickets (see page 340) are sold electronically at www.machupicchu.gob.pe, and at the Cuzco ticket office (Calle Garcilaso 223 y Heladeros, next to Museo de Historia Regional, T084-582030, Monday-Saturday 0700-1930).

### Security

Police patrol the streets and tourist sites, but still be vigilant. Do not walk back to your hotel late at night from a bar or club; call a radio-taxi or ask the doorman to call one for you. You should also take care around San Pedro market (otherwise recommended), in the San Cristóbal area and at out-of-the-way ruins. Also take precautions during Inti Raymi. If robbed, be sure to get a police report for insurance claims.

### Tip...
The best places for views of the Cuzco Valley are San Cristóbal Church, Sacsayhuaman and Limbus Restobar.

Since there are so many sights to see in Cuzco city, not even the most ardent tourist would be able to visit them all. Those with limited time, or who want a whistle-stop tour, should visit the cathedral, Qoricancha, La Compañía de Jesús, San Blas, La Merced, San Cristóbal (for the view) and Sacsayhuaman. If you visit one museum make it the Museo Inka, which has the most comprehensive collection.

## ★Plaza de Armas

The heart of the city in Inca days was Huacaypata (the Place of Tears) and Cusipata (the Place of Happiness), divided by a channel of the Saphi River (no longer visible). Today, Cusipata is Plaza Regocijo and Huacaypata is the Plaza de Armas. This was the great civic square of the Incas, flanked by their palaces, and was a place of solemn parades and great assemblies. Around Plaza de Armas are colonial arcades and four great churches. To the northeast is the early 17th-century baroque **cathedral** ① *US$9 or CRA ticket, daily 1000-1800.* It was built on the site of the Palace of Inca Wiracocha (Kiswarcancha). The high altar is solid silver and the original altar *retablo* behind it is a masterpiece of Andean woodcarving. The cathedral contains two interesting paintings: the first is the earliest surviving painting of the city, depicting Cuzco during the 1650 earthquake; the second, at the far right-hand end of the church, is a local painting of the Last Supper replete with Peruvian details, including *cuy* and *chicha*. In the sacristy are paintings of all the bishops of Cuzco. The choir stalls, by a 17th-century Spanish priest, are a magnificent example of colonial baroque art. The elaborate pulpit is also notable. Much venerated is the crucifix of El Señor de los Temblores, the object of many pilgrimages and viewed all over Peru as a guardian against earthquakes.

The tourist entrance to the cathedral is through the church of **La Sagrada Familia** (also known as Jesús, María y José; 1733), which stands to the left of the cathedral as you face it. Its gilt main altar has been renovated. The far simpler **El Triunfo**, on the right of the cathedral, was the first Christian church in Cuzco, built on the site of the Inca Roundhouse (the Suntur Huasi) in 1536. It has a statue of the Virgin of the Descent that is reputed to have helped the Spaniards repel Manco Inca when he besieged the city in 1536.

On the southeast side of the plaza is the beautiful **La Compañía de Jesús** ① *US$3, students US$1.50, or RBA ticket, Mon-Fri 0900-1700, Sat-Sun 0900-1100, 1300-1700, 1245-1700,*

## Inca stonework

Sacsayhuaman aside, there is much original Inca stonework in the streets of Cuzco, where it is incorporated into the foundations of more recent buildings; the most impressive examples are listed below. True Inca stonework is wider at the base than at the top and features ever-smaller stones as the walls rise, creating a tapering effect. Every wall has a perfect line of inclination towards the centre, from bottom to top. The curved stonework in the Temple of the Sun is probably unequalled anywhere in the world. Doorways and niches are trapezoidal. The Incas clearly learnt that the combination of these techniques helped their structures to withstand earthquakes, which explains why, in the two huge earthquakes of 1650 and 1950, Inca walls stayed standing while colonial buildings tumbled down. Noteworthy Inca stonework is found at the following locations:

Callejón Loreto, below.
West wall of Santo Domingo, below.
Calle Ahuacpinta, page 293.
Calle Hatun Rumiyoc, see page 295.
Calle San Agustin, to the east of the plaza.

built in the 17th century on the site of the Palace of the Serpents (Amarucancha), residence of Inca Huayna Capac. Its twin-towered exterior is extremely graceful, and the baroque interior is rich in fine murals and paintings, with a resplendent altar decorated in gold leaf. Outside the church, look for the **Inca stonework** in the Callejón Loreto, running southeast past La Compañía de Jesús from the main plaza, with the walls of the Acllahuasi (see below) on one side, and the **Amarucancha** on the other.

### Santa Catalina and around

The church, convent and museum of **Santa Catalina** ⓘ *Arequipa at Santa Catalina Angosta, Mon-Sat 0830-1730, Sun 1400-1700,* were built upon the foundations of the **Acllahuasi**, where Inca women chosen for their nobility, virtue and beauty were housed in preparation for ceremonial and domestic duties. The convent is a closed order, but the church and museum are worth visiting. Guided tours by English-speaking students (tip expected) will point out the church's ornate gilded altarpiece and beautifully carved pulpit and the museum's collection of Cuzqueño art.

Around the corner, **Museo Machupicchu** (Casa Concha) ⓘ *Santa Catalina Ancha 320, T084-255535, Mon-Sat 0900-1700, US$7,* features objects found by Hiram Bingham during his initial excavations of Machu Picchu in 1912, which were returned by Yale University to the Peruvian government in 2011-2012.

If you continue down Arequipa from Santa Catalina you come to Calle Maruri. Between this street and Santo Domingo is **Cusicancha** ⓘ *free, Mon-Fri 0715-1300, 1400-1600, sometimes open at weekends,* an open space showing the layout of the buildings as they would have been in Inca times.

### ★ Santo Domingo and Qoricancha

*Mon-Sat 0800-1730, Sun 1400-1700 (closed holidays), Museo Qoricancha US$3.60; church free, multi-lingual guides charge US$11 for a 40-min tour.*

This is one of the most fascinating sights in Cuzco. Behind the walls of a 17th-century Catholic church are the remains of Qoricancha, a complex that formed the centre of the vast Inca society. Its Golden Palace and Temple of the Sun were filled with such fabulous treasures of gold and silver that it took the Spanish three months to melt it all down.

The first Inca, Manco Cápac, is said to have built the temple when he left Lake Titicaca and founded Cuzco with Mama Ocllo. However, it was the ninth Inca, Pachacútec, who transformed it. When the Spaniards arrived, the complex was awarded to Juan Pizarro, the younger brother of Francisco, who willed it to the Dominicans when he was fatally

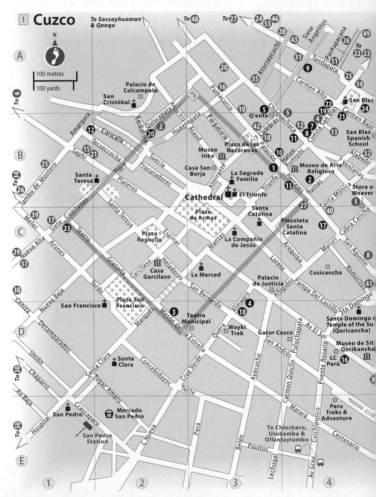

wounded in the Sacsayhuaman siege. The Dominicans ripped much of the complex down to build their church. The baroque cloister has since been excavated to reveal four of the original chambers of the great Inca Temple of the Sun – two on the west have been partly reconstructed in a good imitation of Inca masonry. The finest stonework is in the celebrated curved wall beneath the west end of Santo Domingo. This can be seen (complete with a large crack from the 1950 earthquake) when you look out over the Solar Garden. Excavations have revealed Inca baths below here and more Inca retaining walls. Another superb stretch of late Inca stonework is in Calle Ahuacpinta outside the temple, to the east, or left as you enter.

➡ Cuzco maps
1 Cuzco, page 292
2 Around Plaza de Armas, page 294

**Where to stay** 🛏
1 Albergue Casa Campesina B4
2 Albergue Municipal B2
3 Amaru Colonial B5
4 Amaru Hostal B4
5 Andenes al Cielo B4
6 Andenes de Saphi A1
7 Casa Andina C5
8 Casa Andina Koricancha C4
9 Casa Andina San Blas B5
10 Casa Cartagena A3
11 Casa de la Gringa A4
12 Casa Elena B4
13 Casa San Blas & Tika Bistro B4
14 Casona Les Pleiades A4
15 Cusco Plaza - Saphi B1
16 El Arqueólogo & Divina Comedia Restaurant A3
17 El Mercado C1
18 El Monasterio B3
19 Estrellita C5
20 Flying Dog Hostel A3
21 Hitchhikers B&B Backpackers Hostel B2
22 Hosp El Artesano de San Blas A4
23 Hosp Inka A4
24 Hostal Casa de Campo A3
25 Hostal El Balcón B1
26 Hostal Killipata B1
27 Hostal Kuntur Wasi A3
28 Hostal Pakcha Real A4
29 Hostal Qorichaska C1
30 Hostal Quipu D1
31 Hostal Tikawasi A4
32 Hostería de Anita B4
33 La Encantada A3
34 Loki Cusco B1
35 Los Apus Hotel & Mirador A3
36 Maison de la Jeunesse D4
37 Mallqui Hostal C1
38 Mamá Simona Hostel C1
39 Niños/Hotel Meloc C1
40 Novotel C4
41 Palacio del Inka Luxury Collection C4
42 Palacio Nazarenas B3
43 Pensión Alemana A4
44 Pirwa Backpackers San Blas A5
45 Pirwa Garcilaso D6
46 Quinua Villa Boutique A3
47 Sonesta Posadas del Inca E6
48 Supertramp A3
49 The Blue House A4
50 Tu Casita E1

**Restaurants** 🍴
1 A Mi Manera B3
2 Baco B4
3 Café Cocla D2
4 Café El Ayllu D3
5 Café Punchay A3
6 El Paisa E5
7 Granja Heidi B4
8 Jack's Café B4
9 Juanito's Sandwich Café A4
10 Justina B3
11 Kushka...fé B4
12 Kusikuy B1
13 La Bodega 138 B4
14 La Chomba C5
15 La Cusqueñita E5
16 La Valeriana D4
17 Le Soleil C4
18 Los Toldos D3
19 Macondo A4
20 Orgánika B2
21 Pachapapa B4
22 Panadería El Buen Pastor A4
23 Tacomanía C1
24 The Meeting Place A4

**Bars & clubs** 🍸
25 Km 0 (Arte y Tapas) A4
26 Limbus Restobar A4
27 Museo del Pisco B4

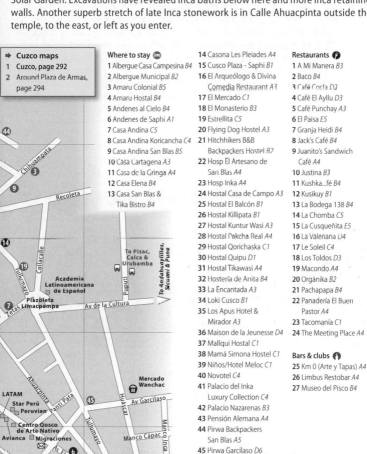

Around the corner from the site (but not part of it), **Museo de Sitio Qorikancha** (formerly Museo Arqueológico) ① *Av El Sol, Mon-Sun 0900-1800, entrance by BTC*, contains a limited collection of pre-Columbian items, Spanish paintings of imitation Inca royalty dating from the 18th century, and photos of the excavation of Qoricancha.

## Southwest of the Plaza de Armas

**The church of La Merced** ① *Plazoleta Espinar, C Mantas, church Mon-Sat 0700-0800, 1700-2000, Sun 0700-1200, 1800-2000; monastery and museum Mon-Sat 0800-1230, 1400-1730, US$3.50*, was first built in 1534 and rebuilt in the late 17th century. Attached is a very fine monastery with an exquisite cloister. Inside the church are buried Gonzalo Pizarro, half-brother of Francisco, and the two Almagros, father and son. The church is most famous for its jewelled monstrance, which is on view in the monastery's museum during visiting hours.

**Museo de Historia Regional** ① *in the Casa Garcilaso, C Garcilaso y Heladeros, daily 0800-1700, entrance by BTC*, tries to show the evolution of the Cuzqueño school of painting. It also contains Inca agricultural implements, colonial furniture and paintings.

**San Francisco** ① *on Plaza San Francisco, 3 blocks southwest of the Plaza de Armas, museum open daily 0900-1800, US$3*, is an austere church reflecting many indigenous influences.

## ② Around Plaza de Armas

➡ Cuzco maps
1 Cuzco, page 292
2 Around Plaza de Armas, page 294

★ Two blocks south of here, **San Pedro market** ① *daily 0900-1800*, is popular with tourists but has only been slightly sanitized for their benefit. It remains a working market and is a pleasant and reasonably safe place to purchase local produce and crafts. In front of the market, the church of **San Pedro** was built in 1688. Its two towers were made from stones brought from an Inca ruin.

## Calle Hatun Rumiyoc

This street, running northeast from the Plaza de Armas, contains some of the most imposing Inca masonry in Cuzco, including the famous 'Stone of 12 angles' (halfway along the street, on the right-hand side going away from the plaza). The huge stone has been precisely cut into a 12-sided polygon in order for it to fit perfectly with the surrounding stones.

The **Museo de Arte Religioso** ① *Hatun Rumiyoc y Herrajes, daily 0800-1800, US$3.60 or CRA ticket*, is housed in the **Palacio Arzobispal**, which was built on the site of an *usnu* or Inca ceremonial platform. The museum contains a collection of colonial paintings and furniture, including the paintings by the indigenous master, Diego Quispe Tito, of a 17th-century Corpus Christi procession that used to hang in the church of Santa Ana.

## ★ San Blas

The San Blas district, uphill from the centre to the northeast, is now firmly on the tourist map, thanks to its shops, galleries and good-value hotels and restaurants. Its main sight is the small, simple church of **San Blas** ① *Plazoleta San Blas, Carmen Bajo, daily 0800-1800, US$3.60 or CRA ticket*, which has a beautiful *mestizo* pulpit, carved from a single cedar trunk; well worth seeing. **Museo Máximo Laura** ① *Santa Catalina Ancha 304, T084-227383, http://museomaximolaura.com, daily 0800-2100*, displays 24 prize-winning exhibits by this celebrated textile artist, with workshop, gallery and shop.

## ★ Museo Inka

*Cuesta del Almirante 103, T084-237380. Mon-Sat 0800-1830. US$4.*

The impressive **Palacio del Almirante**, just north of the Plaza de Armas, houses the Museo Inka, run by the Universidad San Antonio de Abad. The museum exhibits the development of culture in the region from pre-Inca, through Inca times to the present day, with displays of textiles, ceramics, metalwork, jewellery, architecture and technology. Don't miss the collection of miniature

**Where to stay** 🛏
1 Andean Wings *A1*
2 Casa Andina Catedral *C3*
3 Casa Andina
  Cusco Plaza *C2*
4 Cusco Plaza -
  Nazarenas *B3*
5 EcoPackers Hostel *A1*
6 El Procurador del Cusco *A2*
7 Hostal Royal
  Frankenstein *B1*
8 Inkaterra La Casona *B3*
9 Loreto Boutique Hotel *C2*
10 Marqueses *B1*
11 Pariwana *C1*
12 Pirwa Hostels *B1, B2*
13 Sonesta Posadas
  del Inca *B2*
14 The Point *C1*
15 Tierra Viva Cusco Plaza *A3*

**Restaurants** 🍴
1 Barrio Ceviche *B2*
2 Café El Ayllu *C1*
3 Café Halliy *A2*
4 Café Perla *C3*
5 Chicha *B1*
6 Cicciolina *C3*
7 Dolce Vita *C3*
8 Dos por Tres *C1*
9 El Encuentro *A2, C3*
10 Fallen Angel restaurant
  & Guesthouse *B3*

11 Fusi Chicken and Grill *C2*
12 Greens Organic *C3*
13 Incanto *C3*
14 Kión *C3*
15 Kushka...fé *B1*
16 La Bondiet *C1*
17 La Valeriana *C2*
18 Limo *B3*
19 Morena
  Peruvian Kitchen *A2*
20 Mr Soup *B1*
21 Museo del Café *B2*
22 Pucará *B2*
23 Qucharitas *A2*
24 Sara *C3*
25 Tunupa *B2*
26 Yajúú! Juice Bar *B2*

**Bars & clubs** 🍸
27 El Garabato & Ukuku's *B2*
28 Indigo *A2*
29 Los Perros Bar *A2*
30 Mama Africa &
  Inca Rail Ticket Office *B2*
31 Mythology *B3*
32 Norton's Pub *C3*
33 Paddy's Pub *C3*

turquoise figures discovered at Pikillacta and other offerings to the gods. Weaving demonstrations are given in the courtyard.

## Museo de Arte Precolombino

*Plaza de las Nazarenas 231. Daily 0900-2200, US$7, US$3.50 with student card; under same auspices as the Larco Museum in Lima, MAP Café (see Restaurants, page 303).*

Housed in the **Casa Cabrera** on the northwest side of the Plaza de las Nazarenas, this beautiful museum is set around a spacious courtyard and contains many superb examples of pottery, metalwork (largely in gold and silver), woodcarvings and shells from the Moche, Chimú, Paracas, Nazca and Inca cultures. There are some vividly rendered animistic designs, giving an insight into the way Peru's ancient peoples viewed their world and the creatures that inhabited it. Every exhibit carries explanations in English and Spanish. Highly recommended.

Elsewhere on the plaza, the **Convento de las Nazarenas** is now a hotel. You can see the Inca-colonial doorway with a mermaid motif, but ask permission to view the lovely 18th-century frescos inside.

## ★ Sacsayhuaman

*30-min walk from Plaza de las Nazarenas. Daily 0700-1730. Entry with BTC ticket. Students offer free guided tours; give them a tip.*

There are some magnificent Inca walls in this ruined ceremonial centre, on a hill in the northern outskirts. The massive rocks weighing up to 360 metric tons are fitted together with absolute perfection. Three walls run parallel for over 360 m and there are 21 bastions. Sacsayhuaman was thought for centuries to be a fortress, but the layout and architecture suggest a great sanctuary and temple to the Sun, which rises exactly opposite the place previously believed to be the Inca's throne; this was probably an altar, carved out of the solid rock, with broad steps leading to it from either side. The hieratic, rather than the military, hypothesis was supported by the discovery in 1982 of the graves of priests, who would have been unlikely to be buried in a fortress. The precise functions of the site, however, will probably continue to be a matter of dispute as very few clues remain, owing to its steady destruction.

The site survived the first years of the conquest. Pizarro's troops had entered Cuzco unopposed in 1533 and lived safely at Sacsayhuaman, until the rebellion of Manco Inca in 1536 caught them off guard. The bitter struggle that ensued became the decisive military action of the conquest: Manco's failure to hold Sacsayhuaman cost him the war and the empire. The destruction of the hilltop site began after the defeat of Manco's rebellion. The outer walls still stand, but the complex of towers and buildings was razed to the ground. From then until the 1930s, Sacsayhuaman served as a kind of unofficial quarry of pre-cut stone for the inhabitants of Cuzco.

The site can be reached in 30 minutes by walking up Pumacurco from Plaza de la Nazarenas, or from the church of **San Cristóbal**, just north of the centre. The church was built by Cristóbal Paullu Inca to honour his patron saint. Adjacent to San Cristóbal, you can see the 11 doorway-sized niches of the great Inca wall of the **Palacio de Colcampata**. This was Paullu's residence and where, legend has it, the founding Inca Manco Cápac had lived centuries before.

## Beyond Sacsayhuaman

*Take a guide to the sites and visit in the morning for the best photographs. Entry by BTC ticket; carry it with you as there are roving ticket inspectors. To get there take the Pisac bus or the Señor del Huerto city bus from Mercado Rosaspata up to Tambo Machay (US$0.70).*

Along the road from Sacsayhuaman to Pisac, past a radio station, is the temple and amphitheatre of **Qenqo**, which has some of the finest examples of Inca stone carving *in situ*, especially inside the large hollowed-out stone that houses an altar. Four kilometres furthter on the same road is **Puka Pukara**, known as the Red Fort, but more likely to have been a *tambo*, or post-house; it's worth coming here for the wonderful views alone. Nearby is the spring shrine of **Tambo Machay**, which is in excellent condition. Water still flows by a hidden channel out of the masonry wall, straight into a little rock pool traditionally known as the Inca's bath. You can visit the sites on foot, a pleasant walk of at least half a day through the countryside; enquire about safety beforehand, take water and sun protection, and watch out for dogs. Alternatively, catch a bus up, and walk back.

## Rainbow Mountain

*This tour is offered by all low-end agencies in Cuzco, departing 0300 daily, returning 1900, US$25 plus US$3 community entrance fee, typical group size 20-25.*

Since 2016 this previously seldom visited area has become a must for budget travellers seeking surreal selfies. It features a trek along a high ridgeline (up to 5000 m), accessed from the community of Chillca in the Cordillera Vilcanota. The ridge is traversed by colourful mineral bands and there are fine views of Ausangate in good weather. The area is beautiful but has already been impacted by mass tourism. The trek is demanding; you should be acclimatized to altitude before undertaking it. To visit this area safely and responsibly, look for an agency which runs smaller groups and takes more time, such as **Flashpacker** (page 311), **Apus Perú** (page 313) and others.

## Listings Cuzco city *maps pages 292 and 294.*

### Tourist information

**iPerú** is the most reliable source of information. Their main office and information desk is at the airport (T084-237364, iperucusco@ promperu.gob.pe, daily 0600-1700). There is also an iPerú desk on Plaza de Armas (Portal de Harinas 177 at BCP Traveller Point, T084-596159, Mon-Fri 0900-1900, Sat-Sun 0900-1300) and a kiosk next to La Compañía church (T084-216680, Mon-Sat 0900-1300, 1400-1800). Information also available from **iCusco/Dircetur** (Portal Mantas 117-A, next to La Merced church, T084-222032, Mon-Sat 0800-2000, Sun 0800-1300). See also www. aboutcusco.com and www.cuscoonline.com.

The **tourist police** (Plaza Túpac Amaru, Wanchaq, T084-512351/235123) will prepare a *denuncia* (report for insurance purposes) for you. **Indecopi** (Urbanización Constancia Mz A-11-2, Wanchaq, T084-252987, toll-free 24-hr T0800-44040, paragon@indecopi. gob.pe) is the consumer protection bureau.

### Where to stay

Cuzco has hundreds of hotels in all categories but the more expensive ones should nonetheless be booked several months in advance, particularly for the week around Inti Raymi, when prices are greatly increased. Prices given are for the high season in Jun-Aug. When there are fewer tourists, hotels may offer discounts, be sure to ask. Be wary of unlicensed hotel agents who are often misleading about details; their local nickname is *jalagringos* (gringo pullers), or *piratas*. Many places will store your luggage when you go trekking, but always check valuables and possessions before and after depositing them with hotel/hostel staff.

Chain hotels in Cuzco include **Best Western** (www.bestwestern.com), **Casa Andina** (www.casa-andina.com), **JW Marriott** (www.marriott.com), **Novotel** (www.novotel.com) and **Sonesta** (www.sonesta.com). There are also several hostel chains: **Flying Dog** (www.flyingdogperu.com), a huge bustling **Loki** (www.lokihostel.com), **Pirwa** (T084-244315, www.pirwahostelscusco.com) with 4 properties, and **The Point** (www.thepointhostels.com).

## Around the Plaza de Armas

### $$$$ Fallen Angel Guest House
*Pl Las Nazarenas 221, T084-258184,*
*www.fallenangelincusco.com.*
A 4-room luxury hotel above the restaurant of the same name. Each suite is decorated in its own lavish style (with living room, dining room, bathroom, feather duvets, heating), very comfortable and a far cry from the usual adaptation of colonial buildings elsewhere in the city. With all amenities, excellent service, LGBT friendly.

### $$$$ Inkaterra La Casona
*Pl Las Nazarenas 211, T084-234010,*
*www.inkaterra.com.*
A private, colonial-style boutique hotel in a converted 16th-century mansion. 11 exclusive suites, all facilities, concierge service with activities and excursions, highly regarded and the height of luxury.

### $$$ Andean Wings
*Siete Cuartones 225, T084-243166,*
*www.andeanwingshotel.com.*
In a restored 17th-century house, intimate suites, some with jacuzzi, are individually designed (one is accessible for the disabled), spa, restaurant and bar.

### Tip...
Since nights are cold in Cuzco and many hotels have no heating, ask for an *estufa*, a heater which some places will provide for a small extra charge.

### $$$ Loreto Boutique Hotel
*Pasaje Loreto 115, T084-226352,*
*www.loretoboutiquehotel.com.*
Great location; 12 spacious rooms with original Inca walls, upgraded to boutique status. Laundry service, will help organize travel services including guides and taxis, free airport pick-up.

### $$$ Marqueses
*Garcilaso 256, T084-264249,*
*www.hotelmarqueses.com.*
Spanish colonial style, with 16/17th-century style religious paintings and 2 lovely courtyards. Rooms have heavy curtains and some are a little dark; luxury rooms have bath and shower. Buffet breakfast.

### $$$ Tierra Viva Cusco Plaza
*Suecia 345, T084-245858,*
*www.tierravivahoteles.com.*
Boutique hotel in the former residence of Gonzalo Pizarro. Rooms and suites have comfortable beds, heating, minibar, safe, with excellent breakfast. Exemplary service, airport transfers.

### $$$-$$ Cusco Plaza – Nazarenas
*Plaza Nazarenas 181, T084-246161,*
*www.cuscoplazahotels.com.*
Friendly service and good location. Buffet breakfast and café with coffee and snacks. Also runs **Cusco Plaza – Saphi**, Saphi 486, T084-263000.

### $$ EcoPackers Hostel
*Santa Teresa 375, T084-235460,*
*www.ecopackersperu.com.*
Ecologically friendly, well-regarded *hostal* in a colonial *casona*, double rooms with en suite or dorms for 4-18 people, communal kitchen, games room, bar, large-screen TV room, garage for bicycles or motorcycles.

## $$ Pariwana
*Mesón de la Estrella 136, T084-233751,*
*www.pariwana-hostel.com.*
Variety of rooms in a converted colonial
mansion with courtyard, from doubles with
bath to dorms sleeping 14, also girls-only
dorm, restaurant, bar/lounge, English
spoken, lots of activities.

## $ El Procurador del Cusco
*Coricalle 425, Prolongación Procuradores,*
*T084-243559, http://hostelprocurador*
*delcusco.blogspot.com.*
Youth hostel. Basic rooms with or without
bath, upstairs is better, use of the basic
kitchen and laundry area, helpful, good value.

## $ Hostal Royal Frankenstein
*San Juan de Dios 260, 2 blocks from*
*the Plaza de Armas, T084-236999,*
*www.hostal-frankenstein.net.*
Eccentric place but a frequent favourite,
with private or shared bath, hot water, safe,
kitchen, includes breakfast, small charge
for computer, heater and laundry, medical
services, German-owned, German and
English spoken.

## Beyond the plaza, including San Blas

## $$$$ Casa Cartagena
*Pumacurco 336, T084-224356,*
*www.casacartagena.com.*
In a converted monastery and national
heritage building, super-deluxe facilities with
Italian design and colonial features, 4 levels
of suite, **La Chola** restaurant, extensive
complimentary Qoya spa, enriched oxygen
system, and all services to be expected in a
**Luxury Properties** group hotel.

## $$$$ El Mercado
*C Siete Cuartones 306, T084-582640,*
*www.elmercadotunqui.com.*
On the site of a former market close to
the Plaza de Armas, owned by **Mountain
Lodges of Peru**, superior rooms and suites,
restaurant, bar, helpful staff.

## $$$$ El Monasterio (Belmond)
*C Palacios 140, Plazoleta Nazarenas, T084-*
*604000, www.monasteriohotel.com.*
5-star, beautifully restored Seminary of San
Antonio Abad (a Peruvian National Historical
Landmark), including the baroque chapel,
spacious comfortable rooms with all facilities
(some rooms offer an oxygen-enriched
atmosphere), very helpful staff (buffet
breakfast open to non-residents, will fill you
up for the rest of the day), good restaurants,
lunch and dinner à la carte, business centre.

## $$$$ Palacio del Inka Luxury Collection
*Plazoleta Santo Domingo 259, T084-231961,*
*www.libertador.com.pe.*
Real 5-star quality, warm bright rooms and
common areas, especially good service,
**Inti Raymi** restaurant is excellent, live music
in the evening.

## $$$$ Palacio Nazarenas (Belmond)
*Plazoleta Nazarenas 276, T084-582222,*
*www.palacionazarenas.com.*
Boutique hotel in a beautifully restored
former convent. Outdoor swimming pool,
spa, history booklet and cooking classes.

## $$$$-$$$ Casa San Blas
*Tocuyeros 566, just off Cuesta San Blas,*
*T084-237900, www.casasanblas.com.*
An international-standard boutique hotel
with bright, airy rooms decorated with
traditional textiles. Breakfast, served in the
**Tika Bistro** downstairs. Pleasant balcony
with good views, attentive service.

## $$$$-$$$ Quinua Villa Boutique
*Pasaje Santa Rosa A-8, parallel to Tandapata,*
*T084-242646, www.quinua.com.pe.*
A beautiful living museum, 5 different
apartments, each with a different theme
and kitchen, low-season discounts.

## $$$ El Arqueólogo
*Pumacurco 408, T084-232522,*
*www.hotelarqueologo.com.*
Helpful, French and English spoken, heating
extra, will store luggage, garden, cafeteria
and kitchen. Same group as **Vida Tours**

(Ladrillo 425, T084-227750, www.vidatours. com). Traditional and adventure tourism.

### $$$ La Encantada
*Tandapata 354, T084-242206, www.encantadaperu.com.*
Good beds, rooftop spa, fabulous views of the city. Swiss/Peruvian-owned.

### $$$ Los Apus Hotel & Mirador
*Atocsaycuchi 515 y Choquechaca, San Blas, T084-264243, www.losapushotel.com.*
Includes airport transfer, full of character, very clean and smart, central heating, disabled facilities, 2 restaurants, 4th floor terrace.

### $$$ Pensión Alemana
*Tandapata 260, San Blas, T084-226861, www.hotel-cuzco.com.*
Colonial-style modern building. Swiss-owned, welcoming, comfortable, discount in low season.

### $$$-$$ Amaru Hostal Group
*Cuesta San Blas 541, T084-225933, www.amarucolonial.com.*
Private or shared bath. Price includes airport/train/bus pick-up. Oxygen, kitchen for use in the evenings, book exchange. Rooms around a pretty courtyard, good beds, pleasant, relaxing. Same price category and services at: **Amaru Colonial** (Chihuampata 642, San Blas, T084-223521, www.amaruhostal2.com), and **Hostería de Anita** (Alabado 525-5, T084-225499, www.hosteriadeanita.com), safe, quiet, good breakfast. Also has the more economical **Mallqui Hostal** (Nueva Alta 444, T084-231294, www.hostalmallqui.com), with private rooms and gendered dorms.

### $$$-$$ Andenes al Cielo
*Choquechaca 176, T084-222237, www.andenesalcielo.com.*
At the foot of the San Blas district, 15 rooms and a penthouse in renovated historic home, most expensive rooms have fireplaces, all with either balconies or patios, heating. Buffet breakfast, rooftop patio, safe deposit box, free airport pick-up.

### $$$-$$ Casona Les Pleiades
*Tandapata 116-829, T084-506430, www.casona-pleiades.com.*
Small guesthouse in renovated colonial house, cosy and warm, generous hosts, video lounge and book exchange, café, free airport pick-up with reservation, lots of info, low-season discounts.

### $$$-$$ Hostal Casa de Campo
*Tandapata 298 (at the end of the street), T084-244404, www.hotelcasadecampo.com.*
Some of the top rooms have many steps up to them, includes bus/airport/rail transfer with reservations, 10% discount for **Footprint** book owners, safe deposit box, sun terrace, quiet, relaxing, all rooms have great views, Dutch and English spoken, take a taxi after dark.

### $$$-$$ Hostal El Balcón
*Tambo de Montero 222, T084-236738, www.balconcusco.com.*
Warm atmosphere, very welcoming, quiet, laundry, meals on request, English spoken, wonderful views, beautiful garden.

### $$$-$$ Hostal Tikawasi
*Tandapata 491, T084-231609, www.tikawasi.com.*
Includes heating, family-run, lovely garden overlooking the city. Stylish, modern rooms with good views, comfortable beds.

### $$ Albergue Casa Campesina
*Av Tullumayo 274, T084-233466, www.hotelescbc-cusco.com/casacam/.*
Private or shared bath, lovely place, funds support the **Casa Campesina** organization (www.cbc.org.pe), which is linked to local *campesino* communities (see also **Store of Weavers** under Shopping, page 309).

### $$ Andenes de Saphi
*Saphi 848, T084-227561, www.andenesdesaphi.com.*
Set around 3 Inca terraces. Rooms nicely decorated with animal themes. Common room, bright reception area.

## $$ Casa Elena
*Choquechaca 162, T084-241202,*
*www.casaelenacusco.com.*
French/Peruvian hostel, very comfortable,
helpful staff, good choice.

## $$ Hostal Kuntur Wasi
*Tandapata 352-A, San Blas, T084-227570,*
*www.hospedajekunturwasi.com.*
Great views, cheaper without bath, use of
basic kitchen and laundry (both extra), owner
speaks a bit of English and is very helpful and
welcoming, a pleasant place to stay.

## $$ Hostal Qorichaska
*Nueva Alta 458, T084-228974,*
*www.qorichaskaperu.com.*
Rooms are clean and sunny, the older ones
have traditional balconies. Also has dorms,
mixed and gendered. A good choice.

## $$ Hostal Quipu
*Fierro 495, T084-236179, www.hostalquipu.com.*
Small pleasant rooms with private bath and
reliable hot water, sunny patio, modern
kitchen facilities, helpful owner and staff.
Warmly recommended.

## $$ Niños/Hotel Meloc
*Meloc 442, T084-231424,*
*www.ninoshotel.com.*
Modern decor in colonial building. Excellent
breakfast extra, restaurant, laundry service,
luggage store, English spoken, run as part
of the Dutch foundation **Niños Unidos
Peruanos** and all profits are invested in
projects to help street children. Also has
**Niños 2/Hotel Fierro** (C Fierro 476, T084-
254611), with all the same features.

## $$-$ Casa de La Gringa
*Tandapata y Pasñapacana 148, T084-241168,*
*www.casadelagringa.com.*
Uniquely decorated rooms, lots of art and
colour, 24-hr hot water, kitchen, common
areas, heaters, safe homely feeling. See also
**Another Planet** (What to do, page 314).

## $$-$ Mamá Simona Hostel
*Ceniza 364, near San Pedro market,*
*T084-260408, www.mamasimona.com.*

Traditional old house with rooms around a
courtyard, doubles (heating extra) and dorms,
duvets, shared bathrooms, towel rental,
includes breakfast, laundry service, helpful.

## $$-$ Supertramp
*Sapantiana 424B, T084-225783,*
*www.supertramphostel.com.*
In a quiet area, built using recycled materials.
2 rooms with bath (1 has jacuzzi) and several
dorms, bunk beds with privacy curtains and
lockers with electric outlets. Outdoor common
area for breakfast (included) and parties.

## $ Albergue Municipal
*Quiscapata 240 (between Resbalosa and
Arcoiris), T984-252506.*
Municipal youth hostel. Dormitories and
double rooms with shared bath, great views,
small cooking facilities, laundry, luggage
store, very clean, pleasant and good value.

## $ Estrellita
*Av Tullumayo 445, parte Alta, T084-234134.*
Most rooms with shared bath, 2 with private
bath, basic but excellent value, safe parking
available for bikes.

## $ Hitchhikers B&B Backpackers Hostel
*Saphi 440, T084-260079,*
*www.hhikersperu.com.*
Located close to the plaza, mixture of dorms
and 1- to 3-bed private rooms with private
or shared bath, includes breakfast, hot water,
kitchen, lockers.

## $ Hospedaje El Artesano de San Blas
*Suytuccato 790, San Blas, T084-263968,*
*http://hospedaje-el-artesano-de-san-
blas-guest-house-cusco.bedspro.com.*
Many bright and airy rooms overlooking
courtyard, quiet, taxis leave you at Plaza San
Blas, then it's a steep walk uphill for 5-10 mins.

## $ Hospedaje Inka
*Suytuccato 848, San Blas, T084-231995,*
*http://hospedajeinka.weebly.com.*
Spacious rooms with private or shared bath,
wonderful views, very helpful owner, Américo.
Taxis leave you at Plaza San Blas, walk steeply
uphill for 5-10 mins, or phone the *hostal*.

### $ Hostal Killipata
*Killichapata 238, just off Tambo de Montero,*
*T084-236668, hostalkillipata@hotmail.com.*
Family-run lodging with variety of room
sizes, private or shared bath, good showers,
hot water and fully equipped kitchen.
Breakfast is extra.

### $ Hostal Pakcha Real
*Tandapata 300, San Blas, T084-237484,*
*www.hostalpakchareal.com.*
Family-run, hot water, relaxed, with or without
bath. Breakfast included, laundry facilities
extra. Airport/train/bus pick-up, but call
ahead if arriving late.

### $ Maison de la Jeunesse
*Av El Sol, Cuadra 5, Pasaje Grace, Edif San*
*Jorge (down a small side street opposite*
*Museo de Sitio de Qoricancha), T084-235617,*
*hostellingcusco@hotmail.com.*
Double rooms with bath or a bed in a dorm
with shared bath; TV and video room,
lockers, cooking facilities and hot water.
Affiliated to **HI** (www.hihostels.com).

### $ The Blue House
*Kiskapata 291 (parallel and above*
*Tandapata), T084-242407, see Facebook.*
Cosy family *hostal*, good value. Reductions
for longer stays, includes breakfast, hot
shower, views.

### $ Tu Casita
*C Hospital 787, interior 5 (entrance down an*
*alley near San Pedro market), T984-754519,*
*tucasitacusco@gmail.com.*
Dorms, shared bath, 2 kitchens, balcony.
Friendly owner Delcy.

## Restaurants

### Around the Plaza de Armas
There are many good cheap restaurants on
Procuradores, Plateros and Tecseccocha.

### $$$ A Mi Manera
*Triunfo 393, T084-222219.*
Imaginative *Novo Andino* cuisine with open
kitchen. Great hospitality and atmosphere.

### $$$ Barrio Ceviche
*Portal de Harinas 181, Plaza de Armas,*
*T084-226334.*
Coastal Peruvian cuisine, with fresh fish flown
in daily from Lima. Fitting marine decor and
great service.

### $$$ Chicha
*Plaza Regocijo 261, p 2 (upstairs),*
*T084-240520. Daily 1200-2400.*
Specializes in regional dishes created by
restaurateur Gastón Acurio (see under Lima,
Restaurants), Peruvian cuisine of the highest
standards in a renovated colonial house, at
one time the royal mint, tastefully decorated,
open-to-view kitchen, bar with a variety of
*pisco sours*, good service.

### $$$ Cicciolina
*Triunfo 393, 2nd floor, T084-239510.*
*Reservations required for dinner.*
Sophisticated cooking focusing largely on
Italian/Mediterranean cuisine, impressive
wine list. Good atmosphere, great for a
special occasion.

### $$$ Fallen Angel
*Plazoleta Nazarenas 221, T084-258184.*
*Sun from 1500.*
International and *Novo Andino* gourmet cuisine,
great steaks, genuinely innovative interior
design, worth checking out their events.

### $$$ Fusi Chicken and Grill
*Av El Sol 106, T084-233341. Open 1100-2300.*
In the La Merced commercial centre, 2nd floor.
*Novo Andino* and international cuisine in a
chic contemporary setting, fine wines.

### $$$ Greens Organic
*Santa Catalina Angosta 135, upstairs,*
*T084-254753.*
Largely organic, but not wholly vegetarian,
ingredients in fusion cuisine, very good.

### $$$ Incanto
*Santa Catalina Angosta 135, T084-254753.*
*Daily 1100-2400.*
Restaurant has Inca stonework and serves
Italian dishes (pastas, grilled meats, pizzas),

and desserts, accompanied by an extensive wine list. Also Peruvian delicatessen.

### $$$ Kión
*Triunfo 370, T084-431862. Open 1100-2300.*
Traditional *chifa* and regional flavours using Chinese techniques.

### $$$ Limo
*Portal de Carnes 236, p2, T084-240668.*
On 2nd floor of a colonial mansion overlooking the Plaza de Armas, Peruvian cuisine of the highest standard, with strong emphasis on fish and seafood, fine pisco bar, good service and atmosphere.

### $$$ MAP Café
*In Museo de Arte Precolombino, Plaza de las Nazarenas 231, T084-242476. Open for lunch and dinner.*
Haute cuisine approach to traditional dishes using Andean crops, innovative children's menu, minimalist design, top-class food and service.

### $$$ Tunupa
*Portal de Confituría 233, p 2, Plaza de Armas.*
Large restaurant, small balcony overlooking the plaza, international, Peruvian and *Novo Andino* cuisine, good buffet US$15, nicely decorated, cocktail lounge, live music and dance at 1930 and 2130.

### $$$-$$ Morena Peruvian Kitchen
*Plateros 348B, T084-437832. Mon-Sun 1200-2200.*
Modern takes on Peruvian food in a nicely decorated setting, generous portions, good service. Recommended.

### $$ Pucará
*Plateros 309, T084-222027. Mon-Sat 1230-2200.*
Peruvian and international food (no language skills required as a sample plate of their daily menu is placed in the window at lunchtime), nice atmosphere.

### $$ Sara
*Santa Catalina Ancha 370, T084-261691.*
Vegetarian-friendly organic café bistro, stylish and modern setting, menu includes

both traditional Peruvian dishes as well as pasta and other international dishes.

### $ El Encuentro
*Tigre 130 and Santa Catalina Ancha 384. Daily 0800-2200.*
Breakfast, economical *menú* and à la carte. Good vegetarian food, very busy at lunchtime.

## Cafés

### Café Cocla
*Mesón de la Estrella 137. Mon-Fri 0900-1300, 1600-2000, Sat 0900 1400.*
Excellent coffee, also sells organic coffee beans, supports several coffee farmers' cooperatives in the Cuzco region.

### Café El Ayllu
*Almagro 133, and Marqués 263.*
Classical/folk music, good atmosphere, superb range of milk products, wonderful apple pastries, good selection for breakfast, great juices, quick service. A Cuzco institution.

### Café Halliy
*Plateros 357.*
Popular meeting place, especially for breakfast, good for comments on guides, has good snacks and 'copa Halliy' (fruit, muesli, yoghurt, honey and chocolate cake), also good *menú* including vegetarian.

### Café Perla
*Santa Catalina Ancha 304, on the plazoleta.*
Extensive menu of light meals, sandwiches, desserts and coffee, including beans for sale roasted on the premises. Popular.

### Dolce Vita
*Santa Catalina Ancha 366. Open 1000-2100.*
Delicious Italian ice cream.

### Dos por Tres
*Marquez 271. Mon-Sat 0900-2100.*
Popular for over 20 years, great coffee and cakes.

### La Bondiet
*Heladeros 118. Open 0730-2300.*
Upmarket French café with a good selection of sweet and savoury pastries,

*empanadas*, good sandwiches, juices and coffee. A local favourite.

## Museo del Café
*Espaderos 136, around a beautifully restored colonial courtyard.*
Coffee, snacks, sweets as well as delicious, more substantial meals and a chance to get to know the coffee-making process. Coffee accessories for sale.

## Qucharitas
*Procuradores 372.*
Ice cream made right in front of you, with a wide variety of flavours and toppings.

## Yajúú! Juice Bar
*Portal Confituría 249 and Ayacucho 178-2. Daily 0700-2300.*
Fresh inexpensive juices and smoothies as well as sandwiches.

---

## Beyond the plaza, including San Blas

### $$$ Baco
*Ruinas 465, T084-242808.*
Wine bar and bistro-style restaurant, same owner as **Cicciolina**. Specializes in barbecued and grilled meats, also veggie dishes, pizzas and good wines. Unpretentious and comfy, groups welcome.

### $$$ Kusikuy
*Amargura 140, T084-262870.*
High-quality Peruvian food with good ambience. Good for *cuy* (guinea pig); reserve an hour in advance for this.

### $$$ Le Soleil
*C San Agustin 275, in La Lune hotel, T084-240543, www.restaurantelesoleilcusco.com.*
Excellent restaurant using local products to make classic French cuisine.

### $$$ Pachapapa
*Plazoleta San Blas 120, opposite church of San Blas, T084-241318.*
A beautiful patio restaurant in a colonial house, good Cusqueño and other dishes, at night diners can sit in their own, private colonial dining room, attentive staff.

### $$$-$$ Divina Comedia
*Pumacurco 406, T084-437640. Daily 1200-1500, 1800-2200.*
An elegant restaurant just 1 block from El Monasterio hotel, diners are entertained by classical piano and singing. Friendly atmosphere with comfortable seating, perfect for a special night out, reasonable prices.

### $$$-$$ Granja Heidi
*Cuesta San Blas 525, T084-238383, Mon-Sat 1130-2130.*
Delicious yoghurt, granola, ricotta cheese and honey and other great breakfast options. Also vegetarian dishes, a very good midday *menú* and steak at night.

### $$ El Paisa
*Av El Sol 819, T084-501717. Open 0900-1700.*
Typical northern Peruvian dishes including ceviche and goat.

### $$ Jack's Café
*Choquechaca y Cuesta San Blas, T084-254606.*
Excellent varied menu, generous portions, relaxed atmosphere, friendly service, very popular, can get crowded at lunchtime, expect a queue in high season.

### $$ Justina
*Palacios 110. Mon-Sat from 1800.*
Good-value, good-quality pizzeria, with wine bar. It's at the back of a patio.

### $$ Kushka...fé
*Choquechaca 131-A and Portal Espinar 159. Daily 0700-2300.*
Great food in a nice setting, English spoken.

### $$ La Bodega 138
*Herrajes 138, T084-260272.*
Excellent pizza, good salads and pasta. Warm and welcoming. Craft beer.

### $$ La Cusqueñita
*Av Centenario 800, T084-267012.*
A traditional *picantería* serving Cuzco specialities, live music and dance show daily.

### $$ Los Toldos
*Almagro 171, T084-229829 (deliveries).*

Grilled chicken, fries and salad bar, also *trattoria* with home-made pasta and pizza, delivery.

### $$ Macondo
*Cuesta San Blas 571, T084-227887.*
Interesting restaurant with an imaginative menu, good food, well-furnished, gay friendly.

### $$ Orgánika
*Resbalosa 410, T084-237216. Daily 0800-2130.*
Fresh ingredients from their own organic farm in the Sacred Valley. Try the grilled alpaca or the langoustine salad and the delicious combination juices. Sister restaurant **Rúcula** round the corner at Ataúd 266 (1300-2130) also serves pizza.

### $$ Tacomanía
*Teatro 394, T084-597608. Dinner only.*
Serving tacos cooked to order with freshly-made Mexican fillings. Owned by Englishman Nick Garret.

### $$-$ Mr Soup
*Garcilaso 210, 1st floor, T084-253806. Open lunch and dinner, closed Mon.*
Huge bowls of soup from all over the world: udon, goulash, tom ka gai, various Peruvian classics.

### $ Café Punchay
*Choquechaca 229, T084-261504.*
German-owned vegetarian restaurant, with a variety of pasta and potato dishes, good range of wines and spirits, projector for international sports and you can bring a DVD for your own private movie showing.

### $ La Chomba
*Tullumayo 339. Open lunch and dinner.*
Large portions of traditional Peruvian food. Popular with locals, good for tourists seeking a genuine experience.

## Cafés

### Juanito's Sandwich Café
*7 Angelitos 638, San Blas.*
Great grilled veggie and meaty burgers and sandwiches, coffee, tea and hot chocolate.

Juanito himself is a great character and the café stays open late.

### La Valeriana
*Av El Sol 576, and Mantas near Plaza de Armas. Mon-Sat 0700-2200, Sun 0730-2100.*
Good coffee and pastries. Try the *lúcuma* cupcakes.

### Panadería El Buen Pastor
*Cuesta San Blas 579.*
Very good bread, *empanadas* and pastries, proceeds go to a charity for orphans and street children.

### The Meeting Place
*Plazoleta San Blas 630.*
Good coffee, waffles and pastries. Supports various social projects. Popular.

## Bars and clubs

### Bars

### Indigo
*Tecseccocha 415, T084-260271.*
Lounge, cocktail bar and serves Asian and local food.

### Km 0 (Arte y Tapas)
*Tandapata 100, San Blas.*
Mediterranean themed bar tucked in behind San Blas, good snacks and tapas, with live music every night (around 2200).

### Limbus Restobar
*Pasñapakana 84, T084-431282, www.limbusrestobar.com. Mon-Sat 0800-0100, Sun 1200-2400.*
A wide selection of cocktails and decent food – the likes of burgers, pastas and curry; but it's the view you come here for, one of the best in Cuzco.

### Los Perros Bar
*Tecseccocha 436. Open 1100-0100.*
Great place to chill out on comfy couches, excellent music, welcoming, good coffee, tasty meals available (including vegetarian), book exchange, English and other magazines, board games.

## Museo del Pisco
*Santa Catalina Ancha 398, T084-262709, www.museodelpisco.org. Daily 1100-0100.*
A bar where you can sample many kinds of pisco; tapas-style food served.

## Norton's Pub
*Santa Catalina Angosta 116. Daily 0700-0300.*
On the corner of the Plaza de Armas, fine balcony, microbrews, sandwiches and light meals, cable TV, English spoken, pool, darts, motorcycle theme. Very popular.

## Paddy's Pub
*Triunfo 124 on the corner of the plaza. Open 1000-0100.*
Irish theme pub, deservedly popular, good grub.

## Clubs

### El Garabato Video Music Club
*Plateros 316. Daily 1600-0300.*
Dance area, lounge for chilling, bar, live shows 2300-0030 (all sorts of styles) and large screen showing music videos.

### Mama Africa
*Portal de Panes 109.*
Cool music and clubber's spot, good food with varied menu, happy hour till 2300, good value.

### Mythology
*Portal de Carnes 298, p 2.*
Mostly an early '80s and '90s combination of cheese, punk and classic, popular.

### Ukuku's
*Plateros 316. Entry US$1.35.*
Very popular, good atmosphere, good mix of music including live shows nightly.

## Entertainment

**Centro Qosqo de Arte Nativo**, *Av El Sol 604, T084-227901.* Regular nightly folklore show from 1900 to 2030, US$6.
**La Esencia**, *Limacpampa Chico 400, upstairs, T984-169134, www.facebook.com/la esenciacusco.* Nightly music, storytelling, theatre or movies. Serves tea and light snacks.

**Teatro Municipal**, *C Mesón de la Estrella 149 (T084-226203 for information 0900-1300 and 1500-1900).* Plays, dancing and shows, mostly Thu-Sun. They also run classes in music and dancing Jan-Mar which are great value.

## Festivals

**Feb or Mar  Carnival** in Cuzco is a messy affair with flour, water, cacti, bad fruit and animal manure being thrown about in the streets.
**Mon before Easter  El Señor de los Temblores** (Lord of the Earthquakes). Procession starting at 1600 outside the cathedral. A large crucifix is paraded through the streets, returning to the Plaza de Armas around 2000 to bless the tens of thousands of people who have assembled there.
**2-3 May  Vigil of the Cross** takes place at all mountaintops with crosses on them, a boisterous affair.
**Jun  Corpus Christi** (Thu after Trinity Sun). All the statues of the Virgin and the saints from Cuzco's churches are paraded through the streets to the cathedral. The Plaza San Francisco is surrounded by tables with women selling *cuy* (guinea pig) and a mixed grill called *chiriuchu* (*cuy*, chicken, tortillas, fish eggs, water-weeds, maize, cheese and sausage) and lots of Cusqueña beer.
**24 Jun**  The pageant of **Inti Raymi**. The Inca festival of the winter solstice, is enacted in Quechua at 1000 at the Qoricancha, moving on to Sacsayhuaman at 1300. Tickets for the stands can be bought a week in advance from the Emufec office (Santa Teresa 142), US$100-140, less if bought Mar-May. Travel agents can arrange the whole day for you, with meeting points, transport, reserved seats and packed lunch. Those who try to persuade you to buy a ticket for the right to film or take photos are being dishonest. On the night before Inti Raymi, the Plaza de Armas is crowded with processions and food stalls. Try to arrive in Cuzco 15 days before Inti Raymi.
**28 Jul  Peruvian Independence Day.** Prices shoot up during these celebrations.

## A month of festivals

By April most of the corn has been brought in and the large ears of *choclo cusqueño* set out to dry in the sun. May brings a change of climate and new potatoes are ready to be turned into *chuño* and *moraya* (two dehydrated forms of this staple food) as soon as overnight temperatures drop below freezing. If it has been a good harvest then sustenance is assured for the coming year, and the Quechua people are free to turn their attention to other pursuits. In the department of Cuzco June is the month of fiestas.

One of the first celebrations takes place at **Q'eswachaka** during the first weekend of the month, centred on the reconstruction of the Inca rope bridge (see box, page 320).

This is followed by the great pilgrimage of **Q'Olloriti** (page 318), the multitudinous Snow Star Festival held at a sanctuary at 4700 m in the Cordillera Vilcanota near Mahauyani. The festival pays simultaneous homage to a venerated image of Christ and the mountain deity Apu Cinajara. Q'Olloriti builds to a crescendo over two weeks, culminating on the Tuesday after Trinity Sunday (eight weeks after Easter Sunday). Many participants then make their way to the city of Cuzco (the more devout go on foot) for **Corpus Christi**, held two days later on Thursday. All the statues of the Virgin and saints from Cuzco's churches are paraded through the streets to the cathedral and special foods are served.

The second or third weekend in June is the turn of Raqchi (page 319), where the **folklore dance festival** draws participants from all over Peru. Finally, on 24 June, is the greatest celebration of all: **Inti Raymi** (the solstice) in Cuzco, both an enduring link to ancient rites and beliefs as well as a major tourist event. The festivals continue with heavily attended celebrations in mid-July to honour Mamacha Carmen in Paucartambo, Pisac and elsewhere.

In addition to these best known and heavily attended festivities, there are celebrations in towns and villages throughout the department of Cuzco. The dates vary from year to year and you should always confirm these locally in advance.

**Aug** On the last Sun is the **Huarachicoy** festival at Sacsayhuaman, a spectacular re-enactment of the Inca manhood rite, performed in dazzling costumes by boys from a local school.

**8 Sep Day of the Virgin** is a colourful procession of masked dancers from the church of Almudena, at the southwest edge of Cuzco, near Belén, to the Plaza de San Francisco. There is also a splendid fair at Almudena, and a free bull fight on the following day.

**1 Nov All Saints' Day**, celebrated everywhere with bread dolls and traditional cooking.

**8 Dec Day of the Immaculate Conception**. Churches and museums close at 1200.

**24 Dec Santuranticuy**, 'the buying of saints', with a big crafts market in the plaza, very noisy until early hours of the 25th. This is one of the best festivals with people from the mountains coming to celebrate Christmas in Cuzco.

### Shopping

#### Arts and crafts

In the Plaza San Blas and the surrounding area, authentic Cuzco crafts still survive. A market is held on Sat. Many leading artisans welcome visitors. Among fine objects made are biblical figures from plaster, wheatflour and potatoes, reproductions of pre-Columbian ceramics and colonial sculptures, pious paintings, earthenware figurines, festive dolls and wood carvings.

Cuzco is one of the great weaving centres of Peru and excellent textiles can be found at good value. Be very careful of buying gold and silver objects and jewellery in and around Cuzco. Do not buy condor feathers, painted or unpainted, as it is illegal to sell or purchase them. Condors are being killed for this trade. The prison sentence is 4 years.

**Agua y Tierra**, *Cuesta San Blas 595, T084-236466*. Excellent quality crafts from rainforest communities and Ayacucho.

**Factoria La Vicuñita**, *Saphi 818, T084-233890*. Huge selection of alpaca clothing, textiles, ceramics, rugs and jewellery. They can show you how to distinguish between fake and real alpaca items.

**Feria Artesanal Qoricancha**, *Av El Sol, block 4*. Good for cheap crafts.

**Mendívil**, *Plaza San Blas 619 and Hatunrumiyoc 486*. Known for its long-necked statues of saints. Also sells a wide assortment of other crafts.

**Pedazo de Arte**, *Plateros 334B*. A tasteful collection of Andean handicrafts, many designed by Japanese owner Miki Suzuki.

**Seminario**, *inside Museo de Arte Precolombino, Plaza Nazarenas*. Sells the ceramics of Seminario-Behar (see under Urubamba, page 328), plus cotton, basketry, jewellery, etc.

## Books and maps

**Centro de Estudios Regionales Andinos Bartolomé de las Casas**, *Limacpampa Grande 571, T084-234073, www.cbc.org.pe. Mon-Sat 1100-1400, 1600-1900*. Good books on Peruvian history, archaeology, etc.

**Librería Jerusalén**, *Heladeros 143, T984-255033. Open 1030-1400, 1630-1830*. English and Spanish books, maps, guidebooks, postcards, book exchange (2 for 1). Helpful owners César and Diego Chacón.

**Maratón**, *Av de la Cultura 1020, across the street from San Antonio Abad university, T084-225387*. Wide selection of IGN topographical maps, of interest to trekkers and cyclists.

**SBS Libería Internacional**, *Av El Sol 864, T084-248106, www.sbs.com.pe. Mon-Fri 0900-2030, Sat 0930-1330, 1600-2000*. Good selection of books and maps.

## Camping equipment

For renting equipment, check with tour agencies. Check the equipment carefully as it is common for parts to be missing or damaged. A deposit is asked, plus credit card, passport or plane ticket. White gas (*bencina*), US$3 per litre, can be bought at hardware stores and **Camping Rosly**, below. Stove spirit (*alcohol para quemar*) is available at some pharmacies; cooking gas canisters can be found at camping shops.

**Camping Rosly**, *Procuradores 394, T084-248042*. New and second-hand gear sales and rentals; repairs. Owner speaks English.

**Himalaya Outdoor**, *Procuradores 398, T084-286838*. Equipment sales, rentals, repairs, and IGN topographic maps. English spoken.

**Tatoo**, *Espinar 144, T084-236703, www. tatoo.ws*. High-quality hiking, climbing and camping gear, not cheap, but international brand names and their own lines.

## Fabrics and alpaca clothing

**Alpaca Golden**, *Portal de Panes 151, T084-262914*. Also at Plazoleta Nazarenas 175. Designer, producer and retailer of fine alpaca clothing.

**The Center for Traditional Textiles of Cuzco**, *Av El Sol 603, T084-228117, www. textilescusco.org*. A non-profit organization that seeks to promote, refine and rediscover the weaving traditions of the Cuzco area. Tours of workshops, weaving classes, you can watch weavers at work. Also run 3-day weaving courses. Over 50% of the price goes direct to the weaver. Recommended.

**Hilo**, *Carmen Alto 260, T974-222294*. Fashionable items designed individually and handmade on-site. Run by Eibhlin Cassidy, she can adjust and tailor designs.

**Josefina Olivera**, *Portal Comercio 173, Plaza de Armas. Daily 1100-2100*. Sells old textiles and weavings, expensive but worth it to save pieces being cut up to make other item.

**Kuna by Alpaca 111**, *Plaza Regocijo 202, T084-243233, www.kuna.com.pe.* High-quality alpaca clothing with outlets also in hotels **Mariott** and **Palacio del Inka**.

**Store of Weavers (Asociación Central de Artesanos y Artesanas del Sur Andino Inkakunaq Ruwaynin)**, *Av Tullumayo 274, T084-233466.* Store run by 6 local weaving communities, some of whose residents you can see working on site. All profits go to the weavers themselves.

## Food and natural products

**Choco Museo**, *Garcilaso 210, 2nd floor, also at Hatunrumiyoc 480, and in Ollantaytambo, Cuzco T084-244765, www.chocomuseo.com.* Offers chocolate-making classes and runs trips to their cocoa plantation.

**Coca Museum**, *Plaza San Blas 618, T084-501020. Daily 0800-2000.* Shop/museum offers a free tour and sells coca-based products. Information about the history and nutritional value of coca; also about cocaine production.

**Frutas Secas Emilia**, *San Pedro market, Kiosk 1077, southwest side of the market next to one of the entrances. Daily 0900-1800.* Large selection of dried fruit and nuts with good prices; also found at stands in **Wanchaq Market**.

**La Cholita**, *Los Portales Espinar 142B.* Special chocolates made with local ingredients.

**San Isidro**, *San Bernardo 134. Mon-Sat 0900-1300, 1600-2000.* Excellent local dairy products (great natural yoghurt and a variety of cheeses), honey and jams.

## Jewellery

**Cusco Ink**, *Choquechaca 131.* Tattoo and piercing studio. Also sells Peruvian clothing and jewellery including a wide variety of gauges.

**Esma Joyas**, *in the courtyard at Triunfo 393.* Handmade jewellery with interesting designs distinct from other local options.

**Ilaria**, *Portal Carrizos 258, T084-246253.* Branches in hotels **Monasterio**, **Marriott** and at the airport. Recommended for jewellery and silver.

**Inka Treasure**, *Plazoleta Nazarenas 159, T084-262914.* With branches at Portal de Panes 139 and 163. Also at the airport and the airport in Juliaca. Fine jewellery including goldwork, mostly with pre-Columbian designs, and silver with the owner's designs. Tours of workshops at Av Circunvalación, near Cristo Blanco.

**Spondylus**, *Plazoleta San Blas 617 and Cuesta San Blas 505, T084-235227.* A good selection of interesting gold and silver jewellery and fashion tops with Inca and pre-Inca designs.

## Markets

**Wanchaq** (Av Garcilaso, southeast of centre) and **San Pedro market** (see page 295) sell a variety of goods. **El Molino**, beyond the Terminal Terrestre, sells everything under the sun at knock-down prices, but quality is not guaranteed and there are no tourist items; it's fascinating but crowded, so go there by *colectivo* or taxi and don't take valuables.

## Music

**Sabino Huamán**, *Tandapata 370, T984-296440.* Shop and workshop featuring traditional Andean instruments. With advance notice, he can help you create your own custom pan pipe. Recommended for anyone interested in Andean music.

## What to do

There are many travel agencies in Cuzco. The sheer number and variety of tours on offer is bewildering and prices for the same tour can vary dramatically. In general you should only deal directly with the agencies themselves. Do not deal with guides who claim to be employed by agencies listed below without verifying their credentials. Be sure to ask whatever questions you may have in advance. Doing so by email offers the advantage of getting answers in writing but it may also be worth visiting a prospective operator in person to get a feeling for their organization. Competition among agencies can be fierce, but remember that the cheapest option is often not the best. For the latest information, consult other travellers returning from trips. Student discounts are only obtainable with an ISIC card.

City tours cost about US$10-15 for 4 hrs; check what sites are included and that the guide is experienced. Open sightseeing bus tour, about 1 hr, US$7; tickets sold by walking vendors at the Plaza de Armas and the intersection of Heladeros and Mantas. Various 'free' walking tours of Cuzco meet at the Plaza de Armas around midday, the guides expect a minimum tip, ask how much in advance.

In general visitors to Cuzco are satisfied with their tours. Independent travellers should keep in mind, however, that you can do any trek and visit any archaeological site on your own, except for the Inca Trail to Machu Picchu. Visiting independently requires more time, effort and greater language skills than taking a package tour, but it opens the door to a wealth of authentic experiences beyond the grasp of mass tourism.

For a list of recommended Tour operators for Manu, see page 425.

## Cultural tours

**Milla Tourism**, *Urbanización Lucrepata E16, T084-231710, www.millaturismo.com. Mon-Fri 0800-1300, 1500-1900, Sat 0800-1300.* Mystical tours to Cuzco's Inca ceremonial sites such as Pumamarca and the Temple of the Moon. Guide speaks only basic English. They also arrange cultural and environmental lectures and courses.

**Rooftop Kitchen**, *T960-17 835, www.rooftop kitchenperu.com.* Gastronomic tours, include a visit to San Pedro Market and cooking lessons where you prepare your own lunch or dinner using regional ingredients. Cost includes transfers.
See also **Choco Museo**, page 309.

## Inca Trail and general tours

Only a restricted number of agencies are licensed to operate **Inca Trail** trips. **Sernanp** (Oswaldo Baca 402, Urbanización Magisterial, 1 etapa, T084-229297, www.sernanp.gob.pe)

verifies operating permits (see Visitors' tickets, page 289, for Dirección de Cultura office). Unlicensed agencies will sell Inca Trail trips, but pass clients on to the operating agency. This can cause confusion and booking problems at busy times, so book your preferred dates as early as possible in advance. Note also that many companies offer treks as alternatives to the trails to Machu Picchu. These treks are unregulated, so it is up to clients to ensure that the trekking company does not employ the sort of practices (such as mistreating porters, not clearing up rubbish) which are now prohibited on the trails to Machu Picchu. See Essential Inca Trail, page 348.

**Action Valley Adventure Park**, *C Santa Teresa 325, Plaza Regocijo, T954-777400, www.actionvalley.com.* Paragliding, rafting, bungee jumping and other tours and adventure activities.

**Amazon Trails Peru**, *Tandapata 660, T084-437374, or T984-714148, www.amazontrails peru.com.* Excellent trekking tours around the area, including the Inca Trail, Salkantay, Choquequirao and Lares trek with small groups (maximum 8 trekkers) and expert and caring trilingual guides (Santiago Puyo and birder and biologist Nicolás Quinte). Thoroughly recommended. Also well-equipped and well-guided trips to Manu (see page 425).

**Amazonas Explorer**, *see under Rafting, mountain biking, paragliding and trekking, below.* Run a high-quality 5-day/4-night Inca Trail trek, every Tue, Mar-Nov.

**Andean Treks**, *US company, no Cuzco store-front, www.andeantreks.com.* Manager Peter Robertson uses high-quality equipment and satellite phones. Organizes itineraries, from 2 to 15 days with a wide variety of activities in this area and further afield.

**Andina Travel, Treks & Eco-Adventure**, *Plazoleta Santa Catalina 219, T084-251892, www.andinatravel.com.* Eco-agency with more than 10 years' experience operating all local treks. Has a reputation in Cuzco for local expertise and community projects.

**Big Foot**, *Triunfo 392 (oficina 213), T084-233836, www.bigfootcusco.com*. Tailor-made hiking trips, especially in the remote corners of the Vilcabamba and Vilcanota mountains; also the Inca Trail.

**Chaska**, *Garcilaso 265 p 2, of 6, T084-240424, www.chaskatours.com*. Dutch-Peruvian company offering cultural, adventure, nature and esoteric tours. They specialize in the **Inca Trail**, but also llama treks to Lares and treks to Choquequirao.

**Culturas Peru**, *Tandapata 354A, T084-243629, www.culturasperu.com*. Swiss/Peruvian company offering adventure, cultural, ecological and spiritual tours. Also specialize in alternative Inca trails.

**Destinos Turísticos**, *Portal de Panes 123, oficina 101-102, Plaza de Armas, T084-228168, www.destinosturisticosperu.com*. The owner speaks Spanish, English, Dutch and Portuguese and specializes in package tours from economic to 5-star budgets. Advice on booking jungle trips and renting mountain bikes. Very helpful.

**EcoAmerica Peru**, *C Marquez 259, of 8, 2nd floor, T999-705538, www.ecoamericaperu.com*. Associated with **America Tours** (La Paz, Bolivia). Owned by 3 experienced consultants in responsible travel, conservation and cultural heritage. Specializes in culture, history, nature, trekking, biking and birding tours. Knowledgeable guides, excellent customer service for independent travellers, groups or families. Also sell tours and flights to Bolivia.

**Enigma Adventure**, *C Fortunato L Herrera 214, Urbanización Magisterial 1a Etapa, T084-222155,* www.enigmaperu.com. Run by Spaniard Silvia Rico Coll. Well-organized, innovative trekking expeditions including a luxury service, Inca Trail and a variety of challenging alternatives. Also cultural tours to weaving communities, Ayahuasca therapy, climbing and biking.

**Explorandes**, *Paseo Zarzuela Q-2, Huancaro, T084-238380 ext 116, www.explorandes.com*. Experienced high-end adventure company. Arrange a wide variety of mountain treks; trips available in Peru and Ecuador, book through website. Also arranges tours across Peru for lovers of orchids, ceramics or textiles. Award-winning environmental practices.

**Fertur Peru Travel**, *El Sol 803, of 205, T084-221304, www.fertur-travel.com*. Cuzco branch of the Lima tour operator, see page 68.

**Flashpacker Connect Adventure Travel**, *T507-304 0075, www.flashpackerconnect.com*. Specializing in small group tours and treks to Rainbow Mountain, the Ausangate circuit and the Inca Trail.

**Gatur Cusco**, *Puluchapata 140 (a small street off Av El Sol 3rd block), T084-245121, www.gaturcusco.com*. Esoteric, ecotourism, and general tours. Owner Dr José (Pepe) Altamirano is knowledgeable in Andean folk traditions. Excellent conventional tours, bilingual guides and transportation. They can also book internal flights.

**Habitats Peru**, *Condominio La Alborada B-507, Wanchaq, T084-246271, www.habitats peru.com*. Birdwatching and mountain biking trips offered by Doris and Carlos. They also run a volunteer project near Quillabamba.

**Hiking Peru**, *Mantas 113, T984-651414, www.hikingperu.com.* 8-day treks to Espíritu Pampa; 7 days/6 nights around Ausangate; 4-day/3-night Lares Valley Trek.

**Inca Explorers**, *C Peru W-18, Ttio, T084-241070, www.incaexplorers.com.* Specialist trekking agency for small group expeditions in socially and environmentally responsible manner. Also 2-week hike in the Cordillera Vilcanota (passing Nevado Ausangate), and Choquequirao to Espíritu Pampa.

**InkaNatura Travel**, *Ricardo Palma J1, T084-243408, www.inkanatura.com.* Offers tours with special emphasis on sustainable tourism and conservation. Knowledgeable guides.

**Inkayni Tours**, *Triunfo 392, of 214, T084-232817, www.inkayniperutours.com.* Offers trips and treks to Machu Picchu, city tours in Cuzco and alternative treks, such as Salkantay, Lares, Huchuy Qosqo.

**Llama Path**, *Cuichipunco 257, T084-265134, www.llamapath.com.* A wide variety of local tours, specializing in Inca Trail and alternative treks, involved in environmental campaigns and porter welfare. Many good reports.

**Mountain Lodges of Peru**, *T084-243636 (North America T1-877-491-5261, Europe T+44-0-800-014-8886), www.mountainlodgesof peru.com.* Offer lodge-to-lodge treks from one purpose-built lodge to another, including a 7-day Salkantay to Machu Picchu trek and a 5- or 7-day route from Lamay to Ollantaytambo via the Lares Valley (http://laresadventure.com), with flexible options for activities.

**Peru Treks & Adventure**, *Av Pardo 540, T084-222722, www.perutreks.com.* Professional, high-quality tour operators specializing in trekking and cultural tours in the Cuzco region. They pride themselves on good treatment of porters and support staff and have been consistently recommended for professionalism and customer care; a portion of profits go to community projects.

**Q'ente**, *Choquechaca 229, p 2, T084-222535, www.qente.com.* Their Inca Trail service is recommended. Also private treks to Salkantay, Ausangate, Choquequirao and Vilcabamba.

Horse riding to local ruins costs US$35 for 4-5 hrs. Very good, especially with children.

**Sky Travel**, *Santa Catalina Ancha 366, interior 3-C, T084-240141, www.skyperu.com.* English spoken. General tours around city and Sacred Valley. Inca Trail with good-sized double tents and a dinner tent (the group is asked what it would like on the menu 2 days before departure). Other trips include Vilcabamba and Ausangate (trekking).

**Southamerica Planet**, *Garcilaso 210, of 201, T084-241424, www.southamericaplanet.com.* Peruvian/Belgian-owned agency offering the Inca Trail, other treks around Cuzco and packages within Peru, as well as Bolivia and Patagonia.

**Tanager Tours**, *no storefront, T084-237254, Lima T01-669 0825, www.tanagertours.com.* Specializes in birdwatching tours throughout Peru but will also arrange other tours. Book via internet.

**T'ika Trek**, *no storefront, UK T07824-377292, www.tikatrek.com.* UK contact Fiona Cameron lived for many years in Peru and is a keen hiker and biker. With over 10 years in the Cuzco tourism business, Fiona provides high-quality personalized tours all over Peru as well as to the Galápagos Islands (Ecuador). Focus is on small groups and families.

**Trekperu**, *Av República de Chile B-15, Parque Industrial, Wanchaq, T084-261501, www.trekperu.com.* Experienced trek operator as well as other adventure sports. Offers 'culturally sensitive' tours. Cusco Biking Adventure includes support vehicle and good camping gear (but providing your own sleeping bag).

**United Mice**, *Av Pachacútec 424 A-5, T084-221139, www.unitedmice.com.* Inca Trail and alternative trail via Salkantay and Santa Teresa, well-established and reputable. Good guides who speak languages other than Spanish. Discount with student card, good food and equipment. City and Sacred Valley tours and treks to Choquequirao.

**Valencia Travel Cusco**, *Portal de Panes 123, Centro Comercial Ruiseñores, of 306-307, T084-255907, www.valenciatravelcusco.com.*

Specialize in adventure trails, both the classics and the roads less travelled, and immersion homestays.

**Wayki Trek**, *Quera 239, T084-224092, www.waykitrek.net*. Budget travel agency recommended for their Inca Trail service. Owner Americo Aguilar knows the area very well. Treks to several almost unknown Inca sites and interesting variations on the classic Inca Trail with visits to porters' communities. Also treks to Ausangate, Salkantay and Choquequirao.

## Language courses

**Academia Latinoamericana de Español**, www.latinoschools.com; **Acupari**, www.acupari.com; **Amauta Spanish School**, www.amautaspanish.com; **Amigos Spanish School**, www.spanishcusco.com; **Centro Tinku**, www.centrotinku.com (Spanish and Quechua); **Fair Services Spanish School**, www.fairservices-peru.org; **San Blas Spanish School**, www.spanishschoolperu.com.

## Rafting, mountain biking, paragliding and trekking

When looking for an adventure operator please consider more than just the price of your tour. Competition between companies in Cuzco is intense and price wars can lead to compromises in safety. Check the quality of safety equipment (lifejackets, etc) and ask about the number and experience of rescue kayakers and support staff. On large and potentially dangerous rivers like the Apurímac and Urubamba (where fatalities

have occurred), this can make all the difference. Always use a licensed operator.

**Amazonas Explorer**, *Av Collasuyo 910, T084-252846, www.amazonas-explorer.com*. Experts in rafting, stand-up paddle boarding, catamaran sailing, mountain biking, horse riding and hiking. Rafting routes include expeditions to the Apurimac, Cotahuasi and Tambopata rivers. Owner Paul Cripps has great experience. Also offer the classic Inca Trail and alternatives. Group and tailor-made trips. All options are at the higher end of the market. Highly recommended.

**Apumayo**, *Ir Ricardo Palma Ñ-II, Santa Mónica, Wanchaq, T084-246018, www.apumayo.com. Mon-Sat 0900-1300, 1600-2000*. Urubamba rafting (from 0800-1530 every day); 3- to 4-day Apurímac trips. Also mountain biking to Maras and Moray in Sacred Valley, or from Cuzco to the jungle town of Quillabamba. This company also offers tours for disabled people, including rafting.

**Apus Perú**, *Cuichipunco 366, T084-232691, www.apus-peru.com*. Conducts most business by internet, specializes in alternatives to the Inca Trail, strong commitment to sustainability, well organized. Associated with **Threads of Peru** NGO which helps weavers.

**Pachatusan Trek**, *Villa Union Huancaro G-4, B 502, T084-231817, www.pachatusantrek.com*. Offers a wide variety to treks, as alternatives to the Inca Trail, professional and caring staff, "simply fantastic".

**River Explorers**, *Urbanización Kennedy, Av Los Brillantes B36, T084-431116, www.river*

explorers.com. An adventure company offering mountain biking, trekking and rafting trips (on the Apurímac, Urubamba and Tambopata). Experienced and qualified guides with environmental awareness.

**Terra Explorer Peru**, *T084-237352, Urbanización Santa Ursula D4, Wanchaq, www.terraexplorerperu.com.* Offers a wide range of trips from high-end raftingand expeditions to the Apurímac, Colca and Cotahuasi canyons, to trekking the Inca Trail and others, mountain biking, kayaking (including on Lake Titicaca) and jungle trips. All guides are bilingual.

### Shamans and mystical plant experiences

San Pedro and Ayahuasca have been used since before Inca times, mostly as a sacred healing experience. If you choose to experience these plants, only do so under the guidance of a reputable agency or shaman and always have a friend with you who is not partaking. If the medicine is not prepared correctly, it can be highly toxic and dangerous. Never buy from someone who is not recommended; never buy off the streets, and never try to prepare the plants yourself.

**Another Planet**, *Tandapata y Pasñapakana 148, San Blas, T084-241168, www.anotherplanet peru.org.* Run by Lesley Myburgh, who operates mystical and adventure tours in and around Cuzco, and is an expert in San Pedro cactus preparation. She arranges San Pedro sessions for healing in the garden of her house outside Cuzco. Tours meet at **La Casa de la Gringa**, see Where to stay, above.

**Etnikas Travel & Shamanic Healing**, *Av la Cultura 2122 and Recoleta 674, T084-244516, www.etnikas.com.* A shamanic centre offering travel for mind, body and spirit. Offers Ayahuasca sessions in their proper ceremonial context. Expensive but serious in their work.

**Sumac Coca Travel**, *San Agustín 245, T084-260311, www.sumaccoca.com.* Mystical tourism, offering Ayahuasca and San Pedro ceremonies, and also more conventional cultural tourism. Professional and caring.

### Private guides

As most of the sights do not have any information or signs in English, a good guide can really improve your visit. Either arrange this before you set out or contract one at the sight you are visiting. A tip is expected at the end of the tour. Tours of the city or Sacred Valley cost US$50 for half-day, US$65 full day plus transport and entrance fees; a guide to Machu Picchu charges US$80 per day. A list of official guides is held by **Agotur Cusco** (C Heladeros 157, of 34-F, p 3, T084-233457). See also www.leaplocal.org.

## Transport

### Air

The airport (open 0500-2030) is at Quispiquilla, near the bus terminal, 1.6 km from centre, airport information T084-222611/601. There are plans to build a new airport at Chinchero, 23 km northwest of the city (see page 329). The airport can get very busy; check in at least 2 hrs before your flight. Flights may be delayed or cancelled during the wet season. The Arrivals area has ATMs, money exchange booth (poor rates), a medical post, an **iPerú** desk (daily 0600-1700), **Peru Rail** booth, a **Dircetur** desk, restaurant, cafeteria (Oxishot oxygen canisters available here) and a **Tourist Police** booth (open 0500-2000). In the main lobby is the **iPerú** office (open 0600-1700). Hotel representatives and travel agents operate at the airport offering transport to particular hotels for arriving visitors without prior bookings; take your time to choose a hotel at a price you can afford. If you already have a booking, taxis and tourist minibuses meet new arrivals and (should) take you to the hotel of your choice: be insistent. A taxi to and from the airport costs US$5-7 (US$9-12 from the official taxi desk). *Colectivos* (not safe with luggage, white and yellow *Liebre* or blue *Correcaminos*) cost US$0.20 between Plaza San Francisco and the airport; to go to the airport, get on at block 2 of C Ayacucho, by Av El Sol.

To **Lima**, 55 mins, over 40 daily flights with **Avianca/TACA**, **Star Perú**, **LATAM**, **Peruvian Airlines** and **LC Perú**. To **Arequipa**, 30 mins daily with **LATAM**. To **Juliaca** (for Puno), 1 hr daily with **LATAM**. To **Puerto Maldonado**, 30 mins, with **Avianca/TACA**, **LATAM** and **Star Perú**. To **La Paz**, **Peruvian Airlines** and **Amaszonas** (www.amaszonas.com), 1 hr, daily.

## Bus

**Long distance** The busy, often crowded Terminal Terrestre is on Av Vallejo Santoni, block 2 (Prolongación Pachacútec). *Colectivo* from centre US$0.20 (not safe with luggage), taxi US$2-3. Platform tax US$0.50.

To **Lima**, US$35-65, a long ride (20-24 hrs) and worth paying for a comfortable bus. The route is via **Abancay** (US$7, 5 hrs) and **Nazca** (US$30, 13 hrs) on the Pan-American Highway. It is paved, but floods in the wet season often damage large sections. At night, take a blanket or sleeping bag to ward off the cold. Better companies to Lima include: **Molina**, daily at 2000; **Cruz del Sur** at 1400, 1600 and 1800; **Móvil Tours** at 1700 and **Oltursa** at 1600. **Bredde** has most frequent service (5 daily) to Abancay; others include **Expreso Sánchez** and **Celajes**. **Los Chankas** to Abancay at 0730, 1930 and 2000 continues to **Andahuaylas** (US$13.50, 9 hrs) and **Ayacucho** (US$25, 16 hrs).

To **Juliaca**, 344 km, US$5 normal, US$9 semi-cama, US$12.50-17 cama, 5-6 hrs, with **Power** every 2 hrs, 0400-2300; several others. The road is fully paved, but after heavy rain buses may not run. To **Puno**, 388 km, 6-7 hrs; there are 3 levels of service, all via Juliaca: regular, stopping in Juliaca, US$7-12; direct, US$15-27, with **Tour Perú** (www.tourperu.com.pe), **Cruz del Sur** or **Transzela** (www.transzela.com.pe); and

---

### Tip...
If you're prone to travel sickness, take precautions from Cuzco to Abancay on the way to Lima; there are many curves but the scenery is magnificent.

---

tourist service with 5 stops (Andahuaylillas church, Raqchi, Sicuani for lunch, La Raya and Pucará), US$45-50 (includes lunch, may or may not include entry tickets; ask), 10 hrs. Several companies offer the tourist service; all leave from private terminals: **Inka Express** at 0700 from Av 28 de Julio 211, 5th stop Urbanización Ttio, T084-247887, www.inkaexpress.com; **Turismo Mer** at 0700 from Av La Paz A-3, Urbanización El Ovalo, Wanchaq, T084-245171, www.turismomer.com; and **Wonder Perú** at 0700 from Av 28 de Julio R2-1, Urbanización Ttio, Wanchaq, www.wonderperuexpedition.com. In high season, reserve 2 days ahead. **Note** It is advisable to travel by day on the Cuzco-Juliaca-Puno route, the views are great.

To **Arequipa (via Juliaca)**, 521 km, 10-11 hrs, with **Cruz del Sur** at 2000 and 2030, US$37-47; **Cromotex** at 1900 and 2000, US$11-36; **Flores** at 0645 and 2030, US$11; **Power** at 0500 and 1700, US$11; many others, mostly at night. A tourist service direct to **Chivay** on the **Colca Canyon** is offered by **4M Express** (Av 28 de Julio, Urbanización Ttio, Wanchaq, T054-452296, www.4m-express.com), Tue, Thu and Sat at 0700, US$65 (lunch extra); see Colca Canyon Transport, page 248, for details.

Several daily buses between Cuzco and **Puerto Maldonado** bus terminals; **Cruz del Sur** departs from its private terminal at Av Industrial 2126, Santiago; there is also a van service, see page 427. Warning, see tip on this page.

To the **Sacred Valley** There are 2 routes to Urubamba and Ollantaytambo: 1 via Pisac and Calca, the other via Chinchero. It is worth going on one and returning on the other. To **Pisac** (32 km, 1 hr, US$1.50-3), **Calca** (50 km, 1½ hrs, US$1.50) and **Urubamba** (72 km via Pisac and Calca, 2 hrs, US$3), *colectivos* (transfer in Pisac) and minibuses from C Puputi near Av la Cultura (see map, page 292, C6), leave when full 0600-1800. Buses returning from Pisac are often full; last one back leaves around 2000. Taxis charge about US$20 one way to Pisac.

To **Chinchero** (23 km, 45 mins US$2), **Urubamba** (50 km via Chinchero, 1½ hrs, US$2.50), **Ollantaytambo** (70 km via Chinchero and Urubamba, 2 hrs, US$3.50-5), *colectivos* and minibuses from C Pavitos near Av Grau (see map, page 292, E4). Taxi to Ollantaytambo US$22 one way.

## Taxi

In Cuzco taxis are recommended when arriving by air, train or bus. They have fixed prices but you have to stay alert to overpricing (always agree on the price in advance): in the centre US$1.50 (50% more after 2100 or 2200). Safer and more expensive are radio-dispatched taxis with a sign on the roof, including **Aló Cusco** T084-222222, **Ocarina** T084-255000, and many others. With wait time, trips to **Sacsayhuaman**, US$10; to ruins of **Tambo Machay** US$15-20 (3-4 people); day trip US$50-85. **Taxidatum**, T941-764785, www.taxidatum.com. Excellent service, full-day tours of the Sacred Valley, US$60-65. **Miguel Mendoza**, T935-240819, is recommended.

## Train

**PeruRail** uses Estación Wanchaq (Av Pachacúteq, T084-238722, www.perurail.com, ticket sales for all PeruRail services Mon-Fri 0700-1700, Sat, Sun and holidays 0700-1200). There are also **PeruRail** offices at Portal de Carnes 214 and Plaza Regocijo 202,

both open daily 0700-2200, and sales points at the Lima and Cuzco airports (in domestic departures and arrivals, respectively). Purchase tickets well in advance, take your passport or a copy when buying tickets. **Inca Rail** uses Estación San Pedro (Ccascaparo opposite San Pedro Market) for a bus-rail combined service to Machu Picchu via Ollantaytambo, when Poroy station is closed; ticket sales at Portal de Panes 105, Plaza de Armas, T084-581860, www.incarail.com, Mon-Fri 0700-2200, Sat, Sun and holidays 0700-2000.

The *Belmond Andean Explorer*, **PeruRail**'s luxury sleeper trains with cabins with private bath and shower, leave from Wanchaq station. The service includes stops at points of interest; there are also optional excursions at extra cost. These trains do not operate in Feb. The following prices are based on double occupancy. *Spirit of the Water* service to **Puno** (1 day/1 night, US$565-815 pp) departs Tue 1100, stops at Raqchi and La Raya, optional boat tour on Lake Titicaca; *Peruvian Highlands* to **Arequipa** via Titicaca (3 days/2 nights, US$1440-2065 pp), departs Thu 1100, stops at Raqchi, La Raya, excursion on Lake Titicaca (Uros, Taquile and Playa Collata), Saracocha, Sumbay Caves, optional trip to Colca, and Arequipa city tour. Trains to **Machu Picchu** and the **Sacred Valley** leave from Poroy (7.5 km east of the centre), Urubamba, or Ollantaytambo, depending on the season and service, see page 346.

## Upper Vilcanota Valley

head upstream to avoid the crowds

The main road from Cuzco to Lake Titicaca and Arequipa follows the Río Vilcanota upstream to La Raya, the border with the neighbouring department of Puno. Along the route are archaeological sites, fascinating colonial churches, beautiful lakes and the majestic Ausangate massif, where you can do some serious high-altitude trekking.

## Southeast of Cuzco

Between the villages of Saylla and Oropesa are the extensive **Tipón ruins** ⓘ *5-km climb from village, daily 0800-1630, entry only with BTC; take a combi to Oropesa, then a taxi*, which include baths, terraces, irrigation systems, possibly an agricultural laboratory and a temple complex, accessible from a path leading from just above the last terrace. **Oropesa**, whose church contains a fine ornately carved pulpit, is the national 'Capital of Bread'; try the delicious sweet circular loaves known as *chutas*.

## Paucartambo and around

At **Huambutío**, north of the village of Huacarpay, the road divides, with one branch leading northwest to Pisac and the other heading north to **Paucartambo**, in the deep valley of the Río Mapacho, on the eastern slope of Andes. At 2850 m, this pleasant colonial town, 80 km east of Cuzco, has an excellent museum and interesting surroundings (helpful tourist office in the Terminal Terrestre). In the Centro Cultural is the **Museo de los Pueblos** ① *daily 0800-1300, 1500-1800, US$3*, with exhibits on the history, culture and textiles of the region, including the famous **Fiesta de la Virgen del Carmen** (Mamacha Carmen; 15-19 July and smaller one 2-4 February), at which masked dancers enact rituals and folk tales. **Watoqto**, a Killke archaeological site (AD 1200), later occupied by the Incas, is 15 km upriver (taxi US$15 return) and 11 km downstream are the **Chimur** thermal baths (public transport Saturday-Sunday at 0400, US$5 return) and Inca road remnants. You can travel 44 km from Paucartambo to **Tres Cruces**, at the southern edge of **Parque Nacional Manu** ① *entry US$3*, along the Pilcopata road, turning left after 25 km at the Ajcanaco park control point. Come here for the sunrise in May to mid-August, when peculiar atmospheric conditions make it appear that two suns are rising. Tour agencies in Cuzco can arrange transport and lodging or ask at Acjanaco rangers' station (past the control point) to use the Tres Cruces shelter, take warm clothing and sleeping bag. **Trocha Ericson** is a 4-km trail from the Acjanaco control point to Pillahuato, downhill on the road to Pilcopata. **Trocha Unión**, a pre-Hispanic trail, runs 12 km from Tres Cruces to Mirador San Pedro, further along the road to Pilcopata; camping is possible about halfway down.

## Piquillacta

*Daily 0800-1630, entry only with BTC. Buses to Urcos will drop you near the entrance.*

Further on from Huacarpay are the extensive pre-Inca ruins of Piquillacta (which translates as the City of Fleas). This was an administrative centre at the southern end of the Huari Empire. The whole site is surrounded by a wall encompassing many enclosed compounds with buildings of over one storey; it appears that the walls were plastered and finished with a layer of lime. On the opposite side of the highway from Piquillacta is Laguna de Huacarpay (also known as Muina) and the ruins that surround it: Kañarakay, Urpicancha and the impressive Huari aqueduct and Inca gateway of Rumicolca, at the pass just beyond Piquillacta. A guide will help to find the more interesting structures. It's good to hike or cycle and birdwatch around the lake.

## Andahuaylillas to Urcos

*Buses from Cuzco to Urcos leave when full from Av de la Cultura y Pje Carrasco, opposite the Hospital Regional, US$1, 1½ hrs, passing Andahuaylillas en route.*

Andahuaylillas, 32 km southeast of Cuzco, has a lovely shady plaza and beautifully restored early 17th-century **church** ① *daily 0730-1730, on RBA ticket*. It's known as the 'Andean Sistine Chapel', due to its fabulous frescoes. There's also a splendid doorway and a gilded main altar. The next village, **Huaro**, also has a **church** ① *daily 0800-1700, on RBA ticket*, whose interior is entirely covered with colourful frescoes. Urcos, meanwhile, is a chaotic commercial centre and transport hub; beware overcharging for everything here. South of Urcos, stop off at the villages of **Cusipata**, which has an Inca gate and wall, and **Checacupe**, which has a lovely church.

## Cordillera Vilcanota

A spectacular road from Urcos crosses the Eastern Cordillera to Puerto Maldonado in the jungle (428 km, see page 428). Some 82 km from Urcos, near the base of Nevado Ausangate, is the town of **Ocongate**, a friendly regional centre with most services and a good place to prepare for trekking. Beyond Ocongate, **Tinqui** is a smaller, colder town with basic places to stay and eat; it's the starting point for hikes around Ausangate, which, at 6384 m, is the loftiest peak in the Vilcanota range. From Mahauyani, 12 km beyond Tinqui, a wide trail runs 8.5 km up to the sanctuary of **Señor de Q'Olloriti** at 4700 m, where a massive pilgrimage is held during the two weeks leading up to Trinity Sunday (eight weeks after Easter Sunday) and culminating on the following Tuesday. Above the Christian sanctuary are the glaciers of Nevado Cinajara, the original object of devotion and still considered a sacred site. There is good trekking in the area and few visitors outside the festival.

## Ausangate circuit

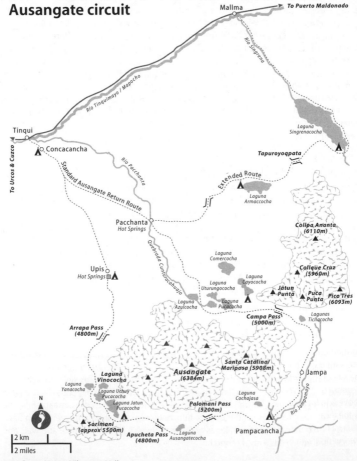

Continuing east, some 47 km after passing the snow line on the Hualla-Hualla Pass, at 4820 m, the super-hot thermal baths of **Marcapata** ① *173 km from Urcos, US$0.20,* provide a relaxing break. Beyond this point, what is arguably the most spectacular road in Peru descends the eastern flank of the Andes towards Puerto Maldonado (see page 428).

★ **Ausangate Trek** ① *Entry US$3.50 at Tinqui plus US$3.50 at each of 3 communities along the route.* The hike around the mountain of Ausangate (6348 m) is spectacular. There are two popular routes requiring three to six days. It is hard going, with two passes over 5000 m and camping above 4000 m, so you need to be fit and acclimatized. Temperatures in high season (April-October) can drop well below zero at night. It is recommended to take a guide and/or *arriero*. *Arrieros* and mules can be hired in Tinqui: US$12 per day for a guide, US$10 per mule, more for a saddle horse. *Arrieros* also expect food. Make sure you sign a contract with full details. Buy supplies in Cuzco or Ocongate. Maps are available at the IGN in Lima (see page 66) and **Maratón** in Cuzco (see page 308). Cuzco agencies and **Hostal Ausangate** (see Where to Stay, below) run tours from about US$120. Bring your own warm sleeping bag. **Miguel Pacsi** (T984-668360, mpacsi1@hotmail.com) has been recommended as a private guide and can help with logistics.

## Acomayo Lakes Circuit

Near the towns of Acomayo and Pomacanchi are four large lakes. To reach the area, take the road that branches off the Cuzco-Puno highway at the little hamlet of Chuquicahuana, between Cusipata and Checacupe. When you reach the first lake, Lago Pomacanchi, take a sharp left along the eastern shore of the lake. You will travel past three more beautiful lakes: Lago Acopia, Lago Asnacocha and Lago Pampamarca. Stop a while beside Lago Pampamarca. Set against the pale green grass banks, serene waters reflect the red soil of the hills behind. The only sound is the occasional splash of an Andean coot. The lakes are most easily visited by car but, given time and patience, they are also accessible by a combination of hiking and public transport from Cuzco or Sicuani. Confirm details locally.

## Q'eswachaka

At Combapata (about 50 km from Urcos on the road to Sicuani) a paved road climbs west for 16 km, through a region of large highland lakes, to the cold regional centre of **Yanaoca** at 3950 m. Yanaoca has simple places to stay and eat, and provides access to the village of Quehue, 20 km further south. Near the village an Inca bridge spans the upper Río Apurímac at Q'eswachaka. The bridge, a UNESCO World Heritage Site, is 28 m long and is made entirely of *q'oya* (a flexible straw), woven and spliced to form cables which are strung across the chasm. The bridge is rebuilt each year in June, during a unique and spectacular four-day event. Cuzco operators offer tours during the festival or you can go on your own at any time of the year, although it's not safe to cross the bridge between December and June.

## Raqchi and around

Continuing on the main road to Sicuani, **Tinta**'s church has a brilliant gilded interior and an interesting choir vault. **Raqchi** is the scene of the region's great folklore festival and also the site of the **Viracocha Temple** ① *daily 0800-1600, US$6, take a bus from Cuzco towards Sicuani, US$3.50.* John Hemming wrote: "What remains is the central wall, which is adobe above and Inca masonry below. This was probably the largest roofed building ever built by the Incas. On either side of the high wall, great sloping roofs were supported by rows of unusual round pillars, also of masonry topped by adobe. Nearby is a complex of barracks-like buildings and round storehouses. This was the most holy shrine to the creator god

## ON THE ROAD
## The last bridge

The great Inca road which connected the vastness of the empire was built not only of monumental stones but also of humble straw. In a land incised by deep chasms and rushing rivers, roads are of little use without bridges, and the greatest Inca suspension bridges were made of straw rope.

The most famous of these, 45 m long and suspended 36 m above the water, crossed the canyon of the Río Apurímac not far from the current road between Cuzco and Abancay. It was first accurately measured and photographed in 1864 by the American explorer George Squire and immortalized 63 years later by Thornton Wilder in his novel, *The Bridge of San Luis Rey*. By then the great bridge was no more; sometime in the 1890s, after over 600 years of existence, it was abandoned and collapsed.

In an environment of intense solar radiation and heavy rainfall during part of the year, straw fibre degrades rapidly so Inca suspension bridges had to be rebuilt on a regular basis. Today that tradition continues in only one place, at Q'eswachaka, also on the Apurímac, about 200 km upstream from the bridge described by Squire and Wilder. Every year in June, two weeks before Inti-Raymi, over 400 families from four communities join forces for four days to reconstruct their Inca bridge using ancestral tools and materials.

Each family is required to contribute 40 arms' length of cord made of twisted *q'oya*, a tough flexible highland straw. Exactly 30 strands of cord are carefully laid out alongside each another and twisted again into a thicker rope, which is, in turn, braided into the heavy cables which form the floor of the bridge. The cables are laboriously tensioned in an impressive effort requiring the brute force of 30 men. Then the taut cables are woven together into a single unit and covered with *chilca* sticks. Thin cords are strung from the handrails, also made of straw rope, to the floor to form the sides of the bridge.

Only the *chacacamayoc* (bridge-master) knows all the secrets of the process, handed down through countless generations of his family, and he constantly supervises the work of his companions. Throughout the construction period, a small but important group of Andean priests make offerings of coca leaves, alcohol and incense to *Pachamama* (Mother Earth) to propitiate a successful and accident-free effort. Even though women prepare most of the original cord, they are strictly forbidden to approach the bridge while it is under construction.

Once complete, the bridge is inaugurated with great ceremony and the event culminates with a day-long festival of food, drink, music and dance. In 2014 the bridge at Q'eswachaka was declared a UNESCO World Heritage Site.

---

Viracocha, being the site of a miracle in which he set fire to the land – hence the lava flow nearby. The landscape is extraordinary, blighted by huge piles of black volcanic rocks."

You can do a homestay here with pottery classes and a walk to the extinct Quimsachata volcano. There is also simple accommodation in the nearby town of **San Pedro**, along the main road to Sicuani. Beyond San Pedro, the road continues southeast to Sicuani, La Raya and the department of Puno.

## Where to stay

### Paucartambo
There are several simple accommodations in town, all are booked a year ahead for the Jul fiesta.

### $ Anka Hostal
*Prolongación Ericson, opposite the terminal, T952-412461.*
Simple rooms with private bath and hot water, no breakfast.

### $ Hospedaje Tres Cruces
*Plazoleta Cuculi, opposite the church, T084-612655.*
Simple rooms with bath, cheaper with shared bath, hot water, covered patio, no breakfast.

### Andahuaylillas to Urcos
These are both in Andahuaylillas; the 1 decent *hostal* in Urcos (**$ El Amigo**, C Carpintero y Jr César Vallejo, T084-307064) is often full.

### $ Hostal Chiss
*C Quispicanchis 216, T984-857294.*
Economical accommodation in a family home with kitchen and washing facilities, private or shared bath, electric shower, some mattresses are poor. Effusively friendly owner, Sr Ladislao Belota.

### $ Hostal El Nogal
*Plaza de Armas, T 977-222727.*
Small place with 3 warm bright rooms, shared bath, electric shower, restaurant.

### Cordillera Vilcanota

### $ Hospedaje Janmarco
*On the left-hand side as you enter Tinqui from Ocongate.*
Simple clean rooms, shared bath with electric shower. Owner Ernesto Jancco is knowledgeable and can arrange guides and pack animals for excursions. **La Casa de Xiomana** next door has good set meals.

### $ Hostal Ausangate
*On the right-hand side as you enter Tinqui from Ocongate, T974-327538, Cuzco T084-227768, ausangate_tour@outlook.com.*
Basic rooms with shared bath, cold water, meals available. Sr Cayetano Crispín, the owner, is knowledgeable and can arrange guides, mules, etc. A reliable source of trekking and climbing information.

### $ Hostal Siesta
*C Libertad 320, Ocongate, T996 030606.*
Pleasant rooms with shared bath, patio, very clean and good value. Helpful owner Sr Raúl Rosas changes US$ at fair rates.

## Festivals

**Jun** Confirm all dates locally. **Q'eswachaka**, during the 1st or 2nd weekend of the month, is a 4-day festival centred on the reconstruction of the Inca rope bridge; **Q'Olloriti**, the multitudinous Snow Star Festival, is held at a sanctuary at 4700 m near Ocongate and Tinqui. It lasts 2 weeks and culminates on the Tue after Trinity Sun; several Cuzco agencies offer tours; on the 2nd or 3rd weekend the **folklore dance festival** in Raqchi draws participants from all over Peru.

## Transport

### Paucartambo
Vehicles to Paucartambo leave as they fill (0300-2000) from the *Paradero Control* in the San Jerónimo neighbourhood of Cuzco: vans, US$3, 2½ hrs; and cars, US$3.60, 2 hrs. **Gallito de las Rocas**, also from San Jerónimo, several daily buses, US$2.45, 3 hrs. From the terminal in Paucartambo to **Pilcopata**, buses pass 0700-0900, US$3, 5 hrs; also buses originating in Cuzco from **Turismo Osmar**, Av Tomasa Ttito Condemayta 1613, near the Coliseo Cerrado, T948-068717. There is more transport to the lowlands on Mon, Wed and Fri, returning Tue, Thu, Sat. To **Tres Cruces**,

a taxi from Paucartambo costs about US$40, alternatively take a bus from Cuzco or Paucartambo bound for Pilcopata to Acjanaco and walk from there. Acjanaco can also be reached taking a combi from Paucartambo to Challabamba (leave when full, US$1, 30 mins) and a pick-up taxi from there (US$12, 45 mins).

## Cordillera Vilcanota

Buses to **Ocongate** (some continue to **Tinqui**) leave from a small terminal on Av Tomasatito Condemayta, corner of the Coliseo Cerrado in Cuzco, every 30 mins, 0430-1800, 3 companies, US$3.25, 3 hrs. Cars are also available from Urcos.

## Cuzco to Choquequirao

stunning views from a 'lost city'

### Abancay road

West of Cuzco a road heads towards Abancay (see page 383) for access to Ayacucho and the central highlands, or Nazca and the coast. There are enough Inca sites on or near this road to remind us that the empire's influence spread to all four cardinal points. Two kilometres before Limatambo, just up from the road, are the ruins of Tarahuasi (76 km from Cuzco, US$6), comprising a very well-preserved Inca temple platform, with 28 tall niches, and a long stretch of fine polygonal masonry. The ruins are impressive, enhanced by the orange lichen which gives the walls a honey colour.

Further along the Abancay road, 100 km from Cuzco, is the exciting descent into the **Apurímac Canyon**, near the former Inca suspension bridge that inspired Thornton Wilder's *The Bridge of San Luis Rey*.

### ★ Choquequirao

*Entry US$18, students US$9.*

Choquequirao is another 'lost city of the Incas', built on a ridge spur almost 1600 m above the Apurímac at 3100 m. It is reckoned to be a larger site than Machu Picchu, but the constructions are more spread out. The main features of Choquequirao are the **Lower Plaza**, considered by most experts to be the focal point of the city. The **Upper Plaza**, reached by a huge set of steps or terraces, has what are possibly ritual baths. A beautiful set of slightly curved agricultural terraces run for over 300 m east-northeast of the Lower Plaza.

The *usnu* (ceremonial platform) is on a levelled hilltop, ringed with stones and giving awesome 360° views. The **Ridge Group**, mostly cleared, is a large collection of unrestored buildings some 50-100 m below the *usnu*. The **Outlier Building**, thought to be the priests' residence, is isolated and surrounded on three sides by steep drops of over 1.5 km into the Apurímac Canyon. It has some of the finest stonework in Choquequirao. The **Llama Terraces** are 200 m below and west of the Lower Plaza, a great set of agricultural platforms beautifully decorated with llamas in white stone. East of the Lower Plaza are two other very large and impressive groups of terraces built on nearly vertical slopes; there is a **Waterfall Temple** located along the southeastern edge of these terraces.

Part of what makes Choquequirao so special is its isolation. At present, the site can only be reached on foot, a tough and exceptionally rewarding trek which attracts fewer than

**Tip...**
Some tours allow insufficient time at Choquequirao (at least one full day is highly recommended), so enquire before you sign up.

50 hikers a day in high season and far fewer at other times. Sadly, there are plans to build a cable car to Choquequirao which would convert it into a mass tourism alternative to Machu Picchu, although construction had not yet begun in 2018.

The route to Choquequirao begins in (San Pedro de) **Cachora**, a village on the south side of the Apurímac, reached by a side road from the Cuzco–Abancay highway, shortly after Saywite. Take an Abancay-bound bus from Cuzco, four hours to the turn-off called Ramal de Cachora, where cars wait for passengers, then it's a 30-minute descent from the road to Cachora village. From the village you need at least a day to descend to the Río Apurímac then another day or two to climb up to Choquequirao, depending on your condition and how much weight you are carrying. Horses can be hired to carry your bags. Allow one or two days at the site. The route is well signed and in good condition, with several nice campsites (some with showers) en route.

You can either return to Cachora the way you came or continue two to four days from Choquequirao to Yanama, and then on to either Huancacalle (see page 352) or to Totora, Santa Teresa and Machu Picchu (see page 339). These treks are all long and demanding. Cuzco agencies offer all-inclusive trekking tours to Choquequirao; some continue to Yanama and Santa Teresa, fewer to Huancacalle.

## Listings Cuzco to Choquequirao

### Where to stay

**$$ Casa de Salcantay**
*200 m below the plaza, Cachora,
1984-2811/1, www.salcantay.com.*
Price includes breakfast, dinner available if booked in advance, very nice comfortable rooms, fantastic views. Dutch/Peruvian-run, Dutch, English, German spoken. Very helpful owners Jan and Giovana can organize treks. Recommended.

**$$ Casa Nostra**
*500 m below Cachora off the road to Capuliyoc,
T958-349949, www.choquequiraotrekk.com.*
Rooms with private bath and dorms, includes breakfast, other meals available, superb views, Italian/Peruvian-run by Matteo and Judith.

**$$ Los Tres Balcones**
*Jr Abancay, Cachora, www.choquequirau.com.*
Hostel designed as start and end-point for the trek to Choquequirao. Breakfast included,

comfortable, hot showers, restaurant and pizza oven, camping. They run an all-inclusive 5-day trek to Choquequirao. May be closed when there is no group, book in advance.

**$ Hospedaje Salcantay**
*1 block above the plaza, Cachora, T958-303055.*
Simple rooms with clean shared bathrooms, warm water, large yard, good value.

### Transport

From the Terminal Terrestre in Cuzco take any bus towards Abancay; **Bredde** has 5 daily, 0600-2030, US$7, 4 hrs, to **Ramal de Cachora**. *Colectivos* from Ramal de Cachora to **Cachora** village, US$1.80, 30 mins, beware overcharging. *Colectivos* also run all day from Prolongación Núñez in Abancay to Cachora, US$3.50, 1½ hrs. **Note** when travelling to Cachora, avoid changing vehicles in Curahuasi, where drivers have attempted to hold up tourists.

# Sacred Valley of the Incas

the Incas' country estates

As the lower Río Vilcanota (also called the Río Urubamba) flows north and west, it waters the agricultural heartland that provided the context for the great city of Cuzco. Here the Incas built country estates, temples, fortresses and other monumental works and, in the process, it became their 'Sacred Valley'.

The name conjures up images of ancient, god-like rulers who saw the landscape itself as a temple; their tributes to this dramatic land survive in places such as Machu Picchu, Ollantaytambo, Pisac and countless others. For the tourist, the most famous sights are now within easy reach of Cuzco and draw massive crowds, but there remains ample scope for genuine exploring, to see lost cities in a less 21st-century setting. If archaeology is not your thing, there are markets to enjoy, birds to watch, trails for mountain biking and a whole range of wonderful places to relax.

West of the towns of the Sacred Valley on a ridge above the Río Vilcanota lies the reason for most tourists' visit to Peru. The once 'lost city' of Machu Picchu has unquestionably been found, but it continues to inspire awe among the over one million visitors it receives each year.

**Best** for
Inca ruins ▪ Markets ▪ Rafting ▪ Relaxing ▪ Trekking

Pisac, Urubamba &
  Ollantaytambo . . . . . . . . . . . 327
Machu Picchu . . . . . . . . . . . . . 339
Inca trails . . . . . . . . . . . . . . . . 347
Vilcabamba & around . . . . . . 352

# Footprint picks

## ★ Pisac, page 327

A small town with amazing ruins and an extremely popular craft market for tourists.

## ★ Huchuy Cuzco, page 328

The impressive ruins of 'little Cuzco' make for an interesting day visit, or they can be reached on a scenic one- or two-day trek from Tambo Machay.

## ★ Maras, page 330

From this village you can walk to both the mysterious Inca-terraced sinkholes at Moray and the ancient salt pans at Salineras.

## ★ Ollantaytambo, page 331

This bustling tourist town has extensive ruins and an intact Inca neighbourhood.

## ★ Machu Picchu, page 339

No amount of mass tourism seems to tarnish the glow of the most famous archaeological site in South America.

## ★ Inca trails, page 347 and 348

As well as the classic trek to Machu Picchu, there are many other fascinating routes to explore.

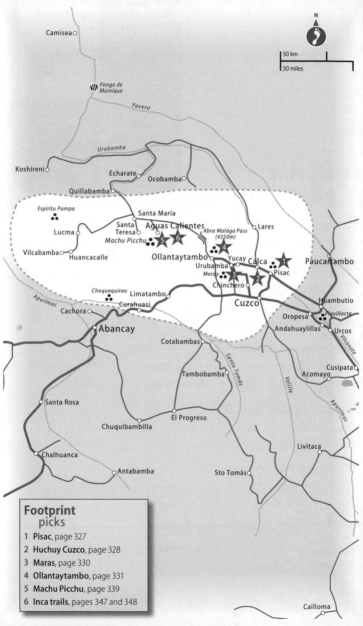

Camisea

*Pongo de Mainique*

*Yavero*

*Urubamba*

Koshireni

Echarate    Ocobamba

Quillabamba

*Espíritu Pampa*    Santa María

Lucma    Santa    Aguas Calientes    Lares
        Teresa
        *Machu Picchu*    5  6    *Abra Malága Pass*
                                    (4350m)
Vilcabamba                    Ollantaytambo    4    Yucay    Calca
        Huancacalle            Urubamba        Yucay        Pisac    Paucartambo
                            *Moray*    3
*Apurímac*        *Choquequirao*    Chinchero                    Huambutío
        Cachora    Limatambo                Cuzco        Oropesa    *Piquillacta*
                Curahuasi                            Andahuaylillas    Urcos

Abancay                                                        Cusipata

            Cotabambas                    *Santa Tomás*        Acomayo

Santa Rosa                                    *Velille*        *Apurímac*
                        Tambobamba

        Chuquibambilla    El Progreso                        Livitaca

Chalhuanca

        Antabamba            Sto Tomás

N
30 km
30 miles

## Footprint
picks

1 **Pisac**, page 327
2 **Huchuy Cuzco**, page 328
3 **Maras**, page 330
4 **Ollantaytambo**, page 331
5 **Machu Picchu**, page 339
6 **Inca trails**, pages 347 and 348

The road from Cuzco that runs past Sacsayhuaman and on to Tambo Machay (see page 297) climbs up to a pass, then continues over the pampa before descending into the densely populated Vilcanota Valley. This road then crosses the river by a bridge at Pisac and follows the north bank to the end of the paved road at Ollantaytambo. It passes through Calca, Yucay and Urubamba, which can also be reached from Cuzco by the beautiful, direct road through Chinchero, see page 329.

### ★ Pisac *Colour map 5, A5.*

Pisac, 30 km north of Cuzco, has a large daily craft market. It is a major draw for tourists who arrive in their droves throughout the day, especially on Sunday. The plaza is packed with vendors and their stalls, and there are many souvenir shops. Each Sunday at 1100 there is a Quechua Mass, preceded by a small procession of the *varayoc* (local dignitaries), held in the church on the plaza, where there is also a small, interesting **Museo Folklórico**. Elsewhere, the **Museo Comunitario Pisac** ① *Av Amazonas y Retamayoc K'asa, museopisac@gmail.com, 0800-1300, 1400-1700, closed Sat, free but donations welcome,*

has a display of village life, created by the people of Pisac. At dusk you may hear, if not see, the *pisaca* (partridges), after which the town is named. The local fiesta, in honour of La Virgen del Carmen, is on 15 July.

High above the town on the mountainside is Pisac's superb **Inca fortress** ① *1½- to 2-hr walk from the plaza (1-hr descent), daily 0800-1600, entry with BTC ticket; upper entrance can be reached by car (combi US$0.75, taxi US$8 each way from Pisac).* Allow at least half a day to enjoy the site at leisure. The path through the ruins is steep in places and climbs about 500 m in 3 km, through very impressive terraces. Follow the direction of the arrows in order to take one route up and a different one down through the ruins. Or you can return to Pisac along the narrow trail in Quebrada Colipala, adjacent to the site. On the eastern side of the ridge, the first group of buildings is Pisaqa, with a fine curving wall. Climb from here to the Inca hospital and on to the central part of the ruins, the Intihuatana group of temples with the most magnificent Inca masonry. Here are palaces of the moon and stars, solstice markers, baths and fine water channels. From Intihuatana, a path leads right, around the hillside Q'Allaqasa,

**Pisac** ↑ Path to Archaeological Site

① Paucartambo ②

Cusco — M Castilla
**Museo Folklórico** ①
San Francisco
Puno ⑤ ③ ⑤
⑦ Arequipa

Pardo — Bolognesi — Grau — Kitamayo
Vigil

Callao

Av Amazonas — Buses to Calca & Urubamba
Buses to Cuzco
*Río Urubamba*

To Calca & Urubamba
To ③ ④ ⑥ Museo Comunitario & Archaeological Site

N
To Cuzco via Chinchero

To Cuzco vía Huambutío

Not to scale

**Where to stay** 🛏
1 Hosp Beho
2 Hosp Kitamayu
3 Melissa Wasi
4 Paz y Luz
5 Pisac Inn
6 Royal Inka Pisac

**Restaurants** 🍴
1 Apus Organic
2 Blue Llama Café
3 Cuchara de Palo
4 Horno Colonial
5 Mullu
6 Sapos Lounge
7 Ulrike's Café

the military area. At this point, a large area of Inca tombs in holes in the hillside can be seen across the valley. The end of the site is Kanchisracay, where the agricultural workers were housed. Road transport approaches from the Kanchisracay end; the drive up from town takes about 20 minutes. Even if you're going by car, do not rush as there is a lot to see and a lot of walking to do.

## ★ Calca and Huchuy Cuzco

The second village on the road from Pisac towards Urubamba is **Lamay**, 7 km away, which has simple places to stay and warm springs nearby that are highly regarded for their medicinal properties. Next is **Calca**, 11 km beyond Lamay at 3000 m, which has a fancier hotel and several simpler ones (a good choice is $ Pakarina Hostal, Avenida Estrada 237, T085-612241), as well as eating places around its large plaza and a bus terminal along the highway. The **Fiesta de la Virgen Asunta** is held here on 15-16 August.

Dramatically located at 3700 m on a flat esplanade on the opposite side of the river (not visible from the valley) are the impressive ruins of a small Inca town, **Huchuy Cuzco** (Little Cuzco). Access by car is along a steep, winding road from Calca or along walking trails from Lamay (good, steep 4-km trail), Calca (difficult 10.5 km), Tambo Machay (about 20 km, one or two days) and Chinchero (18 km, one or two days days), entry US$7. Accommodation is available with families near the ruins and at Pucamarka, towards Tambo Machay. The views are magnificent. The ruins themselves consist of extensive agricultural terraces with high retaining walls and several buildings made from finely wrought stonework and adobe mud bricks.

## Valle de Lares

The Valle de Lares is renowned for its magnificent mountains, lakes and small villages, which make it perfect for trekking and mountain biking, although parts are undergoing rapid development. One route starts near an old hacienda in Huarán (6 km west of Calca at 2830 m), crosses two passes over 4000 m and ends at the hot springs near Lares. From this village, transport runs back to Calca. Alternatively, you can add an extra day and continue to Ollantaytambo, or start in Lares and finish in Yanhuara (between Urubamba and Ollantaytambo). Several agencies in Cuzco offer trekking and biking tours to the region (see pages 310 and 313).

## Yucay

About 3 km east of Urubamba, Yucay has two grassy plazas divided by the restored colonial church of Santiago Apóstol, with its oil paintings and fine altars. On the opposite side from Plaza Manco II is the adobe palace built for Sayri Túpac (Manco's son) when he emerged from Vilcabamba in 1558.

### Urubamba *Colour map 5, A5.*

Like many places along the valley, Urubamba is in a fine setting at 2863 m with snow-capped peaks in view. The main road along the valley skirts the town, and the bridge for the road to Cuzco via Chinchero is just to the east. The large market square is one block west of the main plaza. Calle Berriózabal, on the west edge of town, is lined with pisonay trees and trendy cafés. There are many pottery studios in town, including **Seminario-Bejar Ceramic Studio** ① *Berriózabal 405, T084-201002, www.ceramicaseminario.com.* Pablo Seminario and his workshop have researched pre-Columbian techniques and designs and now use them in their distinctive pottery. The tour of the workshops is highly recommended.

## Chinchero
*Church and archaeological site daily 0800-1600, BTC ticket (see page 289).*

Chinchero (3762 m) is southeast of Urubamba along the more direct (western) road to Cuzco. It is a friendly town with an attractive church (1607) built on an Inca temple. The church has been restored to reveal the full glory of its interior paintings: ceiling, beams and walls are covered in beautiful floral and religious designs. Excavations have revealed many Inca walls and terraces around the town's plaza. Groups from Cuzco come to visit the church, ruins and several touristy textile centres in the town. Much of the area's character will change when the new airport for Cuzco is built nearby.

## Moray and around
*9 km by road west of Maras, BTC ticket (see page 289).*

The beautiful site of Moray comprises three great sinkholes: natural formations lined with fine Inca terracing. Each level is said to have its own microclimate and they have traditionally been described as Inca agricultural laboratories. Subsequent research (*Moray: Inca Engineering Mystery*, by Ruth and Kenneth Wright, 2011), however, suggests that this is unlikely and that the site was in fact part water temple and part royal Inca

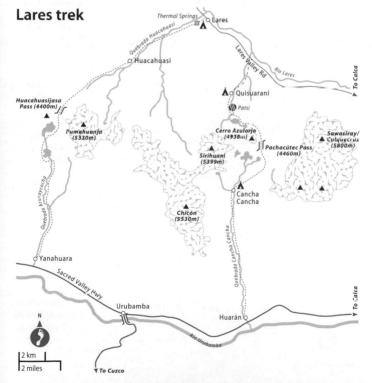

**Lares trek**

estate. It is a very atmospheric place which, many claim, has mystical power, and the scenery is absolutely stunning.

The most interesting way to get to Moray from Urubamba is to walk from **Tarabamba**, 6 km west, where a bridge crosses the Río Urubamba. Turn right after the bridge to reach **Pichingoto**, a tumbled-down village built under an overhanging cliff. Just over the bridge and before the town to the left of a small, walled cemetery is a salt stream. Follow the footpath beside the stream to Salineras, a small village below which are a mass of terraced **Inca salt pans** ① *entry US$3, taxi from Urubamba, US$11*. There are over 5000 *salineras* and they are still in operation. The village of ★ **Maras**, with basic hostels and eateries, is 7 km beyond the salt pans (two-hour walk or 15-minute taxi ride), from where it's 9 km by unmade road or 5 km through the fields to Moray; ask in Maras for the best walking route. Tour companies in Cuzco offer cycle trips to Moray; see Transport, for further details on how to get there. If you're walking to the salt pans and Moray, take water as this side of the valley can be very hot and dry.

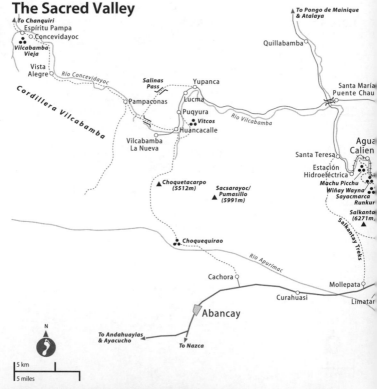

# The Sacred Valley

To Chanquiri
Espíritu Pampa
Concevidayoc
*Vilcabamba Vieja*
Vista Alegre
*Río Concevidayoc*

**Cordillera Vilcabamba**

Pampaconas

*Salinas Pass*

Yupanca
Lúcma
Puqyura
*Vitcos*
Huancacalle

Vilcabamba La Nueva

▲ *Choquetacarpo (5512m)*

*Sacsarayoc/ Pumasillo (5991m)* ▲

Choquequirao

*Río Apurímac*

Cachora

To Pongo de Mainique & Atalaya

Quillabamba

Santa María Puente Chau

*Río Vilcabamba*

Agua Calien
Santa Teresa
Estación Hidroeléctrica
*Machu Picchu*
*Wiñay Wayna*
*Sayacmarca*
*Runkur*
*Salkanta (6271m*
*Salkantay Treks*

Mollepata
Curahuasi
Limatar

Abancay

N

To Andahuaylas & Ayacucho

To Nazca

5 km
5 miles

## ★ Ollantaytambo *Colour map 5, A5.*

The attractive but touristy town of Ollantaytambo is located at 2800 m at the foot of some spectacular Inca ruins and terraces and is built directly on top of an original Inca town. A great many visitors arrive by road from Cuzco to see the ruins and take the train from here to Machu Picchu.

**Tip...**
Traffic around Ollantaytambo train station is chaotic every evening; take care not to be run over on Avenida Ferrocarril.

Entering Ollantaytambo from the east, the road is built along the long Wall of 100 Niches. Note the inclination of the wall, which leans towards the road. Since it was the Incas' usual practice to build their walls leaning towards the interior of the building, it has been deduced that the road, much narrower then, was built inside a succession of buildings. The road leads into the Plaza de Armas. The Inca town, or *Llacta*, on which the present-day town is based, can clearly be seen behind the north side of the plaza, where the original Inca *canchas* (blocks of houses) are almost entirely intact and still occupied. The road out of the plaza leads across a bridge to the colonial church with its enclosed *recinto*. Beyond are Plaza Araccama and the entrance to the archaeological site

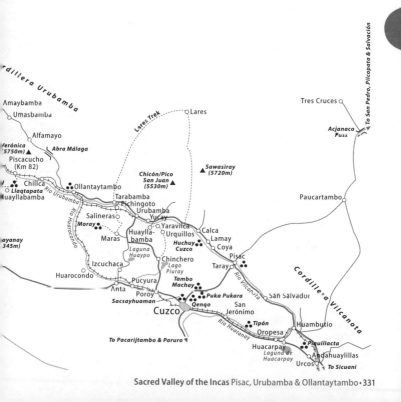

**Ollantaytambo temple fortress** ⓘ *Daily 0800-1600; if possible arrive at 0800, before the other tourists. Admission by BTC visitor's ticket, which can be bought at the site. Guides are available at the entrance.* After crossing the great high-walled trapezoidal esplanade known as 'Mañariki', visitors to Ollantaytambo are confronted by a series of 16 massive, stepped terraces of the very finest stonework. These flights of terraces leading up above the town are superb, and so are the curving terraces following the contours of the rocks overlooking the river. Ollantaytambo was successfully defended by Manco Inca's warriors against Hernando Pizarro in 1536. Manco Inca built the wall above the site and another wall closing the Yucay Valley against attack from Cuzco. Beyond these imposing terraces lies the so-called Temple of Ten Niches. Immediately above this are six monolithic upright blocks of rose-coloured rhyolite, the remains of what is popularly called the Temple of the Sun. The temple was started by Pachacútec, using Colla labourers from Lake Titicaca – hence the similarities of the monoliths facing the central platform with the Tiahuanaco remains. The massive, highly finished granite blocks at the top are worth the climb to see. The Colla are said to have deserted halfway through the work, which explains the many unfinished blocks lying about the site.

There are more Inca ruins in the small area behind the church, between the town and the temple fortress. Most impressive of these is the so-called Baño de la Ñusta (bath of

**Ollantaytambo**

| Where to stay 🛏 | 9 Hostal Plaza | Restaurants 🍴 |
|---|---|---|
| 1 Apu Lodge | Ollantaytambo | 1 Coffee Tree |
| 2 Casa de Wow | 10 Hostal Sauce | 2 Doña Eva |
| 3 El Albergue | 11 Las Orquídeas | 3 Heart's Café & Puka Rumi |
| Ollantaytambo | 12 Pakaritampu | 4 Huatakay |
| 4 Full Moon Lodge | 13 Picaflor Tambo | 5 Il Piccolo Forno |
| 5 Hostal Andean Moon | 14 Sol Ollantay | 6 La Esquina |
| 6 Hostal Chaska Wasi | 15 Tika Wasi Valley | 7 Papa's |
| 7 Hostal El Tambo | | |
| 8 Hostal Iskay II | | |

# BACKGROUND
## Ollantaytambo

When Manco Inca decided to rebel against the Spaniards in 1536, he fell back to Ollantaytambo from Calca to stage one of the greatest acts of resistance to the conquistadors. Hernando Pizarro led his troops to the foot of the Inca's stronghold and, on seeing how well-manned and fortified the place was, described it as "a thing of horror". Under fierce fire, Pizarro's men failed to capture Manco and retreated to Cuzco, but Manco could not press home any advantage. In 1537, feeling vulnerable to further attacks, he left Ollantaytambo for the remote mountainous jungles of Vilcabamba.

the princess) carved from the bedrock. Some 200 m behind the bath, along the face of the mountain, are some small ruins known as Inca Misana, believed to have been a small temple or observatory. A series of steps, seats and niches have been carved out of the cliff. There is a complete irrigation system, including a canal at shoulder level, some 6 inches deep, cut out of the sheer rock face.

On the west side of the main ruins, a two-dimensional 'pyramid' has been identified in the layout of the fields and walls of the valley. A fine 750 m wall aligns with the rays of the winter solstice on 21 June. It can be appreciated from a high point about 3.5 km from Ollantaytambo.

**Listings** Pisac, Urubamba and Ollantaytambo *maps pages 327 and 332.*

## Tourist information

Tourist information is available on the main plaza in Pisac (daily 0800-1700), the bus terminal in Urubamba (Mon-Fri 0745-1630) and the Municipio in Ollantaytambo (T084-204030, ext 207, Mon-Fri 0800-1300, 1400-1700, Sat-Sun 0800-1300).

## Where to stay

### Pisac

**$$$ Melissa Wasi**
*15 mins walk from Pisac Plaza, close to the river, T084-797589, www.melissa-wasi.com.*
A family-run bed and breakfast with rooms and small bungalows. Very homely, English spoken.

**$$$ Royal Inka Pisac**
*Cra Ruinas Km 1.5, T084-263276, www.royalinkahotel.pe.*
Converted hacienda with olympic-size swimming pool (US$3.50 per day), sauna and jacuzzi for guests only, very pleasant,

provides guides. This chain also has **Royal Inkas I** and **II** in Cuzco.

**$$$-$$ Paz y Luz**
*Close to the river, 10-15 mins' walk from Pisac Plaza, T910-598781, www.pazyluzperu.com.*
American-owned, pleasant garden, nicely designed rooms, breakfast included. Diane Dunn offers healing from many traditions (including Andean), sacred tours, workshops and gatherings.

**$$$-$$ Pisac Inn**
*At the corner of Pardo on the plaza, T084-203062, www.pisacinn.com.*
Bright and charming local decor, pleasant atmosphere, private and shared bathrooms, sauna and massage. Good breakfast, the **Cuchara de Palo** restaurant serves meals using local ingredients, plus pizza and pasta, café.

**$$ Hospedaje Kitamayu**
*Federico Zamalloa 424, 5 blocks from main plaza, T984-950891, www.hospedajekitamayucuscoperu.com.*

Pleasant family-run *hospedaje* with simple, bright, comfortable rooms, plenty of warm blankets and hot water, heaters available, charming patio and breakfast room.

### $ Hospedaje Beho
*Intihuatana 114, T084-203001.*
This 1st *hospedaje* in Pisac is a good economy option. Simple rooms with shared or private bath, electric shower, tranquil terrace and garden, kitchen, family-run, good breakfast available, no Wi-Fi.

## Valle de Lares

### $$$ The Green House
*Km 56.8, Huarán, T941-299944,*
*www.thegreenhouseperu.com.*
A charming retreat, only 4 rooms, breakfast included, comfortable lounge, restaurant, small kitchen for guests, beautiful garden, restricted internet. No children under 12. Information on walks and day trips in the area. Activities include hiking, biking, horse riding and rafting. Intimate, beautiful and relaxing.

## Yucay

### $$$$-$$$ Sonesta Posadas del Inca Sacred Valley
*Plaza Manco II de Yucay 123, T084-201107,*
*www.sonesta.com.*
Converted 300-year-old monastery is like a little village with plazas, chapel, 88 comfortable, heated rooms, price includes buffet breakfast. Many activities, canoeing, horse riding, mountain biking, etc. **Inkafe** restaurant is open to all, serving Peruvian, fusion and traditional cuisine with a US$15 buffet.

### $$$ La Casona de Yucay
*Plaza Manco II 104, T084-201116,*
*www.hotelcasonayucay.com.*
This colonial house was where Simón Bolívar stayed during his liberation campaign in 1824. With heating, 2 patios and gardens, **Tika** restaurant and **Apus** bar.

## Urubamba

### $$$$ Casa Andina Private Collection Sacred Valley
*Paradero 5, Yanahuara, between Urubamba and Ollantaytambo, T984-765501, www.casa-andina.com.*
In its own 3-ha estate, with all the facilities associated with this chain, plus **Valle Sagrado Andean Cottage** for family and long-stay accommodation, 'Sacred Spa', gym, planetarium, good restaurant, adventure options.

### $$$$ Río Sagrado (Belmond)
*Km 76 Cuzco–Ollantaytambo Road, 4 km from Urubamba, T084-201631, www.belmond.com.*
Rooms and villas set in beautiful gardens overlooking the river with fine views. **Mayu Wilka** spa, restaurant and bar, offers various packages.

### $$$$ Sol y Luna
*Fundo Huincho, west of town, T084-608930, www.hotelsolyluna.com.*
Award-winning bungalows and suites set off the main road in lovely gardens, pool, excellent gourmet restaurant, wine tastings, spa, handicrafts shop. Also has **Wayra** lounge bar and dining room, open to non-guests, for freshly cooked, informal lunches. Entertainment includes *paso fino* horse shows, contemporary arts and circus shows (open to all). Arranges adventure and cultural activities and traditional tours. Profits go to **Sol y Luna** educational association, www.colegiosolyluna.com.

### $$$$ Tambo del Inka
*Av Ferrocarril s/n, T084-581777, www.luxurycollection.com/vallesagrado.*
A resort and spa on the edge of town, in gardens by the river. Completely remodelled with a variety of rooms and suites, fitness centre, swimming pools, **Hawa** restaurant, bar, business facilities and lots of activities arranged. Has its own train station with departures to Aguas Calientes.

### $$$ Casa Colibrí
*2.5 km from town on road to*
*Ollantaytambo, T084-254852,*
*www.casacolibriecolodge.com.*
Delightful, spacious rooms and *casitas*
made of local stone, wood and adobe, set in
beautiful gardens to attract bees, butterflies
and hummingbirds. Very restful, hammocks,
meditation room, excellent home-grown
food, swings and table tennis, popular with
couples, families and yoga groups.

### $$ Las Chullpas
*Querocancha s/n, 3 km from town,*
*T084-201568, www.chullpas.pe.*
Very peaceful, excellent breakfast, vegetarian
meals, English spoken, natural medicine,
treks, riding, mountain biking, camping
US$3 with hot shower. Mototaxi from town
US$2.50, taxi (ask for Querocancha) US$4.

### $$ Urubamba Homestay
*C Pisagua s/n, T084-201562,*
*www.urubambahomestay.com.*
3 rooms with bath in a private home,
includes breakfast, roof terrace, gardens,
support community projects. British-run
by Keith and Joan Parkin.

### $$-$ Mauru'sTambo del Sol
*Av La Convención 113-B, T084-201352,*
*www.hostaltambodelsol.com.*
Ample modern rooms with bathtubs and
suite with cooking facilities, beautiful garden,
parking, good value.

### $ Hospedaje Buganvilla
*Jr Convención 280, T084-205102,*
*bukanvilla@hotmail.com.*
Sizable rooms with hot water, breakfast
on request, quiet, bright, lovely gardens,
lively owners Raúl and Mónica, good value,
very pleasant.

### $ Hospedaje Los Jardines
*Jr Convención 459, T084-201331, www.*
*hospedajelosjardines.blogspot.co.uk.*
Attractive guesthouse with comfortable
rooms, hot water, non-smoking, delicious
breakfast US$3.25 extra (vegans catered for),

safe, lovely garden, laundry. **Sacred Valley
Mountain Bike Tours** also based here.

## Chinchero

### $$$ La Casa de Barro
*Miraflores 147, T084-306031,*
*www.lacasadebarro.com.*
Modern hotel, with heating, bar, restaurant
serving 'fusion' food using organic local
produce, tours arranged.

### $$ Mi Piuray
*C Garcilaso 187, T084-306029,*
*www.hospedajemipiuraycusco.com.*
Simple rooms around a patio with flowers,
private or shared bath, electric showers,
kitchen facilities, meals on request,
knowledgeable owner.

## Ollantaytambo
There are many hotels but they are
often full, so it's best to book ahead
in high season.

### $$$$ Pakaritampu
*C Ferrocarril 852, T084-204020,*
*www.pakaritampu.com.*
Modern, well-appointed rooms, buffet
breakfast, restaurant and bar, laundry, safe
and room service. Adventure sports can
be arranged. Lunch and dinner are extra.
Excellent quality and service, but room 8
is next to the railway station car park.

### $$$$-$$$ El Albergue Ollantaytambo
*Within the railway station gates,*
*T084-204014, www.elalbergue.com.*
Owned by North American artist Wendy
Weeks. Also has **Café Mayu** in the station
and a very good restaurant using ingredients
from their own organic farm. Characterful
rooms, rustic elegance, some larger than
others, safety boxes, lovely gardens and a
eucalyptus steam sauna. Books and crafts
for sale. Private transport arranged to nearby
attractions and Cuzco airport.

### $$$ Apu Lodge
*Calle Lari, T084-436816, www.apulodge.com.*

On the edge of town, great views of the ruins and surrounding mountains. Run by Scot Louise Norton, good service, quiet, nice garden, good buffet breakfast, can help organize tours and treks.

### $$$ Hostal Sauce
*C Ventiderio 248, T084-204044, www.hostalsauce.com.pe.*
Smart, simple decor and views of the ruins from 3 of the 6 rooms as well as from the dining room, food from own farm.

### $$$ Sol Ollantay
*C Ventiderio 226 by the bridge between the 2 plazas, T084-204130, www.hotelsolollantaytambo.com.*
Tastefully renovated with good views from most rooms, ample rooms with heaters, some with balcony or terrace, buffet breakfast.

### $$$-$$ Picaflor Tambo
*C Lari s/n, T084-436758, www.picaflortambo.com.*
6 comfortable rooms set around a courtyard, charming, a good choice.

### $$$-$$ Tika Wasi Valley
*C Convencion s/n, T084-204166, www.tikawasivalley.com.*
Great location close to the archaeological site, garden, good service and comfortable rooms decorated in 'Inca style'.

### $$ Casa de Wow
*C Patacalle 840, T084-204010, www.casadewow.com.*
Dorms, kitchen facilities, balcony with great view of ruins, English spoken. Organizes tours.

### $$ Full Moon Lodge
*Cruz Esquina s/n, T989-362031, http://fullmoonlodgeperu.com.*
Quiet place away from the centre, rooms with private bath set around a large garden with hammocks and fire pit, also has camp site on Av Estudiantil (US$5 pp). Offers San Pedro experiences.

### $$ Hostal Andean Moon
*Calle del Medio s/n, 3 blocks from Plaza de Armas, T084-204080, www.andeanmoonhostal.com.*
Rooms with wood floors, some with bathtub, heaters, beautiful garden and rooftop views, jacuzzi, bar, luggage storage.

### $$ Hostal Iskay II
*Patacalle 722, T084-434109, www.hostaliskay.com.*
In the Inca town. Great location but car access is difficult. Only 7 rooms, free tea and coffee, use of kitchen. Good reports.

### $$ Las Orquídeas
*Av Ferrocarril 406, T084-204032.*
Fairly small but nice rooms, flower-filled patio, discounts for 2 or more nights, luggage storage.

### $ Hostal Chaska Wasi
*C Principal, 4 blocks east of Plaza de Armas, T084-204045.*
Private rooms and dorms, hammocks, hot showers, free hot drinks, laundry, popular. Owner Katy is very friendly.

### $ Hostal El Tambo
*C Horno, north of the plaza, T984-385770, www.hostaleltambo.com.*
Once past the door you emerge into a lovely garden full of fruit trees and flowers. Small basic rooms for up to 4 people, shared bath downstairs in the courtyard, hot water, breakfast available, good value. Friendly owner.

### $ Hostal Plaza Ollantaytambo
*C Principal s/n, beside the police station on Plaza de Armas, T084-436741, hostalplazaollantaytambo@gmail.com.*
Small modern rooms with private bath and reliable hot water. Variable service, all a bit improvised but great location and value.

### Pisac

#### $$$ Mullu
*Plaza de Armas 352, T084-203073, and Mcal Castilla 375, T084-203182. Tue-Sun 0900-1900.*
Café/restaurant with Peruvian and Asian fusion menu. Has a gallery promoting local artists.

#### $$$-$$ Cuchara de Palo
*In Pisac Inn on Plaza de Armas, T084-203062.*
Gourmet restaurant using local ingredients to make traditional Peruvian food. Cosy atmosphere.

#### $$ Sapos Lounge
*Espinar y Arequipa, T994-647979. Tue-Sun 1500-2300.*
Good pizza and drinks, produce from a local organic farm. Good nightlife spot.

#### $ Apus Organic
*Grau 584, T988-338141.*
Small restaurant serving good organic, vegetarian and vegan food.

### Cafés

#### Blue Llama Café
*Corner of the plaza opposite Pisac Inn, T084-203135.*
Cute, colourful café with a huge range of teas, good coffee, breakfasts, daily *menús*, and board games.

#### Horno Colonial
*Mcal Castilla 572.*
Good wholemeal bread and cheese *empanadas*.

#### Ulrike's Café
*C Pardo 613, T084-203195. Daily 0800-2100.*
The best apple crumble with ice cream, excellent coffee, smoothies and many international dishes. Good value 3-course daily *menú*. Book exchange.

### Urubamba

#### $$$ El Huacatay
*Arica 620, T084-201790, www.elhuacatay.com. Mon-Sat 1230-2130.*
A small restaurant with a reputation for fine, creative fusion cuisine (local, Mediterranean, Asian). Lovely garden setting.

#### $$$ El Maizal
*Av Conchatupa, the main road before the bridge, T984-705211. Daily 1200-1600.*
Country-style restaurant, buffet service with a variety of *Novo Andino* and international choices, beautiful gardens, caters to tour groups.

#### $$$ Tres Keros
*Av Señor de Torrechayoc, T084-201701.*
*Novo Andino* cuisine, try the lamb chops.

#### $$$ Tunupa
*On road from Urubamba to Ollantaytambo, on riverbank, T084-630156. Open 1200-1500.*
Buffet lunch US$15. Same owners as Tunupa in Cuzco, colonial-style hacienda, excellent food and surroundings, pre-Columbian and colonial art exhibitions.

#### $$$-$$ Paca Paca
*Av Mcal Castilla 640, T084-201181. Tue-Sun 1300-2100.*
Varied selection of dishes including Peruvian fusion, also pizza, pleasant inviting atmosphere.

#### $$-$ Guyin
*Comercio 453, T084-608838 for delivery. Daily 1600-2300.*
Pizza, pastas and grill. Popular with local expats.

#### $$-$ Pizza Wasi
*Av Mcal Castilla 857, Plaza de Armas, T084-434751 for delivery. Daily 1200-2300.*
Good pizzas and pastas. Mulled wine served in a small restaurant with nice decor, good value.

#### $ El Edén
*Av Mcal Castilla 960, T084-201605. Mon-Sat 0900-2100.*

Pastries, sandwiches, coffee and juices. Jams and bread to go. Some gluten-free products.

## Ollantaytambo

There are restaurants all over town offering *menú turístico*, pizzas, pastas, juices and hot drinks.

### $$$ Papa's
*C Horno at the plaza, T974-787191.*
*Daily 1100-2100.*
Restaurant and lounge serving Tex-Mex, local dishes, pizzas, soups, salads, and desserts.

### $$$-$$ Puka Rumi
*Av Ventiderio s/n, next to Heart's Café,*
*T084-214828. Daily 0700-2100.*
Serves a variety of international dishes, pizza, salads, upmarket *menu*.

### $$ Coffee Tree
*C del Medio by Plaza de Armas, T084-436734.*
Good coffee and a variety of Peruvian and international dishes. Popular.

### $$ Heart's Café
*Av Ventiderio s/n, T084-436726, www.*
*livingheartperu.org. Open 0700-2100.*
International and Peruvian dishes including vegetarian, box lunch and takeaway available, good coffee. All profits to education and self-help projects in the Sacred Valley. Popular, tasty food but disappointing service.

### $$ Huatakay
*Av Occobamba s/n, 2nd block, T984-397305.*
*Daily 0600-2100.*
Large restaurant serving *menú* and regional specialities à la carte. Pleasant setting. Owns **Quechuas Lodge** on the same street, guests get a discount at the restaurant.

### $$ Il Piccolo Forno
*C del Medio 120, T084-625492.*
*Tue-Sun 1200-2100.*
Very good Italian food and take-away pizza, as well as home-baked bread, pies and cookies. Gluten-free options.

### $$ La Esquina
*C Principal at the corner of Plaza de Armas,*
*T084-204078. Mon-Sat 0700-2100.*
Variety of international dishes, wide selection of pastries and sweets, popular.

### $ Doña Eva
*C Ollantay facing the market.*
*Sun-Fri 0700-2100, Sat 0700-1900.*
Economical *menú* and à la carte, one of the few unpretentious places in town, popular with locals and travellers alike.

## Festivals

### Urubamba
**May-Jun** Harvest months, with many processions following ancient schedules. Urubamba's main festival, **El Señor de Torrechayoc**, takes place around 20 May.
**8 Sep** Chinchero celebrates the **Day of the Virgin**.

### Ollantaytambo
**6 Jan  Bajada de Reyes Magos** (Epiphany) is celebrated with dancing, a bull fight, local food and a fair.
**End-May/early-Jun  Fiesta del Señor de Choquekillca**, patron saint of Ollantaytambo, has his festival 50 days after Easter, with several days of dancing, weddings, processions, masses, feasting and drinking.
**Jun  Ollanta-Raymi**. A colourful festival on the Sun following Inti Raymi.
**29 Oct** The town's anniversary, with lots of dancing in traditional costume and many local delicacies for sale.

## What to do

### Urubamba
**Perol Chico**, *5 km from Urubamba at Km 77,*
*T950-314065/950-314066, www.perolchico.com.*
Dutch/Peruvian-owned and operated stables offering 1- to 11-day horse-riding trips. Good horses, riding is Peruvian *paso* style.

### Ollantaytambo

**Awamaki,** *C La Convención across from the church, T084-436744, www.awamaki.org.* Cultural tours and artisan workshops (dying, weaving, woodcarving) which can be integrated with homestays in local communities. Also adventure tours, volunteering, Spanish and Quechua classes.

## Transport

### Pisac

To **Urubamba**, US$1, 1 hr. To **Cuzco**, 32 km, 1 hr, US$1.50, last one back leaves around 2000; these buses are often full. There are also *colectivos* and minibuses; all leave from C Amazonas near the main bridge.

### Urubamba

The Terminal is on the main road, 3 blocks west of the centre. To **Calca**, US$0.50, 30 mins; and **Pisac**, US$1, 1 hr. To **Cuzco**, by bus, US$1.50, 1½ hrs via Chinchero or 2 hrs via Pisac; by van US$2; by car US$2.50. Frequent vans to **Ollantaytambo**, US$0.50, 30 mins, all leave when full throughout the day.

### Moray and around

Any bus between Urubamba and Cuzco via Chinchero passes the clearly marked turning to Maras (the turn-off is called *El Ramal de Maras*); from the junction taxi *colectivos* charge US$2.50 pp to Maras, or you can walk all the way from here to Moray (see above). There is also public transport from Chinchero to Maras until 1700. A taxi to Moray and the salt pans (from where you can walk back to the Urubamba–Ollantaytambo road) costs US$25, including 1-hr wait.

### Ollantaytambo
#### Bus

Vans leave all day for **Urubamba** from the produce market, 1 block east of the main plaza, US$0.50, 30 mins. Vans to **Cuzco** leave frequently from Av Ferrocarril above the railway station and from the main plaza near the information centre, US$3.50, 1½ hrs. Taxi to Cuzco, US$22.

#### Train

Ollantaytambo is the point of departure for most trains to **Machu Picchu** (see Transport, page 346). The station is a 10- to 15-min walk from the plaza, longer in the early evening when Av Ferrocarril is clogged with vehicles. There are **Perú Rail** and **Inca Rail** ticket offices outside the station and you must have a ticket to be allowed onto the platform unless you are staying at **El Albergue Hotel**.

## ★ Machu Picchu   *Colour map 5, A5.*

**iconic and unmissable**

There is a tremendous feeling of awe on first witnessing Machu Picchu. The ancient citadel (42 km from Ollantaytambo by rail) straddles the saddle of a high mountain (2380 m) with steep terraced slopes falling away to the fast-flowing Vilcanota river snaking its hairpin course far below on the valley floor. Towering overhead is Huayna Picchu, and green jungle peaks provide the backdrop for the whole majestic scene. Machu Picchu is a complete Inca city. For centuries it was buried in jungle, until Hiram Bingham stumbled upon it in 1911. It was then explored by an archaeological expedition sent by Yale University. Take time to appreciate not only the masonry, but also the selection of large rocks used for foundations, the use of water in the channels below the Temple of the Sun and the beauty of the surrounding mountains.

> **Tip...**
> You need time to see the site properly, so try to stay as long as your entry ticket allows.

# Essential Machu Picchu

## Finding your feet

The easiest way to get to Machu Picchu is by train from Poroy (near Cuzco) or Ollantaytambo to Aguas Calientes, from where you can walk or catch a bus to the ruins. Santa Teresa, reached by road from Cuzco via Ollantaytambo, provides alternative access. You can either take the train or walk along the tracks from Estación Hidroeléctrica (10 km from Santa Teresa) to Aguas Calientes. The most strenuous but rewarding way to Machu Picchu is to hike one of the Inca trails (see page 347).

## Tickets

There are two time slots to visit the site: 0600-1200 and 1200-1730. To spend all day at the ruins you must buy both a morning and an afternoon ticket. Both tickets cost the same: Machu Picchu only is 152 soles (US$46), 77 soles (US$23) for university students (see www.machupicchu.gob.pe/items/estudiantes.html for regulations), or 70 soles (US$21) for high school students and children under age 12. To climb Huayna Picchu or Machu Picchu Mountain, visitors of all ages pay an additional 48 soles (US$14.60). When you purchase your ticket for one of the climbs, you must also specify the time you will start. Only 200 people during a time slot are allowed up at Huayna Picchu (access 0700-0800 or 1000-1100) and 400 people during a slot at Machu Picchu Mountain (0700-0800 or 0900-1000). For either climb, it is best to go in the morning and reserve your ticket online in advance at www.machupicchu.gob.pe. You can also pay online (unless you need to show an ISIC card) with Visa or at branches of Banco de la Nación; Centro Cultural de Machu Picchu (Avenida Pachacútec cuadra 1) in Aguas Calientes; Dirección Regional de Cultura in Cuzco (Calle Garcilaso s/n, Monday-Saturday, 0700-1930); offices of PeruRail and Inca Rail in Cuzco, and Hotel Monasterio in Cuzco. Other websites offer tickets for sale at inflated prices. The only place to buy tickets without a previous online reservation is at Dirección Regional de Cultura (see above). Do not buy tickets on the street in Cuzco, they are fake.

## On arrival

The site is open from 0600 to 1730 (also see Tickets, above). Visitors must present their passports, showing details identical to those on their entry tickets. Officially, 5600 visitors are allowed entry each day, but there may be more in high season, April through August. It is best to arrive early, although it is not possible to walk up to the ruins before the first buses arrive. You can deposit your luggage at the entrance for a small fee. Guides are available at the site, US$80 for one to 10 people. Site wardens are also informative.

## Regulations

New rules were implemented in 2017 in an attempt to mitigate overcrowding at the site. They require that all visitors be accompanied by a guide, that they follow one of three established routes without turning back, and that they limit stops at certain places to three to five minutes.

## Advice and precautions

Take your own food, if you don't want to eat at the Sanctuary Lodge self-service restaurant, and take plenty of drinking water. Note that food is not officially allowed into the site and drink can only be carried in canteens/water bottles, not disposable containers. Toilets are only at the entrance. Take insect repellent and wear long sleeves and long trousers. Also take protection against the sun and rain.

# ◉ Machu Picchu

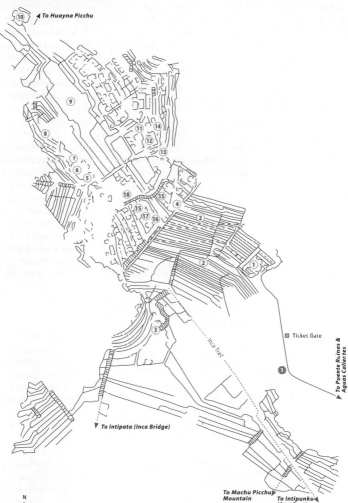

To Huayna Picchu

To Puente Ruinas & Aguas Calientes

Ticket Gate

Inca Trail

To Intipata (Inca Bridge)

To Machu Picchu Mountain

To Intipunku (Sun Gate)

N

50 metres

50 yards

1 Main entrance
2 Terracing 2
3 Watchman's Hut 3

4 Dry moat
5 Temple of the Three Windows
6 Principal Temple
7 Sacristy
8 Intihuatana
9 Main Plaza
10 Sacred Rock

11 Living quarters & workshops
12 Mortar buildings
13 Prison Group & Condor Temple
14 Intimachay
15 Ceremonial baths or Fountains

16 Principal Bath
17 Temple of the Sun
18 Royal Sector

**Where to stay**

1 Machu Picchu Sanctuary Lodge

## Main site

The **main entrance** to the ruins is set at the eastern end of the extensive **terracing** that must have supplied the crops for the city. Above this point to the south is the final stretch of the Inca Trail leading down from **Intipunku** (Sun Gate). From the **Watchman's Hut** you get the perfect view of the city (the one you've seen on all the postcards), laid out before you with Huayna Picchu rising above the furthest extremity. The main path into the ruins comes to a **dry moat**; from here a long staircase goes to the upper reaches of the city, past quarries on the left and roofless buildings on the right which show the construction methods used. Above the main plazas are the **Temple of the Three Windows**, the **Principal Temple** and the **Sacristy**. These buildings were clearly of great importance, given the fine stonework involved. Beyond the Sacristy is the **Intihuatana** or 'hitching-post of the sun', one of the highlights of Machu Picchu. Carved rocks (*gnomons*) such as this are found at all major Inca sites and were the point to which the sun was symbolically 'tied' at the winter solstice, before being freed to rise again on its annual ascent towards the summer solstice. Below the Intihuatana is the **Main Plaza** and, at its northern end a small plaza fronted by the **Sacred Rock**. The outline of this gigantic, flat stone echoes that of the mountains behind it. Southeast of the Main Plaza to the left are several groups of closely packed buildings that were probably **living quarters** and workshops; also in this area are the **Condor Temple** and a cave called **Intimachay**. A short distance to the south is a series of **ceremonial baths**, probably used for ritual bathing. The uppermost, **Principal Bath**, is the most elaborate. Next to it is the **Temple of the Sun**, or Torreón, which was almost certainly used for astronomical purposes. Underneath the Torreón is the **Royal Mausoleum**, which combines a natural cave-like opening with fine masonry. Ascend the stairs south of the Mausoleum to come across a finely constructed two-storey building known as the **Palace of the Princess**; this is likely where priests prepared for ceremonies in the Torreón. North across the stairway from the Torreón is the group of buildings known as the **Royal Sector**.

## Around Machu Picchu

**Huayna Picchu** ① *Access to the main path daily 0700-0800 and 1000-1100; max 200 people per departure. Tickets US$60 (includes entry to Machu Picchu). Check on www.machupicchu. gob.pe or with the Ministerio de Cultura in Aguas Calientes or Cuzco for current departure times and to sign up for a place.* The mountain overlooking the site (on which there are also ruins) has steps to the top for a superlative view of the whole site, but it is not for those who are afraid of heights, and you shouldn't leave the path. The climb takes up to 90 minutes but the steps are dangerous after bad weather. Another trail to Huayna Picchu is via the **Temple of the Moon**, which consists of two caves, one above the other, with superb Inca niches inside. To reach the Temple of the Moon, take the marked trail to the left of the path to Huayna Picchu. It is in good shape, although it descends further than you think it should and there are very steep steps on the way. After the Temple it is safest to return to the main trail to Huayna Picchu, instead of taking a difficult shortcut. The round trip takes about four hours. Before doing any trekking around Machu Picchu, check with an official which paths may be used, or which are one-way.

**Machu Picchu Mountain** ① *2 daily departures, 0700-0800 and 0900-1000, maximum 400 people per departure but they are seldom fully booked. Tickets US$60 (includes entry to Machu Picchu). Check on www.machupicchu.gob.pe or with the Ministerio de Cultura in Aguas Calientes or Cuzco for current departure times and to sign up for a place.* Climbing this mountain is another excellent option and is generally less crowded than Huayna Picchu. It gives a completely different view of the site and surrounding valleys. The route is steep and takes up to three hours.

**Other sights and trails** The famous **Inca bridge** is about 45 minutes along a well-marked trail south of the Royal Sector. The bridge (on which you cannot walk) is spectacularly sited, carved into a vertiginous cliff-face. East of the Royal Sector is the path leading up to **Intipunku** on the Inca Trail (60 minutes, fine views; see page 350).

## Aguas Calientes

The terminus of the tourist rail service to Machu Picchu, Aguas Calientes (official name Machu Picchu Pueblo) has grown from a handful of tin shacks along the railway in the 1980s, into an international resort village with countless multi-storey luxury hotels, restaurants advertising four-for-one happy hours, persistent massage touts and numerous services for the over one million tourists who visit every year. Although it is not to every traveller's taste, it may be worth spending the night here in order to visit the ruins early in the morning. Avenida Pachacútec leads from the plaza to the **thermal baths** ① *at the upper end of town, daily 0500-2000, US$3.50,* which have a communal pool smelling of sulphur that's best early in the morning. There are showers for washing *before* entering the baths; take soap and shampoo, and keep an eye on valuables. The **Museo Manuel Chávez Ballón y Jardín Botánico** ① *near the bridge to Machu Picchu, 25-min walk from town, daily 0900-1600, US$6,* displays objects found at Machu Picchu and local plants. There is also a **Butterfly House** ① *access from Camping Municipal, US$3.50.*

---

**Listings** Machu Picchu *maps pages 341 and 344.*

---

## Tourist information

### iPerú
*Av Pachacútec, by the plaza, Aguas Calientes, T084-211104, iperumachupicchu@promperu. gob.pe. Provides tourist information Mon-Sat 0900-1300, 1400-1800, Sun 0900-1300.*

## Where to stay

**$$$$ Machu Picchu Sanctuary Lodge**
*Reservations as for the Hotel Monasterio in Cuzco, which is under the same management (Belmond), T084-211038, www.belmond.com.*
Comfortable, good service, helpful staff, food well-cooked and presented. Electricity and water 24 hrs a day, prices are all-inclusive, restaurant for residents only in the evening, but the buffet lunch is open to all. Usually fully booked well in advance, but try Sun night when other tourists find Pisac market a greater attraction.

## Aguas Calientes

**$$$$ Casa Andina**
*Av Imperio de los Incas F-34, T084-582950, www.casa-andina.com.*
Luxury chain hotel, rooms with heating and safety boxes, restaurant serving *Novo Andino* cuisine.

**$$$$ Casa del Sol**
*Av Imperio de los Incas 608, on the railroad, T951-298695, www.casadelsolhotels.com.*
5-storey hotel with lift/elevator, different room categories with river or mountain views, nice restaurant, beautiful spa. Shower service and changing room available after check out.

**$$$$ Inkaterra Machu Picchu Pueblo**
*Km 104, 5 mins' walk along the railway from town, T084-211122. Reservations T01-610 0400 in Lima, or Inkaterra La Casona in Cuzco, T084-234010, www.inkaterra.com.*

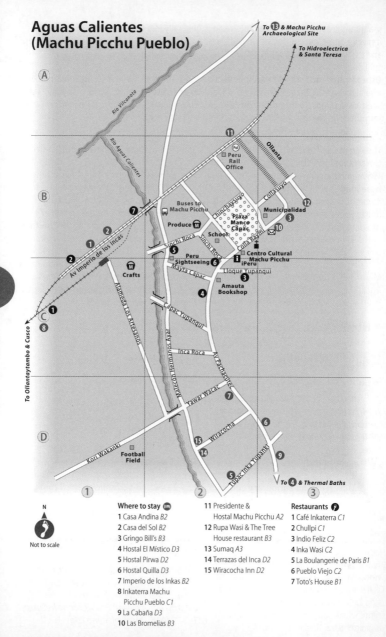

# Aguas Calientes
## (Machu Picchu Pueblo)

To 13 & Machu Picchu Archaeological Site

To Hidroelectrica & Santa Teresa

Río Vilcanota

Río Aguas Calientes

Ollanta

Peru Rail Office

Buses to Machu Picchu

Chinchaysuyo

Collasuyo

Municipalidad

Produce

Plaza Manco Cápac

School

Colla Raymi

Sinchi Roca

Vinchi Roca

Peru Sightseeing

Centro Cultural Machu Picchu

iPeru

Crafts

Mayta Cápac

Lloque Yupanqui

Av Imperio de los Incas

Amauta Bookshop

Capac Yupanqui

Inca Roca

Av Pachacutec

Alameda los Artesanos

Malecón Hernando Ayar

Tawar Wacac

Wiracocha

Korí Wakanki

Football Field

Tupac Inka Yupanki

To Ollantaytambo & Cusco

To 4 & Thermal Baths

N
Not to scale

**Where to stay**
1 Casa Andina B2
2 Casa del Sol B2
3 Gringo Bill's B3
4 Hostal El Místico D3
5 Hostal Pirwa D2
6 Hostal Quilla D3
7 Imperio de los Inkas B2
8 Inkaterra Machu Picchu Pueblo C1
9 La Cabaña D3
10 Las Bromelias B3
11 Presidente & Hostal Machu Picchu A2
12 Rupa Wasi & The Tree House restaurant B3
13 Sumaq A3
14 Terrazas del Inca D2
15 Wiracocha Inn D2

**Restaurants**
1 Café Inkaterra C1
2 Chullpi C1
3 Indio Feliz C2
4 Inka Wasi C2
5 La Boulangerie de Paris B1
6 Pueblo Viejo C2
7 Toto's House B1

Beautiful colonial-style bungalows in village compound surrounded by cloudforest, lovely gardens with a lot of steps between the public areas and rooms, spa, pool, excellent restaurant, offer tours to Machu Picchu, several guided walks on and off the property. Good baggage service to coordinate with train arrivals and departures. Also has the Café Inkaterra by the railway line.

### $$$$ Sumaq Machu Picchu
*Av Hermanos Ayar Mz 1, Lote 3, T084-211059,*
*www.sumaqhotelperu.com.*
Award-winning 5-star hotel on the edge of town, between railway and road to Machu Picchu. Suites and luxury rooms with heating, restaurant, bar, spa.

### $$$ Gringo Bill's
*Colla Raymi 104, T084-211046,*
*www.gringobills.com.*
Pretty rooms, good beds, balconies, train-station pick-up (on foot), lot of coming and going, good restaurant, breakfast from 0500, packed lunch available.

### $$$ La Cabaña
*Av Pachacútec 805, near thermal baths, T084-211048, www.lacabanamachupicchu.com.*
Variety of rooms, café, laundry service, helpful, popular with groups.

### $$$ Presidente
*Av Imperio de los Incas, at the old station, T084-211034, www.hostalpresidente.com.*
Adjoining **Hostal Machu Picchu**, see below, more upmarket but little difference.

### $$$ Wiracocha Inn
*C Wiracocha 206, T084-211088,*
*www.wiracochainn.com.*
Rooms and higher-priced suites, restaurant, helpful, popular with groups.

### $$$-$$ Rupa Wasi
*Huanacaure 105, T084-211101,*
*www.rupawasi.net.*
Charming 'eco-lodge' up a small alley off Collasuyo, laid back, comfortable, great views from the balconies, purified water available, organic garden, good breakfasts, half-board

available, excellent restaurant, **The Tree House**, and cookery classes.

### $$$-$$ Terrazas del Inca
*Wiracocha M-18-4, T084-771529,*
*www.terrazasdelinca.com.*
Includes breakfast, safety deposit box, helpful staff.

### $$ Hostal El Místico
*Av Pachacútec 814, near thermal baths, T084-211051, www.elmisticomachupicchu.com.*
Good breakfast, quiet, new-wave-ish, comfortable.

### $$ Hostal Machu Picchu
*Av Imperio de los Incas 135, T084-211095, hostalmachupicchu.com.*
Functional, quiet, Wilber, the owner's son, has travel information, hot water, nice balcony over the Urubamba, grocery store.

### $$ Hostal Pirwa
*C Túpac Inka Yupanki 103, T084-244315,*
*www.pirwahostelscusco.com.*
In the same group as in Cuzco, Lima and elsewhere.

### $$ Imperio de los Inkas
*Av Pachacútec 602, T084-211105,*
*totemsito@gmail.com.*
Functional, quiet, family-owned *hostal*, group rates, good value.

### $$ Jardines de Mandor
*4 km from Aguas Calientes along the railway to Estación Hidroeléctrica, T940-188155, www.jardinesdemandor.com.*
Relaxed rural lodging with simple rooms and a lovely garden. Camping possible, meals available, a delightful contrast to the buzz of Aguas Calientes.

### $ Hostal Quilla
*Av Pachacútec 705, T084-211009,*
*namdo_28@hotmail.com.*
Adequate functional rooms, small terrace, pizzeria downstairs.

### $ Las Bromelias
*Colla Raymi 102, just off the plaza,*
*T985-935483, on Facebook.*

Rooms with private bath and hot water, some are small, family-run, good value.

## Camping
See **Jardines de Mandor**, above. There is also a campsite (US$6 per tent) in a field by the river, just below the former Puente Ruinas station. It has toilets and cold showers. There's an unpleasant smell from the nearby garbage-processing plant. Do not leave your tent and belongings unattended.

## Restaurants

### Aguas Calientes
The town is packed with eating places which double as bars, many of them are similar-looking pizzerias. Tax is often added as an extra to the bill. Simple economical set meals are served upstairs at the produce market, clean and adequate, daily 0600-1900. See also **The Tree House** restaurant at Rupa Wasi, above.

### $$$ Café Inkaterra
*On the railway, just below the Machu Picchu Pueblo Hotel.*
US$15 for a great lunch buffet with scenic views of the river.

### $$$ Chullpi
*Av Imperio de los Incas 140, T084-211350.*
Traditional Peruvian food with good service.

### $$ Indio Feliz
*C Lloque Yupanqui 103, T084-211090.*
Great French cuisine, excellent value and service, set 3-course meal for US$20, good *pisco sours*, great atmosphere.

### $$ Inka Wasi
*Av Pachacútec 112, T 984-110301.*
Very good choice, has an open fire, full Peruvian and international menu available.

### $$ Pueblo Viejo
*Av Pachacútec 6th block (near plaza), T084-211072.*
Good food in a spacious but warm environment. Price includes use of the salad bar.

### $$ Toto's House
*Av Imperio de los Incas 600, on the railway line across from the craft market, T084-211020.*
Same owners as **Pueblo Viejo**. Good value and quality *menú*, buffet from 1130-1500.

### Cafés

**La Boulangerie de Paris**
*Jr Sinchi Roca by the footbridge.*
*Open 0500-2100.*
Coffee, sandwiches, quiche and great French pastries.

## Transport

### Bus
Buses leave **Aguas Calientes** for Machu Picchu as they fill (long queues) daily 0530-1500, 25 mins, US$24 return, US$12 single, children US$12, valid 48 hrs. The bus stop and ticket office in Aguas Calientes is on Malecón Hermanos Ayar y Av Imperio de los Incas. Tickets can also be bought in advance at **Consettur** in Cuzco (Av Infancia 433, Wanchaq, T084-222125, www.consettur.com), which saves additional queuing when you arrive in Aguas Calientes. Buses return from the ruins to Aguas Calientes daily 0700-1730. The walk up from Aguas Calientes takes 1-2 hrs following a poor path and crossing the motor road (take care). The road is also in poor condition and landslides can cause disruptions.

### Train
2 companies operate services to Machu Picchu, terminating at the station in Aguas Calientes (Av Imperio de los Incas): **PeruRail** (Wanchaq Station, Av Pachacúteq, Cuzco, T084-581414, www.perurail.com) runs trains from Poroy (near Cuzco), from Urubamba

> **Tip...**
> Make sure your train ticket for the return to Cuzco has your name on it (spelt absolutely correctly), otherwise you will have to pay for any changes.

(at 2 hotels: **Río Sagrado** – only for their guests – and **Tambo del Inka** – open to the public), and from Ollantaytambo. **Inca Rail** (Portal de Panes 105, Plaza de Armas, Cuzco, T084-581860, www.incarail.com) runs mostly from Ollantaytambo and 1 daily train from Poroy. Prices and schedules vary depending on the time of year and time of departure. See the following for an overview and consult train company websites for details on a given date. Tickets may be purchased on line, at rail company offices, and as part of tour packages. Book early for high season.

Return tickets are generally more economical than 2 one-way tickets. You require a passport (or copy) to purchase tickets and your original passport to travel to Machu Picchu. High season fares are listed below, they may be slightly cheaper in low season or at different times of day, and all are subject to change. All carriages have a/c and heating, some have panoramic windows. Hot and cold drinks are served in all services, meals only on some trains.

Services may be disrupted in the rainy season, especially Jan-Feb, when trains to some stations may not operate. From Jan through Apr, passengers may be bussed from Cuzco to Urubamba or Ollantaytambo and board trains to Machu Picchu from there. Tourists may not travel on the local trains to Machu Picchu, except from Estación Hidroeléctrica outside Santa Teresa, see page 352.

There are 4 classes of **PeruRail** tourist train: the panoramic **Vistadome** (recommended, US$115-130 one-way from Poroy, US$105 from Urubamba, US$95 from Ollantaytambo); **Expedition**, similar to above but with less visibility and does not include meals (US$70 one-way from Poroy or Ollantaytambo); the upmarket **Sacred Valley** including meals and drinks (US$175 one-way from Urubamba), and the top-of-the-line luxurious **Belmond Hiram Bingham** service with meals, drinks and entertainment (US$525 one way from Poroy). Vistadome and Expedition services are more frequent from Ollantaytambo than from Poroy or Urubamba. For additional **PeruRail** ticket offices, see page 354.

**Inca Rail** offers 3 classes of service: **First Class**, including meals, drinks, entertainment, and private bus from Aguas Calientes to the archaeological site (US$216 one way from Poroy or Ollantaytambo); **360° Class**, uses panoramic carriages and includes meals (US$98-83 one way from Poroy or Ollantaytambo); and **Voyager Class**, including drinks and snacks, a popular economy option (US$79-65 one way from Ollantaytambo). An exclusive private carriage for groups is also available for charter.

## ★ Inca trails

follow in the Incas' footsteps

The most impressive way to reach Machu Picchu is via the centuries-old Inca Trail that winds its way from the Sacred Valley near Ollantaytambo, taking three to five days. What makes this hike so special is the stunning combination of Inca ruins, unforgettable views, magnificent mountains, exotic vegetation and extraordinary ecological variety. The Inca Trail is rugged and steep and you should be in good physical shape. For most hikers, the magnificent views compensate for any weariness, but it is cold at night and weather conditions change rapidly.

### Classic Trail

The trek to Machu Picchu begins for most trekkers at Km 82 on the rail line, **Piscacucho**. In order to reach the trailhead, hikers are transported by their tour operator in a minibus on the road that goes from Ollantaytambo to Quillabamba. At Phiry the road divides; the

# Essential Inca Trail

## Equipment

Take strong footwear, rain gear and warm clothing, extra snacks, water and water-purification supplies, insect repellent, plastic bags, coverings, a good sleeping bag and a torch/flashlight. Equipment is provided by tour agencies, but always check what is included and what must be rented or brought from home. Maps of the trail and area are available from Cuzco bookshops. On most tours, porters will take the heavy gear and you only carry a day-pack.

## Tours

Tour operators taking clients on any of the Inca trails leading to Machu Picchu must be licensed and pass an annual test. **Sernanp** (Avenida Oswaldo Baca C402, Urbanización Magisterio, 1 etapa, T084-229297, www.sernanp.gob.pe) verifies operating permits. Unlicensed

agencies will sell Inca Trail trips, but pass clients on to the operating agency. This can cause confusion and booking problems at busy times. There have been many instances of disappointed trekkers whose bookings did not materialize. Tour operators include transport to the start, equipment and food, as part of the total price for all treks that lead to Machu Picchu. Prices start at about US$600 per person for a four-day/three-night trek on the classic Inca Trail and rise according to the level of service given. If the price is significantly lower, you should be concerned, as the company may be cutting corners. Operators pay US$15 per day for each porter and other trail staff; porters are not permitted to carry more than 20 kg. In principle, groups of up to four independent travellers who do not wish to use a tour operator are allowed to hike the trails if they contract an independent,

**2 Inca Trail**

licensed guide to accompany them, as long as they do not contract any other persons such as porters or cooks. In practice it is hard to find a guide, becuase they are fully occupied working for agencies.

## Tickets

Book your preferred dates as early as possible, several months to a year in advance, depending on the season when you want to go, then confirm nearer the time. Check your operator's cancellation fees before booking. Trail tickets cost US$88.50; university students US$44.60; younger students US$40.90. This is the price for all hiking trails (Km 82 or Km 88 to Machu Picchu, Salkantay to Machu Picchu, and Km 82 or Km 88 to Machu Picchu via Km 104) except for the Camino Real de los Inkas (from Km 104 to Wiñay-Wayna and Machu Picchu), for which the fee is US$67.30,

university students US$34, younger students US$31.80. Tickets can only be purchased by tour operators or guides on behalf of their clients. They are non-refundable and cannot be changed, so make sure you provide accurate passport details to your operator. No tickets are sold at the entrance to any of the routes.

## When to go

July and August is the height of the tourist season but the trail is booked to capacity for most of the year. Check conditions in the rainy season from December to March (note that this can vary from year to year); the weather may be cloudy and the paths are very slippery and difficult in the wet. The trail is closed each February for cleaning and repair.

## Time required

Four days would make a comfortable trip (though much depends on the weather). Allow a further day to see Machu Picchu when you have recovered from the hike. Alternatively, you can take a five-day tour, which reaches Machu Picchu in the afternoon. The first two days of the trail involve the stiffest climbing, so do not attempt it if you're feeling unwell.

## Regulations and precautions

Littering is banned, as is carrying plastic water bottles (canteens only may be carried). Pets and pack animals are prohibited. Groups must use approved campsites only. You cannot take backpacks into Machu Picchu; leave them at the entrance. Leave all your valuables in Cuzco and keep everything inside your tent, even your shoes. Security has, however, improved over the years. Always take sufficient cash to tip porters and guides at the end (S/.50-100 each, but at your discretion).

Map showing: Qorihuayrachina (Km 88, 2600m), To Ollantaytambo, Wayna Q'Ente, Llaqtapata (2288m), To Piscacucho (Km 82) & Chillca, Río Cusichaca, Llulluchapampa, Llulluchayoc (3 White Stones), Huayllabamba (2950m), To Salkantay

left branch follows the north shore of the Río Vilcanota and ends at Km 82, where there is a bridge. Equipment, food, fuel and field personnel reach Km 82 (depending on the tour operator's logistics) for the Sernanp staff to weigh each bundle before the group arrives. Since many groups leave every day, it is convenient to arrive early. An alternative starting point at Km 88, **Qorihuayrachina**, can only be reached by train; it is hardly used.

The walk to **Huayllabamba**, following the Río Cusichaca, needs about three hours and isn't too arduous. Huayllabamba is a popular camping spot for tour groups, but there is another camping place about an hour ahead at **Llulluchayoc** (3200 m). A punishing 1½-hour climb further is **Llulluchapampa**, an ideal meadow for camping. If you have the energy to reach this point, it will make the second day easier because the next stage, the ascent to the first pass, **Warmiwañuska** (Dead Woman's Pass) at 4200 m, is tough; 2½ hours.

Afterwards take the steep path downhill to the **Pacaymayo** ravine. Beware of slipping on the Inca steps after rain. Tour groups usually camp by a stream at the bottom (1½ hours from the first pass). Camping is no longer permitted at **Runkuracay**, on the way up to the second pass. This is a much easier climb to 3900 m, with magnificent views near the summit in clear weather. **Chaquicocha** camp (3600 m) is about 30 minutes past the ruins at **Sayacmarca** (3500 m), about an hour beyond the top of the second pass.

A gentle two-hour climb on a fine stone highway leads through an Inca tunnel to the third pass. Near the top there's a spectacular view of the entire Vilcabamba range, and another campsite. You descend to Inca ruins at **Phuyupatamarca** (3650 m), well worth a long visit.

From there steps go downhill to the magnificent ruins of **Wiñay-Wayna** (2700 m), with impressive views of the cleared terraces of Intipata. There is a campsite here that gets crowded and dirty. After Wiñay-Wayna there is no water and no camping till after Machu Picchu, near Aguas Calientes (see Where to stay, page 343). The path from this point goes more or less level through jungle for two hours before it reaches the steep staircase up to the **Intipunku**, where there's a fine view of Machu Picchu, especially at dawn, with the sun alternately in and out, clouds sometimes obscuring the ruins, sometimes leaving them clear. Groups try to reach Machu Picchu as early as possible to avoid the crowds, but this is usually a futile endeavour and requires a pre-dawn start as well as walking along the edge of the precipice in the dark.

## Camino Real de los Inkas and other options

The **Camino Real de los Inkas** or **Short Inca Trail** starts at Km 104, where a footbridge gives access to the ruins of Chachabamba and the trail, which ascends above the ruins of Choquesuysuy to connect with the main trail at Wiñay-Wayna. This first part is a steady, continuous ascent of three hours (take water). Many people recommend this short Inca Trail. It can be extended into a three-night trek by starting from Km 82, trekking to Km 88, then along the Río Urubamba to Pacaymayo Bajo and Km 104, from where you can join the Camino Real de los Inkas. Alternatively, good day hiking trails from Aguas Calientes run along the banks of the Urubamba.

## Salkantay treks

Two treks involve routes from **Salkantay**: one, known as the **High Inca Trail** joins the classic trail at Huayllabamba, then proceeds as before on the main Trail through Wiñay Wayna to Machu Picchu. To get to Salkantay, you have to start the trek in Mollepata, three hours northwest of Cuzco in the Apurímac Valley. Salkantay to Machu Picchu this way takes three nights and requires an Inca Trail permit and licensed operator.

The second Salkantay route, known as the **Santa Teresa Trek**, takes four days and crosses the 4600-m Salkanatay Pass to reach the Santa Teresa Valley, which you follow to its confluence with the Vilcanota. The goal is the town of Santa Teresa (see page 352). There has long been talk that a trekking permit would also be introduced on this Santa Teresa trek, but no official announcement by the close of this edition.

### Inca Jungle Trail

This route is offered by several tour operators in Cuzco and combines hiking with cycling and other activities. On the first day you cycle downhill from the Abra Málaga Pass on the Ollantaytambo–Quillabamba highway to Alfamayo at 2300 m. This involves three to four hours of riding on the main road with speeding vehicles inattentive to cyclists; it's best to pay for good bikes and back-up on this section. Some agencies also offer white-water rafting in the afternoon or a van ride followed by a hike to Santa María. The second day is a hard 11-km trek from Santa María to Santa Teresa. It involves crossing three adventurous bridges and bathing in the Colcamayo hot springs near Santa Teresa. The third day is a six-hour trek from Santa Teresa to Aguas Calientes along a section of Inca road. Some agencies offer zip-lining near Santa Teresa as an alternative. The final day is a guided tour of Machu Picchu.

# Salkantay treks

## Santa María

A paved road runs from Ollantaytambo to Santa María, sometimes called Puente Chaullay, an important crossroads with basic places to stay and eat. This is a very beautiful journey, with snowy peaks on either side of the valley. The climb to the **Abra Málaga Pass** (4350 m), west of Ollantaytambo, is steep with many tight curves – on the right is a huge glacier. Soon on the left, Nevado Verónica begins to appear in all its huge and snowy majesty. After endless zig-zags and breathtaking views, you reach the pass. The descent to the Vilcanota Valley around Santa María shows hillsides covered in lichen and Spanish moss. From Santa María, roads run to Quillabamba in the lowlands to the north; to Lucma, Pucyura, Huancacalle and Vilcabamba to the west, and to Santa Teresa to the south.

## Huancacalle and around

West of Santa Maria, the tranquil little village of **Huancacalle** is the best base for exploring the last stronghold of the Incas, including the nearby ruins of **Vitcos**, which were the palace of the last four Inca rulers from 1536 to 1572. **Yurac Rumi**, the sacred white rock of the Incas is also here. It is 8 m high and 20 m wide and covered with intricate carvings. The 7-km loop from Huancacalle to Vitcos, the Inca terraces at **Rosaspata**, Yurac Rumi and back to Huancacalle makes a nice half-day hike. Several excellent longer treks begin or end in Huancacalle: from Choquequirao to Vilcabamba Vieja (Espíritu Pampa, see below), and to Machu Picchu via Santa Teresa.

## Towards Vilcabamba Vieja

The road continues west from Huancacalle, 5 km up to the chilly little village of **Vilcabamba**; there's no regular transport but you can hike through the pleasant countryside. There is a mission here run by Italians, with electricity and running water, where you may be able to spend the night; ask for '*La Parroquia*'.

Beyond Vilcabamba the road runs a further 12 km to **Pampaconas**, start of the trail to the **Vilcabamba Vieja** ruins at **Espíritu Pampa**, a vast pre-Inca site with a neo-Inca overlay set in deep jungle at 1000 m. This is where the last Incas held out against the Spanish for nearly 40 years. From Huancacalle a trip to Espíritu Pampa will take three or four days on foot. Give yourself at least a day at the site to soak up the atmosphere before continuing to **Chuhuanquiri** (San Miguel) for transport back to Quillabamba and Cuzco. It is advisable to take local guides and mules, and to enquire in Cuzco and Huancacalle about public safety along the route. Distances are considerable and the going is difficult. The best time of year is May to November. Outside this period it is dangerous as the trails are very narrow and can be thick with mud and very slippery. There are no services along the route; bring all food and supplies including plenty of insect repellent, and take all rubbish with you back to Cuzco for disposal.

## Santa Teresa

South of Santa María, this relaxed little town provides alternative access to Machu Picchu (via Estación Hidroeléctrica; see Transport, below) for those who do not wish to ride the train from Cuzco or Ollantaytambo, and makes a good base for activities in the area. Santa Teresa is located at the confluence of the Ríos Sacsara, Salkantay

**Tip...**

Many Cuzco agencies sell 'Machu Picchu By Car' tours that go through Santa Teresa. You can also reach it by road on your own.

# BACKGROUND

## The last Incas of Vilcabamba

After Pizarro killed Atahualpa in 1532, the Inca empire disintegrated rapidly, and it is often thought that native resistance ended there. But, in fact, it continued for 40 more years, beginning with Manco, a teenage half-brother of Atahualpa.

In 1536, Manco escaped from the Spanish and returned to lead a massive army against them. He besieged Cuzco and Lima simultaneously, and came close to dislodging the Spaniards from Peru. Spanish reinforcements arrived, and Manco fled to Vilcabamba, a mountainous jungle region west of Cuzco that was remote, but still fairly close to the Inca capital, which he always dreamed of recapturing.

The Spanish chased Manco deep into Vilcabamba, but he managed to elude them and continued his guerrilla war, raiding Spanish commerce and keeping alive the Inca flame. Then, in 1544, Spanish outlaws to whom he had given refuge murdered him, ending the most active period of Inca resistance.

The Inca line passed to his sons. The first, a child too young to rule named Sayri Túpac, eventually yielded to Spanish enticements and emerged from Vilcabamba, taking up residence in Yucay near Urubamba in 1558. He died mysteriously    possibly poisoned – three years later.

His brother Titu Cusi, who was still in Vilcabamba, now took up the Inca mantle. Astute and determined, he resumed raiding and fomenting rebellion against the Spanish. But in 1570, Titu Cusi fell ill and died. A Spanish priest was accused of murdering him. Anti-Spanish resentment erupted, and the priest and a Spanish viceregal envoy were killed. Francisco de Toledo, the fifth Viceroy of Peru, reacted immediately, and his troops invaded Vilcabamba for the third and last time in 1572.

A third brother, Túpac Amaru, was now in charge. He lacked his brother's experience and acuity, and his destiny was to be the sacrificial last Inca. The Spanish overran the Inca's jungle capital and dragged him back to Cuzco in chains. There, Túpac Amaru, the last Inca, was publicly executed in Cuzco's main plaza.

The location of the neo-Inca capital of Vilcabamba was forgotten over the centuries, and the search for it provoked Hiram Bingham's expeditions and his discovery of Machu Picchu. Bingham discovered Vilcabama Vieja without realizing it, but the true location at Espíritu Pampa was only pinpointed by Gene Savoy in the 1960s and wasn't confirmed irrefutably until the work of Vincent Lee in the 1980s.

*Sixpac Manco* and *Forgotten Vilcabamba*, both by Vincent Lee (available in Cuzco), have accurate maps of all archaeological sites in the area and describe two expeditions into the region by the author and his party. Gene Savoy's book, *Antisuyo*, is also recommended reading.

and Vilcanota, and its lower elevation at 1600 m creates a warm climate that is a pleasant change from the chill of Cuzco and trekking at high altitude. Many tour groups and independent travellers pass through or spend the night en route to or from Machu Picchu, and several popular treks go through here (see page 347). There are plenty of hotels, restaurants and most services. The **Cocalmayo Thermal Baths** ① *2 km from town along the Río Vilcanota, Wed, Thu, Sat-Mon 0500-2300, Tue and Fri 1600-2300, US$1.75,* have crystal-clear warm pools in a pretty setting and an ice-cold waterfall; free camping nearby (the bugs can be fierce here). There are several zip-lines around town, including Cola de Mono (www.canopyperu.com), which is part of various tour itineraries.

## Listings Vilcabamba

### Tourist information

**Santa Teresa**
There is a tourist information office in the Municipio (Mon-Sat 0800-1700).

### Where to stay and eat

**Huancacalle**
Huancacalle has a few basic shops and eateries, although these are not always open; there's a better selection in Pucyura, 2 km north.

**$ Sixpac Manco**
*Huancacalle, T971-823855.*
A good simple *hostal*, with shared bath, electric shower, large garden, meals on request. It is managed by the Cobos family, who are very knowledgeable about the area and can arrange for guides and pack animals for trekking.

**Santa Teresa**

**$ Casa de Judas**
*Av Calixto Sánchez by the plaza, T974-709058.*
Rooms with private bath and dorm, solar hot water, good value economy option.

**$ Hospedaje El Sol**
*Av Av Calixto Sánchez, T084-637158, hostalelsol@gmail.com.*
Rooms of various sizes, all with private bath and hot water.

**$ Hostal Yacumama**
*C Julio Tomás Rivas, T974-290605.*
Rooms with private bath, hot water, breakfast available, restaurant next door.

### Transport

**Santa María**
To reach Santa María from **Cuzco**, take a Quillabamba-bound van from Av Antonio Lorena by an unnamed street 3 blocks uphill (west) of C Almudena, in the Santiago district, US$9, 4 hrs to Santa María. Cars leave Santa María as they fill throughout the day for **Santa Teresa**, US$3.50, 45 mins. There are also vans from Santa María to **Cuzco** and **Quillabamba** (US$1.75, 1 hr).

**Huancacalle**
Take a van to **Santa María** (see above) and a *colectivo* from there to Huancacalle, US$5.50, 2 hrs; *colectivos* start in Quillabamba, so if they are full, you might have to go to Quillabamba to catch one there. When travelling from Huancacalle to Cuzco you can get off the *colectivo* at Santa María and catch Cuzco-bound transport from there.

**Santa Teresa**
From Santa Teresa market, vans leave for the **Estación Hidroeléctrica** at 0530-0700 and 1200-1430, US$1.75, 30 mins, to meet the local train which runs to **Aguas Calientes**, at 0754, 1500 and 1635; from Aguas Calientes to **Hidroeléctrica** at 0644, 1235 1330; US$31, 40 mins. There is a **PeruRail** office at Santa Teresa market (daily 0500-0720, 1200-1600), but tickets are only sold at the Estación Hidroeléctrica (daily 0500-0720, 1200-1600), which is not much more than a railway siding; tickets are also sold at the Ollantaytambo and Aguas Calientes train stations. You can also walk 11 km along the tracks from Estación Hidroeléctrica to Aguas Calientes, a pleasant 3- to 4-hr hike with great views and many birds, but mind the passing trains.

# Central highlands

Stretching from the southern end of the Cordillera Blanca right up to Cuzco department, this area of stunning mountain scenery and timeless Andean towns and villages is a must for those who appreciate high-quality traditional crafts and off-the-beaten-path travel.

The main highlights include the cities of Huancayo and Ayacucho and the surrounding villages, which are the main production centres for handicrafts. Huancayo is further off the tourist compass but its festivals are very popular. Ayacucho hosts one of the largest and most impressive Holy Week celebrations in Latin America.

If you are seeking refuge from the Andean chill, the road through Tarma to the Selva Central is one of the most impressive in Peru, leading to a relatively unexplored region of the country. More than just fabulous landscapes, this area also hides important pre-Inca sites, such as Kótosh (near Huánuco) and Huari (outside Ayacucho). Stretches of the Capaq Ñan – the Great Inca Road – run from the temple fortress of Huánuco Viejo and up the Yanahuanca Valley, serving as reminders of this imperial causeway. The Spaniards, too, have left their mark, with fine churches and mansions in Ayacucho.

**Best** for
Crafts ■ Festivals ■ Hair-raising journeys ■ Scenery

Lima to Huancayo . . . . . . . . . . 360
Huancayo & the
     Mantaro Valley. . . . . . . . . . . 363
Huancavelica. . . . . . . . . . . . . . 370
Ayacucho & around . . . . . . . . 374
Ayacucho to Cuzco . . . . . . . . . 382
East & north of La Oroya. . . . 385

# Footprint
## picks

★ **Tren Macho**, page 361

Ride the little engine that could, from Huancayo to Huancavelica or vice versa: an exciting, authentic and unpretentious journey.

★ **Mantaro Valley**, page 365

This fertile valley is steeped in the ancient cultures of the Huanca and Inca civilizations.

★ **Ayacucho**, page 374

The city is famous for its Semana Santa celebrations, its splendid market and no fewer than 33 churches.

★ **Huari**, page 377

Visit the first walled urban centre of the Andes, home to the culture that spread across most of Peru from AD 600 to 1000.

★ **Selva Central**, page 385

Between Tarma and La Merced the road drops 2450 m and the vegetation changes dramatically from temperate to tropical.

★ **Huánuco Viejo**, page 388

This was a major Inca city along the Capaq Ñan. It is nicely preserved and receives few visitors.

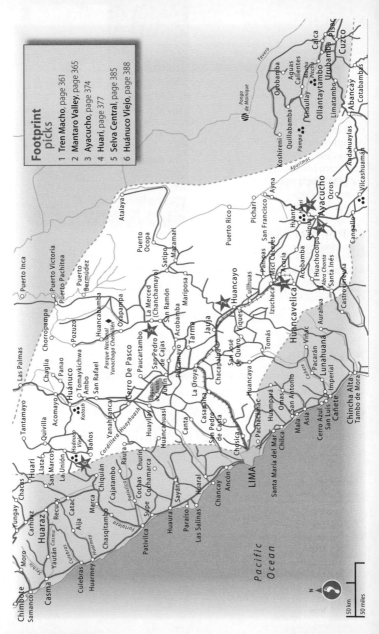

## Footprint picks

1 Tren Macho, page 361
2 Mantaro Valley page 365
3 Ayacucho, page 374
4 Huari, page 377
5 Selva Central, page 385
6 Huánuco Viejo, page 388

Pacific Ocean

50 km
50 miles

N

Chimbote
Samanco
Moro
Casma
Yaután  Casma
Culebras
Culebras
Huarmey  Huarmey
Chasqitambo
Tungay
Carhuaz
Recuay
Huaraz
Aija
Marca
Catac
Pativilca
Las Salinas
Paraíso
Pativilca
Huaral
Sayán
Huaura
Chancay
Ancón
Santa María del Mar
Chilca
Asia
Malá
Oñas
Cañete
Imperial
San Luis
Cerro Azul
Pacarán
Lunahuaná
Tambo de Mora
Chincha Alta
LIMA

Huari
Llatá
Chacas
San Marco
La Unión
Chiquián
Cajatambo
Cochas
Cohhamarca
Churín
Pativilca  Huayhuash
Cordillera Huayhuash
Rauta
Canta
San Pedro de Casta
Chosica
Pachacámac
Huampaní
San Antonio
Yauyos
Aurahua
Castrovirreyna
Yiñac
Huancavelica
Abra Chonta
Santa Inés
Acobamba
Túa
Huachocolpa

Tantamayo
Quivilla
Acomayo
Baños
Huánuco Viejo
Kotesh
Yanahuanca
Huallay
Huancahuasi
Casapalca
Chacapalpa
La Oroya
Jauja
Acobamba
Tarma
San José de Quero
Huancaya
Tomás
San Ramón
La Merced (Chanchamayo)
Mariposa
Satipo
Izcuchaca
Viques
Culhuas
Huancayo
Palmas
Marja  MsC Cáceres
Pampas
Acobamba
Quinua
Huanta
Huari
Huari
Ayacucho
Ocros
Vilcashuamán
Cangallo
Ayacucho
Ayna
San Francisco
Pichari
Puerto Rico
Mazamari
Puerto Ocopa
Oxapampa
Huancabamba
Parque Nacional Yanachaga Chemillén
Pozuzo
Panao
Chaglia
Chorropampa
Las Palmas
Puerto Inca
Puerto Victoria
Puerto Pachitea
Puerto Bermúdez
Atalaya
Koshireni
Quillabamba
Pampa  Machu Picchu
Aguas Calientes
Ollantaytambo
Urubamba
Calca
Pisac
Cuzco
Abancay
Cotabambas
Limatambo
Pisac
Ayahuaylas
Ocros

Huánuco
San Rafael
Ambo
Tomaykichwa
Cerro De Pasco
San Pedro de Cajas
Junín
Palcamayo
Cajas
Paucartambo

Chacra

Yavero
Pongo de Mainique
Apurímac
Mantaro

Huánuco
Huaraz

# **Essential** Central highlands

### Finding your feet

There are several options for getting to the Sierra Central and the views on whichever ascent you choose are beyond compare. The Central Highway and the railway run from Lima to Huancayo (335 km) but there are also paved roads from Pisco to Ayacucho and from Nazca to Abancay. You can also reach the central highlands from Cuzco (via Abancay and Andahuaylas) and from Huaraz (via La Unión and Huánuco), so Lima is not the sole point of access overland. If you prefer to fly, there are flights from Lima to Andahuaylas, Ayacucho, Jauja and Huánuco.

### Getting around

If the infrequent schedules allow, catch the tourist train to Huancayo. You could continue by train to Huancavelica, still in regular service, although the paved road is a quicker. The rest of the region is best explored by bus, by foot, or on a tour. Bear in mind secondary roads in this region tend to be in poor condition, especially in the wet.

### When to go

May to September is the dry season. November to April can be wet and travel can be difficult. Ayacucho's climate is lovely, with warm, sunny days and pleasant balmy evenings.

### Time required

One or two weeks will allow you to see the best of this region, allowing for slow travel on some rough roads.

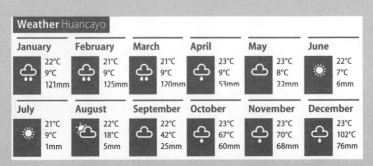

### **Weather** Huancayo

| January | February | March | April | May | June |
|---|---|---|---|---|---|
| 22°C | 21°C | 21°C | 23°C | 23°C | 22°C |
| 9°C | 9°C | 9°C | 9°C | 8°C | 7°C |
| 121mm | 125mm | 120mm | 53mm | 22mm | 6mm |

| July | August | September | October | November | December |
|---|---|---|---|---|---|
| 21°C | 22°C | 22°C | 23°C | 23°C | 23°C |
| 9°C | 18°C | 42°C | 67°C | 70°C | 102°C |
| 1mm | 5mm | 25mm | 60mm | 68mm | 76mm |

The Central Highway more or less parallels the course of the Central Railway between Lima and Huancayo (335 km). With the paving of roads from Pisco to Ayacucho and Nazca to Abancay, there are now more options for getting to the Sierra and the views on whichever ascent you choose are beyond compare. You can also reach the central highlands from Cuzco and Huaraz so Lima is not the sole point of access overland.

## Marcahuasi
*3 hrs' walk from San Pedro de Casta. Entry US$4, pack donkey US$8, horse US$10.*

Up the Santa Eulalia Valley, 40 km beyond **Chosica** (a chaotic town, 45 km east of Lima), is Marcahuasi, a table mountain about 3 km by 1 km at 4000 m, near the village of **San Pedro de Casta**. There are three lakes, a 40-m-high Monumento a la Humanidad and other mysterious lines, gigantic figures, sculptures, astrological signs and megaliths. Their origin is a mystery, although a widely accepted theory is that the formations are the result of wind erosion. The trail to Marcahuasi starts south of the village of San Pedro and climbs southeast. It's three hours' walk to the *meseta*; guides are advisable in misty weather. At shops in San Pedro you can buy everything for the trip, including bottled water. Take all necessary camping equipment for the trek. Tourist information is available at the municipality on the plaza and tours can be arranged with travel agencies in Lima.

## Towards La Oroya
For a while, beyond Chosica, each successive valley looks greener and lusher, with a greater variety of trees and flowers. Between Río Blanco and **Chicla** (Km 127, 3733 m), Inca contour-terraces can be seen quite clearly. After climbing up from **Casapalca** (Km 139, 4154 m), there are glorious views of the highest peaks and of mines at the foot of a deep gorge. The road ascends to the Ticlio Pass, before the descent to **Morococha** and La Oroya. A large metal flag of Peru can be seen at the top of Mount Meiggs; this is not by any means the highest peak in the area, but through it runs the Galera Tunnel, 1175 m long, in which the Central Railway reaches its greatest altitude, 4782 m.

**La Oroya** (3755 m) is the main smelting centre for the region's mining industry. It stands at the fork of the Yauli and Mantaro rivers. Any traveller, but asthmatics in particular, should beware the pollution from the heavy industry, which, combined with the altitude, can cause breathing difficulties. For destinations to the east and north of La Oroya, see page 385.

## Jauja and around
The town of Jauja, founded 1535, 80 km southeast of La Oroya at 3400 m, was Pizarro's provisional capital until the founding of Lima. It has a colourful Wednesday and Sunday market. The **Museo Arqueológico Julio Espejo Núñez** ⓘ *Jr Cusco 537, T064-361163, Mon and Wed 1500-1900, Sun 0900-1200, 1400-1700, donations welcome, knock on door of La Casa del Caminante opposite where the creator and curator lives*, is a quaint but endearing mix of relics from various Peruvian cultures, including two mummies, one still wrapped in the original shroud. The **Cristo Pobre** church is supposedly modelled on Notre Dame and is something of a curiosity. On a hill above Jauja there is a fine line of Inca storehouses, and, on hills nearby, the ruins of Huajlaasmarca, with hundreds of circular stone buildings

## ON THE ROAD

## ★ Railways of the central highlands

Constructed in the late 19th and early 20th centuries, this is one of the highest railways in the world and is a magnificent feat of engineering, with 58 bridges, 69 tunnels and six zigzags, passing beautiful landscapes. It's a great way to travel to the central highlands. The main line runs from Lima, via La Oroya, to Huancayo, and is operated as an irregular tourist service by Ferrocarril Centro Andino (Avenida José Gálvez Barrenechea 566, p 5, San Isidro, Lima, T01-226 6363, www.ferrocarrilcentral. com.pe). The train leaves Lima at 0700, reaching Huancayo around 2000; the return journey begins at 0700, three or four days later. Most departures are on holiday weekends, see the website for the next date. There are *turístico* (US$230 single, US$310 return) and *clásico* fares (US$155 single, US$215 return), sold online and by Lima and Huancayo agencies. Coaches have reclining seats and heating; there's also a restaurant, tourist information, toilets and a nurse with first aid and oxygen.

Beyond Huancayo trains run on a narrow gauge (3 ft) line, 120 km to Huancavelica. This wonderfully authentic Andean train journey remains in regular service and is heavily used by local communities. The leisurely and historic *Tren Macho* and the somewhat faster *Autovagón* navigate 38 tunnels and 15 bridges along their way. There are fine views as the train passes through typical mountain villages where vendors sell food and crafts. In some places, it has to reverse and change tracks. No frills or tourist prices here, just a great ride through the past. For schedules and fares see pages 370 and 373, respectively, and note that they are all subject to change.

from the Huanca culture. There are also ruins near the **Laguna de Paca** ① *3.5 km from Jauja; colectivos from the Terminal, US$0.50*. The western shore is lined with restaurants, many of which offer weekend boat trips, US$1.

On the road south to Huancayo is **Concepción** at 3251 m, with a market on Sunday. From Concepción a branch road (6 km) leads to the **Convent of Santa Rosa de Ocopa** ① *Wed-Mon 0900-1200 and 1500-1800, 45-min tours start on the hour, US$1.25; colectivos from the market in Concepción, 15 mins, US$0.50*, a Franciscan monastery set in beautiful surroundings. It was established in 1725 in order to train missionaries for the jungle. It contains a fine library with over 25,000 volumes, a biological museum and a large collection of paintings.

## Listings Lima to Huancayo

### Tourist information

#### Jauja

**Subgerencia de Turismo**
*At the Municipalidad on the plaza, T064-362075. Mon-Fri 0800-1300, 1400-1700.*
Has pamphlets and general information.

### Where to stay

#### Marcahuasi

Locals in San Pedro de Casta will put you up (**$**); ask at tourist information at the municipality. The best hotel in town is the **$ Marcahuasi**, just off the plaza. Rooms with private or shared bath; it also has a restaurant. There are 2 other restaurants in town.

## Jauja

### $ Hatun Wasi
*Jr Junín 1072, T064-362416.*
Modern multi-storey hotel, good simple rooms, solar hot water after 1100, no breakfast, good value.

### $ Hostal María Nieves
*Jr Gálvez 491, behind school, 1 block from Plaza de Armas, T064-362543.*
Safe, helpful, large breakfast available, hot water on request, small patio, parking. Family-run, older place but well cared for.

## Restaurants

### Towards La Oroya

### $$ El Tambo
*2 km before town on the road from Lima.*
Good trout and frogs legs, local cheese and *manjar*; recommended as the best in and around town; buses on the Lima route stop here.

### Jauja

### $ Quickly's
*Jr Junín 1100. Sun-Fri 1200-2300, Sat 1700-2300.*
*Menú* for lunch, à la carte and sandwiches at night. Clean and friendly.

### $ Yuraq Wasi
*Jr Bolognesi 535. Daily 0900-1600.*
Selection of tasty *menús*, pleasant garden seating, good service, a 'find' for Jauja.

## Transport

Most buses on the Lima–La Oroya route are full when they pass through Chosica.

### Marcahuasi
*Colectivos* for **Chosica** leave from Av Grau, Lima, when full, between 0600 and 2100, US$1. Minibuses to **San Pedro de Casta** leave Chosica from Parque Echenique, opposite market, 0900 and 1500, 4 hrs, US$3.50; return 0700 and 1400.

### Towards La Oroya
To **Lima**, 4½ hrs, US$8. To **Jauja**, 80 km, 1½ hrs, US$2. To **Tarma**, 1½ hrs, US$2.50. To **Cerro de Pasco**, 131 km, 3 hrs, US$3. To **Huánuco**, 236 km, 6 hrs, US$7.50. Buses leave from Zeballos, adjacent to the train station. *Colectivos* also run on all routes.

### Jauja
#### Air
**Francisco Carle** airport is located just outside Jauja. **LC Peru** has 2 daily flights from **Lima**, 45 mins; price includes transfer to Huancayo.

#### Bus
The old train station serves as the bus station. To **Huancayo**, 44 km, 1 hr, US$2.25; combis to Huancayo from 25 de Abril y Ricardo Palma, 1¼ hrs, US$2.50. **Turismo Central** to **Huánuco**, 8 hrs, US$9.50-11. To **Tarma**, US$3, **Turismo Central** has hourly buses from Junín y Tarma, about 10 blocks north of the centre. Also *colectivos* to Tarma from the same corner.

Huancayo is the capital of the Junín region and a major commercial centre for central inland Peru, with a population of over half a million. This busy, over-extended city lies in the Mantaro Valley at 3271 m, surrounded by villages that produce their own original crafts and celebrate festivals all year round. People flock in from far and wide to the important festivals in Huancayo, with an incredible range of food, crafts, dancing and music.

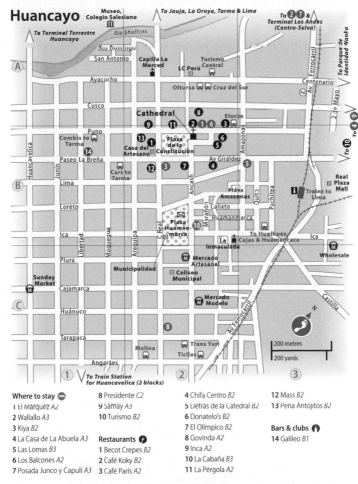

**Where to stay** 🛏
1 El Márquez *A2*
2 Wallallo *A3*
3 Kiya *B2*
4 La Casa de La Abuela *A3*
5 Las Lomas *B3*
6 Los Balcones *A2*
7 Posada Junco y Capulí *A3*
8 Presidente *C2*
9 Samay *A3*
10 Turismo *B2*

**Restaurants** 🍴
1 Becot Crepes *B2*
2 Café Koky *B2*
3 Café París *A2*
4 Chifa Centro *B2*
5 Detrás de la Catedral *B2*
6 Donatelo's *B2*
7 El Olímpico *B2*
8 Govinda *A2*
9 Inca *A2*
10 La Cabaña *B3*
11 La Pérgola *A2*
12 Mass *B2*
13 Peña Antojitos *B2*

**Bars & clubs** 🍸
14 Galileo *B1*

## ON THE ROAD
### Stairway to heaven

High in the central Andes of Peru, along the border between the departments of Lima and Junín, is Pariacaca, a particularly important mountain deity with two splendid summits rising to 5730 m and 5750 m. So great was the importance of this *Apu* (mountain god) that, according to the early 17th-century *Manuscrito de Huarochirí*, all wars were suspended in honour of its annual festival, when faithful from all over the Andean world would flock to visit it.

A great sanctuary on the slopes of Pariacaca was destroyed by the Spaniards in their frenzy to eradicate the old beliefs of the New World; its exact location is today a mystery. The sanctuary of Pariacaca was linked to another of equal importance at Pachacamac on the coast south of Lima by an ancient road – much older than the Inca Empire but greatly enhanced by it. The highest point of the road was crowned with a monumental stairway.

This superb architectural achievement survives to the present day and is located in the **Nor Yauyos Cochas Reserve**, accessed from Jauja, Cañete or Lima. (Some operators in Huancayo offer tours.) The stairway climbs over 300 m, from approximately 4400 to 4700 m above sea level, on 1800 stone steps, each three to four metres wide. Today, it is the focus of efforts to raise awareness of the many wonders still to be found along the *Capaq Ñan* (*Qhapaqñan*), the ancient road network that once linked the four corners of *Tawantinsuyo* – the Inca Empire. The *Capaq Ñan* was declared a UNESCO World Heritage Site in 2014.

## Sights

There is a large neoclassical **cathedral** ① *T064-218051, daily 0800-1200, 1700-1830,* on the always-busy Plaza de Armas/de la Constitución (under renovation since 2016). The weekly Sunday market gives a taste of Huancayo at festival time; it gets going after 0900. Jiron Huancavelica, 3 km long and four stalls wide, sells clothes, fruit, vegetables, hardware, handicrafts and traditional medicines and goods for witchcraft. There is also an impressive daily market behind the railway station and a large handicrafts market on Plaza Huanamarca, between Ancash and Real. For an even wider selection, go to the villages themselves for local handicrafts.

**Yalpana Wasi** ① *Mariscal Castilla 851-853, Chilca district, T064-365318, Mon-Sat 0900-1300, 1500-1800, free admission,* the 'Place of Memory', is a moving modern museum honouring victims of political violence during the Sendero Luminoso campaign (1980-2000). The exhibits and prologue, written by Mario Vargas Llosa, are a "compelling wake-up call to Peruvian society" (Jaime García Heras). The **museum** ① *at the Salesian school, Pje Santa Rosa 229, north of the river in El Tambo, T064-247763, Mon-Fri 0900-1300, 1500-1800, Sat 0900-1200, US$1.50,* has a good collection of ceramics from various cultures, as well as stuffed animals and miscellaneous curiosities. The **Parque de Identidad Wanka** ① *on Jr San Jorge in the Barrio San Carlos northeast of the city, daily 0800-2000, entry free,* is a mixture of surrealistic construction interwoven with native plants and trees and the cultural history of

> **Tip...**
> Huancayo can be a good base to explore the Mantaro Valley while you study Spanish.

the Mantaro Valley. It also has restaurants and craft stalls. On a hillside on the outskirts of town are the impressive, eroded sandstone towers of **Torre-Torre**; take a bus to Cerrito de la Libertad and walk up.

## ★ Mantaro Valley

The whole Mantaro Valley is rich in culture. Near the small town of Huari are the ruins of **Warivilca** ① *5 km from Huancayo, daily 1000-1200, 1500-1700 (museum mornings only), US$1.75, take a micro for Chilca from Av Ferrocaril*, with the remains of a pre-Inca temple of the Huanca tribe. The **Museo de Sitio** on the plaza houses deformed skulls and the modelled, painted pottery of successive Huanca and Inca occupations of the shrine.

East of the Río Mantaro, the villages of **Cochas Chico** and **Cochas Grande** ① *11 km north of Huancayo, micros from the corner of Huancas and Giráldez, US$0.50*, are famous for *mate burilado*, or gourd carving. You can buy samples cheaply direct from manufacturers such as Pedro Veli or Eulogio Medina; ask around. There are beautiful views of the Valle de Mantaro and Huancayo from here.

**Hualahoyo**, near Cochas, has a little chapel with 21 colonial canvases. **San Agustín de Cajas** (8 km north of Huancayo) makes fine hats, and **San Pedro** (10 km) makes wooden chairs. **Hualhuas** (12 km) is known for its fine alpaca weavings which you can watch being made. The weavers take special orders, and small items can be finished in a day; negotiate a price.

The town of **San Jerónimo de Tunan** is renowned for the making of silver filigree jewellery. It has a Wednesday market and a fiesta on the third Saturday in August. There are ruins two to three hours' walk above San Jerónimo, but seek advice before hiking to them.

Situated between Huancayo and Huancavelica, along both the road and railway, **Izcuchaca** is a delightfully tranquil little town (**$ Hotel Santa Eugenia**, Avenida Ferrocarril 245, T09-6491 9910; and other basic hotels, eateries and shops), the site of an impressive colonial bridge over the Río Mantaro. On the edge of town is a fascinating pottery workshop whose machinery is driven by a water turbine. It's a nice hike to the chapel on a hill overlooking the valley (one to 1½ hours each way).

> **Tip...**
> Try the delicious *empanadas de zapallo dulce* (sweet pumpkin pastries) made and sold in Izcuchaca.

## Huancayo to Ayacucho via Huanta

There is a fully paved route to Ayacucho from Huancayo which involves not so much climbing for cyclists. Cross the pass into the Mantaro Valley on the road to **Quichuas**. Then to **Anco** and **Mayocc** (lodging). From here the road crosses a bridge after 10 km and in another 20 km reaches **Huanta** in the picturesque valley of the same name. Huanta celebrates the **Fiesta de las Cruces** during the first week of May. Its Sunday market is huge and interesting. The area is notable as the site of perhaps the oldest known culture in South America, dating from 20,000 years ago. Evidence was found in the cave of **Pikimachay**, 24 km from Ayacucho, off the road from Huanta. The remains are now in Lima's museums.

## Tourist information

The regional office is in Jauja (see page 360).

**Huancayo Municipal Tourist Office**
*Jr Ica esquina Panamá, T064-223623 ext 102, www.munihuancayo.gob.pe. Mon-Fri 0800-1300, 1500-1845.*
Spanish only.

**Indecopi**
*Pje Comercial 474, El Tambo, T01-224 7800 ext 640.*
The consumer protection office.

**Tourist Police**
*Av Ferrocarril 580, T064-219851.*

## Where to stay

The area around many of the upmarket hotels is generally safe but noisy.

### Huancayo

**$$$ El Marquez**
*Puno 294, T064-219202, www. elmarquezhuancayo.com.*
Efficient, popular with local business travellers, attentive service, heaters in rooms, parking.

**$$$ Presidente**
*C Real 1138, T064-235419, http://huancayo. hotelpresidente.com.pe.*
Large, modern, classy hotel, safe, restaurant, helpful staff, convention centre.

**$$$ Turismo**
*Ancash 729, T064-231072, www.turismo. hotelpresidente.com.pe.*
Restored colonial building, same owner as Presidente, with more atmosphere, elegant, rooms quite small, quiet area, buffet breakfast.

**$$-$ Samay**
*Jr Florida 285 (cdra 9 de Giráldez), T064-655937, www.samayperu.com.*

Rooms with private or shared bath, quiet (unless the little football field next door is being used), breakfast, laundry and kitchen facilities, garden, nice terraces on 3rd floor, helpful staff.

**$$-$ Kiya**
*Giráldez 107, T064-214955, www.hotelkiya.com.pe.*
Comfortable although ageing, spectacular view of the plaza, hot water, helpful staff, no breakfast.

**$$-$ Posada Junco y Capulí**
*Julio Tello 414, El Tambo neighbourhood, T064-244368, www.posadajuncoycapuliperu.com.*
Small charming place located about 2 km from Plaza de la Constitución, convenient to shops and services. Simple, comfortable, quiet rooms, includes very good breakfast.

**$ Hostal Wallallo**
*Chavín 283, Urbanización La Alborada, El Tambo, T064-388 015, reservaswallallo@ gmail.com.*
Modern hostel, rooms with private bath, hot water, heaters available, patio, includes breakfast, other meals on request, laundry facilities, airport transfers available, attentive service.

**$ La Casa de la Abuela**
*Prolongación Cusco 794 y Gálvez, T064-223303, www.incasdelperu.org/casa-de-la-abuela.*
Doubles with or without private bath and dorms, quiet area, 10-min walk from centre. Hot shower, breakfast, laundry facilities, meals available, sociable staff, owner speaks English, good meeting place, games room, free pick-up from bus station if requested in advance. Discount for **Footprint** readers.

**$ Las Lomas**
*Giráldez 327, T064-237587, laslomashostal@hotmail.com.*
Small hostel in a central (noisy) location, basic rooms, hot water, good value, can arrange tours, no breakfast.

## $ Los Balcones
*Jr Puno 282, T064-214881, www. losbalconeshuancayo.com.pe.*
Comfortable rooms, restaurant, hot water, helpful staff, elevator (practically disabled-accessible). View of the back of the cathedral.

### Huancayo to Ayacucho via Huanta

### $ Gran Hotel Imperial
*Jr Miguel Untiveros 257, Huanta, T066-322748, granhotelimperial@gmail.com, on Facebook.*
Decent rooms with private bath and hot water, very friendly and helpful, good value. Several places to eat around the corner.

## Restaurants

### Huancayo
Breakfast is served in Mercado Modelo from 0700. Better, more expensive restaurants serve typical dishes for about US$6, drinks can be expensive. Lots of cheap restaurants along Av Giráldez, and a large food court in Real Plaza mall.

### $$$ Detrás de la Catedral
*Ancash 335 (behind cathedral as name suggests), T064-212969. Mon-Sat 0700-2300.*
Old-style elegant atmosphere, excellent regional dishes. Charcoal grill in the corner keeps the place warm on cold nights. Considered by many to be the best in town.

### $$ El Olímpico
*Giráldez 199, T064-588705, www.restauranteolimpico.com. Mon-Sat 0700-2230, Sun 0700-2000.*
Long-established, one of the more upscale establishments offering *comida criolla* and international dishes; the real reason to go is the owner's model car collection displayed in glass cabinets.

### $$ La Cabaña
*Av Giráldez 675, T064-223303. Daily 1700-2330.*
Pizzeria, restaurant and bar, pastas, grill, juices and ice cream, wide variety of dishes, casual atmosphere, home delivery.

### $$ Peña Antojitos
*Puno 591, T064 202244. Daily 0730-0330.*
Attractive, atmospheric pizzeria/bar with live music some nights.

### $$-$ Donatelo's
*Puno 287.*
Good pizza and pasta place, Wi-Fi, popular.

### $ Chifa Centro
*Giráldez 238 and at Av Leandra Torres 240, T064-217575. Daily 1300-2315.*
Large Chinese restaurant, good food, service and atmosphere.

### $ Govinda
*Jr Cusco 289. Mon-Sat 0830-1730.*
Vegetarian restaurant and café, good service, sells natural products. Nice tranquil atmosphere with no blaring TV, good concert videos instead.

### $ La Pérgola
*Puno 444, overlooking the plaza. Daily 0800-2200.*
An oldie with a pleasant atmosphere, tasty 4-course *menú*.

### $ Mass
*Real 549 and on block 10 of Real.*
A clean place for *pollo a la brasa* with fast service.

### Cafés

### Becot Crepes
*Av Real 471.*
A good ice cream parlour.

### Café Koky
*Ancash y Puno, Ancash 235, and Real Plaza Mall. Daily 0700-2300, lunch 1230-1530.*
Good breakfasts, lunches, sandwiches, cappuccino and pastries, fancy, free Wi-Fi.

### Café París
*Puno 254 and Arequipa 265.*
Sofá-café and restaurant, good food and atmosphere, many sweets, *menú* at midday.

### Inca
*Puno 530.*

Popular *fuente de soda*, with coffee, Peruvian food, desserts, milkshakes.

## Bars and clubs

### Huancayo

**Galileo Disco-Pub**
*Paseo La Breña 376.*
Live music Wed through Sat, good atmosphere.

## Festivals

There are so many festivals in the Mantaro Valley that it is impossible to list them all. Nearly every day of the year there is some sort of celebration in one of the villages. See also Festivals, page 18, and Public holidays, page 500.

**1-6 Jan New Year** has many celebrations, including **La Huaconada** dance festival in Mito.
**20 Jan San Sebastián y San Fabián,** recommended in Jauja.
**Feb** There are carnival celebrations for the whole month, with highlights including **Virgen de la Candelaria** and **Concurso Nacional de Huaylash**.
**Mar-Apr Semana Santa**, with impressive Good Fri processions.
**3-8 May Fiesta de los Shapis** in Chupaca.
**May Fiesta de las Cruces** throughout the whole month.
**13 Jun Virgen de las Mercedes**.
**22-30 Jun San Juan Bautista**.
**24-25 Jul Santiago**.
**4-15 Aug San Juan de Dios**.
**16 Aug San Roque**.
**30 Aug Santa Rosa de Lima**.
**8 Sep Virgen de Cocharcas**.
**15-18 Sep Virgen de la Natividad**.
**23-24 Sep Virgen de las Mercedes**.
**4th week of Sep Tourism week**.
**18-30 Oct** Celebrations for **El Señor de los Milagros**.

## Shopping

All crafts are made outside Huancayo in the many villages of the Mantaro Valley, or in Huancavelica. The villages are worth a visit to learn how the items are made.

## What to do

### Huancayo
**Language courses**
**Exclusive English**, *Jr Huancas 626, of 204, T064-636421, admin@exclusivenglishperu.com.* Small-group Spanish and English classes. Hindi lessons also available, as well as yoga and meditation. Friendly dynamic owners Jessica and Dinesh.

### Tour operators
**A & R American Travel** *Plaza Constitución 122, of 2 (next to the cathedral), T064-397281, T964-602647.* Wide range of classical and more adventurous tours in the Mantaro Valley and the central jungle. Transport and equipment rental available, sells flight tickets. Most group-based day tours start at US$8-10 pp.

**Hidden Perú**, *no storefront, T964-164979, andinismo_peru@yahoo.es*. Marco Jurado Ames is a mountain guide who organizes adventure and cultural trips in the Andes and Amazon Basin, for 1-12 days with trekking in the Mantaro Valley, Huaytapallana and Pariacaca ranges; mountain biking, walking and mountaineering in Cuzco and Huaraz.
**Incas del Perú**, *Av Giráldez 675, T064-223303, www.incasdelperu.org*. Jungle, biking and hiking trips throughout the region as well as day trips to the Mantaro Valley. Also arranges flight/train tickets and language and volunteer programmes (Spanish for beginners, US$50 for 5 days or US$185 per week, including accommodation at **Hostal La Casa de La Abuela** and all meals at La Cabaña); also home-stays and weaving, traditional music, Peruvian cooking and lots of other things. Very popular and recommended.
**Peruvian Prime**, *Plaza Constitución 122, p 2, of 1, next to the cathedral, T064-213069*. Tours of the Mantaro Valley, plus day trips up to the Huaytapallana Nevados above Huancayo, plus long, 16-hr excursions to Cerro de Pasco and Tarma.

## Transport

### Huancayo
### Bus
**Terminal Terrestre Huancayo** for buses to most destinations is 3 km north of the centre in the Parque Industrial. **Terminal Los Andes** (also known as **Terminal Centro-Selva**; Av Ferrocarril 151) serves mainly the central highlands and the jungle. Some companies have their own terminal in the centre, including **Turismo Central** (Jr Ayacucho 274, T064-583716). Most buses to the Mantaro Valley leave from several places around the market area, and from Av Ferrocarril. Buses to **Huallhuas** and **CaJas** leave from block 3 of Pachitea. Buses to **Cochas** leave from Amazonas y Giráldez.

There are regular buses to **Lima**, 6-7 hrs on a good paved road, US$13-25 with **Oltursa**. Other recommended companies with frequent service include **Turismo Central**, **Mega Bus** (Av Mariscal Castilla 1520) and **Cruz del Sur** (Terminal Los Andes). Travelling by day is recommended for the fantastic views and for safety, although most major companies go by night (take warm clothing).

To **Ayacucho**, 319 km, 9-10 hrs, US$13 with **Molina** (C Angaráes 334, T064-224501), 3 a day, recommended; 1 a day with **Turismo Central** (via Huanta) US$10-22; also **Ticllas** and **Etucsa** from Terminal Terrestre, US$5-10. There are 2 routes: one via Huanta, mostly paved; and the other via Huancavelica, partly paved with the remainder in poor condition, very difficult in the wet. Take warm clothing.

To **Huancavelica**, 147 km, 3 hrs, US$5. Many buses daily, including **Transportes Yuri** (Ancash 839, Centro Comercial of 204), 3 a day. The road is paved and offers a delightful ride, much more comfortable than the train (if you can find a driver who will not scare you to death). Shared taxis from Av Real cuadra 12, US$8 (US$10 at weekends), negotiable.

To **Cerro de Pasco**, 255 km, 5 hrs, US$7.50. Several departures. Alternatively, take a bus to La Oroya, about every 20 mins from Terminal Los Andes, or a shared taxi, US$5, 2 hrs. From La Oroya there are regular buses and *colectivos* to Cerro, US$8. The road to La Oroya and on to Cerro is paved and in good condition. To **Huánuco**, 7 hrs, **Turismo Central**, twice daily, US$20, good service.

To **Tarma**, **Lobato** and **America** from Terminal Los Andes, 5 hrs, US$10; some continue to **La Merced**. Also **Turismo Central** to La Merced, US$19. Minibuses and cars from outside the terminal, to Tarma US$6, to La Merced US$12, 3 hrs.

To **Yauyos**, cars at 0500 from Plaza de los Sombreros, El Tambo, US$7.50. It is a poor road with beautiful mountain landscapes before dropping to the valley of Cañete; cars go very fast.

To **Jauja**, 44 km, 1 hr. *Colectivos* and combis leave every few mins from Terminal Los Andes, US$2.50. Taxi to Jauja US$15, 45 mins.

To **Tingo María** and **Pucallpa**, daily with Turismo Central, US$27.

### Train
For the Ferrocarril Centro Andino and general background, see Railways of the central highlands, page 361. The station for **Huancavelica** is in the suburb of Chilca (15 mins by taxi from the centre, US$2). *Autovagón*, US$4, 3 hrs (to **Izcuchaca**, US$3, 1½ hrs), Tue, Thu, Sat 0630, plus Fri 1200 and Sun 1800; *Tren Macho*, US$2.75-4, 5 hrs, Mon, Wed, Fri at 0630. Be at the station at least 30 mins before departure.

## Huancavelica  *Colour map 3, C5.*

**an authentic colonial mountain town**

Huancavelica is a tranquil, friendly and attractive town of 50,000 inhabitants at 3676 m, surrounded by huge, rocky mountains. It was founded in the 16th century by the Spanish to exploit rich deposits of mercury and silver, but it remains predominantly an indigenous town. There are beautiful mountain walks in the surrounding area.

# Huancavelica

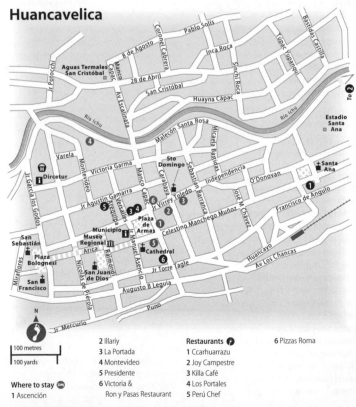

| 100 metres | |
|---|---|
| 100 yards | |

**Where to stay** 🛏
1 Ascención

2 Illariy
3 La Portada
4 Montevideo
5 Presidente
6 Victoria &
  Ron y Pasas Restaurant

**Restaurants** 🍴
1 Ccarhuarrazu
2 Joy Campestre
3 Killa Café
4 Los Portales
5 Perú Chef

6 Pizzas Roma

## Sights

On the Plaza de Armas, the **Catedral de San Antonio**, built in 1673, has an altar considered to be one of the finest examples of colonial art in Peru. Also very impressive are the five other churches in town, including **Santo Domingo** built in 1601 (Toledo y Carabaya), **San Francisco** (Plaza Bolognesi) built in 1774, with no less than 11 altars, and **San Sebastián** (Plaza Bolognesi). Unfortunately, most are closed to visitors outside early-morning mass. The **Ministerio de Cultura** ① *Plazoleta San Juan de Dios, Arica y Raimondi, T01-618 9393 ext 7022*, is a good source of information on festivals, archaeological sites, history, etc. It also runs courses and lectures on music and dancing, and has a small but interesting **Museo Regional** ① *US$0.60, Mon-Fri 0830-1300, 1430-1700*, with exhibits of archaeology, anthropology and popular art.

Bisecting the town is the Río Ichu. South of the river is the main commercial centre. On the hillside north of the river are the **San Cristóbal thermal baths** ① *Av Escalinata y 28 de Abril, daily 0600-1700, US$0.50 for private rooms, water not very hot (26º C), US$0.30 for the hot public pool, also hot showers, take a lock for the doors*. The pedestrian walkway up to the baths on Av Escalinata is full of figures illustrating the village festivals of the region and their typical characters. There are also thermal baths in Secsachaca, 1 km from town. The Potaqchiz hill, just outside the town, gives a fine view; it's about one hour walk up from San Cristóbal.

Excursions from Huancavelica include the abandoned **Santa Bárbara mine** and nearby village of **Sacsamarca**, 4 km southwest the city and accessible by vehicle or on foot, a demanding day-hike. The small town of **Yauli**, 14 km east of Huancavelica, has an interesting Saturday market (*colectivos* from Terminal Pampa Amarilla, Avenida Huancavelica y Sebastián Barranca, leave as they fill, US$1.50).

## Huancavelica to Ayacucho

There are three options for this journey, all spectacular. For details of bus and train service, see Transport, page 373.

The fully paved route (247 km via **Santa Inés**) is high, rarely dropping below 4000 m for 150 km, with great views and many lakes along the way. Out of Huancavelica the road climbs steeply south with switchbacks between herds of llamas and alpacas grazing on rocky perches. Around Pucapampa (Km 43) is a plateau at 4500 m, where the rare ash-grey alpaca can be seen. Snow-covered mountains are passed as the road climbs to 4853 m at the Abra Chonta Pass, 23 km before Santa Inés. By taking the turn-off to Huachocolpa at Abra Chonta and continuing for 3 km you'll reach one of the highest drivable passes in the world, at 5059 m. Near Santa Inés are two large lakes (Lagunas Orcococha and Choclococha) which can be visited in about 2½ hours. The Abra de Apacheta (4750 m) is 52 km beyond Santa Inés, on the main Pisco–Ayacucho road. The rocks here are all the colours of the rainbow, and running through this fabulous scenery is a violet river. You can combine a tour to Santa Inés with the trip to Ayacucho (eg with **Paccari Tours**, see page 373).

A second route to Ayacucho runs 55 km north from Huancavelica to **Izcuchaca** (see page 365), in the Mantaro Valley. From Izcuchaca, an unpaved road, narrow and dangerous, follows the Río Mantaro west (downstream) for 110 km before leaving the canyon to head south to Huanta and Ayacucho.

Another adventurous route to Ayacucho is via **Lircay** (simple, unnamed *hostal* at Sucre y La Unión, with bath and hot water) and **Julcamarca** (with a colonial church and the very basic **Hostal Villa Julcamarca**, near the plaza), along dirt roads with beautiful scenery all the way.

## Tourist information

**Dircetur**
*Pje Miraflores 280, p4, T067-452938,*
*www.dirceturhuancavelica.gob.pe.*
*Mon-Fri 0800-1300, 1430-1730.*
Good maps and leaflets, very helpful.

**Municipal Tourist Office**
*Plaza de Armas, www.turismohuanca*
*velica.com. Daily 0700-1300, 1400-2200.*
Also houses the **Policía de Turismo**.
Can arrange for local guides.

## Where to stay

**$$$ Presidente**
*Plaza de Armas, T067-452760,*
*www.hotelpresidente.com.pe.*
Lovely colonial building, higher-priced suites
available, ample common areas, heating,
parking, safe, laundry, buffet breakfast, very
good restaurant (small and old-fashioned)
and café.

**$$ Illariy**
*Jr Carabaya 344, T067-369028,*
*illariyhotel@hotmail.com.*
Convenient near Plaza de Armas, clean
and quiet, good rooms, excellent buffet
breakfast, helpful.

**$$ Victoria**
*Virrey Toledo esquina Manco Capac,*
*by the plaza, T067-555123,*
*hotelvictoriahvca@gmail.com.*
New section with ample comfortable rooms
and common areas. Upstairs rooms are
bright, older ones are basic.

**$ Ascención**
*Jr Manco Capac 481 (Plaza de Armas),*
*T067-453103.*
Very comfortable, wooden floors, with
or without bath, hot water, good value,
no breakfast.

**$ La Portada**
*Virrey Toledo 252, T067-451050.*
Large rooms with private bath or small, basic
rooms upstairs with shared bath. Lots of
blankets, unlimited coca tea, friendly helpful
staff, good value.

**$ Montevideo**
*Av Malecón Santa Rosa 168, T967-980638.*
Clean basic rooms. 4th floor terrace has great
views of the river and *malecón*.

## Restaurants

**$$-$ Pizzas Roma**
*Manco Capac 568, T067-452608.*
*Open 1800-2300.*
Smells delicious, friendly staff,
delivery available.

**$$-$ Ron y Pasas**
*Virrey Toledo y Manco Capac, near the plaza.*
*Mon-Fri 0700-2300, Sun 1800-2300.*
Breakfast, good *menú ejecutivo* at midday
(go early), à la carte at night. Attentive service,
upmarket for Huancavelica. Recommended.

**$ Ccarhuarrazu**
*Av Celestino Manchego Muñoz 492.*
Big bright *pollería* downstairs (daily
1200-2400), good value *menú* served
on 3rd floor (daily 0700-1600), both
are tasty and very popular.

**$ Joy Campestre**
*Av de los Incas 870.*
*Comida criolla* and regional dishes served in a
leisurely country environment.

**$ Perú Chef**
*Agustín Gamarra esquina Arequipa.*
*Mon-Sat 0800-1500.*
Part of a cooking school, offers varied *menú*
with Peruvian dishes.

## Cafés

### Killa Café
*Virrey Toledo, on Plaza de Armas opposite the cathedral. Mon-Sat 0800-1200, 1600-2200.*
Good coffee, sandwiches and drinks, free Wi-Fi, nice and cosy.

### Los Portales
*Virrey Toledo 158, on Plaza de Armas. Mon-Sat 0700-2200, Sun 0700-1300.*
Nice cafeteria in a colonial building with courtyard. Good breakfast, sandwiches and coffee, giant fruit extracts (try the apple extract).

## Festivals

**4-8 Jan  Fiesta de los Reyes Magos y los Pastores**.
**2nd Sun in Jan  Fiesta del Niño Perdido**.
**20 Jan-mid Mar  Patun Pukllay Carnavales**, celebration of the 1st fruits from the ground (harvest).
**Mar/Apr  Semana Santa** (Holy Week).
**End May-Jun  Toro Pukllay** festival.
**May and Aug  Fiesta de Santiago** in all communities.
**22-28 Dec  Los Laijas** or **Galas** (scissors dance). This event is on UNESCO's World Heritage list.

## Shopping

Huancavelica is a major craft centre, with a wide variety of goods produced in surrounding villages. Handicraft sellers congregate on the 4th block of Victoria Garma and under Plaza Santa Ana (*sótano*). Most handicrafts are transported directly to Lima, but you can still visit craftsmen in neighbouring villages.

## What to do

**Cielo Azul**, *Jr Manuel Ascencio Segura 140, on the plaza (former municipal tourism office), T967-718802.* City tours and many others, US$10-30 pp for a group of 6.

**Paccari Tours**, *Av Ernesto Morales 637, T978-978828, www.paccaritours.com.* Offers city tours (also by bike), visits to Uchkus Inkañan archaeological site, boating on one of the lakes, alpaca herding on the Puna, and historic mine tours. Owner Daniel Páucar is very helpful.
**Willka Tours**, *Jr Carabaya 199, T967-758007, www.willkatours.com.* Variety of local tours.

## Transport

### Bus
There is a Terrapuerto bus terminal in Ascensión, next to the Esalud Hospital II in the west end of town. Many bus companies also have offices on, and leave from the east end of town, around Parque M Castilla (Santa Ana), between Manchego and O'Donovan.

To **Huancayo**, 147 km, 5 hrs, US$4, paved road, hourly with **Ticllas** (Av de los Incas 195, T067-452787). Also shared taxis all day from Av Machego Muñoz y González Prada and from the Terrapuerto, US$8 Mon-Thu, US$10 Fri-Sun, 3½ hrs. Most buses to Huancayo go on to **Lima**, 445 km, 10-12 hrs US$12, including **Molina** (Manchego 608, T067-481236) daily at 2000. Another route to Lima is via **Pisco**, 269 km, 6 hrs, US$9. To **Ica**, US$12, 7-8 hrs, 1900 daily with **Oropesa** (Manchego 948, 067-368427). Buy your ticket a day in advance. The road is poor until it joins the Ayacucho—Pisco road, beyond which it is paved. Most of the journey is done at night; be prepared for sub-zero temperatures in the early morning as the bus passes snowfields, then temperatures of 25-30°C as you descend to the coast. Shared taxis to Pisco (US$11, 5 hrs) and Ica (US$14, 6 hrs) leave when full from Av Manchego Muñoz by Plaza Santa Ana.

### Train
Station at Av Ferrocarril s/n, T067-452898, Mon-Fri 0530-1400, Sat 0530-0900. From Huancavelica to **Huancayo**, *Autovagón*, US$4, 3 hrs (to **Izcuchaca**, US$3, 1½ hrs), Mon, Wed, Fri at 0630, plus Fri at 1800;

*Tren Macho*, US$2.75-4, 5 hrs, Tue, Thu, Sat at 0630. Be at the station at least 30 mins before departure. See also Railways of the central highlands box, page 361.

## Huancavelica to Ayacucho

Along the paved road, the only direct transport from Huancavelica to Ayacucho is with **Molina**; it passes through from Huancayo daily around midnight (see their address above, office open 0700-2030, buy ticket in advance), US$10, 6 hrs. Otherwise go to **Rumichaca**, a crossroads with only a couple of foodstalls and filthy toilets, on the Pisco–Ayacucho road; **San Juan Bautista**, 0430, 4 hrs, then take a minibus to Ayacucho, 3 hrs.

To **Izcuchaca**, **Ticllas** hourly, US$2.20, 2 hrs, continuing to Huancayo; or ride the *Tren Macho* (see above). For Ayacucho, **Señor de Ataco** passes through Izcuchaca twice daily, US$4.60, 5 hrs on a narrow, dangerous road with heavy lorry traffic.

The 3rd option is to take a taxi or *colectivo* from Huancavelica with **Transportes 5 de Mayo** (Av Sebastián Barranca y Cercado) to the small village of **Lircay,** US$7.55, 2½ hrs. **Transportes 5 de Mayo** continues from Lircay hourly (starting 0430) to **Julcamarca**, 2½ hrs, US$6. From Julcamarca plaza, take a minibus to Ayacucho, US$4, 2 hrs.

---

## ★ Ayacucho and around   *Colour map 5, A4.*

**indigenous handicrafts and colonial churches**

The city of Ayacucho (population 200,000), the capital of its department, is famous for its hugely impressive Semana Santa celebrations, its splendid market and, not least, its plethora of churches – 33 of them no less – giving the city its alternative name La Ciudad de las Iglesias. A week can easily be spent enjoying Ayacucho and its hinterland. The climate is lovely, with warm, sunny days and pleasant balmy evenings. It is a hospitable, tranquil place, where the inhabitants are eager to promote tourism. It also boasts a large, active student population. Ayacucho is a large city but the interesting churches and colonial houses are all fairly close to the Plaza Mayor. Barrio Santa Ana, home to many artisans' studios, is further away to the south; you can take a taxi or walk.

The decisive Battle of Ayacucho was fought on the Pampa de Quinua (see page 378), on 9 December 1824, bringing Spanish rule in Peru to an end. In the middle of the festivities, the Liberator Simón Bolívar decreed that the city be named Ayacucho, 'Place of the Souls', instead of its original name, Huamanga.

### Sights

**Plaza Mayor** The city is built round the Plaza Mayor, with the cathedral, Municipalidad, Universidad Nacional de San Cristóbal de Huamanga (UNSCH) and various colonial mansions facing on to it. The **cathedral** ① *open for Mass Mon-Sat 1830, Sun 1000 and 1830, 45-min guided tours Mon-Sat 0900-1200, 1600-1800, US$3,* built in 1612, has superb gold-leaf altars. It is beautifully lit at night. On the north side of the Plaza Mayor, at Portal de la Unión 37, is the **Casona de los Marqueses de Mozobamba del Pozo**, also called Velarde-Alvarez. Restored as the **Centro Cultural de la UNSCH**, it hosts frequent artistic and cultural exhibitions; see the monthly Agenda Cultural. Jirón Asamblea is pedestrianized for its first two blocks north of the plaza; on a parallel street is **Santo Domingo** (1548) ① *9 de Diciembre, block 2, Mass daily 0630-0730, visits 0900-1200 with advance booking.* Its fine façade has triple Roman arches and Byzantine towers.

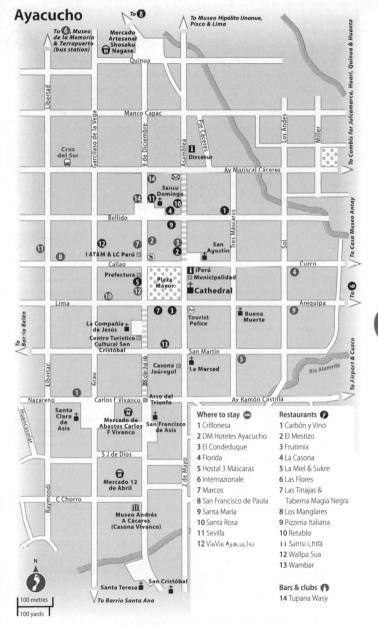

# Ayacucho

To 8

To 6, Museo de la Memoria & Terrapuerto (bus station)

To Museo Hipólito Unanue, Pisco & Lima

To Combis for Julcamarca, Huari, Quinua & Huanta

Mercado Artesanal Shosaku Nagase

Quinua

Libertad

Garcilaso de la Vega

9 de Diciembre

Manco Capac

Pje Cáceres

Asamblea

Los Andes

Miller

Directur

Cruz del Sur

Av Mariscal Cáceres

To Casa Museo Antay

14

Santo Domingo

14

11

4

10

1

Tres Máscaras

Sol

Bellido

9

San Agustín

11

12

7

2

LATAM & LC Perú

8

2

3

Cuzco

Callao

Prefectura

5

Plaza Mayor

iPerú

Municipalidad

4

To 6

10

12

Cathedral

Arequipa

Lima

7

3

Tourist Police

Buena Muerte

9

La Compañía de Jesús

Centro Turístico Cultural San Cristóbal

13

San Martín

To Airport & Cuzco

To Barrio Belén

Libertad

Grau

28 de Julio

Casona Jaúregui

La Merced

5

Río Alameda

Nazareno

Carlos F Vivanco

Arco del Triunfo

Av Ramón Castilla

Huancasolar

1

Santa Clara de Asís

Mercado de Abastos Carlos F Vivanco

San Francisco de Asís

S J de Dios

Raymondi

C Chorro

Mercado 12 de Abril

2 de Mayo

Museo Andrés A Cáceres (Casona Vivanco)

N

100 metres
100 yards

Santa Teresa

San Cristóbal

To Barrio Santa Ana

## Where to stay
1 Crillonesa
2 DM Hoteles Ayacucho
3 El Condeduque
4 Florida
5 Hostal 3 Máscaras
6 Internazionale
7 Marcos
8 San Francisco de Paula
9 Santa María
10 Santa Rosa
11 Sevilla
12 ViaVia Ayacucho

## Restaurants
1 Carbón y Vino
2 El Mestizo
3 Frutimix
4 La Casona
5 La Miel & Sukre
6 Las Flores
7 Las Tinajas & Taberna Magia Negra
8 Los Manglares
9 Pizzeria Italiana
10 Retablo
11 Sarhsi Chifa
12 Wallpa Sua
13 Wambar

## Bars & clubs
14 Tupana Wasy

## BACKGROUND
## Ayacucho

The city was founded on 9 January 1539 by the invading Spaniards, who named it San Juan de la Frontera. This was changed to San Juan de la Victoria after the Battle of Chupas, when the king's forces defeated the rival Almagrist faction. Despite these Spanish titles, the city always kept its original name of Huamanga. It became an important base for the army of Simón Bolívar in his triumphant sweep south from the Battle of Junín. It was here, on the Pampa de Quinua, on 9 December 1824, that the decisive Battle of Ayacucho was fought, bringing Spanish rule in Peru to an end.

Bolívar decreed that the city be named Ayacucho, meaning 'Place of the Dead'. For much of the 1980s and early 1990s, this title seemed sadly appropriate as the Shining Path terrorized the local populace, severely punishing anyone they suspected of siding with the military. Those painful times are long past but the memory of the many victims is commemorated at the moving and recommended **Museo de Anfasep** (Asociación Nacional de Familiares de Secuestrados Detenidos y Desaparecidos del Perú), Prolongación Libertad 1229, in the north of the city, 15 minutes' walk or a mototaxi ride from Mercado Artesanal Shosaku Nagase. Entry is free but a donation is appreciated.

**Beyond the plaza** Jr 28 de Julio is pedestrianized for two blocks south of the plaza. A stroll down 28 de Julio leads to the prominent **Arco del Triunfo** (1910), which commemorates victory over the Spaniards. Through the arch is the church of **San Francisco de Asís** (1552) ① *28 de Julio, block 3, open for Mass Mon-Sat 0700-0800, 1800-1900*. It has an elaborate gilt main altar and several others. Across 28 de Julio from San Francisco is the **Mercado de Abastos Carlos F Vivanco**, the packed central market. As well as household items and local produce, look out in particular for the stalls dedicated to cheese, breads and fruit juices. West of the market, **Santa Clara de Asís** ① *Jr Grau, block 3, open for Mass 0630-0730*, is renowned for its beautifully delicate coffered ceiling and for housing an image of Jesús Nazareno, patron of Huamanga. It is open for the sale of sweets and cakes made by the nuns; go to the door at Nazareno 184, which is usually open.

One block east of Jirón 28 de Julio, the 16th-century church of **La Merced** ① *2 de Mayo, open for Mass 1000-1200, 1700-1900*, is the second oldest in the city. The high choir is a good example of the simplicity of churches in the early period of the viceroyalty. The private **Casona Jaúregui**, opposite, is also called **Ruiz de Ochoa** after its original owner. Its outstanding feature is its doorway, which has a blue balcony supported by two fierce beasts with erect penises.

On the fifth block of 28 de Julio is the late 16th-century **Casona Vivanco**, which houses the **Museo Andrés A Cáceres** ① *Jr 28 de Julio 508, Mon-Fri 0900-1300, 1500-1700, US$0.70*. The museum has baroque painting, colonial furniture, republican and contemporary art, and exhibits on Mariscal Cáceres' battles in the War of the Pacific. Further south still, on a pretty plazuela, is **Santa Teresa** (1683) ① *28 de Julio, block 6, daily Mass 0630-0730, plus Thu 1500-1700*, with its monastery. The nuns here sell sweets and crystallized fruits and a *mermelada de ají*, made to a recipe given to them by God; apparently it is not *picante* (spicy). **San Cristóbal** ① *Jr 28 de Julio, block 6*, was the first church to be founded in the city (1540), and is one of the oldest in South America. Its roof has collapsed and only the façade remains.

The city of Huari had a population of 50,000 and reached its apogee in AD 900. Its influence spread throughout much of Peru: north to Cajamarca; along the north coast to Lambayeque; south along the coast to Moquegua; and south across the sierra to Cuzco. Before the Inca invasion, the Huari formed a *chanca* – a confederation of ethnic groups – and populated the Pampas river and an area west of the Apurímac. This political agreement between the peoples of Ayacucho, Andahuaylas, Junín and Huancavelica was seen by the Incas in Cuzco as a threat. The Incas fought back around 1440 with a bloody attack on the Huari on the Pampa de Ayacucho, and so began a period of Inca domination. The scene of this massacre is still known as *Rincón de los Muertos*.

The **Casa Museo Joaquín López Antay** ① *Jr Cuzco 424, T956-695466, Tue-Sat 1600-2000,* is located in the home of a well-known local artist who excelled in the creation of *retablos*. **Museo de Antropología y Arqueología Hipólito Unanue** ① *Av Independencia 508, T66-318305, Tue-Sun 0900-1300, 1500-1700,* is a small, very well organized private museum with Wari ceramics and other artefacts.

**Barrio Santa Ana** For a fascinating insight into Inca and pre-Inca art and culture, a visit to Barrio Santa Ana is a must. Here, about 200 families have workshops making *artesanías*: textiles, *retablos*, ceramics and work in stone. Their work is distributed through the galleries in the barrio. A good grasp of Spanish is essential to appreciate the galleries fully. Note that the galleries in the barrio are closed on Sunday. Visit **Julio Gálvez** ① *Plazoleta Santa Ana 120, T066-314278,* for remarkable jewellery and sculptures in alabaster (*piedra de huamanga*). Also see Handicrafts, page 381.

### North of Ayacucho

★ **Huari** ① *22 km from Ayacucho, archaeological site open daily 0900-1300, 1400-1700, museum closed Mon; entry US$1.50, guides (Spanish only) US$6 per group. Vans leave all day from Terminal Huari-Quinua (Jr Ricardo Palma esquina Santos Chocano in Jesús de Nazareno district), US$1.25 (more in shared taxis and at weekends), 40 mins; or take a tour (US$11 pp).*
A good road north from Ayacucho leads to this impressive 1600-ha site dates from the 'Middle Horizon' (AD 600-1000), when the Huari culture spread across most of Peru. This was the first walled urban centre in the Andes. The huge irregular stone walls are up to 3- to 4-m high, and rectangular houses and streets can be made out. The most important activity here was artistic: ceramics, gold, silver, metal and alloys such as bronze, which was used for weapons and for decorative objects. The ruins now lie in an extensive *tuna* (prickly pear) cactus forest (don't pick the fruit, it is covered in tiny spines). The site museum is good. Only two percent of the site has been excavated.

**Tip...**

For a moving insight into the recent history of this region and the violence surrounding the Sendero Luminoso campaign, visit Museo de la Memoria de ANFASEP (Prolongación Libertad 1229 (cuadra 14), in the north of the city, T066-317170, www.anfasep.org.pe, Monday-Friday 0900-1300, 1500-1800, Saturday 0900-1300, US$0.60).

**Quinua** ① *37 km northeast of Ayacucho, a further 25 mins, US$1.50, or US$2 from Ayacucho; for a little extra you can ask the driver to go all the way to the 'Obelisco'.* Vans to Huari continue to this village, which has a charming cobbled main plaza; many of the buildings have been restored. There is a small market on Sunday. The village's handicrafts are recommended, especially its ceramics; **San Pedro Ceramics**, at the foot of the hill, and **Mamerto Sánchez** (Jirón Sucre) should be visited, but there are many others. Most of the houses have miniature ceramic churches on the roof. The **Fiesta de la Virgen de Cocharcas** is celebrated around 8 September. Nearby, on the **Pampa de Quinua** ① *entry US$0.60* (part of a 300-ha Santuario Histórico), a 44-m-high obelisk commemorates the Battle of Ayacucho in 1824. A reenactment of the battle is held on 9 December, with college students playing the roles of Royalist and South American soldiers.

Trips of about six hours can be arranged to Huari, La Quinua village and the Santuario Histórico for US$18 per person (minimum three people).

## Vilcashuamán and beyond
*Full-day tours to these sites cost US20 pp for 8 passengers, departing 0600. Alternatively, travel by van from Terminal Zona Sur, Av Cuzco 350 (daily 0200-1600, return 0700-1700, 3½ hrs, US$4.50) and stay overnight in one of the several basic but clean hotels ($).*

The Inca ruins of **Vilcashuamán** are 120 km to the south of Ayacucho. Vilcashuamán was an important Inca provincial capital at the crossroads where the main road from Cuzco to the central coast met the empire's north–south highway. There are several monumental Inca buildings, including an intact *usnu*, a flat-topped pyramid which was used for religious ceremonies. The village of Vischongo is one hour from Vilcashuamán; it has a market on Wednesday. Other attractions in the area include **Intihuatana**, Inca baths of fine masonry, near a lake about one hour uphill from the village, and *Puya raymondii* plants at Titankayoq, two hours' walk from Vischongo.

Further afield in the department of Ayacucho, off the main road between Nazca and Cuzco but also accessible from Ayacucho city, is the beautiful and seldom-visited **Sondondo Valley**, see page 213.

## Listings Ayacucho and around *map page 375.*

### Tourist information

**Dircetur**
*Asamblea 481, T066-312548. Mon-Fri 0730-1430.*
Friendly and helpful.

**iPerú**
*Jr Cuzco 108, T066-318305, iperuayacucho@ promperu.gob.pe. Mon-Sat 0900-1800, Sun 0900-1300.*
Very helpful. Also has an office at the airport, open only when flights arrive.

**Tourist police**
*Jr Sol 480, T066-315892. Daily 0800-2000.*

### Where to stay

**$$$ DM Hoteles Ayacucho**
*Jr 9 de Diciembre 184, T066-312202, www.dmhoteles.pe.*
Large, elegant hotel with comfortable rooms, some suites have balconies overlooking the plaza. Buffet breakfast, restaurant, bar, *cafetería*, conference rooms, parking, helpful staff.

**$$$-$$ Internazionale**
*Urbanización María Parado de Bellido Mz O, Lt 1, Emadi, T066-314701, www. internazionalehotel.pe.*
Business-oriented, 5 mins' drive from the centre, modern, junior suites with jacuzzi

and roof terrace with great view of the city. Restaurant, parking, helpful staff.

## $$$-$$ ViaVia Ayacucho
*Portal Constitución 4, Plaza de Armas, T066-316014, www.viavia.world/ayacucho.*
Single, double and triple rooms with private bath, solar hot water 24 hrs, TV room, Peruvian/Belgian owners, Spanish, Dutch and English spoken. The attached restaurant/café overlooks the plaza, live music Fri-Sat. Popular and busy. 2nd location, **ViaVia Alameda** (Alameda Valdelirios 720), slightly cheaper, with restaurant, bar and ice cream parlour.

## $$ San Francisco de Paula
*Jr Callao 270, T066-312353, www. hotelsanfranciscodepaula.com.*
A bit like a museum with hallways filled with handicrafts and a nice patio, mirador (terrace with views), restaurant, parking, popular choice. Comfortable rooms and suites, some with jacuzzi. Includes breakfast Mon-Sat.

## $$ Santa María
*Jr Arequipa 320, T066-314988, www.jianhoteles.com.pe.*
Ample comfortable rooms and nice common areas, attentive service, buffet breakfast, good quality and value.

## $$ Santa Rosa
*Jr Lima 166, T066-314614, www.hotelsantarosa.com.pe.*
Lovely colonial courtyard in building with historical associations, roof terrace, warm rooms, attentive staff, car park, computers for guests, cash only, good restaurant with good value *menú*.

## $$ Sevilla
*Jr Libertad 631, T066-314388, www.hotelsevillaperu.com.*
Convenient location, comfortable rooms with fridge, microwave and abundant hot water, nice courtyard and common areas, includes buffet breakfast, friendly helpful staff.

## $$-$ El Condeduque
*Jr Asamblea 159, T066-316231, elcondeduquehotel@hotmail.com.*
Colonial-style, ample rooms with private bath, hot water, nice common areas, good central location, includes breakfast, good value.

## $$-$ Marcos
*9 de Diciembre 143, T066-316867.*
Comfortable, modern, in a cul-de-sac half a block from the plaza, quiet, hot water, laundry, includes breakfast in the *cafetería*.

## $ Crillonesa
*C Nazareno 165, T066 312350, hotelcrillonesa@outlook.com, www.hotelcrillonesa.com.*
Good rooms, hot water, laundry facilities, common areas decorated with local crafts, great views from roof terrace, near produce market but reasonably quiet, volunteer opportunities. Owner Carlos Manco is very friendly, helpful and has loads of information. Good value, warmly recommended.

## $ Florida
*Jr Cuzco 310, T066-312565.*
Small, central location, pleasant, quiet, patio with flowers, solar showers, breakfast extra.

## $ Hostal 3 Máscaras
*Jr 3 Máscaras 194, T066-312921, www.hoteltresmascaras.galeon.com.*
Newer rooms with bath better, but with less character, than the old ones without, nice colonial building with patio, hot water, breakfast extra, car park.

## Restaurants

Ayacucho has its own regional gastronomy, specialities include *cuy chactado* (deep-fried guinea pig) and *puca picante* (red-hot spicy beetroot and potatoes). For a cheap, healthy breakfast, try *maca*, a drink of maca tuber, apple and quinoa, sold outside the market opposite Santa Clara, 0600-0800.

## $$ El Mestizo
*Jr Cuzco 241, near Plaza Mayor.*
*Mon-Sat 0830-2230.*

Restaurant, café and art gallery serving regional specialities, vegetarian and international dishes, good midday *menú*. Tranquil atmosphere in a colonial *casona*.

### $$ Las Flores
*Jr José Olaya 106, Plaza Conchopata, east of city in the 'gourmet neighbourhood', T066-316349. Daily 1100-1900.*
Specializes in *cuy chactado* and other regional dishes. Taxi US$1.50 from centre.

### $$ Las Tinajas
*Portal Independencia 65, T066-310128. Open 1200-2400.*
Chicken grill and bar, large balcony overlooking the main square, very popular, good service.

### $$ Sukre
*Portal Constitución 8, upstairs. Daily 0800-2330.*
Upmarket Peruvian dining, regional and national dishes à la carte, good location overlooking the Plaza de Armas.

### $$-$ La Casona
*Jr Bellido 463. Open 1200-1700, 1830-2130.*
Dining under the arches and in the dining room, regional specialities, try their *puca picante, mondongo* and *cuy*, and a wide menu.

### $$-$ Los Manglares
*Av 26 de Enero 415, T066-315900. Open 1030-1600.*
The best-established *cevichería* of several on this avenue, also does home delivery.

### $ Carbón y Vino
*Jr Bellido 593. Mon-Sat 0830-2300 .*
Good-value midday *menú*, juices and sandwiches in the morning, pasta and pizza at night.

### $ Pizzeria Italiana
*Jr Bellido 486, T066-317574. Daily 1700-2300.*
Pizzeria with a huge wood-burning oven. Also good pastas.

### $ Retablo
*Jr Asamblea 219, T066-528453.*

Chicken, meat, burgers and more in a large modern locale. Always full with locals, good value.

### $ Samsí Chifa
*9 de Diciembre 212-217. Mon-Sat 1300-1600, 1800-2230, Sun 1300-2200.*
Good popular Chinese serving *menú* and à la carte.

### $ Wallpa Sua
*Jr Garcilazo de la Vega 240.*
A good chicken place, also with *parrillas*.

### $ Wambar
*San Martín 403, upstairs. Daily.*
Generous portions of grilled chicken with native Andean potatoes and *qapchi de queso*. Live music Sat-Sun.

## Cafés

### Centro Turístico Cultural San Cristóbal
*28 de Julio 178.*
Has some expensive cafés including **Lalo's** (café, pizza delivery service and bar) and **Café New York** (coffee specialists) other restaurants and craft shops. There are tables in the pleasant courtyard.

### Frutimix
*Portal Independencia 56, and Jr 9 de Diciembre 427.*
Shakes, frappés (Baileys, chocolate or frapuccino), modern and tasty.

### La Miel
*Portal Constitución 11-12, on the plaza. Daily 1000-2300.*
Good coffee, hot drinks, juices, shakes, cakes and snacks, also ice creams.

## Bars and clubs

### Taberna Magia Negra
*Portal Independencia 65A. Mon-Sat 1600-2400.*
Craft beer with varied folk and rock music.

### Tupana Wasy
*Jr 9 de Diciembre 213, 3rd floor, and Jr 9 de Diciembre 270.*

Live contemporary and traditional Andean music. Several other bars in the same area.

## Festivals

The area is well known for its festivals throughout the year. Almost every day there is a celebration in one of the surrounding villages; check with the tourist office.

**Feb  Carnaval**. Reported to be a wild affair.
**Mar/Apr  Semana Santa** begins on the Fri before Holy Week. There follows one of the world's finest Holy Week celebrations, with candle-lit nightly processions, floral 'paintings' on the streets, daily fairs (the biggest on Easter Sat), horse races and contests among peoples from all over central Peru. Prices double and all accommodation is fully booked for months in advance. Many people offer beds in their homes during the week. Look out for notices on the doors and in windows of transport companies.
**25 Apr  Anniversary of the founding of Huamanga province**.
**9 Dec  Reenactment of the Battle of Ayacucho** on the Pampa de Quinua.

## Shopping

### Handicrafts
Ayacucho is a good place to buy local crafts including filigree silver, which often uses *mudéjar* patterns. Also look out for little painted nativity scenes, carvings in local alabaster, harps, or the pre-Inca tradition of carving dried gourds. The most famous goods are carpets and retablos. In both weaving and retablos, scenes of recent political strife have been added to more traditional motifs. For carpets, go to Barrio Santa Ana (see page 377). Also recommended is **Familia Pizarro** (Jr Perú 102, Barrio Belén), who produce textiles, *piedra huamanga* (sculptures in local alabaster) and carnival masks of good quality; all pieces are individually made. They also have rooms for

visitors to stay and take classes. Edwin Pizarro (T966-180666) creates amazing altarpieces.

### Markets
**Mercado 12 de Abril**, *Chorro y San Juan de Dios*. For fruit and vegetables.
**Shosaku Nagase**, *Jr Quinua y Av Maravillas, opposite Plazoleta de María Parado de Bellido*. A large handicraft market.

## What to do

**A&R Tours**, *Jr 9 de Diciembre 130*, T066-311300, www.viajesartours.com. *Daily 0800-2000*. Offers tours in and around the city.
**Fly Travel**, *Jr 9 de Diciembre 118*, T066-313282, flytravel_ayp@hotmail.com. Offers tours along 2 main circuits. To the north: Wari–Quinua–Huanta; south: Vilcashuamán–Cangallo.
**Morochucos Rep's**, *Jr 9 de Diciembre 136*, T066-317844. Dynamic company in business for over 30 years, with tours locally and to other parts of Peru, flight, train and bus tickets.
**Urpillay Tours**, *28 de Julio 262 (Plaza More), of 8*, T066-315074. All local tours and flight tickets.
**Wari Tours**, *Lima 138*, T066-311415. Local tours.
**Willy Tours**, *Jr 9 de Diciembre 209*, T066-314075. Personal guides, also handles flight and bus tickets.

## Transport

### Air
The airport is to the east of the city along Av Castilla. Taxi from airport to city centre, US$3.

To/from **Lima**, 55 mins, with **LATAM** (Jr 9 de Diciembre 107) and **LC Peru** (Jr 9 de Diciembre 139, T066-312151).

### Bus
Large long-distance bus terminal **Terrapuerto "Libertadores de América"** (Av Javier Pérez de Cuéllar s/n, T066-312666) is 10 mins northwest of centre. All bus companies are here, and **Cruz del Sur** also has its own terminal in the centre (Av Mcal Cáceres 1264, T066-312813).

To **Lima**, 8-10 hrs on a good paved road, via Ica, several companies US$13-37, including Expreso **Molina** (T066-312984), 7 daily, 5 in the evening; **Cruz del Sur,** US$26 *regular*, US$37 *suite* and *VIP* services; **Móvil Tours**, 1000 and 2100-2200; **Tepsa,** US$25, at 2200; **Internacional Palomino** (T066-313899), morning service, US$13-26; **Los Chankas** T066-401943), at 2000, US$10-16. For **Pisco**, 332 km, take an Ica/Lima bus and get out at San Clemente (10 mins from Pisco), 5 hrs, same fare as Ica; then take a bus or van.

To **Cuzco**, with **Los Chankas**, vans at 0720 to Andahuaylas, US$9, transfer there; buses at 2000 direct to Cuzco, US$18, some continue to Puerto Maldonado. Also **Señor De Huanca**.

To **Huancayo**, 319 km, 8-9 hrs, US$10-13, 3 daily with **Molina**, also **Turismo Central** (T066-317873), US$13 at 2030. The views are stunning.

For **Huancavelica**, Expreso Molina at 2100, US$9, 7 hrs, continuing to Huancayo, you must pay the full fare to there; also **Turismo Central** at 2030. Vans to Huancavelica via Rumichaca with **Transportes Nevados** (T645-108211), US$10, Mon, Thu, Sat at 0430; or take a bus or combi to Rumichaca, US$4.50, 3 hrs, to try to catch the 1030 bus from Rumichaca to Hunacavelica, US$4.50, 3 hrs, confirm departure time locally. **Señor de Ataco** to **Izcuchaca**, US$4.60, 5 hrs on a narrow, dangerous road, at 0900 and 2030, where you can catch a bus or train to Huancvelica. Also see Huancavelica to Ayacucho, page 371.

stop to stretch your legs on the journey to Cuzco

Beyond Ayacucho are two growing highland cities, Andahuaylas and Abancay, which are possible stopping or bus-changing places on the road to Cuzco. The road towards Cuzco climbs out of Ayacucho and crosses a wide stretch of high, treeless *páramo* before descending through Ocros to the Río Pampas. It then climbs up to Chincheros, 158 km from Ayacucho, and Uripa, which has a good Sunday market. Ayacucho to Andahuaylas is 261 km on a paved road. It's in good condition when dry, but landslides may occur in the wet. The scenery is stunning. Daytime buses stop for lunch at Chumbes, which has a few restaurants, a shop selling fruit, bread and *refrescos*, and some grim toilets.

### Andahuaylas

Andahuaylas is about 80 km further on, at 3000 m in a fertile valley. It offers pleasant scenery, worthwhile excursions and a good Sunday market. A small **Museo Arqueológico** ① *inside the estadio, Mon-Fri 0800-1300,1400-1700, free*, has a nice collection of pre-Columbian objects, including mummies.

To visit **Laguna de Pacucha**, take a *colectivo* from Avedida Los Chankas, half a block from the market (US$1, 20 minutes), continuing to Sóndor (US$1.50), 40 minutes from Adahuaylas. On the shore of the lake is the quiet town of Pacucha, which has a couple of basic *hostales* and various places to eat (most open at weekends). A road follows the north shore of the lake and climbs to **Sóndor** ① *entry US$0.60*, 9 km from Pacucha (taxi from Andahuaylas US$10). This Inca archaeological site at 3300 m has various buildings and small plazas leading up to a conical hill with concentric stone terracing and, at the summit, a large rock or *intihuatana*. **Sóndor Raymi** is celebrated here each year on 18-19 June. The site can be enjoyed at leisure in one to two hours. In addition to the fine archaeology, the views are lovely. Archaeologists recently dated human bones from

Sóndor to 1400 BC. Transport returns to Andahuaylas via Pacucha until about 1800, or you can walk back along the lakeshore to Pacucha in two to four hours and pick up transport there, also until about 1800. Confirm latest return time locally. It is slightly shorter to walk along the north side of the lake.

## Abancay

Nestled between mountains in the upper reaches of a glacial valley, the town of Abancay is first glimpsed from many kilometres away. It is capital of the department of Apurimac, an important mining area. Abancay's major attraction is the **Santuario Nacional de Ampay** ⓘ *5 km north of town on a paved road (take a colectivo to Tamburco and ask the driver where to get off), entry US$9*. It has two lakes called Ankasccocha (3200 m) and Uspaccocha (3820 m), a small rapidly receding glacier on Ampay mountain (5235 m), and a forest of endemic *Intimpa* trees (*Podocarpus glomeratus,* the only conifer native to Peru). There are two hiking trails and it's a two-day trek up to the glacier, with overnight camping.

## Saywite

*3 km from the main road, Km 49 from Abancay. US$4, students US$2.*

Beyond the town of Curahuasi, 126 km before Cuzco, is the large carved rock of Saywite. It is a UNESCO World Heritage Site. The principal monolith is said to represent the three regions of jungle, sierra and coast, with the associated animals and Inca sites of each. It is fenced in, but ask the guardian for a closer look. It was defaced, allegedly, when a cast was taken, breaking off many of the animals' heads. Six further archaeological areas stretch away from the stone and its neighbouring group of buildings.

## Listings Ayacucho to Cuzco

## Tourist information

### Andahuaylas

Dircetur
*Jr Túpac Amaru 365.*

### Abancay

**Dircetur**
*Av Arenas 121, p1, T083-321664,
www.dirceturapurimac.gob.pe.*
Has maps, flyers, and lots of information, friendly service.

**SERNANP**
*Prolongación Cusco 923, Urbanización Las Torres, T083-322233.*
Information about Santuario Nacional de Ampay.

## Where to stay

### Andahuaylas

**$ Conquistador**
*Jr Guillermo Cáceres 450, T083-205525.*
Modern multi-storey building, comfortable rooms, private bath, hot water, a good choice.

**$ El Encanto de Apurímac**
*Jr Ramos 401, T083-723527, and a newer branch at Jr Guillermo Cáceres 132, T083-205513, www.hotelencantodeapurimac.com.*
Small clean rooms with private bath, hot water, front rooms bigger but noisy, includes simple breakfast at nearby *chifa* **El Dragón**, helpful staff, good value.

**$ Sol de Oro**
*Jr Juan A Trelles 164, T083-421152.*
Older place but well maintained. Warm rooms with wooden floors, includes

breakfast, restaurant, pleasant common areas, elevator.

## Abancay

### $$-$ El Peregrino Apart Hotel
*Jr Andrés Caceres 390, T083-502610, www.aparthotelperegrino.com.*
Small modern hotel in a quiet part of town, 10-min walk from the centre. Comfortable rooms and beds, reliable hot water, includes good breakfast, excellent service.

### $$-$ Turistas
*Av Díaz Barcenas 600, T083-321017, www.turismoapurimac.com.*
The original building is in colonial style, rooms a bit gloomy, breakfast not included. Newer rooms on top floor (best) and in new block are more expensive, including breakfast. Good restaurant ($$), wood-panelled bar, parking.

### $ Imperial
*Díaz Barcenas 517, T083-321538.*
Great beds, hot water, spotless, very helpful, parking, good value, cheaper without bath or breakfast.

## Restaurants

### Andahuaylas

### $$ D'Marce
*Jr Ricardo Palma 340, Plaza de Armas. Daily 0800-2200.*
Good-looking innovative restaurant/café, upmarket for Andahuaylas.

### $$-$ Il Gatto
*Jr Guillermo Cáceres 334. Daily 1800-2400.*
A warm pizzeria, with wooden furniture, pizzas cooked in a wood-burning oven.

### $ El Dragón
*Jr Juan A Trellas 279.*
A popular *chifa* serving huge portions, good value (same owner as **Hoteles El Encanto de Apurímac**).

### Abancay

### $ Café Matias
*Av Arenas 160.*
Nice café/bar serving sandwiches, snacks and light meals. Newspapers are available to read.

### $ Focarela Pizzería
*Díaz Bárcenas 533-535, T083-322036.*
Simple but pleasant decor, pizza from a wood-burning oven, fresh, generous toppings, popular.

## What to do

### Abancay
**Apurimak Tours**, *at Hotel Turistas, see Where to stay.* Run local tours and 1- and 2-day trips to Santuario Nacional de Ampay: 1-day, 7 hrs, US$40 pp for 1-2 people (cheaper for more people). Also a 3-day trip to Choquequirao including transport, guide, horses, tents and food, just bring your sleeping-bag, US$60 pp. The hotel can also put you in touch with Carlos Valer, a very knowledgeable and kind guide.

## Transport

### Andahuaylas
**Air**
The airport is 17 km from town along the road to Huancabamba, combi US$1. To/from **Lima**, 4 flights a week with **LC Perú**.

**Bus**
**Expreso Los Chankas** (Av José María Arguedas y Jr Trelles,T983-727657) is the main bus company and most transport leaves from their terminal or nearby, including all of the following; several others along the same road. To **Ayacucho**, US$9, 5-6 hrs, at 0430, 1100, 2030. Shared taxis to Ayacucho, US$15, 4 hrs . To **Abancay**, shared taxis (US$7.50) and vans (US$5), 3 hrs, every 30 mins. To **Cuzco**, US$10, 9 hrs, at 1945 and 2030. To **Lima** via Ayacucho, US$19-25, 16 hrs, at 1300, 1500, 1700. On all night buses, take a blanket.

## Abancay

The Terminal Terrestre is on Av Pachacútec, on the west side of town. Taxi to centre, US$1, or it's a steep walk. All buses leave from Terminal Terrestre but several companies have offices on or near the El Olivo roundabout at Av Díaz Bárcenas y Gamarra; others are on Av Arenas.

To **Cuzco**, 195 km, 4½ hrs, US$14-18, with **Bredde** (Gamarra 423, T083-321643), 5 a day; **Molina** (Gamarra 422, T083-322646), 3 a day; **San Jerónimo**, at 2130; **Los Chankas** (Díaz Bárcenas 1011, El Olivo, T083-321485) and several others. To **Lima**, **Oltursa**, US$66, or **Tepsa** US$71; several others. The scenery en route is dramatic, especially as it descends into the Apurímac Valley and climbs out again. To Andahuaylas, **Molina** at 2330; **San Jerónimo** at 2130; **Señor de Huanca** (Av Arenas 198, T083-322377), 3 a day; also Los Chankas.

## East and north of La Oroya

east to the jungle or north to Cordillera Blanca

A paved road heads north from La Oroya towards Cerro de Pasco and Huánuco. Just 25 km north of La Oroya a branch turns east towards Tarma, then descends to the little-visited jungles of the Selva Central. This is a really beautiful run. North of La Oroya the road crosses the great heights of the Junín pampa and the mining zone of Cerro de Pasco, before losing altitude on its way to the Huallaga Valley. On this route you can connect by road to the Cordillera Blanca via La Unión.

### ★ Selva Central

Founded in 1534, **Tarma** (60 km from La Oroya) has a charming Plaza de Armas and is notable for its Semana Santa celebrations (see Festivals, page 391) and its locally made fine flower-carpets. The town is noisy and dirty, mainly of interest as a transport hub, but the surrounding countryside offers some worthwhile excursions. **Acobamba**, a small town 9 km along the road to San Ramón (see below), provides access to the **Santuario de Muruhuay**, 2 km away, which has a venerated image of Christ painted on the rock behind the altar. High-quality weavings are produced in **San Pedro de Cajas**, about 27 km northwest of Tarma, where you can visit the workshop of the Ulloa Bailón family (Calle San Pedro 1007, T964-243816), among others. There are petroglyphs at **Pintish Machay**, a good day-hike from the village of **Huaricolca**, 15 km south of Tarma along the road to Jauja.

Beyond Tarma the road is steep and crooked but there are few places where cars cannot pass one another. In the 80 km from Tarma to La Merced the road runs between great overhanging cliffs as it drops 2450 m and the vegetation changes dramatically from temperate to tropical. The first town in Chanchamayo Province is **San Ramón**, 11 km before La Merced. It has several hotels (**$$$-$**) and restaurants, and there are regular combis and *colectivos* between the two towns. **La Merced** lies in the fertile Chanchamayo Valley. Asháninka *indígenas* can usually be found around the central plaza selling bows, arrows, necklaces and trinkets. There is a festival in the last week of September. There are several hotels (**$$-$**) and restaurants.

About 25 km from La Merced along the road to **Oxapampa**, a road turns northeast to Villa Rica, centre of an important coffee-growing area. From here, a poor dirt road continues northeast to **Puerto Bermúdez**. This authentic jungle town, at the geographic centre of Peru, has grown up along the now seldom-used airstrip. It lies on the Río Pichis, an affluent of the Pachitea, and is a great base for exploring further into the Selva Central, with trips upriver to the Asháninka community. Tours are arranged by **Albergue Cultural Humboldt** (see Where to stay, below). To go further downriver to Pucallpa, there is road transport via Ciudad Constitución, about US$20 over two stages.

## Pampas de Junín
The road north from La Oroya runs up the Mantaro Valley through canyons to the wet and mournful Junín pampa at over 4250 m, one of the world's largest high-altitude plains. An obelisk marks the battlefield where the Peruvians under Bolívar defeated the Spaniards in 1824 (celebrated on 6 August annually). Blue peaks line the pampa in a distant wall. This windswept sheet of yellow grass is bitterly cold and the only signs of life are the youthful herders with their sheep and llamas. The road follows the east shores of Lago Junín. The town of **Junín** lies some distance south of the lake and has the desolate feel of a high *puna* town, bisected by the railway; it has several basic hotels. The **Junín National Reserve** ① *US$9, ticket from Sernanp in Junín, Jr San Martín 138, T064-344146*, protects one of the best birdwatching sites in the central Andes where the giant coot and even flamingos may be spotted. It is easiest to visit from the village of Huayre, 5 km south of Carhuamayo, from where it is a 20-minute walk down to the lake. Fishermen are usually around to take visitors out on the lake.

## Cerro de Pasco and around *Colour map 3, B4.*
This long-established mining centre, 130 km from La Oroya, is not attractive, but is nevertheless very friendly. Copper, zinc, lead, gold and silver are mined here, and coal comes from the deep canyon of Goyllarisquisga, 42 km north of Cerro de Pasco. It is the highest coal mine in the world and its name translates as the 'place where a star fell'. The town is sited between Lago Patarcocha and the huge abyss of the mine above which its buildings and streets cling precariously. Nights are bitterly cold here at 4330 m. Southwest of Cerro de Pasco by 40 km is **Santuario Huayllay (Bosque de Piedras)** ① *information from Sernanp in Junín, US$1; camping permitted*. These unique weathered limestone formations at 4100-4600 m are in the shape of a tortoise, elephant, alpaca, and more. They can be explored on 11 tourist circuits through the rock formations. The village of **Huallay** is 6 km southwest of the sanctuary; it has a municipal hostel and other hotels. A festival of sports and music is held here on 6-8 September. Minibuses to Huallay depart from Cerro de Pasco's terminal throughout the day, about one hour (US$1); last return 1800.

## Huánuco and around *Colour map 3, B4.*
The Central Highway from Cerro de Pasco continues northeast another 528 km, fully paved, to Pucallpa, the limit of navigation for large Amazon river boats. The sharp descent along the nascent **Río Huallaga** is a tonic to travellers suffering from *soroche*. The road drops 2436 m in the 100 km from Cerro de Pasco to Huánuco, most of it in the first 32 km. From the bleak high ranges the road plunges below the tree line offering great views. The only town of any size before Huánuco is **Ambo**. Huánuco itself (population 175,000) is located on the Upper Huallaga and has an interesting Saturday morning market. Situated between the highlands and jungle at 1894 m it has a particularly pleasant climate but the city centre is noisy, its streets clogged with cars and mototaxis. The **Museo Regional** ① *2 de Mayo y Tarapacá, Mon-Fri 0900-1300, 1500-1800*, is located in a nicely restored colonial building.

Located 5 km west of Huánuco on the road to La Unión is **Kótosh** ① *daily 0800-1700, US$1.50, guides available (in Spanish)*; (mototaxi from Huánuco, US$1.50). Investigations suggest that this archaeological site, at an altitude of 1912 m, was occupied for over

2000 years. Six distinct phases of occupation have been identified, the oldest of which dates back some 4000 years. The Temple of Crossed Hands dates from 2000 BC and was once regarded as the 'oldest temple in the Americas'.

Off the road to La Unión, 75 km from Huánuco, is the large archaeological site of **Garu** ① *daily 0800-1700, US$1.50,* an important centre of the **Yarowilca** culture. To get there, take a tour from Huánuco or a *colectivo* to Choras from Jirón Tarapacá 283 (US$6, 2½-three hours) and it's half an hour's walk from there. Further afield, in the **Upper Marañón** region are other widely dispersed Yarowilca sites, see box, page 388.

The small town of **Churubamba** (21 km from Huánuco off the road to Tingo María, *colectivo* from the Mercado Central, US$1.25), has a small **municipal museum** ① *US$1, daily 0900-1300, 1400-1600,* displaying mummies and ceramics, well-known Semana Santa celebrations, and provides access to Bosque Unchog, a cloudforest reserve with many birds, including the endemic golden-backed mountain tanager.

Huánuco can be an alternative jumping off point for trekking in the **Cordillera Huayhuash** and local operators offer tours.

## La Unión and around

From Huánuco, a spectacular but narrow road leads to La Unión, capital of Dos de Mayo district. It's a regional supply centre with a couple of simple hotels and restaurants:

Huánuco

**Where to stay** 🛏
1 Cuzco
2 Grand Hotel Huánuco
3 Grima
4 Imperial
5 Plaza

6 Santorini

**Restaurants** 🍴
1 Don Carlos
2 La Olla de Barro
3 Pizzería Don Sancho
4 Sol de Mayo
5 Valle del Pillco

## ON THE ROAD
### The Upper Marañón

One of Peru's most important rivers and a major tributary of the Amazon, the **Río Marañón** arises from Lago Lauricocha at 3850 m above sea level, between the Cordilleras Huayhuash and Raura. For approximately 150 km of its 1700-km course, the deep canyon of the Upper Marañón runs northward to form the boundary between the departments of Ancash and Huánuco. This area of striking landscapes and varied ecological zones, has since 2015 been the scene of fresh archaeological interest and new botanical discoveries. It is also ideally suited to off-the-beaten-path travel and trekking.

Between approximately AD 1000 and 1450, the **Yarowilca** culture thrived along both rims of the Upper Marañón, one of many ethnic groups who inhabited the region following Huari fragmentation. In the 15th Century, they were incorporated into the Inca Empire but Spanish chroniclers documented Yarowilca culture into the colonial period. Spread along ridgetops high above the rushing waters of the Río Marañón are many impressive stone structures, ranging from isolated towers to complete settlements, in various states of preservation. The Yarowilca citadels and tombs share some similarities with those of the Chavín, Huari, Chachapoyas and Inca. Buildings reach up to five stories in height, with a characteristic architectural style of 'windows' which may have displayed mummy bundles. Few sites have been extensively studied or granted official protected status and all have been disturbed by *huaqueros* (looters). The sites are mostly known to local communities who can guide visitors through their remote areas, long overlooked by Peruvians and foreigners alike.

Among the few better-known archaeological sites of the Upper Marañón are those accessed from the friendly town of **Tantamayo**, five to six hours from Huánuco along a rough dirt road (US$11 by shared taxi or 4WD pick-up). **Hospedaje Maro** ($), in Tantamayo, T01-672 6181, T987-412702, offers basic accommodation, meals, and plenty of helpful advice about visiting nearby sites by owners Eladio and Consuelo Marticorena. These include **Susupillo**, a walled compound with towers and an elaborate four-storey building; **Piruro**, a large complex with an imposing five-storey building; and **Japayán**, spectacularly situated high above the Marañón with views all the way to the Cordillera Blanca.

At present, the Upper Marañón has minimal tourist infrastructure but visits can be organized by Huánuco agencies, or undertaken by independent travellers with plenty of time, patience and curiosity. For more information about tours and services, contact Miquer Cornelio, **High Tours** (www.hightours.pe, see page 391); about archeology and botany, John Ingham (john.ingham1@gmail.com). Also see Alexis Mantha: *Territoriality, social boundaries and ancestor veneration in the central Andes of Peru*, Journal of Anthropological Archaeology, 28(2009): pp158-176.

**$ Hostal Imperial** (Jirón Huánuco 250, T942-746677) and **Chifa Huerta** are good choices. On the pampa above La Unión are the large and impressive Inca ruins of ★ **Huánuco Viejo** (or **Huánuco Pampa**) ⓘ *entry US$1.50*, a great temple-fortress with residential quarters. The site has examples of very fine Inca stonework comparable with those in Cuzco. It is the only major Inca settlement on the Capac Ñan (Royal Inca Road) not to have been built over by a colonial or modern town. It's 9 km from La Unión, 2½ hours' walk or a taxi from La Unión will charge US$6.50-9.50 with wait.

A good fragment of Inca Road can be seen and walked from Colpa, 6 km from La Unión (mototaxi US$1.50) along the road to Huallanca and Huaraz. Cross the river on the footbridge at Colpa and climb north along the ancient stone stairway.

## Listings East and north of La Oroya *map page 387.*

### Tourist information

#### Selva Central

**Dircetur**
*In La Merced, Pardo 110, San Ramón, T064-331265.*

**Tourist office**
*On the plaza in Tarma, Arequipa 259, T064-638750. Mon-Fri 0800-1300, 1500-1800.*
Very helpful, mostly Spanish spoken; see also www.tarma.info.

#### Huánuco and around

A website giving local information is www.webhuanuco.com.

**Dircetur office**
*On the plaza, Gen Prado 716, T062-512980. Mon-Fri 0900-1200.*
Crafts for sale all day.

**Subgerencia de Turismo**
*In the Municipalidad, General Prado 750, p3, www.munihuanuco.gob.pe. Mon-Fri 0730-1530.*
Some English spoken, has a city map and pamphets.

### Where to stay

#### Selva Central
#### Tarma

**$$$ Hacienda Santa María**
*2 km out of town at Vista Alegre 1249, Sacsamarca, T064-321232.*
A beautiful (non-working) 17th-century hacienda, beautiful gardens and antique furniture. Includes breakfast. Excellent guides for local day trips.

**$$$ Los Portales**
*Av Castilla 512, T064-321411, www.losportaleshoteles.com.pe.*
On the edge of town, hot water, heating, 1950s building with old furnishings, includes breakfast, good restaurant.

**$$$-$$ Hacienda La Florida**
*6 km from Tarma, T064-341041, www.haciendalaflorida.com.*
18th-century working hacienda owned by German/Peruvian couple Inge and Pepe, who also arrange excursions. Variety of rooms sleeping 1-4, adjoining family rooms, dorm for groups and an independent house; all with hot water, meals available, lots of home-grown organic produce. Also camping for US$5.

**$$ Los Balcones**
*Jr Lima 370, 064-323600.*
Good location near the plaza, all rooms are non-smoking, some with balcony and frigobar, indoor parking.

**$$ Normandie**
*Beside the Santuario de Muruhuay, Acobamba, T064-341028, Lima T01-365 9795, www.hotelnormandie.com.pe.*
Rooms with hot water, bar, restaurant, tours offered.

**$ Hospedaje Residencial El Dorado**
*Huánuco 488, T064-321914, www.hospedajeeldoradotarma.com.*
Hot water, ample rooms set round a patio, 1st floor better, includes simple breakfast, safe, welcoming, secure parking. Older place but well cared for.

## $ Tampu Wasi
*Jr Amazonas 798, T064-321744, and*
*Jr Huánuco 235, T064-323128.*
Rooms with private bath, electric shower,
parking. Nice place, good value.

## Puerto Bermúdez

### $ Albergue Cultural Humboldt
*By the river port (La Rampa), T063-963-*
*722363, http://alberguehumboldt.free.fr.*
The owner, Basque writer Jesús, has created
a real haven for backpackers, with maps,
library and book exchange. Rooms sleep
1-3, or there are hammocks and tents. Meals
available, Spanish and Peruvian food. Jesús
arranges tours, from day trips to camping
and trekking in primary forest.

## Pampas de Junín

Carhuamayo is the best place to stay
when visiting the reserve. **Gianmarco**
(Maravillas 454) and **Patricia** (Tarapacá 862)
are the best of several basic *hostales*. There are
numerous restaurants along the main road.

## Cerro de Pasco and around

### $ Hostal Arenales
*Jr Arenales 162, near the bus station,*
*T063-723088.*
Modern, TV, hot water in the morning.

### $ Señorial
*Jr San Martín 1, in the district of San Juan,*
*5 mins north of Cerro by taxi, T063-422802,*
*hotelsenorial@hotmail.com.*
The most comfortable in town, hot water,
fine view across the mine pit.

### $ Welcome
*Av La Plata 125, opposite the entrance to the*
*bus station, T063-721883.*
Some rooms without window, hot water 24 hrs.

## Huánuco and around

The centre has many hotels in all price
categories, several good choices on Dámaso
Beraún near the plaza. Most front rooms
have traffic noise.

### $$$ Grand Hotel Huánuco (Inka Comfort)
*Dámaso Beraún 775, Plaza de Armas, T062-*
*512410, www.grandhotelhuanuco.com.*
Colonial-style hotel, 1940s elegance,
large rooms, older ones are dark, those
in new section are better, some are
wheelchair accessible. Ample common
areas, buffet breakfast, restaurant, pool,
parking, free airport transfers, attentive
staff. A Huánuco classic.

### $$$-$$ Grima
*Dámaso Beraún 880, T062-513649,*
*http://grimahotel.pe.*
Modern multi-storey hotel with large, clean,
airy rooms, excellent hot water, spacious
common areas. Includes good buffet
breakfast but no restaurant.

### $$-$ Santorini
*Dámaso Beraún 993, T062-515130.*
Bright clean rooms with frigobar, parking,
good value, no breakfast.

### $ Cuzco
*Huánuco 616, T942-015429.*
Large centrally located hotel, rooms with
private bath and hot water, patio, restaurant,
ample parking, no breakfast.

### $ Imperial
*Huánuco 581, T062-514758.*
Simple rooms with private bath, hot water,
helpful staff, a decent economy option,
no breakfast.

### $ Plaza
*Dámaso Beraún 832, T062-635160.*
Very clean rooms, some are small, private
bath, reliable hot water, common areas,
attentive staff, no breakfast.

## Restaurants

## Selva Central
## Tarma

### $ Chavín
*Jr Lima 270 at Plaza de Armas. Daily 0730-2230.*
Very good quality and variety in set meals
(weekdays only), also à la carte.

**$ Chifa Roberto Siu**
*Jr Lima 569 upstairs.*
A good option for Chinese food, popular with locals.

**$ Comedor Vegetariano**
*Arequipa 695. Open 0700-2100, but closed Fri after lunch and Sat.*
Vegetarian, small and cheap, sells great bread.

## Cerro de Pasco and around

**$ Los Angeles**
*Jr Libertad, near the market.*
Excellent *menú* for US$1.50. Recommended.

**$ San Fernando**
*Bakery in the plaza. Opens at 0700.*
Great hot chocolate, bread and pastries.

## Huánuco and around

**$$ La Olla de Barro**
*Gral Prado 860. Daily 0700-1530.*
Varied *comida criolla*, large portions, upmarket for Huánuco.

**$$-$ Pizzería Don Sancho**
*Prado 645. Daily 1830-2330.*
Said to make the best pizzas in town.

**$$-$ Sol de Mayo**
*28 de Julio, 894. Daily 0700-1700.*
Good varied *menú*, generous portions, mid-range prices, popular.

**$ Don Carlos**
*Dámaso Beraún 815.*
*Mon-Sat 0700-1000, 1200-1530.*
Breakfast and economical midday *menú* with several daily choices, attentive service.

**$ Valle del Pillco**
*Abtao 658. Mon-Sat 0700-2100, Sun 0700-1600.*
Small place serving tasty vegetarian meals, varied *menú*.

## Festivals

### Selva Central
**Mar/Apr** The **Semana Santa** celebrations at Tarma are spectacular, with a very colourful Easter Sun morning procession in the main plaza. Accommodation is hard to find at this time, but you can apply to the Municipalidad for rooms with local families.

### Pampas de Junín
**6 Aug** Colourful ceremony to commemorate the **Batalla de Junín** (1824), which was fought on the nearby Pampas de Junín, marking a decisive victory in favour of the independence of Peru and South America. The town fills with visitors, prices rise and hotel rooms are scarce.

### Huánuco and around
**7-8 Jan** **Festival de los Negritos** with dancers from from all over the department; dances start before Christmas.
**20-25 Feb** **Carnaval Huanuqueño**.
**3 May** **La Cruz de Mayo**.
**10-16 Aug** **Anniversary of Huánuco**.
**28-29 Oct** **Señor de Burgos**, the patron of Huánuco.

### La Unión and around
**27 Jul** **Fiesta del Sol**. Major annual festival at Huánuco Viejo. Lodgings in La Unión are almost impossible to find at this time.

## What to do

### Selva Central
**Tarma**
**Max Aventura**, *Jr 2 de Mayo 682, T064-323908, www.maxaventuraperu.com.* Reliable operator offering tours around Tarma, Lago Junín, and into the Chanchamayo region. Uses good vehicles.

### Huánuco and around
**High Tours**, *Jr Dámaso Beraún 849, T062-517203, www.hightours.pe.* Local, regional and Peru wide tours including trekking in the Cordillera Huayhuash, rafting, and Upper Marañón archaeological sites. Enthusiastic, attentive service.

## Transport

### Tarma
#### Bus
Most buses and vans leave from the Terminal Terrestre at the west end of Jr Lima. Some companies also have private terminals. Beware overcharging by *colectivo* drivers. To **Lima**, 231 km (paved and congested with heavy traffic), 6-9 hrs, US$10-15, with the following companies: **Transportes Junín** (Amazonas 669; in Lima at Av Nicolás Arriola 198, T01-224 9220), 6 a day, with *bus cama* at night; **Trans La Merced** (in Lima at Av 28 de Julio 1581, La Victoria), 3 a day; **Trans Los Canarios** (Jr Amazonas 694), 2 daily starting in Tarma; **Transportes Chanchamayo** (Callao 1002, T064-321882), 2 a day, en route from Chanchamayo. To **Jauja**, US$2, and **Huancayo**, US$3, from the stadium, 0800-1800, every 1½ hrs; also **Trans Los Canarios** about 1 per hr, 0500-1800, and **Trans Junín** at 1200 and 2400; *colectivos* depart when full from Callao y Jauja, 2 hrs, US$4, and 3 hrs, US$6, respectively. To **Cerro de Pasco**, **Empresa Junín** (Amazonas 450), 4 a day, 3 hrs, US$2.50; also *colectivos* when full, 2 hrs, US$4. To **La Oroya, buses** leave from opposite the Terminal, 1 hr, US$1.50, while *colectivos* leave from petrol station on Av Castilla block 5, 45 mins, US$2. To **San Ramón**, US$1.75, 1½ hrs, with **Trans Junín**, 4 a day, continuing to La Merced, US$2.75, 2 hrs; vans US$1.75, and *colectivos*, US$4, depart from the stadium to La Merced. Combis and *colectivos* run along Jr Huánuco by the Mercado Modelo to **Acobamba** and up to **Muruhuay**, 15 mins, US$0.30 and US$0.45 respectively.

### Chanchamayo
#### Air
Flights leave from San Ramón. There is a small airstrip where **Aero Montaña**, T064-331074 has air taxis that can be chartered (*viaje especial*) to the jungle towns, with a maximum of 3 people, but you have to pay for the pilot's return to base. Flights cost US$250 per hr. **Puerto Bermúdez** takes 33 mins. You can also just go to the air base, across the river, on the east side of town.

#### Bus
Many buses go to La Merced from **Lima**: **Expreso Satipo, Junín, La Merced** and **Chanchamayo** each have several buses during the day, US$8 *regular*, US$11 *cama* upper level, US$12.50 *cama* lower level, 7-8 hrs. To **Tarma**, with **Transportes Angelitos/San Juan**, hourly, 2½ hrs, US$1.75, or *colectivos*, just over 1 hr, US$4. To **Puerto Bermúdez**, **Empresa Transdife** and **Villa Rica** have 4WD pick-ups between 0400 and 0600 and may pick up passengers at their hotels. You must purchase tickets in advance, the vehicles get very full, US$14 in front, US$8 in the back (worth spending the extra money), 8-10 hrs or more.

### Cerro de Pasco and around
There is a large bus station. To **Lima** several companies including **Carhuamayo** and **Transportes Apóstol San Pedro**, hourly 0800-1200, plus 4 departures 2030-2130, 8 hrs, US$8. If there are no convenient daytime buses, you could change buses in La Oroya. Buses leave when full, about every 20-30 mins, to **Carhuamayo** (1 hr, US$1), **Junín** (1½ hrs, US$1) and **La Oroya** (2½ hrs, US$2); *colectivos* also depart with a similar frequency, 1½ hrs, US$2.50, to La Oroya. To **Tarma**, **Empresa Junín**, at 0600, 1500, 3 hrs, $2.50; *colectivos* also depart hourly, 1½ hrs, US$4. To **Huancayo**, various companies leave throughout the day, 5 hrs, US$4. To **Huánuco**, buses and cars leave when full, about half hourly, 2½ hrs and 1½ hrs, US$2 and US$4 respectively.

### Huánuco and around
#### Air
The airport is just north of the city (T062-513066). Daily flights to/from **Lima** with **StarPerú** (28 de Julio 1015, T062-519595) and 2 a day with **LCPeru** (Jr Crespo y Castillo 614, T062-280357).

## Bus

To **Lima**, most buses leave 2030-2200, some also in the morning, 9-10 hrs, US$12-15 regular, US$17-19 *semi-cama*, US$20-28 *cama*; **Bahía Continental** (recommended, Valdizán 718, T062-519999), 4 daily including 1030; **GM** (28 de Julio 535, T962-813906), 8 daily including 0830; and **Turismo Real** (28 de Julio 580, T062-518022), 3 daily. To **Cerro de Pasco**, US$2, 3 hrs; *colectivos* US$4, 2 hrs, all leave when full from Ovalo Carhuayna on the north side of the city. To **Huancayo**, US$9.50-11, 8 hrs, with **Turismo Central** (Tarapacá y Abtao, www.turismocentral.com.pe), at 2130 and 2200; also to **La Merced** US$14, 6½ hrs, at 1930. *Colectivos* run to **Tingo María**, from block 10 of Gen Prado close to Puente Calicanto, US$6, 3 hrs, many companies including **Empresa de Automóviles No 5**

(recommended, Gen Prado 1085, T962-877272); also several vans including **Express San Juan** (Carreterra Central y Jr Llica), every 40 mins, US$3. For **Pucallpa**, **Turismo Central,** US$9.50-17, 9 hrs, at 2030 and 2100, or take a *colectivo* to Tingo María and transfer there. To **La Unión** on a narrow road, cars from several companies on Tarapacá between San Martín and Huayllaco, US$9.25, 3½ hrs, leave when full throught the day.

## La Unión and around

To **Huánuco**, several *colectivo* companies along Jr Comercio leave as they fill throughout the day, US$9, 3-4 hrs. To Huaraz on a fully paved, winding mountain road with beautiful scenery, with **Rápido**, Jr Comercio opposite the small bus terminal, US$4.50, 4 hrs, at 0300, 1100, 1300.

# Amazon Basin

fabulous flora and fauna

The Amazon Basin covers a staggering 4,000,000 sq km and the Peruvian Amazon is home to a diversity of life unequalled anywhere on Earth. It is this immense diversity which makes the jungle a paradise for nature lovers, be they scientists or simply curious amateurs.

The area is home to countless plants and animals, including 2000 species of fish and 300 mammals. It also has over 10% of the world's 8600 bird species and, together with the adjacent Andean foothills, 4000 butterfly species. At the same time, petroleum exploitation, illegal gold mining and logging, unsustainable agriculture and ranching, as well as uncontrolled colonization from the highlands are all perennial threats.

The two major tourist areas in the Peruvian Amazon are the northern and southern jungles. Northeastern Peru is dominated by vast floodplains and rivers. The southern Amazon is dominated by the floodplains of smaller meandering rivers and the most striking features are former river channels that have become isolated as oxbow lakes. The southern jungle is world famous for its clay licks, which offer unsurpassed birdwatching opportunities.

**Best** for
Ecotourism ▪ River trips ▪ Wildlife watching

Northern Amazon . . . . . . . . . . 398
Southern Amazon . . . . . . . . . . 418

# Footprint picks

## ★ Pacaya-Samiria Reserve, page 404

Travel by boat through this two-million-hectare reserve to see countless species of mammal, bird and fish, many of them endangered.

## ★ Iquitos, page 407

The isolated yet bustling jungle city is a world-apart from the rest of Peru and an excellent base for exploring the northern jungle; don't miss the market in Belén.

## ★ Manu Biosphere Reserve, page 419

A massive conservation area encompassing wildlife zones from 200 to 4100 m above sea level. Stay at a jungle lodge to experience the reserve's extraordinary natural diversity.

## ★ Tambopata National Reserve, page 429

Along the Río Tambopata are famous *collpas* (clay licks) and oxbow lakes amid virgin rainforest, both ideal places for birdwatching and wildlife observation.

N

100 km
100 miles

ECUADOR          COLOMBIA

Pantoja
Curaray
Copal Urco
Napo
Marsella
San Jacinto
Andoas
Tigre
Intuto
Mazán
Amazonas
Indiana
Iquitos
Pebas
Caballococha
San Pablo
Leticia
Santa Rosa
Trompeteros
Morona
Pastaza
Nauta
Borja
Marañón
San Ramón
Lagunas
Reserva Nacional
Pacaya-Samiria
BRAZIL
Balsapuertos
Yurimaguas
Ucayali
Moyobamba
Lamas
Tarapoto
Huallabamba
Pampas de Sacramento
Tocache Nuevo
L. Yarinacocha
Pucallpa
Aucayacu
La Morada
Aguaytía
Tournavista
Tingo María
Huaraz
Acomayo
Huánuco
Huancabamba
Atalaya
Cerro
De Pasco
San
Ramón
Mazamari
Iñapari
Iberia
Junín
Tarma
La Oroya
Jauja
Manu
Biosphere
Reserve
Madre Dios
Boca Manu
Boca
Colorado
Puerto
Maldonado
LIMA
Huancayo
Itahuanía
Shintuya
Laberinto
Huancavelica
Ayna
Atalaya
Bahuaja-Sonene
National Park
Tambopata
National Reserve
Ayacucho
Calca
Cuzco
Urcos
Ica
Nazca

**Footprint**
picks

1  **Pacaya-Samiria Reserve**, page 404
2  **Iquitos**, page 407
3  **Manu Biosphere Reserve**, page 419
4  **Tambopata National Reserve**, page 429

# Essential Amazon Basin

## Getting around

Iquitos is the main transport and tourism hub in the northern Amazon. It has an airport with flights to/from Lima and several river ports; the main ports for long-distance services are Puerto Henry and Puerto Masusa, north of the centre. When travelling from the highlands, the roads end at Yurimaguas on the Río Huallaga and at Pucallpa on the Río Ucayali. From these towns onward transport is by riverboat.

In the southern Amazon the main hub is Puerto Maldonado, which has an airport with flights to/from Lima and Cuzco. Buses and tours from Cuzco travel either via Atalaya and Itahuania to reach Manu National Park, or via Quincemil and Mazuko on the Interoceanic Highway to reach Puerto Maldonado. Beyond Puerto Maldonado, the Interoceanic Highway continues to the border at Iñapari and on into Brazil.

## When to go

April to October is the dry season; September is the best month to see flowers and butterflies in the northern jungle. November to March or April is the rainy season and can be oppressively hot; there are also more mosquitoes in the wet season. Expect some rain at any time of year.

## Time required

Allow one week to explore the northern jungle and one week in the southern jungle.

### Tip...
When travelling in the Peruvian Amazon, make sure you are properly equipped. Take a sun hat, long-sleeved shirt, rain poncho, rubber boots on jungle trips, binoculars, a torch or headlamp, sun block, and insect repellent. Also a mosquito net if heading into remote areas.

## Weather Iquitos

| Month | High | Low | Rainfall |
|-------|------|-----|----------|
| January | 31°C | 22°C | 260mm |
| February | 30°C | 22°C | 250mm |
| March | 30°C | 22°C | 290mm |
| April | 30°C | 22°C | 300mm |
| May | 30°C | 22°C | 260mm |
| June | 29°C | 22°C | 300mm |
| July | 29°C | 21°C | 160mm |
| August | 30°C | 22°C | 160mm |
| September | 31°C | 22°C | 190mm |
| October | 31°C | 22°C | 230mm |
| November | 31°C | 22°C | 240mm |
| December | 31°C | 22°C | 250mm |

# Northern
Amazon

Cooled by winds sweeping down from the Andes but warmed by its jungle blanket, this region contains important tropical flora and fauna. It is a very varied landscape, with grasslands and tablelands of scrub-like vegetation, inaccessible swamps and forests up to 2000 m above sea level. The principal means of communication is by the many rivers, the most important being the Amazon, which rises high up in the Andes as the Marañón, then joins the Ucayali to become the longest river in the world. The northern tourist area is based on the River Amazon itself around thebig busy city of Iquitos. Although it has lost its rubber-boom dynamism, Iquitos is still at the heart of life on the river. There are jungle lodges upstream and down, each with its own speciality and level of comfort, but none is more than half a day away by fast boat. To get right into the wilds, head for Peru's largest national reserve, Pacaya-Samiria, accessed by boat from Iquitos or from the little town of Lagunas.

## Huánuco to Tingo María

The road to Tingo María from Huánuco, 135 km, is fully paved and filled with heavy lorry traffic. Some 25 km beyond Huánuco it begins a sharp climb to the Carpish tunnel (2707 m), after which a descent of 58 km brings it to the Río Huallaga again; it then continues along the river to Tingo María. Travel by day to enjoy the lovely views.

## Tingo María

Tingo María (population approximately 50,000) is beautifully situated on the Río Huallaga near its confluence with the Río Monzón. The Cordillera Azul, the jungle-covered front range of the Andes, separates this striking transition zone from the Amazon lowlands to the east. At 650 m above sea level the climate is warm but not oppressive (annual rainfall 2650 mm) and nights are pleasantly fresh. Starting around 2005, crop substitution programs replaced much of the coca leaf grown in the area with coffee and cocoa. **Choco Passion** (T991-235028), open to visitors in the nearby town of Bella, is one of several co-operatives producing high-quality chocolate. In 2018 Tingo María and surroundings were safe, tranquil and increasingly popular with Peruvian vacationers. A nice shady spot for a stroll is the 4-ha **Jardín Botánico** ① *Enrique Pimentel cuadra 3, at the end of Alameda Perú, Mon-Fri 0700-1430, US$0.50.*

**Parque Nacional Tingo María** ① *4800 ha, entry US$9.25 sold at visitors sites and valid for 2 days, park office at Elias Mabama 290, Barrio Tupac Amaru, T062-563559, Mon-Fri 0800-1300, 1500-1800,* includes the large **Cueva de las Lechuzas** (Km 5 on the road to Bella, mototaxi US$0.60), where many oilbirds and bats roost. The national park protects the formation known as **La Bella Durmiente** (the Sleeping Beauty, visible from all over town), with hiking trails through forest filled with birds, butterflies and waterfalls. Take a *colectivo* (US$0.60) from behind the market to Gloriapata where a suspension bridge (Puente 3 de Mayo) crosses the Río Huallaga to the ranger station and the start of a 5-km hike to **Cataratas Gloriapata** and **Sol Naciente**. You can trek all the way across the park in two or three days from Gloriapata to Cueva de las Lechuzas, advance arrangements and guide required (US$15 per person), bring all your own supplies.

## Tingo María to Pucallpa

From Tingo María a fully paved road continues 255 km to Pucallpa. It climbs over the Cordillera Azul, the watershed between the Huallaga and Ucayali rivers. Travel by day for great views as you go from the high jungle to the Amazon Basin. When the road was being surveyed it was thought that the lowest pass over the Cordillera Azul was over 3650 m high, but then an old document was discovered, stating that a Father Abad had found a pass through these mountains in 1757. As a consequence, the road goes through the **Boquerón del Padre Abad**, a gigantic gap 4 km long and 2000 m deep. Beyond the pass the road runs along the floor of a magnificent canyon. It is a beautiful trip through luxuriant jungle, ferns and sheer walls of bare rock, punctuated by occasional waterfalls plunging into the roaring torrent below. Further east the road goes over the flat pampa, with few bends, to the town of **Aguaytía**, from where it continues for 160 km to Pucallpa.

## Pucallpa *Colour map 3, A5.*

Pucallpa is a rapidly expanding jungle city (population 220,000) on the Río Ucayali, navigable by vessels of 3000 tons from Iquitos, 533 nautical miles away. Different 'ports' are used depending on the level of the river; they are mostly mud banks without any facilities (see Transport, page 403). The economy of the area is based on timber, relentlessly depleting the rainforest, as well as an oil refinery, fishing and boat building. Pucallpa is very hot, the dry season is June to November and it rains from December to May. In the Parque Natural de Pucallpa the **Museo Regional** ⓘ *Cra Federico Basadre Km 4.2, Mon-Fri 0800-1630, Sat and Sun 0900-1730, park entry US$1.50*, has examples of Shipibo ceramics, as well as some delightful pickled snakes and other reptiles.

### Lago Yarinacocha
*Northeast of Pucallpa, 20 mins by colectivo or bus along Jr Ucayali, US$1.50, or 15 mins by taxi.*

The main attraction in this area is Lago Yarinacocha, an oxbow lake linked to the Río Ucayali by a canal at the northern tip of its west arm. Pink river dolphins (*bufeo colorado*) can be seen here. **Puerto Callao**, also known as **Yarinacocha** or **Yarina**, is the main town at the southern tip, reached by road or tour boat (US$3 per person, minimum US$15 per boat) from Pucallpa. There are many restaurants and bars here and it gets crowded at weekends.

**Pucallpa**

Where to stay
1 Antonio's
2 Arequipa
3 Barbtur
4 Grand Hotel Mercedes
5 Komby

Restaurants
1 C'est si Bon

200 metres
200 yards

From the town, a road continues along the western arm to **San José**, **San Francisco** and **Santa Clara** (bus US$3 from Yarina). The area is populated by the Shipibo people, who make ceramic and textile crafts. The area between the eastern arm of the lake and the Río Ucayali has been designated a reserve and incorporates the beautifully located **Jardín Botánico Chullachaqui** ① *free, reached by boat from Puerto Callao to Pueblo Nueva Luz de Fátima, 45 mins, then a 1-hr walk, guides available in Puerto Callao.*

## Listings From Huánuco to Pucallpa *map page 400.*

### Tourist information

#### Tingo María

**Municipal tourist office**
*Alameda Perú 525, T062-562058,*
*www.munitingomaria.gob.pe.*
*Mon-Fri 0800-1300, 1430-1715.*
Very helpful.

#### Pucallpa

**Dircetur**
*Jr 2 de Mayo 111, T061-575110.*
*Mon-Fri 0730-1300, 1330-1515.*

**Gobierno Regional de Ucayali**
*GOREU; Raimondi block 220, T061-575018.*

### Where to stay

#### Tingo María
There are many hotels in all categories. Those in the centre, especially along the main avenue, Alameda Perú, are often noisy.

**$$$-$$ Shushupe**
*Av Alameda Perú 362, T062-284505,*
*www.shushupehotel.pe.*
Modern and comfortable but rather small rooms with fan and frigobar, rooftop pool and terrace with nice views, excellent buffet breakfast, attentive staff, discounts in low season, opened in 2018.

**$$ Albergue Ecológico Villa Jennifer**
*Km 3.4 Monterrico, Castillo Grande, 10 mins from town and the airport, T962-603509,*
*www.villajennifer.com.*
Pleasant older rooms surrounded by 10 ha of land with lots of birdlife. Includes breakfast,

restaurant, 2 pools, mini-golf, birdwatching, tours to local sites. Danish/Peruvian-owned.

**$$ Madera Verde**
*Av Universitaria s/n, out of town on the road to Huánuco, near the University, T062-561800,*
*www.maderaverdehotel.com.pe.*
Older wooden chalets, cabins and rooms in beautiful surroundings, breakfast included, restaurant, 2 swimming pools, small zoo.

**$ Nueva York**
*Av Alameda Perú 553, T062-562406,*
*info@hotelnuevayork.com.pe.*
Ample rooms and common areas, private bath, refurbished in 2017, central location, no breakfast.

**$ Tingo María**
*Av Ucayali 528, T062 283474,*
*hoteltingomaria@gmail.com.*
Very clean rooms with private bath and fan, some have hot water, cheaper on top floor with cold water, small patio/garden, ample parking, friendly, family-run, good value, no breakfast.

#### Pucallpa
There is a **Casa Andina** (www.casa-andina.com) in town.

**$$$-$$ Grand Hotel Mercedes**
*Raimondi 610, T061-575120,*
*www.granhotelmercedes.com.*
Pucallpa's first hotel, still family-run, with some refurbished rooms, modern facilities with old-fashioned ambiance, includes breakfast, hot water, a/c, fridge, pool, restaurant.

## $$ Antonio's
*Jr Progreso 545, T061-573721,*
*www.antonioshotel.com.pe.*
A variety of rooms and prices, garden,
pool, jacuzzi, parking, airport pick-up.

## $$ Komby
*Ucayali 360, T061-571562,*
*http://kombypucallpa.com.*
Cold water, fan or a/c, ample rooms, pool,
very noisy street but back rooms are quiet,
good value, free airport pick-up.

## $$-$ Arequipa
*Jr Progreso 573, T061-571348,*
*www.hostal-arequipa.com.*
Good, a/c or fan, breakfast, comfortable,
safe, restaurant, pool.

## $ Barbtur
*Raimondi 670, T061-572532.*
Cheaper without bath, central, good beds,
cold water, friendly but noisy.

---

### Lago Yarinacocha

## $$$ pp Yarina Ecolodge (Pandisho Amazon Ecolodge)
*North of the village of 11 de Agosto, towards*
*the northern tip of the eastern shore of the*
*west arm, T061-799214 (in Pucallpa, Pasaje*
*Bolívar 261, T961-994227).*
Full board, good resort with cabins by the
lakeshore, includes packages of varying
length and rainforest expeditions. Also has
a lodge in Pacaya-Samiria, Amazon Green.

### Restaurants

#### Tingo María
Local specialities include jungle river fish
such as *paiche* and *dorado*, as well as *tacacho*
made with mashed green bananas.

## $$ El Encanto de la Selva
*Av Alameda Perú 288, T062-562848,*
*also upstairs in the Mercado Modelo.*
*Daily 0700-2300.*
Variety of typical jungle fare à la carte. Open
kitchen, good food, presentation and service.
The *dorado saltado* is recommended.

## $$-$ El Carbón
*Av Raimondi 435, T062-564255, www.*
*elcarbonrestobar.com. Daily 1200-2400.*
*Menú ejecutivo* at lunchtime as well as
à la carte all day, VIP room in back with river
views (à la carte only). Tasty dishes, attentive
service, live music Fri-Sun night. Popular.

## $ Vegetariano
*Jr Monzón 468. Sun-Thu 0700-2230,*
*Fri 0700-1500.*
Good vegetarian *menú* with generous
portions and a variety of options.

---

### Pucallpa

## $$ Parillada
*Jr Tacna y San Martín.*
Grill serving a variety of meats and regional
specialities such as *cecina con tacacho*.

## $$-$ C'est si bon
*Jr Independencia 560 y Pasaje Zegarra,*
*Plaza de Armas. Daily 0800-2400.*
Cafeteria serving chicken, snacks, drinks,
sweets and ice cream.

### Festivals

#### Tingo Maria
**24 Jun  San Juan** is celebrated here and
throughout the Peruvian Amazon.

#### Pucallpa
**Feb  Carnival.**
**24 Jun  San Juan.**
**Oct**  Ucayali regional fair.

### Shopping

#### Pucallpa
Many Shibipo women carry and sell their
products around Pucallpa and Yarinacocha.
For local wood carvings visit the workshop
of **Agustín Rivas** (Jr Tarapacá 861/863,
above a small restaurant; ask for it), whose
work is made from huge tree roots.
**Artesanías La Anaconda** (Pasaje Cohen
by Plaza de Armas) has a good selection
of indigenous crafts.

## What to do

### Pucallpa
**Usko Ayar Amazonian School of Painting**,
*Jr LM Sánchez Cerro 465-467, T958-623871,
see Facebook page.* Located in the house of
artist and healer Pablo Amaringo, who died
in 2009, the renowned school provides art
classes for local people and is dependent
upon selling their art. It welcomes overseas
visitors for short or long stays to study
painting and learn Spanish and/or to teach
English to Peruvian students.

## Transport

### Tingo María
**Air**
To/from **Lima** daily with **LCPerú**
(Av Raymiondi 571, T062-561672) and
3 weekly with **ATSA** (www.atsaairlines.com,
local agent Tropical Tours, T961-556335).

### Bus
Most transport companies are along
Jr Raimondi and Jr Pimentel. To
**Huánuco**, US$6, 3 hrs, many companies
including **Empresa de Automóviles
No 5** (recommended, Jr Raimondi 108,
T962-875252); also several vans including
**Express San Juan** (Raimondi cuadra 5),
every 40 mins, US$3. To **Lima**, 12 hrs, regular
US$15.50, *semi-cama* US$18-21, *cama* US$22-
32; with **Bahía Continental** (recommended,
Pimentel 188, T962-622746) at 0730, 1900,
1930; **Tepsa** (Raimondi 686, T989-015475) at
1930; **Turismo Central** (Raimondi cuadra 9,
T062-562668, www.turismocentral.com.pe)
at 1900; **GM Internacional** (Av Raimondi 740,
T062-561895, www.gminternacional.com.pe)
at 1900 and 1945. To **Pucallpa**, US$6-7,
5-6 hrs, with **Transmar** (Pimentel 147,
T062-564733, www.transmar.com.pe)
around 0600, and **Turismo Central** around
0730, both originate in Lima; also *colectivos*
including **Pizana Express** (Raimondi 128,
T062-561087), **Turismo Ucayali** (Av Tito
Jaime 215, T062-564193) and **Selva Express**
(Av Tito Jaime 218, T062-562380), US$14,

4½ hrs. To **Tarapoto** (paving in progress in
2018 between Tocache and Juanjui), US$17,
10 hrs, with **Transmar**, Mon, Wed, Fri; and
**Transamazónica** (Pimentel 148) daily, both
originate in Pucallpa and pass Tingo María
around 2400; also vans with **Pizana Express**,
US$21.50, 9 hrs, at 0400 and 0900.

### Pucallpa
**Air**
To **Lima** and **Iquitos**, daily 1 hr, with **LATAM**
(Jr Tarapacá 805, T061-579840), **Peruvian**
(Independencia 324, T061-505655) and
**Star Perú** (7 de Junio 865, T061-590585).
To **Tarapoto**, 3 weekly with each of **SAETA**
(www.saetaperu.com) and **North American**
(T961-717276, www.northamerican.pe), they
also fly to regional destinations. Airport taxis
charge US$6 to town; other taxis charge US$3.

### Bus
Bus terminal at Km 4 on the road to Tingo
María, car and van terminal at Km 6, some
companies have city offices for ticket sales.
To **Lima**, several companies, US$24-28 *semi-
cama*, US$29-35, *cama*, 18 hrs; **Tepsa** at 1400,
**GM** at 1430 and **Transmar** (T061-579778,
www.transmar.com.pe). To **Tingo María**,
take **Turismo Central** or **Transmar** on their
service to Lima; for *colectivos* see Tingo
María transport, above. To **Tarapoto**, US$22,
15-16 hrs; **Transamazónica** at 1800 daily,
**Transmar** Tue, Thu, Sat.

### Riverboat
Boats to all destinations dock around
Puerto Inmaculada, 2 blocks downriver
from the Malecón Grau, at the bottom of
Jr Inmaculada, unless the water level is very
high, in which case they dock at Puerto
Manantay, 4 km south of town. A mototaxi
to any of the ports costs US$0.75 from the
Plaza de Armas; taxis charge US$3.

To **Iquitos** down the Ucayali and Amazon
rivers, 3-4 days, longer if the water level is
low when larger boats must travel only by
day, hammock US$40, berth US$140 double.
**Henry** is a large company with departures

Mon, Wed, Fri and Sat from Puerto Henry at the bottom of Jr Manco Capac, by Jr Arica; their newer boats, *Henry 6* and *7*, have some cabins with private bath. Another good boat is *Pedro Martín 2* sailing from Puerto Inmaculada. You must ask around for the large boats to Iquitos. Departure times are marked on chalk boards on the deck. Schedules seem to change almost hourly. Do not pay for your trip before you board the vessel, and only pay the captain. Some boat captains may allow you to live on board for a couple of days before sailing. See also Getting around, page 489.

## Yurimaguas and Pacaya-Samiria

explore the waterways and wetlands

The Río Huallaga winds northwards for 930 km from its source to the confluence with the Marañón. The Upper Huallaga is a torrent, dropping 15.8 m per km between its source and Tingo María. In contrast, the Lower Huallaga moves through an enervation of flatness. Its main port, Yurimaguas, lies below the last rapids and only 150 m above the Atlantic Ocean yet is distant from that ocean by over a month's voyage. Between the Upper and Lower rivers lies the Middle Huallaga, the third of the river that is downstream from Tingo María and upstream from Yurimaguas.

### Yurimaguas *Colour map 1, B5.*
Yurimaguas is connected by road with the Pacific coast, via Tarapoto (120 km) and Moyobamba (see page 182). It's a very relaxed jungle town and, as the roadhead on the lower Río Huallaga, is an ideal starting point for river travel in the Peruvian Amazon. A colourful Mercado Central is open every morning, full of fruit and jungle animals, many, sadly, for the pot. The town's patron saint, La Santísima Virgen de las Nieves, is celebrated from 5 to 15 August each year, which coincides with tourism week. Excursions in the area include the gorge of Shanusi and the lakes of Mushuyacu and Sanango.

> **Tip...**
> There are several banks with ATMs in town and **Casa de Cambio Progreso** (Progreso 117) changes US$ cash.

### ★ Reserva Nacional Pacaya-Samiria *Colour map 2, C2.*
*SERNANP, Jorge Chávez 930/942, Iquitos, T065-223555, Mon-Fri 0700-1300, 1500-1700. Entry US$2 for 1 day, US$23 for 3 days, US$46 for 7 days, payable at the ranger stations.*

Northeast of Yurimaguas, this vast reserve is bounded by the rivers Marañón and Ucuyali, narrowing to their confluence near the town of Nauta. At 2,080,000 ha, it is the country's second-largest protected area. The reserve's waterways and wetlands provide habitat for several cats (including puma and jaguar), manatee, tapir, river dolphins, giant otters, black cayman, boas, 269 species of fish and 449 bird species. Many of the animals found here are in danger of extinction. There are 208 population centres in the area of the reserve, 92 within the park, the others in the buffer zone. Five native groups plus colonos live in the region.

The reserve can only be visited with an authorized guide arranged through a tour operator or a local community tourism association. Native guides generally speak only Spanish and native tongues. Most of the reserve is off-limits to tourists, but eight areas have been set up for visitors. These have shelters or camping areas; conditions are generally simple and may require sleeping in hammocks. Trips are mostly on the river and often include fishing. Four circuits are most commonly offered. All are rich in wildlife.

The basin of the Yanayacu and Pucate rivers is the most frequently visited area and includes Laguna El Dorado, an important attraction. This area is accessed from **Nauta** on the Marañón, 1½ to two hours by paved road from Iquitos. It's three hours by *peque peque* or 1½ hours by *deslizador* from Nauta to the reserve. Note that Nauta has pirate guides, so it's best to arrange a tour with an operator.

The middle and lower Samiria is accessed from **Leoncio Prado** (which has a couple of *hospedajes*), 24 hours by *lancha* from Iquitos along the Marañón. Several lakes are found in this area.

The lower Pacaya, mostly flooded forest, is accessed from **Bretaña** on the Canal de Puinahua, a shortcut on the Ucayali, 24 hours by *lancha* from Iquitos. This area is less frequently visited than others.

The Tibilo-Pastococha area in the western side of the park, also in the Samiria Basin, is accessed from **Lagunas**, on the Río Huallaga. It's 10-12 hours by *lancha* or three hours by *deslizador* from Yurimaguas, 17 hours by *deslizador* from Nauta and 48 hours by *lancha* from Iquitos. All river traffic from Yurimaguas to Iquitos stops here.

Another way of visiting the reserve is on a cruise, sailing along the main rivers on the periphery of the park. These tours are offered by some Iquitos operators.

## Listings Yurimaguas and Pacaya-Samiria

### Tourist information

**Yurimaguas**
Ask for information at the **Municipalidad Provincial de Alto Amazonas** (Plaza de Armas 112-114, T065-351213), or see www.yurimaguas.net.

**Pacaya-Samiria Reserve**
General information and a list of authorized community associations and operators is found on the reserve's web page, at the reserve office in Iquitos and at **iPerú** in Iquitos.

### Where to stay

**Yurimaguas**

**$$$-$$ Río Huallaga**
*Arica 111, T065-353951,*
*Facebook: RioHuallagaHotel.*
Pleasant modern hotel overlooking the river, safety box, pool, bar, cinema, rooftop restaurant with lovely views.

**$$-$ Hostal Luis Antonio**
*Av Jaúregui 407, T352062, hostal_luis_*
*antonio@hotmail.com (also on Facebook).*
Cold water, small pool, a/c at extra cost, breakfast, very helpful.

**$$-$ Posada Cumpanama**
*Progreso 403, T065-352905, http://*
*posadacumpanama.blogspot.com.*
Rooms cheaper with shared bath, breakfast extra, tastefully decorated, pool, very pleasant.

**$ Hostal Akemi**
*Jr Angamos 414, T065-352237,*
*www.hostalakemi.com.*
Decent rooms with hot water, cheaper without a/c, some with frigobar, restaurant, pool, helpful owner, good value.

**$ Hostal El Caballito**
*Av Jaúregui 403, T065-352427.*
Cold water, small bathroom, fan, pleasant, good value.

## $ Hostal El Naranjo

*Arica 318, T065-352650.*
A/c or fan, hot water, frigobar, small pool,
with restaurant.

### Pacaya-Samiria Reserve

#### $$$$ Pacaya Samiria Amazon Lodge

*www.pacayasamiria.com.pe; office at
Urbanización Las Palmeras 09, Iquitos,
T065-225769.*
Hatuchay hotel group. Beautifully designed
lodge on a hill overlooking the Marañón,
just inside the reserve but close to road
and town. All buildings in indigenous style,
with balconies and en suite bathrooms,
restaurant, bar. Community visits and
specialist birdwatching trips included in
the price, but boat trips (also included) can
be long. Camping trips can be arranged
deeper inside the reserve. Packages start at
US$520 pp for 3-day/2-night programme.

#### $$$ Ecological Jungle Trips &
Expeditions Tours

*www.ecologicaljungletrips.com;
office at Putumayo 163 p 2, Iquitos,
T965-783409/942-643020.*
Delfín Lodge, 2½ hrs from Nauta on the
Río Yarapa, is the base for tours to Pacaya-
Samiria, 10 rooms. Programmes from 3 days
to 7 days, tailored according to the interests
of the guests.

$ Basic places in Nauta include **Nauta Inn**
(Manuel Pacaya by Laguna Sapi Sapi, T065-
411025) and **Plaza Inn** (Marañón 365, T65-
411735, with bath, some rooms with a/c).

$ Basic places in Lagunas include **Eco**
(Jr Padre Lucero, near cemetery, T065-
503703); **Hostal Paraíso Verde** (Carrión
320, ½ block from the plaza, T941 809988,
www.hostalparaisoverde.com, with fan and
electric shower); **Samiria** (Jr José Cárdenas,
near the market).

## What to do

### Yurimaguas

**Huayruro Tours**, *Río Huallaga Hotel,
Yurimaguas; also at Alfonso Aiscorbe 2 in
Lagunas, T065-401186, www.peruselva.com.*
Tours to lakes, day and multi-day trips to
Pacaya-Samiria.

### Pacaya-Samiria

Community associations in many of the
villages around the reserve run tours.
Community tours cost about US$70 pp
per day, compared to US$80 minumum for
agency tours arranged in Iquitos. Make sure
you know exactly what is included (park fees,
lodging, food, transport, guide), what the
trip involves (canoeing, walking, hunting,
fishing) and the type of accommodation.
In the community of San Martín de Tipishca
in the Samiria Basin are **Asiendes** (Asociación
Indígena en Defensa de la Ecología Samiria),
T965-861748, asiendesperu@hotmail.com
(asiendes.peru on Facebook) and **Casa
Lupuna**. 5 associations operate in Lagunas;
a tour operator is **Huayruro Tours** (see above).
In Bretaña, the **Gallán family** offer tours.

## Transport

### Yurimaguas
#### Air
**SAETA** (www.saetaperu.com) flies Mon, Wed,
Fri, to Iquitos and Tarapoto.

#### Bus
The road to Tarapoto is paved. To Lima, with
**Paredes Estrella** (Mariscal Cáceres 220),
0830 daily, 32-34 hrs, US$38.50, via **Tarapoto**
(US$4), **Moyobamba** (US$7.75, 5-6 hrs),
**Pedro Ruiz** (US$17.50), **Chiclayo** (US$27) and
**Trujillo** (US$33). Also **Ejetur**, 0500 to Lima.
Faster than the bus to Tarapoto are: **Gilmer
Tours** (C Victor Sifuentes 580), frequent mini-
buses, US$5.75, 2½ hrs; cars (eg **San Martín**)
US$7.75; and combis (**Turismo Selva**, Mcal
Cáceres 3rd block) US$4.

**Riverboat**
There are 6 docks in all. To **Iquitos**, *lanchas* from Embarcadero La Boca, 3 days/2 nights, best is **Eduardo/Gilmer** (Elena Pardo 114, T065-352552; see under Iquitos, Transport).

To **Lagunas** for Pacaya-Samiria Reserve, from Embarcadero Abel Guerra at 0900, US$11.55, 10 hrs. Also *rápidos* to Lagunas and Nauta (1½ hrs by *colectivo* from Iquitos, US$4), see Iquitos Transport, page 416.

see Iquitos Transport, page 416.

## ★ Iquitos and around  Colour map 2, B4.

*unique jungle city and gateway to the Amazon*

Iquitos stands on the west bank of the Amazon and is the main city (population 500,000) of Peru's jungle region. Some 800 km downstream from Pucallpa and 3646 km from the mouth of the Amazon, the city is completely isolated except by air and river. Its first wealth came from the rubber boom in the late 19th century and early 20th century, but now the main economic activities are logging, commerce, petroleum and tourism. The atmosphere of the city is completely different from the rest of Peru: hot, dirty, colourful, noisy and congested with the tens of thousands of mototaxis and motorcycles that fill the streets. Iquitos is the main starting point for tourists wishing to explore Peru's northern jungle. Here you can experience the authentic Amazon, from the chaotic streets of the city to the pink dolphins and Victoria regia water lilies of the river and its waterways. Iquitos has many good restaurants.

### Sights
The incongruous **Iron House/Casa de Fierro** stands on the Plaza de Armas, designed by Eiffel for the Paris exhibition of 1889. It is constructed entirely of iron trusses and sheets, bolted together and painted silver and was supposedly transported from Paris by a local rubber baron. It now houses a pharmacy. Of special interest in the city are the older buildings, faced with *azulejos* (glazed tiles). They date from the rubber boom of 1890 to 1912, when the rich merchants imported tiles from Portugal and Italy and ironwork from England to embellish their homes. **Museo Amazónico** ① *Malecón Tarapacá 386, T065-234221, Mon-Sat 0800-1300, 1430-1730, Sun 0800-1230, free, some guides speak English, tip expected*, in the Prefectura, has displays of native art and sculptures by Lima artist Letterstein. Also worth visiting is the **Museo de Culturas Indígenas Amazónicas** ① *Malecón Tarapacá 332, T065-235809, daily 0800-1930, US$5.25*, the private museum of Dr Richard Bodmer, who owns the **Casa Morey** hotel (see below). It celebrates cultures from the entire Amazon region; ask here about historic Amazonian boats, such as **Barco Ayapua** ① *Plaza Ramón Castilla, T065-236072, US$5*, an early 20th-century vessel from the rubber boom era, fully restored for visits, expeditions and short trips. The waterfront by Malecón Maldonado, known as 'Boulevard', is a pleasant place for a stroll and gets busy on Friday and Saturday evenings.

**Belén**, the picturesque, lively waterfront district, is an authentic part of Amazon river life, but is not safe at night. Most of its huts were originally built on rafts to cope with the river's 10 m change of level during floods from January to July; now they're more commonly built on stilts. Arrive by 0700 to see people arriving with their forest fruits and fish to sell in the **Belén market**. On Pasaje Paquito are bars serving local sugar cane rum and places where shamans buy medicinal plants and other items for their ceremonies. The main plaza has a bandstand made by Eiffel. In the high season canoes can be hired on the waterfront for a tour of Belén, US$3 per hour. To get there take a mototaxi to Los Chinos and walk down to the port.

## Around Iquitos

When the river is low (June-September), there is a pleasant beach, with white sand and palms, at **Tipishca** on the Río Nanay, reached in 20 minutes by boat from Puerto de Santa Clara near the airport; it gets quite busy at weekends. **Santa Rita**, reached from Puerto

**Iquitos**

To **9**, Explorama Tours & ports (Embarcadero Turístico, Masusa & Bellavista)

To **4** & offices of rápidos to Brazil

To **13**

To **3**

Craft Kiosks

Pevas

Nauta

Napo

Putumayo

Indecopi **3**

Plaza de Armas, Iron House, Casá de Hierro

Cathedral

Calvo de Araujo

Boulevard

Mercado Artesanal Anaconda

Mercado Central

Colombian Consulate

Sgto Lores

Muyuna

LATAM

Peruvian Airlines

Museo de Culturas Indígenas Amazónicas

Brazilian Consulate

Museo Amazónico

Morona

Supermarket

Río Itaya

Brasil

Ricardo Palma

Malecón Tarapacá

To Immigration

Av M Cáceres

San Martín

Plaza de 28 de Julio

Ucayali

Bermúdez

To Airport & Nauta

To Belén & Market

N

200 metres

200 yards

**Where to stay** 🛌
1 Best Western
2 Casa Andina
3 Casa Linda
4 Casa Morey
5 Double Tree by Hilton
6 El Sitio
7 Green Track Hostel
8 Hostal El Colibrí
9 La Casa Fitzcarraldo
10 La Casona
11 Las Amazonas Inn
12 Marañón
13 Nativa Apartments
14 Victoria Regia

**Restaurants** 🍴
1 Amazon Bistro
2 Antica Pizzería
3 Chef Paz
4 Chez Maggy Pizzería
5 El Carbón
6 El Sitio
7 Espresso Café
8 Festejo
9 Fitzcarraldo
10 Helados La Muyuna
11 Huasaí
12 La Gran Maloca
13 La Mona
14 María's Café
15 Mitos y Cubiertos
16 Norma Mía
17 Panadería Tívoli
18 Yellow Rose of Texas

**Bars & clubs** 🍸
19 Arandú
20 Ikaro
21 Karma
22 Noa Noa

## BACKGROUND
## Rubber barons

The conquest and colonization of the vast Amazon Basin was consolidated by the end of the 19th century with the invention of the process of vulcanizing rubber. Many and varied uses were found for this new product and demand was such that the jungle began to be populated by numerous European and North American immigrants who came to exploit this resource boom.

The rubber tree grew wild in the Amazon but the indigenous peoples were the only ones who knew the forests and could find this coveted tree. The exporting companies set up business in rapidly expanding cities along the Amazon, such as Iquitos. They sent their slave hunters out into the surrounding jungle to find the native labour needed to collect the valuable rubber resin. These people were completely enslaved; their living conditions were intolerable, and they perished in their thousands, leading to the extinction of many indigenous groups.

An especially notable figure from the rubber boom was Carlos Fermín Fitzcarrald, the Peruvian-born son of a sailor from the United States. He was accused of spying during the 1879 war between Peru and Chile and fled to the Amazon where he lived for many years among the indigenous people.

Thanks to Fitzcarrald, the isthmus between the basin of the Ucayali river and that of the Madre de Dios was discovered. Before this, no natural form of communication was known between the two rivers. The first steamships to go up the Madre de Dios were carried by thousands of indigenous workers across the 8-km stretch of land that separated the two basins. Fitzcarrald, one of the region's richest men, died at the age of 36 when the ship on which he was travelling sank.

The rubber barons lived in the new Amazonian cities. Every imaginable luxury was imported for their use: latest Parisian fashions for the women; finest foreign liqueurs for the men; even the best musical shows were brought over from the Old World. But after the boom came the bust: the heyday of Amazon rubber came crashing to an end in 1912 when rubber grown in the French and British colonies in Asia and Africa began to compete on the world market.

Perhaps Peru's 21st-century mining barons should take note…

de Pampa Chica, on a turn-off from the airport road, is quieter. Also near the airport is the village of **Santo Tomás**. To get there turn left just before the airport, then take another left 300 m further on, then it's about 4 km to the village; mototaxi from Iquitos US$5. It has a nice lake for swimming and renting canoes; beaches appear when the river is low, from July to September. The restaurants at the lake are very basic, so it's best to take your own food.

**Pilpintuhuasi Butterfly Farm** ⓘ *near the village of Padre Cocha, T065-232665, www. amazonanimalorphanage.org, Tue-Sun 0900-1600, guided tours at 0930, 1100, 1330 and 1500, US$5, students US$3, includes guided tour*, has butterflies, a small, well-kept zoo and a rescue centre, run by Austrian biologist Goody Sperrer. (Next door is another butterfly farm run by Goody's ex-husband.) To get there catch a *colectivo* from Bellavista to Padre Cocha (20 minutes), then walk 15 minutes from there. If the river is high, speedboats can reach Pilpintuhuasi directly from Iquitos, US$25 return including waiting time; pay at the end.

The **Centro de Rescate Amazónico** ① *Km 4.5 on the road to Nauta, www.centrode rescateamazonico.com, Mon 1200-1500, Tue-Sun 0900-1500, 1-hr guided tour US$6, students US$3, must show ID*, is where orphaned and injured manatees and other aquatic mammals and wildlife are nursed until they can be released. It's a good place to see these endangered species. Further along the road to Nauta are several *balnearios*.

## Allpahuayo-Mishana Reserve
*SERNANP, Jorge Chávez 930/942, Iquitos, T065-223555. Mon-Fri 0700-1300, 1500-1700, reserve fees US$8.50, students US$6.25.*

On the Río Nanay, some 25 km south of Iquitos by the Nauta road or two hours by boat from Bellavista, this reserve protects the largest concentration of white sand jungle (varillales) in Peru. Part of the Napo ecoregion, it has one of the highest levels of biodiversity in the Amazon Basin. Among several endangered species are two primates and several endemic species. The area is rich in birds: 475 species have been recorded. Within the reserve at Km 25 is **Zoocriadero BIOAM**, a good birdwatching circuit in land belonging to the Instituto Nacional de Innovación Agraria (INIA). Just beyond is the **Jardín de Plantas Medicinales y Frutales** ① *Km 26.8, daily 0800-1600, guiding 0800-1000*; with over 2400 species of medicinal plants. At Km 28, **El Irapay Interpretation Centre** ① *Mon-Sat 0830-1430*, has a trail to Mishana village by the river.

## Border with Brazil and Colombia
*Lanchas* and *rápidos* make the journey downriver to the tri-border. Details on exit and entry formalities change frequently, so when leaving Peru, check in Iquitos first at **Immigration** ① *Mcal Cáceres 18th block, T065-235371, Mon-Fri 0800-1615*, or with the **Capitanía** at the port. Boats stop in **Santa Rosa** for Peruvian exit formalities. Santa Rosa has various simple hotels ($): Bellavista, half a block past immigration, with private bath, Diana and Las Hamacas are all reported adequate. Motorized canoes cross the river from Santa Rosa to **Tabatinga** (Brazil, passports stamped at **Policia Federal**), which is adjacent to **Leticia** (Colombia, passports stamped at the airport).

> **Tip...**
> Reais and pesos colombianos are accepted in all three towns; soles are seldom used. There are ATMs in Tabatinga and Leticia, and the latter is the best place to change cash.

> **Tip...**
> If you are only visiting any of the towns for the day, there is no need to get stamped-in, but always keep your passport with you. Remember that Leticia and Santa Rosa are one hour behind Tabatinga.

**Consulates in Iquitos**: Brazil ① *Sargento Lores 363, T065-235151, cg.iquitos@itamaraty. gov.br. Mon-Fri 0800-1400*, visas issued in two days; **Colombia** ① *Calvo de Araújo 431, T065-231461, http://iquitos.consulado.gov.co, Mon-Fri 0800-1400*.

## Tourist information

www.iquitosnews.com and www.iquitos
times.com have articles, maps and information.

### Indecopi
*Putumayo 464, T065-243490.*
*Mon-Fri 0830-1630.*
Contact if you have a complaint about service.

### iPerú
*Jr Napo 161, of 4, T065-236144, iperuiquitos@*
*promperu.gob.pe. Mon-Sat 0900-1800,*
*Sun 0900-1300.*
Also has a desk at the airport, open at flight
times. If arriving by air, go to this desk first to
get a list of hotels, a map and advice about
the touts outside the airport.

### Tourist police
*Sargento Lores 834, T065-242081*
Contact to report a crime.

## Where to stay

Information on jungle lodges is given under
What to do, below, as many work closely or
exclusively with particular tour operators.
Around Peruvian Independence Day
(27 and 28 Jul) and Easter, Iquitos can get
crowded and flight prices rise at this time.

Chain hotels include: **Best Western** (www.
bestwestern.com), **Double Tree by Hilton**
(www.hilton.com), and **Casa Andina** (www.
casa-andina.com).

### $$$ Casa Morey
*Raymondi y Loreto, Plaza Ramón Castilla,*
*T065-231913, www.casamorey.com.*
Boutique hotel in a beautifully restored
historic rubber-boom period mansion. Great
attention to detail, includes airport transfers,
ample comfortable rooms, pool, good
library, good service, an excellent choice.

### $$$ Victoria Regia
*Ricardo Palma 252, T065-231983,*
*www.victoriaregiahotel.com.*

Free map of city, safe deposit boxes in rooms,
good restaurant, indoor pool.

### $$$-$$ La Casa Fitzcarraldo
*Av La Marina 2153, T065-601138,*
*http://casafitzcarraldo.com.*
Prices vary according to room. Includes
breakfast and airport transfer, with Wi-Fi,
satellite TV, minibar, 1st-class restaurant,
treehouse, pool in lovely gardens, captive
animals. The house is the home of Walter
Saxer, the executive-producer of Werner
Herzog's famous film, lots of movie and
celebrity memorabilia.

### $$$-$$ Marañón
*Fitzcarrald y Nauta 289, T065-242673,*
*http://hotelmaranon.com.*
Multi storey hotel, spotless comfortable
rooms, a/c, convenient location, small pool.

### $$$-$$ Nativa Apartments
*Nanay 144, T065-600270,*
*https://nativaapartments.com.*
Bright suites with kichenette and
apartments, a/c, no breakfast,
complementary tea and coffee.
Very attentive owner and staff.

### $$ La Casona
*Fitzcarrald 147, T065-234 394,*
*www.hotellacasonaiquitos.com.pe.*
In building dating from 1901, now
modernized, hot water, fan or a/c,
breakfast extra, kitchen facilities, small
patio, pool, popular with travellers.
Opposite, at Fitzcarrald 152, is **Hostal La
Casona Río Grande**, with smaller rooms,
fan. Transport to either from the airport
with advance reservation.

### $$ Las Amazonas Inn
*Ricardo Palma 460, T065-225367,*
*www.lasamazonasinn2.com.*
Simple rooms with electric shower, a/c,
kitchen facilities, breakfast available,
airport transfers included, friendly owner.

### $$-$ Casa Linda
*Napo 818, T065-231533, http://*
*residenciacasalinda.com.*
Good hotel in a quiet area, rooms with a/c,
private bath, hot water, frigobar.

### $$-$ Hostal El Colibrí
*Raymondi 200, T065-241737,*
*hostalelcolibri@hotmail.com.*
1 block from the plaza and 50 m from the
river so can be noisy, nicely refurbished
house, a/c or fan, hot water, gym, secure,
good value, breakfast extra, helpful staff.

### $ Green Track Hostel
*Ricardo Palma 516, T950-664049,*
*www.greentrack-hostel.com.*
Pleasant hostel, 4- to 6-bed dorms with a/c
or fan, private rooms with and without bath,
free pick-up with advanced booking, terrace,
Brazilian breakfast, English spoken, helpful
owners, tours arranged to Tapiche Reserve
(see page 416).

### $ El Sitio
*Ricardo Palma 541, T065-234932.*
Fan, private bath, cold water, good value.

## Restaurants

Local specialities include *a la Loretana*
dishes (prepared with local spices),
*inchicapi* (chicken, corn and peanut
soup), *cecina* (fried dried pork), *tacacho*
(fried green banana served with meat
or chicken, mashed into balls and eaten
for breakfast or tea), *juane* (chicken, rice,
olive and egg, seasoned and wrapped in
bijao leaves and sold in restaurants) and
the *camu-camu*, an acquired taste fruit,
said to have one of the highest vitamin C
concentrations in the world. Avoid eating
endangered species, such as paiche,
caiman, turtle or chonta (wild palm heart)
which are sometimes on menus.

For a good local breakfast, go to the **Mercado**
**Central**, C Sargento Lores, where there are
several kiosks outside, popular and cheap.
Try the local *jugo de cocona*, a tart fruit juice.

### $$$ Al Frío y al Fuego
*On the water, go to Embarcadero Turístico*
*(El Huequito) and a boat will pick you up,*
*T065-224862. Mon 1830-2300, Tue-Sat 1130-*
*1600 and 1830-2300, Sun 1130-1600.*
Good upscale floating restaurant with
regional specialities and a pool.

### $$$ Fitzcarraldo
*Malecón Maldonado 103 y Napo.*
Smart, typical food, also pizza, good pastas
and salads.

### $$$ La Gran Maloca
*Sargento Lores 170, opposite Banco Continental.*
*Closes 2000 on Sun, other days 2300.*
A/c, high-class regional food.

### $$$-$$ Amazon Bistro
*Malecón Tarapacá 268, T065-242918.*
*Mon-Sat 0600-0100, Sun 0700-1400.*
Upscale French bistro/bar on the
waterfront, drinks, snacks, breakfasts
and meal of the day. Goof food, trendy
and popular. Belgian/Peruvian-run. Live
music at weekends.

### $$$-$$ Chef Paz
*Putumayo 468, T065-241277.*
*Mon-Sat 0800-midnight.*
Excellent food including fish, shellfish,
meat dishes, local specialities and their
own jungle sushi.

### $$$-$$ Festejo
*Morona 287, T065-242660. Tue-Sat 1200-2200,*
*Sun 1200-1700.*
Very good Peruvian cooking, modern
decor, a/c.

### $$ Yellow Rose of Texas
*Putumayo 180. Open 24 hrs so you can wait*
*here if arriving late at night.*
Varied food including local dishes, Texan
atmosphere, good breakfasts, lots of
information, also has a bar, Sky TV and
Texan saddle seats.

### $$-$ Antica Pizzería
*Napo 159. Sun-Thu 0700-2400,*
*Fri-Sat 0700-0100.*

"The best pizza in town" and Italian dishes, pleasant ambiance especially on the upper level.

### $$-$ Chez Maggy Pizzería
*Raymondi 177. Daily 1800-0100.*
Wood-fired pizza and home-made pasta.

### $ El Carbón
*La Condamine 115. Open 1900-2300 only.*
Grilled meats, salads, regional side dishes such as *tacacho* and *patacones*.

### $ El Sitio
*Sargento Lores 404. Mon-Sat 1930-2230.*
A simple place for *anticuchos* for all tastes including vegetarian, popular.

### $ Huasaí
*Fitzcarrald 131. Open 0715-1615, closed Mon.*
Varied and innovative menu, popular, good food and value, go early.

### $ Mitos y Cubiertos
*Napo 337, by the plaza. Mon-Sat midday only.*
Generous lunches, good value.

## Cafés

### Espresso Café
*Jr Próspero 418, p2, http://espressocafe.com.pe. Daily 1700-2400.*
Upscale café-bar in a nicely decorated rubber-boom-era house. A variety of coffees and teas, gourmet sandwiches and snacks, desserts, art exhibits.

### Helados La Muyuna
*Jr Próspero 621 and on Napo near Malecón.*
Good natural jungle fruit ice cream.

### La Mona
*Jr Nauta 656. Mon 1630-2300, Tue-Sat 0730-1200, 1630-2300, Sun 0800-1200, 1700-2300.*
Café with a peaceful terrace with plants. Serves coffee, juices, sandwiches. Nice atmosphere and decor.

### María's Café
*Nauta 292. Tue-Sun 0800-1230.*
Breakfasts, sandwiches, burgers, coffee and cakes, with desserts of the day.

### Norma Mía
*La Condamine 153.*
Doña Norma has been making delicious cakes for over 30 years, also sells ice cream.

### Panadería Tívoli
*Ricardo Palma, block 3.*
A variety of good bread and sweets.

## Bars and clubs

Local drinks include: *chuchuhuasi*, made from the bark of a tree, which is supposed to have aphrodisiac properties (for sale at Arica 1046), *cola de mono* (a cocktail with milk and coffee) and *siete raíces* (aguardiente mixed with the bark of 7 trees and wild honey), sold at **Musmuqui** (Raymondi 382), Mon-Sat from 1900.

### Arandú
*Malecón Maldonado.*
Good bar with nice views of the river.

### Ikaro
*Putumayo 341.*
Good bar, Spanish rock music. Also has internet.

### Karma
*Napo 138.*
Cocktails and rock music, has a happy hour.

### Noa Noa
*Pevas y Fitzcarrald.*
Popular disco with cumbia and Latin music.

## Festivals

**5 Jan** Founding of Iquitos.
**Feb-Mar** Carnival.
**Jun** Tourist week is the 3rd week.
**24 Jun** San Juan, the most important festival.
**28-30 Aug** Santa Rosa de Lima.
**8 Dec** Immaculate Conception (La Purísima), celebrated in Punchana, near the docks, Bellavista and Nanay.

## Shopping

### Handicrafts

Hammocks in Iquitos cost about US$20. **Mercado Artesanal Anaconda**, by the waterfront at Napo is good for Amazon handicrafts, but be sure not to buy items that contain animal products. Also try the **Asociación de Artesanos El Manguaré**, which has kiosks on Jr Pevas, block 1. **Mercado Artesanal de Productores** (4 km from the centre in the San Juan district, on the road to the airport; take a *colectivo*) is the cheapest in town with more choice than elsewhere.

For jungle clothing and equipment, visit **Comisesa** (Arica 348), and **Mad Mick's Trading Post** (Putumayo 163, top floor, next to the Iron House).
**La Restinga**, *Raymondi 254, T065-221371, larestinga@gmail.com.* This association sells T-shirts, books and soaps made by children. It also runs literacy workshops in Belén on Tue and Thu from 1430-1800, at which you can volunteer.

## What to do

### Jungle tours

Agencies arrange 1-day or longer trips to places of interest with guides speaking some English. Take your time before making a decision, research what is on offer and don't be bullied by the hustlers at the airport or on the street. Buy your tour at the operator's office. Find out all the details of the trip and food arrangements before paying (a minimum of US$50 per day). Several companies have their own lodges, providing various levels of accommodation in the heart of the jungle (see below). Downriver from Iquitos you find more comfort (electricity, air conditioning, swimming pool, internet, cell phone coverage) and tours often include visits to native communities and to Isla de los Monos, where monkeys and other animals can be seen. Upriver along the Amazon and its tributaries conditions are more primitive (solar powered or no electricity, no internet

> **Tip...**
> Some tours include visits to a Monkey Island (Isla de Monos), which claims to be a rescue centre for animals but often has animals that have been captured in the wild. Similarly, trips to Yagua or Bora indigenous communities merely provide a show of costume and dancing. Think twice about visiting such 'attractions'.

or phone). In this more scarcely populated area, there are better chances of seeing animals in the wild.

### River cruises

There are several agencies that arrange river cruises in well-appointed boats with large picture windows. Most go to the Pacaya-Samiria region and depart from Nauta, very few go towards Brazil. There are 3-to 7-night cruises. Day tours and charters are also available. Luxury cruises cost about US$2400-4000 for 3 nights/4 days, more economical vessels about US$1400-1900 for the same period. Among the luxury boats are the *Aria* (www.aquaexpeditions.com), *Delfín I, II and III* (www.delfinamazoncruises.com), *Cattleya* and *Zafiro* (www.junglexperiences.com). More economical boats include *Amatista* and *La Perla* (same group as *Zafiro*), *Arapaima* (www.amazonexpeditioncruises.com), *Dawn on the Amazon I* (see Tour operators, below, cruises to Allpahuayo Mishana Natural Reserve, US$225 pp per day), *La Estrella Amazónica* and *Queen Violeta*. Contact companies like **Amazon River Expeditions** (www.amazonriverexpeditions.com) **Amazon Voyagers** (www.amazoncruise.net) or **Rainforest Cruises** (www.rainforestcruises.com), for options. Alternatively, speed boats for river trips can be hired by the hour or day at the **Embarcadero Turístico**, at the intersection of Av de la Marina and Samánez Ocampo in Punchana. Prices vary greatly, usually US$15-20 per hr, US$80 for speedboat, and are negotiable.

## Shaman experiences

Iquitos is an important place for Ayahuasca tourism. There are legitimate shamans as well as charlatans. **Karma Café** (Napo 138; see above) is the centre of the scene in town. See also the work of Alan Shoemaker (**Soga del Alma**, Rómulo Espinar 170, Iquitos 65, alanshoemaker@hotmail.com), who holds an International Amazonian Shamanism Conference every year (www.vineofthesoul.org).

## Tour operators and jungle lodges

**Cumaceba Amazonia Tours**, *Putumayo 184 in the Iron House, T065-232229, www. cumaceba.com.* Overnight visits to Cumaceba Lodge, 35 km from Iquitos, and tours of 1-4 nights to the Botanical Lodge on the Amazon, 80 km from Iquitos, birdwatching tours, Ayahuasca ceremonies.

**Curuhuinsi Eco Adventure Tours & Expeditions**, *T965-013225, www.facebook. com/CuruhuinsiEcoAdventureToursExpeditions.* **Gerson Pizango** is a local, English-speaking and award-winning guide who will take you to his village 2½ hrs by boat, from where you can trek and camp or stay and experience village life. Expert at spotting wildlife and knowledgeable about medicinal plants, he offers interesting and varied expeditions benefitting the community. In the village, accommodation is in a hut by the riverside where there are pink and grey dolphins. A private room with mosquito net costs US$50-70 pp per day depending on length of trip and size of party, includes food, water, camping gear, boots, raincoats, torches, binoculars, fishing rods, machetes.

**Dawn on the Amazon**, *Malecón Maldonado 185 y Nauta, T065-223730, www.dawnonthe amazon.com.* Offers a variety of day tours around Iquitos by land or river (US$85 pp per day) and custom-made cruises. Also has a good café/restaurant in town (http://dawnontheamazoncafe.com).

**Explorama Tours**, *by the riverside docks on Av La Marina 340, T065-252530, www. explorama.com.* The biggest and most

established operator, with over 40 years' experience. Frequently recommended. Their lodges are:

**Ceiba Tops**, 40 km (1½ hrs) from Iquitos, a comfortable resort with 75 a/c rooms with electricity, hot showers, good food, pool with hydromassage and beautiful gardens. Walks and excursions, a recommended jungle experience for those who want their creature comforts, US$340 pp for 1 night/2 days.

**Explorama Lodge** at Yanamono, 80 km from Iquitos, 2½ hrs from Iquitos, has palm-thatched accommodation with separate bathroom and shower facilities connected by covered walkways, cold water, no electricity, good food and service. US$455 for 3 days/2 nights.

**Explornapo Lodge** at Llachapa on the Sucusai creek (a tributary of the Napo), is in the same style as Explorama Lodge, but is further away from Iquitos, 160 km (4 hrs by river or a 15-min ride from Mazán), and is set in 105,000 ha of rainforest, so is better for seeing wildlife, US$1120 for 5 days/4 nights. Nearby is the impressive canopy walkway 35 m above the forest floor and 500 m long. It is associated with the Amazon Center for Tropical Studies (ACTS), a scientific station, only 10 mins from the canopy walkway.

**Explor Tambos**, 2 hrs from Explornapo, offer more primitive accommodation, 8 shelters for 16 campers, bathing in the river.

**Heliconia Lodge**, Ricardo Palma 242; contact T01-421 9195, www.heliconialodge. com.pe. On the Río Amazonas, 80 km downriver from Iquitos, surrounded by rainforest, islands and lagoons, this is a beautiful place for resting, birdwatching, looking for pink dolphins, jungle hikes. Organized packages 3 days/2 nights, US$282. Good guides, food and flexible excursions according to guest's requirements. The lodge has hot water, electricity for 5 hrs each day, pool and a traditionally rustic yet comfortable design.

**Muyuna Amazon Lodge**, Putumayo 163, ground floor, T065-242858, T995-918964, www.muyuna.com. 140 km upstream from

Iquitos on the Río Yanayacu, before San Juan village. 1- to 5-night packages available. 2 nights/3 days is US$400 pp all-inclusive for 2-10 people. Trusted guides, high-quality accommodation, solar electricity, hot water, good food and service, kayak and paddle boards; very well organized, flexible and professional. Amenities are constantly updated with new ecological considerations. Birdwatching (400 species might be seen in a 4 day tour) and camping trips into the forest. This area is less spoilt than some other parts of the forest downstream. **Centro de Rescate Amazónico** (see page 410) has released manatees here. Highly recommended. **Tapiche Reserve**, *Ricardo Palma 516, T065-600805/950-664049, office at Green Track Hostel (see above), www.tapichejungle.com*. On the Río Tapiche, a tributary of the Ucayali, 11 hrs up river from Iquitos. Fully screened wood cabins with thatched roofs, custom designed trips according to the visitor's interests, 4-day/3-night and 5-day/4-night tours offered.

## Transport

### Air
Francisco Secada Vigneta airport, T065-260147 is southwest of the city; a taxi to the airport costs US$10; *mototaxi* (motorcycle with 2 seats), US$3.25. Most buses from the main road outside the airport go through the centre of town, US$0.75. To **Lima**, daily, with **LATAM** (direct or via Tarapoto), **Peruvian Airlines** and **Star Perú** (direct or via Tarapoto, also daily to Pucallpa) and Avianca/TACA. The military **Grupo Aéreo 42** fly occasionally to Santa Rosa.

### Bus
To **Nauta**, **Trans del Sur** from Libertad y Próspero, daily 0530-1900, US$3.10, 2 hrs; also vans from Av Aguirre cuadra 14 by Centro Comercial Sachachorro, which leave when full, US$4, 1½ hrs.

### Riverboat
For general hints on river travel, see page 489. For information about boats, go to the corresponding ports of departure for each destination, except for speed boats to the Brazil/Colombian border which have their offices clustered on Raymondi block 3. When river levels are very high departures may be from alternative places.

*Lanchas* leave from Puerto Henry and Masusa, 2 km north of the centre, a dangerous area at night. The 1st night's meal is not included. Always deal directly with boat owners or managers, avoid touts and middle-men. All fares are negotiable. If arriving in Iquitos on a regular, slow boat, take extreme care when disembarking. Things get very chaotic at this time and theft and pickpocketing is rife. Some of the newer boats have CCTV to deter theft. *Deslizadores* or *rápidos* leave from Embarcadero Turístico or Nauta (see below).

To **Pucallpa**, 4-5 days upriver along the Amazon and Ucayali (can be longer if the water level is low), larger boats must travel only by day, hammock US$40, berth US$140 double. **Henry** (T065-263948) is a large company with 4 departures per week from Puerto Henry; *Henry 5, 6* and *7* have some cabins with bath. Another good boat is *Pedro Martín 2* from Puerto Masusa.

To **Yurimaguas** by *lancha*, 3-4 days upriver along the Amazon, Marañón and Huallaga, hammock space US$40, berth US$119-134 double. The **Eduardo/Gilmer** company, T065-960404, with 8 boats is recommended, sailing from Puerto Masusa several times a week, except Sun; *Eduardo I* and *Gilmer IV* have berths with bath for US$192. By *rápido* from Nauta, with **Rápido NR** (C Puerto Principal, Nauta, T953-998980), 20 hrs navigation upstream, US$40 includes a meal, snack and overnight lodging in Lagunas; all basic. The reverse, downstream, journey is 12 hrs, US$38, no overnight in Lagunas.

To **Santa Rosa** (on the border with **Brazil** and **Colombia**), the most convenient way to travel is by *rápido*, 8-10 hrs downriver,

US$60, from the Embarcadero Turístico (always confirm departure point in advance) at 0530 Tue-Sun; be at the port 0445 for customs check, board 0500-0530. (In the opposite direction, boats leave Santa Rosa Tue-Sun at 0400 and take 10-12 hrs upstream; if you're coming from Brazil or Colombia get your immigration entry stamp the day before.) *Rápidos* carry life jackets and have bathrooms; a simple breakfast and lunch are included in the price. Luggage limit is 15 kg. Purchase tickets in advance from company offices in Iquitos: **Golfinho** (Raymondi 378, T065-225118, www. transportegolfinho.com) and **Transtur** (Raymondi 384, T065-221356). *Lanchas* to Santa Rosa, which may continue to Islandia, leave from the Puerto Pesquero or Puerto Masusa (enquire at T065-250440), Mon-Sat at 1800, 2-3 days downriver, US$31 in hammock, US$50 in cabin; in the other direction they depart Santa Rosa Mon-Sat at 1200.

To reach the border with **Ecuador** you go to **Pantoja**, 5-7 days upriver on the Napo, a route requiring plenty of time, stamina and patience. There are irregular departures once or twice a month, US$38, plus US$3 per day for a berth if you can get one; for details call **Radio Moderna** in Iquitos (T065-250440), or T065-830055 (a private phone in Pantoja village). The vessels are usually cargo boats that carry live animals, some of which are slaughtered en route. Crowding and poor sanitation are common. Once in Pantoja, there is no public transport to **Nuevo Rocafuerte** (Ecuador), so you must hire a private boat, about US$60. To shorten the voyage, or to visit the jungle towns along the way, go to **Indiana**, daily departures from **Muelle de Productores** in Iquitos, US$5, 45 mins, then take a mototaxi to **Mazán** on the Río Napo. From Mazán, there are also *rápidos* to **Santa Clotilde**, US$31 includes a snack, 4-5 hrs, information from **Familia Ruiz** in Iquitos (T065-251410). There have been unconfirmed reports of *rápidos* operating from Mazán or Santa Clotilde all the way to **Pantoja** (about 36 hrs from Mazán, US$60), enquire locally.

# Southern
## Amazon

The southern selva is mostly in Madre de Dios department, which contains the Manu National Park (2.04 million ha), the Tambopata National Reserve (274,690 ha) and the Bahauja-Sonene National Park (1.1 million ha). The forest of this lowland region (altitude 260 m) is technically called subtropical moist forest, which means that it receives less rainfall than tropical forest and is dominated by the floodplains of its meandering rivers. The most striking features are the former river channels that have become isolated as oxbow lakes. These are home to black caiman and giant otter and a host of other species. Other rare species living in the forest are jaguar, puma, ocelot and tapir. There are also howler monkeys, capybara, macaws, guans, currasows and the giant harpy eagle.

As well as containing some of the most important flora and fauna on Earth, the region also harbours gold-diggers, loggers, hunters, drug smugglers and oil-men, whose activities endanger the unique rainforest. Moreover, the construction of the Interoceánica, a road linking the Atlantic and Pacific oceans via Puerto Maldonado and Brazil, has brought more uncontrolled colonization in the area, as seen so many times before throughout the Amazon.

The trip over the Andes from Cuzco to the lowlands is long, the road is in places hair-raising and breathtaking, and the scenery is magnificent. Check about road conditions in the rainy season.

From Cuzco you climb up to the Huancarani Pass (very cold at night) then drop to Paucartambo (see page 317) in the valley of the Río Mapacho. The road then ascends to the Acjanaco Pass (also cold at night), one access to the highland section of Manu (see Tres Cruces, page 317), after which it follows the Río Cosñipata down to the cloudforest around **San Pedro** (part of Manu's Cultural Zone, includes a 5060 ha Perú Verde Reserve, excellent birding including a cock-of-the-rock lek, several lodges), before reaching the lowlands at **Patria**, an area of coca production, followed by **Pilcopata**, at 650 m, a supply town on the border between the departments of Cuzco and Madre de Dios. Beyond Pilcopata is the turn-off for **Atalaya**, the first village on the Alto Madre de Dios River and tourist port from where tours depart for Boca Manu and the park; there are basic lodgings and restaurants here.

The route continues to **Salvación** (575 m), with some simple *hostales* and restaurants, the most pleasant town along this road. Just north of town is a national park office. **Cocha Machuhuasi** ① *1.5 km from town, entry US$1.50*, a municipal nature reserve with many birds, caymans and some mammals, has a small lake with punts and walking trails around it. From Salvación the road continues north, always along the east bank of the Alto Madre de Dios to Santa Cruz, with a park ranger station; nearby is the access for the Río Palotoa and the **Pusharo Petroglyphs** ① *entry US$15*, within the national park. Next is the turn-off for **Shintuya**, with thermal baths and community tourism and volunteering opportunities run by **Proyecto Oteri** (T082-812966 ask for Wili Corisepa, oteriproyect@gmail.com). Continuing on the road is **Itahuanía**, centre of an agricultural area with basic services and *hostales*. Next is **Shipitiari** (a couple of restaurants and a very basic lodging on the southeast shore of the river). In 2018, a poor road reached **Nuevo Edén** and the road cut, not yet transitable, reached **Diamante**. Where river transport starts depends on the road condition at the time, as rain often disrupts wheeled transport. There is no scheduled boat service to continue downriver. There may be cargo boats leaving for either Boca Manu or Boca Colorado on the Río Madre de Dios, but only when the boat is fully laden.

## ★ Manu Biosphere Reserve
### Peru's premier wildlife-watching destination

Few other reserves on the planet can compare with Manu for the diversity of life forms; it holds over 1000 species of bird and covers an altitudinal range from 200 m to 4100 m above sea-level. Giant otters, jaguars, ocelots and 13 species of primate abound in this pristine tropical wilderness; uncontacted indigenous tribes are present in the more remote areas, as are indigenous groups with limited access.

The reserve is one of the largest conservation units on Earth, encompassing the complete drainage of the Manu River. It is divided into the **Manu National Park** (1,716,295 ha), which only government-sponsored biologists and anthropologists may visit with permits from

# Essential Manu Biosphere Reserve

## Access to Manu

The Multi-Use Zone of Manu Biosphere Reserve is accessible to anyone and several lodges exist in the area. The Reserved Zone is accessible by permit only, available from the Manu National Park office in Cuzco; entry is strictly controlled and visitors must visit the area under the auspices of an authorized operator with an authorized guide. Permits are limited and reservations should be made well in advance. There is very little permanent accommodation in the Reserved Zone but several companies have tented safari camp infrastructures, some with shower and dining facilities, but all visitors sleep in tents. The entrance fee to the Reserved Zone is S/150 per person (about US$45) and is included in package tour prices.

Tours to Manu usually enter by road, overnighting in a lodge in the cloudforest, and continue by boat (the route is described below). It is this journey from the highlands down through the various strata of habitat that sets it apart from many other visits to the jungle. At the end of the tour, passengers either return overland or fly back to Cuzco from Puerto Maldonado. There is an airstrip at Diamante, near Boca Manu, but

## Tip...

It is not possible to arrange last-minute trips to the Reserved Zone of the national park from Boca Manu. Owing to park regulations, all arrangements, including permits, must be made in advance from Cuzco, Lima, or abroad.

there are no regular flights from Cuzco. Ask the tour operators in Cuzco if your tour will go overland or by air.

## When to go

The climate is warm and humid, with a rainy season from Novemer to March and a dry season from April to October. Cold fronts from the South Atlantic, called *friajes*, are characteristic of the dry season, causing temperatures to drop to 15-16°C during the day and to 13°C at night. Always bring a sweater at this time. The best time to visit is during the dry season when there are fewer mosquitoes and the rivers are low, exposing the beaches. This is also a good time to see birds nesting and to view animals at close range, as they stay close to the rivers and are easily seen. A pair of binoculars is essential and insect repellent is a must.

the Ministry of Agriculture in Lima; the **Reserved Zone** (257,000 ha) within the national park, which is set aside for applied scientific research and ecotourism; and the **Cultural** or **Multiple Use Zone** (92,000 ha), a buffer area which contains acculturated native groups and colonists along the Alto Madre de Dios and its tributaries, where the locals still employ their traditional way of life. Among the ethnic groups in the Cultural Zone are the Mashco-Piro and the Yine, while the Harakmbut and Matsiguenka are mostly in the Reserved Zone. Also within the biosphere reserve are the **Nahua-Kugapakori Reserved Zone**, set aside for these two nomadic native groups, which is the area between the headwaters of the Río Manu and headwaters of the Río Urubamba, to the north of the Alto Madre de Dios; the **Megantoni Sanctuary**, in the foothills of the Ausangate range, north of Quillabamba and to the west of the national park; and, to the east of the national park, the **Amarakaeri Communal Reserve**, see below. Associated with Manu are other areas protected by conservation groups, or local people (for example the **Blanquillo** and **Manu Wildlife Center** reserves) and some cloudforest parcels along the road.

## Boca Manu and the Reserved Zone

Boca Manu (365 m) is the connecting point between the rivers Alto Madre de Dios, Manu and Madre de Dios. It is a friendly village with basic places to stay and eat and reasonably supplied shops. On the south bank across the river, by an indigenous community, is an airstrip. La Isla del Valle is a Matsiguenka community (1 km from town) and La Cocha (2 km away) is an oxbow lake with giant otters, birds and other fauna.

Boca Manu is the entrance to the **Manu Reserved Zone** and to go further you must be part of an organized group. The park ranger station and an interpretation centre

# Manu Biosphere Reserve

**Where to stay** 🛏
1 Amazonia Lodge
2 Casa Matsiguenka
3 Cloud forest lodges
4 Erika Lodge
5 Manu Learning Centre
6 Manu Wildlife Center
7 Pantiacolla Lodge
8 Romero Lodge
9 Tambo Blanquillo Lodge
10 Yanayacu Lodge
11 Yine Lodge

Cultural Zone ▨

are located in Limonal, upstream along the Río Manu. You need to show your permit here. Upstream on the Río Manu you pass Cocha Juárez after three or four hours. You can continue to Cocha Otorongo in 2½ hours and Cocha Salvador, a further 30 minutes. The latter is the biggest lake with plenty of wildlife. From here it is two to three hours to Pakitza, the entrance to the National Park Zone, only accessible to biologists with a special permit. Beyond is Cocha Casu with a biological station.

## Boca Manu to Puerto Maldonado via Boca Colorado

*There is no regular passenger service between Boca Manu and Boca Colorado from where there is transport to Puerto Maldonado; see Transport, page 437.*

The Madre de Dios River flows southeast from Boca Manu. South of the river is the 402,335-ha **Amarakaeri Communal Reserve** ⓘ *headquarters at Jr Cajamarca 946, Puerto Maldonado, T082-571505, rcamarakaeri@sernanp.gob.pe*, protecting a variety of ecosystems in the watersheds of the Madre de Dios and Colorado rivers. Adjacent to Amarakaeri, in an area very rich in wildlife, with important macaw and mammal clay licks and several oxbow lakes, are a couple of private reserves: **Manu Wildlife Center** ⓘ *www.inkanatura.com/manu-tours-and-lodges*, with 16,190 ha, and **Tambo Blanquillo** ⓘ *http://tamboblanquillo.com*, with 10,000 ha; both have lodges (see Where to stay) and canopy observation towers. Visitors get here on packaged tours. Downstream from the reserves the devastation from informal gold mining becomes evident until you reach **Boca Colorado**, a mining supply centre with accommodation, restaurants (**Milenium** is good), shops, internet and boats for hire; lone women travellers should be careful here. From Colorado you can take a van to Puerto Carlos (one hour, basic accommodation), cross the Inambari river (10 minutes), then take another van to Puerto Maldonado (two hours, see Transport) or Mazuko (1½ hours).

## Cuzco to Puerto Maldonado via Mazuko

One branch of the Interoceánica highway runs Cuzco–Urcos–Quincemil–Mazuko–Puerto Maldonado. The changing scenery en route is magnificent.

**Quincemil**, 240 km from Urcos, is a centre for alluvial gold-mining with many banks. Hunt Oil is building a huge oil and gas facility here; its exploration controversially overlaps the Amarakaeri Communal Reserve.

Puente Inambari is the junction of three sections of the Interoceanic Highway, from Cuzco, Puerto Maldonado and Juliaca (see Puno to the jungle, page 280). However, this is only a small settlement and transport stops 16 km further north at **Mazuko**. In the evenings, Mazuko is a hive of activity as temperatures drop and the buses arrive.

The highway beyond Mazuko cuts across lowland rainforest, large areas of which have been cleared by migrants engaged in small-scale gold mining. Their encampments of plastic shelters, shops and prostibars now line the highway for several kilometres around La Pampa (known as Km 108). A worthwhile stop on the route is the **Parador Turístico Familia Méndez** ⓘ *Km 410, 85 km (1 hr) from Puerto Maldonado, T962-352668,* which prepares local dishes from home-grown ingredients and has wood cabins (**$**), camping and a trail network in the surrounding forest (walking tour available).

## Tourist information

### Manu National Park Office
*Av Cinco los Chachacomos F2-4, Larapa
Grande, San Jerónimo, Cuzco, T084-274509,
www.visitmanu.com. Mon-Fri.*
Issues permits for the Reserved Zone.

NGOs working in the area which provide
information include: **Amazon Conservation
Association** (ACCA, Cuzco, T084-222329,
Puerto Maldonado, T082-573543, www
amazonconservation.org); **Perú Verde**
(Cuzco, T084-226392, www.peruverde.
org); **Pronaturaleza** (Lima T01-271 2662,
Puerto Maldonado T082-571585, www.
pronaturaleza.org).

## Where to stay

Most jungle lodges are booked as package
deals for 3 days, 2 nights, or longer, with
meals, transport and guides; see websites
for offers. Some lodges in the Cultural
Zone, including those in the cloudforest
area accept independent travellers. Many
lodges in the Cultural Zone use generators
to provide a few hours of electricity for
light and charging batteries, a few use solar
power. In the Reserved Zone, solar power
is used, tent camps may not have electricity.

### Cloudforest lodges

### Cock of the Rock Lodge
*South of Puente San Pedro,
www.inkanatura.com.*
Very nice cabins with private or shared bath,
hot water, lovely grounds and common
areas, camping platform with shower.
The fanciest lodge in the area.

### Manu Paradise Lodge
*Km 181.6, just north of Puente San Pedro,
T084-224156, www.manuparadiselodge.com.*
Nice setting by the river, well-kept grounds

and rooms with bath and hot water, includes
dinner and breakfast.

### Orquídeas de San Pedro Lodge
*On a trail 10 mins upriver from the bridge along
the Río San Pedro, www.manuadventures.com.*
Rustic basic cabins with mosquito nets,
shared bath.

### Posada San Pedro Lodge
*1.5 km north of Puente San Pedro,
http://pantiacolla.com*
Rustic but very clean wood cabins with
mosquito nets, shared bath with hot
showers, pleasant common areas and
grounds.

### Tambo Paititi
*On a trail 20 mins upriver from the bridge along
the Río San Pedro, www.perudiscovery.com/en/.*
Rustic basic cabins with mosquito nets,
shared bath.

### Alto Madre de Dios lodges

### Amazonia Lodge
*20 mins by boat from Atalaya, T084-816131,
www.amazonialodgeperu.com; in Cuzco at
Calle Tandapata 660, San Blas T084-137371.*
An old tea hacienda set in 350 ha of primary
rainforest, famous for its bird diversity
and fine hospitality, a great place to relax,
also nice for children. Price range **$$$** pp
including meals, rooms with shared or
private bath, birding and natural history
tours available. Bookings through Cuzco
office, contact in advance to arrange for
transfer or guide.

### Erika Lodge
*25 mins from Atalaya, www.
manuadventures.com.*
Set in a 900-ha reserve with a range of
altitudes. Offers basic accommodation and
is cheaper than the other, more luxurious
lodges. Also has a canopy zip-line. Contact
**Manu Adventures** (see page 426).

## Manu Learning Centre
*Fundo Mascoitania, 45 mins by boat from Atalaya, www.crees-manu.org.*
A 600-ha reserve within the Cultural Zone, see **Crees Tours**, under What to do, below.

## Pantiacolla Lodge
*30 mins downriver from Shintuya, http://pantiacolla.com.*
Set in 900 ha of forest with great altitude range in a transition zone between cloudforest and rainforest. Owned by the Moscoso family. Book through **Pantiacolla Tours** (see page 426).

## Yanayacu Lodge
*On the southeast bank of the river, about 1 hr by boat upstream from Diamante village.*
Using local river transport to arrive at the lodge rates are very reasonable, prices depend on length of stay. Nearby is a small parrot *collpa* (clay lick). The lodge also offers several different itineraries in Manu.

## Cuzco to Boca Manu

### $ Don Pocho
*At the north end of town, Itahuanía, T996-547050.*
Simple with shared bath and cold water. Owner offers transport.

### $ Gallito de las Rocas
*Av Cusco s/n, Pilcopata, T952-490712, gallitorocas@hotmail.com.*
Bright rooms in clean wooden house, private or shared bath, cold water, a good option.

### $ Hospedaje Sulema
*In the centre, Itahuanía, T082-830674.*
Simple place, friendly owner Sra Eulogia.

### $ Los Amigos
*Los Amigos s/n, behind the hospital, Salvación, T974-907909.*
Simple but clean rooms, private or shared bath, cold water, quiet location.

### $ Oteri
*Shintuya, T082-812966, Oteriote on Facebook.*

Homestay with Wili Corisepa and Isabel Poo, part of a community project.

## Boca Manu
Community phones: T082-834099, 082-830600. Several basic family-run *hospedajes*, ask at the shops by the plaza.

### $ El Albergue
*2 blocks from the river.*
Simple rooms with shared bath, cold water, courtyard, caters to groups.

### $ Yine Lodge
*Next to Boca Manu airport.*
A cooperative project run between **Pantiacolla Tours** and the Yine community of Diamante, who operate their own tours into their community and surroundings.

## Manu National Park Reserved Zone
Several tour operators have camp tents around Cocha Salvador or Cocha Otorongo.

### Casa Matsiguenka (Machiguenga)
*Near Cocha Salvador, http://matsiguenka. weebly.com. In Cuzco, Av El Sol 627B, of 305, T084-225595.*
Traditional Matsiguenka-style cabins each with 3 rooms with private bath, shared showers, solar lighting. Run by 2 local communities which also offer 4- to 7-day tours.

### $ Romero Lodge
*Near Limonal, www.crees-manu.org.*
Traditional wooden lodge with thatched roof, rooms with bath and hot shower. See **Crees Tours**, page 425.

## Boca Manu to Boca Colorado
## Madre de Dios Lodges

### Manu Wildlife Center
*On the left (northeast) bank, 2 hrs down the Río Madre de Dios from Boca Manu, 3 hrs up from Boca Colorado.*
Book through **Manu Expeditions** (www. manuexpeditions.com), which runs it in conjunction with the conservation group **Perú Verde**. 22 double cabins, with private

bathroom and hot water. Also canopy towers for birdwatching and a tapir lick.

## Tambo Blanquillo Lodge
*On the right bank of the Madre de Dios, 30 mins downstream from Manu Wildlife Center (see above). In Lima: Av Nicolás de Piérola 265, Barranco, T01-249 9342, http://tamboblanquillo.com.*
Comfortable wooden cabins with bath, hot shower and fan and a traditional style *maloca* with 20 rooms with shared bath, solar electricity. A 10-min boat ride to the access trail to the famous Blanquillo macaw lick, 4- to 6-day tours. Volunteer opportunities available.

## Boca Colorado

### $ Hospedaje Colorado
*Across from the high school, past the bus station.*
Among the newer hotels in Boca Colorado, built in 2016.

### $ Hospedaje Fiori
*Av Madre de Dios s/n, 1 block from the plaza, T997-277668.*
Simple rooms with mosquito nets, private or shared bath, cold water.

## What to do

Beware of pirate operators on the streets of Cuzco who offer trips to the Reserved Zone of Manu and end up halfway through the trip changing the route "due to emergencies", which, in reality means they have no permits to operate in the area. Some unscrupulous tour guides will offer trips to see the uncontacted tribes of Manu; on no account make any attempt to view these very vulnerable people.

The following companies in Cuzco organize trips into the Multiple Use and Reserved Zones; contact them for more details. See also **Manu Tambopata Travel**, listed with Local (Puerto Maldonado) tour operators, below.

**Amazon Trails Peru**, *Tandapata 660, San Blas, Cuzco, T084-437374, or T984-714148, www.amazontrailsperu.com.* Operated by ornithologist Abraham Huamán, who has many years' experience guiding in Manu, and his German wife, Ulla Maennig. Well-organized tours to the national park and Blanquillo clay lick, with knowledgeable English-speaking guides, good boatmen and cooks, small groups, guaranteed departure dates. Runs 2 lodges in Manu. Also offers trekking in the Cuzco area, see page 310.
**Bonanza Tours**, *Suecia 343, Cuzco, T084 507871, www.bonanzatoursperu.com.* 4- to 8-day tours to Manu with local guides, plenty of jungle walks and camp-based excursions with good food. Tours are high quality and good value.
**Crees Tours**, *Urbanización Mcal Gamarra B-5, Zona 1, Cuzco, T084-262433, and 7/8 Kendrick Mews, London SW7 3HG, T+44 (0)20-7581 2932, www.crees-manu.org.* Tours

from 4 days/3 nights to 9 days/8 nights to the **Manu Learning Centre**, a lodge accommodating 24 guests, 45 mins from Atalaya by boat. The lodge has all en suite rooms with hot showers; food is produced locally in a bio-garden. All tours spend the 1st night at the **Cock of the Rock Lodge**, on the road from Paucartambo to Atalaya. Tours are associated with the **Crees Foundation** (www.crees-foundation.org), a fully sustainable organization which works with immigrant and indigenous communities to reduce poverty and protect biodiversity in the rainforest.

**Expediciones Vilca**, *Plateros 359, Cuzco, T084-244751*. Offers tours at economical prices.

**Greenland Peru**, *Celascso Astete C-12, Cuzco, T084-246572, www.greenlandperu.com*. Fredy Domínguez is an Amazonian and offers good-value trips to Manu with comfortable accommodation and transport and excellent food cooked by his mother. Experienced, knowledgeable and enthusiastic, and he speaks English.

**InkaNatura**, *Ricardo Palma J1, Cuzco, T084-243408; in Lima T01-203 5000, UK T0800-234 8659, USA/Canada T1-888-870 7378, www.inkanatura.com*. Tours to **Manu Wildlife Centre** (see page 424) and to **Sandoval Lake Lodge** and **Heath River Wildlife Center** in the Tambopata Reserve (see Lodges on the lower Río Madre de Dios, page 432) with emphasis on sustainable tourism and conservation. Knowledgeable guides. They also run treks in Cuzco area and tours in the Titicaca area and northern Peru.

**Manu Adventures**, *Plateros 356, Cuzco, T084-261640, www.manuadventures.com*. This company operates one of the most physically active Manu programmes, with options for 1 hr of whitewater rafting on the way to **Erika Lodge** on the Río Alto Madre de Dios, where they operate a canopy walkway and zip-line.

**Manu Expeditions and Birding Tours**, *Jr Los Geranios 2-G, Urbanización Mariscal Gamarra, 1a Etapa, Cuzco, T084-225990, www.manuexpeditions.com*. Owned by ornithologist Barry Walker, 3 trips available to Manu National Park and **Manu Wildlife Center**, plus specialized birding tours in several South American countries and trekking and horse riding tours in the Cuzco area.

**Oropéndola**, *Av Circunvalación s/n, Urbanización Guadalupe Mz A Lte 3, Cuzco, T084-241428, www.oropendolaperu.org*. Guide Walter Mancilla Huamán is an expert on flora and fauna. 5-, 7- and 9-day tours. Good reports of attention to detail and to the needs of clients.

**Pantiacolla Tours**, *Garcilaso 265, interior, p 2, of 12, Cuzco, T084-238323, www.pantiacolla. com*. Run by Marianne van Vlaardingen and Gustavo Moscoso. They have tours to the cloudforest, the **Pantiacolla Lodge** (see Where to stay, page 424) and also 7- and 9-day tours to the Reserved Zone. Pantiacolla works with indigenous communities and supports the Federación de Nativos de Madre de Dios.

### Transport

Tour companies usually use their own vehicles for the overland trip from Cuzco to Manu, but it is possible to do it independently. Some companies offer the option to fly from Cuzco to Boca Manu in a charter flight, at an additional cost.

#### Air

There is an airfield at the indigenous community across the river from Boca Manu. There are no commercial flights from Cuzco, only those chartered by tour operators. Irregular light-aircraft flights from Boca Manu to **Puerto Maldonado**, operated by the Pucallpa based company **North American** (T995-734281, www.northamerican.pe) are intended for the local population and subsidized by the government; they may take tourists if they have space. Ask at the Municipalidad in Boca Manu, the flights are scheduled one month at a time, according to demand (about 2 flights per week).

## Road and river

In 2018, the road from Cuzco was paved almost to Paucartambo, beyond is a good dirt road. It is passable in the rainy season, but there are usually some landslides that close the road for a few hours, a day, occasionally longer. Take repellent and some food and water. Most transport to this area leaves from Control de San Jerónimo, across from the police station, south of Cuzco (reached by Satélite city bus from San Francisco or by taxi, about US$6, 1 hr). Transport that starts elsewhere also passes the San Jerónimo stop. The following leave from San Jerónimo unless otherwise noted. To **Pilcopata Gallito de las Rocas**bus at 0500, **Apu Coñahuay** at 1700, US$7.50, 8 hrs; vans bound for Salvación (see below) take passengers to Pilcopata, US$9, 6 hrs. Trucks to Pilcopata run Mon, Wed, Fri, returning Tue, Thu, Sat, 9 hrs in wet season, less in the dry. To **Salvación**, vans leave from PRONAA, Av República del Perú, Primer Paradero, San Sebastián, south of Cuzco, most at 1100 and a few at 1600, US$12, 7-8 hrs; **Villa Salvación** (T990-420222), **Amazon Tours** (T984-802628, also has a kiosk at Control San Jerónimo), **Corazón Serrano** (T957-698111) and **Manu Express** (T932-756510). Book ahead; return to Cuzco at the same times. Salvación to **Shintuya**, Sr Cotayo, bus at 0600, US$2.45, 1½ hrs, return around 0730. Between Pilcopata and Salvación, Sr Yuyo, van, US$6 pp, 1½ hrs; also on Mon, Wed, Fri, Sr Cotayo's bus from Salvación at 1100, return from Pilcopata at 1600, US$2.45. Other than the bus to Shintuya, there is no scheduled service to continue north from Salvación. Depending on demand, Don Pocho (T996-547050, Itahuanía), offers transport north, most reliably in the evening Mon, Wed, Fri, enquire with Silvia at Transportes Villa Salvación (T942-144622); to **Itahuanía**, US$7.60, 2½ hrs; to **Shipitiare**, US$10.60, 3 hrs; to **Nuevo Edén** about US$12.60, 3½ hrs; beware of overcharging. Pick-ups can also be hired, enquire at **Transportes Corazón Serrano**.

To reach **Boca Manu**, enquire in Salvación which port is being used at the time (it depends on the state of the road). Time and patience are required at the port to get a boat, ask around and be attentive, sometimes they stop briefly. If they are taking cargo, you will have to wait for the boat to be fully laden. Itahuanía–Boca Manu in a shared boat is US$7.50; a private, chartered boat would be over US$100; Shipitiare–Boca Manu, US$6, 3 hrs; Diamante–Boca Manu, about US$4, 45 mins-1 hr. Boats may also leave from the port at the roadhead directly for Boca Colorado on the Río Madre de Dios (from Itahuanía, about 9 hrs, US$20).

There is no scheduled boat service from Boca Manu to **Boca Colorado**. Shared service costs US$9-12 and to charter a boat about US$300. Boats can be hired to go upriver from Boca Colorado with **Express Wari** (Av El Puerto, T958-966014) and others.

To reach **Puerto Maldonado** from Boca Colorado, vans leave the bus terminal for Puerto Carlos, US$6, 1 hr, for the ferry across the Inambari River, US$1.50, 10 mins; vans then run on an unpaved road to Santa Rosa (basic accommodation), the junction with the Cra Interoceánica, to go either northeast to Puerto Maldonado, US$7.60, 2 hrs, or south to Mazuko, US$4.55, 1½ hr. In Puerto Maldonado, contact **Turismo Boca Colorado** (Tacna 342, T082-573435) or **Expediciones Colorado Manu** (Av Ernesto Rivero 952, T946-693201). From Mazuko there is transport to Cuzco, Puno and Juliaca.

Puerto Maldonado (approximate population 80,000), overlooking the confluence of the Tambopata and Madre de Dios rivers, is an important base for visiting the southeastern jungles of the Tambopata Reserve or departing for Bolivia or Brazil. Because of the gold mining and timber industries, it is a busy town and the immediate surrounding jungle is now cultivated.

A bridge, part of the Interoceánica highway which continues north to the borders with Brazil and Bolivia, spans the Río Madre de Dios. Lovely sunsets are seen from the bridge and especially from the 47-m-high **mirador** ① *Av Madre de Dios y Av Fitzcarrald, 15 blocks west*

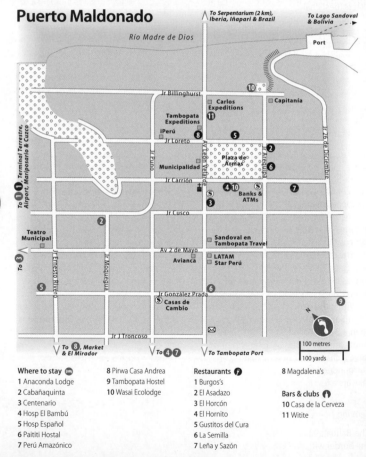

**Puerto Maldonado**

Where to stay
1 Anaconda Lodge
2 Cabañaquinta
3 Centenario
4 Hosp El Bambú
5 Hosp Español
6 Paititi Hostal
7 Perú Amazónico
8 Pirwa Casa Andrea
9 Tambopata Hostel
10 Wasai Ecolodge

Restaurants
1 Burgos's
2 El Asadazo
3 El Horcón
4 El Hornito
5 Gustitos del Cura
6 La Semilla
7 Leña y Sazón
8 Magdalena's

Bars & clubs
10 Casa de la Cerveza
11 Witite

of the plaza, 0700-2030, closed Wed, US$1. In and around town are a butterfly farm (www.perubutterfly.com) and a serpentarium (Serpentario Tropifauna on Facebook).

**Tip...**
Try the locally grown Brazil nuts (*castañas*) sold in the markets and shops of Puerto Maldonado. The harvest is from March to June, and the crop tends to be good on alternate years.

## Jungle tours from Puerto Maldonado

A multi-day trip to a jungle lodge is the best way to experience the forest and see fauna. There are also many community tourism projects around Puerto Maldonado accessed by road and/or river. Attractions in the buffer zone of the Tambopata Reserve, include **Lago Tres Chimbadas** ① *entry US$4.50, 0600-1700, access from Puerto Vicente in the village of Infierno, then a 45-min boat ride and a 30-min walk*, a small oxbow lake (2 km long) rich in wildlife including giant river otters (best chance to see them in early morning), caymans and many birds.

Along the **lower Madre de Dios**, also in the national reserve's buffer zone, are small private reserves with lodges in all price categories. In this area is **Lago Valencia**, 60 km from Puerto Maldonado near the Bolivian border (four hours there, eight hours back, or by road). It is a large oxbow lake, 15 km long, with lots of wildlife and many excellent beaches and islands within an hour's boat ride. Mosquitoes are voracious, though. If you're camping, take food and water. For a cycling tour to Lago Valencia, see Lupuna Lodge, page 433.

To the north of Puerto Maldonado, the **Río Las Piedras** drainage also offers opportunities to visit rich forest. The area is reached by a five-hour drive followed by boat travel. Several NGOs work in the region; see www.arbioperu.org, http://conservetheamazon.org and www.tamanduajungle.com.

## ★ Tambopata National Reserve

*Sernanp, Jr Cajamarca 946, Puerto Maldonado, T082-571247, rntambopata@sernanp.gob.pe.*

The 274,690 ha Tambopata National Reserve (TNR) lies between the rivers Madre de Dios, Tambopata and Heath. The area was first declared a reserve in 1990 and is a very reasonable alternative for those who do not have the time or money to visit Manu. It is a close rival in terms of seeing wildlife and boasts some superb oxbow lakes. Other highlights are the famous clay licks or *collpas*, where macaws and parrots gather to eat minerals which allow them to digest otherwise toxic seeds and fruits; most renowned are **Collpa Chuncho** ① *entry US$20* and **Collpa Colorado** ① *entry US$30*, visited in five-day tours. There are a number of lodges here which are excellent for lowland rainforest birding and fauna observation. The reserve must be visited with an authorized tour operator (see What to do, page 436).

Within the park and relatively close to Puerto Maldonado is the beautiful and tranquil **Lago Sandoval** ① *entry US$9*, a 30-minute boat ride along the Río Madre de Dios, and then a 3-km walk into the jungle; the first kilometre on a raised wooden walkway, but boots are advisable. You must go with a tour operator and start very early in order to have a chance to see giant river otters. The 3-km-long lake is very rich in fauna and it is surrounded by beautiful forest including *aguaje* palms and very tall kapoks. Around the lake are a few lodges.

## Bahuaja Sonene National Park

*Sernanp, Libertad 1189, Puno, T051-363960, daranibar@sernanp.gob.pe, fee US$54 for 7-day visit.*

The Bahuaja-Sonene National Park, declared in 1996, stretches from the Heath River on the border with Bolivia across the Tambopata and includes the Pampas del Heath tropical grasslands. There are no facilities in the park. Visits only with tour operators who offer seven-day rafting trips along the Río Alto Tambopata, downriver from Putina Punco, in the department of Puno (see page 281), camping on the shore of the river and finishing at the Tambopata Research Centre (TRC). It is an adventurous trip involving paddling through grade III and IV rapids. Sernanp has a list of authorized operators, it includes **Amazonas Explorer** and **River Explorers**, see Cuzco operators, pages 310 and 313. **Collpa Heath** ① *entry US$6*, salt lick can be accessed by boat from Puerto Maldonado, along the lower Madre de Dios then up-river on the Heath; **InkaNatura** (page 426) and **Manu Tambopata Travel** (page 436) arrange tours. There are lodges in the park's buffer zone, **InkaNatura** has a lodge on the Río Heath, the **Heath River Wildlife Center** ① *www.inkanatura.com*.

## To Iberia and Iñapari

Frequent public transport runs to Iberia and Iñapari on the border with Brazil. No primary forest remains along this section of the Interoceánica, only secondary growth and small *chacras* (farms). There are lumber towns and a few picturesque *caseríos* (settlements) that serve as processing centres for the brazil nut.

# Tambopata National Reserve & Bahuaja-Sonene National Park

**Where to stay** 🛌
1 Casa de Hospedaje Mejía
2 Eco Amazonia Lodge
3 El Corto Maltés
4 Estancia Bello Horizonte
5 Explorers Inn
6 Hacienda Tambopata
7 Inkaterra Reserva

Amazónica Lodge
8 Lupuna Lodge
9 Monte Amazónico Lodge Lago Sandoval
10 Posada Amazonas Lodge
11 Refugio Amazonas Lodge
12 Sandoval Lake Lodge
13 Tambopata Eco Lodge

14 Tambopata Research Centre
15 Wasaí Tambopata Lodge

**Iberia**, Km 168, a small, quiet town, has a few simple hotels, including **$ Casa Blanca** (José Aldamis 848,T972-702204, with private bath, cold water, fan and a small garden); Las Castañuelas serves good breakfasts and lunches. Many birds and, at times, monkeys can be seen along the road across the Río Tahuamanu at dawn.

**Iñapari**, at the end of the road, Km 235, is a tranquil spread out border town with all services, connected by a suspension bridge to Brazil.

**Crossing to Brazil** Public transport stops near immigration (open 0700-1900 daily), 1 km before the centre of Iñapari and the international bridge (mototaxi US$0.30). Brazilian entry/exit stamps are given by Polícia Federal (open 0700-1900), just outside **Assis Brasil** (mototaxi from Iñapari US$1.20). The only exchange facilities at the border are in Iñapari: opposite immigration and around the plaza, and at Banco de la Nación, at the plaza, which also has an ATM, but rates are better in Cobija (Bolivia) and Puerto Maldonado. There is a paved road from Assis Brasil to Brasiléia, where you can cross to Cobija (Bolivia), or carry on to Rio Branco. There is no official crossing from Peru to Bolivia here, you must continue to Brasiléia.

---

**Listings** Puerto Maldonado and around *maps pages 428 and 430.*

## Tourist information

### Puerto Maldonado

#### Immigration
*Av 15 de Agosto 658, T082-571069.*
*Mon-Fri 0800-1600, Sat 0800-1200.*

#### iPerú
*Jr Loreto 390, a block from the plaza, T082-571830, iperuptomaldonado@promperu.gob.pe. Mon-Sat 0900-1800, Sun 0900-1300.*
Also has desks at the airport (open for arrivals) and the terminal terrestre (irregular hours). Very helpful.

## Where to stay

### Cuzco to Puerto Maldonado via Mazuko Quincemil
Most accommodation is right along the highway, with lots of traffic noise.

#### $$ La Casona
*200 m from the plaza, T999-859080.*
Nice hotel with a large garden, good birdwatching, camping possible, terrace, dining room, includes breakfast, other meals on advance request, parking for small vehicles. Opened in 2017.

#### $ Hospedaje Las Rosas
*Along the highway to Mazuko, 5 mins from the plaza, T931-823640.*
4-storey concrete building, rooms with fan and shared bath, parking. Opened in 2017.

### Mazuko

#### $ Hostal Valle Sagrado
*Plaza de Armas, T941-467463.*
Rooms with fan, parking.

---

### Puerto Maldonado

#### $$$-$$ Wasaí Puerto Maldonado Ecolodge
*Jr Guillermo Billinghurst s/n, T082-572290, www.wasai.com.*
In a beautiful location overlooking the Madre de Dios, with forest surrounding bungalows and suites, with a/c, also simpler double rooms with bath and dorms (US$12 pp), small pool with waterfall, massage (US$30 per hr), good restaurant (local fish a speciality), bar. Includes buffet breakfast and transfers, bicycles. Helpful, family-run, they can organize local tours and also have a lodge on the Río Tambopata (see page 435).

## $$ Cabañaquinta
*Jr Moquegua 422, T082-571045,*
*www.cabanaquinta.com.*
A/c or fan, frigobar, laundry, free drinking
water, good restaurant, garden with pool,
very comfortable, airport transfers. Request
a room away from the highway.

## $$ Centenario
*Av Dos de Mayo 744, T082-574731,*
*www.hotelcentenario.com.pe.*
Modern hotel 7 blocks from the plaza,
bright ample rooms with a/c or fan and
frigobar, good views from upper floors,
restaurant, terrace with pool, parking,
English spoken. Facilities open to non-
guests with advance reservation.

## $$ Paititi Hostal
*Jr González Prada 290 y Av León Velarde,*
*T082-574667, www.paititihostal.com.*
Ample rooms with a/c or fan, those in
front are bright but get street noise,
good breakfast, gym, attentive staff.

## $$ Perú Amazónico
*Jr Ica 269, T082-571799,*
*www.peruamazonico.com.*
Very nice modern hotel, comfortable rooms
with a/c, fan and frigobar, parking, bicycle
rentals. Recommended.

## $$-$ Pirwa Casa Andrea
*Jr Moquegua y Tacna, T082-637785.*
Bright clean rooms and dorms (US$9)
with a/c or fan, large patio, terrace with
hammocks, good service, safe
motorcycle parking. Can arrange airport
trasfers and tours. Opened in 2017.

## $ Anaconda Lodge
*600 m from airport, T982-728518,*
*www.anacondajunglelodge.com.*
With private or shared bath, Swiss/Thai-
owned bungalows, hot showers, swimming
pool, breakfast available. Thai restaurant,
pizza workshop (arrange a day ahead), tours
arranged, camping (US$6 pp), very pleasant,
family atmosphere.

## $ Hospedaje El Bambú
*Jr Puno 837, T082-639399.*
Basic and small but well-kept rooms with
bath and fan, family atmosphere, breakfast
and juices not included in price but served
in dining room. A good budget option.

## $ Hospedaje Español
*González Prada 670, T082-572381.*
Simple economical rooms with or without
fan, set back from the road, in a quiet part
of town.

## $ Tambopata Hostel
*Jr González Prada 161, T082-574201,*
*www.tambopatahostel.com.*
Private rooms with or without bath and
unisex or mixed dorms (US$10 pp), terrace
with hammocks, pool, kitchen facilities. Nice
atmosphere, they also organize 1- to 5-day
tours to Tambopata.

---

## Around Tambopata National Reserve
Most jungle lodges are booked as package
deals with meals, transport and guides.
Prices given below are per person for 3 days,
2 nights, unless indicated otherwise. They are
all subject to change, see lodges' websites
for current offers.

### Lodges on the lower Río Madre de Dios

#### Casa de Hospedaje Mejía
*US$180. Close to Lago Sandoval, T082-573372;*
*contact Sandoval en Tambopata Travel,*
*see Local tour operators, page 436.*
Attractive but basic rustic lodge, full board
can be arranged, canoes are available.
In the same family and also by the lake
is **Maloka Sandoval Lodge**, www.
malokasandovallodge.com.

#### Eco Amazonia Lodge
*US$325. 1 hr downriver from Puerto*
*Maldonado. Office at Av 26 de Diciembre 435,*
*T082-573491; also have offices in Lima and*
*Cuzco, www.ecoamazonia.com.pe.*
Basic bungalows and dormitories set in a
4450-ha private reserve with trails, good for

birdwatching, has its own Monkey Island with animals taken from the forest.

### El Corto Maltés
*On south shore of the river, Billinghurst 229, Puerto Maldonado, T082-573831, www. cortomaltes-amazonia.com.*
On the Madre de Dios, halfway to Sandoval which is the focus of most visits, private reserve with trails and clay lick. Thatched cabins with water, huge dining room, pool, Ayahuasca ceremonies, well run.

### Estancia Bello Horizonte
*US$250-290. 18 km northeast of Puerto Maldonado towards the border, Loreto 252, T082-572748, www.estanciabellohorizonte.com.*
In a nice stretch of forest overlooking the old course of the Madre de Dios, now a huge *aguajal* (swamp) populated with macaws. A small lodge with bungalows for 30 people, with private bath, hot water, pool. Transport, all meals and guide (several languages offered) included, US$250-280 for 3 days/2 nights. The lodge belongs to **APRONIA**, an organization that trains and provides employment for orphaned children. Suitable for those wanting to avoid a river trip.

### Inkaterra Reserva Amazónica Lodge
*US$335-530. 45 mins by boat down the Madre de Dios, Calle Asunción Nicole s/n – ex ENAPU, T082-573534, Puerto Maldonado, in Lima T01-610 0400, in Cuzco, T084-234010, www.inkaterra.com.*
Tastefully redecorated hotel in the jungle with suites and bungalows, solar power, good food in huge dining room supported by a big tree. Jungle tours in its own 10,000-ha reserve, 30-40 m-high canopy walk; also tours to Lago Sandoval. In the same group and with the same high standards and style is **Inkaterra Hacienda Concepción**, 30 mins by boat from Puerto Maldonado (before Isla de los Monos), with cabins and a 6 room lodge. They also run **Inkaterra Guides Field Station**, 1 hr from Puerto Maldonado, a guides training centre and more rustic lodge for visitors and researchers.

### Lupuna Lodge
*US$130. On the north shore of the river, 13 km (40 mins by boat) from Puerto Maldonado, can also be reached by road and a short walk, T943-524714 (Spanish), 928-841740 (English, German), UK bookings T7800-829652 (Eduardo), www.lupunavacations.com.*
Small private reserve (90 ha) and family farm, 3 rustic screened cabins with bath and cold water, mosquito nets, tasty food with homegrown produce. Spanish, English or German guiding on forest trails and nearby attractions including a clay lick, a good economy option with personalized service. Also offer half- to 3-day cycling tours, including a trip to Lago Valencia.

### Monte Amazónico Lodge Lago Sandoval
*US$180. On the south shore of the river, near Lago Sandoval, 60 mins by boat from Puerto Maldonado, reserve through Carlos Expeditions, see Local tour operators, page 436, http://carlosexpeditions.com.*
Screened rooms and cabins with mosquito nets and bath, ample common areas include a pool, Ayahuasca ceremonies (US$60 pp).

### Sandoval Lake Lodge
*1 km beyond Mejía on Lago Sandoval. Book through InkaNatura, www.inkanatura.com.*
Usual access is by canoe after a 3-km walk or rickshaw ride. Lodge overlooking the lake, huge bar and dining area, electricity, hot water. InkaNatura also has a lodge on the Río Heath, the **Heath River Wildlife Center**, about 4½ hrs from Puerto Maldonado by boat, but journey times depend on river levels. Just 10 mins from the lodge is a large macaw and parrot clay lick. In the vicinity you can visit both jungle and savannah and in the latter are many endemic bird species. **InkaNatura** runs tours which combine both lodges.

### Lodges on the Río Tambopata
Lodges on the Tambopata are reached by vehicle to Puerto Nuevo port, 20 km upriver

from Puerto Maldonado by the community of Infierno, then by boat. Over 20 small lodges and *casas de hospedaje* along the Tambopata river are grouped together under the names: **Tambopata Ecotourism Corridor** and **Tambopata Homestays**, iPerú has a current listing for these. See lodge websites for prices of packages offered, check whether entry fees to the reserve are included.

### Explorers Inn
*US$370. 58 km from Puerto Maldonado (2½ hrs up the Río Tambopata; 1½ hrs return); Av Circunvalación, Terminal Terrestre, p2, of 111, Puerto Maldonado, T082-573029, www.explorersinn.com.*
Just before the La Torre control post, adjoining the TNR, in the part where most research work has been done, this is one of the best places in Peru for seeing jungle birds (580 plus species have been recorded, they have their own clay lick and a 42-m viewing tower) and butterflies (1230 plus species). There are also giant river otters, but you probably need more than a 2-day tour to benefit fully from the location. Tours through the adjoining community of La Torre. The guides are biologists and naturalists undertaking research in the reserve. They provide interesting wildlife treks.

### Hacienda Tambopata
*US$350. On the north shore of the river, near Collpa Chuncho (included), 60 mins by boat from Puerto Maldonado, reserve through*

*Carlos Expeditions, see Local tour operators below, http://carlosexpeditions.com.*
Screened rooms and cabins with mosquito nets and bath, some with jacuzzi.

### Rainforest Expeditions Lodges
*Approximately US$625, varies with lodge and programme, many packages and add-ons available. Operate 3 top-of-the-line lodges on the Tambopata River, office at Av Aeropuerto Km 6, La Joya, Puerto Maldonado, T082-572575, in Lima T01-7196422, in Cusco T984-705266, USA and Canada T1-877-231 9251, www.perunature.com.*

### Posada Amazonas Lodge
*2 hrs from Puerto Maldonado, 45 mins from Puerto Nuevo.*
A collaboration between the tour operator and the local native community of Infierno. Attractive rooms with hot showers, visits to Lake Tres Chimbadas, with good birdwatching including the Tambopata *collpa*. Offers trips to a nearby indigenous primary healthcare project where a native healer gives guided tours of the medicinal plant garden. Service and guiding is very good.

### Refugio Amazonas Lodge

*3½ hrs from Puerto Maldonado, 2 hrs from Puerto Nuevo, close to Lago Condenado.*
Bungalows within a private reserve, large en suite rooms with mosquito nets, hot water, well designed and run, large open dining area, atmospheric with a resort feel. Visits to El Chuncho clay lick, 30-m observation tower.

### Tambopata Research Centre

*7 hrs from Puerto Maldonado, 4 hrs from Refugio Amazonas.*
The company's more intimate, but very comfortable lodge, inside the Tambopata Reserve. Rooms and suites with private toilet and shared hot showers. Top-end suites have a private outdoor deck and tub. The lodge is next to the famous Colorado macaw clay lick and a visit to El Chuncho lick is also included. Surrounded by outstanding jungle (includes 5 habitats). Excellent guides.

### Tambopata Eco Lodge

*US$437. On the Río Tambopata; reservations office at Nueva Baja 432, Cuzco, T084-245695; operations office Jr Javier Heraud, Urbanización Los Lirios, Puerto Maldonado, T082-571392, www.tambopatalodge.com.*
Rooms with solar-heated water, good guides, excellent food. Trips go to Lake Condenado, some to Lake Sachavacayoc, and to the Collpa de Chuncho, guiding mainly in English and Spanish, naturalists programme provided.

### Wasaí Tambopata Lodge

*US$426. Río Tambopata, 120 km (4½ hrs by boat) upriver from Puerto Maldonado or 1½ hrs by van and 1 hr walking; In Lima T01-436 8792, or Jr Guillermo Billinghurst, Puerto Maldonado, T997-516352, www.wasai.com.*
Rustic cabins with bath, cold water, kayaking, zip-line, fishing, photography tours, mystic tours, wildlife observation, volunteering, tours to the Collpa de Chuncho and Lago Sandoval, guiding in English and Spanish. Also run a tent camp further upstream and a hotel in Puerto Maldonado (see above).

### To Iberia and Iñapari

#### $ Hospedaje Casa Blanca
*Av José Aldamiz 848, Iberia, T972-702204.*
Simple rooms with or without bath, electric shower, fan, small garden, breakfast available, helpful owners, a good choice.

#### $ Hospedaje Delta
*Jr Jaime Troncoso 439, Iberia, T987-332968.*
Multi-storey building, small rooms with bath, cold water, no breakfast.

#### $ Hospedaje Milagritos
*Av León Velarde, near the international bridge, Iñapari, T965-041533.*
Very clean functional rooms with bath, cold water, a/c, cheaper with fan.

#### $ Iñapari
*Av Acre s/n, Iñapari, T948-573604.*
A variety of rooms and prices, with or without bath, a/c or fan, Wi-Fi in common area.

## Restaurants

### Puerto Maldonado

#### $$ Burgos's
*Av Sinchi Roca y Calle Las Chimicuas, near Terminal Terrestre, T082-573653, www.burgosrestaurant.com. Daily 1100-2300.*
Serves a choice of regional and international dishes, wine list. Upmarket for Puerto Maldonado. Groups should reserve ahead.

#### $$-$ El Asadazo
*Arequipa 209, east side of the plaza.*
Popular *menú* at lunchtime, great sandwiches later in the day, cool bar in the evening.

#### $$-$ El Horcón
*Av León Velarde 361, T082-574029. Daily 1800-0100.*
Good pizza, also Italian and Mexican dishes and grill, delivery.

#### $$-$ El Hornito
*Jr Carrión on the plaza and 2 other locations. Open from 1800.*
Cosy, good pizzas, busy at weekends.

### $$-$ Leña y Sazón
*Jr Carrion 135, 2nd location at Av Madre de Dios 285, T994-692360. Daily 1230-2400, Sat until 0100.*
Chicken and beef grilled on a wood fire, cocktails, wines, patio, play area for kids.

### Gustitos del Cura
*Loreto 258, Plaza de Armas, and José María Grain 105. Open 1900-1300, 1600-1900, closed Tue.*
Ice cream and juice parlour offering unusual flavours, snacks, sweets, vegetarian dishes. Run by the NGO APRONIA working with homeless teenagers. Also at Ucayali y 28 de Julio (closed Mon) and at C José María Grain 105, with river views.

### La Semilla
*Jr Arequipa 281, Plaza de Armas, upstairs. Mon-Fri 0900-2200, Sat 1000-2200.*
Healthy sandwiches, salads, crêpes, pizza, juices and coffee. Book exchange, games, Wi-Fi, helpful with local information. Canadian/French-run.

### Magdalena's
*Loreto 300, Plaza de Armas. Daily 0600-2300.*
Café, choice of bread, *empanadas*, sweet and savoury pastries, sandwiches, coffee, juices. A popular breakfast spot among tourists.

## Bars and clubs

### Puerto Maldonado

### Casa de la Cerveza
*On the plaza adjoining El Hornito. Daily 1000-0100.*
Nearest thing to a pub in Puerto Maldonado, rock music, sports on large screen TV, burgers and snacks.

### Witite
*Av León Velarde 151. Daily from 2200.*
A popular disco playing varied music.

## What to do

### Puerto Maldonado
### Boat hire
Boat hire may be arranged at Puerto Capitanía.

### Local tour operators
Many operators are located on the pedestrian section of Av León Velarde between the plaza and the bridge.
**Carlos Expeditions**, *Av León Velarde 119, T082-571320, www.carlosexpeditions.com.* Run by Carlos Borja Gama who speaks several languages, offers traditional tours and specialist birdwatching and photography tours. Also runs the Monte Amazónico lodges near Laguna Sandoval and along the Río Tambopata. Popular with backpackers. Opening its own hostel in Puerto Maldonado in 2018.
**Manu Tambopata Travel**, *Jr San Martín 775, T082-573755, http://manutambopata travel.com.* 3- to 8-day tours in Manu and Tambopata reserves. Include a trip to the Río Heath area.
**Paquetes Turísticos Municipales**, *at the Municipalidad, Av León Velarde 230, Plaza de Armas, T983-336618.* Medio ambiente y Turismo at the Municipalidad organizes group day tours to nearby attractions (including Lago Sandoval) at weekends and holidays. A good choice for those who have little time.
**Sandoval en Tambopata Travel**, *Av León Velarde 487, Plaza de Armas, T082-573372, www.malokasandoval.com.* Run by the Mejía brothers who speak English and French and offer tours to Sandoval Lake and their lodges: **Casa de Hospedaje Mejía** and **Ceiba Lodge Sandoval**.
**Tambopata Expeditions**, *Av León Velarde 160, T987-590164.* Tours to attractions in the Tambopata Reserve and surroundings including Sandoval, Valencia and Tres Chimbadas lakes, also adventure tours like kayaking, canopy and zip-lines. Operate **Tambopata Hostel** in town and **Collpas Tambopata Inn**, http://tambopatajungle.

com, abutting the Tambopata Reserve. Popular with backpackers.

## Tambopata National Reserve

For tours to the Tambopata Reserve, see Lodges on the lower Río Madre de Dios, Lodges on the Río Tambopata and Local tour operators, all above.

## Transport

### Cuzco to Puerto Maldonado: via Urcos and Mazuko
#### Bus and van

The Interoceánica is paved all the way. There are many daily buses between the Cuzco and Puerto Maldonado bus terminals, US$9-12 económico, US$12-21 semi-cama, US$21-24 cama, 10-11 hrs. The more reliable companies include **Cruz del Sur** (from its private terminal in Cuzco at 2100), **Móvil** (0900 – the only daytime option, 1800, 2030), and **Transzela** (2100); there are many others (2000-2100). Van companies that run to Mazuko, also offer service to Cuzco (US$18). Vans run between **Mazuko** and Puerto Maldonado 0300-2200, with **Express Turismo** (Av Tacna con Piura, Puerto Maldonado, T973-581284; Av Inambari in Mazuko) and **Expediciones Colorado Manu** (see page 427; in Cuzco, Av Alameda Pachacútec 427, T946-693203), US$7.60, 3 hrs. Several buses also run daily along the Interoceanic Highway from Arequipa and Juliaca, crossing the altiplano and joining the Cuzco–Puerto Maldonado section at Puente Inambari, south of Mazuko.

### Puerto Maldonado
#### Air

To **Lima**, daily with **LATAM** (León Velarde 503), direct and via Cuzco, **Avianca/ TACA** (2 de Mayo 313), via Cuzco and **Star Perú** (León Velarde 505) direct and via Cuzco. Mototaxi from town to airport, US$3.75, taxi US$6, 8 km.

**Warning...**
Avoid nightime travel to and from Puerto Maldonado as violent robberies have occured on this route.

#### Bus and van

The Terminal Terrestre is at Jr Atahualpa and Circunvalación Norte, 4 km northwest of the plaza; taxi to the centre US$2.75, mototaxi US$1.80. The better companies are listed, there are others. To **Cuzco**, see Cuzco to Puerto Maldonado via Mazuko, above (note warning, above); buses leave Puerto Maldonado at same time as departures from Cuzco. To **Juliaca**, via Mazuko, San Gabán and Macusani, US$10.60-15, 12 hrs, with **Santa Cruz** (T951-289800) at 1430, 1730; **Realeza** (T984 901945) at 1900; **Julsa** at 1530; **Mendivil** at 1630; **Wayra** (T940-213859) at 1700; **Power** (T977-648208) at 1600; the last 4 continue to **Arequipa**, US$18-24, 16 hrs. To **Juliaca**, with **Santa Cruz**, 3 daily, US$14-15, 11-12 hrs; several other companies. To **Puno**, with **Reyna**, at 1900, US$14-15, 11-12 hrs.

For **Boca Manu** and **Salvación** take a colectivo to **Boca Colorado** and then hire a boat or take a cargo boat to Boca Manu and further to Nuevo Edén or beyond (no fixed schedule). From Salvación there is transport to Cuzco.

To **Brazil**: to **Iberia**, 2½ hrs, US$4.55, and **Iñapari**, 3½ hrs, US$7.60, vans 0330-1900 daily, from Jr Ica block 5 y Jr Piura, by Mercado Modelo; recommended companies are **Turismo Imperial** and **Turismo Real Dorado**.

#### Car and motorcycle hire

**Las Anclas**, Gonzales Prada 380, T983-766618, motorcycles cost US$1.50-3 per hr plus US$15 security deposit, pick-up including 300 km costs US$280 per day, plus US$300 security deposit. Passport and driver's licence plus copies must be shown. English and German spoken.

# Background

History . . . . . . . . . . . . . . . . . . . . . . . . . .439
Modern Peru . . . . . . . . . . . . . . . . . . .452
People . . . . . . . . . . . . . . . . . . . . . . . . .455
Culture . . . . . . . . . . . . . . . . . . . . . . . .459
Land & environment . . . . . . . . . . .474
Books . . . . . . . . . . . . . . . . . . . . . . . . . 482

# History

## Pre-Columbian history

Despite Peru's formidable geographical barriers and frequent natural disasters, archaeologists have uncovered a pre-Columbian history of highly advanced societies that prevailed against these awesome odds. The coastal desert from Lambayeque department south to Paracas has revealed an 'American Egypt', although this has meant a bias towards the coastal region and a reliance on the contents of tombs for information. Knowledge of these tombs often only comes to light following their looting by *huaqueros* (grave robbers), incited by demand from the international antiquities market.

The Incas told the Spaniards that before they established their Tawantinsuyo Empire, the land was overrun by primitives constantly at war with one another. There were, in fact, many other civilized cultures dating back to before 2000 BC. The most accomplished of these were the Chavín and Sechín (circa 900-200 BC), the Paracas-Nazca (circa 200 BC-AD 500), the Huari-Tiahuanaco (circa 750 BC-AD 1000), and the Moche-Chimú (200 BC-AD 1400).

### Early settlement

It is generally accepted that the earliest settlers in Peru were related to people who had crossed the Bering Straits from Asia and drifted through the Americas from about 20,000 BC. However, theories of early migrations from across the Pacific and Atlantic have been rife since Thor Heyerdahl's raft expeditions in 1947 and 1969-1970.

The earliest evidence of human presence has been found at three sites: Pikimachay near Ayacucho, Pachamachay in Junín and the Guitarrero Cave in the Callejón de Huaylas. All have a radiocarbon date prior to 9000 BC. It had been thought that village settlement in Peru, on the central coast at Pampa, dated from 2500 BC. The theory was that, between these two dates, people lived nomadically in small groups, mainly hunting and gathering but also cultivating some plants seasonally. Domestication of llamas, alpacas and guinea pigs also began at this time, particularly important for the highland people around the Titicaca Basin. **Caral**, however, has overturned many of the accepted tenets of Peruvian archaeology for this period. Caral is a city, 20 km from the coast in the Supe Valley whose date is about 2600 BC. It is a monumental construction and appeared to be easily the oldest city in South America until this claim was disputed by the Miravalles site in the department of Cajamarca. Caral flourished for some 500 years. The evidence points to complex urban society beginning much earlier than previously thought and the city seems to have had a primarily religious, rather than warlike purpose. If these deductions are correct, they also upset some long-held beliefs about city-building worldwide being principally bellicose rather than peaceful.

The abundant wealth of marine life produced by the Humboldt Current, especially along the north coast, boosted population growth and settlement in this area. Around 2000 BC climatic change dried up the lomas ('fog meadows'), and drove sea shoals to deeper water. People turned to farming and began to spread inland along river valleys.

### Origins of Andean civilization

From the second millennium BC to around the first century BC is known as the Formative Period (also called Preceramic Period VI and Initial Period) when the first signs of the high culture of Andean society appeared. During this period sophisticated irrigation and canal systems were developed, farming productivity increased and communities had more time to devote to building and producing ceramics and textiles. The development of pottery also led to trade and cultural links with other communities. Distribution of land and water to the farmers was probably organized by a corporate authority, and this may have led to the later 'Mit'a' labour system developed by the Incas.

Above all, this period is characterized by the construction of centres of urban concentration (Caral notwithstanding) that promoted labour specialization and the development of cultural expression. The earliest buildings built were *huacas*, adobe platform mounds, centres of cult or sacred power. Huaca Florida was the largest example of this period, near the Río Rimac, later replaced by Huaca Garagay as a major centre for the area. Similar centres spread along the north coast, such as El Aspero and Piedra Parada.

During this period, however, much more advanced architecture was being built at **Kótosh**, in the central Andes near Huánuco. Japanese archaeological excavations there in the 1960s revealed a temple with ornamental niches and friezes. Some of the earliest pottery was also found here, showing signs of influence from southern Ecuador and the tropical lowlands, adding weight to theories of Andean culture originating in the Amazon. Radiocarbon dates of some Kótosh remains are as early as 1850 BC.

## Chavín and Sechín

For the next 1000 years or so up to circa 900 BC, communities grew and spread inland from the north coast and south along the northern highlands. Farmers still lived in simple adobe or rough stone houses but built increasingly large and complex ceremonial centres, such as at Las Haldas in the Casma Valley (dated at 1700 BC). As farming became more productive and pottery more advanced, commerce grew and states began to develop throughout central and north-central Peru, with the associated signs of social structure and hierarchies.

Around 900 BC a new era was marked by the rise of two important centres; **Chavín de Huántar** in the central Andes and **Sechín Alto**, inland from Casma on the north coast (some date the latter from 1600 BC).

Chavín was the first of several 'horizon styles' that were of the greatest importance in Peru and had very widespread influence. The other later ones, the Huari-Tiahuanaco and the Inca, were pan-Peruvian, affecting all parts of the country. The chief importance of Chavín de Huántar was not so much in its highly advanced architecture as in the influence of its cult coupled with the artistic style of its ceramics and other artefacts. The founders of Chavín may have originated in the tropical lowlands as some of its carved monoliths show representations of monkeys and felines.

Objects with Chavín traits have been found all along the coast from Piura to the Lurin Valley south of Lima, and its cult ideology spread to temples around the same area. Richard L Burger of Yale University has argued that the extent of Chavín influence has been exaggerated. Many sites on the coast already had their own cult practices and the Chavín idols may have been simply added alongside. There is evidence of an El Niño flood that devastated the north coast around 500 BC. Local cults fell from grace as social order was disrupted and the Chavín cult was snatched up as a timely new alternative.

## Chavín cult

The Chavín cult was paralleled by the great advances made at this time in textile production and in some of the earliest examples of metallurgy (whose origins have been attributed to gold, silver and copper ornaments found in graves in Chongoyape, near Chiclayo, which show Chavín-style features). But earlier evidence has been discovered in the Andahuaylas region, dating from 1800 to 900 BC. The religious symbolism of gold and other precious metals and stones is thought to have been an inspiration behind some of the beautiful artefacts found in the central Andean area. The emergence of social hierarchies also created a demand for luxury goods as status symbols.

The cultural brilliance of Chavín de Huántar was complemented by its contemporary, **Sechín**. This huge granite-faced complex near Casma, 370 km north of Lima, was described by JC Tello as the biggest structure of its kind in the Andes. According to Michael Moseley of Harvard University, Chavín and Sechín may have combined forces, with Sechín as the military power that spread the cultural word of Chavín, but their influence did not reach far to the south where the Paracas and Tiahuanaco cultures held sway.

## Upper Formative Period

The Chavín hegemony, which is also known as the Middle Formative Period (or Early Horizon), broke up around 300 BC. The 'unity' of this period was broken and the initial phase of the regional diversification of Andean cultures began. The process of domestication of plants and animals culminated in the Upper Formative Period. Agricultural technology progressed leading to an economic security that permitted a considerable growth in the centres of population. Among the many diverse stylistic/cultural groups of this period are: the Vicus on the north coast; Salinar in the Chicama Valley; Paracas Necrópolis on the south coast; and Huarás in the Ancash highlands.

**Paracas Necrópolis** was the early phase of the Nazca culture and is renowned for the superb technical quality and stylistic variety in its weaving and pottery. The mantos (large, decorated cloth) rank amongst the world's best, and many of the finest examples can be seen in the museums of Lima. The extreme dryness of the desert here has preserved the textiles and ceramics in the mummies' tombs which have been excavated.

Paracas Necrópolis is, in fact, a cemetery located on the slopes of Cerro Colorado, in the Department of Ica, from which 429 funerary bundles were excavated. Each bundle is a mummy wrapped in many fine and rough textiles. Paracas Necrópolis corresponds to the last of the 10 phases into which Paracas ceramics have been divided. The previous ones, known as Paracas Cavernas, relate to the Middle Formative Period and were influenced by the Chavín cult.

## Nazca culture

The Regional Development Period up to about AD 500, was a time of great social and cultural development. Sizable towns of 5000-10,000 inhabitants grew on the south coast, populated by artisans, merchants, government administrators and religious officials.

One of the most famous cultures of this period, or indeed of pre-Columbian history was the Nazca. The Nazca Lines are a feature of the region. Straight lines, abstract designs and outlines of animals are scratched in the desert surface forming a lighter contrast that can be seen clearly from the air. There are many theories as to how and why the lines were made but no explanation has yet been able definitively to establish their place in Peruvian history; for further details, see page 210). There are similarities between the style of some of the line patterns and that of the pottery and textiles of the same period. It is clear from the scale of the lines and the quality of the work that they were important to the Nazca culture.

In contrast to the quantity and quality of the Nazca artefacts found, relatively few major buildings belonging to this period have been uncovered in the southern desert. Dos Palmas is a complex of rooms and courtyards in the Pisco Valley, while Cahuachi in the Nazca Valley is a large area including adobe platforms, pyramids and a 'wooden Stonehenge' cluster of preserved tree trunks. Among the recently excavated sites are the architectural complex of Los Molinos, with large buildings, patios and passages, and the necropolis of La Muña, both near Palpa. As most of the archaeological evidence of the Nazca culture came from their desert cemeteries, little is known about the lives and social organization of the people. Alpaca hair found in Nazca textiles, however, indicates that there must have been strong trade links with highland people.

## Moche culture

Nazca's contemporaries on the north coast were the militaristic Moche who, from about AD 100-800 built up an empire whose traces stretch from Piura in the north to Casma, beyond Chimbote, in the south. The Moche built their capital in the middle of the desert, outside present day Trujillo. It features the pyramid temples of the Huaca del Sol and Huaca de la Luna (see page 116). The Moche roads and system of way stations are thought to have been an early inspiration for the Inca network. The Moche increased the coastal population with intensive irrigation projects. Skillful engineering works were carried out, such as the La Cumbre canal, still in use today, and the Ascope aqueduct.

The Moche's greatest achievement, however, was its artistic genius. Exquisite ornaments in gold, silver and precious stones were made by its craftsmen. Moche pottery progressed through five stylistic periods, most notable for the stunningly lifelike portrait vases. A wide variety of ceremonial and everyday scenes were created in naturalistic ceramics, telling us more about Moche life than is known about other earlier cultures, and perhaps used by them as 'visual aids' to compensate for the lack of a written language.

A spectacular discovery of a Moche royal tomb at **Sipán** was made in February 1987 by Walter Alva, director of the Brüning Archaeological Museum, Lambayeque. Reports of the excavation in the National Geographic magazine (October 1988 and June 1990), talked of the richest unlooted tomb in the New World (see page 133). The find included semi-precious stones brought from Chile and Argentina, and seashells from Ecuador (the Moche were also great navigators).

The cause of the collapse of the Moche Empire around AD 600-700 is unknown, but it may have been started by a 30-year drought at the end of the sixth century, followed by one of the periodic El Niño floods (identified by meteorologists from ice thickness in the Andes) and finished by the encroaching forces of the Huari Empire. The decline of the Moche signalled a general tipping of the balance of power in Peru from the north coast to the southern sierra.

## Huari-Tiahuanaco

The ascendant Huari-Tiahuanaco movement, from circa AD 600-1000, combined the religious cult of the Tiahuanaco site in the Titicaca Basin, with the military dynamism of the Huari, based in the central highlands. The two cultures developed independently but, as had occurred with the Chavín-Sechín association, they are generally thought to have merged compatibly.

Up until their own demise around AD 1440, the Huari-Tiahuanaco had spread their empire and influence from Cajamarca and Lambayeque in the north and across much of southern Peru, northern Bolivia and Argentina. The Huari introduced a new concept in urban life, the great walled urban centre, the best example of which is their capital city, 22 km north of Ayacucho (see page 92). They also made considerable gains in art and technology, building roads, terraces and irrigation canals across the country.

The Huari-Tiahuanaco ran their empire with efficient labour and administrative systems that were later adopted and refined by the Incas. Labour tribute for state projects had been practised by the Moche and was further developed now. But the empire could not contain regional kingdoms who began to fight for land and power. As control broke down, rivalry and coalitions emerged, and the system collapsed.

## Chimú culture

After the decline of the Huari Empire, the unity that had been imposed on the Andes was broken. A new stage of autonomous regional or local political organizations began. Among the cultures corresponding to this period were the Kuélap, centred in the Chachapoyas region (see page 171), and the Chimú.

The Chimú culture had two centres. To the north was Lambayeque, near Chiclayo, while to the south, in the Moche Valley near present-day Trujillo, was the adobe walled city of Chan Chán. At 20 sq km, this was the largest pre-Hispanic Peruvian city (see page 117).

Chimú has been classified as a despotic state that based its power on wars of conquest. Rigid social stratification existed and power rested in the hands of the great Lord Siquic and the Lord Alaec. These lords were followed in social scale by a group of urban couriers who enjoyed a certain degree of economic power. At the bottom were the peasants and slaves. In AD 1450, the Chimú kingdom was conquered by the Inca Túpac Yupanqui.

## Inca Dynasty

The origins of the Inca Dynasty are shrouded in mythology. The best known story reported by the Spanish chroniclers talks about Manco Cápac and his sister rising out of Lake Titicaca, created by the Sun as divine founders of a chosen race. This was in approximately AD 1200. Over the next 300 years the small tribe grew to supremacy as leaders of the largest empire ever known in the Americas. The four territories of Tawantinsuyo, united by Cuzco as the umbilicus of the universe, were: Chinchaysuyo, north and northwest; Cuntisuyo, south and west; Collasuyo, south and east; Antisuyo, east.

At its peak, just before the Spanish Conquest, the Inca Empire stretched from the Río Maule in central Chile, north to the present Ecuador-Colombia border, containing most of Ecuador, Peru, western Bolivia, northern Chile and northwest Argentina. The area was roughly equivalent to France, Belgium, Holland, Luxembourg, Italy and Switzerland combined (980,000 sq km).

Legen has it that the first Inca ruler, Manco Cápac, moved to the fertile Cuzco region and established Cuzco as his capital. Successive generations of rulers were fully occupied with local conquests of rivals, such as the Colla and Lupaca to the south, and the Chanca to the northwest. At the end of Inca Viracocha's reign the hated Chanca were finally defeated, largely thanks to the heroism of one of his sons, Pachacútec Inca Yupanqui, who was subsequently crowned as the new ruler.

From the start of Pachacútec's own reign in AD 1438, imperial expansion grew in earnest. With the help of his son and heir, Topa Inca, territory was conquered from the Titicaca Basin south into Chile, and all the north and central coast down to the Lurin Valley. The Incas also subjugated the Chimú, their highly sophisticated rivals on the coast (see above). Typical of the Inca method of government, some of the Chimú skills were assimilated into their own political and administrative system, and some Chimú nobles were even given positions in Cuzco.

Perhaps the pivotal event in Inca history came in AD 1527 with the death of the ruler, Huayna Capac. Civil war broke out in the confusion over his rightful successor. One of his legitimate sons, Huáscar, ruled the southern part of the empire from Cuzco. Atahualpa, Huáscar's half-brother, governed Quito, the capital of Chinchaysuyo. In 1532, soon after Atahualpa had won the civil war, Francisco Pizarro arrived in Tumbes with 167 conquistadors, a third of them on horseback. Atahualpa's army was marching south, probably for the first time, when he clashed with Pizarro at Cajamarca.

Francisco Pizarro's only chance against the formidable imperial army he encountered at Cajamarca was a bold stroke. He drew Atahualpa into an ambush, slaughtered his guards, promised him liberty if a certain room were filled with treasure, and finally killed him on the pretext that another Inca army was on its way to free him. Pushing on to Cuzco, Pizarro was at first hailed as the executioner of the traitorous Atahualpa, who had ordered the death of Huáscar in AD 1533. Panic followed, however, when the conquistadors set about sacking the city. The Spanish fought off with difficulty an attempt by Manco Inca to recapture Cuzco in 1536.

## Empire building

Enough remains today of their astounding highways, cities and agricultural terracing for people to marvel and wonder how they accomplished so much in so short a time. They seem to have been amazingly energetic, industrious and efficient – and the reports of their Spanish conquerors confirm this hypothesis.

They must also have had the willing cooperation of most of their subject peoples, most of the time. In fact, the Incas were master diplomats and alliance-builders first, and military conquerors only second, if the first method of expansion failed. The Inca skill at generating wealth by means of highly efficient agriculture and distribution brought them enormous prestige and enabled them to 'out-gift' neighbouring chiefs in huge royal feasts involving ritual outpourings of generosity, often in the form of vast gifts of textiles, exotic products from distant regions, and perhaps wives to add blood ties to the alliance. The 'out-gifted' chief was required by the Andean laws of reciprocity to provide something in return, and this would usually be his loyalty, as well as a levy of manpower from his own chiefdom.

Thus, with each new alliance the Incas wielded greater labour forces and their mighty public works programmes surged ahead. These were administered through an institution known as *mit'a*, a form of taxation through labour. The state provided the materials, such as wool and cotton for making textiles, and the communities provided skills and labour.

*Mit'a* contingents worked royal mines, royal plantations for producing coca leaves, royal quarries and so on. The system strove to be equitable, and workers in such hardship posts as high altitude mines and lowland coca plantations were given correspondingly shorter terms of service.

## Organization

Huge administrative centres were built in different parts of the empire, where people and supplies were gathered. Articles such as textiles and pottery were produced there in large workshops. Work in these places was carried out in a festive manner, with plentiful food, drink and music. Here was Andean reciprocity at work: the subject supplied his labour, and the ruler was expected to provide generously while he did so.

Aside from *mit'a* contributions there were also royal lands claimed by the Inca as his portion in every conquered province, and worked for his benefit by the local population. Thus, the contribution of each citizen to the state was quite large, but apparently, the imperial economy was productive enough to sustain this.

Another institution was the practice of moving populations around: inserting loyal groups into restive areas, and removing recalcitrant populations to loyal areas. These movements of *mitmakuna*, as they were called, were also used to introduce skilled farmers and engineers into areas where productivity needed to be raised.

## Communications

The huge empire was held together by an extensive and highly efficient highway system. There were an estimated 30,000 km of major highway, most of it neatly paved and drained, stringing together the major Inca sites. Two parallel highways ran north to south, along the coastal desert strip and the mountains, and dozens of east-west roads crossing from the coast to the Amazon fringes. These roadways took the most direct routes, with wide stone stairways zig-zagging up the steepest mountain slopes and rope suspension bridges crossing the many narrow gorges of the Andes. The north-south roads formed a great axis that eventually came to be known as **Capaq Ñan** – 'Royal', or 'Principal Road', in Quechua – which exceeded in grandeur not only the other roads, but also their utilitarian concept. They became the Incas' symbol of power over men and over the sacred forces of nature. So marvellous were these roads that the Spaniards who saw them at the height of their glory said that there was nothing comparable in all Christendom.

Every 12 km or so there was a *tambo*, or way station, where goods could be stored and travellers lodged. The *tambos* were also control points, where the Inca state's accountants tallied movements of goods and people. Even more numerous than *tambos*, were the huts of the *chasquis*, or relay runners, who continually sped royal and military messages along these highways.

The Inca state kept records and transmitted information in various ways. Accounting and statistical records were kept on skeins of knotted strings known as *quipus*. Numbers employed the decimal system (although Italian engineer Nicolino De Pasquale claimed in 2006 the number system was based on 40), and colours indicated the categories being recorded. An entire class of people, known as *quipucamayocs*, existed whose job was to create and interpret them. Neither the Incas nor their Andean predecessors had a system of writing as we understand it, but there may have been a system of encoding language into *quipus*. Archaeologists are studying this problem today. History and other forms of knowledge were transmitted via songs and poetry. Music and dancing, full of encoded information that could be read by the educated elite, were part of every major ceremony and public event information was also carried in textiles, which had for millennia been the most vital expression of Andean culture.

## Textiles

Clothing carried insignia of status, ethnic origin, age and so on. Special garments were made and worn for various rites of passage. It has been calculated that, after agriculture, no activity was more important to Inca civilization than weaving. Vast stores of textiles were maintained to sustain the Inca system of ritual giving. Armies and *mit'a* workers were partly paid in textiles. The finest materials were reserved for the nobility, and the Inca emperor himself displayed his status by changing into new clothes every day and having the previous day's burned.

Most weaving was done by women, and the Incas kept large numbers of 'chosen women' in female-only houses all over the empire, partly for the purpose of supplying textiles to the elite and for the many deities, to whom they were frequently given as burned offerings. These women had other duties, such as making *chicha* – the Inca corn beer that was consumed and sacrificed in vast quantities on ceremonial occasions. They also became wives and concubines to the Inca elite and loyal nobilities. And some may have served as priestesses of the moon, in parallel to the male priesthood of the sun.

## Religious worship

The Incas have long been portrayed as sun-worshippers, but it seems that they were mountain-worshippers too. Research has shown that Machu Picchu was at least partly dedicated to the worship of the surrounding mountains, and Inca sacrificial victims have been excavated on frozen Andean peaks at 6700 m. In fact, until technical climbing was invented, the Incas held the world altitude record for humans.

Human sacrifice was not common, but every other kind was, and ritual attended every event in the Inca calendar. The main temple of Cuzco was dedicated to the numerous deities: the Sun, the Moon, Venus, the Pleiades, the Rainbow, Thunder and Lightning, and the countless religious icons of subject peoples which had been brought to Cuzco, partly in homage, partly as hostage. Here, worship was continuous and the fabulous opulence included gold cladding on the walls, and a famous garden filled with life-size objects of gold and silver. Despite this pantheism, the Incas acknowledged an overall Creator God, whom they called Viracocha. A special temple was dedicated to him, at Raqchi, about 100 km southeast of Cuzco. Part of it still stands today.

## Military forces

The conquering Spaniards noted with admiration the Inca storehouse system, still well-stocked when they found it, despite several years of civil war among the Incas. Besides textiles, military equipment, and ritual objects, they found huge quantities of food. Like most Inca endeavours, the food stores served a multiple purpose: to supply feasts, to provide during lean times, to feed travelling work parties, and to supply armies on the march.

Inca armies were able to travel light and move fast because of this system. Every major Inca settlement also incorporated great halls where large numbers of people could be accommodated, or feasts and gatherings held, and large squares or esplanades for public assemblies.

Inca technology is usually deemed inferior to that of contemporary Europe. Their military technology certainly was. They had not invented iron-smelting, and basically fought with clubs, palmwood spears, slings, wooden shields, cotton armour and straw-stuffed helmets. They did not even make much use of the bow and arrow, a weapon they were well aware of. Military tactics, too, were primitive. The disciplined formations of the Inca armies quickly dissolved into melees of unbridled individualism once battle was joined. This, presumably, was because warfare constituted a theatre of manly prowess, but was not the main priority of Inca life. Its form was ritualistic. Battles were suspended by both sides for religious observance. Negotiation, combined with displays of superior Inca strength, usually achieved victory, and total annihilation of the enemy was not on the agenda.

## Architecture

Other technologies, however, were superior in every way to their 16th century counterparts: textiles; settlement planning; and agriculture in particular with its sophisticated irrigation and soil conservation systems, ecological sensitivity, specialized crop strains and high productivity under the harshest conditions. The Incas fell short of their Andean predecessors in the better-known arts of ancient America – ceramics, textiles and metalwork – but it could be argued that their supreme efforts were made in architecture, stoneworking, landscaping, roadbuilding, and the harmonious combination of these elements.

These are the outstanding survivals of Inca civilization, which still remain to fascinate the visitor: the huge, exotically close-fit blocks of stone, cut in graceful, almost sensual curves; the astoundingly craggy and inaccessible sites encircled by great sweeps of Andean scenery; the rhythmic layers of farm terracing that provided land and food to this still-enigmatic people. The finest examples of Inca architecture can be seen in the city of Cuzco and throughout the Sacred Valley. As more evidence of Inca society is uncovered each year, our knowledge of these remarkable people can only improve.

## Ruling elite

The ruling elite lived privileged lives in their capital at Cuzco. They reserved for themselves and privileged insiders certain luxuries, such as the chewing of coca, the wearing of fine vicuña wool, and the practice of polygamy. But they were an austere people, too. Everyone had work to do, and the nobility were constantly posted to state business throughout the empire. Young nobles were expected to learn martial skills, as well as read the quipus, speak both Quechua and the southern language of Aymara, and know the epic poems.

The Inca elite belonged to royal clans known as *panacas*, which each had the unusual feature of being united around veneration of the mummy of their founding ancestor – a previous Inca emperor, unless they happened to belong to the *panaca* founded by the Inca emperor who was alive at the time. Each new emperor built his own palace in Cuzco and amassed his own wealth rather than inheriting it from his forebears, which perhaps helps to account for the urge to unlimited expansion.

This urge ultimately led the Incas to overreach themselves. Techniques of diplomacy and incorporation no longer worked as they journeyed farther from the homeland and met ever-increasing resistance from people less familiar with their ways. During the reign of Wayna Cápac, the last emperor before the Spanish invasion, the Incas had to establish a northern capital at Quito in order to cope with permanent war on their northern frontier. Following Wayna Cápac's death came a devastating civil war between Cuzco and Quito, and immediately thereafter came the Spanish invasion. Tawantisuyo, the empire of the four quarters, collapsed with dizzying suddenness.

## Conquest and after

Peruvian history after the arrival of the Spaniards was not just a matter of conquistadors versus Incas. The vast majority of the huge empire remained unaware of the conquest for many years. The Chimú and the Chachapoyas cultures were powerful enemies of the Incas. The Chimú developed a highly sophisticated culture and a powerful empire stretching for 560 km along the coast from Tumbes south to present-day Lima. Their history was well-recorded by the Spanish chroniclers and continued through the conquest possibly up to about 1600. The Kuélap/ Chachapoyas people were not so much an empire as a loose-knit "confederation of ethnic groups with no recognized capital" (Morgan Davis *Chachapoyas: The Cloud People*, Ontario, 1988). But the culture did develop into an advanced society with great skill in roads and monument building. Their fortress at Kuélap was known as the most impregnable in Tawantinsuyo. It remained intact against Inca attack and Manco Inca even tried, unsuccessfully, to gain refuge here against the Spaniards.

In 1535, wishing to secure his communications with Spain, Pizarro founded Lima, near the ocean, as his capital. The same year Diego de Almagro set out to conquer Chile. Unsuccessful, he returned to Peru, quarrelled with Pizarro, and in 1538 fought a pitched battle with Pizarro's men at the Salt Pits, near Cuzco. He was defeated and put to death. Pizarro, who had not been at the battle, was assassinated in his palace in Lima by Almagro's son three years later.

For the next 27 years each succeeding representative of the Kingdom of Spain sought to subdue the Inca successor state of Vilcabamba, north of Cuzco, and to unify the fierce Spanish factions. Francisco de Toledo (appointed 1568) solved both problems during his 14 years in office: Vilcabamba was crushed in 1572 and the last reigning Inca, Túpac Amaru, put to death.

For the next 200 years the Viceroys closely followed Toledo's system, if not his methods. The Major Government – the Viceroy, the Audiencia (High Court), and *corregidores* (administrators) – ruled through the Minor Government (indigenous chiefs put in charge of large groups of natives), a rough approximation to the original Inca system.

## Towards independence

There was an indigenous rising in 1780, under the leadership of an Inca noble, José Gabriel Condorcanqui, who called himself Túpac Amaru II. He and many of his lieutenants were captured and put to death under torture at Cuzco. Another indigenous leader in revolt suffered the same fate in 1814, but this last flare-up had the sympathy of many of the locally born Spanish, who resented their status, inferior to the Spaniards born in Spain, the refusal to give them any but the lowest offices, the high taxation imposed by the home government, and the severe restrictions upon trade with any country but Spain.

Help came to them from the outside world. José de San Martín's Argentine troops, convoyed from Chile under the protection of Lord Cochrane's squadron, landed in southern Peru on 7 September 1820. San Martín proclaimed Peruvian independence at Lima on 28 July 1821, though most of the country was still in the hands of the Viceroy, José de La Serna. Bolívar, who had already freed Venezuela and Colombia, sent Antonio José de Sucre to Ecuador where, on 24 May 1822, he gained a victory over La Serna at Pichincha.

San Martín, after a meeting with Bolívar at Guayaquil, left for Argentina and a self-imposed exile in France, while Bolívar and Sucre completed the conquest of Peru by defeating La Serna at the battle of Junín (6 August 1824) and the decisive battle of Ayacucho (9 December 1824). For over a year there was a last stand in the Real Felipe fortress at Callao by the Spanish troops under General Rodil before they capitulated on 22 January 1826. Bolívar was invited to stay in Peru, but left for Colombia in 1826.

## Post-independence Peru

Following independence Peru attempted a confederation with Bolivia in the 1830s but this proved temporary. Then, in 1879 came the disastrous War of the Pacific, in which Peru and Bolivia were defeated by Chile and Peru lost its southern territory.

### Economic change

Peru's economic development since independence has been based upon the export of minerals and foodstuffs to Europe and the United States. Guano, a traditional fertilizer in Peru and derived from the manure of seabirds, was first shipped to Europe in 1841. In the three decades that followed it became an important fertilizer in Europe and by the early 1860s over 80% of the Peruvian government's revenues were derived from its export. Much of this income, though, went to pay off interest on the spiralling national debt. By the 1870s the richer deposits were exhausted and cheaper alternatives to guano were being discovered. One of these was nitrates, discovered in the Atacama desert, but Peru's defeat by Chile in the War of the Pacific ensured that she would lose her share of this wealth.

After the decline of guano, Peru developed several new exports. In the 1890s the demand in Europe and USA for Amazonian rubber for tyres and for use in electrical components led to a brief boom in both the Brazilian and Peruvian Amazon. The Peruvian industry was based around the port of Iquitos. This boom was short-lived as cheaper rubber was soon being produced from plantations in the East Indies. Peru's colonial mineral exports, gold and silver, were replaced by copper, although ownership was mainly under control of foreign companies, particularly the US-based Cerro de Pasco Copper Corporation and Northern Peru Mining. Oil became another important product, amounting to 30% of Peruvian exports by 1930. Further exports came from sugar and cotton, which were produced on coastal plantations.

## Social change

Independence from Spanish rule meant that power passed into the hands of the Creole elite with no immediate alternation of the colonial social system. The *contribución de indígenas* (the colonial tribute collected from the native peoples) was not abolished until 1854, the same year as the ending of slavery.

Until the 1970s land relations in the sierra changed very little, as the older landholding families continued to exert their traditional power over 'their' peones. The traditional elite, the so-called '44 families', were still very powerful, though increasingly divided between the coastal aristocracy with their interests in plantation agriculture and trade, and the serrano elite, more conservative and inward looking.

The pattern of export growth did, however, have major social effects on the coast. The expansion of plantation agriculture and mining led to the growth of a new labour force; this was supplied partially by Chinese indentured labourers, about 100,000 of whom arrived between 1855 and 1875, partly by the migration of indigenous people from the sierra and partly by the descendants of black slaves.

## Political developments

### 19th century

For much of the period since independence Peruvian political life has been dominated by the traditional elites. Political parties have been slow to develop and the roots of much of the political conflict and instability which have marked the country's history lie in personal ambitions and in regional and other rivalries within the elite.

The early years after independence were particularly chaotic as rival *caudillos* (political bosses) who had fought in the independence wars vied with each other for power. The increased wealth brought about by the guano boom led to greater stability, though political corruption became a serious problem under the presidency of José Rufino Echenique (1851-1854) who paid out large sums of the guano revenues as compensation to upper-class families for their (alleged) losses in the Wars of Independence. Defeat by Chile in the War of the Pacific discredited civilian politicians even further and led to a period of military rule in the 1880s.

### Early 20th century

Even though the voting system was changed in 1898, this did little to change the dominance of the elite. Voting was not secret so landowners herded their workers to the polls and watched to make sure they voted correctly. Yet voters were also lured by promises as well as threats. One of the more unusual presidents was Guillermo Billinghurst (1912-1914) who campaigned on the promise of a larger loaf of bread for five cents, thus gaining the nickname of 'Big Bread Billinghurst'. As president he proposed a publicly funded housing programme, supported the introduction of an eight hour working day and was eventually overthrown by the military who, along with the elite, were alarmed at his growing popularity among the urban population.

**The 1920s** This decade was dominated by Augusto Leguía. After winning the 1919 elections Leguía claimed that Congress was plotting to prevent him from becoming president and induced the military to help him close Congress. Backed by the armed forces,

Leguía introduced a new constitution which gave him greater powers and enabled him to be re-elected in 1924 and 1929. Claiming his goal was to prevent the rise of communism, he proposed to build a partnership between business and labour. A large programme of public works, particularly involving building roads, bridges and railways, was begun, the work being carried out by poor rural men who were forced into unpaid building work. The Leguía regime dealt harshly with critics: opposition newspapers were closed and opposition leaders arrested and deported. His overthrow in 1930 ended what Peruvians call the *Oncenio* or 11-year period.

The 1920s also saw the emergence of a political thinker who would have great influence in the future, not only in Peru but elsewhere in Latin America. José Carlos Mariátegui, a socialist writer and journalist, argued that the solution to Peru's problems lay in the reintegration of the indigenous people through land reform and the breaking up of the great landed estates.

**The formation of APRA** Another influential thinker of this period was Víctor Raúl Haya de la Torre, a student exiled by Leguía in 1924. He returned after the latter's fall to create the Alianza Popular Revolucionaria Americana (APRA), a political party which called for state control of the economy, nationalization of key industries and protection of the middle classes, which, Haya de la Torre argued, were threatened by foreign economic interests.

In 1932 APRA seized control of Trujillo; when the army arrived to deal with the rising, the rebels murdered about 50 hostages, including 10 army officers. In reprisal the army murdered about 1000 local residents suspected of sympathizing with APRA. APRA eventually became the largest and easily the best-organized political party in Peru, but the distrust of the military and the upper class for Haya de la Torre ensured that he never became president.

A turning point in Peruvian history occurred in 1948 with the seizure of power by General Manuel Odría, backed by the coastal elite. Odría outlawed APRA and went on to win the 1950 election in which he was the only candidate. He pursued policies of encouraging export earnings and also tried to build up working class support by public works projects in Lima. Faced with a decline in export earnings and the fall in world market prices after 1953, plus increasing unemployment, Odría was forced to stand down in 1956.

In 1962 Haya de la Torre was at last permitted to run for the presidency. But although he won the largest percentage of votes he was prevented from taking office by the armed forces who seized power and organized fresh elections for 1963. In these the military obtained the desired result: Haya de la Torre came second to Fernando Belaúnde Terry. Belaúnde attempted to introduce reforms, particularly in the landholding structure of the sierra; when these reforms were weakened by landowner opposition in Congress, peasant groups began invading landholdings in protest.

At the same time, under the influence of the Cuban revolution, terrorist groups began operating in the sierra. Military action to deal with this led to the deaths of an estimated 8000 people. Meanwhile Belaúnde's attempts to solve a long-running dispute with the International Petroleum Company (a subsidiary of Standard Oil) resulted in him being attacked for selling out to the unpopular oil company and contributed to the armed forces' decision to seize power in 1968.

## The 1968 coup

This was a major landmark in Peruvian history. Led by General Juan Velasco Alvarado, the Junta had no intention of handing power back to the civilians. A manifesto issued on the day of the coup attacked the 'unjust social and economic order' and argued for its replacement by a new economic system 'neither capitalist nor communist'. Partly as a result of their experiences in dealing with the insurgency, the coup leaders concluded that agrarian reform was a priority.

Wide-ranging land reform was launched in 1969, during which large estates were taken over and reorganized into cooperatives. By the mid-1970s, 75% of productive land was under cooperative management. The government also tried to improve the lives of shanty-town dwellers around Lima, as well as attempting to increase the influence of workers in industrial companies. At the same time efforts were made to reduce the influence of foreign companies. Soon after the coup, IPC was nationalized, to be followed by other transnationals including ITT, Chase Manhattan Bank and the two mining giants Cerro de Pasco and Marcona Mining. After a dispute with the US government, compensation was agreed.

Understandably, opposition to the Velasco government came from the business and landholding elite. The government's crack-down on expressions of dissent, the seizure of newspapers and taking over of TV and radio stations all offended sections of the urban middle class. Trade unions and peasant movements found that, although they agreed with many of the regime's policies, it refused to listen and expected their passive and unqualified support. As world sugar and copper prices dropped, inflation rose and strikes increased. Velasco's problems were further increased by opposition within the armed forces and by his own ill-health. In August 1975 he was replaced by General Francisco Morales Bermúdez, a more conservative officer, who dismantled some of Velasco's policies and led the way to a restoration of civilian rule. Velasco Alvarado's land reforms marked a watershed in 20th-century Peruvian history, and he remains a hero to many *campesinos*.

Belaúnde returned to power in 1980 by winning the first elections after military rule. His government was badly affected by the 1982 debt crisis and the 1981-1983 world recession, and inflation reached over 100% a year in 1983-1984. His term was also marked by the growth of the Maoist movement **Sendero Luminoso** (Shining Path) and the smaller, Marxist **Movimiento Revolucionario Túpac Amaru** (MRTA).

Initially conceived in the University of Ayacucho, Shining Path gained most support for its goal of overthrowing the whole system of Lima-based government from indigenous highlanders and migrants to urban shanty towns. The activities of Sendero Luminoso and the MRTA were effectively curtailed after the arrest of both their leaders in 1992: Víctor Polay of MRTA and Abimael Guzmán of Sendero Luminoso. Although Sendero did not capitulate, many of its members in 1994-1995 took advantage of the Law of Repentance, which guaranteed lighter sentences in return for surrender, and freedom in exchange for valuable information. Meanwhile, MRTA was thought to have ceased operations.

In 1985 APRA, in opposition for over 50 years, finally came to power. With Haya de la Torre dead, the APRA candidate Alan García Pérez won the elections and was allowed to take office by the armed forces. García attempted to implement an ambitious economic programme intended to solve many of Peru's deep-seated economic and social problems. He cut taxes, reduced interest rates, froze prices and devalued the currency. However, the economic boom that this produced in 1986-1987 stored up problems as increased incomes were spent on imports. Moreover, the government's refusal to pay more than 10% of its foreign debt meant that it was unable to borrow. In 1988 inflation hit 3000% and unemployment soared. By the time his term of office ended in 1990 Peru was bankrupt and García and APRA were discredited.

# Modern Peru

## The Fujimori years

In presidential elections held over two rounds in 1990, **Alberto Fujimori** defeated the novelist **Mario Vargas Llosa** (see box, page 468). Fujimori, the son of Japanese immigrants and former dean of an agricultural college without an established political network behind him, failed to win a majority in either the senate or the lower house. Lack of congressional support was one of the reasons behind his dissolution of congress and the suspension of the constitution in 1992.

A new constitution was drawn up in 1993. Among its articles were the establishment of a single-chamber congress, the designation of Peru as a market economy and the favouring of foreign investment. Fujimori stood for re-election in 1995 and won by a resounding margin, about 65% of the votes cast. But the government's success in most economic areas did not appear to accelerate the distribution of funds for social projects. Rising unemployment and the austerity imposed by economic policy continued to cause hardship for many, despite the government's stated aim of alleviating poverty.

Dramatic events in 1996 thrust several of these issues into sharper focus: 14 Túpac Amaru terrorists infiltrated a reception at the Japanese Embassy in Lima, taking 490 hostages. Most were eventually released and negotiations pursued during a stalemate that lasted six months. The president took sole responsibility for the successful, but risky assault that freed all the hostages (one died of heart failure) and killed all the terrorists. By not yielding to Túpac Amaru, Fujimori regained much popularity.

But this masked the fact that no steps had been taken to ease social problems. It also deflected attention from Fujimori's plans to stand for a third term. Local and international observers voiced concern over his increasingly autocratic tendencies and state domination of the media. The opposition candidate boycotted the election and Fujimori won unopposed, but with scant approval.

The next bombshell was the airing of a secretly shot video showing Fujimori's close aide and head of the National Intelligence Service, Vladimiro Montesinos, handing US$15,000 to a congressman to persuade him to switch allegiances to Fujimori's coalition. Although Montesinos initially evaded capture, investigators began to uncover the extent of his empire, which held hundreds of senior figures in its web. His activities encompassed extortion, money-laundering, bribery, intimidation, alleged arms and drugs dealing and possible links with the CIA and death squads. Swiss bank accounts in his name were found to contain about US$70 million. In early 2001 he was captured in Venezuela and returned to Peru where he was tried on, and convicted of, a multitude of charges.

Fujimori fled to Japan from where, on 20 November 2000, he sent Congress an email announcing his resignation. An interim president, **Valentín Paniagua**, was sworn in, and the government set about uncovering the depth of corruption associated with Montesinos and Fujimori. In 2004, prosecutors sought to charge exiled Fujimori with authorizing death squads at Barrios Altos (1991) and La Cantuta (1992) in which 25 people

## BACKGROUND

### The high price of minerals

Since 2006 Peru has enjoyed unaccustomed social and political tranquility, due in large measure to an impressive economic boom. Various sectors of the Peruvian economy are thriving, among them tourism, but the current blush of prosperity is largely due to the high world price of minerals which has encouraged widespread exploitation of the country's extensive ore deposits.

Peru's rapidly growing economy has drawn much praise from the international economic community and allowed successive governments to increase funding for social programmes. But are these fat years really the best of times? The view from the ground, voiced by intellectuals, villagers and parish priests, among others, is "maybe not". Alongside the environmental upheaval caused by some of the world's largest open-pit mines, the social consequences of all the mining revenue have been less than positive.

Communities near the mines receive a *canon minero*, their own direct share of mining royalties, and the influx of this easy money has fostered unprecedented corruption in local governments. Cronies of those in office are appointed to sinecures and many people have abandoned their traditional activities, such as agriculture, to take on do-nothing municipal positions.

The seemingly endless flow of funds is squandered on showy but senseless projects, such as an oversize sports stadium for a tiny village, while more basic needs like sanitation are ignored. At the national level, one sees a great burst of vacuous consumer spending without any indication that the mining revenues are being re-invested in sustainable development.

Can you guess what will happen after the boom goes bust?

died. This followed the Truth and Reconciliation Committee's report (2003) into the civil war of the 1980s and 1990s, which stated that over 69,000 Peruvians had been killed and multiple atrocities had been committed by insurgent groups and government forces alike.

With attempts to extradite Fujimori from Japan coming to nothing, prosecution could not proceed. Meanwhile Fujimori declared that he would be exonerated and stand again for the presidency in 2006. To this end he flew to Chile in November 2005 with a view to entering Peru, but the Chilean authorities jailed him for seven months and then held him on parole until an extradition request was finally approved in 2007. In December of that year the first of several trials began, Fujimori being charged with, but strenuously denying, the Barrios Altos and La Cantuta murders, kidnapping and corruption. He was found guilty of human rights abuses in 2009 and sentenced to 25 years in prison. Further convictons followed, but, despite his controversial time in power, advancing age and ill health, he still retains some popularity and was eventually pardoned and freed in 2017. His daughter, Keiko, has become a major political player and ran a close second in 2011 and 2016 presidential elections (see below).

## From Fujimori to Vizcarra

In the 2001 presidential elections, **Alejandro Toledo**, a former World Bank official of humble origins defeated ex-president Alan García. He pledged to heal the wounds that

## Constitution and government

Peru has a single chamber 120-seat congress. Men and women over 18 are eligible to vote, and registration and voting is compulsory until the age of 70. Those who do not vote are fined. The president, to whom is entrusted the executive power, is elected for five years. Since the Regionalization Law of 2002, Peru's territory has been divided into 26 units: 25 *regiones*, formerly called *departamentos* (a term that remains in common use) plus the Province of Lima. The regiones are subdivided into *provincias*, which are in turn made up of *distritos*. There are 195 *provincias* and 1840 *distritos* in Peru.

had opened in Peru during Fujimori's tenure, but his presidency was marked by slow progress on both the political and economic fronts. Nor could Toledo escape charges of corruption; accusations that he and his sister orchestrated voter fraud were upheld by a congressional commission. He completed his term of office but has been answering to additional corruption charges ever since, and subsequently left Peru to avoid detention.

The 2006 elections were again contested by Alan García and **Ollanta Humala**, a former military officer and unsuccessful coup leader who claimed support from Venezuela's Hugo Chávez and Evo Morales of Bolivia. García won in the second round, in part because many were suspicious of the 'Chávez factor' and the latter's interference in Peruvian affairs. Many were equally suspicious of García's ability to overcome his past record as president, but it turned out that the former populist had changed his stripes. In 2006 he signed a free trade agreement with the USA, which came into effect in 2009. The Peruvian economy showed exceptionally strong growth throughout most of his time in office, based almost exclusively on high international mineral prices, and mining interests became a dominant force in Peru. Some of the mining revenues eventually trickled down to the poorer segments of society. After completing his term of office, García, like many of his predecessors, faced investigation on corruption charges.

In 2011, Ollanta Humala again ran for the presidency, this time with a more polished image and more moderate rhetoric than in the past. He defeated Keiko Fujimori in the second round with 51.5% of the vote. Humala had obtained the support of intellectuals and urban middle-class Peruvians, in addition to his traditional power base among poorer rural dwellers. Once in office, he quickly disappointed his former supporters with policies catering precisely to the international corporate interests (especially in the mining sector) whose influence he had previously decried. But with the economy still booming and his strengthening of various social programmes, he did not face much effective opposition.

Having completed a lacklustre term of office, Humala and his wife, Nadine Heredia, were arrested in 2017 on corruption charges, the third recent ex-president of Peru to face prosecution.

Presidential elections in 2016 brought **Pedro Pablo Kuczynski** (better known as 'PPK'), an economist with a corporate and political career dating back to the 1960s, to office following an extremely narrow (50.1%) victory over Keiko Fujimori. At age 77, he became the oldest president of Peru but his time in office was short-lived and unimpressive. Having pardoned ex-president Fujimori at the end of 2017, he resigned in March 2018 to avoid impeachment over a vote-buying scandal in Congress. He was succeeded by vice president **Martín Vizcarra**, former governor of the department of Moquegua, who is scheduled to hold office until the next presidential elections in 2021.

# People

Peruvian society today is a melting pot of Native Andeans, Afro-Peruvians, Spanish, immigrant Chinese, Japanese, Italians, Germans and, to a lesser extent, indigenous Amazon tribes. The total population was estimated to be 31.2 million in 2015 (INEI projected data), with an annual average growth rate of 1.6%. The urban population represents 73% of the total.

## Criollos and mestizos

The first immigrants were the Spaniards who followed Pizarro's expeditionary force. Their effect, demographically, politically and culturally, has been enormous. They intermarried with the indigenous population and the children of mixed parentage were called *mestizos*. The Peruvian-born children of Spanish parents were known as *criollos*, though this word is now used to describe people who live on the coast, regardless of their ancestry, and coastal culture in general.

## Afro-Peruvians

Peru's black community is based on the coast, mainly in Chincha, south of Lima, and also in some working-class districts of the capital. Their forefathers were originally imported into Peru in the 16th century as slaves to work on the sugar and cotton plantations on the coast. The black community represents between 2-5% of the total population. See also page 456.

## Asian immigrants

There are two main Asian communities in Peru, the Japanese and Chinese. Large numbers of poor Chinese labourers were brought to Peru in the mid-19th century to work in virtual slavery on the guano reserves on the Pacific coast and to build the railroads in the central Andes. The culinary influence of the Chinese can be seen in the many *chifas* found throughout the country.

The Japanese community, now numbering some 100,000, established itself in the first half of the 20th century. The normally reclusive community gained prominence when Alberto Fujimori, one of its members, became the first president of Japanese descent outside Japan anywhere in the world. During Fujimori's presidency, many other Japanese Peruvians took prominent positions in business, central and local government. The nickname 'chino' is applied to anyone of Oriental origin.

## Europeans

Like most of Latin America, Peru received many emigrés from Europe seeking land and opportunities in the late 19th century. The country's wealth and political power remains concentrated in the hands of this small and exclusive class of whites, which also consists of the descendants of the first Spanish families. There still exists a deep divide between people of indigenous and European descent and the old colonial snobbery persists.

## Peru's indigenous people

Peru has a substantial indigenous population, only smaller as a percentage of the total than Bolivia and Guatemala of the Latin American republics. From 1980 to 2000, highland communities bore the brunt of the conflict between Sendero Luminoso and the security forces, which caused tens-of-thousands of deaths and mass migration from

# BACKGROUND
## The Afro-Peruvian experience since 1532

The first person of African descent to arrive in the Americas came in 1492 with Christopher Columbus. He was a mulatto from Spain and a free man. During the next three centuries an estimated 15 million Africans arrived in the Americas as slaves. Francisco Pizarro brought the first black slaves to Peru. They were present at the capture of Atahualpa in Cajamarca in 1532 and saved the Spanish during Manco Inca's siege of Cuzco in 1536, when they put out the fire engulfing the great hall of Sunturwasi, where the conquistadors had taken refuge.

When Hernando de Soto returned to Spain in 1534 bearing Atahualpa's gold and silver ransom, he asked the crown for permission to take 100 slaves back to Peru. By 1550, their number had risen to 3000 – half of whom lived in Lima – and by 1640 to 30,000. In total, between 1532 and 1816, an estimated 100,000 African slaves were transported to Peru.

They were sent to replace an indigenous labour force ravaged by the destruction of its sociopolitical infrastructure and by European diseases. Some worked in the cities as servants, artisans or porters, others in the mines of Huancavelica or Potosí and the majority toiled on the coast in sugar cane plantations, cotton fields and vineyards.

Indigenous and African workers transformed Peru into the richest of all the Spanish colonies in the 16th and 17th centuries. Many fortunes, including that amassed by the Jesuits, were made using slave labour. The ownership of black slaves was a status symbol and even some Afro-Peruvians who had achieved their own freedom subsequently acquired slaves.

The location of Afro-Peruvian communities today reflects the colonial distribution of black labour. They are concentrated in the coastal areas once dominated by the great haciendas: Chincha, Cañete and Ica; the northern departments of Lambayeque and Piura, and the cities, especially Lima. Here, the vibrant culture created by slaves from diverse African heritages lives on in local art, music, dance, religion, food and folklore.

The wars of independence spread the libertarian ideal of emancipation. Promised their freedom, hundreds of Afro-Peruvians joined the republican armies, only to find their situation little changed in 1821 under the fledgling government. In 1854, Generals Ramón Castilla and José Rufino Echenique engaged in civil war and were in need of troops. To attract black recruits Echenique offered freedom to those who would join him and, in reply, Castilla announced the abolition of slavery, paying off landowners with awards raised from guano exports.

The 25,000 black slaves freed in 1854 were received by society with contempt and remained oppressed by labour laws. Racism continues to live on today. Colour is still identified with inferiority in everyday attitudes and in the poverty and marginalization of black communities and their lack of representation in government. Over 150 years after abolition, those who shared the hardships of the conquistadors have still not shared in either their glory or their wealth.

the countryside to provincial cities or to Lima. Many indigenous groups are also under threat from colonization, development and mining. Long after the end of Spanish rule, discrimination is still a fact of life for many native Peruvians.

## Quechua
Although predominantly an agricultural society, growing potatoes and corn as their basic diet, they are no longer outside the money economy. Today, there remain two enduring legacies of Inca rule; their magnificent architecture and their language, Quechua, which, although predating the Incas themselves, has become synonymous with the descendants of their subjects. Quechua is one of the key channels of continuity with the captivating pre-European past and indigenous identity of the Andes. Sadly, that continuity still takes the form of a distinctly underprivileged status in relation to the dominant Spanish and it is only the remoteness of many Quechua speakers which has preserved the language in rural areas. This isolation has also helped preserve many of their ancient traditions and beliefs. Most Quechua speakers today are bilingual but Quechua is still losing ground to Spanish. It remains primarily a spoken, in-group language, strongly bound up with the distinct indigenous identity, but unlike the Aymara (see below), the seven million or so Quechua-speakers have generally been much less successful in asserting themselves. There is no real sense of unity between the disparate groups of speakers scattered through Ecuador, Peru and Bolivia. Some recent developments in these three countries have at last been more positive. The language is now increasingly written and is being fitfully introduced in primary education, though the impact of Spanish, and polemics about standardization, continue to have a very disruptive effect. At least some Quechua-speaking communities, in Peru and elsewhere, are gradually recovering a long-deserved semblance of pride in their native tongue and culture.

## Aymara
Prior to Inca rule Tiahuanaco on Lake Titicaca was a highly organized centre for one the greatest cultures South America has ever witnessed: the Aymara people. Today, the shores of this lake and the plains that surround it remain the homeland of the Aymara. The majority live in Bolivia, the rest are scattered on the southwestern side of Peru and northern Chile. The climate is so harsh on the *altiplano* that, though they are extremely hard working, their lives are very poor. They speak their own unwritten language, Aymara. More so than the scattered group of different peoples that speak Quechua, the Altiplano Aymara people form a compact group with a clear sense of their own distinct identity and in many respects have been able to preserve more of their indigenous traditions and belief system.

## Amazonian peoples
Before the arrival of the Europeans, an estimated six million people inhabited the Amazon Basin, comprising more than 2000 tribes or ethnic-linguistic groups who managed to adapt to their surroundings through the domestication of a great variety of animals and plants, and to benefit from the numerous nutritional, curative, narcotic and hallucinogenic properties of thousands of wild plants.

It's not easy to determine the precise origin of these aboriginal people. What is known, however, is that since the beginning of colonial times this population slowly but constantly decreased, mainly because of the effect of western diseases such as influenza and measles. This demographic decline reached dramatic levels during the rubber boom of the late 19th and early 20th centuries, due to forced labour and slavery.

Today, in the Amazon Basin, the indigenous population is calculated at approximately two million inhabitants making up 400 ethnic groups, of which approximately 200,000-250,000 live in the Peruvian jungle. Within the basin it is possible to distinguish at least three large conglomerates of aboriginal societies: the inhabitants of the *várzea*, or seasonally flooded lands alongside the large rivers (such as the Omagua, Cocama and Shipibo people); the people in the interfluvial zones or firm lands (such as the Amahuaca, Cashibo and Yaminahua) and those living in the Andean foothills (such as the Amuesha, Asháninka and Machiguenga).

Indigenous Amazonians began to be decimated in the 16th century, and so were the first endangered species of the jungle. These communities still face threats to their traditional lifestyles, notably from timber companies, gold miners and multinational oil and gas companies. There appears to be little effective control of deforestation and the intrusion of colonists who have taken over native lands to establish small farms. And though oil companies have reached compensation agreements with local communities, previous oil exploration has contaminated many jungle rivers, as well as exposing inhabitants to risk from diseases against which they have no immunity.

# Culture

## Religion

Inca spirituality was displaced by Roman Catholicism from the 16th century onwards, the conversion of the inhabitants of the 'New World' to Christianity being one of the stated aims of the Spanish conquistadors. Today, statistics vary between 81% and 89% of the population declaring itself Catholic.

One of the first exponents of Liberation Theology, under which the Conference of Latin American Bishops in 1968 committed themselves to the 'option for the poor', was Gustavo Gutiérrez, from Huánuco. This doctrine caused much consternation to orthodox Catholics, particularly those members of the Latin American church who had traditionally aligned themselves with the oligarchy. Gutiérrez, however, traced the church's duty to the voiceless and the marginalized back to Fray Bartolomé de las Casas.

The Catholic Church faced a further challenge to its authority when President Fujimori won the battle over family planning and the need to slow down the rate of population growth. Its greatest threat, however, comes from the proliferation of evangelical Protestant groups throughout the country. Some 6% of the population now declare themselves Protestant and one million or more people belong to some 27 different non-Catholic denominations.

Although the vast majority of the population ostensibly belongs to the Roman Catholic religion, in reality religious life for many Peruvians is a mix of Catholic beliefs imported from Europe and indigenous traditions based on animism, the worship of deities from the natural world such as mountains, animals and plants.

## Arts and crafts

Peru has a rich variety of handicrafts. Its geographic division into four distinct regions – coast, mountains, valleys and Amazon Basin – coupled with cultural differences, has resulted in numerous variations in technique and design. Each province, even each community, has developed its own style of weaving or carving.

The Incas inherited 3000 years of skills and traditions: gold, metal and precious stonework from the Chimú; feather textiles from the Nazca; and the elaborate textiles of the Paracas. All of these played important roles in political, social and religious ceremonies. Though much of this artistic heritage was destroyed by the Spanish conquest, the traditions adapted and evolved in numerous ways, absorbing new methods, concepts and materials from Europe while maintaining ancient techniques and symbols.

### Textiles and costumes

Woven cloth was the most highly prized possession and sought after trading commodity in the Andes in pre-Columbian times. It is, therefore, not surprising that ancient weaving traditions have survived. In the ninth century BC camelid fibre was introduced into weaving on the south coast. This allowed the development of the textiles of the Paracas culture that consist of intricate patterns of animalistic, supernatural and human forms embroidered onto dark backgrounds. The culture of the Chancay valleys cultivated cotton for white and beige dyed patterned cloth in preference to the camelid fibres used by the

Paracas and Nazca cultures. The Incas inherited this rich weaving tradition. They forced the Aymaras to work in *mit'as* or textile workshops. The ruins of some enormous *mit'as* can be seen at the temple of Raqchi, south of Cuzco (see page 319). Inca textiles are of high quality and very different from coastal textiles, being warp-faced, closely woven and without embroidery. The largest quantities of the finest textiles were made specifically to be burned as ritual offerings – a tradition which still survives. The Spanish, too, exploited this wealth and skill by using the mitas and exporting the cloth to Europe.

**Prior to Inca rule** Aymara men wore a tunic (*llahua*) and a mantle (*llacata*) and carried a bag for coca leaves (*huallquepo*). The women wore a wrapped dress (*urku*) and mantle (*iscayo*) and a belt (*huaka*); their coca bag was called an *istalla*. The *urku* was fastened at shoulder level with a pair of metal *tupu*, the traditional Andean dress-pins. Inca men had tunics (*unkus*) and a bag for coca leaves called a *ch'uspa*. The women wore a blouse (*huguna*), skirts (*aksu*) and belts (*chumpis*), and carried foodstuffs in large, rectangular cloths called *llicllas*, which were fastened at the chest with a single pin or a smaller clasp called a *ttipqui*. Women of the Sacred Valley now wear a layered, gathered skirt called a *pollera* and a *montera*, a large, round, red Spanish type of hat. Textiles continue to play an important part in society. They are still used specifically for ritual ceremonies and some even held to possess magical powers. One of the most enduring of these traditions is found among the Aymara people of Taquile island on Lake Titicaca.

## Textile materials and techniques

The Andean people used mainly alpaca or llama wool. The former can be spun into fine, shining yarn when woven and has a lustre similar to that of silk, though sheep's wool came to be widely used following the Spanish conquest. A commonly used technique is the drop spindle. A stick is weighted with a wooden wheel and the raw material is fed through one hand. A sudden twist and drop in the spindle spins the yarn. This very sensitive art can be seen practised by women while herding animals in the fields.

Spinning wheels were introduced by Europeans and are now prevalent owing to increased demand. In Ayacucho and San Pedro de Cajas, centres of the cottage textile industry, the wheel is the most common form of spinning. Pre-Columbian looms were often portable and those in use today are generally similar. A woman will herd her animals while making a piece of costume, perhaps on a backstrap loom, or waist loom, so-called because the weaver controls the tension on one side with her waist with the other side tied to an upright or tree. The pre-Columbian looms are usually used for personal costume while the treadle loom is used by men for more commercial pieces.

The skills of dyeing were still practised virtually unchanged even after the arrival of the Spanish. Nowadays, the word *makhnu* refers to any natural dye, but originally was the name for cochineal, an insect that lives on the leaves of the nopal cactus. These dyes were used widely by pre-Columbian weavers. Today, the biggest centre of production in South America is the valleys around Ayacucho. Vegetable dyes are also used, made from the leaves, fruit and seeds of shrubs and flowers and from lichen, tree bark and roots.

## Symbolism

Symbolism plays an important role in weaving. Traditionally every piece of textile from a particular community had identical symbols and colours that were a source of identity as well as carrying specific symbols and telling a story. One example is on the island of Taquile where the Inti (sun) and Chaska (Venus) symbols are employed as well as motifs such as fish and birds, unique to the island.

Animal figures dominated the motifs of the Chavín culture and were commonly used in Paracas textiles. Specimens of cotton and wool embroidery found in Paracas graves often show a puma as a central motif. Today, this and other pre-Columbian motifs are found on many rugs and wall-hangings from the Ayacucho region. Other symbols include Spanish figures such as horses and scenes depicting the execution of Túpac Amaru.

## Pottery

The most spectacular archaeological finds in South America have been made in Peru. The Nazca culture (100 BC-AD 900) excelled in polychrome painting of vessels with motifs of supernatural beings, often with strong feline characteristics, as well as birds, fish and animals. Many of the Nazca ceramic motifs are similar to those found in Paracas textiles.

Moche or Mochica vessels combined modelling and painting to depict details of Moche daily life. Human forms are modelled on stirrup spout vessels with such precision that they suggest personal portraits. The Moche also excelled in intricate linear painting often using brown on a cream base.

Inca ceramic decoration consists mainly of small-scale geometric and usually symmetrical designs. One distinctive form of vessel that continues to be made and used is the arybola. This pot is designed to carry liquid, especially *chicha*, and is secured with a rope on the bearer's back. It is believed that arybolas were used mainly by the governing Inca elite and became important status symbols. Today, Inca style is very popular in Cuzco and Pisac.

With the Spanish invasion many indigenous communities lost their artistic traditions, others remained relatively untouched, while others still combined Hispanic and indigenous traditions and techniques. The Spanish brought three innovations: the potter's wheel, which gave greater speed and uniformity; knowledge of the enclosed kiln; and the technique of lead glazes. The enclosed kiln made temperature regulation easier and allowed higher temperatures to be maintained, producing stronger pieces. Today, many communities continue to apply pre-Hispanic techniques, while others use more modern processes.

## Jewellery and metalwork

Some of the earliest goldwork originates from the Chavín culture – eg the Tumi knife found in Lambayeque. These first appeared in the Moche culture, when they were associated with human sacrifice. Five centuries later, the Incas used Tumis for surgical operations such as trepanning skulls. Today, they are a common motif.

The Incas associated gold with the Sun. However, very few examples remain as the Spanish melted down their amassed gold and silver objects. They then went on to send millions of indigenous people to their deaths in gold and silver mines.

During the colonial period gold and silver pieces were made to decorate the altars of churches and houses of the elite. Metalworkers came from Spain and Italy to develop the industry. The Spanish preferred silver and strongly influenced the evolution of silverwork during the colonial period. A style known as Andean baroque developed around Cuzco embracing both indigenous and European elements. Silver bowls in this style – *cochas* – are still used in Andean ceremonies.

**False filigree** This was practised by some pre-Hispanic cultures. The effect of filigree was obtained with the use of droplets or beads of gold. True filigree work developed in the colonial period. Today, there are a number of centres. Originally popular in Ayacucho, the tradition continues in the small community of San Jerónimo de Tunan, near Huancayo.

Here, silversmiths produce intricate filigree earrings, spoons and jewellery boxes. Catacaos near Piura also has a long tradition of filigree work in silver and gold.

**Seeds, flowers and feathers** These continue to be used as jewellery by many Amazonian peoples. Pre-Hispanic cultures also favoured particular natural materials; eg the sea shell spondylus was highly revered by the Chavín and Moche. It was found only along part of the Ecuadorean coast and must have been acquired through trade. The western fashion for natural or ethnic jewellery has encouraged production, using brightly coloured feathers, fish bones, seeds or animal teeth.

## Woodcarving

Wood is one of the most commonly used materials. Carved ceremonial objects include drums, carved sticks with healing properties, masks and the Incas' *keros* – wooden vessels for drinking *chicha*. Keros come in all shapes and sizes and were traditionally decorated with scenes of war, local dances, or harvesting coca leaves. The Chancay, who lived along the coast between 100 BC and AD 1200, used *keros* carved with sea birds and fish. Today, they are used in some Andean ceremonies, especially during Fiesta de la Cruz, the Andean May festival.

Glass mirrors were introduced by the Spanish, although the Chimú and Lambayeque cultures used obsidian and silver plates, and Inca *chasquis* (messengers) used reflective stones to communicate between hilltop forts. Transporting mirrors was costly so they were produced in Lima and Quito. Cuzco and Cajamarca then became centres of production. In Cuzco the frames were carved, covered in gold leaf and decorated with tiny pieces of cut mirror. Cajamarca artisans, meanwhile, incorporated painted glass into the frames.

## Gourd-carving

Gourd-carving, or *mate burilado*, as it is known, is one of Peru's most popular and traditional handicrafts. It is thought even to predate pottery – engraved gourds found on the coast have been dated to some 4500 years ago. During the Inca empire gourd-carving became a valued art form and workshops were set up and supported by the state. Gourds were used in rituals and ceremonies and to make poporos – containers for the lime used while chewing coca leaves. Today, gourd-carving is centred around the small communities of Cochas Grande and Chico, near Huancayo.

The information on arts and crafts in this guidebook has been adapted from *Arts and Crafts of South America*, by Lucy Davies and Mo Fini, published by Tumi, 1994. **Tumi** ⓘ *Unit 2, Ashmead Business Centre, Ashmead Road, Keynsham, Bristol BS31 1SX, T0117-986 9216*, the Latin American Craft Centre, specializes in Andean and Mexican products and produces cultural and educational videos for schools. **Tumi Music** ⓘ *www.tumi.com*, specializes in different rhythms of Latin America.

## Music and dance

The music of Peru can be described as the very heartbeat of the country. Peruvians see music as something in which to participate, and not as a spectacle. Just about everyone, it seems, can play a musical instrument or sing. Just as music is the heartbeat of the country, so dance conveys the rich and ancient heritage that typifies much of the national spirit. Peruvians are tireless dancers and dancing is the most popular form of entertainment. Unsuspecting travellers should note that once they make that first wavering step there will be no respite until they collapse from exhaustion.

Each region has its own distinctive music and dance that reflects its particular lifestyle, its mood and its physical surroundings. The music of the sierra, for example, is played in a minor key and tends to be sad and mournful, while the music of the lowlands is more up-tempo and generally happier. Peruvian music divides at a very basic level into that of the highlands (Andina) and that of the coast (Criolla). For a celebration of many Peruvian dance styles, see the film *Soy Andina* and its accompanying website www.soyandina.com. Made by Mitch Teplitsky in 2007 it documents two women, both living in the USA, rediscovering their roots in Peru through its music and traditions.

## Highlands

When people talk of Peruvian music they are almost certainly referring to the music of the Quechua- and Aymara-speaking people of the highlands that provides the most distinctive Peruvian sound. The highlands themselves can be very roughly subdivided into some half dozen major musical regions, of which perhaps the most characteristic are Ancash and the north, the Mantaro Valley, Cuzco, Puno and the Altiplano, Ayacucho and Parinacochas.

**Musical instruments** Before the arrival of the Spanish in Latin America, the only instruments were wind and percussion. Although it is a popular misconception that Andean music is based on the panpipes, guitar and charango, anyone who travels through the Andes will realize that these instruments only represent a small aspect of Andean music. The highland instrumentation varies from region to region, although the harp and violin are ubiquitous. In the Mantaro area the harp is backed by brass and wind instruments, notably the clarinet. In Cuzco it is the charango and quena and on the *altiplano* the sicu panpipes.

The *quena* is a flute, usually made of reed, characterized by not having a mouthpiece to blow through. As with all Andean instruments, there is a family of quenas varying in length from around 15-50 cm. The sicu is the Aymara name for the *zampoña*, or panpipes. It is the most important pre-Hispanic Andean instrument, formed by several reed tubes of different sizes held together by knotted string. Virtually the only instrument of European origin is the Charango. When stringed instruments were first introduced by the Spanish, the indigenous people liked them but wanted something that was their own and so the charango was born. Originally, they were made of clay, condor skeletons and armadillo or tortoise shells.

**Highland dances** The highlands are immensely rich in terms of music and dance, with over 200 dances recorded. Every village has its fiestas and every fiesta has its communal and religious dances.

*Comparsas* or *cuadrillas* are organized groups of dancers who perform for spectators dances following a set pattern of movements to a particular musical accompaniment, wearing a specific costume. They have a long tradition, having mostly originated from certain contexts and circumstances and some of them still parody the ex-Spanish colonial masters.

One of the most notable is the comical Auqui Auqui (*auqui* is Aymara for old man). The dance satirizes the solemnity and pomposity of Spanish gentlemen from the colonial period. Because of their dignified dress and manners they could appear old, and a humped back is added to the dancers to emphasize age. These little old men have long pointed noses, flowing beards and carry crooked walking sticks. They dance stooped, regularly pausing to complain and rub aching backs, at times even stumbling and falling. Another dance parody is the Contradanza, performed in the highlands of La Libertad.

Many dances for couples and/or groups are danced spontaneously at fiestas throughout Peru. These include indigenous dances which have originated in a specific region and ballroom dances that reflect the Spanish influence. One of the most popular of the indigenous dances is the **Huayno**, which originated on the *altiplano* but is now danced throughout the country. It involves numerous couples, who whirl around or advance down the street arm-in-arm, in a Pandilla. During fiestas, and especially after a few drinks, this can develop into a kind of uncontrolled frenzy.

Two of the most spectacular dances to be seen are the **Baile de las Tijeras** (scissor dance) from the Ayacucho/Huancavelica area, for men only, and the pounding, stamping **Huaylas** for both sexes. Huaylas competitions are held annually in Lima and should not be missed. Also very popular among indigenous and/or mestizo people are the Marinera, Carnaval, Pasacalle, Chuscada (from Ancash), Huaylas, Santiago and Chonguinada (all from the Mantaro) and Huayllacha (from Parinacochas).

**Urban and other styles** Owing to the overwhelming migration of peasants into the barrios of Lima, most types of Andean music and dance can be seen in the capital, notably on Sundays at the so-called 'Coliseos', which exist for that purpose. This flood of migration to the cities has also meant that the distinct styles of regional and ethnic groups have become blurred. One example is **Chicha music**, which comes from the *pueblos jóvenes*, and was once the favourite dance music of Peru's urban working class. Chicha is a hybrid of Huayno music and the Colombian Cumbia rhythm – a meeting of the highlands and the tropical coast.

**Tecno-cumbia** originated in the jungle region with groups such as Rossy War, from Puerto Maldonado, and Euforia, from Iquitos. It is a vibrant dance music which has gained much greater popularity across Peruvian society than *chicha* music ever managed. There are now also many exponents on the coast such as Agua Marina and Armonía 10. Many of the songs comment on political issues and Fujimori used to join Rossy War on stage. Tecno-cumbia has evolved into a more sophisticated form with wider appeal across Peruvian society. Listen to Grupo 5, from Chiclayo, for instance.

## Coast

**Música Criolla** The music from the coast, could not be more different from that of the sierra. Here the roots are Spanish and African. The immensely popular **Valsesito** is a syncopated waltz that would certainly be looked at askance in Vienna and the **Polca** has also undergone an attractive sea change. Reigning over all is the **Marinera**, Peru's national dance, a splendidly rhythmic and graceful courting encounter and a close cousin of Chile's and Bolivia's Cueca and the Argentine Zamba, all of them descended from the Zamacueca. The Marinera has its 'Limeña' and 'Norteña' versions and a more syncopated relative, the Tondero, found in the northern coastal regions, is said to have been influenced by slaves brought from Madagascar. All these dances are accompanied by guitars and frequently the cajón, a resonant wooden box on which the player sits, pounding it with his hands. Some of the great names of 'Música Criolla' are the singer/composers Chabuca Granda and Alicia Maguiña, the female singer Jesús Vásquez and the groups Los Morochucos and Hermanos Zañartu.

**Afro-Peruvian** Also on the coast is the music of the small but influential black community, the 'Música Negroide' or 'Afro-Peruano', which had virtually died out when it was resuscitated in the 1950s, but has since gone from strength to strength, thanks to Nicomedes and Victoria Santa Cruz who have been largely responsible for popularizing this black music and making it an essential ingredient in contemporary Peruvian popular music. It has all the qualities to be found in black music from the Caribbean – a powerful, charismatic beat, rhythmic and lively dancing, and strong percussion provided by the cajón and the quijada de burro, a donkey's jaw with the teeth loosened. Its greatest star is the Afro-Peruvian diva Susana Baca. Her incredible, passionate voice inspired Talking Head's David Byrne to explore this genre further and release a compilation album in 1995, thus bringing Afro-Peruvian music to the attention of the world. Other notable exponents are the excellent Perú Negro, one of the best music and dance groups in Latin America, and the singer Eva Ayllón. In the footsteps of the dynamic Gotan Project (Argentine musicians who have taken a radical approach to the interpretation of the tango), Novalima, a group of internationally based Peruvian musicians, have produced new arrangements of many classic Afro-Peruvian tracks (see www.novalima.net). Some of the classic dances in the black repertoire are the Festejo, Son del Diablo, Toro Mata, Landó and Alcatraz. In the last named one of the partners dances behind the other with a candle, trying to set light to a piece of paper tucked into the rear of the other partner's waist.

## Festivals

*Fiestas* (festivals) are a fundamental part of life for most Peruvians, taking place the length and breadth of the country and with such frequency that it would be hard to miss one, even during the briefest of stays. This is fortunate, because arriving in any town or village during these frenetic celebrations is a great Peruvian experience.

With over 3000 fiestas, there are too many to mention them all. The main national ones are described on page 18, and details of local fiestas are given under the listings for each town.

### Meaning of fiestas

It is only when they don their extravagant costumes and masks and drink, eat and dance to excess that the indigenous Peruvians show their true character. The rest of the time they hide behind a metaphorical mask of stony indifference as a form of protection against the alien reality in which they are forced to live. When they consume alcohol and coca and start dancing, the pride in their origins resurfaces. This allows them to forget the reality of poverty, unemployment and oppression and reaffirms their will to live as well as their unity with the world around them.

The object of the fiesta is a practical one, such as the success of the coming harvest or the fertility of animals. Thus the constant eating, drinking and dancing serves the purpose of giving thanks for the sun and rain that makes things grow and for the fertility of the soil and livestock, gifts from Pachamama, or Mother Earth, the most sacred of all gods. The first drop of each glass of *chicha* (maize beer) or other alcoholic drink is traditionally spilled as an offering to her.

The participants in the dances that are the central part of the fiesta are dressed in garish, outlandish costumes and elaborate masks, each one depicting a character from popular myth. Some of these originate in the colonial period, others survive from the Inca Empire or even further back. Often the costumes caricature the Spanish. In this way, the indigenous people mock those who erased their heritage.

## Quechua

The fact that the Incas had no written texts in the conventional European sense and that the Spaniards were keen to suppress their conquest's culture means that there is little evidence today of what poetry and theatre was performed in pre-conquest times. It is known that the Incas had two types of poet, the *amautas*, historians, poets and teachers who composed works that celebrated the ruling class' gods, heroes and events, and *haravecs*, who expressed popular sentiments. There is strong evidence also that drama was important in Inca society.

Written Quechua even today is far less common than works in the oral tradition. Although Spanish culture has had some influence on Quechua, the native stories, lyrics and fables retain their own identity. Not until the 19th century did Peruvian writers begin seriously to incorporate indigenous ideas into their art, but their audience was limited. Nevertheless, the influence of Quechua on Peruvian literature in Spanish continues to grow.

## Colonial period

In 16th-century Lima, headquarters of the Viceroyalty of Peru, the Spanish officials concentrated their efforts on the religious education of the new territories and literary output was limited to mainly histories and letters.

Chroniclers such as Pedro Cieza de León (*Crónica del Perú*, published from 1553) and Agustín de Zárate (*Historia del descubrimiento y conquista del Perú*, 1555) were written from the point of view that Spanish domination was right. Their most renowned successors, though, took a different stance. Inca Garcilaso de la Vega was a mestizo, whose *Comentarios reales que tratan del origen de los Incas* (1609) were at pains to justify the achievements, religion and culture of the Inca Empire. He also commented on Spanish society in the colony. A later work, *Historia General del Perú* (1617) went further in condemning Viceroy Toledo's suppression of Inca culture. Through his work, written in Spain, many aspects of Inca society, plus poems and prayers have survived.

Writing at about the same time as Inca Garcilaso was Felipe Guaman Poma de Ayala, whose *El primer nueva corónica y buen gobierno* (1613-1615) is possibly one of the most reproduced of Latin American texts (eg on T-shirts, CDs, posters and carrier bags). Guaman Poma was a minor provincial Inca chief from Ayacucho province whose writings and illustrations, addressed to King Felipe III of Spain, offer a view of a stable pre-conquest Andean society (not uniquely Inca), in contrast with the unsympathetic colonial society that usurped it.

In the years up to Independence, the growth of an intellectual elite in Lima spawned more poetry than anything else. As criollo discontent grew, satire increased both in poetry and in the sketches that accompanied dramas imported from Spain. The poet Mariano Melgar (1791-1815) wrote in a variety of styles, including the yaraví, the love-song derived from the pre-Columbian *harawi* (from *haravek*). Melgar died in an uprising against the Spanish but played an important part in the Peruvian struggle from freedom from the colonial imagination.

## After Independence

After Independence, Peruvian writers imitated Spanish *costumbrismo*, sketches of characters and lifestyles from the new Republic. The first author to transcend this fashion was Ricardo Palma (1833-1919), whose inspiration, the *tradición*, fused *costumbrismo* and

Peru's rich oral traditions. Palma's hugely popular *Tradiciones peruanas* is a collection of pieces which celebrate the people, history and customs of Peru through sayings, small incidents in mainly colonial history and gentle irony.

Much soul searching was to follow Peru's defeat in the War of the Pacific. Manuel González Prada (1844-1918), for instance, wrote essays fiercely critical of the state of the nation: *Páginas libres* (1894), *Horas de lucha* (1908). José Carlos Mariátegui, the foremost Peruvian political thinker of the early 20th century, said that González Prada represented the first lucid instant of Peruvian consciousness. He also wrote poetry, some Romantic, some, like his *Baladas peruanas*, an evocation of indigenous and colonial history, very pro-Indian, very anti-White.

## 20th-century prose

Mariátegui himself (1895-1930), after a visit to Europe, considered the question of Peruvian identity. His opinion was that it could only be seen in a global context and that the answer lay in Marxism. With this perspective he wrote about politics, economics, literature and the indigenous question (see *Siete ensayos de interpretación de la realidad peruana*, 1928).

Other writers had continued this theme. For instance Clorinda Matto de Turner (1854-1909) intended to express in *Aves sin nido* (1889) her "tender love for the indigenous people" and hoped to improve their lot. Regardless of the debate over whether the novel achieves these aims, she was the forerunner by several years of the 'indigenist' genre in Peru and the most popular of those who took up González Prada's cause.

Other prose writers continued in this vein at the beginning of the 20th century, but it was Ciro Alegría (1909-1967) who gave major, fictional impetus to the racial question. Like Mariátegui, Alegría was politically committed, but to the APRA party, rather than Marxism. Of his first three novels, *La serpiente de oro* (1935), *Los perros hambrientos* (1938) and *El mundo es ancho y ajeno* (1941), the last named is his most famous.

Contemporary with Alegría was José María Arguedas (1911-1969), whose novels, stories and politics were also deeply rooted in the ethnic question. Arguedas, though not *indígena*, had a largely Quechua upbringing and tried to reconcile this with the Hispanic world in which he worked. This inner conflict was one of the main causes of his suicide. His books include *Agua* (short stories, 1935), *Yawar fiesta* (1941), *Los ríos profundos* (1958) and *Todas las sangres* (1964). They portray different aspects of the confrontation of indigenous society with the changing outside world that impinges on it.

In the 1950s and 1960s, there was a move away from the predominantly rural and indigenist to an urban setting. At the forefront were, among others, Mario Vargas Llosa, Julio Ramón Ribeyro, Enrique Congrains Martín, Oswaldo Reynoso, Luis Loayza, Sebastián Salazar Bondy and Carlos E Zavaleta. Taking their cue from a phrase used by both poet César Mora and Salazar Bondy (in an essay of 1964), "Lima, la horrible", they explored all aspects of the city, including the influx of people from the sierra. These writers incorporated new narrative techniques in the urban novel, which presented a world where popular culture and speech were rich sources of literary material, despite the difficulty in transcribing them.

Many writers, such as Vargas Llosa (see box, page 468), broadened their horizons beyond the capital. His novels after *La ciudad y los perros* encompassed many different parts of the country. An additional factor was that several writers spent many years abroad, Vargas Llosa himself, for instance, and Ribeyro (1929-1994). The latter's short stories, though mostly set in Lima, embrace universal themes of delusion and frustration. The title story of *Los gallinazos sin pluma* (1955), a tale of squalor and greed amid the city's

## BACKGROUND
## Mario Vargas Llosa

The best known of Peru's writers, Mario Vargas Llosa was born in 1936 in Arequipa and educated in Cochabamba (Bolivia), from where his family moved to Piura. After graduating from Lima's Universidad de San Marcos, he won a scholarship to Paris in 1958 and then, from 1959 to 1974, lived first in Paris then in London in voluntary exile. He was one of the leading figures in the so-called 'Boom' in Latin American writers in the 1960s and is regarded as an author of the highest international standing. In 2010, while teaching at Princeton University in the US, he was awarded the Nobel Prize for Literature, "for his cartography of structures of power and his trenchant images of the individual's resistance, revolt and defeat". At the time, he said "This Nobel goes to Latin American literature. It is a recognition of everything that surrounds me." Much has been written about his personal life, and his political opinions have been well documented, but it is for his novels that Vargas Llosa is best known.

The first three – *La ciudad y los perros* (1963), *La casa verde* (1966) and *Conversación en la Catedral* (1969) – with their techniques of flashback, multiple narrators and different interwoven stories, are an adventure for the reader. Meanwhile, the humorous books, like *Pantaleón y las visitadoras* (1973) and *La tía Julia y el escribidor* (1977) cannot be called lightweight. *La guerra del fin del mundo* (1981) marked a change to a more direct style and an intensification of Vargas Llosa's exploration of the role of fiction as a human necessity, extending also to political ideologies. *La fiesta del chivo* (2000) is another fictionalized account of historical events, this time the assassination of President Trujillo of the Dominican Republic in 1961 and the intrigue and fear surrounding his period in office. It is a gripping story, widely regarded as one of his best. More recently he has written *Travesuras de la niña mala* (2006; The Bad Girl), which the author called his first 'love story', and *El sueño del celta* (2010; The Dream of the Celt) about the Irishman Roger Casement.

Vargas Llosa has always maintained that in Peruvian society the writer is a privileged person who should be able to mix politics and literature as a normal part of life. This drive for authenticity led to his excursion into national politics. He stood as a presidential candidate in 1990, losing to Alberto Fujimori. He has since taken Spanish citizenship (2007) and has homes in Lima, Paris, Madrid and London.

In 2014 the Casa Museo Vargas Llosa opened at his birthblace in Arequipa (see page 226). Here, in innovative holographic displays, the writer himself tells about the highlights of his life and career.

rubbish tips, has become a classic, even though it does not contain the irony, pathos and humour of many of his other stories or novels.

Other writers of this period include Manuel Scorza (1928-1983), who wrote a series of five novels under the general title of *La guerra silenciosa* (including *Redoble por Rancas*, *El jinete insomne*, *La tumba del relámpago*) which follow the tradition of the indigenist struggle, and also emphasize the need to defend indigenous society with growing militancy if necessary.

Alfredo Bryce Echenique (born 1939) has enjoyed much popularity following the success of *Un mundo para Julius* (1970), a brilliant satire on the upper and middle classes of Lima. His other novels include *Tantas veces Pedro* (1977), *La última mudanza de Felipe Carrillo* (1988), *No me esperen en abril* (1995), *Dos señoras conversan* (1990), *La amigdalitis de Tarzan* (2000) and *El huerto de mi amada*, which won the Premio Planeta (Barcelona) in 2002. Other contemporary writers of note are: Rodolfo Hinostroza (born 1941), novelist, playwright and poet, whose books include *Cuentos de Contranatura* (1972) and *Extremo occidente* (2002); Mario Bellatín (born 1960 in Mexico but educated in Peru), among whose works are the excellent short novels *Salón de belleza* (1994) and *Damas chinas* (1995); Jaime Bayly (born 1965), who is also a journalist and TV presenter. His novels include *Fue ayer y no me acuerdo, Los últimos días de la prensa, No se lo digas a nadie, La noche es virgen* and *Y de repente, un ángel*.

Recent trends for novelists include confronting the violence and the after-effects of the Sendero Lumnioso/MRTA and Fujimori/Montesinos period, with powerful, neorealist novels and stories. Among the best examples are Alonso Cueto (born 1954), *Grandes miradas* (2003), *La hora azul* (2005); and Santiago Roncagliolo (born 1975), see *Abril rojo* (2006). His newest book is *Tan cerca de la vida*, published in 2010. Another new voice is Daniel Alarcón, born in Lima in 1977 but brought up in Birmingham, Alabama, whose first collection of stories, *War by Candlelight* (*Guerra en la penumbra* – 2005) is set almost entirely in Lima but is written in English. His first novel, *Lost City Radio* (2007) tells the story of a radio presenter, whose most popular show unites people separated by civil war, and her relationship with a young boy who comes in person to deliver such a message. Another strand is writing about the reality of immigrant communities in Lima, such as Augusto Higa Oshiro's novel, *Final del porvenir* (1992), and Siu Kam Wen's stories in *El tramo final* (2009).

## 20th-century poetry

At the end of the 19th century, the term Modernism was introduced in Latin America by the Nicaraguan Rubén Darío, not to define a precise school of poetry, but to indicate a break with both Romanticism and Realism. In Peru one major exponent was José Santos Chocano (1875-1934), who labelled his poetry 'mundonovismo' (New Worldism), claiming for himself the role of Poet of South America. He won international fame (see, for example, *Alma América*, 1906), but his star soon waned.

A much less assuming character was José María Eguren (1874-1942) who, feeling alienated from the society around him, sought spiritual reality in the natural world (*Simbólicas*, 1911; *La canción de las figuras*, 1916; *Poesías*, 1929). It has been said that with Eguren the flourishing of Peruvian 20th century poetry began.

Without doubt, the most important poet in Peru, if not Latin America, in the first half of the 20th century, was César Vallejo. Born in 1892 in Santiago de Chuco (Libertad), Vallejo left Peru in 1923 after being framed and briefly jailed in Trujillo for a political crime. In 1928 he was a founder of the Peruvian Socialist Party, then he joined the Communist Party in 1931 in Madrid. From 1936 to his death in Paris in 1938 he opposed the fascist takeover in Spain. His first volume was *Los heraldos negros* in which the dominating theme of all his work, a sense of confusion and inadequacy in the face of the unpredictability of life, first surfaces. *Trilce* (1922), his second work, is unlike anything before it in the Spanish language. The poems contain (among other things) made-up words, distortions of syntax, their own internal logic and rhythm, graphic devices and innovative uses of sounds, clichés and alliterations. *Poemas humanos* and *España, aparta de mí este cáliz* (written as a result of Vallejo's experiences in the Spanish Civil War) were both published posthumously, in 1939.

In the 1960s writers began to reflect the broadening horizons of that increasingly liberal decade, politically and socially, which followed the Cuban Revolution. One poet who embraced the revolutionary fervour was Javier Heraud (born Miraflores 1942). His early volumes, *El río* (1960) and *El viaje* (1961) are apparently simple in conception and expression, but display a transition from embarking on the adventure of life (the river) to autumnal imagery of solitude. In 1961 he went to the USSR, Asia, Paris and Madrid, then in 1962 to Cuba to study cinema. He returned to Peru in 1963 and joined the Ejército de Liberación Nacional. On 15 May 1963 he was shot by government forces near Puerto Maldonado. Heraud's friend César Calvo, now living in Cuba, is a poet and essayist.

Other major poets born in the early 20th century are Emilio Adolfo Westphalen (1911) and Jorge Eduardo Eielson (see his book *Celebración*). Others who began to publish in the 1960s were Luis Hernández (1941-1977), Antonio Cisneros (born 1942) and Marco Martos (born 1942).

In the 1970s, during the social changes propelled by the Velasco regime (1968-1975), new voices arose, many from outside Lima, eg the Hora Zero group (1970-1973 – Enrique Verástegui, Jorge Pimentel, Juan Ramírez Ruiz), whose energetic poetry employed slang and obscenities and other means to challenge preconceptions. Other poets of the 1970s and after include José Watanabe (1946-2007), a film-maker as well as poet, with *Album de familia* (1971), *Historia natural* (1994) and the anthology *Elogio del Refrenamiento* (2004). Renato Cisneros (born 1976) is a poet (*Ritual de los prójimos*, 1998; *Maquina fantasma*, 2002), novelist (*Nunca confíes en mí*, 2010) and blogger (*Busco novia*, see www.renatocisneros.net).

**Women poets and novelists** In addition to Clorinda Matto de Turner (see page 467), modern writers worth checking out are: Blanca Varela (1926-2009), who was married to sculptor Fernando de Szyszlo (see page 473), published volumes of poetry from 1959 (*Ese puerto existe*) to her anthology *Como Dios en la nada* (covering 1949-1998). Her work was championed by the Mexican Octavio Paz, among others. Carmen Ollé (born 1947) introduced a style of writing that is regarded as feminist and confessional. Her best known poetry collection is *Noches de adrenalina* (1981), while her prose includes *Las dos caras del deseo* (1994) and *Una muchacha bajo su paraguas* (2002). Giovanna Pollarolo is a poet, short story writer and screenwriter (born 1952) whose collections include *Huerto de olivos*, 1982, *Entre mujeres solas*, 1996, *La ceremonia de adios*, 1997 and *Atado de nervios*, 1999. Rocio Silva Santiesteban (born 1967) has published short stories as well as the poetry collections *Asuntos circunstanciales* (1984), *Este oficio no me gusta* (1987) and *Mariposa negra* (1996). Laura Riesco's (1940-2008) novel *Ximena de dos caminos* (1994) is an episodic tale of a young girl growing up in the Sierra, experiencing the clash between the oral culture of the local people who look after her, the mining company her father works for, city people who visit and the life of the coast where she goes on holiday. Younger poets of note are: Ericka Ghersi (born 1972), *Zenobia y el anciano* (1994), *Contra la ausencia* (2002), Rosella di Paolo (born 1960), *Piel alzada* (1993), *Tablillas de San Lázaro* (2001) among other collections, and Marita Troiano, whose works include *Mortal in puribus* (1996) and *Secreto a veces* (2003). Novelists include Alina Gadea (born 1966), with *Otra vida para Doris Kaplan* (2009), and Giselle Klatic (born 1976), *Alguien que me quiera* (2010).

# Fine art and sculpture

The Catholic church was the main patron of the arts during the colonial period. The churches and monasteries that sprang up in the newly conquered territories created a demand for paintings and sculptures, met initially by imports from Europe of both works of art and of skilled craftsmen, and later by home-grown products.

## Colonial period

An essential requirement for the inauguration of any new church was an image for the altar and many churches in Lima preserve fine examples of sculptures imported from Seville during the 16th and 17th centuries. Not surprisingly, among the earliest of these are figures of the crucified Christ, such as those in the cathedral and the church of La Merced by Juan Martínez Montañés, one of the foremost Spanish sculptors of the day, and that in San Pedro, by his pupil Juan de Mesa of 1625. Statues of the Virgin and Child were also imported to Lima from an early date, and examples from the mid-16th century survive in the cathedral and in Santo Domingo by Roque de Balduque, also from Seville although Flemish by birth.

Sculptures were expensive and difficult to import, and as part of their policy of relative frugality the Franciscan monks tended to favour paintings. In Lima, the museum of San Francisco now houses an excellent collection of paintings imported from Europe, including a powerful series of saints by Zubarán, as well as other works from his studio, a series of paintings of the life of Christ from Ruben's workshop and works from the circles of Ribera and Murillo.

The Jesuits commissioned the Sevillian artist Juan de Valdés Leal to paint a series of the life of St Ignatius Loyola (1660s) which still hangs in San Pedro. The cathedral museum has a curious series from the Bassano workshop of Venice representing the labours of the monks and dating from the early 17th century. Another interesting artistic import from Europe that can still be seen in San Pedro (see Lima Churches) are the gloriously colourful painted tile decorations (azulejos) on the walls of Dominican monastery, produced to order by Sevillian workshops in 1586 and 1604.

Painters and sculptors soon made their way to Peru in search of lucrative commissions including several Italians who arrived during the later 16th century. The Jesuit Bernardo Bitti (1548-1610), for example, trained in Rome before working in Lima, Cuzco, Juli and Arequipa, where examples of his elegantly Mannerist paintings are preserved in the Jesuit church of the Compañia.

Another Italian, Mateo Pérez de Alesio worked in the Sistine Chapel in Rome before settling in Peru. In Lima the Sevillian sculptor Pedro de Noguera (1592-1655) won the contract for the choirstalls of the cathedral in 1623 and, together with other Spanish craftsmen, produced a set of cedar stalls decorated with vigorous figures of saints and biblical characters, an outstanding work unmatched elsewhere in the viceroyalty.

## Native artists

European imports, however, could not keep up with demand and local workshops of Creole, mestizo and indigenous craftsmen flourished from the latter part of the 16th century. As the Viceregal capital and the point of arrival into Peru, the art of Lima was always strongly influenced by European, especially Spanish models, but the old Inca capital of Cuzco became the centre of a regional school of painting that developed its own characteristics.

A series of paintings of the 1660s, now hanging in the Museo de Arte Religioso in Lima (see page 39), commemorate the colourful Corpus Christi procession of statues of the local patron saints through the streets of Cuzco. These paintings document the appearance of the city and local populace, including Spanish and Inca nobility, priests and laity, rich and poor, Spaniard, indígena, African and mestizo. Many of the statues represented in this series are still venerated in the local parish churches. They are periodically painted and dressed in new robes, but underneath are the original sculptures, executed by native craftsmen. Some are of carved wood while others use the pre-conquest technique of maguey cactus covered in sized cloth.

A remarkable example of an indigenous Andean who acquired European skills was Felipe Guaman Poma de Ayala whose 1000-page letter to the King of Spain celebrating the Andean past and condemning the colonial present contained a visual history of colonial and precolonial life in the Andes.

One of the most successful native painters was Diego Quispe Tito (1611-1681) who claimed descent from the Inca nobility and whose large canvases, often based on Flemish engravings, demonstrate the wide range of European sources that were available to Andean artists in the 17th century. But the Cuzco School is best known for the anonymous devotional works where the painted contours of the figures are overlaid with flat patterns in gold, creating highly decorative images with an underlying tension between the two- and three-dimensional aspects of the work. The taste for richly decorated surfaces can also be seen in the 17th- and 18th-century frescoed interiors of many Andean churches, as in Chinchero, Andahuaylillas and Huaro, and in the ornate carving on altarpieces and pulpits throughout Peru.

Andean content creeps into colonial religious art in a number of ways, most simply by the inclusion of elements of indigenous flora and fauna, or, as in the case of the Corpus Christi paintings, by the use of a setting, with recognizable buildings and individuals.

Changes to traditional Christian iconography include the representation of one of the Magi as an Inca, as in the painting of the Adoration of the Magi in San Pedro in Juli. Another example is that to commemorate his miraculous intervention in the conquest of Cuzco in 1534, Santiago is often depicted triumphing over indigenous people instead of the more familiar Moors. Among the most remarkable 'inventions' of colonial art are the fantastically over-dressed archangels carrying muskets which were so popular in the 18th century. There is no direct European source for these archangels, but in the Andes they seem to have served as a painted guard of honour to the image of Christ or the Virgin on the high altar.

## Independence and after

Political independence from Spain in 1824 had little immediate impact on the arts of Peru except to create a demand for portraits of the new national and continental heroes such as Simón Bolívar and San Martín, many of the best of them produced by the mulatto artist José Gil de Castro (died Lima 1841). Later in the century another mulatto, Pancho Fierro (1810-1879) mocked the rigidity and pretentiousness of Lima society in lively satirical watercolours, while Francisco Laso (1823-1860), an active campaigner for political reform, made the Andean people into respectable subjects for oil paintings.

It was not until the latter part of the 19th century that events from colonial history became popular. The Museo de Arte in Lima (see Lima, page 45) has examples of grandiose paintings by Ignacio Merino (1817-1876) glorifying Columbus, as well as the gigantic romanticized 'Funeral of Atahualpa' by Luis Montero (1826-1869). A curious late flowering of this celebration of colonial history is the chapel commemorating Francisco Pizarro in Lima cathedral which was redecorated in 1928 with garish mosaic pictures of the conqueror's exploits.

Impressionism arrived late and had a limited impact in Peru. Teofilo Castillo (1857-1922), instead of using the technique to capture contemporary reality, created frothy visions of an idealized colonial past. Typical of his work is the large 'Funeral Procession of Santa Rosa' of 1918, with everything bathed in clouds of incense and rose petals, which hangs in the Museo de Arte, in Lima. Daniel Hernández (1856-1932), founder of Peru's first Art School, used a similar style for his portraits of Lima notables past and present.

## 20th century to today

During the first half of the 20th century, Peruvian art was dominated by figurative styles and local subject matter. Political theories of the 1920s recognized the importance of Andean indigenous culture to Peruvian identity and created a climate which encouraged a figurative indigenista school of painting, derived in part from the socialist realism of the Mexican muralists. The movement flourished after the founding of the Escuela de Bellas Artes in 1920. José Sabogal (1888-1956) is the best known exponent of the group which also included Mario Urteaga (1875-1957), Jorge Vinatea Reinoso (1900-1931), Enrique Camino Brent (1909-1960), Camilo Blas (1903-1984) and Alejandro González (1900-1984). Their work can be seen in the Museo de Arte and the Museo Banco Central de Reserva in Lima.

The Mexican muralist tradition persisted into the 1960s with Manuel Ugarte Eléspuru (1911) and Teodoro Núñez Ureta (1914), both of whom undertook large-scale commissions in public buildings in Lima. Examples of public sculpture in the indigenist mode can be seen in plazas and parks throughout Peru, but it was in photography that indigenism found its most powerful expression. From the beginning of the century photographic studios flourished even in smaller towns. Martín Chambi (1891-1973) is the best known of the early 20th-century Peruvian photographers but there were many others, including Miguel Chani (1860-1951) who maintained the grandly named Fotografía Universal studios in Cuzco, Puno and Arequipa.

From the middle of the century artists have experimented with a variety of predominantly abstract styles and the best known contemporary Peruvian painter, Fernando de Szyszlo (1925) has created a visual language of his own, borrowing from Abstract Expressionism on the one hand and from pre-Columbian iconography on the other. His strong images, which suggest rather than represent mythical beings and cosmic forces, have influenced a whole generation of younger Peruvian artists. Look for his monument, Intihuatana 2000, near the sea in Miraflores.

Other leading figures whose work can be seen in public and commercial galleries in Lima include Venancio Shinki, Tilsa Tsuchiya, José Tola, Ricardo Weisse, Ramiro Llona and Leoncio Villanueva. Carlos Revilla, whose wife is his muse and principal subject of his painting, is clearly influenced by Hieronymous Bosch, while Bill Caro is an important exponent of hyperrealism. Víctor Delfín, a painter and sculptor (with beautiful work in iron) can be visited at his house in Barranco (Domeyko 366). His piece, The Kiss (El beso), is in the Parque del Amor in Lima. Pedro Azabache (from Trujillo) is a disciple of José Sabogal; his work is much broader in scope than the indigenism of his mentor. There are many other new artists whose work could be mentioned (Luz Letts, Eduardo Tokeshi, Carlos Enrique Polanco, Bruno Zepilli, Christian Bendayan – try to contact him in Iquitos, Flavia Gandolfo, Claudia Coca) and there are plenty of galleries in Lima with representative exhibitions. There is a museum of contemporary art in Barranco, Lima. One striking modern piece outside Lima is the mosaic mural at the Ciudad Universitaria UNT in Trujillo, which, at almost 1 km long, is the longest mosaic mural in the world.

# Land &
# environment

## Geography

Peru is the third largest South American country, the size of France, Spain and the United Kingdom combined, and presents formidable difficulties to human habitation. Virtually all of the 2250 km of its Pacific coast is desert. From the narrow coastal shelf the Andes rise steeply to a high plateau dominated by massive ranges of snow-capped peaks and gouged with deep canyons. The heavily forested and deeply ravined Andean slopes are more gradual to the east. Further east, towards Brazil and Colombia, begin the vast jungles of the Amazon Basin.

### Geology

The geological structure of Peru is dominated by the Nazca Plate beneath the Pacific Ocean, which stretches from Colombia in the north southwards to mid Chile. Along the coastline, this Plate meets and dives below the mass of the South American Plate that has been moving westwards for much of the Earth's geological history. Prior to the middle of the Tertiary Period, say 40 million years ago, marine sediments suggest that the Amazon Basin drained west to the Pacific, but from that time to the present, tectonic forces have created the Andes range the length of the continent, forming the highest peaks outside the Himalayas. The process continues today as shown by the earthquakes and active volcanoes and, in spite of erosion, the mountains still grow higher.

### Coast

The coastal region, a narrow ribbon of desert 2250 km long, takes up 11% of the country and holds 44% of the population. It is the economic heart of Peru, consuming most of the imports and supplying half of the exports. When irrigated, the river valleys are extremely fertile, creating oases that grow cotton throughout the country, sugar-cane, rice and asparagus in the north, and grapes, fruit and olives in the south. At the same time, the coastal current teems with fish, and Peru has on occasion had the largest catch in the world.

Not far beyond the border with Ecuador in the north, there are mangrove swamps and tropical rainforest, but southwards this quickly changes to drier and eventually desert conditions. South of Piura is the desert of Sechura, followed by the dry barren land or shifting sands to Chimbote. However, several rivers draining the high mountains to the east more or less reach the sea and water the highly productive 'oases' of Piura, Trujillo, Cajamarca and Chimbote.

South of Chimbote, the Andes reach the sea, and apart from a thin strip of coastland north of Lima, the coastal mountains continue to the Chilean border at Arica. This area receives less rain than the Sahara, but because of the high Andes inland, over 50 Peruvian rivers reach the sea, or would do naturally for at least part of the year. As in the north, there are oases in the south, but mostly inland at the foot of the mountains where the river flow is greatest and high sunshine levels ensure good crop production.

The climate of this region depends almost entirely on the ocean currents along the Pacific coast. Two bodies of water drift northwards, the one closest to the shore, known as the Humboldt Current, is the colder, following the deep sea trench along the edge of the Pacific Plate. The basic wind systems here are the South-East Trades crossing the continent from the Atlantic, but the strong tropical sun over the land draws air into Peru from the Pacific. Being cool, this air does no more than condense into mist (known as the *garúa*) over the coastal mountains. This is sufficient to provide moisture for some unusual flora but virtually never produces rain, hence the desert conditions. The mixing of the two cold ocean currents, and the cloud cover that protects the water from the strongest sunlight, creates the unique conditions favourable to fish, notably sardines and anchovy, giving Peru an enormous economic resource. In turn, the fish support vast numbers of seabirds whose deposits of guano have been another very successful export for the country. This is the normal situation; every few years, however, it is disrupted by the phenomenon known as 'El Niño'.

## Highlands

The highlands, or la sierra, extend inland from the coastal strip some 250 km in the north, increasing to 400 km in the south. The average altitude is about 3000 m and 50% of Peruvians live there. Essentially it is a plateau dissected by dramatic canyons and dominated by some of the most spectacular mountain ranges in the world.

## Mountains

The tallest peaks are in the Cordillera Blanca (Huascarán; 6768 m) and the neighbouring Cordillera Huayhuash (Yerupajá; 6634 m). Huascarán is often quoted as the second highest point in South America after Aconcagua, but this is not so; there are some five other peaks on or near the Argentina-Chile border over 6770 m. The snowline here, at nine degrees south, is around 5000 m, much lower than further south. For example, at 16 degrees south, permanent snow starts at 6000 m on Coropuna (6425 m). Peru has more tropical glaciers than any other country in South America, but in recent years scientists have recorded rapid shrinkage of snow and glaciers from Peruvian peaks. This loss is blamed on global warming.

The reasons for this anomaly can be traced again to the Humboldt current. The Cordillera Blanca is less than 100 km from the coast, and the cool air drawn in depresses temperatures at high altitudes. Precipitation comes also from the east and falls as snow. Constant high winds and temperatures well below freezing at night create an unusual microclimate and with it spectacular mountain scenery, making it a mecca for snow and ice mountaineers. Dangers are heightened by the quite frequent earthquakes causing avalanches and landslides which have brought heavy loss of life to the valleys of the region. In 1970, 20,000 people lost their lives when Yungay, immediately west of Huascarán, was overwhelmed.

## Canyons

Equally dramatic are the deep canyons taking water from the high mountains to the Pacific. The Colca Canyon, about 100 km north of Arequipa, has been measured at 3200 m from the lower rim to the river, more than twice as deep as the Grand Canyon. At one point it is overlooked by the 5227 m Señal Yajirhua peak, a stupendous 4150 m above the water level. Deeper even than Colca is the Cotahuasi Canyon, also in Arequipa Department, whose deepest point is 3354 m. Other canyons have been found in this remote area yet to be measured and documented.

In spite of these ups and downs, which cause great communications difficulties, the presence of water and a more temperate climate on the plateau has attracted people throughout the ages. Present day important population centres in the highlands include Cajamarca in the north, Huancayo in central Peru and Cuzco in the south, all at around 3000 m. Above this, at around 4000 m, is the 'high steppe' or *puna*, with constant winds and wide day/night temperature fluctuations. Nevertheless, fruit and potatoes (which originally came from the puna of Peru and Bolivia) are grown at this altitude and the meagre grasslands are home to the ubiquitous llama and alpaca.

## Volcanoes

Although hot springs and evidence of ancient volcanic activity can be seen almost anywhere in Peru, the southern part of the sierra is the only area where there are active volcanoes. These represent the northernmost of a line of volcanoes which stretch 1500 km south along the Chile-Bolivia border to Argentina. Sabancaya (5977 m), just south of the Colca Canyon, is currently active, often with a dark plume downwind from the summit. Beyond the Colca Canyon is the Valle de los Volcanes, with 80 cinder cones rising 50-250 m above a desolate floor of lava and ash. There are other dormant or recently active volcanoes near the western side of Lake Titicaca – for example Ubinas – but the most notable is El Misti (5822 m), which overlooks Arequipa. It is perfectly shaped, indicating its status as active in the recent geologic past. Some experts believe it is one of the most potentially dangerous volcanoes in South America. Certainly a major eruption would be a catastrophe for the nearby city.

## Lake Titicaca

The southeastern border with Bolivia passes through Titicaca, with about half of the lake in each country. It is the largest lake in South America (ignoring Lake Maracaibo in Venezuela, which is linked to the sea) and at 3812 m, the highest navigable body of water in the world. It covers about 8300 sq km, running 190 km northwest to southeast, and is 80 km across. It lies in a 60,000 sq km basin between the coastal and eastern Andes that spread out southwards to their widest point at latitude 18 degrees south.

The average depth is over 100 m, with the deepest point recorded at 281 m. Twenty-five rivers, most from Peru, flow into the lake and a small outlet leaves the lake at Desaguadero on the Bolivia-Peru border. This takes no more than 5% of the inflow, the rest is lost through evaporation and hence the waters of the lake are slightly brackish, producing the totora reeds used to make the mats and balsa boats for which the lake dwellers are famed.

The lake is the remnant of a vast area of water formed in the Ice Age known as Lake Ballivián. This extended at least 600 km to the south into Bolivia and included what is now Lake Poopó and the Salar de Uyuni. Now the lake level fluctuates seasonally, normally rising from December to March and receding for the rest of the year but extremes of 5 m between high and low levels have been recorded. This can cause problems and high levels in the late 1980s disrupted transport links near the shoreline. The night temperature can fall as low as -25°C but high daytime temperatures ensure that the surface average is about 14°C.

## Eastern Andes and Amazon Basin

Almost half of Peru is on the eastern side of the Andes and about 90% of the country's drainage is into the Amazon system. It is an area of heavy rainfall with cloudforest above 3500 m and tropical rainforest lower down. There is little savannah, or natural grasslands, characteristic of other parts of the Amazon Basin.

There is some dispute on the Amazon's source. Officially, the mighty river begins as the Marañón, whose longest tributary rises just east of the Cordillera Huayhuash. However, the longest journey for the proverbial raindrop, some 6400 km, probably starts in southern Peru, where the headwaters of the Apurímac (Ucayali) flow from the snows on the northern side of the Nevado Mismi, near Cailloma.

With much more rainfall on the eastern side of the Andes, rivers are turbulent and erosion dramatic. Although vertical drops are not as great – there is a whole continent to cross to the Atlantic – valleys are deep, ridges narrow and jagged and there is forest below 3000 m. At 1500 m the Amazon jungle begins and water is the only means of surface transport available, apart from three roads which reach Borja (on the Marañón), Yurimaguas (on the Huallaga) and Pucallpa (on the Ucayali), all at about 300 m above the Atlantic which is still 4000 km or so downstream. The vastness of the Amazon lowlands becomes apparent and it is here that Peru bulges 650 km northeast past Iquitos to the point where it meets Colombia and Brazil at Letícia. Development and especially road construction are ongoing threats to the unique natural and cultural environments of the Peruvian Amazon.

## Climate

### Coast
On the coast summertime is from December to April, when temperatures range from 25° to 35°C and it is hot and dry. Wintertime is May to November, when the temperature drops a bit and it is cloudy.

The coastal climate is determined by the cold sea-water adjoining deserts. Prevailing inshore winds pick up so little moisture over the cold Humboldt current, which flows from Antarctica, that only from May to November does it condense. The resultant blanket of sea-mist (called *garúa*) extends from the south to about 200 km north of Lima. It is thickest to the south as far as Chincha and to the north as far as Huarmey, beyond which it thins and the sun can be expected to break through.

### Sierra
From April-October is the dry season. It is hot and dry during the day, around 20°-25°C, and cold and dry at night, often below freezing. From November to April is the wet season, when it is dry and clear most mornings, with some rainfall in the afternoon. There is a small temperature drop (18°C) and not much difference at night (15°C).

### Selva
April to October is the dry season, with temperatures up to 35°C. In the jungle areas of the south, a cold front can pass through at night. November to April is the wet season. It is humid and hot, with heavy rainfall at any time.

## Flora and fauna

Peru is a country of great biological diversity. The fauna and flora are to a large extent determined by the influence of the Andes, the longest uninterrupted mountain chain in the world, and the mighty Amazon river, which has the largest volume of any river in the world. Of Earth's 32 known climate zones Peru has 28, and of the 117 recognized microclimates Peru has 84. Some 17% of the surface area of Peru is protected. Throughout the country there are 216 protected natural areas, including 76 national parks and reserves, 18 regional reserves and 122 private reserves.

## ON THE ROAD

### Viringo

If you go to a Peruvian museum at a coastal archaeological site, you may see an elegant dog with a long, thin nose and arched neck near the entrance. It might be a bit shy, and, if the weather is cold, it may be wearing a little woollen jacket. This is because the dog has no hair.

The Peruvian hairless, or *viringo*, is a rare breed today, but in Inca times was a companion animal whose main job was to warm his master s bed. The Chavín, Moche and Chimú cultures represented it on their ceramics, but its origins are unknown. The most likely theory is that it accompanied the first migrants to the Amercian continent from Asia. In its most common, hairless form, it has no fleas and no smell.

Breeders note that it needs protection against the sun and the cold, but there is also a coated variety (called 'powder puff' in the dog world).

In recognition of the importance of this dog in its history, the Peruvian government decreed in Law number 27537 that every site museum on the coast must have at least one *viringo* on the premises.

In 2006 archaeologists announced the discovery of over 40 mummified dogs at tombs of the Chiribaya people in the Ilo Valley, dating from AD 900-1350. They weren't *viringos*, but a distinct breed, christened 'Chiribaya shepherds' because, it is supposed, they herded llamas.

## Natural history

This diversity arises not only from the wide range of habitats available, but also from the history of the continent. South America has essentially been an island for some 70 million years joined only by a narrow isthmus to Central and North America. Land passage played a significant role in the gradual colonization of South America by species from the north. When the land-link closed these colonists evolved to a wide variety of forms free from the competitive pressures that prevailed elsewhere. When the land-bridge was re-established some four million years ago a new invasion of species took place from North America, adding to the diversity but also leading to numerous extinctions. Comparative stability has ensued since then and has guaranteed the survival of many primitive groups like the opossums.

## Coast

The coastal region of Peru is extremely arid, partly as a result of the cold Humboldt current (see Climate, above). The paucity of animal life in the area between the coast and the mountains is obviously due to this lack of rain, though in some areas intermittent lomas, which are areas of sparse scrubby vegetation caused by moisture in the sea mist. The plants which survive provide ideal living conditions for insects which attract insectivorous birds and humming birds to feed on their nectar. Cactuses are abundant in northern Peru and provide a wooded landscape of trees and shrubs including the huarango (*Prosopis juliflora*). Also common in the north is the algorrobo tree – 250,000 ha were planted in 1997 to take advantage of the El Niño rains. Algorrobo forests (*algorrobales*), scrub thicket (*matorrales*) and coastal wetlands each provide habitat for some 30 species of birds. Mammals include foxes, three species of deer and six species of dogs from pre-Columbian times.

## Andes

From the desert rise the steep Andean slopes. In the deeply incised valleys Andean fox and deer may occasionally be spotted. Herds of domestic llamas and alpacas graze the high plateaus as well their wild cousins the vicuñas and guanacos. Mountain caracara and Andean lapwing are frequently observed soaring, and there is always the possibility of spotting flocks of mitred parrots or even the biggest species of hummingbird in the world (*Patagonia gigas*). The most emblematic bird is the Andean condor.

The Andean zone has many lakes and rivers and countless swamps. Exclusive to this area short-winged grebe and the torrent duck which feeds in the fast flowing rivers, and giant and horned coots. Chilean flamingo frequent the shallow soda lakes. The puna, a habitat characterized by tussock grass and pockets of stunted alpine flowers, gives way to relict elfin forest and tangled bamboo thicket in this inhospitable windswept and frost-prone region. Occasionally the dissected remains of a Puya plant can be found; the result of the nocturnal foraging of the rare spectacled bear. There are quite a number of endemic species of rodent including the viscacha, and it is the last stronghold of the chinchilla. Here pumas roam preying on the herbivores which frequent these mountain – pudu, a tiny Andean deer or guemal and the mountain tapir.

## Tropical Andes

The elfin forest gradually grades into mist enshrouded cloudforest at about 3500 m. In the tropical zones of the Andes, the humidity in the cloudforests stimulates the growth of a vast variety of plants particularly mosses and lichens. The cloudforests are found in a narrow strip that runs along the eastern slopes of the spine of the Andes. It is these dense, often impenetrable, forests clothing the steep slopes that are important in protecting the headwaters of all the streams and rivers that cascade from the Andes to form the mighty Amazon as it begins its long journey to the sea. This is a verdant world of dripping epiphytic mosses, lichens, ferns and orchids that grow in profusion despite the plummeting overnight temperatures. The high humidity resulting from the 2 m of rain that can fall in a year is responsible for the maintenance of the forest and it accumulates in puddles and leaks from the ground in a constant trickle that combines to form myriad icy, crystal-clear streams that cascade over precipitous waterfalls. In secluded areas, orange Andean cock-of-the-rock give their spectacular display to females in the early morning mists. Woolly monkeys are also occasionally sighted as they descend the wooded slopes. Mixed flocks of colourful tanagers are commonly encountered as are the golden-headed quetzal and Amazon umbrella bird.

## Amazon Basin

At about 1500 m there is a gradual transition to the vast lowland forests of the Amazon Basin, which are warmer and more equable than the cloudforests clothing the mountains above. The daily temperature varies little during the year with a high of 23-32°C falling slightly to 20-26°C overnight. This lowland region receives some 2 m of rainfall per year most of it falling from November to April. The rest of the year is sufficiently dry, at least in the lowland areas to inhibit the growth of epiphytes and orchids that are so characteristic of the highland areas. For a week or two in the rainy season the rivers flood the forest. The zone immediately surrounding this seasonally flooded forest is referred to as terre firme forest.

The vast river basin of the Amazon is home to an immense variety of species. The environment has largely dictated their lifestyle. Life in or around rivers, lakes, swamps and forests depend on the ability to swim and climb – amphibious and tree-dwelling animals are common. Once, the entire Amazon Basin was a great inland sea and the river still contains mammals more typical of the coast, eg manatees and dolphins.

Here in the relatively constant climatic conditions animal and plant life has evolved to an amazing diversity over the millennia. It has been estimated that 3.9 sq km of forest can harbour some 1200 vascular plants, 600 species of tree, and 120 woody plants. Here, in these relatively flat lands, a soaring canopy some 50 m overhead is the powerhouse of the forest. It is a habitat choked with strangling vines and philodendrons among which mixed troupes of squirrel monkeys and brown capuchins forage. In the high canopy small groups of spider monkeys perform their lazy aerial acrobatics, whilst lower down, cling to epiphyte-clad trunks and branches, groups of saddle-backed and emperor tamarins forage for blossom, fruit and the occasional insect prey.

The most accessible part of the jungle is on or near the many meandering rivers. At each bend of the river the forest is undermined by the currents during the seasonal floods at the rate of some 10-20 m per year leaving a sheer mud and clay bank, whilst on the opposite bend new land is laid down as broad beaches of fine sand and silt.

A succession of vegetation can be seen. The fast growing willow-like Tessaria first stabilizes the ground enabling the tall stands of *caña brava* Gynerium to become established. Within these dense almost impenetrable stands the seeds of rainforest trees germinate and over a few years thrust their way towards the light. The fastest growing is a species of Cercropia that forms a canopy 15-18 m over the *caña* but even this is relatively short-lived. The gap in the canopy is quickly filled by other species. Two types of mahogany outgrow the other trees forming a closed canopy at 40 m with a lush understory of shade tolerant Heliconia and ginger. Eventually even the long-lived trees die off to be replaced by others providing a forest of great diversity.

## Jungle wildlife

The meandering course of the river provides many excellent opportunities to see herds of russet-brown capybara – a sheep-sized rodent – peccaries and brocket deer. Of considerable ecological interest are the presence of oxbow lakes, or *cochas*, since these provide an abundance of wildlife that can easily be seen around the lake margins. The best way to see the wildlife, however, is to get above the canopy. Ridges provide elevated view points. From here, it is possible to look across the lowland floodplain to the foothills of the Andes, some 200 km away. Flocks of parrots and macaws can be seen flying between fruiting trees and troupes of squirrel monkeys and brown capuchins come very close.

The lowland rainforest of Peru is particularly famous for its primates and giant otters. Giant otters were once widespread in Amazonia but came close to extinction in the 1960s owing to persecution by the fur trade. The giant otter population in Peru has since recovered and is now estimated to be at least several hundred. Jaguar and other predators are also much in evidence. Although rarely seen their paw marks are commonly found along the forest trails. Rare bird species are also much in evidence, including fasciated tiger-heron and primitive hoatzins.

The (very) early morning is the best time to see peccaries, brocket deer and tapir at mineral licks (collpa). Macaw and parrot licks are found along the banks of the river. Here at dawn a dazzling display arrives and clambers around in the branches overhanging the clay-lick. At its peak there may be 600 birds of up to six species (including red and green macaws, and blue-headed parrots) clamouring to begin their descent to the riverbank where they jostle for access to the mineral rich clay. A necessary addition to their diet that may also neutralize the toxins present in the leaf and seed diet. Rare game birds such as razor billed curassows and piping guans may also be seen.

A list of over 600 species has been compiled. Noteworthy are the black-faced cotinga, crested eagle, and the Harpy eagle, the world's most impressive raptor, easily capable of taking an adult monkey. Mixed species flocks are commonly observed containing from 25 to 100-plus birds of perhaps 30 species including blue dacnis, blue-tailed emerald, bananaquit, thick-billed euphoria and the paradise tanager. Each species occupies a slightly different niche, and since there are few individuals of each species in the flock, competition is avoided. Mixed flocks foraging in the canopy are often led by a white-winged shrike, whereas flocks in the understorey are often led by the bluish-slate antshrike.

# Books

## Culture and history

**Bingham, Hiram** *Lost City of the Incas (illustrated edition, with introduction by Hugh Thomson, Weidenfeld & Nicolson, London, 2002).*

**Bowen, Sally** *The Fujimori File. Peru and its President 1990-2000 (2000).* A very readable account of the last decade of the 20th century; it ends at the election of that year so the final momentous events of Fujimori's term happened after publication. Bowen has also written, with Jane Holligan, *The Imperfect Spy: the Many Lives of Vladimiro Montesinos* (2003), Peisa.

**Hemming, John** *The Conquest of the Incas (1970).* The one, invaluable book on the period of the conquest.

**MacQuarrie, Kim** *The Last Days of the Incas (2007, Piatkus).* A thrilling account of the events that led to the Incas' final resistance and of the explorers who have tried to uncover the secrets of their civilization.

**Morrison, Tony** *Qosqo. The Navel of the World (1997, Condor Books).* Cuzco's past and present with an extensive section of photographs of the city and its surroundings. *Pathways to the Gods: The Mystery of the Andes Lines* (1978), Michael Russell, obtainable in Lima; and *The Mystery of the Nasca Lines* (1987), nonesuch Expeditions, with an intro by Marie Reiche.

**Mosely, Michael E** *The Incas and their Ancestors: The Archaeology of Peru (2001, Thames and Hudson).*

**Muscutt, Keith** *Warriors of the Clouds: A Lost Civilization in the Upper Amazon of Peru (1998, New Mexico Press).* Excellent coffee table book and Chachapoyas memoir; also refer to its website (www.chachapoyas.com).

**Starn, Orin, Carlos Iván Degregori, and Robin Kirk** *The Peru Reader (2nd edition, 2005),* Duke Univeristy Press. A good collection on history, culture and politics.

**Urton, Gary** *The Social Life of Numbers (1997, University of Texas Press).* On the significance and philosophy of numbers in Andean society. Related to Urton's other studies on khipus and Inca mythology.

## Capaq Ñan, the Royal Inca Road

**Espinosa, Ricardo** *La Gran Ruta Inca, The Great Inca Route (2002, Petróleos del Perú).* A photographic and textual record of Espinosa's walk the length of the Camino Real de los Incas, in Spanish and English. He has also walked the length of Peru's coast, described in *El Perú a toda Costa (1997 Editur).* The same company has published **Zarzar, Omar**, *Por los Caminos del Perú en Bicicleta.*

**Muller, Karin** *Along the Inca Road (2000, National Geographic).* A Woman's Journey into an Ancient Empire.

**Portway, Christopher** *Journey Along the Andes (1993, Impact Books).* An account of the Andean Inca road.

## Non-Peruvian Fiction

**Matthiessen, Peter** *At Play in the Fields of the Lord (1965).*

**Shakespeare, Nicholas** *The Vision of Elena Silves (1989).*

**Thubron, Colin** *To the Last City (2002, Chatto & Windus).*

**Vltchek, Andre** *Point of No Return (2005, Mainstay Press).*

**Wilder, Thornton** *The Bridge of San Luis Rey (1941, Penguin).*

## Travel

**Murphy, Dervla** *Eight Feet in the Andes (1983).*

**Parris, Matthew** *Inca-Kola (1990).*

**Shah, Tahir** *Trail of Feathers (2001).*

**Simpson, Joe** *Touching the Void (1997, Vintage).* A nail-biting account of Simpson's accident in the Cordillera Huayhuash.

**Thomson, Hugh** *The White Rock (2002 Phoenix).* Describes Thomson's own travels in the Inca heartland, as well as the journeys of earlier explorers. *Cochineal Red: Travels through Ancient Peru (2006 Weidenfeld & Nicolson),* explores pre-Inca civilizations.

## Trekking and climbing

**Biggar, John** *The Andes. A Guide for Climbers (1999, Andes Publishing).*

**Gómez, Antonio, and Tomé, Juan José** *La Cordillera Blanca de Los Andes (1998, Desnivel).* Spanish only, climbing guide with some trekking and general information, available locally. Also *Escaladas en los Andes. Guía de la Cordillera Blanca (1999, Desnivel).* (Spanish only), a climbing guide.

**Kunstaetter, Robert and Daisy** *Trekking Peru (2017, Mountaineers Books).* The latest trekking guide, see www.trekkingperu.org.

**Ricker, John F** *Yuraq Janka, Cordilleras Blanca and Rosko (1977, The Alpine Club of Canada, The American Alpine Club).*

**Sharman, David** *Climbs of the Cordillera Blanca of Peru (1995, Whizzo).* A climbing guide, available locally, as well as from **Cordee** in the UK and **Alpenbooks** in the USA.

## Wildlife

**Clements, James F and Shany, Noam** *A Field Guide to the Birds of Peru (2001, Ibis).*

**Schulenberg, Thomas S, Stotz, Douglas F, et al** *Birds of Peru (2007, Helm).* A comprehensive field guide.

**TReeS** *(PO Box 33153, London, NW3 4DR, www.tambopata.org.uk)* publish *Tambopata – A Bird Checklist, Tambopata – Mammal, Amphibian & Reptile Checklist* and *Reporte Tambopata;* they also produce tapes and CDs of *Jungle Sounds* and *Birds of Southeast Peru* and distribute other books and merchandise.

**Valqui, Thomas** *Where to Watch Birds in Peru (2004).* Describes 151 sites, how to get there and what to expect once there.

**Walker, Barry, and Jon Fjeldsa** *Birds of Machu Picchu.*

# Practicalities

Getting there .................. 485
Getting around ............... 488
Essentials A-Z ................. 494

# **Getting** there

## Air

### From Europe

There are direct flights to **Lima** from Amsterdam (**KLM** via Bonaire), Madrid (**Iberia**, **Air Europa** and **LATAM**) and Paris (**Air France**). From London, Frankfurt, Rome, Milan, Lisbon or other European cities, the best connections are made in Madrid, or via Brazilian or US gateways.

### From North America

Miami is the main gateway to Peru, together with Atlanta, Dallas, Houston, Los Angeles and New York. There are flights, though not all are direct, with **American**, **Delta**, **LATAM**, **Avianca**, **Copa** and **AeroMéxico**. Daily connections can be made from almost all major North American cities. From Toronto and Montreal, **Air Canada** flies direct to Lima. COPA offers connections from Montreal and Toronto to Lima via Panama City.

### From Australia, New Zealand and South Africa

You can fly from Auckland to Lima via Santiago, Chile, with **LATAM**. Also from Auckland to Buenos Aires with **Air New Zealand** and on from there to Lima. Alternatively, fly to Los Angeles and travel down. From Johannesburg, make connections in Buenos Aires or São Paulo.

### From Latin America

There are regular flights to Peru from most South American capitals. The **LATAM** group has the most routes to Lima within the continent. **Avianca** also has extensive coverage, including to Central America and Mexico. **COPA** offers many useful connectiontions through Panama City.

### Airport information

With the exception of a few flights between Cuzco and Santiago (Chile) or La Paz (Bolivia), all international flights arrive at **Jorge Chávez Airport** in Callao ⓘ *16 km from the centre of Lima, T01-511 6055, www.lap.com.pe.* For details of facilities in the airport and onward transport, see page 70. Lima airport is very busy and the city's congested trafic often causes ground transport delays, always give yourself extra time. Airlines recommend that you arrive up to three hours before international flights and 90 minutes before domestic flights. Check-in closes one hour before departure for international flights, 30 minutes for domestic flights, after which you may not be permitted to board. Check your airline's website for current requirements.

The *aduana* (customs) process is relatively painless and efficient (a push-button, red light/green light system operates for customs baggage checks – see also Customs, page 494).

### Baggage allowance

The weight limit for baggage varies between airlines. You should therefore find out from the carrier exactly how much weight you are permitted. In general, the maximum weight of checked-in baggage will be 23 kg. You may find that allowances are different for each direction of your journey. Checked and carry-on luggage are normally restricted by both size and weight. At busy times of the year it can be very difficult and expensive

## TRAVEL TIP
## Packing for Peru

A good principle is to take half the clothes and twice the money that you think you will need. As you pack for your trip to Peru, keep in mind the joy of travelling light and remember that many of the following articles are available locally. Always take out a good travel insurance policy to cover your belongings (see page 497).

Listed here are those items most often recommended by other travellers. These include strong shoes, waterproof clothing and waterproof treatment for leather footwear. An inflatable travel pillow and wax earplugs are vital for long bus trips and noisy hotels. Also important are flip-flops, which can be worn in showers to avoid both athlete's foot and electric shocks, and a sheet sleeping bag for use in cheap hotels.

Other useful things include: a clothes line, a nailbrush, a water bottle, a universal sink plug of the flanged type that will fit any waste-pipe, string, a pocket knife (don't carry it in your hand luggage when flying), an alarm clock, candles (for power cuts), a torch/ flashlight or headlamp, pocket mirror, suitable chargers and adaptors for recharging all your electronic kit, a padlock for the doors of the cheapest hotels, a small first-aid kit, sun hat, lip salve with sun protection, contraceptives, waterless soap, wipes and a small sewing kit. Always carry toilet paper, especially on long bus trips. The most security conscious may also wish to include a length of chain and padlock for securing luggage to a bed or bus seat. Contact lens wearers note that lens solution can be difficult to find in Peru; ask for it in a pharmacy, rather than an opticians.

to bring items such as bikes and surfboards along. Airlines may let you pay a penalty for overweight baggage, but you should verify this in advance. Do not assume that you can bring extra luggage. The usual weight limit for domestic flights is also 23 kg per person, but can be considerably less on some airlines or if the plane is small.

### Airport taxes
Airport taxes are included in the price of flight tickets, not paid at the airport. When making a domestic connection in Lima, you don't have to pay airport tax; contact airport personnel to be escorted to your departure gate.

## Road and river

Peru has land and river borders with neighbouring countries and they are heavily used, see Border crossings box, page 491. Taking an international bus is usually (but not always) more expensive than travelling to and from the border on domestic bus routes.

### Car
You must have an international driving licence and be over 21 to drive in Peru. If you bring your own vehicle into the country, you must provide proof of ownership. Officially you cannot enter Peru with a vehicle registered in someone else's name, but it may be possible with a notarized letter of authorization in Spanish (at the discretion of the customs officer). There are two recognized documents for taking a vehicle into South America: a *carnet de passages* issued jointly by the Fedération Internationale de l'Automobile (FIA-Paris) and the **Alliance Internationale de Tourisme** (AIT-Geneva), and the *Libreta de*

*Pasos por Aduana* issued by the **Federación Interamericana de Touring y Automóvil Clubs** (FITAC). Officially, Peru requires one or the other, but it is seldom asked for. Nevertheless, motorists seem to fare better with one than without it.

*SOAT (Seguro Obligatorio para Accidentes de Tránsito)* is a compulsory insurance that covers people injured in road accidents. Transit police regulary ask to see proof that you have it. It can be purchased at major border crossings but only during regular business hours, not weekends or holidays. Insurance for the vehicle against accident, damage or theft is best arranged in the country of origin, but it is difficult to find agencies who offer this service. The **Touring y Automóvil Club del Perú** ① *Av Trinidad Morán 698, Lince, T01-614 9999*, offers help to visiting motorists and particularly to members of the leading motoring associations in many countries.

# **Getting** around

## Air

Peru is bigger than you think. If you only have a couple of weeks, travelling by air is the sensible option. It allows access to most major regions and means you can spend more time at your destination and less getting there. On the downside, you will see less of the country and will meet fewer people than if you travel overland.

Carriers serving major cities are **Star Perú** ① *T01-705 9000, www.starperu.com*, **LATAM** ① *T01-213 8200, www.latam.com*, **Avianca** ① *T01-511 8222, www.avianca.com*, **Peruvian Airlines** ① *T01-716 6000, www.peruvianairlines.pe*, **Viva Air** ① *T01-7050107, www.vivaair. com/pe*, and **LC Peru** ① *T01-204 1313, www.lcperu.pe*. The latter also flies to smaller airports as do **ATSA** ① *T01-717 3268, www.atsaairlines.com* and **SAETA** ① *T042- 587893, www. saetaperu.com*.

Prices vary greatly between airlines, with **LATAM** being the most expensive for non-Peruvians. Prices often increase at holiday times (Semana Santa, May Day, Inti Raymi, 28-29 July, Christmas and New Year), and for elections. During these times and the northern hemisphere summer, seats can be hard to come by, so book early. Flight schedules and departure times may change. In the rainy season delays and cancellations are more common and flights to jungle regions may be less reliable. It is best to allow an extra day between national and international flights, especially in the rainy season. Be at the airport well ahead of your flight.

## Rail

There are just a few lines of interest to most travellers. The first is Cuzco–Machu Picchu, on which two companies operate services: **PeruRail** ① *www.perurail.com*, and **Inca Rail** ① *www.incarail.com*; the second and third are Puno–Cuzco and Cuzco–Arequipa, run by **PeruRail**. **PeruRail** also offers occasional tourist service, mostly at holiday times, along the Ferrocarril Central between Lima and Huancayo. A wonderfully authentic Andean train journey, heavily used by local communities, remains in regular service between Huancayo and Huancavelica. Train buffs might also enjoy riding the short cross-border line between Tacna and Arica (Chile).

## River

On almost any trip to the Amazon Basin, a boat journey will be required at some point, either to get you to a jungle lodge, or to travel between river ports.

### Motorized canoes

Motorized canoes with canopies usually take passengers to jungle lodges. They normally provide life jackets and have seats that aren't very comfortable on long journeys, so a cushion may come in handy. They are open to the elements, so take a waterproof to keep you dry and warm. The breeze can be a welcome relief from the heat and humidity in the daytime, but it can be cold in the early morning, and, if there is any rain about, it will blow into your face. You sit very close to the water and you soon learn to respect the driver's knowledge of the river.

## Public river transport

There are various types of vessel: a *lancha* is a large riverboat; a *rápido* or *deslizador* is a speedboat (increasingly common on long-haul routes); a *yate* is a small to medium wooden *colectivo*, usually slow, and a *chalupa* is a small motor launch used to ferry passengers from the *lanchas* to shore. A *peque-peque* is any boat with a two-cycle outboard engine with a long propeller shaft, specialized for shallow water and very common in the Peruvian Amazon. Standards are variable and not all vessels are safe or reliable; always look over several of them and talk to the staff before choosing. The best *lanchas* are on the Iquitos–Pucallpa and Iquitos–Yurimaguas routes.

**Practicalities** Departure times are marked on a chalk-board on each vessel. All say '*sin falta*' ('without fail') but that does not necessarily mean the boat leaves at that time, nor even on that day. How long the trip takes depends on the water level, the weather, the size and state of the engine, the amount of cargo (boats go very loaded from Pucallpa to Iquitos), how long they wait at intermediate ports, and whether you're going upstream or downstream. Always allow extra time for your journey. A flexible attitude and an ability to speak Spanish are both essential.

Boats travel near shore upstream and in the middle of the river downstream. To flag down a boat at intermediate points along the river, use a white sheet during the day or strong light at night; sometimes they don't bother stopping even when they see you are calling. Pay the captain or *mestre* (manager) on the boat; avoid touts. On some boats, staff collect the fares in the middle of the first night, once passengers are all in their hammocks.

**Sleeping and eating on board** Accommodation on *lanchas* is either in a cabin for two or four passengers (on the best boats some cabins have a/c and private bath), which will be more expensive than slinging your hammock on deck. Some boats have two classes of hammock space. It may be possible to sleep on board ahead of departure or if you arrive in the middle of the night. The quality of your experience depends largely on the level of crowding and hygiene, especially if you're travelling hammock class.

Food on boats is of variable quality, often monotonous, and sometimes meagre; you need to take your own plate, cutlery and cup, plenty of drinking water (the silt in the rivers will clog filters; purifying tablets may not kill all pathogens), extra snacks and seasonings. Local produce can sometimes be purchased on route. There is usually (not always) a bar on board (often expensive) serving beer, soft drinks and a few snacks. Departures are after sunset and the first night's meal is not included.

You need to take a bag for your rubbish (rather than chucking it overboard), toilet paper, mosquito repellent and long-sleeved shirts/long trousers for after dusk. DEET is the best mosquito repellent but it will be washed directly into the river and it is lethal to most fish. Thieves are a problem; do not leave any possessions out of your sight, not even your shoes under your hammock at night. Also take great care of your belongings when embarking and

> **Tip...**
> If you choose to sleep in a hammock, hang it away from lightbulbs, which aren't switched off at night and attract all sorts of strange insects, and away from the engines, which usually emit noxious fumes and, of course, noise. Do try to find somewhere sheltered from the cold, damp night breeze. Take a rope for hanging your hammock, plus string and sarongs for privacy. Use a double fabric (not string) hammock for warmth; you may need a blanket as well.

disembarking. Women travellers can expect the usual unwanted attention; it becomes more uncomfortable when you are confined to a small boat.

## Road

Although Peru's geography is dominated by the Andes, one of the world's major mountain ranges, great steps have been taken to improve major roads and enlarge the paved network linking the Pacific coast with the highlands and jungle. The most important development has been the completion of two branches of the fully paved *Carretera Interoceánica*, which runs from the Pacific port of Ilo to Puerto Maldonado and on to the Brazilian border at Iñapari. New and improved roads continue to enhance the country's transportation infrastructure, but they also rapidly become corridors of deforestation and cause more accidents due to speeding. Regardless of road quality, travelling at night or in bad weather should be avoided whenever possible.

It is always worth taking some time to plan an overland journey in advance, checking which roads are finished, which have roadworks and which will be affected by the weather. Smaller mountain roads are often dirt, some good, some very bad, especially on the eastern slopes. The highland and jungle wet season, from mid-October to late March, can seriously hamper travel in these regions, with heavy rainfall and the ensuing landslides making roads impassable. This makes for slow travel and frequent breakdowns, so allow extra time. You should check road conditions before you travel with locals (not with bus companies, who only want to sell tickets), as accidents are more common at these times. Finally, bear in mind that extended overland travel is not really an option if you only have a few weeks' holiday.

### Major routes

Note that many paved roads in Peru charge tolls, which vary depending on the size of the vehicle. The Pan-American Highway runs north–south through the coastal desert and is mostly in very good condition. Also paved and well-maintained is the direct road that branches off the Pan-American at Pativilca and runs up to Huaraz and on to Caraz. The northern route from Chiclayo through to Tarapoto and Yurimaguas is fully paved, as is the spur to the Ecuadorean border via Jaén. Cajamarca has a paved connection to the coast and the Central Highway from Lima to Pucallpa is fully paved. There is also a paved road from La Oroya to Tarma and Satipo. South of Lima, there's the paved 'Liberatores' highway from Pisco to Ayacucho. From Nazca to Abancay and on to Cuzco is fully paved. This is the main route from Lima to Cuzco. The main roads into the Sacred Valley from Cuzco are also paved. The Cuzco–Puno highway is fully paved and is a fast, comfortable journey. The paved road continues along the south shore of Lake Titicaca to Desaguadero on the Bolivian border. From there the paving runs down the western slope of the Andes to Moquegua and the coast. Also in the south, the road that runs into the sierra to Arequipa is paved and in good condition. From Arequipa the road to Puno is paved. Roads from Arequipa to Mollendo and Matarani are also excellent.

### Bus services

Services all along the coast to the north and south as well as inland to Huancayo, Pucallpa, Ayacucho and Huaraz are generally good, but on long-distance journeys it is advisable to pay extra and travel with a reliable company. There are many different bus companies, but the larger ones are better organized, leave on time and do not wait until the bus is full. Cruz del Sur, Móviltours and Oltursa are among the best bus lines covering large parts of

## TRAVEL TIP
### Border crossings

The main entry points into Peru by land and river are as follows:

From Bolivia  Desaguadero (the town has the same name on both sides of the border; see page 266) and Kasani–Yunguyo on the southeastern side of Lake Titicaca (see page 266). There is also an unpaved crossing on the north shore, from Puerto Acosta to Tilali (see page 284).

From Chile  Arica–Tacna (see page 254).

From Ecuador  At Huaquillas–Aguas Verdes (see page 148); Macará–La Tina (see page 146); La Balsa (Zumba)–Namballe (see page 189); and Nuevo Rocafuerte–Pantoja, a river crossing on the Río Napo (see page 417).

From Brazil  The Assis Brasil–Iñapari crossing (see page 431) is part of the Interoceanic highway. There is also a river crossing in the Amazon from Tabatinga (Brazil) and Leticia (Colombia) to Santa Rosa in Peru (see page 410).

the country. **Cruz del Sur** accepts Visa cards and gives 10% discount to ISIC and Under 26 cardholders (you may have to insist). There are also many smaller but still excellent bus lines that run only to specific areas. An increasing number accept internet bookings and you may find good deals on their websites. For a centralized information and booking sites, visit www.redbus.pe. Whatever the standard of service, accidents and hold-ups on buses do occur, especially at night; it is best to travel by day whenever possible, both for safety and to enjoy the outstanding views.

All major companies operate modern buses with two decks on interdepartmental routes. The first deck is called *bus cama;* the second, *semi-cama.* Both have seats that recline, but *bus cama* seats go back further than *semi-cama.* These buses usually run overnight and are more expensive than ordinary buses which tend to run earlier in the day. Many buses have toilets and show movies. Each company has a different name for its regular and *cama* or *ejecutivo* services. With the better companies you will get a receipt for your luggage, which will be locked under the bus. On local buses watch your luggage and never leave valuables on the luggage rack or floor, even when on the move. If your bus breaks down and you are transferred to another line and have to pay extra, keep your original ticket for a refund from the first company.

Most bus terminals charge a usage fee of about US$0.50 which you pay at a kiosk before boarding. Many also charge a small fee for use of the toilet. Take a blanket or warm jacket when travelling in the mountains. It is possible to buy food on the roadside at long-distance bus stops.

Light vehicles operate on many shorter routes, up to about five hours, and are increasingly popular, replacing bus service altogether in some areas. These may be minibuses, modern vans, older combis, or cars. The latter are called colectivos or *autos* and are usually faster (often too fast) and more expensive than the others. Luggage space is more limited than on buses, but these light vehicles make it possible, in

**Tip...**
Prices of bus tickets rise by 60-100%, two or three days before Semana Santa, 28 July (Independence Day – Fiestas Patrias), Christmas and special local events. Tickets are sold out two or three days in advance at this time and transport is hard to come by.

many cases, just to turn up and travel within an hour or two. They usually leave only when full although some adhere to a regular schedule. They go almost anywhere in Peru; most firms have offices. Book a day in advance and they may pick you up at your hotel.

## Car

You must have an international driving licence and be over 21 to drive in Peru. For other rules on bringing a car into Peru, see page 486.

**Fuel** Prices fluctuate over time and are higher in remote areas; current prices are posted on www.facilito.gob.pe. In mid-2018 90 octane petrol/gasoline cost about US$3.60; 95 octane, US$3.89; 97 octane, US$4.06. Diesel cost US$3.57.

**Car hire** The minimum age for renting a car is 25. If renting a car, your home driving licence will be accepted for up to six months. Prices reflect high costs and accident rates. Hotels and tourist agencies will tell you where to find cheaper rates, but you will need to check that the car has such basics as spare wheel, toolkit and functioning lights, etc. A test drive is recommended before signing any contracts. It can be much cheaper to rent a car in a town in the Sierra for a few days than to drive from Lima; also note that you may have to return the car to the same office where you picked it up..

## Hitchhiking

Hitchhiking in Peru is neither easy nor risk-free. A female traveller should not hitch by herself. Besides, you are more likely to get a lift if you are with a partner, whether they are male or female. The best combination is a male and female together. Positioning is also key: try toll points, although these are often far from towns. You are usually expected to pay for a ride, so always check in advance.

## Motorcycling and cycling

**Motorcycling** The motorbike should be off-road capable. Get to know the bike before you go; ask the dealers in your country what is likely to go wrong with it, and arrange a link whereby you can get parts flown out to you. Get the book for international dealer coverage from your manufacturer, but don't rely on it, since they frequently have few or no parts for modern, large machinery. An Abus D lock or chain will keep the bike secure and a cheap alarm will give you peace of mind if you have to leave the bike outside a hotel at night. Many hotels will allow you to bring the bike inside (see accommodation listings for details); look for hotels that have a courtyard or more secure parking. Never leave luggage on the bike overnight or while unattended. Passport, international driving licence and bike registration document are necessary. Riders fare much better with a *carnet de passages* than without it.

**Cycling** Unless you are planning a journey almost exclusively on paved roads – when a high-quality touring bike would suffice – a mountain bike is strongly recommended. The good-quality ones (and the cast-iron rule is **never** to skimp on quality) are incredibly tough and rugged, with low gear ratios for difficult terrain, wide tyres with plenty of tread, disk brakes, sealed hubs and bottom bracket and a low centre of gravity for improved stability. A chrome-alloy frame is a desirable choice over aluminium as it can be welded if necessary. Although touring bikes, and to a lesser extent mountain bikes and spares, are available in the larger cities, remember that most locally manufactured goods are of variable quality and rarely last. (Shimano parts are generally the easiest to find.) Buy everything you possibly can before you leave home.

Remember that you can always stick your bike on a bus, canoe or plane to get yourself nearer to where you want to go. This is especially useful when there are long stretches of major road ahead, where all that awaits you are hours of turbulence as the constant stream of heavy trucks and long-haul buses zoom by. It is possible to rent a bike for a few days, or join an organized tour for riding in the mountains. You should check, however, that the machine you are hiring is up to the conditions you will be encountering, and that the tour company is reliable.

Visit www.warmshowers.org for a hospitality exchange for touring cyclists. A related organization is Cyclo-Camping International ⓘ www.cci.asso.fr.

## Taxi

Taxi prices in the mountain towns are fixed at about US$1-1.50 for journeys in the urban area. Fares are not fixed in Lima, although some drivers work for companies that do have standard fares. Ask locals what the price should be and always set the price beforehand; expect to pay US$3-5 in the capital. The main cities have radio taxis that can be hired by phone; these charge a little more, but are usually reliable and safe. Many taxi drivers work for commission from hotels. Choose your own hotel and get a driver who is willing to take you there. Taxis at airports are much more expensive; seek advice about the price in advance. In most places it is cheaper to hail a cab that has just dropped a passenger in the departures area or walk out of the airport to the main road and flag down a cab; but this may not be safe (it is out of the question in Lima), especially at night.

Another common form of public transport is the mototaxi, a three-wheel motorcycle with an awning covering the double-seat behind the driver. Luggage space is limitted and fares are about US$1.

## Maps

Lima 2000's *Mapa Vial del Perú* (1:2,200,000) is probably the best overall map of Peru, highly recommended even if you are not driving. It is sold by bookshops in Lima but is harder to find outside the capital, see www.lima2000.com.pe. Maps are available from the Instituto Geográfico Nacional in Lima (see page 66), and online from the Ministerio de Transporte y Comunicaciones ⓘ www.mtc.gob.pe/transportes/caminos/normas_carreteras/mapas_viales.html. Maratón in Cuzco (see page 308) sells IGN topographic maps covering most of Southern Peru.

Very good tourist maps of the Cordilleras Blanca and Huayhuash, as well as Cuzco, the Sacred Valley, Arequipa and surroundings, by Felipe Díaz, are available in many book shops in Huaraz, Cuzco and Arequipa. The Österreichischer Alpenverein ⓘ www.alpenverein.at, publishes three excellent trekking maps of the region: Cordillera Blanca Nord 0/3a and Cordillera Blanca Süd 0/3b at 1:100,000; Cordillera Huayhuash 0/3c at 1:50,000. All are usually available in Huaraz and Lima, but best bought outside Peru. The Cordillera Huayhuash map, 1:50,000 (second edition, 2004) by the Alpine Mapping Guild is also recommended and is available in Huaraz at Café Andino. Trekking maps for several regions of Peru can be obtained from Trekking Peru ⓘ www.trekkingperu.org.

# Essentials A-Z

## Accidents and emergencies

**Police** T105, www.pnp.gob.pe (Policía
Nacional del Perú); **Emergency medical
attention (Cruz Roja)** T115; **Fire** T116; these
are meant to be nationwide but do not
work in all locations. **Tourist police**, Plaza
Túpac Amaru, Wanchaq, Cuzco, T084-
512351/235123; Jr Moore 268, Magdalena,
38th block of Av Brasil, Lima, T0800-
22221 nationwide toll-free; Lima T01-460
1060/0844, daily 24 hrs. They are friendly,
helpful and speak English and some German.

## Bargaining

Sooner or later almost everyone has to
bargain in Peru. Remember to do so in a
friendly and courteous manner – always with
a smile. In a country where the majority of
people live below the poverty line, foreigners
are seen as rich, even if they are backpackers
or students. In order to bring prices down, it
is extremely helpful to speak at least some
Spanish and know the fair price.

You should not bargain in restaurants,
department stores, expensive hotels or airline
offices. However, prices almost everywhere
else are negotiable. If you think a lower price
is appropriate in a cheaper hotel, ask for 'una
rebajita, por favor' ('a little discount, please').
You can negotiate the price of a tour booked
through a travel agency, but not an aeroplane,
bus or train ticket. In fact, you will probably
get a better price directly from the airline.

Bargaining is expected when you are
shopping for artwork, handicrafts, souvenirs,
or even food in the market. Remember,
though, that most of the handicrafts, including
alpaca and woollen goods, are made by
hand. Keep in mind, these people are making
a living and the 50c you save by bargaining
may buy the seller 2 loaves of bread. You
want the fair price not the lowest one.

## Customs and duty free

**On arrival** Customs inspection is carried
out at airports after you clear immigration.
Such inspection is not usually carried out at
land borders but there is often a customs
post or spot check further inside Peru.

Visitors to Peru can bring in a limited
amount of tobacco, alcohol and new articles
for personal use or gifts. The VAT for items
that are not considered duty-free but are still
intended for personal use is generally 18%.
Personal items such as laptops, cameras,
bicycles, hiking and climbing equipment
and anything else necessary for adventure
sports are exempt from taxes and should
be regarded as personal effects that will not
be sold or left in Peru. Anything that looks
like it's being brought in for resale, however,
could cause you trouble at customs.

**Goods shipped to you** Customs duties
must be paid on all goods (except for
documents) shipped to Peru. It is better
to bring anything you think you will need
with you when you travel, rather than
having it sent to you later on.

**On departure** All airline baggage is
inspected by security personnel and sniffed
by dogs for drugs. Never transport anything
you have not packed yourself, as you will be
held responsible for the contents. It is also
prohibited to take any archaeological pieces
or specimens of wild plants or animals
out of the country without a permit.

## Disabled travellers

As in most developing countries, facilities
for the disabled traveller are sadly lacking.
Wheelchair ramps are a rare luxury and
getting a wheelchair into a bathroom or
toilet is almost impossible, except in some
of the more upmarket hotels. The entrance

to many cheap hotels is up a narrow flight of stairs. Pavements are often in a poor state of repair (everybody should look out for uncovered manholes and other unexpected traps). There are similarly few facilities and services for visually and hearing-impaired travellers, but experienced guides can often provide tours with individual attention. Disabled Peruvians obviously have to cope with these problems; they mainly rely on the help of others to get on and off public transport and generally move around.

Having said that, the Peruvian government has fostered accessible tourism, and some travel companies (such as **Apumayo** in Cuzco; see page 313) now specialize in exciting holidays, tailor-made for individuals depending on their level of disability.

The **Society for Accessible Travel and Hospitality** (SATH, www.sath.org), and has lots of advice on how to travel with specific disabilities, plus listings and links.

## Drugs

Illegal drugs are the most common way for foreigners to get into serious trouble in Peru. Some people come specifically to consume or buy drugs and may have the false impression that the country is permissive in this regard. This is not the case. While drugs are easily available, anyone caught in possession will be assumed to be a trafficker. Drug use or purchase is punishable by 8 to 15 years' imprisonment and the number of foreigners in Peruvian prisons on drug charges is increasing. If arrested on any charge, the wait for trial in prison can take up to a year and is particularly unpleasant. Be wary of anyone approaching you in a club and asking where they can score – the chances are they'll be a plain-clothes cop. Likewise, never respond to offers by anyone selling drugs on the street anywhere.

Tricks employed to get foreigners into trouble over drugs include slipping a packet of cocaine into the money you are exchanging, being invited to a party or somewhere involving a taxi ride, or simply being asked on the street if you want to buy cocaine. In all cases, a plain-clothes 'policeman' will discover the planted cocaine – in your money, at your feet in the taxi – and will ask to see your passport and money. He will then return them, minus a large part of your cash. Do not get into a taxi in these circumstances, do not show your money and try not to be intimidated. Being in pairs is no guarantee of security, and single women may be particularly vulnerable. Beware also thieves dressed as policemen asking to see your passport and wanting to search for drugs; note that drug searches are only permitted if prior paperwork is done.

Many places in the Amazon and elsewhere offer experiences using the psychoactive Ayahuasca or the San Pedro cactus, often in ceremonies with a shaman. Although these are legal, be sure to choose a reputable tour operator or shaman; do not go with the first person who offers you a trip. There are plenty of websites for starting your research. Single women should not take part.

In Cuzco and Aguas Calientes many clubs and bars offer coupons for free entry and a free drink. The drinks are made with the cheapest, roughest alcohol; always watch your drink being made and never leave it unattended.

## Electricity

220 volts AC, 60 cycles throughout the country, except Arequipa (50 cycles). Most 4- and 5-star hotels have 110 volts AC. Plugs are either American flat-pin or twin flat and round pin combined.

## Embassies and consulates

For all Peru embassies and consulates abroad and for all foreign embassies and consulates in Peru, see http://embassy.goabroad.com.

## Health

### Before you travel

See your GP or travel clinic at least 6 weeks before departure for general advice on travel risks and vaccinations. Try phoning a specialist travel clinic if your own doctor is unfamiliar with health in Peru. Make sure you have sufficient medical travel insurance, get a dental check, know your own blood group and, if you suffer a long-term condition such as diabetes or epilepsy, obtain a **Medic Alert** bracelet (www.medicalert.co.uk).

### Vaccinations and anti-malarials

Confirm that your primary courses and boosters are up to date. It is advisable to vaccinate against polio, tetanus, typhoid, hepatitis A and, for more remote areas, rabies. Yellow fever vaccination is obligatory for tropical lowland areas but not for the Pacific coast or the highlands. If you plan to visit the jungle, specialist advice should be taken on the best anti-malarials to take before you leave.

### Health risks

The major risks posed in the region are those caused by insect disease carriers such as mosquitoes and sandflies. The key parasitic and viral diseases are malaria, dengue fever, and in some areas South American trypanosomiasis (Chagas' disease). **Malaria** is a danger throughout the lowland tropics and coastal regions. **Dengue fever** is particularly hard to protect against as the mosquitoes can bite throughout the day as well as at night (unlike those that carry malaria). Also spread by mosquitoes, **zika virus** is considered a risk in areas below 2000 m. Try to wear clothes that cover arms and legs and also use effective mosquito repellent. Mosquito nets dipped in permethrin provide a good physical and chemical barrier at night. **Chagas' disease** is spread by the faeces of a bug called the *vinchuca* or *chirimacha* which occurs in the north-central highlands and, with a much greater

prevalence, in southwestern Peru. Sandflies spread **leishmaniasis**, a serious skin disease; it is called *uta* in northern Peru.

Some form of **diarrhoea** or intestinal upset is almost inevitable, the standard advice is always to wash your hands before eating and to be careful with drinking water and ice. If you have any doubts about the water then boil it or filter and treat it. In a restaurant buy bottled water or ask where the water has come from. Food can also pose a problem. Be wary of salads if you don't know whether they have been washed or not, undercooked meat, reheated foods or food that has been left out in the sun having been cooked earlier in the day. There is a simple adage that says 'wash it, peel it, boil it or forget it'. The key treatment for diarrhoea is rehydration. Try to keep hydrated by taking the right mixture of salt and water. This is available as oral rehydration salts (*sales de rehidratación oral*) in ready-made sachets, or can be made up by adding a teaspoon of sugar and half a teaspoon of salt to a litre of clean water. If diarrhoea persists for several days or you develop additional symptoms, see a doctor.

There is a threat of **tuberculosis** (TB) and BCG vaccine is not guaranteed protection. Avoid unpasteurized dairy products and try not to let people cough and splutter all over you. Another risk, especially to campers and small children, is that of the **hanta virus**, which is carried by some forest and riverine rodents. Symptoms are a flu-like illness which can lead to complications. Try as far as possible to avoid rodent-infested areas, especially close contact with rodent droppings.

One of the most common problems for travellers in the highlands is **altitude sickness**. Acute mountain sickness can strike from about 3000 m upwards and is more likely to affect those who ascend rapidly (for example by plane) and those who over-exert themselves. Smokers and those with underlying heart and lung disease are often hardest hit. The sickness presents with headache, lassitude, dizziness, loss of appetite, nausea and vomiting. Insomnia is common and often associated with a suffocating feeling when lying down in bed. If the symptoms are mild, the treatment is to rest from your trip, take it easy for the first few days and drink plenty of water. Should symptoms be severe and prolonged it is best to descend to a lower altitude immediately and re-ascend, if necessary, slowly and in stages.

It is essential to get acclimatized to the thin air of the Andes before undertaking long treks or arduous activities. No one should attempt to climb over 5000 m until they have spent at least a week at around 3000 m and then a couple of nights at 4000 m. Agencies who offer 2-day climbs without adequate acclimatization are not to be trusted.

The altitude of the Andes also means that strong **protection from the sun** is always needed, regardless of how cool it may feel. Always use sunblock and a hat. Mountaineers should use glasses that provide 100% UV protection. In fact a good pair of sunglasses and a high-factor sunscreen are recommended in all parts of Peru.

### If you get sick

Make sure you have adequate insurance (see below). Contact your embassy or consulate for a list of recommended doctors and dentists who speak your language, or at least some English. Your hotel may also be able to recommend good local medical services.

**Arequipa** Clinic Arequipa SA, Puente Grau y Av Bolognesi, T054-599000, www. clinicarequipa.com.pe. Fast and efficient with English-speaking doctors and all hospital facilities. Paz Holandesa, Villa Continental, C 4, No 101, Paucarpata, T054-432281, www.pazholandesa.com. Dutch and English spoken, 24-hr service. Highly recommended.

**Cuzco** Hospital Regional, Av de la Cultura, T084-227661, emergencies T084-223691; Clínica Pardo, Av de la Cultura 710, T084-240387, 24 hrs daily, highly regarded and expensive, works with international insurance companies, some English-speaking staff;

Clínica Paredes, Calle Lechugal 405, T084-225265, www.sos-mg.com. 24 hrs daily, excellent service, emergency doctors speak good English.

**Iquitos** Clínica Ana Stahl, Av la Marina 285, T065-250025, www.clinicaanastahl.org.pe.

**Lima** Clínica Anglo Americana, Alfredo Salazar 350, San Isidro, T01-616 8900, www. angloamericana.com.pe, stocks yellow fever and tetanus; Clínica Internacional, Jr Washington 1471 y Paseo Colón (9 de Diciembre), T01-619 6161, www.clinica internacional.com.pe, good, clean and professional, consultations up to US$35, no inoculations; Instituto de Medicina Tropical, Av Honorio Delgado 430 near the Pan-American Highway in the Cayetano Heredia Hospital, San Martín de Porres, T01-482 3903, good for check-ups after jungle travel. Clínica Good Hope, Malecón Balta 956, Miraflores, T01-610 7300, www.goodhope. org.pe, has been recommended, will make visits to hotels; prices similar to US.

### Further information
Centres for Disease Control and Prevention (USA), www.cdc.gov.
Department of Health advice for travellers (UK), www.gov.uk/foreign-travel-advice.
Fit for Travel (UK), www.fitfortravel.scot. nhs.uk, a site from Scotland providing a quick A-Z of vaccine and travel health advice requirements for each country.
National Travel Health Network and Centre (NaTHNaC), www.nathnac.org.
World Health Organisation, www.who.int.

### Insurance

We strongly recommend that you invest in a good insurance policy that covers you for theft or loss of possessions and money, the cost of medical and dental treatment, cancellation of flights, delays in travel arrangements, accidents, missed departures, lost baggage and lost passport. Be sure to check on inclusion of 'dangerous activities' if you plan on doing any. These generally include climbing, diving, skiing, horse riding, parachuting, even trekking. You should always read the small print carefully. Not all policies cover ambulance, helicopter rescue or emergency flights home.

There are a variety of policies to choose from, so it's best to shop around. Your travel agent can advise on the best deals available. Reputable student travel organizations often offer good-value policies. Travellers from North America can try the **International Student Insurance Service (ISIS)**, which is available through **STA**, T800-7814040, www.statravel.com. Companies worth trying in Britain include **Direct Line Insurance**, T0845-246 8704, www.directline.com, and the **Flexicover Group**, T0800-093 9495, www.flexicover.net. Some companies will not cover those over 65. The best policies for older travellers are through **Age UK**, T0845-600 3348, www.ageuk.org.uk.

## Language

The official language is **Spanish**. Quechua, an Andean language that predates the Incas, is spoken by millions of people in the *sierra*, and some have little or no knowledge of Spanish. Quechua has been given some official status and there is much pride in its use, but it is seldom taught in schools. Another highland indigenous language is **Aymara**, used in the area around Lake Titicaca. The jungle is home to a plethora of languages, but Spanish is spoken in all but the remotest areas. **English** is not spoken widely, except by those employed in the tourism industry (eg hotel, tour agency and airline staff).

## LGBT travellers

Online resources for gay travellers in Peru are http://lima.queercity.info/index.html (a good site in English, with lots of links and information) and www.gayperu.com. The latter also has a tour operator in Miraflores, T01-447 3366, www.gayperutravel.com.

There are gay-friendly places in Cuzco, but the scene is not very active there. This does not mean, however, that there is hostility towards gay and lesbian travellers. As a major tourist centre that welcomes a huge variety of visitors, Cuzco is probably more open to gay travellers than anywhere in Peru.

## Money

*US$1 = S/3.28; £1 = S/4.36; €1 = S/3.85 (Jul 2018).*
### Currency
The sol (s/) is divided into 100 céntimos. Notes in circulation are: S/200, S/100, S/50, S/20 and S/10. Coins: S/5, S/2, S/1, S/0.50, S/0.20, S/0.10 and S/0.05 (rare). Some prices are quoted in dollars (US$) in more expensive establishments. You can pay in soles, however. Try to break down large notes whenever you can as there is a shortage of change in some places, especially small towns. Taxi drivers are notorious in this regard – one is simply told 'no change'. Do not accept this excuse.

### Checking for forgeries
Forged US$ notes and forged soles notes and coins are in circulation. Always check your money when you change it, even in a bank (including ATMs). Hold sol notes up to the light to inspect the watermark and that the colours change according to the light. The line down the side of the bill spelling out the bill's amount should appear green, blue and pink. Fake bills are only pink and have no hologram properties. There should also be tiny pieces of thread in the paper (not glued on). In parts of the country, forged S/2 and S/5 coins are in circulation. The fakes are slightly off-colour and the engraving is rough. Posters in public places explain what to look for in forged soles. See also www.bcrp.gob.pe, under **Billetes y Monedas**.

### Credit cards, ATMs and banks
Visa (by far the most widely accepted card in Peru), MasterCard, American Express and Diners Club are all accepted. There

is often an 8-12% commission for credit card charges. Bank exchange policies vary from town to town, but as a general rule the following applies (but don't be surprised if a branch has different rules): **BCP** (Mon-Fri 0900-1800, Sat 0900-1300) changes US$ cash to soles; cash advances on Visa in soles only; VíaBCP ATM with US$2 surcharge for Visa/Plus, MasterCard/Cirrus, Amex. **BBVA Continental** changes US$ cash to soles; B24 ATM for Visa/Plus has US$5 charge. **Interbank** (Mon-Fri 0900-1815, Sat 0900-1230) changes US$ cash to soles for US$5 per transaction up to US$500; branches have **Global Net** ATMs (see below). **Scotiabank** (Mon-Fri 0915-1800, Sat 0915-1230) changes US$ cash to soles, cash advances on MasterCard; ATM for Visa, MasterCard, Maestro and Cirrus. There are also **Global Net** and **Red Unicard** ATMs that accept Visa, Plus and MasterCard, Maestro and Cirrus (the former makes a charge per transaction). ATMs usually have a maximum withdrawal limit of between US$140 and US$200. It is safest to use ATMs at bank branches during banking hours. At public places like shopping malls, at night and on Sun there is more chance of the transaction going wrong. Most ATMs allow you to request either soles or US$ and their use is widespread. Availability decreases outside large towns. In smaller towns, always take some cash. Businesses displaying credit card symbols may not necessarily accept the cards.

#### Currency exchange

All banks' exchange rates are considerably less favourable than *casas de cambio* (exchange houses). Long queues and paperwork may be involved. US$ and euros are the only currencies which should be brought into Peru from abroad (take some small bills). There are no restrictions on foreign exchange. Few banks change euros. Some banks ask to see 2 documents with your signature for changing cash. Always count your money in the presence of the cashier. A repeatedly recommended *casa de cambio* is **LAC Dolar**, Jr Camaná 779, 1 block from Plaza San Martín, p 2, T01-428 8127, also at Av La Paz 211, Miraflores, T01-242 4069. Open Mon-Sat 1000-1800, good rates, very helpful, safe, fast, reliable, 2% commission on cash, will come to your hotel if you're in a group. Another recommended *casa de cambio* is **Virgen P Socorro**, Jr Ocoña 184, T01-428 7748. Open daily 0830-2000, safe, reliable and friendly. In Lima, there are many *casas de cambio* on and around Jr Ocoña off the Plaza San Martín. You can check the current exchange rate at **www.bcrp.gob.pe**, but remember that it will be a little lower outside Lima. **Moneygram**, Ocharan 260, Miraflores, T01-447 4044, is a safe and reliable agency for sending and receiving money. Locations throughout Lima and the provinces. Exchanges most world currencies, but check their rates and commissions. Soles can be exchanged into US$ at the exchange desks at Lima airport (poor rates), and you can change soles for US$ or the currency of the neighbouring country at most borders.

There is no real advantage in changing money on the street, but should you choose to do so, it does avoid paperwork and queuing. Use only official street changers, such as those around Parque Kennedy and down Av Larco in Miraflores (Lima). They carry ID cards and wear a green vest. Check your soles before handing over your US$ or euros, check their calculators, etc, and don't change money in crowded areas. If using their services, think about taking a taxi after changing to avoid being followed.

In Cuzco, many *casas de cambio* are concentrated along Av El Sol near the Plaza de Armas (see Cuzco map, page 292), so it is easy to shop around and compare rates before changing.

> **Tip...**
> There is no real advantage in changing money on the street and there is a greater chance of getting counterfeit soles.

## Cost of travelling

The average budget is US$45-60 pp a day for living fairly comfortably, including transport, based on 2 people travelling together. Your budget will be higher the longer you stay in Lima and Cuzco and depending on how many internal flights you take. Rooms range from US$7-11 pp for the most basic *alojamiento* to US$20-40 for mid-range places, to over US$90 for more upmarket hotels (more in Lima or Cuzco). Living costs in the provinces are 20-50% below those in Lima and Cuzco.

## National parks

Peru has 190 protected natural areas, including national parks and private reserves, covering 17% of the country's surface area. For information about national parks see **Servicio Nacional de Areas Naturales Protegidas por el Estado (Sernanp)**, Calle Diecisiete 355, Urbanización El Palomar, San Isidro, Lima, T01-717 7500, www.sernanp. gob.pe. See also Sernanp's app.

## Opening hours

**Banks**: see under Money, above. Outside Lima and Cuzco banks may close 1200-1500 for lunch. **Government offices**: Jan-Mar Mon-Fri 0830-1130; Apr-Dec Mon-Fri 0900-1230, 1500-1700, but these hours change frequently. **Offices**: 0900-1700; most close on Sat. **Shops**: 0900 or 1000-1230 and 1500 or 1600-2000. In the main cities, supermarkets do not close for lunch and Lima has several that are open 24 hrs.

## Post

The central Lima post office is on Jr Camaná 195 near the Plaza de Armas. Mon-Fri 0730-1900, Sat 0730-1600. In Miraflores the main post office is on Av Petit Thouars 5201 (same hours). There are many small branches around Lima and in the rest of the country, but they may be less reliable. For express service: **EMS**, next to central post office in downtown Lima, T01-533 2020.

## Public holidays

Most businesses such as banks, airline offices and tourist agencies close for the official holidays, while supermarkets and street markets usually stay open. Sometimes holidays that fall during mid-week will be moved to the following Mon to make a long weekend. See also Festivals, page 18.

1 Jan  New Year.
6 Jan  Bajada de Reyes.
1 May  Labour Day.
29 Jun  San Pedro y San Pablo.
28-29 Jul  Independence (Fiestas Patrias).
7 Oct  Battle of Angamos.
24-25 Dec  Christmas (Navidad).

## Safety

The greatest risk for travellers in Peru is the distressing frequency of road accidents; see page 490 for important advice on road and bus safety.

In terms of personal safety Peru is not a particularly dangerous country to travel in, but it is by no means crime free. You can minimize the risks by being aware of possible problems and by using a mixture of common sense and vigilance. For up-to-date public safety information contact the **tourist police** (see Accidents and emergencies, page 494), your embassy or consulate or fellow travellers.

### On the street

Take local advice about being out at night, but do not assume that daytime is necessarily safer. You should be on your guard during festivals, at markets and wherever there are crowds. Care should be taken at all times and in most parts of Lima.

Be especially careful when using ATMs and when arriving at or leaving from bus and train stations. Do not set your bag down without putting your foot on it, even just to double check your tickets. Be wary of accepting food, drink, sweets or cigarettes from unknown people on buses or trains; they may be drugged. Ruses involving 'plainclothes policemen' are infrequent, but it is worth knowing that the real police only have the right to see your passport (not your money, tickets or hotel room).

## Personal belongings

Keep all documents secure and hide your main cash supply in different places or under your clothes. Keep cameras in bags, take spare spectacles and don't wear wristwatches or jewellery. If you wear a shoulder-bag, carry it in front of you. Backpacks can be covered with a sack (a plastic one will also keep out rain and dust). Make photocopies or scans of important documents to leave at home with family or friends and send yourself an email containing details of your documents, insurance, itinerary, tickets, addresses, etc, which you can access in an emergency. Where there is no safe or locker in your room, you should be able to leave valuables in the hotel's safe-deposit box, but keep a record of what you have deposited. If none of these options is available, lock everything in your luggage and secure that in your room.

If you lose your valuables or have them stolen, always report it to the police and obtain a report for insurance purposes. Double check that all reports written by the police actually state your complaint. The **tourist police** in Lima are excellent (see Accidents and emergencies, page 494).

## Senior travellers

Those in good health should face no special difficulties travelling in Peru, but it is very important to know and respect your own limits and to give yourself sufficient time to acclimatize to altitude in the highlands. Senior discounts are not common in Peru.

## Smoking

Smoking is not permitted on buses nor in restaurants. A few better hotels have non-smoking rooms or are entirely non-smoking.

## Students travellers

Students can obtain very few reductions in Peru with an international students' card, except in and around Cuzco where such discounts are more common. To be any use in Peru, the card must bear the owner's photograph. An ISIC card can be obtained in Lima from **Intej**, Av San Martín 240, Barranco, T01-247 3230; they can also change flight itineraries bought with student cards. For other locations see www.intej.org and www.isic.org.

## Taxes

VAT/IGV/IVA is 18%.

## Telephone and Wi-Fi

*Country code+51.*
There are a diminishing number of independent phone offices, *locutorios*, in Lima and other cities as well as coin-operated payphones, but mobile (cellular) phones are by far the most common form of telecommunication. In larger cities you can purchase a SIM card (*un chip*) for US$1.50 (much more at Lima airport) for any of the main mobile carriers: **Bitel, Claro, Entel** and **Movistar**. You must show your passport; Claro is easiest, for the other you have to go to their main office in town. You get a Peruvian mobile phone number and can purchase credit (*recarga*) anywhere for as much or as little as you like. There are many pre-paid calling plans including unlimited voice, text and data. Mobile phone numbers (*celulares*) have 9 digits, landlines (*fijos*) have 7 digits in Lima, 6 elsewhere, plus an area code (e.g. 01 for Lima, 084 for Cuzco). When calling a landline from a mobile phone, you must include the area code.

Free Wi-Fi is standard at even the most basic hotels in tourist areas and at better hotels everywhere. Some cafés and public areas also have connectivity. Skype, WhatsApp, and similar services on Wi-Fi-enabled devices are the most economical form of international communication from Peru.

## Time

GMT-5.

## Tipping

**Restaurants**: service is included in the bill, but tips can be given directly to the waiter for exceptional service. **Taxi drivers**: none (bargain the price down, then pay extra for good service). **Trekking**: if going on a trek or tour, it is customary to tip the guide as well as the cook and porters.

## Toilets

Most Peruvian toilets are adequate, but the further you go from main population and tourist centres, the poorer the facilities. In cheap hotels, the toilets may not have seats. Always carry extra toilet paper or tissues with you. Used toilet paper and feminine hygiene products should not be flushed down the pan, but placed in the receptacle provided. This applies even in quite expensive hotels; when in doubt ask.

## Tourist information

Tourism promotion and information is handled by **PromPerú**, Edif Mincetur, C Uno Oeste 50, p 13 y 14, Urbanización Córpac, San Isidro, T01-616 7300, or Av República de Panamá 3647, San Isidro, T01-616 7400, www.promperu.gob.pe. See also www. peru.travel. PromPerú runs an information and assistance service, **iPerú**, T01-574 8000 (24 hrs). Main office: Jorge Basadre 610, San Isidro, Lima, T01-616 7300 or 7400, WhatsApp +51-944-492314 (24 hrs), iperulima@promperu.gob.pe, Mon-Fri 0830-1830. Also a 24-hr office at Jorge Chávez airport, and throughout the country. Service is generally excellent. For PromPerú apps, see www.peru.travel.

There are tourist offices of varying quality in most towns, usually run by the municipality. Outside Peru, information can be obtained from Peruvian embassies/consulates. **Indecopi** T01-224 7777 (in Lima), T0800-44040 (in the Provinces), www.indecopi. gob.pe, is the government consumer protection and tourist complaint bureau. They are friendly, professional and helpful.

### Useful websites

**www.caretas.com.pe** The most widely read weekly magazine, *Caretas*.
**www.leaplocal.org** Recommends good quality guides, helping communities benefit from socially responsible tourism.
**www.peruthisweek.com** Informative guide and news service in English for people living in Peru.
**www.peruviantimes.com** The *Andean Air Mail* & *Peruvian Times* internet news magazine.

### Tour operators

Peru-based operators are given in the text in the relevant chapter.

## UK and Ireland

Contact the **Latin American Travel Association (LATA)**, 46 Melbourne Rd, London SW19 3BA, www.lata.org, for useful country information and a list of all UK tour operators specializing in Latin America.

**Amazing Peru**, T0800-088 5370, T1-800-704 2915 (USA and Canada), www.amazingperu.com. Professional and well-organized tours to Peru, with knowledgeable guides.

**Andean Trails**, T0131-467 7086, www.andeantrails.co.uk. For mountain biking, trekking and other adventure tours.

**Discover South America Ltd**, T01273 921655, www.discoversouthamerica.co.uk. British-Peruvian owned operator offering tailor-made and classic holidays in South America. Specialist in off-the-beaten-track locations in Peru. ATOL-protected flights and packages from the UK.

**Dragoman**, T01728-861133, www.dragoman.com. Overland camping and/or hotel journeys throughout South America.

**Exodus Travels**, T020-3811 4311, www.exodus.co.uk. Experienced in adventure travel, including cultural tours, trekking and biking holidays.

**Explore**, T01252-883691, www.explore.co.uk. Highly respected operator. They offer small-group tours in Peru. Well executed.

**Fairtravel4u**, The Netherlands, T0615-292565, www.fairtravel4u.org. Tailor-made real-world tours in Peru, Bolivia and Ecuador.

**High Places**, T011-4352 0060, www.highplaces.co.uk. Trekking and mountaineering trips.

**Journey Latin America**, T020-8747 8315, www.journeylatinamerica.co.uk. The world's leading tailor-made specialist for Latin America, running escorted tours throughout the region; they also offer a wide range of flight options.

**KE Adventure Travel**, T01768-773966, www.keadventure.com. Specialist in adventure tours, including family trekking trips in and around Cuzco and Machu Picchu.

**Last Frontiers**, T01296-653000, www.lastfrontiers.com. South American specialists

offering tailor-made itineraries, plus family holidays and honeymoons.

**Llama Travel**, T020-7263 3000, www.llamatravel.com. Promises high-quality holidays to Latin America at the lowest possible prices.

**Naturetrek**, T01962-733051, www.naturetrek.co.uk. Birdwatching tours throughout the continent, also botany, natural history tours, treks and cruises.

**Oasis Overland**, T01963-530113, www.oasisoverland.co.uk. Small-group trips to Peru and overland tours throughout South America.

**Peruvian Secrets**, T01248-852089, www.peruviansecrets.co.uk. A leading specialist tour operator to Peru.

**Reef and Rainforest Tours**, T01803-866965, www.reefandrainforest.co.uk. Specialists in tailor-made and group wildlife tours.

**Select Latin America**, T020-7407 1478, www.selectlatinamerica.co.uk. Quality tailor-made holidays and small group tours.

**The South America Specialists**, T01252-306555, www.thesouthamericaspecialists.com. A luxury travel site for travel to South America with hotel reviews, photos and videos.

**STA Travel**, T0333-321 0099, www.statravel.co.uk. 55 branches in the UK. Low-cost flights and tours, good for students.

**Steppes Latin America**, T01285-601759, www.steppestravel.com. Tailor-made itineraries for destinations throughout Peru.

**Trailfinders**, T020-7368 1200, www.trailfinders.com. 32 branches throughout the UK. For flights and tours.

**Tribes Travel**, T01473-890499, www.tribes.co.uk. The associated charitable foundation aims to relieve poverty in indigenous communities.

### North America

**Ladatco**, T1-800 327 6162, www.ladatco.com. 'Themed' explorer tours based around the Incas, mysticism, etc.

**Peru For Less**, T1-817 230 4971, www.peruforless.com. Customized tours to Peru.

**Puchka Peru**, www.puchkaperu.com. Specializes in textiles, folk art and market tours.

**Tambo Tours**, USA, T1-888-2-GO-PERU (246 7378), www.2GOPERU.com. Long-established adventure and tour specialist with offices in Peru and the US. Customized trips to the Amazon and archaeological sites of Peru.

**Wildland Adventures**, T800-345 4453, www.wildland.com. Specializes in cultural and natural history tours to the Andes and Amazon.

### Australia

**Adventure World**, T1300-295049, www.adventureworld.com.au. Escorted group tours, locally escorted tours and packages to Peru.

**Contours Travel**, T03-9328 8488, www.contourstravel.com.au. Tours to Peru and throughout South and Central America.

## Visas and immigration

No visa is necessary for citizens of EU countries, most Asian countries, North and South America, and the Caribbean, or for citizens of Andorra, Belarus, Finland, Iceland, Israel, Liechtenstein, Macedonia, Moldova, Norway, Russian Federation, Serbia and Montenegro, Switzerland, Ukraine, Australia, New Zealand and South Africa. Tourists are granted up to 183 days stay on arrival in Peru by air or land. The length of stay is subject to an annual maximum (183 days) as well as the discretion of the immigration officer. The number of days is stamped into your passport and you may also be given a computer-generated slip with the same information. If you are given this on arrival, keep it in your passport until you leave the country, if not then you can can download and print one from www.migraciones. gob.pe (click on Consulta de TAM Virtual). The head office of Migraciones in Lima is at Av España 730, Breña, T01-200 1000, Mon-Fri 0830-1600; their website (above) has detailed information in several languages. They also have offices in all departmental capitals but offer few services of interest to most tourists.

Keep ID, preferably a passport, on you at all times. You must present your passport when reserving travel tickets. To avoid having to show your passport, you can photocopy the important pages of your passport – including the immigration stamp, and have it legalized by a 'Notario público'.

### Tourist visas

For citizens of countries not listed above (including Turkey), visas cost US$37.75 or equivalent, for which you require a valid passport, a departure ticket from Peru (or a letter of guarantee from a travel agency), 2 colour passport photos, 1 application form and proof of economic solvency. Tourist visas are valid for 183 days.

### Student visas

These must be requested from Migraciones (address and website above) once you are in Peru. In addition to completing the general visa form you must have proof of adequate funds, affiliation to a Peruvian educational institution, a letter of consent from parents or tutors if you are a minor.

### Extensions

Extensions of stay may be obtained online from www.migraciones.gob.pe (click on Prórroga de Permanencia en Línea) up to a maximum of 183 days. The fee of US$3.60 must first be paid at Banco de la Nación.

## Weights and measures

Metric.

## Women travellers

Generally women travellers should find visiting Peru an enjoyable experience. However, machismo is alive and well here; you should be prepared for this and try not to overreact. When you set out, err on the side of caution until your instincts have adjusted to the customs of a new culture.

It is easier for men to take the friendliness of locals at face value; women may be subject to much unwanted attention. To minimize this, do not wear revealing clothing. If politeness fails, do not feel bad about showing offence and departing. When accepting a social invitation, make sure that someone knows the address and the time you left. Ask if you can bring a friend (even if you do not intend to do so).

# Footnotes

Basic Spanish for travellers . . . . . .507
Index . . . . . . . . . . . . . . . . . . . . . . . .512
About the authors . . . . . . . . . . . . .520
Acknowledgements . . . . . . . . . .521
Credits. . . . . . . . . . . . . . . . . . . . . . .522

# Basic Spanish for travellers

Learning Spanish is a useful part of the preparation for a trip to Latin America and no volumes of dictionaries, phrase books or word lists will provide the same enjoyment as being able to communicate directly with the people of the country you are visiting. It is a good idea to make an effort to grasp the basics before you go. As you travel you will pick up more of the language and the more you know, the more you will benefit from your stay.

## General pronunciation

Whether you have been taught the 'Castilian' pronunciation (*z* and *c* followed by *i* or *e* are pronounced as the *th* in think) or the 'American' pronunciation (they are pronounced as *s*), you will encounter little difficulty in understanding either. Regional accents and usages vary, but the basic language is essentially the same everywhere.

### Vowels

- *a*  as in English *cat*
- *e*  as in English *best*
- *i*  as the *ee* in English *feet*
- *o*  as in English *shop*
- *u*  as the *oo* in English *food*
- *ai*  as the *i* in English *ride*
- *ei*  as *ey* in English *they*
- *oi*  as *oy* in English *toy*

### Consonants

Most consonants can be pronounced more or less as they are in English. The exceptions are:

- *g*  before *e* or *i* is the same as *j*
- *h*  is always silent (except in *ch* as in *chair*)
- *j*  as the *ch* in Scottish *loch*
- *ll*  as the *y* in *yellow*
- *ñ*  as the *ni* in English *onion*
- *rr*  trilled much more than in English
- *x*  depending on its location, pronounced *x*, *s*, *sh* or *j*

## Spanish words and phrases

### Greetings, courtesies

hello *hola*
good morning *buenos días*
good afternoon/evening/night
 *buenas tardes/noches*
goodbye *adiós/chao*
pleased to meet you *mucho gusto*
see you later *hasta luego*
how are you? *¿cómo está?/¿cómo estás?*
I'm fine, thanks *estoy muy bien, gracias*
I'm called... *me llamo...*
what is your name? *¿cómo se llama?/*
 *¿cómo te llamas?*
yes/no *sí/no*
please *por favor*

thank you (very much) *(muchas) gracias*
I speak Spanish *hablo español*
I don't speak Spanish *no hablo español*
do you speak English? *¿habla inglés?*
I don't understand *no entiendo/*
*no comprendo*
please speak slowly *hable despacio por favor*
I am very sorry *lo siento mucho/disculpe*
what do you want? *¿qué quiere?/¿qué quieres?*
I want *quiero*
I don't want it *no lo quiero*
good/bad *bueno/malo*
leave me alone *déjeme en paz/*
 *no me moleste*

## Questions and requests

Have you got a room for two people?
*¿Tiene una habitación para dos personas?*
How do I get to_? *¿Cómo llego a_?*
How much does it cost?
*¿Cuánto cuesta? ¿cuánto es?*
I'd like to make a long-distance
phone call *Quisiera hacer una llamada
de larga distancia*
Is service included? *¿Está incluido el servicio?*
Is tax included? *¿Están incluidos los impuestos?*

When does the bus leave (arrive)?
*¿A qué hora sale (llega) el autobús?*
When? *¿cuándo?*
Where is_? *¿dónde está_?*
Where can I buy tickets?
*¿Dónde puedo comprar boletos?*
Where is the nearest petrol station?
*¿Dónde está la gasolinera más cercana?*
Why? *¿por qué?*

## Basics

bank *el banco*
bathroom/toilet *el baño*
bill *la factura/la cuenta*
cash *el efectivo*
cheap *barato/a*
credit card *la tarjeta de crédito*
exchange house *la casa de cambio*
exchange rate *el tipo de cambio*

expensive *caro/a*
market *el mercado*
note/coin *le billete/la moneda*
police (policeman) *la policía (el policía)*
post office *el correo*
public telephone *el teléfono público*
supermarket *el supermercado*
ticket office *la taquilla*

## Getting around

aeroplane *el avión*
airport *el aeropuerto*
arrival/departure *la llegada/salida*
avenue *la avenida*
block *la cuadra*
border *la frontera*
bus station *la terminal de autobuses/
camiones*
bus *el bus/el autobús/el camión*
collective/fixed-route taxi *el colectivo*
corner *la esquina*
customs *la aduana*
first/second class *primera/segunda clase*
left/right *izquierda/derecha*
ticket *el boleto*
empty/full *vacío/lleno*
highway, main road *la carretera*
immigration *la inmigración*
insurance *el seguro*

insured person *el/la asegurado/a*
to insure yourself against *asegurarse contra*
luggage *el equipaje*
motorway, freeway *el autopista/la carretera*
north, south, east, west *norte, sur,
este (oriente), oeste (occidente)*
oil *el aceite*
to park *estacionarse*
passport *el pasaporte*
petrol/gasoline *la gasolina*
puncture *el pinchazo/la ponchadura*
street *la calle*
that way *por allí/por allá*
this way *por aquí/por acá*
tourist card/visa *la tarjeta de turista*
tyre *la llanta*
unleaded *sin plomo*
to walk *caminar/andar*

## Accommodation

air conditioning *el aire acondicionado*
all-inclusive *todo incluido*
bathroom, private *el baño privado*
bed, double/single *la cama matrimonial/
sencilla*

blankets *las cobijas/mantas*
to clean *limpiar*
dining room *el comedor*
guesthouse *la casa de huéspedes*
hotel *el hotel*

noisy *ruidoso*
pillows *las almohadas*
power cut *el apagón/corte*
restaurant *el restaurante*
room/bedroom *el cuarto/la habitación*
sheets *las sábanas*

shower *la ducha/regadera*
soap *el jabón*
toilet *el sanitario/excusado*
toilet paper *el papel higiénico*
towels, clean/dirty *las toallas limpias/sucias*
water, hot/cold *el agua caliente/fría*

## Health

aspirin *la aspirina*
blood *la sangre*
chemist *la farmacia*
condoms *los preservativos, los condones*
contact lenses *los lentes de contacto*
contraceptives *los anticonceptivos*
contraceptive pill *la píldora anti-conceptiva*
diarrhoea *la diarrea*

doctor *el médico*
fever/sweat *la fiebre/el sudor*
pain *el dolor*
head *la cabeza*
period/sanitary towels *la regla/
las toallas femeninas*
stomach *el estómago*
altitude sickness *el soroche*

## Family

family *la familia*
friend *el amigo/la amiga*
brother/sister *el hermano/la hermana*
daughter/son *la hija/el hijo*
father/mother *el padre/la madre*

husband/wife *el esposo (marido)/la esposa*
boyfriend/girlfriend *el novio/la novia*
married *casado/a*
single/unmarried *soltero/a*

## Months, days and time

January *enero*
February *febrero*
March *marzo*
April *abril*
May *mayo*
June *junio*
July *julio*
August *agosto*
September *septiembre*
October *octubre*
November *noviembre*
December *diciembre*

Monday *lunes*
Tuesday *martes*
Wednesday *miércoles*

Thursday *jueves*
Friday *viernes*
Saturday *sábado*
Sunday *domingo*

at one o'clock *a la una*
at half past two *a las dos y media*
at a quarter to three *a cuarto para las tres/
a las tres menos quince*
it's one o'clock *es la una*
it's seven o'clock *son las siete*
it's six twenty *son las seis y veinte*
it's five to nine *son las nueve menos cinco*
in ten minutes *en diez minutos*
five hours *cinco horas*
does it take long? *¿tarda mucho?*

## Numbers

one *uno/una*
two *dos*
three *tres*
four *cuatro*
five *cinco*
six *seis*
seven *siete*

eight *ocho*
nine *nueve*
ten *diez*
eleven *once*
twelve *doce*
thirteen *trece*
fourteen *catorce*

fifteen *quince*
sixteen *dieciséis*
seventeen *diecisiete*
eighteen *dieciocho*
nineteen *diecinueve*
twenty *veinte*
twenty-one *veintiuno*
thirty *treinta*

forty *cuarenta*
fifty *cincuenta*
sixty *sesenta*
seventy *setenta*
eighty *ochenta*
ninety *noventa*
hundred *cien/ciento*
thousand *mil*

**Food**
See also Menu reader, page 33.
avocado *la palta*
baked *al horno*
bakery *la panadería*
banana *la banana*
beans *los frijoles/las habichuelas*
beef *la carne de res*
beef steak *el lomo*
boiled rice *el arroz blanco*
bread *el pan*
breakfast *el desayuno*
butter *la manteca*
cake *la torta*
chewing gum *el chicle*
chicken *el pollo*
chilli or green pepper *el ají/pimiento*
clear soup, stock *el caldo*
cooked *cocido*
dining room *el comedor*
egg *el huevo*
fish *el pescado*
fork *el tenedor*
fried *frito*
garlic *el ajo*
goat *el chivo*
grapefruit *la toronja/el pomelo*
grill *la parrilla*
grilled/griddled *a la plancha*
guava *la guayaba*
ham *el jamón*
hamburger *la hamburguesa*
hot, spicy *picante*
ice cream *el helado*
jam *la mermelada*
knife *el cuchillo*

lemon *el limón*
lobster *la langosta*
lunch *el almuerzo/la comida*
meal *la comida*
meat *la carne*
minced meat *la carne picada*
onion *la cebolla*
orange *la naranja*
pepper *el pimiento*
pasty, turnover *la empanada/el pastelito*
pork *el cerdo*
potato *la papa*
prawns *los camarones*
raw *crudo*
restaurant *el restaurante*
salad *la ensalada*
salt *la sal*
sandwich *el bocadillo*
sauce *la salsa*
sausage *la longaniza/el chorizo*
scrambled eggs *los huevos revueltos*
seafood *los mariscos*
soup *la sopa*
spoon *la cuchara*
squash *la calabaza*
squid *los calamares*
supper *la cena*
sweet *dulce*
to eat *comer*
toasted *tostado*
turkey *el pavo*
vegetables *los legumbres/vegetales*
without meat *sin carne*
yam *el camote*

## Drink

beer *la cerveza*
boiled *hervido/a*
bottled *en botella*
camomile tea *la manzanilla*
canned *en lata*
coffee *el café*
coffee, white *el café con leche*
cold *frío*
cup *la taza*
drink *la bebida*
drunk *borracho/a*
firewater *el aguardiente*
fruit milkshake *el batido/licuado*
glass *el vaso*
hot *caliente*
ice/without ice *el hielo/sin hielo*
juice *el jugo*
lemonade *la limonada*
milk *la leche*
mint *la menta*
rum *el ron*
soft drink *el refresco*
sugar *el azúcar*
tea *el té*
to drink *beber/tomar*
water *el agua*
water, carbonated *el agua mineral con gas*
water, still mineral *el agua mineral sin gas*
wine, red *el vino tinto*
wine, white *el vino blanco*

## Key verbs

| to go | ir |
|---|---|
| I go | *voy* |
| you go (familiar) | *vas* |
| he, she, it goes, you (formal) go | *va* |
| we go | *vamos* |
| they, you (plural) go | *van* |

| to have (possess) | tener |
|---|---|
| I have | *tengo* |
| you (familiar) have | *tienes* |
| he, she, it, you (formal) have | *tiene* |
| we have | *tenemos* |
| they, you (plural) have | *tienen* |
| there is/are | *hay* |
| there isn't/aren't | *no hay* |

| to be | ser | estar |
|---|---|---|
| I am | soy | estoy |
| you are | eres | estás |
| he, she, it is, you (formal) are | es | está |
| we are | somos | estamos |
| they, you (plural) are | son | están |

(*ser* is used to denote a permanent state, whereas *estar* is used to denote a positional or temporary state.)

This section has been assembled on the basis of glossaries compiled by André de Mendonça and David Gilmour of South American Experience, London, and the Latin American Travel Advisor, No 9, March 1996.

# Index

*Entries in bold refer to maps*

## A

Abancay 322, 383
Abra Málaga pass 352
accidents 494
accommodation 28
  price codes 28
Achoma 243
Acobamba 385
Acomayo Lakes Circuit 319
Acora 265
Aguas Calientes 279, 343, **344**
Aguas Verdes 148
Aguaytía 399
Ahuashiyacu Falls 184
air travel 485, 488
Alca 250
Alis 197
Allpahuayo-Mishana Reserve 410
alpaca clothing 25
Alpamayo Trek 14
Amantaní 276
Amarakaeri Communal Reserve 422
Amarucancha 291
Ambo 386
Anapia 276
Anco 365
Andagua 249
Andahuaylas 382
Andahuaylillas 317
Andamarca 213
Aplao 249
Apurímac Canyon 322
architecture 446
Arco Deustua 263
Area de Conservación Regional Cordillera Escalera 183
Arequipa 222, **224**, **226**, **228**
  rafting 237
Arte y Joyas Arqueológicas del Perú 133
arts and crafts 459
Assis Brasil 431
Atalaya 419
Atuncolla 264
512·Index

Ausangate Trek **318**, 319
Ayacucho 374, **375**
  Barrio Santa Ana 377
Ayaviri 279
Aymaña 281
Aymara, language 498
Azángaro 280

## B

Bagua Grande 188
Baños Termales San Mateo 182
Barco Ayapua 407
bargaining 494
birdwatching 19
Boca Colorado 422
Boca Manu 421
bodegas 202
books 482
Boquerón del Padre Abad 399
border crossings 491
  Bolivia 284
  Brazil 410, 431
  Chile 254
  Colombia 410
  Ecuador 146, 148
Bosque de Cañoncillo 120
Bosque de Protección Alto Mayo 182
Bretaña 405
bus travel 490

## C

Cabanaconde 243, **244**
Cachora 323
Cahuachi 212
Cajabamba 159
Cajamarca 158, 161, **161**
  Archaeological and Ethnological Museum 162
Calca 328
Caleta La Cruz 147
Callán Pass 110
Callejón de Huaylas 94
Camino Real de los Inkas 350
Campiña de Moche 117
camping 29

Campo de la Alianza 254
Cañete 196
canoes 488
Cañón del Pato 110
canyons 475
Capac Ñan 364
Caral 108, 439
Caraz 95, **95**, **96**
Carhuaz 94
car hire 492
Carretera Binacional 253
Carretera Interoceánica 490
Casapalca 360
Casma 109, 110
Catac 90
Catacaos 143
Cataneo 168
Cataratas de Sipia 250
Cataratas Gloriapata 399
Ccotos 264
Celendín 168
Central Railway 361
Centro de Rescate Amazónico 410
Cerro Amaru 159
Cerro Baúl 253
Cerro Blanco 212
Cerro de Pasco 386
Cerro La Raya 134, 135
Cerro San Cristóbal 45, 46
Chacas 92
Chachani 228
Chachapoyas **169**, 171, **171**, **189**
Chala 213
Chalhuanca 213
Chan Chán 117
Chaparrí Reserve 134
Chaquicocha 350
Chauchilla 212
Chavín de Huántar 91
Checacupe 317
Chicla 360
Chiclayo 130, **131**
Chifrón 264
Chimbote 109

Chimur 317
Chinata 174
Chincha Alta 198
Chinchero 329
Chipuric 173
Chivay 241
Choquequirao 322
Chorrillos 54
Chucuito 265
Chuhuanquiri 352
Chullo 242
Chuquibamba 249
Churca 250
Churubamba 387
climate 17
climbing 19
Cocachimba 173
Cocalmayo Thermal Baths 353
Cocha Machuhuasi 419
Cochas Chico 365
Cochas Grande 365
Colán 143
Colca Canyon 241
Collpa Chuncho 429
Collpa Colorado 429
Collpa Heath 430
colonial houses 225
community tourism 20
Concepción 361
Copacabana 284
Coporaque 241
Cordillera Blanca 78
Cordillera Carabaya 280
Cordillera Escalera 184
Cordillera Huayhuash
  101, **102**, 387
Cordillera Vilcanota 318
Corire 249
Cotahuasi 250
Cotahuasi Canyon 249
Court of Inquisition 42
Cristo Pobre 360
Cruz del Cóndor 242, 243
Cuartel Huain 101
Cueva de las Lechuzas 399
cuisine 30
Cuispes 174
culture 459
Cumbe Mayo 163
Cusicancha 291

Cusipata 317
customs 494
Cutimbo 264
Cuzco 286, **292**, **294**
  Calle Hatun Rumiyoc 295
  listings 297
  Museo de Arte
    Precolombino 296
  Museo Inka 295
  Plaza de Armas 290
  Qoricancha 291
  San Blas 295
  Santa Catalina 291
  Santo Domingo 291
cycling 492

### D

Darwin, Charles 44
Desaguadero 266, 284
Diamante 419
disabled travellers 494
diving 20
dress 47
drink 31
drugs 495
duty free allowance 494

### E

EcoMuseo Molino de Piedra
  San José 173
Ekeko 270
El Brujo 118
El Candelabro 199
El Carmelo 202
El Carmen 116
El Castillo de Lamas 184
El Catador 202
electricity 495
El Edén 159
El Irapay Interpretation Centre
  410
El Misti 228
El Molinete 168
El Purgatorio 134
El Triunfo 290
embassies and consulates 495
Escallani 264
Espíritu Pampa 352
Estaquería 212

### F

Ferreñafe 136
festivals 18, 465
food 30
Fundo Chincheros 263

### G

Garu 387
geography 474
Gibbs-Ricketts house 225
Gocta 173
Gocta waterfall 173
government 454

### H

handicrafts 25
hang-gliding 21
Hatun Infiernillo 243
health 496
High Inca Trail 350
history 439
hitchhiking 492
hospedajes 28
hotels 28
  price codes 28
Huaca Arco Iris 118
Huacachina 201
Huaca de las Balsas 135
Huaca del Sol 116
Huaca El Dragón 118
Huaca El Mirador 135
Huaca La Esmeralda 118
Huaca Larga 135
Huaca Las Estacas 135
Huaca Pintada 135
Huaca Pucllana 50
Huacho 108
Hualahoyo 365
Hualhuas 365
Huallamarca 49
Huallanca 109
Huallay 386
Huamachuco 159
Huambocancha 163
Huambutío 317
Huancacalle 352
Huancas 172
Huanca Urco 172
Huancavelica 370, **370**

Huancaya 197
Huancayo 363, **363**
Huanchaco 118, **119**
Huanta 365
Huánuco 386, **387**
Huaquillas 148
Huaraz 79, **80**, **82**
  Cathedral 79
  Museo Arqueológico de
    Ancash 79
  Sala de Cultura SUNARP 79
Huari 92, 377
Huaricolca 385
Huarmey 109
Huaro 317
Huayhuash trekking circuit 101
Huayllabamba 350
Huayna Picchu 342
Huchuy Cuzco 328
Huembo 181
Humay 198

**I**

Iberia 431
Ica 200
Ichupampa 241
Ilave 265
Iñapari 431
Inca bridge 343
Inca fortress 327
Inca Jungle Trail 351
Inca Kola 54
Incas 443
Inca salt pans 330
Inca stonework 291
Inca Trail 347, **348**
Incawasi 196
Inkatiana 276
insurance 497
Intihuatana 378
Intipunku 343, 350
Iquitos 407, **408**
  Belén 402
Isla Foca 143
Islas Ballestas 200
Isla Suasi 281
Itahuanía 419
Izcuchaca 365, 371

**J**

Jaén 188
Jalca Grande 168
Jardín Botánico Chullachaqui
    401
Jardín de Plantas Medicinales y
    Frutales 410
Jauja 360
Juanjui 184
Judiopampa 250
Julcamarca 371
Juli 265
Juliaca 278
Julio C Tello Site Museum 199
Junín 386
Junín National Reserve 386

**K**

Karajía 173
kayaking 20
Kótosh 386
Kuélap 170
Kuélap cable car 170
Kuntur Wasi 163

**L**

La Balsa 189
La Bella Durmiente 399
La Calera 241
La Caravedo 202
La Casita de mi Abuela 94
La Catedral 199
La Congona 168
Lago Sandoval 429
Lago Tres Chimbadas 429
Lago Valencia 429
Lago Yarinacocha 400
La Grama 159
Laguna 69 95
Laguna Azul 184
Laguna Chinancocha 95
Laguna Churup 81
Laguna de los Cóndores 168
Laguna de Paca 361
Laguna Orconcocha 95
Laguna Parón 97
Lagunas 405
Lagunas de Llanganuco 95
Lagunilla 199

Lake Titicaca 265
La Mansión del Fundador 227
Lamas 184
Lamay 328
Lambayeque 132
  Brüning Archaeological
    Museum 132
La Merced 385
Lampa 278
Lamud 173
language 498
La Oroya 360
La Paz 284
La Raya 279
La Recoleta 225
Lari 241
La Ruta de los Lagares 202
La Ruta del Pisco 253
Las Cattleyas 184
Las Pocitas 147
La Unión 387
Leoncio Prado 405
Leticia 410
Levanto 172
Leymebamba 168
LGBT travellers 498
Lima 34, **38**, **43**
  Alameda Chabuca Granda 42
  Archbishop's Palace and
    museum 39
  Barranco 51, **52**, 54
  beaches 54
  Breña 46
  Casa de Jarava or Pilatos 40
  Casa de la Gastronomía
    Nacional Peruana 40
  Casa de la Literatura 40
  Casa de la Rada 40
  Casa de las Trece Monedas
    40
  Casa de Osambela 42
  Casa Solariega de Aliaga 39
  cathedral 39
  Centro Comercial Larcomar
    49
  Circuito Mágico del Agua 45
  Desamparados railway
    station 40
  El Olivar 49
  Goyeneche 40
  Gran Hotel Bolívar 45

Gran Parque Cultural de Lima 45
House of the Mamaconas 54
Instituto de Arte Contemporáneo 45
La Merced 44
Las Nazarenas 42
listings 55
Lugar de la Memoria, la Tolerancia y la Inclusion Social (LUM) 50
MATE (Asociación Mario Testino) 53
Mateo Salado archaeological site 46
Miraflores 49, **50**, 54
Museo Banco Central de Reserva 40
Museo de Arte de Lima 45
Museo de Arte Italiano 45
Museo de Arte Religioso 39
Museo del Congreso y de la Inquisición 41
Museo de Sitio Bodega y Quadra 40
Museo Metropolitano 45
Oquendo 42
Palacio de Gobierno 39
Palacio de la Exposición 45
Palacio Torre Tagle 40
Parque de la Exposición 45
Parque de la Muralla 40
Parque de la Reserva 45
Parque del Amor 49
Parque Kennedy 49
Parque Salazar 49
Pasaje Ribera el Viejo 39
Plaza Bolívar 41
Plaza de Acho 45
Plaza de Armas (Plaza Mayor) 39
Plaza San Martín 44
Pueblo Libre 46
Puente de los Suspiros 51
Puente de Piedra 45
San Agustín 42
San Borja 46
San Francisco 40
San Isidro 49
San Pedro 40
San Pedro market 295
Santo Domingo 42
Santuario de Santa Rosa 42
shanty towns 48
Surco 46
Lircay 371
literature 466
Llachón 264
Llahuar 244
Llapay 196
Llulluchapampa 350
Llulluchayoc 350
Los Baños del Inca 162
Luicho 250
Lunahuaná 196
Luquina Chico 265
Luya 173

## M

Maca 243
Machu Picchu 339, **341**
Machu Picchu Mountain 342
Macusani 280
Madrigal 241
Malecón Benavides 147
Máncora 147
Mancos 94
Mantaro Valley 365
Manu Biosphere Reserve 419
Manu National Park 419, **421**
Manu Reserved Zone 421
Manu Wildlife Center 422
maps 493
Maranganí 279
Maras 330
Marca Huamachuco 159
Marcahuasi 360
Marcapata 319
Maria Reiche Centre 210
Maria Reiche Planetarium 210
Maria Reiche Planetarium and Observatory 241
Mayocc 365
Mazuko 280, 422
Megantoni Sanctuary 420
Mendoza 172
menu reader 33
MN Coya 264
Moche culture 113
Moho 281
Molino de Sabandía 227
money 498
Monsefú 131
Montevideo 168
Moquegua 253
Moray 329
Morococha 360
Morro de Calzada 183
Mórrope 133
motorcycling 492
Moyobamba 182, **182**
MS Ollanta 264
Museo Amazónico 407
Museo Andrés A Cáceres 376
Museo Antonini 209
Museo Arqueológico Amano 49
Museo Arqueológico y Etnológico 162
Museo Arqueológico Bruning 132
Museo Arqueológico Julio Espejo Núñez 360
Museo Banco Central de Reserva 40
Museo Carlos Dreyer 262
Museo Comunitario Pisac 327
Museo Contisuyo 253
Museo de Antropología y Arqueología Hipólito Unanue 377
Museo de Arqueología, Trujillo 116
Museo de Arqueología Universidad Católica de Santa María UCSM 226
Museo de Arte Colonial, Cajamarca 162
Museo de Arte Colonial Pedro de Osma 53
Museo de Arte Contemporáneo de Arequipa 226
Museo de Arte Contemporáneo de Lima (MAC Lima) 53
Museo de Arte de Lima 45
Museo de Arte Italiano 45
Museo de Arte Moderno, Trujillo 116
Museo de Arte Precolombino, Cuzco 296

Museo de Arte Religioso, Lima 39

Museo de Arte Religioso, Cuzco 295

Museo de Arte Virreinal, Arequipa 225

Museo de Culturas Indígenas Amazónicas 407

Museo de la Coca y Costumbres, Puno 263

Museo de la Nación, Lima 46

Museo de la República, Trujillo 116

Museo de las Tumbas Reales de Sipán 132

Museo del Congreso y de la Inquisición 41

Museo del Juguete, Trujillo 116

Museo de los Pueblos 317

Museo de Moche, Trujillo 116

Museo de Oro del Perú, Lima 46

Museo de Sitio Bodega y Quadra 40

Museo de Sitio Huaca Rajada 134

Museo de Sitio Qorikancha 294

Museo de Zoología de Juan Ormea 116

Museo Folklórico, Pisac 327

Museo Haya de la Torre (Casa del Pueblo), Trujillo 116

Museo Hermógenes Mejía Solf 188

Museo Histórico de Paracas 200

Museo Histórico Municipal, Arequipa 225

Museo Huacas de Moche 117

Museo Inka, Cuzco 295

Museo Kampac 279

Museo Larco de Lima 47

Museo Leymebamba 168

Museo Los Chankas 184

Museo Machupicchu 291

Museo Manuel Chávez Ballón y Jardín Botánico 343

Museo María Reiche 210

Museo Máximo Laura 295

Museo Médico Belén 162

Museo Metropolitano 45

Museo Municipal Vicús 143

Museo Municipal Wamachuko 159

Museo Nacional Chavín 92

Museo Nacional de Antropología, Arqueología e Historia 47

Museo Nacional Sicán 136

Museo Santa Ana 171

Museo Santuarios Andinos 223

Museo Silvo-agropecuario 162

Museo Taurino 45

music 462

## N

Nahua-Kugapakori Reserved Zone 420

Namballe 189

Narihuala Archaeological Site 143

national parks 500

Nauta 405

Nazca Lines 210

Nazca town 209, **209**

Nevado Mismi 242

Nor Yauyos Cochas Reserve 364

Nuevo Edén 419

## O

Ocongate 318

Ocucaje 202

Ollantaytambo 331, **332**

Ollantaytambo temple fortress 332

Olleros 90

Olmos 136

Oropesa 316

Orquideario Waqanki 182

Owlet 181

Oxapampa 385

## P

Pacasmayo 120

Pacaymayo 350

Pachacámac 53

Pacha Mama 276

Pacha Tata 276

packing 486

Paita 143

Palma, Ricardo 49

Pampaconas 352

Pampa de Quinua 378

Pampamarca 250

Pampas de Junín 386

Paracas National Reserve 198, 199

Paramonga 109

parapenting 21

Paredones ruins and aqueduct 210

Pariacoto 110

Parjugsha 173

Parque de Identidad Wanka 364

Parque de la Locomotora 254

Parque Nacional Bahuaja-Sonene 281, 429, **430**

Parque Nacional Cerros de Amotape 147

Parque Nacional Cordillera Azul 184

Parque Nacional Huascarán 77

Parque Nacional Manu 317

Parque Nacional Tingo María 399

Patria 419

Paucartambo 317

pedal boats 263

Pedro Ruiz 181

Península de Capachica 264

pensiones 28

people 455

photography 26

Phuyupatamarca 350

Pichingoto 330

Picota 184

Pikimachay 365

Pilcopata 419

Pilpintuhuasi Butterfly Farm 409

Pimentel 131

Pinchollo 243

Pintish Machay 385

Piquillacta 317

Pisac 327, **327**

Piscacucho 347

pisco 31

Pisco 198

Piscobamba 93

Piura 142, **142**

police 501

Pomabamba 93
Pomata 266
Porcón 163
price codes 28
public holidays 500
Pucallpa 399, **400**
Pucará 279
Puente Callalli 242
Puente Iñambari 280
Puente Santo Tomás 168
Puerto Acosta 284
Puerto Bermúdez 385
Puerto Callao 400
Puerto Chicama 120
Puerto de Tahuishco 182
Puerto Eten 132
Puerto Inca 213
Puerto Maldonado 428, **428**
Puka Pukara 297
Puno 262, **262, 280**
  Buque Museo Yavarí 263
Punta Cacanan Pass 101
Punta Olímpica 92
Punta Sal 147
Pusharo Petroglyphs 419
Putina 281
Putina Punco 281
Puya raimondii 97, 98
Puyca 250

**Q**

Qenqo 297
Q'eswachaka 319
Qoricancha 291
Qorihuayrachina 350
Quebrada de Lunahuaná 196
Quechua, language 498
Quechualla 250
Queshque Gorge 91
Quichuas 365
Quincemil 422
Quinua 378
Quiocta cave 173

**R**

rafting 22, 237
rail travel 488
Rainbow Mountain 297
Raqchi 319
Reiche, Maria 211

religion 459
Reserva Nacional del Titicaca 281
Reserva Nacional de San Fernando 213
Reserva Nacional Pacaya-Samiria 404
Reserva Nacional Pampa Galeras Bárbara D'Achille 213
Reserva Paisajística Nor Yauyos-Cochas (RPNYC) 197
restaurants 32
  price codes 28
Rímac 45
Río Huallaga 386
Río Las Piedras 429
Río Majes Valley 249
Río Marañón 388
river travel 486, 488
road travel 486, 490
Rosaspata 352
Ruiz de Ochoa 376
Runkuracay 350
Ruta del Pisco 198

**S**

Sacsamarca 371
Sacsayhuaman 296
safety 500
Salkantay 350, **351**
Salvación 419
San Agustín de Cajas 365
San Bartolo 168
San Carlos 174
San Cristóbal 296
San Cristóbal thermal baths 371
Sandia 281
San Gabán 280
Sangalle 243
San Ignacio 188
San Jerónimo de Tunan 365
San Juan Bautista 226
San Juan del Oro 281
San Lázaro 225
San Luis 92
San Marcos 92
San Pablo de Valera 173
San Pedro 320, 365, 419
San Pedro de Cajas 385
San Pedro de Casta 360

San Pedro de Mórrope 133
San Pedro de Utac 168
San Ramón 385
Santa Apolonia hill 162
Santa Bárbara mine 371
Santa Catalina 291
Santa Cruz Valley 97
Santa Inés 371
Santa María 264, 352
Santa Rita 408
Santa Rosa 132, 279, 410
Santa Teresa 352, 376
Santa Teresa Trek 351
Santo Tomás 409
Santuario de Muruhuay 385
Santuario Huayllay (Bosque de Piedras) 386
Santuario Nacional de Ampay 383
Santuario Nacional los Manglares de Tumbes 147
Santuario Tabaconas-Namballe 188
Santuario y Reserva Nacional Calipuy 120
San Vicente de Cañete 196
Sauce 184
Sayacmarca 350
Saywite 383
Sechín 109
Sechura Desert 133
Selva Central 385
Shintuya 419
Shipitiari 419
shopping 25
Sibayo 242
Sicán (El Santuario Histórico Bosque de Pómac) 136
Sicuani 279
Sihuas 93
Sillustani 264
Sipán 133
Sistema de Islas, Islotes y Puntas Guaneras (SIIPG) National Reserve 200
Sol Nasciente 399
Sondondo Valley 213, 378
Sóndor 382
Spanish, language 498
student travellers 501
Sucuni 281

Sullana 146
Sumbay 242
surfing 22

## T

Tabatinga 410
Tacama 202
Tacna 254
Tambo Blanquillo 422
Tambo Colorado 198
Tambo Machay 297
Tambopata National Reserve 429, **430**
Tantamayo 388
Tapay 241, 244
Taquile 274
Tarabamba 330
Tarapoto 183, **183**
Tarma 385
tax 501
taxis 493
telephone 501
Ticonata 264
Tilali 281, 284
Tingo 227
Tingo María 399
Tingo Viejo 170
Tinqui 318
Tinta 319
Tipón ruins 316
tipping 502
Tocache 184
Tomepampa 250
Torata 253
Toro Muerto 249
Torre-Torre 365
train travel 488
transport 485-493
trekking 14, 23, 88, 96, 243
Tres Cruces 317
Tristan, Flora 44, 47
Trocha Ericson 317

Trocha Unión 317
Trujillo 112, **114**
Tschudi, Jean Jacques 44
Túcume 134
Túcume Viejo 135
Tumbes 147
Tumshukaiko 96
Tuti 242

## U

Ubilón 168
Universidad de Trujillo 114
Upper Cañete Valley 196
Upper Marañón 387
Uros Islands 274
Urubamba 328

## V

vaccinations 496
Valle de Lares 328, **329**
Valle de los Volcanes 249
Vargas Llosa, Mario 226, 468
Velinga 250
Ventanillas 162
Ventanillas de Combayo 163
Ventanillas de Otusco 162
Ventarrón 134
Vichayito 147
Vilcabamba 352
Vilcabamba Vieja 352
Vilcanota Valley 316
Vilcashuamán 378
Vilcauta 266
Viñas Queirolo 202
Vitcos 352
volcanoes 476
volunteering 24
von Humboldt, Alexander 44

## W

Wanglic 173
Warivilca 365

Warmiwañuska 350
Watoqto 317
Wayku 184
Wayrasacha 183
Wi-Fi 501
Willkawain 80
Wiñay-Wayna 350
Winchos 98
wineries 202
Wiracochapampa 159
women travellers 505

## Y

Yalape 172
Yalpana Wasi 364
Yanahuara 226
Yanama 93
Yanaoca 319
Yanque 242
Yarina 400
Yarinacocha 400
Yarowilca 387, 388
Yasila 143
Yauli 371
Yauyos 196
Yerbabuena 168
youth hostels 29
Yucay 328
Yumbilla 174
Yumina 227
Yungay 94, **96**
Yunguyo 266, 284
Yurac Rumi 352
Yurimaguas 184, 404
Yuspique 276

## Z

Zaña 130
Zepita 266
Zona Reservada de Tumbes 148
Zorritos 147

## FOOTPRINT

### Features

A blooming century 97
A fashion for passion 47
A lasting tradition 276
A month of festivals 307
Ancient apparel 235
An economic mess 199
Appeasing the gods 227
Arequipa's gastronomy 232
Arriving at night 71
A tale of fish and demons 135
Border crossings 491
Constitution and government 454
Court of Inquisition 42
Gastronomic Lima 60
Guardian of the Lines 211
How deep is that canyon? 243
Impressions of Lima 44
Inca Kola 54
Inca stonework 291
King Kong in Lambayeque 132
Lampa: living in the past 279
Like the fish and birds of the water 275
Lima's shanty towns 48
Mario Vargas Llosa 468

Masters of sculpture 113
Menu reader 33
Old Lord of Sipán 133
Packing for Peru 486
Pisco: a history in the making 201
Pot luck 270
Rafting around Arequipa 237
Railways of the central highlands 361
Rubber barons 409
Sacred lake 265
Stairway to heaven 364
Textiles and trepanation 200
The Afro-Peruvian experience since 1532 456
The high price of minerals 453
The Huari influence 377
The last bridge 320
The last Incas of Vilcabamba 353
The stone gods of Chavín 91
The Upper Marañón 388
Trekking and climbing in the cordilleras 88
Vikings in the cloudforest? 172
Viringo 478

### Advertisers' index

Amazonas Explorer, Peru 313
Amazon Trails Peru, Peru 425
Andina Travel, Peru 311
Café Andino, Peru 85
Crillon Tours, Bolivia 271
ECOAN, Peru 181
Exclusive English, Peru 368
Fairtravel4u, The Netherlands 502
Fertur Peru Travel, Peru 69
Journey Latin America, UK inside back cover

Kuntur Adventure & Tourism (K.A.T.), Peru 238
Llama Travel, UK 504
Oasis Overland, UK 504
Peter Frost, Peru 290
Rainforest Expeditions, Peru 434
Runa Turismo, Peru 140
Select Latin America, UK 503
Trekking Peru, Peru 23
Vamos Expeditions, Peru 68
Vilaya Tours, Peru 179

# **About** the authors

### Robert and Daisy Kunstaetter

Robert and Daisy's experience with Peru goes back to the 1980s. Even so, it was not until they spent 18 months trekking and travelling throughout the country, covering 1400 km on foot between 2013 and 2015, that they began to really feel comfortable with it. Daisy hails from neighbouring Ecuador, Robert from Canada, and they had regularly travelled in Peru for work and play. But it was in both their natures as well as the nature of Peru that they had to walk the land in order to understand it.

Over the preceding years and miles, Robert and Daisy had become regular correspondents for Footprint, helping to update annual editions of the *South American Handbook*. Based in Ecuador since 1993, they have been closely involved with tourism there as well as in Peru and Bolivia. They are authors, co-authors, contributors to, and cartographers for numerous Footprint guidebooks. They have also written trekking guides to Ecuador and Peru. Their most recent explorations have taken them to remote areas along the upper reaches of the Río Marañón.

Robert and Daisy's learning experience with Peru continues and, in the words of a close friend and colleague, there remain at least three lifetimes-worth of ground for them to cover.

### Correspondents

**Chris Benway** Originally from the USA, Chris lives in Huaraz with his wife Isabel and their two sons. He runs a popular café and provides logistic support for mountaineering groups and expeditions. Chris updated Huaraz and parts of the Cordillera Blanca.

**Rob Dover** Rob came to Peru from England and lives in Chachapoyas with his wife Sadie and their daughter Charlotte. He is a very experienced guide and leads tours throughout the region. Rob updated Cajamarca and Chachapoyas.

**Leo Duncan** Having lived in Canada and Ecuador, Leo makes his home in Cuzco. He collaborated with his father, Peter Frost, on their *Exploring Cuzco* guidebook and has an in-depth knowledge of the intricacies of this complex region. Leo updated Cuzco and the Sacred Valley.

**Ricardo Espinosa** Ricardo was born in Lima and lives in Caraz with his wife Analee and their son Zat. He is a legendary *caminante* (trekker) and has written well-known accounts of his epic journeys: along the entire desert coast of Peru (*El Perú a toda Costa*,1997); and from Quito (Ecuador) to La Paz (Bolivia) along the great Inca road that traverses the highlands of Peru (*La Gran Ruta Inca*, 2002). Ricardo updated the South coast and Caraz.

**Annelies Hamerlinck, Pablo Moreno and Alvaro Montoya** Annelies, originally from Belgium, and Pablo, from Lima, run a popular tour agency in Lima, specializing in tailor-made programs. Along with their colleague Alvaro, they undertook the daunting task of updating Peru's seemingly boundless capital city.

**Klaus Hartl** Klaus grew up in the Czech Republic and Germany and divides his time between Arequipa, where his wife and two sons live, and the jungle outside Puerto Maldonado. An accomplished cyclist, bicycle tour leader, trekker and traveller, Klaus updated Arequipa, the Colca canyon, and the Southern jungle.

**Dinesh and Jessica Pol** Dinesh, originally from India, and Jessica from Huancayo, make their home in the latter city where they run a language school. They updated the Huancayo section.

**Julio Porras** Julio's roots are in Piura. He lives in Chiclayo and works as a tour guide throughout the north coast, specializing in bicycle and nature tours as well as the region's many archaeological attractions. Julio updated Chiclayo, Piura and Tumbes.

**Martijn Steijn** Originally from The Netherlands, Martijn divides his time between Huanchaco and Vilcabamba (Ecuador). He organizes and guides custom-made tours throughout Ecuador, Peru and Bolivia. Martijn updated Trujillo and Huanchaco.

# Acknowledgements

When we (Robert and Daisy) first arrived in Lima in 1988 there was a strict curfew in force. Friends needed a special permit and had to fly a white flag from their car in order to pick us up at the airport. The peaceful, prosperous and heavily visited Peru described in this book is a far cry from those dark days and it is with much satisfaction that we have witnessed its evolution. At the same time, we are dismayed by the rising tide of unsustainable development in Peru and struck by the irony of all the narrowly focused mass tourism in a country with so much to offer and ideally suited to independent travel.

Peru is too complex to be seen exclusively through our eyes, however, and we are grateful to our correspondents for their diverse points of view. This dedicated multinational team of travel professionals and professional travellers has worked hard to share an intimate knowledge of their common home. They are listed above and we thank them warmly.

Additional editorial contributions were made by Alberto Cafferata, Ana Lucía Espinosa, John and Julia Forrest, Jaime García-Heras and Francisco Romero. We thank all our companions from the 2018 Upper Marañón expedition led by John Ingham. They include Michell and Miquer Cornelio, Eladio and Consuelo Marticorena, Daniel Montesinos, Daniela Raillard, Gisela Sancho, Brayan Sotil, and Jesús Valdívia. Others who have helped us in various ways while we researched and wrote this edition include Constantino Aucca, Baruch and Aviva Aziza, Marta Giraldo, John Gorfinkel, Miguel de Kergariou, Duver Loayza, Analee Merino, Marcelo Naranjo, Percy Sánchez and Analía Sarfaty. We likewise acknowledge the very kind and unfailingly competent assistance of iPerú throughout the country.

This 10th edition of the *Peru Handbook* is built on the hard work of several generations of Footprint travel writers and editors, including Ben Box and Alan Murphy. They laid the solid foundations upon which the current title is built. We thank the entire Footprint editorial and production team, including Felicity Laughton, Emma Bryers, Kevin Feeney, John Hendry, Kirsty Holmes, John Sadler and Debbie Wylde.

# Credits

**Footprint credits**
**Project editor**: Felicity Laughton
**Production and layout**: Emma Bryers
**Maps**: Kevin Feeney and Robert Kunstaetter
**Colour section**: John Hendry

**Publisher**: John Sadler
**Marketing**: Kirsty Holmes

**Photography credits**
**Front cover**: David Ionut/Shutterstock.com
**Back cover top**: SL-Photography/
Shutterstock.com
**Back cover bottom**: Mikadun/
Shutterstock.com
**Inside front cover**: Robert and Daisy
Kunstaetter; vitmark/Shutterstock.com.

**Colour section**
**Page 1**: Richard Constantinoff/Shutterstock.com. **Page 2**:
Diego Grandi/Shutterstock.com. **Page 4**: Skreidzeleu/
Shutterstock.com, Mikadun/Shutterstock.com. **Page 5**:
age fotostock/Superstock.com, Diego Grandi/Shutterstock.
com, Jess Kraft/Shutterstock.com, Christian Vinces/
Shutterstock.com, John Kershner/Shutterstock.com. **Page 6**:
mehdi33300/Shutterstock.com, Serjio74/Shutterstock.
com, saiko3p/Shutterstock.com. **Page 7**: sharptoyou/
Shutterstock.com, cge2010/Shutterstock.com, Robert
and Daisy Kunstaetter, Christian Vinces/Shutterstock.com.
**Page 10**: Mikadun/Shutterstock.com. **Page 11**: VarnaK/
Shutterstock.com. **Page 12**: marktucan/Shutterstock.com.
**Page 13**: Christian Vinces/Shutterstock.com. **Page 14**:
3523studio/Shutterstock.com, kesterhu/Shutterstock.
com. **Page 15**: Michal Knitl/Shutterstock.com, Robert and
Daisy Kunstaetter, Erik Hausted Larsson/Shutterstock.com.
**Page 16**: Milton Rodriguez/Shutterstock.com.

**Duotones**
**Page 34**: Neale Cousland/Shutterstock.com.
**Page 74**: Grant Dixon/Superstock.com.
**Page 104**: Fotos593/Shutterstock.com.
**Page 154**: Terry Carr/Dreamstime.com.
**Page 192**: John Kershner/Shutterstock.com.
**Page 218**: Elzbieta Sekowska/Shutterstock.com.
**Page 258**: Elzbieta Sekowska/Shutterstock.com.
**Page 286**: Elzbieta Sekowska/Shutterstock.com.
**Page 324**: Anton_Ivanov/Shutterstock.com.
**Page 356**: Robert and Daisy Kunstaetter.
**Page 394**: Dirk Ercken/Shutterstock.com.

**Publishing information**
Footprint Peru
10th edition
© Compass Maps Ltd
October 2018

ISBN: 978 1 911082 55 2
CIP DATA: A catalogue record for this book
is available from the British Library

® Footprint Handbooks and the
Footprint mark are a registered
trademark of Compass Maps Ltd

Published by Footprint
5 Riverside Court
Lower Bristol Road
Bath BA2 3DZ, UK
T +44 (0)1225 469141
footprinttravelguides.com

Every effort has been made to ensure that
the facts in this guidebook are accurate.
However, travellers should still obtain advice
from consulates, airlines, etc about travel
and visa requirements before travelling.
The authors and publishers cannot
accept responsibility for any loss, injury
or inconvenience however caused.

Printed in India
Print and production managed by
Jellyfish Solutions

# Distance chart

Distances in kilometres
1 kilometre = 0.62 miles

| Arequipa | | | | | | | | | | | | | | | |
|---|---|---|---|---|---|---|---|---|---|---|---|---|---|---|---|
| 1078 | Ayacucho | | | | | | | | | | | | | | |
| 1860 | 1394 | Cajamarca | | | | | | | | | | | | | |
| 515 | 597 | 1957 | Cuzco | | | | | | | | | | | | |
| 2195 | 1729 | 335 | 2292 | Chachapoyas | | | | | | | | | | | |
| 1773 | 1307 | 260 | 1870 | 622 | Chiclayo | | | | | | | | | | |
| 1308 | 257 | 1150 | 854 | 1485 | 1063 | Huancayo | | | | | | | | | |
| 1417 | 951 | 857 | 1514 | 1192 | 770 | 707 | Huaraz | | | | | | | | |
| 706 | 372 | 1154 | 803 | 1489 | 1067 | 602 | 711 | Ica | | | | | | | |
| 997 | 556 | 856 | 1153 | 1186 | 763 | 299 | 517 | 303 | Lima | | | | | | |
| 1982 | 1516 | 496 | 2079 | 831 | 209 | 1272 | 979 | 1276 | 973 | Piura | | | | | |
| 1048 | 1130 | 2490 | 533 | 2825 | 2403 | 1387 | 2047 | 1336 | 1637 | 2612 | Puerto Maldonado | | | | |
| 326 | 986 | 2186 | 389 | 2573 | 2099 | 1243 | 1743 | 1032 | 1542 | 2308 | 922 | Puno | | | |
| 284 | 1306 | 2144 | 799 | 2479 | 2057 | 1592 | 1701 | 990 | 1293 | 2266 | 1332 | 610 | Tacna | | |
| 2022 | 1100 | 294 | 1663 | 629 | 207 | 856 | 563 | 860 | 557 | 416 | 2196 | 1892 | 1850 | Trujillo | |
| 2265 | 1799 | 750 | 2362 | 1114 | 492 | 1555 | 1262 | 1559 | 1299 | 283 | 2895 | 2591 | 2549 | 699 | Tumbes |

# Index

## A
5 A5 Abancay
5 A5 Aguas Calientes
6 B2 Amantaní
4 A4 Andahuaylas
5 A5 Anta to Curahuasi
5 C6 Arequipa
5 B/C6 Arequipa to Chivay
1 B2 Ayabaca
5 A4 Ayacucho

## B
5 B2 Ballestas Islands
3 B3 Baños Termales Monterrey

## C
5 B5 Cabanaconde
1 C3 Cajamarca
3 C3 Callao
3 B4 Canta
3 A2 Caraz
3 B2 Carhuaz
3 B2 Casma to Huaraz via Pariacoto
3 B3 Catac to Chavín
3 B4 Cerro de Pasco
3 A3 Chacas
1 C4 Chachapoyas
3 A1 Chan Chán
3 C3 Chancay Valley
3 B5 Chanchamayo
3 B3 Chavín
3 B3 Chavín de Huantar
1 C2 Chepén
1 C2 Chiclayo
1 C3 Chilete
3 A2 Chimbote
3 A2 Chincha Alta
5 A5 Chinchero
5 B6 Chivay
5 A5 Choquequirao
3 B3 Churín
6 B1 Colca Canyon
3 B3 Cordillera Blanca
5 A6 Cordillera Vilcanota
3 B3/4 Cordilleras Huayhuash & Raura
5 B5 Cotahuasi Canyon
5 A5 Cuzco city

## E
3 A1 El Brujo
5 C6 El Misti and Chachani

## F
1 C2 Ferreñafe and Sicán

## G
1 C4 Gran Vilaya

## H
3 B3 Huacho
3 B3 Huallanca
3 A2 Huamachuco
1 B2 Huancabamba
5 A4/5 Huancacalle to Esprítu Pampa
3 C5 Huancavelica
3 C5 Huancayo
3 A1 Huanchaco
5 A4 Huanta Valley
3 B4 Huánuco
3 B3 Huaraz
3 B2/3 Huaraz to Caraz
3 B3 Huari

## I
5 B2 Ica
2 B4 Iquitos

## J
1 B3 Jaén
3 C4 Jauja
6 B2 Juliaca
3 B4 Junín

## K
1 C4 Kuélap and Tingo

## L
3 C4 La Oroya
3 B3 La Unión
1 B6 Lagunas
1 C2 Lambayeque
1 C4 Levanto
1 C4 Leymebamba
5 A1 Lima
6 B2 Los Uros

## M
5 A5 Machu Picchu ruins
1 B1 Máncora
3 B2 Mancos and around
4 C4 Manu Biosphere Reserve
6 C1 Mollendo
1 C2 Monsefú
6 C2 Moquegua
1 C2 Mórrope
1 B5 Moyobamba

## N
5 B3 Nazca
3 B3 Nazca Lines
1 B4 Nuevo Cajamarca

## O
5 A5 Ollantaytambo
3 B4 Oxapampa

## P
5 B2 Paracas Peninsula
1 C2 Pimentel
5 B2 Pisac
3 B2 Pisco
3 A3 Piscobamba
1 B1 Piura
3 A3 Pomabamba
5 A5 Pucallpa
3 B5 Puerto Bermúdez
1 C2 Puerto Etén
6 A3 Puerto Maldonado
6 B2 Puno

## Q
5 A2 Quebrada de Lunahuaná
5 A5 Quillabamba and around

## R
5 B6 Raqchi
2 C2 Reserva Nacional Pacaya-Samiria
1 B5 Rioja

## S
3 A3 San Luis
3 C4 San Pedro de Casta
1 C2 Santa Rosa
3 B2 Sechín
1 B2 Sechura Desert
5 A6 Shintuya
5 B6 Sicuani
6 B2 Sillustani
1 C2 Sipán
5 A1/2 South to Cañete
1 B1 Sullana

## T
6 C2 Tacna
1 B1 Talara
6 A3 Tambopata National Reserve
3 B3 Tantamayo
1 C5 Tarapoto
3 C4 Tarma
3 A4 Tingo María
3 A2 To Sihuas and beyond
3 A1 Trujillo
1 C2 Túcume
1 A2 Tumbes

## U
5 A5 Urubamba

## Y
3 B4 Yanahuanca
3 A2 Yungay
5 C6 Yura
1 B5 Yurimaguas

## Z
1 C2 Zaña

# Footprint Mini Atlas
# Peru

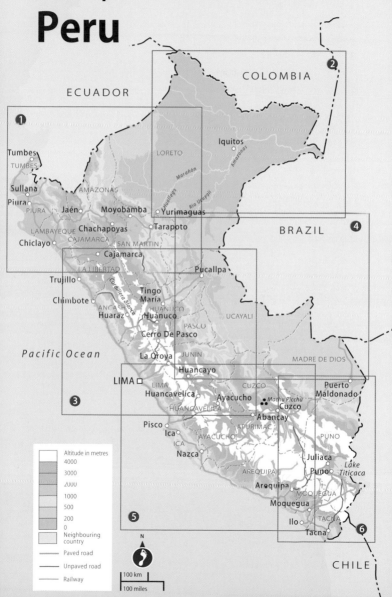

ECUADOR

COLOMBIA

❷

❶

Tumbes
TUMBES

Sullana

Piura
PIURA

Jaén

Moyobamba

Chachapoyas

Chiclayo
LAMBAYEQUE  CAJAMARCA  SAN MARTIN

Cajamarca

LA LIBERTAD

Trujillo

Chimbote

Tingo
María

Huaraz
ANCASH  HUÁNUCO

Huánuco

Cerro De Pasco
PASCO

La Oroya
JUNIN

LORETO

Iquitos

Marañón

Yurimaguas

Tarapoto

Pucallpa

UCAYALI

BRAZIL

❹

Pacific Ocean

LIMA ☐
LIMA

Huancayo

Huancavelica
HUANCAVELICA

Ayacucho

Machu Picchu
CUZCO

Cuzco

Abancay

MADRE DE DIOS

Puerto
Maldonado

❸

Pisco

Ica
ICA

Nazca

AYACUCHO

APURIMAC

PUNO

Juliaca

Puno
AREQUIPA

Lake
Titicaca

Arequipa

MOQUEGUA

Moquegua

Ilo
TACNA

❺

Tacna

❻

CHILE

| Altitude in metres | |
|---|---|
| | 4000 |
| | 3000 |
| | 2000 |
| | 1000 |
| | 500 |
| | 200 |
| | 0 |
| | Neighbouring country |

Paved road
Unpaved road
Railway

N

100 km
100 miles

# Map 1

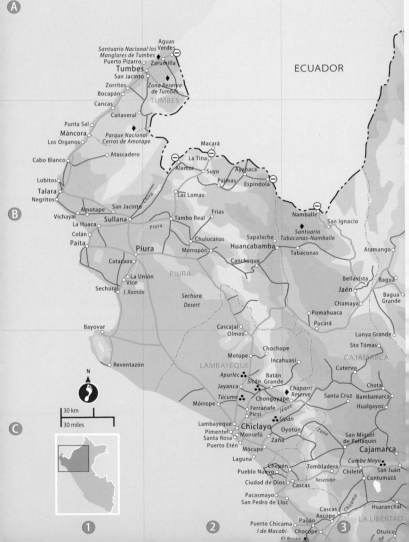

Pacific Ocean

**A**

Aguas Verdes
Santuario Nacional los Manglares de Tumbes
Puerto Pizarro
**Tumbes**
San Jacinto
Zarumilla

**ECUADOR**

Zorritos
Bocapán
Zona Reserva de Tumbes
Cancas
TUMBES
Cañaveral

Punta Sal
**Máncora**
Los Organos
Parque Nacional Cerros de Amotape

Cabo Blanco
Atascadero
Macará

Lobitos
La Tina
**Talara**
Alamor
Suyo
Ayabaca
Negritos
Paimas
Espíndola

**B**
Amotape
San Jacinto
Las Lomas
Vichayal
**Sullana**
Tambo Real
Frías
Namballe
San Ignacio

La Huaca
Piura
Colán
Chulucanas
Sapalache
Santuario Tabaconas-Namballe
**Paita**
**Piura**
Morropón
**Huancabamba**
Tabaconas
Aramango

Catacaos
Canchaque
Bellavista
Bagua

La Unión
**Jaén**
Vice
Chamaya
Bagua
Sechura
L. Ramón
PIURA
Grande

Sechura
Desert
Pomahuaca
Pucará

Bayovar
Cascajal
Olmos
Lunya Grande
Sto Tómas

Reventazón
Motupe
Chochope
Cuervo
CAJAMARCA

Incahuasi
LAMBAYEQUE
Apurlec
Batán
Grande
Chota
Jayanca
Sicán
Chaparri
Reserve
Santa Cruz
Bambamarca

**Túcume**
Chongoyape
Hualgayoc
Mórrope
Ferreñafe
Picsi
Sipán

**C**
Lambayeque
**Chiclayo**
Oyotún
San Miguel de Pallaques
Pimentel
Santa Rosa
Monsefú
Zaña
**Cajamarca**

Puerto Etén
Mócupe
Cumbe Mayo
San Juan
Laguna
Chepén
Tembladera
Chilete
Contumazá

Pueblo Nuevo
Reservoir
Ciudad de Dios
Cascas

Pacasmayo
San Pedro de Lloc
Cascas
Huaranchal
Ascope

Puerto Chicama
Paiján
I de Macabí
Chocope
Otusco
El Brujo
LA LIBERTAD

N

30 km
30 miles

**1**  **2**  **3**

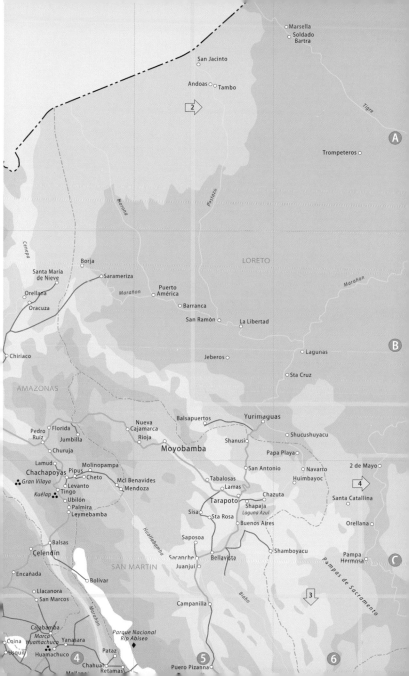

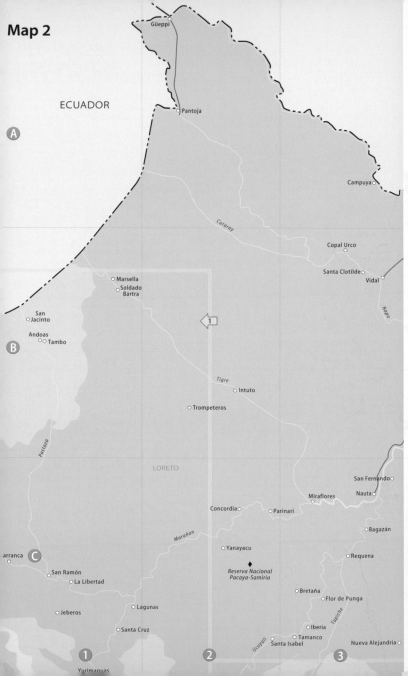

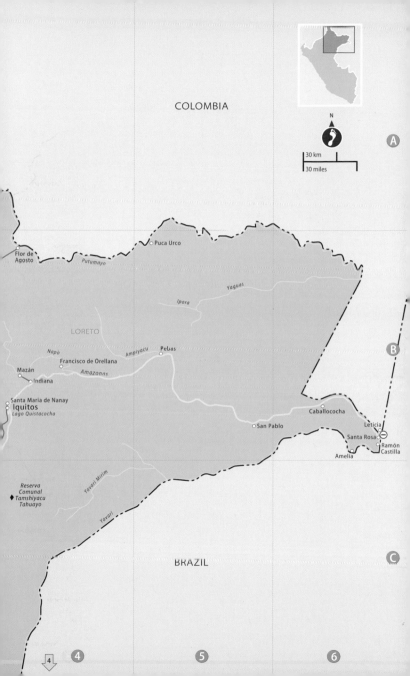

COLOMBIA

N

30 km
30 miles

A

Flor de
Agosto

Puca Urco

*Putumayo*

*Yaguas*

*Ipora*

LORETO

*Napo*

Francisco de Orellana

*Ampiyacu*

Pebas

B

Mazán

*Amazonas*

Indiana

Santa Maria de Nanay

Iquitos

*Lago Quistacocha*

Caballococha

San Pablo

Leticia

Santa Rosa

Ramón
Castilla

Amelia

*Yavari Mirim*

Reserva
Comunal
Tamshiyacu
Tahuayo

*Yavari*

BRAZIL

C

4

4

5

6

# Map 4

LORETO

Orellana

Conamaná

Cerro do Canchyauya

Pampas de Sacramento

Sierra Contamana

Abuja

L Yarinacocha   **Pucallpa**

Masisea

Von Humboldt   Honoria   L Chauya Cocha

San Alejandro   Ganzo Azul

Pachitea   Tournavista   L Inuria

Aguaytía

HUANUCO

Puerto Inca

UCAYALI

Chorropampa   Ciudad Constitución

Puerto Victoria

Puerto Pachitea

Pozuzo

Curanja

Puerto Bermúdez

Palcazú

Huancabamba   PASCO

Neguachi

Oxapampa   Atalaya   Ucayali

Villa Rica

San Lus de Shuaro

La Merced (Chanchamayo)   Pichanaki   Puerto Ocopa   Shepahua

San Ramón

Palcamayo   Satipo   Tambo

Acobamba   JUNIN   Mazamari   CUZCO

Tarma   Mariposa

Huairicolca

Jauja   Comas

hacapalpa   Concepción

San José   Chupaca

Camisea

Huancayo

BRAZIL

Esperanza

Curanja

Iñapari

Iberia

San Lorenzo

Alerta

Las Piedras

MADRE DE DIOS

Manu
Biosphere
Reserve

Madre de Dios

Mavila

4

5

Boca Manu

6

Planchón

30 km

30 miles

N

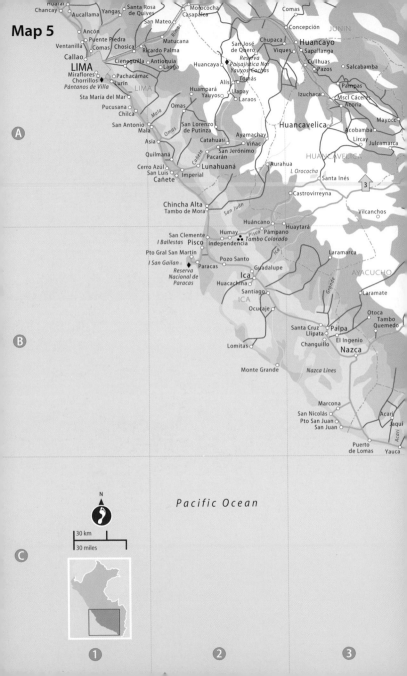